CU01276790

Northamptonshire Archaeology, 41, 2021

The Archaeology of Medieval Northampton

Edited by Andy Chapman

Contents

Produced and printed for the Society by 4word Limited, Bristol

Northamptonshire Archaeology, **41**, 2021, 1–3

Introduction

The archaeology of medieval Northampton

by Andy Chapman

Preamble

For me, this medieval Northampton special edition has been 45 years in the making. It was a darkening early evening in October 1976 when I stepped off a train at Northampton Station, walked across the forecourt and, loaded down as I was with a large rucksack, I must have passed the relocated postern gate from the castle without noticing it while on my way up Black Lion Hill and along Marefair and Gold Street. I passed Barclaycard House, a brash and bold example of modern brutalist architecture, and crossed The Drapery and the Market Square to stand outside the locked doors of the Grosvenor Centre, wondering how I was to get to the Bus station that I had been told was on the other side.

I was arriving to join the digging team of the Northampton Development Corporation Archaeological Unit on a three-month contract to work on the excavation of the Briar Hill Neolithic causewayed enclosure. At the time this was just another short-term stopover in the life of a circuit digger, having already similarly passed through Cambridge, Chesterfield, Chelmsford, Derby and various other locations in England, Northern Ireland and Central France over the previous three years or so while learning the craft of field archaeology.

After being in Northampton for a few months digging at Briar Hill I had still learnt little about the archaeology of the town itself, but one day Mike Shaw explained to me the importance of the area around the station both in terms of the late Saxon archaeology and the medieval castle. 'Castle!', I exclaimed in disbelief, 'what castle?'. At that time I wouldn't have dreamt that 45 years later I would not only still be living in Northampton, but that in 2013 I would have excavated the very station forecourt that I had walked over in 1976 in total ignorance of what might lie beneath.

Editing *Northamptonshire Archaeology*

Despite the attempt to provide a thematic journal with volume 37 in 2012, where the first half of the volume was focussed on Neolithic and Bronze Age archaeology, a journal editor is necessarily largely at the mercy of the contributors, who stubbornly insist on providing a wide diversity of material covering all periods.

However, in the early 2010s a chance meeting in the library of the Society of Antiquaries with John Williams, the head of the Northampton Development Corporation Archaeological Unit from the early 1970s to its closure in the mid-1980s, opened up the possibility of perhaps achieving at least one volume with a clear theme, namely, the archaeology of medieval Northampton.

At the time there was much attention being given to the proposals for building a new station, and to the royal castle that had largely been levelled towards the end of the 19th century to provide a location for the station and its extensive goods yard, now the station car park. But at the same time the fascinating story of the pre-Conquest origins of the town, as revealed by the work of the NDC from the mid-1970s to mid-1980s, appeared to have been largely forgotten within the public discussion of the history of Northampton.

I am afraid that life and events have schemed to delay getting this much promised volume to completion, and it has had to wait until my retirement finally provided a little more space and time. And then through 2020 and 2021 Covid-19 came along and with it lockdowns and a new way of life. However, we finally have a volume, and through time it has grown into some 500 pages, and I hope at least some will agree that it has been worth the wait. We also hope that it will have sufficient public interest to generate sales beyond NAS membership and institutional subscribers. I must also apologise for the fact that the report on Northampton Castle is now in two parts, with the second forthcoming for the next journal, but otherwise publication might have been delayed until well into 2022.

The Archaeology of medieval Northampton

In this volume, following a brief diversion into flint scatters, we will examine aspects of the medieval archaeology of Northampton, with much of the volume focussed on the western end of the town to cover its pre-Conquest origins and the royal castle that was built over part of Anglo-Saxon Hamtun.

Anglo-Saxon Hamtun

While much of the volume comprises excavation reports, John Williams provides us with a synthetic overview of the archaeology of the pre-Conquest town. This centres on the spectacular discoveries of the Middle Saxon timber and stone halls that lay between the early churches of St Peter and St Gregory (Fig 1). The accompanying mortar mixers are themselves considered in their national and international context in an appendix. In another appendix Michael Shaw, who, like me, arrived in Northampton as a young archaeologist in 1976 to work for the NDC, has examined medieval pottery distribution across the town. The results lend support to the double street pattern theory as defining the northern and eastern defences of the late Saxon town, by showing how pottery dating to the 11th century occurs in quantity only within the double street pattern. In a further appendix radiocarbon dates from the 1980s are recalibrated and tabulated in the modern format to make a contribution to the reconsideration of the dating of the timber hall. We now move its date of construction from around the mid-8th century AD to between the later 7th to early 8th century AD, although the large error margins on these old dates still limit what we can achieve with a high degree of confidence.

The overview of the Anglo-Saxon town is followed by a site report on the pre-castle deposits that lay beneath the area of the Outer Bailey of the castle that was excavated in 2013 in advance of the building of the new station. This was a marginal area, close to the river and the late Saxon West Bridge. If town defences continued around the western side of the town, this area would have lain on the slope below them, which might explain why for much of the 11th to mid-12th century it was a dumping ground for the bones from butchery waste.

The pre-Conquest section comes to an end with a short article reporting a radiocarbon date for the buried soil beneath the late Saxon clay bank of the original town defences, although the broad 10th century date has failed to discriminate between the period of Danish control from the late 9th to the early 10th century, and the re-conquest by Edward the Elder in the early 10th century.

Northampton Castle

And then we come to that old royal castle, which the town has done such a good job of removing almost entirely from its topography. The intention had been that this volume would contain a complete overview of the history and archaeology of the castle, based on work that I originally undertook in the mid-1980s for the NDC in an attempt to produce a report on Dr John Alexander's excavations in the early 1960s.

However, having put that report aside earlier in 2021 to ensure that all the other contributions were ready for publication, time and space caught up with me. It became evident that finding the time and energy to complete the castle report would take me to, probably, to the end of November. At the same time, with other articles being typeset it became evident that with the full report on the castle the volume would run to some 550 pages or more. I therefore made the decision that it would be preferable to bring the volume to a more speedy, and slightly thinner conclusion, by presenting only the first half of the castle report in this volume; comprising a broad overview of the survey and excavation work that has recorded the castle ruins, and an overview of the history and topography of the castle, with only the pre-castle archaeology approached in more detail. The more detailed record of the archaeology, particularly for the 1960s excavations of the north-east corner of the Inner Bailey and the nearby Castle Hill, will now appear in the next volume of the journal.

There is, though, a separate full excavation report on the work in the Outer Bailey in 2013 in advance of the new station, which includes coverage of the events of the 19th century, with progressive encroachment leading to the final clearance in 1879–80 for the new railway.

The Green

The Northampton Development Corporation Archaeological Unit had an excellent publication record, but at its demise in the mid-1980s there were a couple of excavations within the heart of the late Saxon town that remained unpublished. The middle-late Saxon and medieval deposits at The Green had been something of a disappointment, in contrast to the spectacular uncovering of the Middle Anglo-Saxon timber and stone halls, with their mortar mixers, to the immediate north in earlier excavations (Fig 1). However, the site did produce the best evidence we have of the early post-medieval tanning industry that once dominated this quarter of the town, and this aspect of the site was moved on to publication in the 1990s. A report on the medieval phases was drafted in the late 1980s but then stalled in the early 1990s and never made it to publication. The existing draft has now been resurrected to fill this gap in the NDC publication record. If the comparable draft texts for the St Gregory Street excavations can be located, it is hoped that that too might be brought to publication to complete the NDC set.

The Northampton Jewry

We move across to the heart of the medieval town, the market place, to look at the location of the medieval Jewry, and specifically the location of the synagogue. This section of the report comprises three articles: Marcus Roberts looks at the documentary evidence relating to the Jewry and uses map regression to suggest a specific location for the synagogue, with the location subsequently examined by Ground Penetrating Radar (GPR), which has located the possible presence of surviving below ground features, some below cellar level, that might relate to below ground remains of the synagogue.

To put this paper in context, there is also a summary report on the archaeological watching brief undertaken by Northamptonshire Archaeology (now MOLA Northampton) on the demolition of the Fish Market and the limited survival of earlier archaeological deposits. In a third paper I question some of the assumptions made by Marcus Roberts in his map regression, but also demonstrate that even if the Marcus Pierce map that his analysis is based on is treated with more caution, an alternative exercise in map regression produces essentially the same result for the suggested location of the synagogue.

Cow Lane and the new Museum

The central part of the volume ends with a report on excavations at Cow Lane (Swan Street) by MOLA Northampton, which provided a sequence of activity from earlier quarry pits through to a 19th-century foundry, and a study of the buildings of the old County Gaol, latterly offices of Northamptonshire County Council and now within the recently opened refurbished and extended Northampton Museum and Art Gallery.

Northampton Notes

Given the recent publication by MOLA of the excavations at Angel Street, which produced a workshop where they were producing stylised chess pieces in antler, and the recovery in the 19th century of a chess piece from the castle, I couldn't resist putting these together to provide an article on medieval stylised chess pieces, a subject that I have been fortunate enough to be able to publish articles on several times over the years.

Thanks must go to Graham Cadman for short notes on various aspects of the town landscape: the Postern Gate from the castle, the town mill and the town jetties. There is also a note with a link to a 3D image of the structure of the Greyfriars Bus Station.

County Notes

Moving outside Northampton, there is a study of the topical subject of social distancing, in this case extended into death though a victim of leprosy buried in a corner of the churchyard at Furnells manor, Raunds, The rest of the county notes comprises three short contributions all related to medieval pottery including the production centres around Stanion and Glapthorn in the north-east of the county.

Obituaries

We must also sadly note that we have never had so many obituaries in a single issue before, covering a range of people and ages. They all had an impact on the archaeology of Northamptonshire, and many also had a long involvement with both the society and the journal.

Northamptonshire Archaeology online

Finally, we must note that lockdown in 2020 did provide an opportunity for me to work on the huge database that was required by the Archaeology Data Service (ADS) in order to put all the material from the past 40 volumes online, as reported in the Recent Publications section, which also contains a lengthy list of publications that have appeared in the past couple of years.

The next volume

Material is already accumulating for the next edition, which may even appear before the end of 2022, but perhaps I shouldn't be making such promises giving how many years this volume has been in gestation.

Andy Chapman BSc MCIfA FSA
11 October 2021

Fig 1: Looking south from the roof of the former Barclaycard House on Marefair in the 1970s, showing St Peter's church right, Hazelrigg house centre foreground, and the corner of Gregory Street centre left. The area behind Hazelrigg House was the location for major excavations from the early 1970s to the early 1980s that explored the middle Anglo-Saxon 'palaces' and the post-medieval tannery on The Green. Compare to *Archaeology and the Changing Face of Northampton*, page 10

Northamptonshire Archaeology, **41**, 2021, 5–15

Brave New World:
Northampton Development Corporation and Archaeology 1970–85

by

John H Williams

Summary

In 1968 Northampton was designated an area of considerable expansion under the New Towns Act of 1946, with the Master Plan for development being approved in 1970. In the same year an archaeologist was appointed by Northampton Development Corporation and from then an expanding team undertook archaeological investigations within the town and surrounding area designated for development until the demise of the Corporation in 1985. The paper looks at the organisational and planning context of the Corporation's archaeological work and reflects on some of the results of this work.

Introduction

This short contribution has been written in response to an invitation by Andy Chapman, as editor of *Northamptonshire Archaeology*, to complete the series of articles contained in volume 38 of the journal, which looked back over the growth of archaeology in Northamptonshire (Moore 2015; Chapman 2015a & 2015b).

It has been a pleasure to reminisce on the early days of my professional involvement in archaeology, but at the same time quite a challenge to recall accurately the precise sequence of events and their associated details, beyond the archaeological results contained within the published reports of excavations. Nonetheless, in looking back at the broad sweep of events, I can recognise the 1970s as a period of considerable development pressure and profound change within the archaeological world, with Northampton Development Corporation (hereafter NDC) being among the earliest 'governmental' bodies to embrace archaeology within the development process.

The organisational and planning framework

On 3 February 1965 the Government announced its intention to expand Northampton, using the machinery of the New Towns Act of 1946, and on 14 February 1968 the Northampton New Town (Designation) Order was made. The Minister of Housing and Local Government made the order establishing NDC on 30 August in the same year and the Master Plan for development was approved on 24 September 1970 (Barty-King 1985, 21, 54, 59, 84; see also Brown 1990, 184ff).

In one of the meetings held by the new General Manager, Dr John Weston, in November 1969, Harold Frost, a local architect and keen amateur archaeologist who had assisted Dr John Alexander on his excavations on Northampton castle, raised the question of the impact of the proposed development on archaeological remains. A consequence of this was the appointment in 1970 of Dennis Mynard to undertake excavations in advance of development works. Dennis moved on to Milton Keynes Development Corporation in 1971 and I became the NDC archaeologist in September 1971, staying until 1984, a year before the impending winding up of NDC. Dennis, with the assistance of John Small, had established a Sites and Monuments Record for the development area, which in those days comprised a map and simple card system, and had undertaken medieval excavations at the Mayorhold and St Andrew's priory in the town and at Thorplands (Romano-British) and Moulton Park (Iron Age) in the Eastern District. Before, however, looking further at the archaeological achievements of the NDC team perhaps it is appropriate to consider further the context of its establishment.

In 1970 there was only a handful of archaeological field officers in the whole of the country and a comprehensive national network of archaeological units and planning archaeologists was very much a vision for the future. There had been increasing concern during the 1960s at the unmitigated destruction of important archaeological remains, particularly within the country's historic urban centres, leading to the birth of 'rescue archaeology'. The formation of the organisation Rescue at the beginning of the 1970s was a clear manifestation of the archaeological issues of the time, which were vividly encapsulated, not without controversy, in its dramatic logo of trilithons, of Stonehenge type, being carried off in the bucket of a powerful mechanical excavator. *The Erosion of History*, which provided a disturbing overview of the impact of development on the historic towns of England, Wales and Scotland, was published by the Council for British Archaeology's Urban Research Committee in 1972 (Heighway 1972). If one looks at maps showing the provision of field archaeologists in the country in 1970 (where the NDC archaeologist is, however, omitted) and 1976 one can see that NDC was very much at the forefront in realising the need to embrace archaeological concerns within the development process, while at the same time recognising its value for public relations (Jones 1984, 6–7).

There was little in the NDC Master Plan about archaeology (which was written indeed before the appointment of an archaeologist), with, generically, only Scheduled Ancient Monuments being mentioned as potential constraints and Hunsbury hillfort appearing as a focal point in a proposed country park, more, it would appear, on account of its landscape contribution than its archaeological significance. The Master Plan was, however, modified subsequently when medieval village earthworks were recognised at Upton in 1972. The housing allocation for the site was transferred, with the earthworks becoming open space and indeed scheduled (Williams 1977, 68–9).

In respect of the centre of the town the Planning Proposals (1968, 99, 110 viii; Williams 1977, 69) stated that:

> 'The centre still retains its medieval circular plan form and its grain of narrow side streets and pedestrian ginnels or jetties opening into the expanse of the Market Square';

also that:

> 'Careful attention should be given to the retention of the character of Northampton centre. In this connection the churches, open spaces, narrow lanes and Market Square are of particular importance and new buildings should be in scale with the existing fabric'.

Matching conservation of the historic environment with the social and economic imperatives of the present is always a challenge and Northampton has few buildings predating the fire of 1675 that consumed much of the town, but it is a pity that so much of the character represented on John Speed's plan of 1610 has been lost.

In terms of implementation of the development proposals outside the existing urban area NDC for the most part acquired and owned the land to be built on before selling it on to the developer; it was thus in a position to control the development process and the incorporation of archaeological work into the programme, and this it did on a number of sites in the Eastern and Southern Districts. In the case of the Briar Hill causewayed enclosure, discovered by aerial photography in 1972 and subsequently scheduled, it was possible, following geophysical survey and trial trenching, to conduct extensive excavations totalling 150 weeks spread over four winter seasons between 1974 and 1978. During trial trenching it had been established that the site was badly eroded by ploughing and the case for preservation was therefore considerably weakened. The excavation was largely funded by an adjustment of the value of the land as a result of the anticipated cost of the archaeological constraint (Williams 1977, 72; Bamford 1985, 2).

Within the town archaeological investigation was initially carried out as a result of the goodwill of the developer, St Peter's Street being a notable example which was achieved with the considerable cooperation of Metropolitan Estates (see below and Williams *et al*

this volume). By 1977, however, formal conditions were being placed within planning consents by the Borough Council, as planning authority, as follows:

> 'Provision shall be made in the phasing and construction of the work for archaeological investigations to be made in accordance with further details to be agreed with the council before clearance of any part of the site and during construction stages proper protection shall be afforded to the archaeological works over a period to be agreed with the Council which shall in any event not exceed six months from the commencement of such investigations.'

This was very much an early use of an archaeological planning condition (Williams 1977, 71; see also Hedges 1977, 42ff) but developer funding as formalised in PPG16 was some way in the future.

For most of the life of NDC's archaeological unit there was a permanent staff of seven, supplemented by others on short-term contracts and volunteers. Core funding was supplied by NDC with project funding coming from the Department of the Environment, which then housed the Inspectorate of Ancient Monuments; its inspectors were most supportive of the work being undertaken, with the Ancient Monuments Laboratory assisting greatly with geophysical survey and environmental and metallurgical analyses. The role of the Borough Council in the planning process has already been mentioned and it was also helpful in providing other support and indeed accommodation, in keeping with the archaeological spirit of the time, for temporary digging staff.

After the new NDC and Borough Council offices at Cliftonville House had been commissioned, the NDC archaeological unit was housed in a hexagonal cottage that formed part of Thorplands Farm, an early to mid-19th-century model farm, the rest of the complex being the home of the NDC tree nursery.

Archaeological results

To return to the archaeology itself, in the Eastern District excavation continued on the Moulton Park Iron Age site in 1971–2 (Fig 1) and an Iron Age double-ditched enclosure at Blackthorn was completely stripped in 1972–3 (Fig 2) (Williams 1974). The Thorplands Romano-British site was revisited in 1974 (Fig 3) (Hunter and Mynard 1977).

In the Southern District, following a geophysical survey, excavation had commenced on the Briar Hill Neolithic causewayed enclosure in 1974 (Fig 4–6). In addition to the interrupted circuits of the Early Neolithic causewayed enclosure there was also a Late Neolithic horseshoe-shaped timber structure; an undated but possibly Late Neolithic pit alignment; a Middle Bronze Age cremation cemetery; three small Iron Age enclosures; Roman pit groups; and early Anglo-Saxon sunken-featured buildings (Fig 5). Such palimpsest landscapes are typical of Northamptonshire and the Nene valley.

Today drones are being increasingly used not only for taking aerial site photographs but also to provide vertical

Fig 1: The late Iron Age causeway, with a facing of herringbone stonework, perhaps early 1st-century AD, set across one of the enclosure ditches at Moulton Park (see Williams 1974, 16–17)

Fig 3: A Romano-British stone round building at Thorplands, probably late 3rd-century

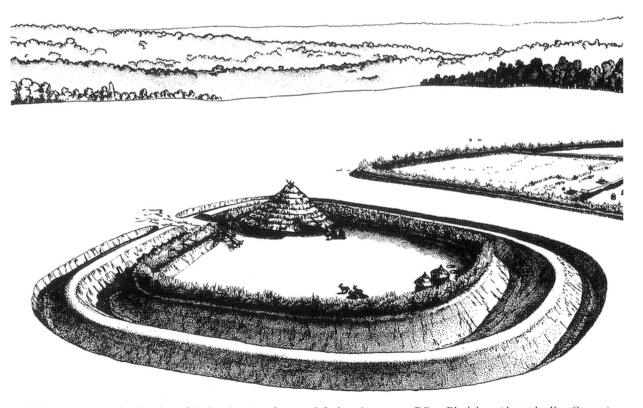

Fig 2: A reconstruction drawing of the late Iron Age farmstead, 2nd- to 1st-century BC, at Blackthorn (drawn by Ken Connor)

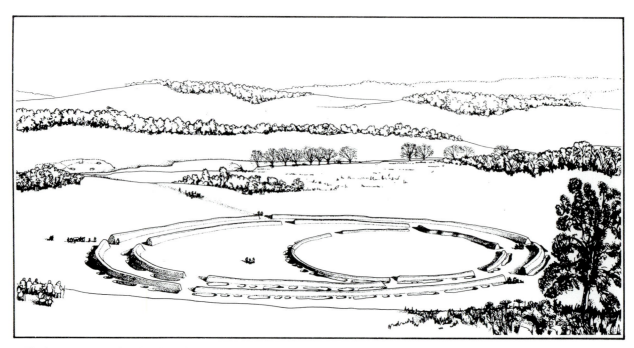

Fig 4: A reconstruction drawing of the earthworks of the Neolithic causewayed enclosure at Briar Hill (drawn by Ken Connor)

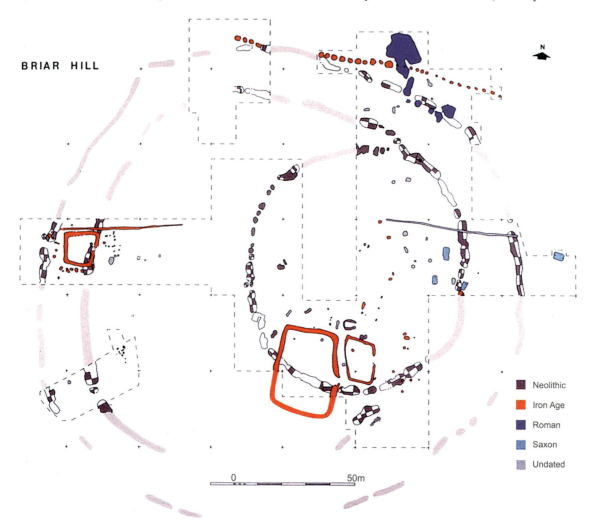

BRIAR HILL

N

Neolithic
Iron Age
Roman
Saxon
Undated

0   50m

Fig 5: Plan of the Briar Hill causewayed enclosure, showing the successive phases of occupation from Neolithic to Anglo-Saxon
(drawn by Andy Chapman)

Fig 6: Cleaning of the weathered ironstone surface at Briar Hill with the photographic quadrupod tower to the left (photo by Andy Chapman)

Fig 7: The bath-suite hypocaust of the Romano-British villa at Hunsbury

shots to aid site planning; on Briar Hill the cleaned subsoil was photographed in units of 4 x 4m using a 7.5m high collapsible quadrupod tower, modelled on a prototype of Philip Mayes, with a hoist and self-levelling plate for the twin reflex camera which was operated by an air-release cable (Fig 6). The square black and white photographs produced were printed at 1:40 and assembled into a mosaic, to form a key component of the planning system.

The weathered ironstone subsoil made it a difficult site to excavate but Helen Bamford and her team teased out the subtleties of the recutting of the interrupted ditch system by excavating opposing quadrants to provide both longitudinal and transverse sections of the ditch segments.

Less extensive excavations and watching briefs were undertaken in both the Eastern and Southern Districts and salvage recording was carried out on the site of the Romano-British small town at Duston and on the bath suite of a small Romano-British villa at Hunsbury (Fig 7), the villa proper being partly excavated subsequently. Notes on all this work can be found in the various issues of *Northamptonshire Archaeology* and in the Royal Commission on Historical Monuments *Archaeological Sites and Churches in Northampton* (RCHM 1985).

My first foray into medieval archaeology in Northampton itself was in 1972 in respect of Greyfriars, the medieval Franciscan house north-east of the Market Square, on the site to be developed for the Greyfriars Shopping Centre and the new bus station (Williams 1978). While archaeological levels survived well below the 19th-century streets, the adjoining street frontages had unfortunately been heavily cellared. A lasting memory, however, is that of arriving on a Monday morning, after a successful open day at the weekend, to discover the site robbed of the medieval encaustic tiles that had been on view in situ.

The view of the Greyfriars site (Fig 8) demonstrates one of the problems of excavating in some parts of

Northampton (but contrasts with the much less disturbed St Peters Street), with deep Victorian or earlier post-medieval cellars cutting down through and destroying earlier archaeological deposits on either side of the streets where stratigraphy was better preserved. Certainly it made interpretation of the friary remains more difficult.

In 1972–3 trial trenching was undertaken to the north of St Peter's Street with encouraging results. There was an absence of cellarage to disturb the archaeological levels and it was decided to excavate the frontages to the north and south of the street and thereby investigate the development of a medieval urban neighbourhood. The remains of ten medieval plots with their associated houses and other structures were revealed (Fig 9 and see the double-page spread: Archaeology and the Changing Face of Northampton) but more exciting was the uncovering of late Saxon settlement and then three middle Anglo-Saxon mortar mixers, the first to be recognised as such (Williams J H 1979; Williams *et al*, this volume, 25–77), and other remains of the same date. The excavations lasted from June 1973 through to June 1974.

As a result of the pre-Conquest discoveries a policy decision was made to prioritise the investigation of sites in the south-west quadrant of the town in order to reveal as clearly as possible the layout, chronology and dynamics

Archaeology and the Changing Face of Northampton (i)

1973

2018

1 St Peter's church 2 Hazelrigg House 3 St Peter's Street excavations 1972-82
4 The Green excavations 1983 5 Marefair excavations 1977
6 Chalk Lane excavations 1975-78 7 Northampton Castle excavations 1961-64
8 Black Lion public house 9 Gregory Street excavation 1978 10 St Gregory's church
11 Green Street excavations 1995-96 12 Riverside development zone
13 Barclaycard House/Sol Central 14 Northampton Station excavations 2013

Archaeology and the Changing Face of Northampton (ii)

The designation of Northampton as a New Town would have a considerable impact on both the surrounding countryside and the historic core of the town. Apart from the churches of St Peter, All Saints, the Holy Sepulchre and St Giles, and St John's hospital no medieval standing structures had survived, largely as a result of a series of fires that devastated the town, including those of 1516 and 1675. The castle had also largely been levelled for the (Castle) Station in the late 19th century. Nonetheless the grain of the medieval town in its historic street plan, as recorded in 1610 on John Speed's map of Northampton (RCHM 1985, 51) had survived into the 20th century and key elements of it, such as Market Square, still conjure up the past. The medieval core of the town is, however, now bisected north-south by the Horsemarket dual carriageway and east-west by a multi-storey car-park and the vacant site of the former Greyfriars bus station.

In the south-west of the town, the focus of the pre-Norman Conquest settlement, the St Peter's Way dual carriageway was a major intrusion in 1959, but changes to the urban fabric in the last fifty years, excepting the Barclaycard House/Sol Central development, which although substantial fitted into the existing street grid, have been more subtle but nonetheless significant. It is interesting to compare an air-photograph taken in 1973 at the start of the St Peter's Street excavations with today's Google Earth view (see facing page) and reflect not only on the appearance of this quarter but also on the programme of archaeological work by NDC in the 1970s and 80s, and continuing to today.

The sole surviving historic buildings are the fine Norman church of St Peter (**1**) and the elegant 17th-century mansion of Hazelrigg House (**2**). Excavations commenced in St Peter's Street (**3**) in 1973, while buildings were still standing on the south side of the street (as on the aerial view). Investigations continued to the south and then to the north in 1976 and 1980-82; high-status middle Anglo-Saxon timber and stone halls were uncovered.

To the north of Marefair (**5**), where there is today green space, more Anglo-Saxon and medieval structures were found in 1977.

Further work to the south of St Peter's Street in 1983, at The Green, revealed remains of a 15th- to 17th-century tannery (**4**). The whole of this area is now occupied by offices and housing.

In Chalk Lane (**6**) council offices were cleared and Anglo-Saxon levels excavated in 1975-78, partly beneath the levelled bailey bank of Northampton castle. Castle remains surviving to the north had been investigated in the early 1960s (**7**). The site is currently a car-park with the area to the north under grass. To the west of the Black Lion public house (**8**), Anglo-Saxon and medieval levels were revealed in 1982 ahead of development for offices. Redevelopment was also anticipated on both sides of Gregory Street (**9**). Excavations to the south in 1978-9 uncovered late Saxon timber buildings as well as middle Anglo-Saxon graves, which suggest that St Gregory's church to the north (**10**) was in existence at this time. The site, now partly a car park, is crucial for understanding Anglo-Saxon Northampton and thorough investigation is essential if development eventually materialises.

Archaeological work continued following the winding up of the NDC in 1984. At Green Street (**11**) in 1995-6 late Saxon and medieval defences were discovered, and these would continue into the proposed new Riverside development (**12**). Excavations prior to the replacement of Barclaycard House by Sol Central in 2002 (**13**) were limited in scale, but did uncover important Anglo-Saxon remains, and more should still be preserved on the site. Although the coming of the railway removed much of Northampton castle, excavations in 2013 (**14**) prior to the building of a new station, have revealed buildings within the outer bailey as well as earlier, late Saxon features.

Today the historic landscape of south-west Northampton may be largely an imagined one, but St Peter's church stands proud as a reminder of former glories and archaeology still has important tales to tell.

Fig 8: The Greyfriars site in the final phase of excavations in 1972, looking west, with Princess Street to the south (left), Albert Street to the east (foreground) and trenches along Greyfriars Street (centre). Part of the Greyfriars church lay under Princess Street and one of the claustral ranges was below Greyfriars Street; the two trenches visible there were the survivors of a line of four

of the pre-Norman Conquest settlement over an extended area (see the double-page spread: Archaeology and the Changing Face of Northampton). Excavations were therefore undertaken, in response to perceived development pressures, in Chalk Lane in 1975–8 (Williams and Shaw, 1981), Marefair in 1977 (Williams F 1979), Gregory Street in 1978 (Williams 1982, 22–24), St Peters Gardens, really an extension northwards of the St Peter's Street excavations, in 1980–2 (Williams *et al* 1985), Black Lion Hill in 1982 (Shaw 1985) and the Green 1983 (Shaw 1996; Shaw this volume, 257–304). Of major significance was the discovery of two further mortar mixers and the large, middle Anglo-Saxon, high-status, timber and stone halls (see Williams *et al*, this volume, 25–77) but the work more generally extended our knowledge of pre-Conquest Northampton. The stone hall is still without parallel in this country. The excavation of the middle Anglo-Saxon levels was particularly challenging. Considerable patience, a keen eye and a ready feel for subtle textural variations in the archaeological deposits was needed to distinguish the orange-brown weathered ironstone infill of a construction trench for a timber building from the orange-brown weathered ironstone subsoil into which the rapidly infilled trench had been cut.

In addition to the investigations in the south-west quarter of the town smaller-scale work was undertaken elsewhere within medieval Northampton (see various reports and notes in *Northamptonshire Archaeology*). On the margins of the south-west quarter, these works included the salvage

recording of a Saxo-Norman Northampton ware kiln site during road improvements to Horsemarket in 1971, and the uncovering, during the widening of Horseshoe Street in 1974, of a medieval stone building filled with charnel lying some 60m north-east of church of St Gregory (Williams 1982, 48, fig 33).

The 1970s were a period of intense 'rescue' archaeology nationally and there was considerable debate about the value of excavating sites just because they were threatened, the most frequently cited case being that of investigating areas of intercutting medieval rubbish pits. A conscious attempt was made in Northampton to place development-led archaeology within a research framework. It is disappointing to me in this respect that in the excavations at the Sol Central site in 1998–2002 middle Anglo-Saxon levels were only selectively reached, within areas where construction impact could clearly be anticipated (Miller *et al*, 2005). It is very much a key site and it is to be hoped that such levels have survived beneath the massive superstructure, to be investigated in advance of the next development cycle on the site: certainly that must be the assumption. Another massively important site is that of St Gregory's church on the south side of Marefair. Thorough archaeological investigation is absolutely essential in advance of any development in order to clarify the interpretation and context of the middle Anglo-Saxon halls to the east of St Peter's church.

Fig 9: The north side of St Peter's Street in 1973, looking west, showing the walls of 15th-century houses

Post-excavation work and publication

Publication of the results of the archaeological work both within the town and also the surrounding area was seen to be important from the start and NDC created its own monograph series for major sites (Fig 10) (Bamford 1985; Willliams 1974; Williams J H 1979; Williams *et al* 1985), as well as supporting the newly formed Northamptonshire Archaeological Society through placing a succession of excavation reports within *Northamptonshire Archaeology*. Members of the archaeological team also worked closely with the staff of the Royal Commission on Historical Monuments to produce *An Inventory of Archaeological Sites and Churches in Northampton* (RCHM 1985).

In terms of post-excavation work mention should be made of the medieval pottery type series devised by Mike McCarthy and subsequently developed and enhanced by Mary Gryspeerdt and Varian Denham, which, with refinement, is still being used, a testament to the initial rigour of the work (see also Shaw in Williams *et al* this volume, 57–63). Collaboration with the University of Bradford's Department of Archaeology saw neutron activation analysis of St Neots type ware, investigation of organic residues in medieval pottery and computer seriation of flint data from Briar Hill undertaken by means of MA dissertations and CASE studentships, NDC sponsoring two of

the latter. At the same time thought was being given to the analysis of the stratigraphic sequence using what was commonly referred to as the Winchester or Harris matrix (Harris 1979). While the technique has developed subsequently and is now commonplace, the St Peter's Street volume (Williams J H 1979) was a very early demonstration of the practical and, indeed, the non-computer-aided use of the stratigraphic matrix.

It is perhaps easy to forget in the current digital world the laborious nature of archaeological recording, analysis and reporting in earlier times. Only towards the end of the lifespan of NDC were relatively simple computers beginning to make an appearance, with a single BBC B computer with 64k RAM and 100k floppy discs being utilised for simple word-processing. Perhaps recognising the times and as an aid to the employment prospects of its staff after its forthcoming demise, NDC arranged for those interested to undertake the City and Guilds certificate in computer literacy, the syllabus including some BASIC programming.

Understanding medieval Northampton could not be achieved solely through archaeology and there is a need to look at the documentary record. We were very fortunate to have the benefit of courses in palaeography at the University of Leicester's Adult Education Centre in Barrack Road provided by Professor Geoffrey Martin, a specialist in urban history who subsequently became Keeper of the Public Records. It was only in retirement, however, twenty years after leaving Northampton that the full fruits of this work saw the light of day in a publication through the Northamptonshire Record Society (Williams 2014).

The NDC also promoted more widely the work of the archaeological team, and indeed Northampton's rich historic past. An exhibition was created for an initial showing at the Northampton Show of 1979, coinciding with the launch of the publication of *Northampton – The First 6000 Years* (Williams and Bamford 1979) (Figs 10 & 11). The display subsequently transferred to Northampton's Central Museum and Art Gallery before a two-month stay at Birmingham Museum and Art Gallery. The NDC also provided funding towards a new display gallery at the Central Museum and Art Gallery, which remains in place within the new extended museum that opened in 2021. *Saxon and Medieval Northampton* was another publication for a non-specialist audience (Williams 1982).

Some further thanks and reflections

It would be difficult to mention all permanent, semi-permanent and temporary staff who contributed to the work of the NDC, not forgetting the many specialists who, sometimes without payment, reported on various categories of finds. In addition to those referred to previously in the text Andrew Boddington, Andy Chapman, Christine and Dave Farwell, Richard Hunter, Mike Shaw, Frances Williams and Tim Yates led or supervised projects in the field, Gwynne Oakley was responsible for finds processing and we were lucky to have the fine drafting skills of Ken Connor for publication drawings and reconstructions; he

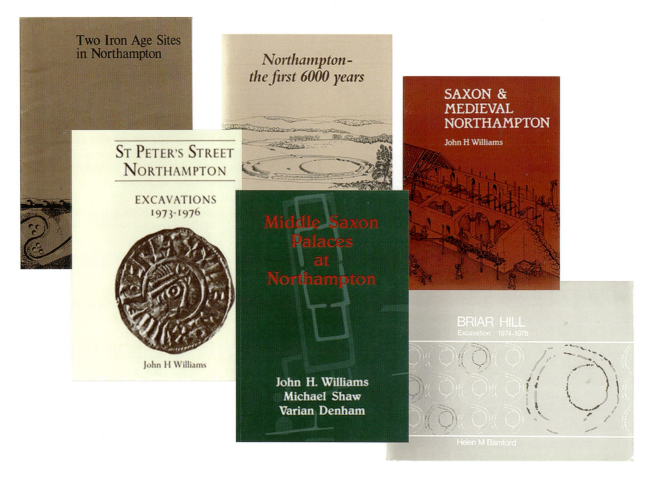

Fig 10: Monographs and other publications produced by Northampton Development Corporation

Fig 11: The NDC funded an exhibition display seen here at the Northampton Show in 1979 housed in its own tent

also with painstaking care chipped away with hammer and chisel the various layers of mortar mixer 3, thereby unravelling its mysteries. Their skill, dedication and good humour bring back many fond memories.

Today, when public sector archaeology is becoming increasingly under pressure, it is also pleasing to recall the ongoing support of the NDC board, chief officers and staff more generally at a pioneering time in development-led archaeology. Their help and, in many cases, their enthusiasm for a vision of a new Northampton which at the same time embraced its important history, helped to make things happen and this indeed provides important lessons for the present.

Bibliography

Bamford, H M, 1985 *Briar Hill, Excavation 1974–1978,* NDC Archaeological Monog, **3**

Barty-King, H, 1985 *Expanding Northampton,* Secker & Warburg

Brown, C, 1990 *Northampton 1835–1985, Shoe Town, New Town,* Phillimore

Chapman, A, 2015a Forty years of Northamptonshire Archaeological Society and its journal *Northamptonshire Archaeol,* **38**, 23–8

Chapman, A, 2015b A short history of Northamptonshire Archaeology, *Northamptonshire Archaeol,* **38**, 29–38

Harris, E C, 1979 *Principles of Archaeological Stratigraphy,* Academic Press

Hedges, J, 1977 Development control and archaeology, *in* Rowley and Breakell 1977, 32–51

Heighway, C, (ed) 1972 *The Erosion of History: archaeology and planning in towns: a study of historic towns affected by modern development in England, Wales and Scotland,* Council for British Archaeology

Hunter, R, and Mynard, D, 1977 Excavations at Thorplands near Northampton, 1970 and 1974 *Northamptonshire Archaeol,* **12**, 97–154

Jones, B, 1984 *Past imperfect: the story of rescue archaeology*, Heinemann Educational Books

Miller, P, Wilson, T, with Harward, C, 2005 *Saxon, medieval and post-medieval settlement at Sol Central, Marefair, Northampton*, MoLAS Monog, **27**

Moore, R, 2015 The development of archaeology in Northamptonshire to 1980 *Northamptonshire Archaeol*, **38**, 5–22

Planning Proposals 1968 *Expansion of Northampton – Planning Proposals*

RCHM 1985 *An Inventory of the Historical Monuments in the County of Northampton, Volume V, Archaeological Sites and Churches in Northampton*, Royal Commission on Historical Monuments England

Rowley, R T, and Breakell, M, (eds) 1977 *Planning and the Historic Environment, II, papers presented to a conference in Oxford, 1977, Oxford*

Shaw, M, 1985 Excavations on a Saxon and medieval site at Black Lion Hill. *Northamptonshire Archaeol*, **20**, 113–38

Shaw, M, 1996 The excavation of a late 15th- to 17th-century tanning complex at The Green, Northampton, *Post-medieval Archaeol*, **30**, 63–127

Shaw, M, 2021 Excavations at The Green, Northampton, 1983: the Anglo-Saxon and medieval phases, *Northamptonshire Archaeol*, **41**, 257–304

Williams, F, 1979 Excavations on Marefair, Northampton, 1977, *Northamptonshire Archaeol*, **14**, 38–79

Williams, J H, (ed) 1974 *Two Iron Age Sites in Northampton*, NDC Archaeological Monog, **1**

Williams, J H, 1977 Planning and the historic environment in a new town, *in* Rowley and Breakell 1977, 65–74

Williams, J H, 1978 Excavations at Greyfriars, Northampton 1972 *Northamptonshire Archaeol*, **13**, 96–160

Williams, J H, 1979 *St Peter's Street, Northampton, Excavations 1973–1976*, NDC Archaeological Monog, **2**

Williams, J H, 1982 *Saxon and Medieval Northampton*, Northampton Development Corporation

Williams, J H, 2014 *Town and Crown: the Governance of Later Thirteenth-Century Northampton*, Northamptonshire Record Society

Williams, J H, and Bamford, H, 1979 *Northampton – The first 6000 years*, Northampton Development Corporation

Williams, J H, and Shaw, M, 1981 Excavations in Chalk Lane, Northampton, 1975–1978 *Northamptonshire Archaeol*, **16**, 87–135

Williams, J H, Shaw, M, and Denham, V, 1985 *Middle Saxon Palaces at Northampton*, NDC Archaeological Monog, **4**

Williams, J H, Shaw, M, and Chapman, A, 2020 Anglo-Saxon Northampton Revisited, *Northamptonshire Archaeol*, **41**, 25–77

Unless otherwise stated photographs in this paper are by the author

Northamptonshire Archaeology, **41**, 2021, 17–24

Prehistoric Northampton: A circular ring ditch and flint scatters

by

Andy Chapman

Summary

An arc of ditch excavated at St Peter's Street in the 1970s may have been part of a ring ditch with an internal diameter of c.23m, probably dating to the Late Neolithic/ Early Bronze Age and either an Early Bronze Age round barrow or some other form of Late Neolithic/Early Bronze Age monument. The ditch fills produced small scraps of pottery and a small mixed flint assemblage, while the snail assemblage indicated the presence of local scrub or woodland. A complete but damaged collared urn, buried 35m to the east within a shallow depression, may have been an accessory vessel to a lost satellite cremation burial. A small flint assemblage from the excavations at Northampton Station in 2013 is described and related to more extensive flint scatters from nearby sites and at Duston to the west. The assemblages indicate a specific Mesolithic presence at Chalk Lane, but also span the Neolithic to Early Bronze Age. It is suggested that these concentrations of flint to the north of the river Nene may define parts of a zone of enhanced flint deposition centred on the Briar Hill causewayed enclosure to the south of the river. They may at least partly derive from periodic temporary gatherings of people in the vicinity of the enclosure. It has previously been postulated by the author that there were similar zones of enhanced flint deposition around the Dallington causewayed enclosure, Northampton, and the Cardington causewayed enclosure, Bedford.

Introduction

The urban centre of Northampton is an unlikely location for the survival of significant evidence of Neolithic and Bronze Age activity, and particularly so within the Anglo-Saxon town where there is more than a thousand years of continuous occupation. However, two notable occurrences are described in this paper. Firstly, a length of curving ditch located during the St Peter's Street excavations in the mid-1970s (Williams 1979) may have been the eastern side of a circular ring ditch monument of the Late Neolithic to Early Bronze Age, the mid-3rd to mid-2nd millennium BC (NGR SP 7500 6037). Secondly, excavations at this western end of town, overlooking the main course of the river Nene to the south and a major tributary to the west, have produced significant quantities of worked flint ranging in date from the Mesolithic through the Neolithic to the Late Neolithic/Early Bronze Age. The most recent assemblage, from excavations within the outer bailey of Northampton Castle in 2013, the

site of the new railway station, is described in detail (NGR SP 7477 6043), while the later periods of activity are also described in this volume (Chapman 79–127 and 191–255). Other assemblages from the area are summarised and quantified before providing a possible explanation for the density of deposition in this area.

The broader environs of the Borough of Northampton include three major monuments of the Neolithic to Early Bronze Age. There is a Neolithic causewayed enclosure at Dallington Grange (SP 725 635), largely unexcavated, lying on the limits of the modern borough to the west of the town (Chapman 2019), but this is too distant to relate to contemporary material from the historic town centre. To the south of the river on the south-western margins of the town at Banbury Lane (SP 725582), a triple-ring ditch system of the Middle Neolithic contained a pit filled with disarticulated human bone from more than 150 individuals, forming the largest mortuary assemblage of this date from the UK (Yates *et al* 2012). This site lies close to the Wootton Brook, but is hidden from the town centre by the slopes of Hunsbury Hill to the north-east.

This leaves a single known prehistoric monument that would have been visible from the area of the historic town centre, and that is the Neolithic causewayed enclosure at Briar Hill (SP 736592), on the lower slopes below the Iron Age hillfort of Hunsbury Hill (Bamford 1985). This enclosure was a focal point from the Early Neolithic to Early Bronze Age. A Middle Bronze Age cremation cemetery within the encircling ditch systems indicates its continuing importance after active maintenance and recutting of the ditches had been abandoned. The Briar Hill enclosure lay some 1.6km south-west of St Peter's church directly facing Upton and Duston on the northern slopes of the Nene valley, where there were further concentrations of worked flint spread over an extensive area at a distance of around 1.2km.

Acknowledgements

The impetus for this short study has been the work of John Williams and Michael Shaw in reassessing the evidence for the Anglo-Saxon origins of Northampton, including the church and hall complex focussed on the area around St Peter's church, as published in this volume (Williams *et al* 25–77), which has drawn attention to a length of prehistoric ditch at St Peter's Street.

Much of the evidence quoted derives from the work of the Northampton Development Corporation (NDC)

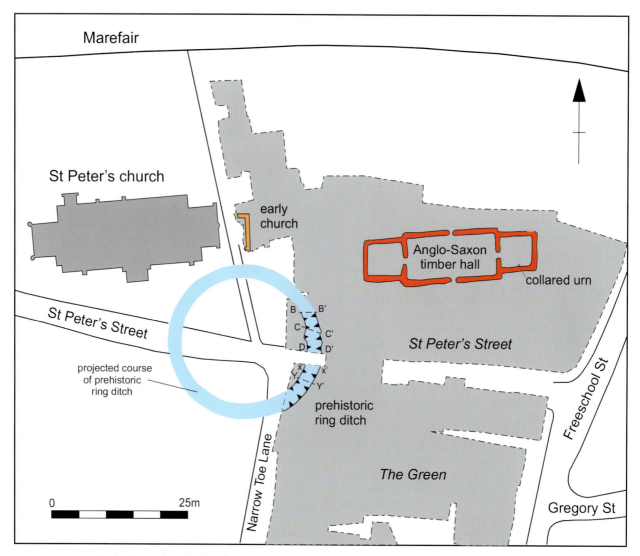

Fig 1: The prehistoric ring ditch in relation to St Peter's church and the Middle Saxon timber hall

Archaeological Unit, which was led by John Williams from the early 1970s to the mid-1980s (Williams this volume 5–15). The paper draws on and summarises evidence from the original excavation reports by the NDC, including flint and prehistoric pottery reports by Helen Bamford and Jon Humble. The analysis of the small flint assemblage from recent work at Northampton Station within the outer bailey of Northampton Castle was conducted by the author for Northamptonshire Archaeology, with the report prepared under its successor, MOLA (Museum of London Archaeology) Northampton. Illustrations are by Andy Chapman, modified from original sources.

The prehistoric ring ditch at St Peter's Street

The ring ditch

At the western end of the St Peter's Street excavation, a length of curvilinear ditch appears to have a formed a 100° sector (c.28%) of a probable circular ring ditch with a projected internal diameter of c.23m (Fig 1: Williams 1979, figs, 7, 8, 41 and 74). The ditch was 2.7–3.2m wide and up to 1.4m deep. It had a U-shaped profile; a flat base 1.5m wide and steep sides with later erosion of the upper edges. The single section that does not show a recut (Fig 2, Section B-B'), at the northern end of the excavated length, shows the western inner edge as the more heavily eroded, and a similar pattern is evident, if less clearly so, in the other sections. This indicates that there was a more rapid accumulation of primary fill against the outer edge of the ditch, which might suggest the presence of an external bank, as in a classic henge of the Late Neolithic/ Early Bronze Age.

The primary fills comprised sands and fine shaley ironstone, and minimal limestone. One section (Fig 2, C-C') shows a narrow steep-sided recut from the top of the lower secondary fill, with the ditch still a substantial earthwork, while two sections further south, X-X' and Y-Y', show a recut from a much higher level, through upper secondary fill, and section D-D' appears to show successive recuts both from high in the fills. However, the sections are all consistent in the nature of the recut as being fully within the original ditch, narrow and steep-sided, c.0.8m wide at the base and perhaps 1.2m wide at the top, with later erosion of the upper edges, and bottoming either on or a little above the base of the original ditch. Having recognised the presence of the recut during excavation of the northern half of the arc, on the southern half it was possible to excavate the recut as a separate feature.

The fills of the recut again comprised sands and shalely ironstone, but they also contained quantities of limestone up to large blocks, which would not have been available from the immediately local geology. This suggests that limestone had been brought to site, most likely to form a revetment to the sides of a bank or mound set close to the ditch. The disposition of the limestone does not clearly indicate which side of the ditch it has come from; with section C-C' showing an accumulation against the inner edge of the recut and section D-D' an accumulation against the outer edge. The evidence for the location of an adjacent bank or of a central mound is therefore both uncertain and equivocal, but it seems likely that one or the other would have existed.

The minute sherds of pottery from the ditch fills could not be dated. Of the total site flint assemblage of 176 pieces, 25 were from the ditch fills, and the general concentration of residual flint was across the western half of the site around and above the ring ditch (H Bamford in Williams 1979, 290–295. The overall analysis indicated that it was not a homogeneous group; with some probable Mesolithic material although the bulk of the assemblage was broadly Neolithic including implement types dating to the Late Neolithic/Early Bronze Age.

A good snail assemblage from the fills was of shade loving species, with open-county forms absent (J G Evans in Williams 1979, 338–39), indicating that the area was probably covered with dense scrub or woodland, with little disturbance by agriculture: a landscape most appropriate for a context pre-dating the Iron Age.

A further flint assemblage of similar size, 158 worked flints, was recovered from the adjacent site, St Peter's Gardens, and also showed a general concentration across the western half of the site, closest to the ring ditch (J L Humble in Williams et al 1985, 71). This assemblage also contained a Mesolithic element, and two of the four other classifiable implements, a waisted tool and a straight-edged flake knife, were types found only in Late Neolithic/Early Bronze Age contexts.

A collared urn from St Peter's Gardens

An almost complete Early Bronze Age collared urn was found lying on its side in a shallow depression, 0.48m diameter by 0.14m deep, beneath the eastern annex of the Middle Saxon timber hall (Fig 1). The uppermost portion of the neck and collar were missing, presumably as a result of later ground disturbance, indicating that it had been deposited as a complete vessel (J L Humble in Williams et al 1985; 46, fig 29, loose plan of Trench AA: Phase, and Microfiche).

The urn stands 161mm high, with the mouth 135mm in diameter, the shoulder 147mm in diameter and the base 71mm in diameter (Fig 3). The exterior and the interior of the neck are brown, and the remainder of the interior

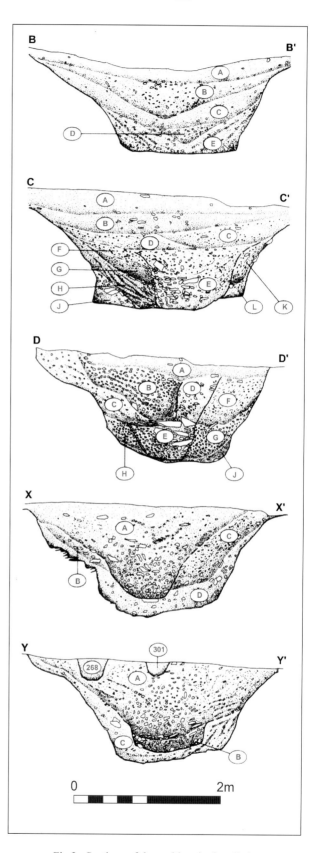

Fig 2: Sections of the prehistoric ring ditch

Fig 3: The Early Bronze Age collared urn from
St Peter's Garden

grey. The collar is 41mm deep, decorated with multiple lines of incised herringbone motif. The elongated neck/upper body is 45mm deep, decorated with upright filled triangles and smaller inverted filled triangles filling the gaps, all incised most probably with the same implement as used on the collar. The shoulder/carination is decorated with a row of fingertip impressions, most of which include a crescentic groove from a fingernail impression. The lower body is undecorated. The vessel can be described as a tripartite Form II collared urn of the primary series (Longworth 1984, 21, 27).

It would seem likely that the collared urn had served as an accessory vessel to a nearby but lost cremation burial of the Early Bronze Age, which was probably a satellite burial to the ring ditch monument 35m to the west.

The St Peter's Street prehistoric monument; discussion

While the evidence is far from clear-cut, it does seem likely that the ring ditch at St Peter's Street would probably broadly date to the Late Neolithic/Early Bronze Age (c.2500–1500BC), with nearby activity within this date range evidenced by the collared urn of the Early Bronze Age from the St Peter's Garden excavations.

The worked flint assemblages from St Peter's Street and St Peter's Gardens total 334 pieces. The distribution is concentrated towards the western end of both sites, which suggests deposition was focussed on and around the ring ditch. As discussed below, the worked flint spans a wide range of dates, including a Mesolithic element, some earlier Neolithic material and continuing into the Early Bronze Age. At least the Mesolithic material must be residual, pre-dating the ring ditch. The same is probably also true of the early Neolithic component, although the size of this group cannot be accurately estimated, leaving

only the Late Neolithic/Early Bronze Age element as contemporary with the monument itself.

Given the imprecise dating of the ring ditch, it is difficult to characterise the form of this monument. The steep-sided U-shaped ditch is more characteristic of the Neolithic, with Early Bronze Age round barrow ditches tending to be more V-shaped. The suggestion from the differential erosion of the upper edges of ditch suggested the possibility of an external bank, but the ditch fills provided no support for this supposition. Also, the projected internal diameter of 23m is on the large size for a single ditch round barrow, but far from impossibly so.

One possibility is that this was a henge monument of the Late Neolithic/Early Bronze Age, but this monument type is uncommon in Northamptonshire. The only excavated example at Priors Hall, Corby (Chapman and Jones 2012), was 32m in diameter with an entrance to the south-east, and clear indication in the ditch fills of the former presence of an external bank. However, in recent years excavations in the Midland counties have been finding continuous ring ditch monuments, typically dating to the Early Bronze Age, c.2000–1500BC, which do not appear to be round barrows, although there may be associated, but not central, burials. They appear to be allied to the henge tradition while not necessarily possessing either single or opposing entrances or external banks. These are often classed as hengiform monuments, but they really demand classification as a distinct regional form, perhaps in much the same way as the early Neolithic oval mortuary enclosures of the Nene valley, as seen at Grendon, Tansor, Aldwincle (Chapman 2012a, fig 3) and Peterborough, Orton Meadows (Mackreth 2020), are allied to but distinct from the long barrow tradition, and also deserve to be recognised as a distinct regional group.

There are examples of such continuous ring ditches from Wasperton, Warwickshire in the west, where the southern ring ditch was 23m in diameter, with a U-shaped ditch 3.5–6.5m wide by 1.7m deep (Hughes and Crawford 1995), to Bedford in the east with a U-shaped ring ditch, c.33m in diameter and up to 1.5m deep and 5–6m wide as a result of heavy erosion of the upper edges in a sandy natural, with a mortuary pit set just inside the ditch (Chapman and Chapman 2017, figs 2.1 & 2.5).

Lacking further evidence for this particular example, no firm conclusion can be reached, leaving the St Peter's Street ring ditch as of probable Late Neolithic/Early Bronze Age date and either a round barrow burial mound or another monument form, perhaps serving a similar role to classic henge monuments.

Flint scatters in the environs of the Briar Hill causewayed enclosure

Worked flint from excavations at Northampton Station 2013

A total of 46 struck flints (Table 1) were recovered from the excavation at Northampton Station in 2013 (Chapman this volume 79–127 and 191–255). They came from a wide range of contexts typically in small numbers. The pre-castle buried soil produced 16 flints, with 13 of these, over a quarter of the total (28.3%), from deposit (206), the only extensive area of the buried soil taken down by hand, using mattock and spade, with most of the rest removed by machine excavation. This indicates that if more of the buried soil had been removed by hand the quantity of recovered flint would have increased significantly.

Table 1: Quantification of flint by period context

Context type	Period	Total	%
Soil horizon	Pre-castle	16	34.8
Other contexts	Pre-castle	18	39.1
All contexts	*Pre-castle*	*34*	*73.9*
All contexts	*Castle*	*11*	*23.9*
U/S		*1*	*2.2*
Total		46	

Thirty-four flints (73.9%), came from pre-castle deposits, and 11 (23.9%) from medieval castle deposits, indicating that the major disturbance of the pre-existing soils occurred in the pre-castle period, with the material in the medieval castle deposits probably largely derived from further re-deposition through disturbance of the pre-castle deposits. A similar distribution of residual flint through deposits of later periods has been seen at other sites in the town.

The flint assemblage

The raw material is typically vitreous flint, with the occasional piece opaque and stony. The colour is usually brown to grey-brown or grey to grey-black. As noted with other local flint assemblages from the county, brown-coloured flint appears most frequently on diagnostic pieces dating to the Early Neolithic, such as blades derived from prepared blade cores, but rarely on items likely to date to the Late Neolithic/Early Bronze Age. This apparent Early Neolithic preference for paler brown flint has also been noted at Irchester Roman town, Chester Farm, where targeted excavations examined a soil horizon beneath the Roman level that produced Late Mesolithic and Early Neolithic assemblages with a significant proportion manufactured in brown flint (Chapman 2012b).

Cores and core rejuvenation flakes provide an unusually high proportion of the material at 10.8% (Table 2); at the Briar Hill causewayed enclosure they formed 6.9% of a large primary assemblage (Bamford 1985, 63, table 4). This suggests that knapping was being carried out at this location. A core rejuvenation flake is struck from a large blade core in grey flint, 60mm long, of the Early Neolithic, with the flake detached from the opposite end to a prepared platform from which long narrow blades had been struck. The two cores are both small, at 20mm and 30mm long, typical of Late Neolithic/Early Bronze Age flint working, using local flint from the river gravels to produce small squat flakes.

Flakes form the largest group, at 41.3%. While many of these are squat and irregular, suggesting a Late Neolithic/Early Bronze Age date, some were evidently from prepared blade cores. Of particular interest is a blade-like flake, 65mm long, which tapered to a rounded end but

had been struck from a blade core in grey flint. One edge has random edge damage and the other has sparse edge damage but also finer worn edge 'damage', possibly a heavily used and worn serrated edge.

The smallest bladelet is 18mm long by 8mm wide, and many other blades are also small, with intact examples at 25–30mm long by 10–12mm wide, while others at up to 15mm wide are broken. Over half of the blades show extensive edge damage from use as cutting blades, and in some instances this use damage may obscure well-worn serrated edges; with serrated blades characteristic of Early Neolithic assemblages. Many of these small blades are in brown flint. Included with the blades is a parallel-sided rod, with a triangular section, 50mm long and 10mm wide.

The only identified tool is a side scraper, 30mm in diameter, although a further four pieces show some marginal edge retouch, with some of these broken and too incomplete to identify a tool type.

Table 2: The worked flint assemblage

Flint type	No	%
Core	2	4.3
Core rejuvenation flake	3	6.5
Flake	19	41.3
Flake utilised	1	2.2
Blade/bladelet	7	15.2
Blade/bladelet utilised	8	17.4
Scraper (side)	1	2.2
Misc. retouch	4	8.7
Shattered piece	1	2.2
Total	46	100.0

Chronology

The high percentage of blades, some of which were probably serrated, indicates an early date for a proportion of the assemblage. While many of the blades are small, it is suggested that this derives from the small size of the likely raw material, flint nodules obtained from the local glacial gravels often exposed along the river margins. None of these small blades exhibit fine microlithic-style retouch, so it is suggested that an Early Neolithic date is most appropriate, while the presence of small squat flakes indicates a continuation into the Late Neolithic/Early Bronze Age.

Other flint assemblages from Northampton

Larger assemblages of worked flint have been recovered from other excavations at the west end of Northampton, with a total of nearly 4000 pieces from seven excavations (Table 3).

At Chalk Lane, the most northerly site, on a levelled length of the Inner bailey bank of the castle, produced by far the greater part of the total, with 3123 worked flints recovered (Bamford in Williams and Shaw 1981, 126–130). This partly reflects the extensive area of buried subsoil that had been protected from later disturbance by virtue of the overlying castle bank, with much of this deposit also being excavated by hand. The buried soils at Chalk Lane parallel the buried soils at Northampton Station, at the south-western extremity of the castle site, where only a small area of buried soil was excavated by hand. The numerical disparity between Chalk Lane and the other sites was, therefore, partly but probably not totally, a product of differing site formation processes.

The Chalk Lane assemblage included a substantial group of Mesolithic microliths, 65, forming nearly a quarter (23.6%) of the total of 279 implements. This quantity probably denotes the presence of Mesolithic occupation here or directly nearby. The remainder of the implements comprise a few other probable Mesolithic forms, and a number of characteristic Late Neolithic/Early Bronze Age types, with this date range also confirmed by the presence of some Beaker pottery (Bamford in Williams and Shaw 1981, 108). Earlier Neolithic elements were scarce but present, with two possible leaf-shaped arrowheads and six serrated blades.

In addition to Chalk Lane, other sites in Northampton also produced some Mesolithic flints, as did Duston and the Briar Hill enclosure itself. However, of interest here is that the assemblages from the town also showed that flint deposition had been a long-term ongoing process from the Mesolithic/Early Neolithic through to the Late Neolithic/Early Bronze Age.

Worked flint from Duston

There is also a large assemblage of worked flint, including Mesolithic material, from around Duston, some 1.7km to the west of the town centre (RCHME 1985, 28–38).

"Between 1904 and 1912 approximately 25,000 worked flints, including retouched implements, flakes, blades and cores were collected from topsoil over about 70 hectares, chiefly S. of the Weedon Road. The exact provenance of many of these finds is not recorded, but the greatest concentration appears

to have been within an area around SP 731605. The retouched implements in Northampton Museum known or thought to have come from this site are types diagnostic of Mesolithic, Neolithic and Early Bronze Age industries. The number and density of finds indicate a domestic settlement or settlements from at least the Neolithic period onwards" (RCHME 1985, Microfiche catalogue: Duston, 249–251).

The Neolithic worked flint included leaf-shaped arrowheads, fragments of polished flint axes, and a polished stone axe of Group VI, from Great Langdale, Cumbria is probably also from this area. The specifically Late Neolithic/Early Bronze Age material includes barbed-and-tanged arrowheads, plano-convex and straight-edged knives, and also a perforated stone axehead.

The worked flint from the Briar Hill causewayed enclosure

A total of over four thousand worked flints were recovered during the partial excavation of the causewayed enclosure, with a further one thousand recovered from the overlying ploughsoil (Bamford 1985, 60–91). The site also produced seventeen flakes and fragments from Neolithic polished stone axes from Cornwall (1 flake); Great Langdale, Cumbria (14 flakes) and Craig Lwyd, Wales (1 large fragment), and part of a perforated hammer from Leicestershire.

The worked flint assemblage includes a Mesolithic component, with 18 microliths which are closely comparable to the microliths from both Chalk Lane and Duston, with some elements indicative of earlier Mesolithic industries and others of the later Mesolithic (Bamford 1985, 76). However, the bulk of the assemblage spans the Neolithic to Late Neolithic/Early Bronze Age, and a small group associated with the Middle Bronze Age cremation cemetery.

Table 3: Quantification of flint recovered from sites in Northampton

Site Name (Year)	Quantity	Comment	Date range
Chalk Lane (1975–78)	3123	9% from prehistoric features	Strong Mesolithic element Late Neolithic/Early Bronze Age
Marefair (1977)	269	69% from EM Saxon layers	Mesolithic-Early Bronze Age
Sol Central (1998–2002)	10		Neolithic-Early Bronze Age
St Peter's Street (1972–73)	176	25 (14%) from prehistoric ditch 31% from EM Saxon layers Concentrated at W end of site	Some Mesolithic element Mainly Neolithic
St Peter's Gardens 'The Palaces' (1980–82)	158	Concentrated at W end of site	Mesolithic element, Neolithic to Early Bronze Age
Black Lion Hill (1982)	46	All residual	Neolithic-Early Bronze Age
Northampton Station (2013)	46	74% from pre-Castle deposits and buried soil	Early Neolithic-Late Neolithic/EBA
Total	**3828**		
Briar Hill Causewayed enclosure (1974–78)	4359 1006	Excavation Ploughsoil collection	Mesolithic to Early Bronze Age

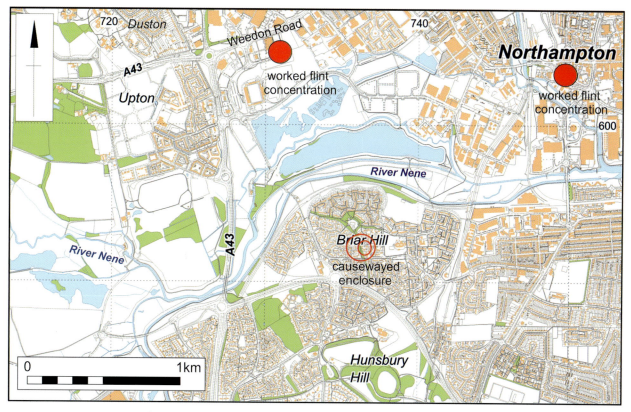

Fig 4: The Briar Hill causewayed enclosure in relation to the flint scatters

A zone of enhanced flint deposition

The author has previously argued that there were probably zones of enhanced flint deposition around both the Cardington causewayed enclosure, Bedford (Chapman and Chapman 2017, 137) and the Dallington causewayed enclosure, Northampton (Chapman 2019, 43–44). At Bedford the flint scatter, comprising 391 pieces, lay 1.5–2.1km west of the Cardington causewayed enclosure, largely occurring as residual finds on the eastern half of the site in features of Roman and later date but, most interestingly, not in association with large and small diameter ring ditches dated to the Early Bronze Age that lay on the western part of the site. Both of these Bedford sites also lay close to the Elstow Brook. At Dallington Grange the fills of a pit alignment 0.7–1.1km west of the causewayed enclosure produced 87 pieces of worked flint, presumably derived from a pre-existing surface scatter; while a comparable length of pit alignment and other features 1.6–1.9km north-west of the enclosure, at Harlestone Quarry, produced only 18 worked flints.

The suggestion from both Bedford and Dallington is that zones of enhanced flint deposition may have extended up to 1.5–2.0km from a focal causewayed enclosure, with local topography, including river courses and line of site being determining factors for variations in the maximum distance of enhanced deposition. The distances of around 1.2km and 1.6km from Duston and the west end of the town to the Briar Hill causewayed enclosure are in close agreement, although the location of fordable river crossings may have made the practical distances a little longer, but perhaps still within the 2km distance seen at Bedford.

At Northampton, a portion of all three flint scatters is of Mesolithic date, pre-dating the causewayed enclosure, so deposition at this date should be unrelated as the monument did not then exist: unless, of course, a pre-existing Mesolithic focus had influenced the choice of location for the Neolithic enclosure. That is another possible story to follow, but one that cannot be considered here.

It may be that the quantities of Neolithic to Early Bronze Age flint deposited at both Duston and around the west end of Northampton relate purely to local settlement. But if causewayed enclosures were, as is generally assumed, focal points in the landscape that attracted people from far and wide to periodic, perhaps seasonal, gatherings, then there does appear to be grounds to suggest that these unexpectedly high numbers of flint were perhaps at least partly the product of such periodic gatherings, marking what might be termed the temporary camp sites of those visiting the enclosure. Places at which flints were knapped, utilised and lost over the extended period of time, Early Neolithic to Early Bronze Age, around 2000 years, during which the enclosure was a major feature within the local landscape. Indeed, camping on the north flanks of the Nene valley, with a view of the enclosure on the southern flanks, would seem an ideal location.

Bibliography

Bamford, H, 1985 *Briar Hill: Excavation 1974–1978*, Northampton Development Corporation (NDC) Archaeol Monog, **3**

Chapman, A, 2012a Towards a new prehistory, *Northamptonshire Archaeol*, **37**, 7–18

Chapman, A, 2012b The worked flint, in I Meadow 2012, 43–45

Chapman, A, 2017 The worked flint, *in* A Chapman and P Chapman 2017, 40–46

Chapman, A, 2019 Flint distribution in the vicinity of the Dallington Neolithic Causewayed Enclosure, Northampton, *Northamptonshire Archaeol*, **40**, 33–45

Chapman, A, 2021a Late Saxon and Saxo-Norman occupation beneath the outer bailey of Northampton Castle, *Northamptonshire Archaeol*, **41**, 79–127

Chapman, A, 2021b Excavation within the Outer Bailey of Northampton Castle, 2013–15, *Northamptonshire Archaeol*, **41**, 191–255

Chapman, A, and Chapman, P, 2017 *Bronze Age Monuments and Bronze Age, Iron Age, Roman and Anglo-Saxon landscapes at Cambridge Road, Bedford*, Archaeopress Archaeol

Chapman, A, and Chapman, P, 2017 *Bronze Age Monuments and Bronze Age, Iron Age, Roman and Anglo-Saxon landscapes at Cambridge Road, Bedford*, Archaeopress Archaeol

Chapman, A, and Jones, C, 2012 An Early Bronze Age henge and a Middle Bronze Age ditch system at Priors Hall, Kirby Lane, Corby, *Northamptonshire Archaeol*, **37**, 37–67

Hughes, G, and Crawford, G, 1995 Excavations at Wasperton, Warwickshire 1980–1985, Introduction and Part 1: the Neolithic and Early Bronze Age, Trans of the Birmingham and Warwickshire Archaeol Soc, **99**, 9–45

Mackreth, D, 2020 *Prehistoric burials in Orton Meadows, Peterborough*, Nene Valley Archaeol Trust/East Anglian Archaeol, **173**

Meadows, I, 2012 *Targeted archaeological excavations at Chester Farm Irchester, Northamptonshire, September 2011*, Northamptonshire Archaeology report, **12/75**

RCHME 1985 *An Inventory of the Historical Monuments in the County of Northampton, V, An Inventory of Archaeological Sites and Churches in Northampton*, Royal Commission on Historical Monuments, England

Williams, J H, 1979 *St Peter's Street, Northampton: Excavations 1973–1976*, NDC Archaeol monog, **2**

Williams, J, 2021 Brave new World: Northampton Development Corporation and Archaeology 1970–85, *Northamptonshire Archaeol*, **41**, 5–15

Williams, J H, and Shaw, M, 1981 Excavations in Chalk Lane, Northampton, 1975–1978 *Northamptonshire Archaeol*, **16**, 87–135

Williams, J H, Shaw, M, and Chapman, A, 2021 Anglo-Saxon Northampton Revisited, *Northamptonshire Archaeol*, **41**, 25–77

Northamptonshire Archaeology, **41**, 2021, 25–77

Anglo-Saxon Northampton Revisited

by

John H Williams, Michael Shaw and Andy Chapman

Summary

The paper reviews archaeological work relating to the development of Anglo-Saxon Northampton during the past almost fifty years. A major series of excavations was undertaken between 1973 and 1982 to the north and south of Marefair, with further investigations, particularly to the east, being subsequently spread across the area enclosed by and immediately outside the medieval town walls. Early Anglo-Saxon settlement was represented by a few sunken-featured buildings. By the middle of the 8th century and possibly as early as the late 7th century a large timber hall was erected immediately to the east of St Peter's church, to be replaced, perhaps early in the 9th century, by an even more substantial stone hall, which remains without parallel in Anglo-Saxon England. Five mortar mixers were associated. Contemporary churches almost certainly lay to the west at St Peter's and to the east at St Gregory's. The paper reassesses the ongoing debate as to whether the complex represents a minster complex or a royal or high-status estate centre. The evidence for Danish occupation at the end of the 9th century and the subsequent development of Northampton in the late Saxon period is then considered. Three appendices look at: how an analysis of the distribution of the major pottery types of the period contributes to understanding the development of settlement at Northampton up to the Norman Conquest; whether advances in radiocarbon analysis and calibration can refine the previous chronology put forward for Anglo-Saxon Northampton; and how early medieval mortar mixers, first identified as such at Northampton, can now be seen to have a wide distribution both in Britain and continental Europe. An opportunity is taken to publish, for the first time in colour, photographs of a number of the most significant excavations.

Introduction

The early 1970s, following the establishment of an archaeological unit within Northampton Development Corporation (Williams 2021, this volume 5–15), saw the start of what has become a major ongoing programme of archaeological work within the town of Northampton, now approaching some fifty years. With the winding-up of the Development Corporation in 1985 the responsibility for investigation transferred to Northamptonshire County Council's archaeological unit. In the early 1990s, in the wake of the onset of commercial archaeology and competitive tendering, the unit, rebranded as

Northamptonshire Archaeology, continued its lead role, although other organisations including MoLAS (Museum of London Archaeology Service), Oxford Archaeology and Cotswold Archaeology also won a share of the contracts. Northamptonshire Archaeology remained within the county council until early 2015, when it was taken over by what was by then MOLA (Museum of London Archaeology), to become MOLA Northampton. The first two authors directed or were responsible for most of the significant excavations during the earlier part of this period and the third author, alongside Jim Brown and Iain Soden, continued the campaign within Northamptonshire Archaeology and MOLA Northampton.

While the work has almost entirely been generated by the development process, nonetheless an emphasis has been placed on seeking to maintain a research-based approach relating to the origins and early development of the town, and the results have certainly changed our perceptions of how Anglo-Saxon Northampton evolved. Considerable discussion has been stimulated, and it is still ongoing, particularly in respect of the status of the large timber and stone halls immediately to the east of St Peter's church, but also relating to the topographical development of the late Saxon town. With surprisingly limited comparative evidence from sites where one might expect to see a similar historical trajectory (cf Hall 1989; 2001) the debate will continue. Nonetheless, given that some significant work has been undertaken in the years since the last detailed synthesis it seems an appropriate time to revisit the town's early history, both critically appraising the Northampton data and seeking to draw on current thinking about Anglo-Saxon urban origins.

The main part of this paper is a synthetic review, bringing together the evidence from all the sites within and immediately outside the medieval town walls (Figs 1 and 2 and Table 1). As part of this work one of the authors has undertaken a quantitative analysis of key pottery types that are very much linked to the town's chronological development, and has demonstrated how this material underpins and reinforces the conclusions developed in the main body of the paper. A summary of the methodology and key outcomes are outlined in Appendix 1. With advances in the calibration of radiocarbon dates it is also appropriate to reconsider those obtained from Anglo-Saxon Northampton, in Appendix 2, with revised dates included in the main narrative. Northampton was the first site on which early medieval mechanical mortar mixers were recognised, since when their distribution can be seen to have extended across Europe, the main concentrations lying in Britain, southern Germany, Switzerland and Tuscany in Italy. As the literature relating to many of these

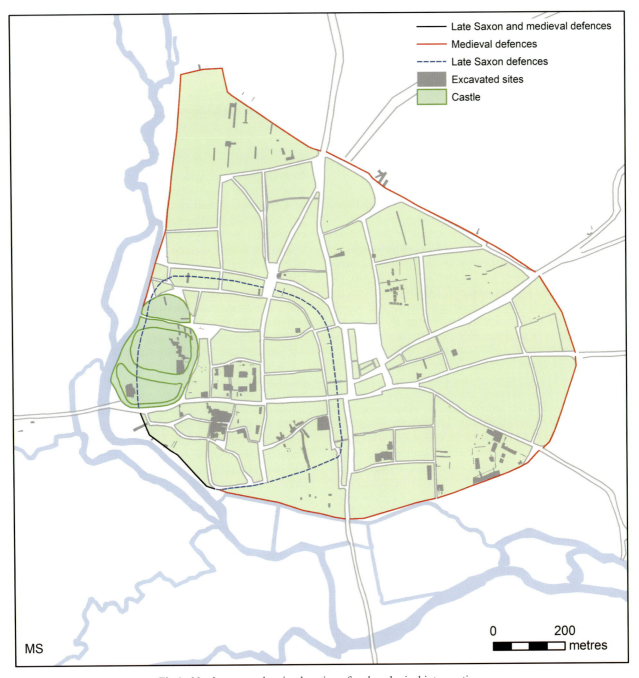

Fig 1: Northampton, showing location of archaeological interventions

sites is not readily accessible in this country, Appendix 3 provides a listing of examples known to 2020, together with a discussion on changing views on what the mixers would have looked like and how they would have worked.

Within this paper, following current Society for Medieval Archaeology guidelines, 'early Anglo-Saxon' and 'middle Anglo-Saxon' have been used for referring to the periods AD 410 – 650 and AD 650 – 850 respectively, but 'early-middle Saxon (EMS)' has been applied to the pottery of that period as being the term that has long been adopted for pottery of that date in Northamptonshire. The two approaches have been variously utilised by others in works appearing in the bibliography.

Acknowledgements

A review of almost fifty years of archaeological work, much of which the authors were personally involved in in one way or another, brings back fond memories of the far too numerous to mention individuals and organisations to whom we are indebted in various ways over the years. In particular, we would wish to thank those who participated in the field investigations and subsequently in post-excavation work and synthesis, as well as those who facilitated the work.

Figures 1–5, 9, 25, 27–29 and 37–39 were compiled and drawn by Michael Shaw. Figures 10, 30, 33 and 42

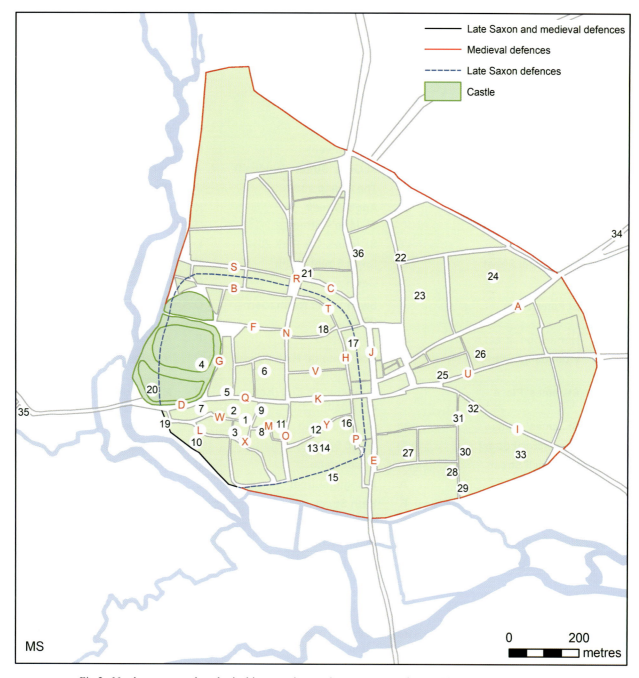

Fig 2: Northampton: archaeological interventions and street names referenced in the paper (see Table 1)

were redrawn by Andy Chapman. Figure 41 was drawn by Kenneth Connor and Figure 36 by Alex Thompson (née Thorne). Photographs 6–8, 11–24, 31–32, 34, 47–48 were taken by John Williams, 35 by Iain Soden and 43–46 by Alessandro Fichera. We are grateful to Alessandro Fichera for permission to publish these photographs. John Williams is grateful to him also for his invaluable discussions on mortar mixer reconstructions and he also wishes to thank Sophie Hüglin for providing information on a number of excavated mortar mixers. Michael Shaw would like to thank Northamptonshire Archaeology for providing copies of unpublished excavation and ceramic reports and Andy Heald of AOC Archaeology for supplying a copy

of the pottery report on their excavations at The Ridings. The figures prepared by Michael Shaw also form part of a broader study of medieval towns, including Northampton (see Shaw 2021a).

John Blair and Martin Biddle have read earlier versions of this paper and we are grateful for their various helpful comments. The authors, however, must accept responsibility for the views expressed in the published paper.

Unpublished client reports produced by commercial archaeological organisations, such as Northamptonshire Archaeology and MOLA Northampton, are denoted in the bibliography as, eg Northamptonshire Archaeology report. Digital copies may be available online through

Table 1: List of site names and street names (see Fig 2)

Site No.	Site name	Site No.	Site name	Letter	Street name
1	St Peter's Street	21	Mayorhold	E	Bridge Street
2	St Peter's Gardens/ Anglo-Saxon 'Palaces'	22	Newlands	F	Castle Street
3	The Green	23	Greyfriars	G	Chalk Lane
4	Chalk Lane	24	The Convent	H	College Street
5	Marefair	25	St Giles' Street (Guildhall)	I	Derngate
6	Sol Central (Marefair)	26	The Riding sites	J	Drapery
7	Black Lion Hill	27	Angel Street/ St John's Street	K	Gold Street
8	Gregory Street	28	St John's Car Park 2012	L	Green Street
9	Freeschool Street	29	Swan Street South	M	Gregory Street
		30	Cow Lane	N	Horsemarket
10	St Peter's Way	31	Swan Street North (Derngate A)	O	Horseshoe Street
11	Horseshoe Street A	32	Derngate B	P	Kingswell Street
12	Woolmonger Street	33	Northampton High School for Girls sites	Q	Marefair
13	St James' Place	34	St Edmund's End (Kettering Road)	R	Mayorhold
14	St James' Square	35	St James' End	S	Scarletwell Street
15	Commercial Street	36	46–50 Sheep Street	T	Silver Street
16	Kingswell Street	**Letter**	**Street name**	U	St Giles's Street
17	College Street	A	Abington Street	V	St Katherine's Street
18	Moat House Hotel	B	Bath Street	W	St Peter's Street
19	Green Street	C	Bearward Street	X	The Green
20	Northampton Station	D	Black Lion Hill	Y	Woolmonger Street

the Archaeology Data Service (ADS) Grey Literature Library, or by application to the issuing organisation or at the Northamptonshire Historic Environment Record (HER). Reports issued by Northamptonshire Archaeology are held by MOLA Northampton.

Northampton *c*.400–680

Prior to the Anglo-Saxon settlement discussed in this paper the area at the west of Northampton had seen sporadic activity over the centuries. To the south of St Peter's church was a possible round barrow or other prehistoric monument represented by a ring ditch, with a Bronze Age collared urn found 35 metres to the east. To the north-west was an extensive prehistoric flint scatter of Mesolithic to early Bronze Age date. There was also a scatter of Roman coins, pottery and tiles but no structural evidence. Marefair, the east-west road which presently bisects this area, possibly follows the line of a Roman

road between Duston and Irchester but there is no firm evidence for this (Williams *et al* 1985, 9, 46; Williams 1979, 137; Williams and Shaw 1981, 90; Williams 1984, 114; Chapman 2021a, this volume, 17–24).

Structures

Structural evidence for the period between *c*.400 and 680 is fragmentary and difficult to interpret, as might be expected for the earliest levels of an intensively occupied urban site (Fig 3). For example, in the area of the middle Anglo-Saxon timber and stone halls more than half of the earliest levels had been removed by later activity, especially the excavation of rubbish pits in medieval times (Williams *et al* 1985, Phase 1 plans). Five small early Anglo-Saxon sunken-featured buildings have been excavated within Northampton, three to the east of St Peter's church and two in Chalk Lane. Radiocarbon analysis indicates a date range spanning the

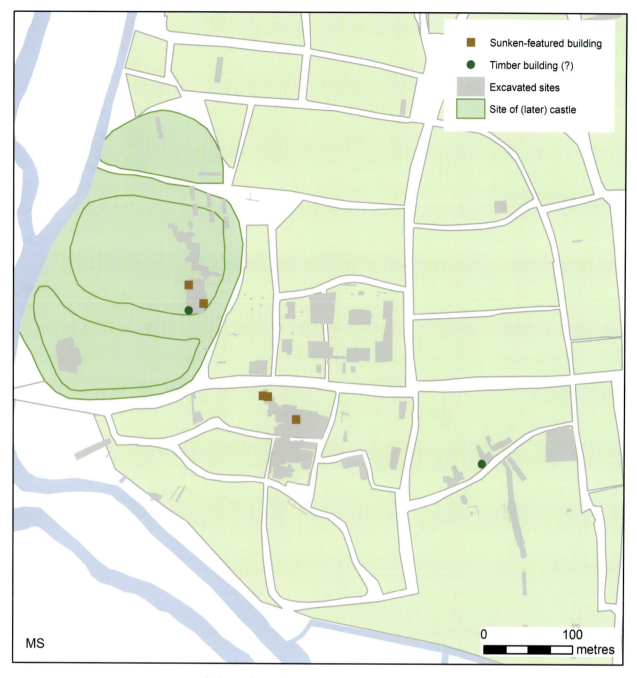

Fig 3: Early Anglo-Saxon Northampton *c.*400–680

period between the early 5th and the late 8th century. One to the east of St Peter's church has been dated to the 5th to mid-6th century (Cal AD 410–540, 68% confidence, Har-5557, Table 3, 1) and the two in Chalk Lane to the mid-6th to mid-8th century (Cal AD 545–640, 68% confidence, Har-3688/89; Cal AD 650–770, 68% confidence, Har-3935, Table 3, 2 and 3). The structures most probably date to the 6th or 7th century. There were also postholes suggesting contemporary post-built structures in Chalk Lane and in Woolmonger Street (Williams *et al* 1985, 9, 15, 38; Williams and Shaw 1981, 95; Soden 1998–99, 70–1; Walker *et al* 1985).

Finds

The evidence from the finds is also tantalisingly imprecise. The main pottery types were black gritty wares together with some chaff-tempered wares (see Appendix 1 for details). Quite large amounts have been recovered but, with forms and fabrics changing little during the early and middle Anglo-Saxon periods, it is difficult to establish how much of the pottery found in the areas of these buildings should be associated with them and how much belongs rather to the period of the middle Anglo-Saxon halls and associated structures (see below). It can be noted, however, that the largest concentrations of early to middle

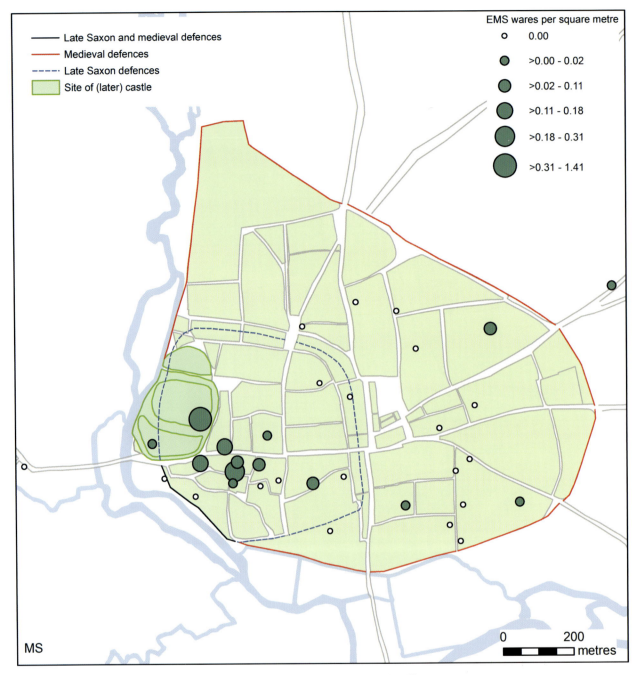

Fig 4: Distribution of early-middle Saxon (EMS) pottery

Saxon (EMS) pottery were found within the infill deposits of the early Anglo-Saxon sunken-floored buildings, and further that the assemblages in these areas contained over thirty sherds of decorated and bossed pottery vessels of funerary type, clearly belonging to the early, pagan Anglo-Saxon period (Gryspeerdt 1981, 108; Williams *et al* 1985, 50). St Peter's Street produced a fine disc composite brooch of late 5th- or early 6th-century date and a bronze finger ring of similar date, The Green produced a further disc brooch, also of late 5th- or early 6th-century date, and Woolmonger Street a small equal-armed brooch, possibly 5th-century; a fragment of claw-beaker, perhaps 6th-century, was found on Woolmonger Street and further

fragments of early Anglo-Saxon glass on Marefair (Oakley *et al* 1979, 248, 250; Soden 1998–9, 73; Hylton 1998–9, 97; Hunter and Oakley 1979, 74). We can thus confirm the presence of early Anglo-Saxon occupation in the south-west quarter of Northampton, principally in the area between Chalk Lane to the west and Woolmonger Street to the east, possibly from the 5th century onwards, although the status of this occupation is uncertain (Fig 4).

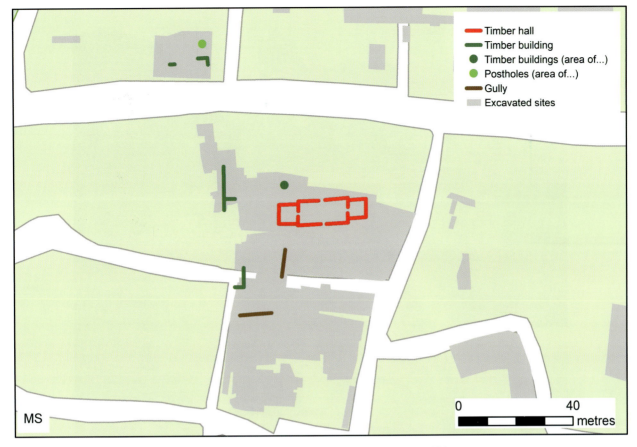

Fig 5: Middle Anglo-Saxon Northampton, *c*.680–820

Cemeteries

A number of early Anglo-Saxon cemeteries were located in the vicinity of Northampton, with the largest two being that about 4.5km to the west, just beyond the Roman small town at Duston and that excavated by MOLA in 2019 at Overstone Gate, about 7.5km to the north-east; there were others at St Andrew's Hospital and Hardingstone to the east and south-east. Scattered settlement activity has been identified across a similar area (RCHM 1985, 40; Williams *et al* 1985, 38; Williams 1984, 115; Williams 1977, 1ff). There is, however, little to indicate any particular importance for the locality and it is possible that we have in Northampton one, or more than one, of the type of early Anglo-Saxon sites that are ubiquitous in Northamptonshire at this time, especially along the Nene valley (Parry 2006, 91–4, 274; Shaw 1993–4). Given the wide date range of the features and finds, we may also be seeing an example of 'settlement drift', common at early Anglo-Saxon sites elsewhere, such as Mucking (Hamerow 1993, 86–91).

Northampton *c*.680–875

The great timber hall complex

By the middle of the 8th century and possibly as early as the late 7th century a large timber hall had been erected on the St Peter's Street site (Figs 5–8). It measured, to the centre line of its wall-trenches *c*.29.4m long by 8.35m wide; a central double-square element, with central opposing doorways in the long sides, was *c*.16.7m long by 8.35m wide, and there were annexes, approximately 6.35m square, at each end. The positions of the individual posts within the substantial wall-trenches, which were about 1.0m wide and 1.0m+ deep, could be identified as ghosts or voids. Those along the long sides were regularly placed 0.6m apart, with post-positions in the south walls matching those in the north walls; the span between opposing pairs in the north and south walls of the main hall was consistent, not varying by more than 0.1m.

The hall was clearly a very substantial, well-carpentered structure of sophisticated design. There was some evidence that the eastern annexe narrowed just a little towards its east end (Williams *et al* 1985, 9ff) and John Blair wonders whether this apparent slight tapering reflects the angle-sided hall tradition (John Blair pers comm; Blair 2018, 286; cf Blair 2015), although the examples noted in Blair 2015 are somewhat later than the Northampton hall. Re-evaluation of the radiocarbon dates suggests that it may have been constructed at the end of the 7th century or soon after (Appendix 2; Williams *et al* 1985, 26, 38; Walker *et al*, 1985, 65).

To the west and south-west of the hall were the remains of further post-in-trench timber buildings and to the north-west was extensive but enigmatic evidence for a sequence of much smaller ones, again of post-in-

Fig 6: The large Middle Anglo-Saxon timber hall from the east, with St Peter's church beyond

trench construction. Their orientation seemed to respect that of the hall, although the longer axes of these structures were perhaps set at right angles to it (Williams *et al* 1985, 9ff). A smallish building represented by similar post-in-trench construction was excavated to the west of St Peter's Church and radiocarbon-dated to the 7th or 8th century (Cal AD 625–770, 68% confidence, Har-5560; see Table 3, 4; Walker *et al* 1985; Shaw 1985, 116). To the north of Marefair was the corner of a further trench-built timber structure, but of somewhat different character; in the centre of the slot were 'many irregular and ambiguous patches and lenses of different sands' but vertical planks, perhaps of mature oak, could be identified lining

the outside of the north-south slot. At the time of excavation it was queried whether they formed the retaining elements of a turf-, cob- or wattle-filled wall, but perhaps we should now see the structural technique as related to that employed in a number of robust plank-built halls within great-hall complexes (Williams F 1979, 43, plates 9 and 10; cf McBride 2020, 119). No definite structures relating to this period were found in Chalk Lane, at Sol Central (although this might not be significant on this site given that excavation here may only in places have reached an appropriate depth), on Gregory Street or on Woolmonger Street.

Fig 7: The large Middle Anglo-Saxon timber hall from the east, with the excavators standing in the corners of the main modules of the hall

Fig 8: Timber hall construction trench sections: a) post-pipe surviving as a void, north-west corner of central module (context AA465.8); b) truncated section along north side of hall, east of the central entrance, showing the regular spacing of the uprights and the compacted weathered ironstone infill of the trench (Scales 0.5m)

The great timber hall rebuilt in stone

Probably at about the turn of the 9th century the great timber hall was superseded by an even larger one in stone (Figs 9–16). Indeed the latter was very much a direct replacement of the former in that the south and east walls of the stone building lay directly on top of the south and east walls of the timber hall (Fig 10). The large rectangular hall measured 37.5m x 11.5m. The foundations, robbed for the most part, were 1.2m wide and 0.6m deep and composed of neatly laid limestone and ironstone set in earth. The walls above were probably bonded with mortar and faced, at least on the inside, with plaster, coated with a white lime-wash. The overall length of the building was increased to 43.4m by the addition of two rooms at its western end. One room was wrapped around the north-west corner of the hall and the other, smaller one, of simple rectangular form, nestled in the angle formed by the south wall of this extension and the west wall of the hall. The foundations were a little narrower and shallower than those of the hall and less well constructed. A construc-

tion date around 820 was suggested in the excavation report; reassessment of the radiocarbon dates has not really refined the chronology (Appendix 2; Williams *et al* 1985, 26; Walker *et al* 1985, 65). Allowing a reasonable life-span for the timber hall, with the stone hall clearly a direct replacement, the most likely construction date for the stone hall would appear to be in the final part of the 8th or perhaps the beginning of the 9th century.

About 8m to the west of the extended hall was the east wall of a further stone building which continued westwards under the present St Peter's church, and it is interpreted as belonging to an early phase of the church (Figs 17–18). The building measured just over 6m north-south. The rubble foundations were similar in size and character to those of the extension to the main hall. The inner face of the east wall was again mortar-rendered and there were traces of a lime-mortar floor. There were no contemporary graves. While the east wall of this building may be an addition to a more substantial building, the main body of which lies further to the west, what has been

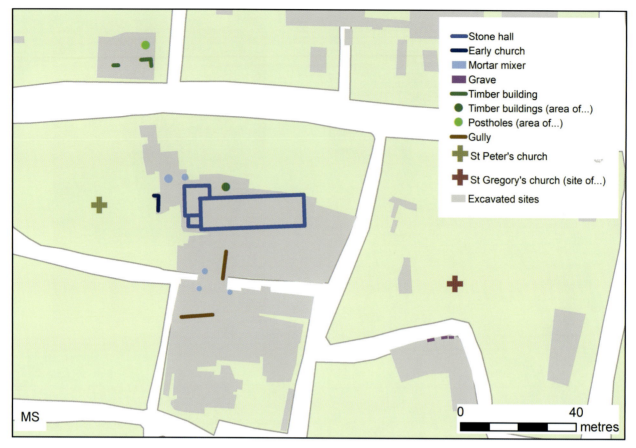

Fig 9: Middle Anglo-Saxon Northampton *c*.800–875

excavated is certainly less substantial than the remains of the stone hall, perhaps indicating that the latter formed the main component of the complex.

The mortar mixers and their significance

The remains of five mortar mixers were found, two to the north-west of the stone hall and three to the south (Figs 19–24; see also Appendix 3). They were probably used for the construction of the stone buildings. Over seventy such mortar mixers are now known, spread across Europe, but with the main concentrations in Switzerland, southern Germany, Tuscany and Britain. The vast majority date from the 8th to the 11th century and are associated with high-status secular and ecclesiastical sites.

Bede, in a celebrated passage, records Benedict Biscop travelling to France in 674 to return with *cementarii* to build a church in stone after the Roman fashion [at Wearmouth] (*Benedictus oceano transmisso Gallias petens, cementarios qui lapideam sibi ecclesiam juxta Romanorum ... morem facerent*) (Bede, *Lives of the Abbots*, 401). *Cementarii* have normally been translated as masons, as in the Loeb edition of the *Lives* above, but Bede, in his *On Ezra and Nehemiah* (*CCSL* 273; DeGregorio, 55), defines *cementarii* as those who make mortar from gypsum or lime [*alt.* limestone] in order to bind stones together (*cementarii sunt qui cementa ad conglutinandos lapides ex gypso vel calce faciunt*). The *cementarii* are there

contrasted with the *latomi* who cut stones and the difference in role of the *latomi* and the *cementarii* is maintained later in the text, the former preparing stones and the latter mortar, although the *cementarii* might lay the stones in mortar. In writing allegorically about the building of the church community Bede describes the *latomi* as fitting stones to their neighbours by squaring them (*quadrando circumpositis lapidibus aptant*) (*CCSL* 273); he compares the *cementarii*, in binding together squared and polished stones with a pouring or spreading of mortar (*infusione cementi*), to preachers joining together with the bond of love those whom they educate (*CCSL* 274).

It would seem that the expertise required in preparing mortar was recognised as a specialist craft function. Presumably this involved both lime burning and the subsequent mixing of lime mortar; although there is no mention in the passages of Bede quoted as to whether any mechanical device was used in mixing the mortar it would not be unreasonable to see an itinerant *cementarius* travelling with skills in both lime burning and the mechanical mixing of mortar.

Sophie Hüglin has queried whether there could be any link between mortar mixers and *magistri/maestri commacini*, a group of builders and craftsmen renowned from the mid-7th to 8th century onwards, *commacini* having been variously interpreted as 'from Como' or 'with machines' (2011, 202). Irrespective of the specifics of that particular argument, it is important to note the extensive networks maintained by monastic institutions across

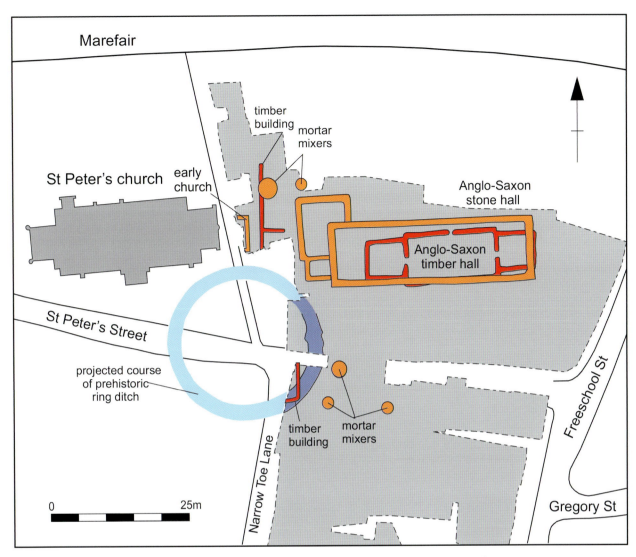

Fig 10: The relationship between the timber and stone halls and other main features

Europe, which would have facilitated the ready diffusion of craft techniques and skills as well as personnel (Bianchi 2011, 15). The mixers, which clearly seem to underpin the high status of the Northampton complex, are discussed further in Appendix 3 below.

Burials on the site of St Gregory's church

About 50m to the east of the stone hall, and immediately to the south of the site of St Gregory's church, four graves were excavated, all aligned west-east. Three radiocarbon dates, the earliest having a large error value, suggest that burial had begun by the late 7th to early 8th century, and that the area was still in use for burial between the late 9th and late 10th century, a range of up to 300 years (Grave C315, Cal AD 580–770, 68% confidence, Har-4390; Grave C410, Cal AD 670–780, 53% confidence, Har-4810; Grave C408, Cal AD 860–980, 50% confidence, Har-4809; Table 2, 21–3). The radiocarbon dates would indicate that the graves were contemporary with the timber and stone halls, raising the possibility that

there was a church or chapel in this location, even at this relatively early date. John Blair has noted that 'dedications to Gregory the Great can be expected to originate at the end of the 7th century or in the first half of the 8th, when the cult was at its height in England' (1996, 105).

The extent of middle Anglo-Saxon settlement

Present evidence would seem to indicate that middle Anglo-Saxon settlement was unenclosed and concentrated very much in the area between St Peter's Street and Chalk Lane. A number of gullies discovered during the St Peter's Street, The Green and Black Lion Hill excavations are perhaps best interpreted as boundary ditches. No traces have been found of defences immediately surrounding this area and there are no reasonable grounds for supporting John Blair's suggestion that the 'Lee line' (see below 55) might define a very large example of the sort of monastic enclosure that he postulates for Cheddar (1996, 98–100), nor for endorsing the thesis put forward by Jeremy Haslam, and more recently by Steven Bassett, that Northampton was part of a system of 8th- or early 9th-century Mercian defended settlements (Haslam 1987, 84; Bassett 2007, 80).

The artefactual evidence associated with the middle Anglo-Saxon structural remains was surprisingly limited, given their undoubted status and importance. As regards ceramics the clearly middle Saxon Maxey-type ware was present only in small quantities and its distribution therefore needs to be treated with care. Nevertheless, there was a concentration in the St Peters Street / Marefair / Chalk Lane / Gregory Street area (Fig 25) so we may be seeing here a true reflection of the extent of middle Anglo-Saxon settlement. The apparent high density beneath the town defences at Green Street has been discounted since fourteen of the fifteen sherds found came from a single vessel. Coin evidence from contexts allowing association with the halls consisted of two sceattas, dating to c.750, and a rare silver penny of Berhtwulf of Mercia (838–851) (Archibald et al 1979, 243; Archibald and Metcalf 1985, 64). Additionally, but found in later contexts, were a possibly late 8th-century shrine mount (Fig 26), a stylus of similar date and a disc-headed bone pin of middle Anglo-Saxon date (Oakley et al 1979, 254, 260, 310). There was some limited evidence for iron-working, as well as for copper-working on the Marefair site (Cleere 1979; Cleere 1985, 70; Bayley 1979a and 1979b; Cleere and Oakley 1979).

Understanding Northampton's middle Anglo-Saxon status: comparative evidence

When the excavations were published the halls were interpreted as belonging to a 'palace' or royal administrative centre, a *villa regalis* from where the king's authority could be exercised and where dues could be gathered; it would have been part of a 'hierarchical network of centres ... of which only a few would have served as more than the most temporary residence for the royal entourage on its progress, but which would have had permanent roles as *capita* of royal estates under the control of a reeve or even a member of the royal family' (Williams 1984, 124).

John Blair has subsequently challenged this interpretation, stressing the role of minsters as proto-urban centres and arguing rather that the halls were more likely to belong to an ecclesiastical, minster complex: he feels that the conception of minsters as secondary to royal *villae* sites uneasily with their independence and argues that, although by the 11th century it was common for minsters and royal vills to be juxtaposed, it was debatable which came first. More specifically he suggests that the Northampton halls' topographical location in the crook of a river confluence was typical of that chosen for a minster; that royal sites tended to be short-lived while minsters continued to provide focal points for and articulate with the countryside; that finds from the site are typical of a minster site; and that the halls lay between two churches, St Peter's and St Gregory's, paralleling the linear arrangement of churches in many minster complexes (1996, 98ff; 2005, 267). As others have argued more recently (Loveluck 2013, 171; Hen 2009, 331) perhaps too much emphasis has been placed on the dynamics of minster organisation

as a force for change socially and economically, at the expense of other influences. Martin Carver, again critical of the overuse of the minster hypothesis, suggests that the creation of the late Saxon burh at Stafford took its inspiration from an awareness of still surviving, if ruined, Roman fortresses and an admiration of things Roman (2010, 128, 143). It is appropriate, therefore, to re-examine the case for the status of the halls in the light both of John Blair's and others' observations, and also comparative data emerging from recent archaeological and historical research.

The focus of early and middle Anglo-Saxon activity at Northampton, to the east and north-west of the present St Peter's church, is on a bluff of high ground in the angle of the river Nene and one of its tributary streams. The site very much overlooks the valley of the Nene and the present church is well visible to approaching travellers, particularly those coming from the south and the west. Such a prominent location advertises itself well and while minsters were often located in similar positions (Blair 1992, 227) it was also an eminently suitable location for the head of a secular, perhaps royal estate. Perhaps we should also note the prehistoric ring ditch which lay only 10m to the south-west of the large timber hall, with the construction trench of a perhaps contemporary building cutting the infilled ring ditch (Fig 10). The 'appropriation' of prehistoric monuments, in particular barrows, in Anglo-Saxon England and their relationship to a number of elite sites of power and authority has been noted; among the 'great hall complexes' (see below) Yeavering (Northumberland), Sutton Courtenay (Oxfordshire), Lyminge (Kent), Hatton Rock (Warwickshire), Long Wittenham (Oxfordshire) and Cowage Farm (Wiltshire) are all associated with one or more such monuments (Semple 2013, 207; Blair 2013, 113; Thomas 2017, 97; Thomas 2018, 269; McBride 2020, 66).

Northampton's large timber hall, in terms of its scale, at 29.4m x 8.35m, and in plan, with its central main unit and annexes at each end, most nearly resembles halls at Yeavering, A1(b) 25m x 7m; A3(a) 30m x 9.9m, Atcham (Shropshire) 23m x 8m and 26m x 9m, Sprouston, (Roxburghshire) c.23.5m x 9m, Milfield (Northumberland) c.33m x 9.8m and Long Itchington, (Warwickshire) c.30.5m x 8.2m (White and Young 2020; Hope-Taylor 1977, 46–51, 55–8, 141–6; St Joseph 1975, 293–5; St Joseph 1982; Hope-Taylor 1977, 13; McBride 2020, 129). While Yeavering and Milfield can be identified as royal sites there is nothing in the historical record concerning the status of Atcham and Sprouston. We can also consider Lyminge, Cowdery's Down (Hampshire), Sutton Courtenay and elsewhere where there were large halls without double annexes (Thomas 2017, 2018; Millett et al 1983, 215, 248, McBride 2020; Austin 2017). The Northampton hall was clearly a high-status structure and very much comparable with the examples above which are now, with their associated buildings, collectively identified as 'great hall complexes' (Blair 2018, 114; Austin 2017; McBride 2020).

There are indications that double-annexed halls are late in the great-hall sequence (McBride 2020, 88, 124, 128). Adam McBride considers the 'new style' of annexed halls emerging in the early to middle 7th century to be less robust than earlier versions (2020, 124) and John

Fig 11: The western part of the middle Anglo-Saxon stone hall from the south-east, with St Peter's church in the background

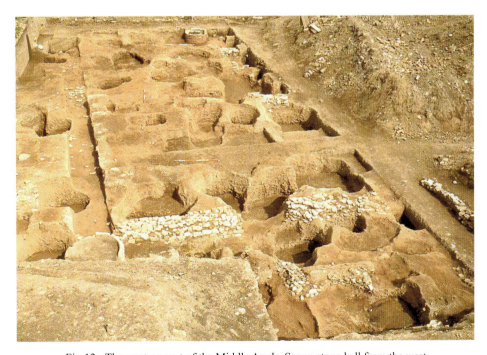

Fig 12: The western part of the Middle Anglo-Saxon stone hall from the west

Fig 13: Foundations of the south-west corner
of the stone hall (scale 0.5m)

Fig 15: Section across the foundations of the west
end of the stone hall

Fig 14: Section across the foundations of the west
end of the stone hall

Fig 16: Section through the foundations of the annexe of the
stone hall composed of loosely packed uncoursed rubble

Fig 17: The middle Anglo-Saxon stone building extending westwards under St Peter's church. The north wall of the building can
be seen in section, cut into the ironstone subsoil at the right of the photograph, with a thin mortar floor level to its left. The south
wall can be seen in section at the left of the photograph (scale 2m)

Fig 18: The south-east corner of the middle Anglo-Saxon building extending westwards under St Peter's church. Two courses of stone wall can be seen above rubble foundations

Fig 21: Mortar mixer 3 before the removal of the mortar residues; voids in the central ridge, running left to right, indicate where the paddles were located (scale 0.5m)

Fig 19: Mortar mixer 1; note the central posthole and the impressions of the peripheral wattlework (scale 0.5m)

Fig 22: Mortar mixer 3 after the removal of the upper mortar level, with the paddle holes in the central ridge clearly visible, along with concentric grooves in the lower mortar residue

Fig 20: Mortar mixer 2, with impressions of the peripheral wattlework visible in the mortar residues (scale 0.5m)

Fig 23: The remains of mortar mixer 4; note concentric grooves around the central posthole (scale 0.5m)

Fig 24: The fragmentary remains of mortar mixer 5, which, unlike the other mixers, was constructed at ground level rather than in a cut. Below and to the right of the central posthole can be seen a band of mortar residue within the mixer, with wattlework impressions around its outer edge. An orange band then marks the truncated remains of a retaining bank for the mixing bowl and the further mortar spread is outside the mixer (Scale 2m)

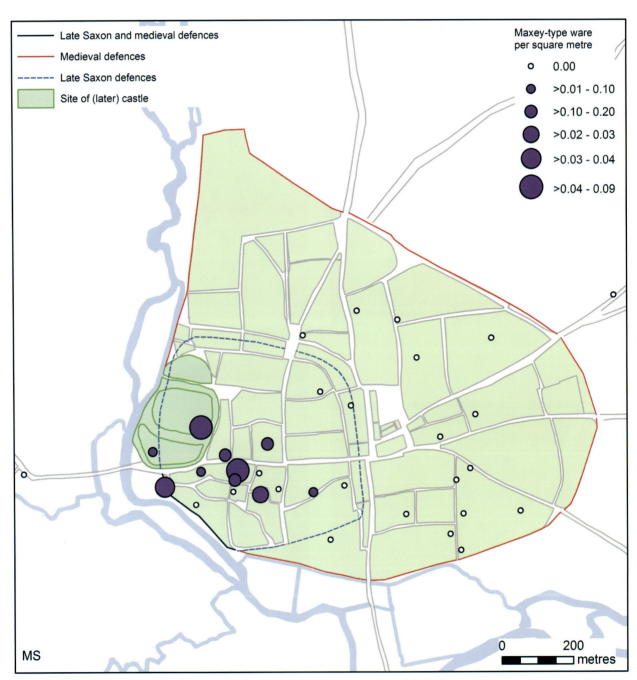

Fig 25: Maxey type pottery distribution

Fig 26: The copper-alloy shrine-mount from St Peter's Street
(25mm diameter)

Blair refers to the Northampton hall as small and rather lightweight (2013, 185). It needs to be underlined that the Northampton hall is very similar in size to the other annexed halls noted above, has substantial foundation trenches over a metre deep and is of sophisticated design, based on matching pairs of posts in the facing long walls (Williams *et al* 1985, 9–15, 28–31). Indeed we can note in the great cathedrals of the Middle Ages that less stone can show increasing mastery of materials and techniques.

While, because of the constraints of excavating within an urban environment, the main focus at Northampton has been on the double-annexed hall, for which we have a virtually complete plan, there are sufficient archaeological remains from adjacent areas to suggest that it was but one, if perhaps the major, component of a more extensive area of timber buildings. There can be no certainty as to which of the various middle Anglo-Saxon timber buildings were contemporary, but it can be noted that they extend over an area at least 150m east-west by 100m north-south and all seem to follow or be at right angles to a single alignment. Although the evidence is inevitably more fragmentary than on rural sites it is possible to see elements of a 'planned' layout which it is suggested is characteristic of great hall complexes (cf McBride 2020, 39).

The 'great hall complexes' have been linked with a short-lived, ostentatious display of royal and aristocratic power in the 7th century and they were seemingly abandoned by the early 8th century or their estate centre role, as for example at Lyminge, may have been assumed by minsters (Blair 2018, 131; Thomas 2018, 266ff). It is difficult, however, on many sites accurately to determine how long occupation continued into the 8th century (Austin 2017, 61; McBride 2020, 56). The potential re-dating of the Northampton timber hall to the turn of the 8th century might perhaps suggest that it and its associated structures were another somewhat late example of the great hall phenomenon. The earlier the date, however, that is assigned to the timber hall, and particularly its demise, the earlier the date that needs to be given to the stone hall that succeeds it. The latter was clearly a direct and thus seemingly immediate replacement of the former, its east wall sitting on the line of the timber hall's east wall, with its south wall likewise respecting the line of the timber hall's south wall (Fig 10); there is little sign of modification or repair of the hall and its earthfast posts would have had a limited lifespan. The stone hall would not appear, however, to be earlier than the early 9th century, possibly the very end of the 8th century. The annexed hall at Brandon, Suffolk (Tester *et al* 2014, 48) and the possible one (U3) at Whitehall, London (Cowie and Blackmore 2008, 93; Rob Cowie pers comm) are later than those belonging to 'great hall complexes' but their construction trenches are far less substantial than either that at Northampton or those of the great halls. Indeed the Whitehall structure would appear to be defined only by two post positions and the edge of the clay floor.

Northampton's stone hall remains, for the time being, without parallel in England, the closest comparable structures that were not specifically churches being the main domestic ranges at Bede's monastery at Jarrow, Co Durham. It can be noted, however, that Building A there, *c*.28m by 8m, and Building B, 18.5m by 8m, were rather smaller than the Northampton hall at 37.5m by 11.5m and their walls, varying between 0.61m and 0.76m wide, were rather less substantial (Cramp 2005, 187ff). John Blair suggests that the position of the stone hall between the churches of St Peter and St Gregory brings to mind the axial linearity of a number of church complexes, but no example is adduced of a building that was not a church forming the central component of such an arrangement and there is no reason to regard the Northampton hall as a church. Indeed, if the timber hall is accepted as a 'great hall', with the stone hall being so clearly a direct replacement, what are the implications for the status of the stone hall?

For structures similar to the stone hall we have to look to the Carolingian empire and continental Europe. When the Northampton hall was first published it was noted that, while the hall was certainly not part of building complexes on the same scale as the great Frankish palaces at Aachen, Ingelheim, Samoussy and Quiercy, there were similarities with Zurich Lindenhof, Frankfurt, Paderborn, Mikulčike and Naranco (Williams *et al* 1985, 31; Hugot 1965; Thordeman, 1979; Rauch 1976; Vogt 1948; Weise 1923, 5–83; Stamm 1955; Winkelman 1972; Poulik 1975; Haupt 1916; Lobbedy 2003, 143ff; Gai 2001). A key element on all these sites was a great rectangular hall or *aula* where the royal 'court' or that of an important lord might assemble, where audiences might be held and officials carry out their responsibilities, including the administration of justice, and where ceremonial functions or feasting might take place. The hall at Zurich Lindenhof measured 30m by at least 16m externally, that at Frankfurt 26.5m by 12.2m internally and that at Paderborn 30.9m by 10.3m, all shorter than that at Northampton. The layout of the Paderborn site in its first stone phase dating to the last quarter of the 8th century, with stone hall set on a similar orientation, but not the same axis, as that of the church of The Saviour, just over 20m away, is very similar to that at Northampton (Gai 2001, 203). It can be noted, however, that the Northampton hall did not have the opulence provided by the marble and porphyry veneers witnessed at Aachen, Ingelheim, Paderborn and Compiegne (Loveluck 2013, 115), but Northampton certainly lacked the presence of a major local Roman site suitable for plundering.

In addition to 'palaces' we can see a capacity to build in stone at some more modest high-status Carolingian-period sites. For example, at Mayenne a rectangular stone building, constructed around AD 900, has survived within the fabric of the later chateau. It measured 10.7m by 7.7m internally, and stood 10.5m high to its eaves. A 4m-square tower, with a smaller rectangular tower adjoining it, possibly for stairs, was attached to the hall, in a manner somewhat reminiscent of the additional rooms at Northampton. Subsequently the building acquired covered external verandas on two sides (Early 2003). One can also note the transformation of the seigneurial site at Le Thier d'Olne, near Liège, in the 9th century, when a multi-roomed building measuring 25.8m by 17.5m, perhaps of timber on stone foundations, replaced an earlier, somewhat simpler, timber structure. A central area has been interpreted as an *aula*, but, in the absence of a made floor, could it in fact have been an open court-yard around which ranges of rooms were disposed? The complex also embraced a chapel (Witrouw 2006, 277 ff). At Petegem, about 30km south-west of Ghent, a timber building was replaced in the first half of the 9th century by a stone hall, to which a chamber was subsequently added. The structure measured 10.9m wide internally by more than 15.4m long. At Ename, a little to the north-east, chamber, hall and chapel were arranged in linear fashion within a single stone structure 36m long by 11m wide that was constructed in the 10th century (Callebaut 1994). We can also note royal houses, well-built of stone, in the model survey of five Carolingian estates, as contained in the *Brevia Exempla*, dating to somewhere around AD 800 (Loyn and Percival 1975, 102). John Blair may argue that the very real Carolingian influences on English politics and culture during the 8th to 10th century (see for example Story 2003, 257ff) have been overemphasised at the expense of ignoring fundamental and continuing Scandinavian character (Blair 2018, 228 and pers comm) but perhaps we should remember that the finest surviving manifestation of Carolingian style church-building in England is to be found at Brixworth, just six miles to the north of Northampton.

Discussion about the status of sites of this date and their secular or ecclesiastical affiliations has focused not only on the structures but also on the richness of the finds' assemblages either in terms of production or 'conspicuous consumption'. The Northumbrian monastic site of Whitby is notable for the quantity, quality and range of artefacts (Webster 1991, 141; Wormald 1982, 79), but at Jarrow and Monkwearmouth, Co Durham, among the relatively large collection of copper alloy and silver objects there are 'no examples of fine metalwork ... and little which distinguishes the artefacts from those from secular sites' (Cramp *et al*, 2006,230), although there was a specialist workshop area at Jarrow for a variety of crafts (Cramp

2005, 232, 241); Hartlepool, Co Durham, is notable for the mould and crucible fragments producing high quality silver and copper alloy objects (Bayley 1988, 184; Cramp 1988 187). Further south, at Eynsham, Oxfordshire, while there was evidence for copper-alloy-, iron- and textile-working, the associated finds were unexceptional (Dodd and Hardy 2003, 470ff). At St Augustine's, Canterbury, there was clear evidence for intensive metal-working and other craft activity (Hicks 2015, 117). Fine metal-working was a characteristic of Irish monastic sites (Ryan 1988, 44). In terms of high-status secular sites the 7th-century great hall complex at Lyminge, which is clearly royal, displays a rich finds' collection (Thomas 2017, 105) and field survey of the admittedly exceptional East Anglian royal site at Rendlesham, near Sutton Hoo, has recovered an unprecedented wealth of coins, metalwork and other finds (Minter *et al* 2016, 37), but the material culture from the central areas of great hall complexes is unexceptional (McBride 2020, 50).

Against this background there has been considerable debate on the status of the sites of Flixborough, North Lincolnshire, and Brandon, Suffolk, and the 'conspicuous consumption' witnessed by their finds' assemblages. At Flixborough there was no large hall but rather a series of smaller buildings, mostly between 13m and 15m in length, arranged in linear fashion on higher ground. Large quanti-ties of domestic livestock were consumed and feasting is perhaps evidenced by the presence of numerous glass drinking vessels imported from continental Europe, along-side coinage and pottery. The excavator interpreted the various buildings as being occupied by different compo-nents of an extended aristocratic family (Loveluck 2007; 2013, 128). Brandon, like Flixborough, is undocumented in the contemporary historical record; in the 8th and 9th centuries there was dense settlement over the more than a hectare investigated, which probably comprised a third of the historical site. A number of halls were excavated as well as a church and a cemetery. Again there was conspic-uous consumption of livestock, there was a rich finds assemblage, and glass drinking vessels were being broken, indicating a scenario which the excavator suggests would have been 'consistent with an aristocratic lifestyle, but not necessarily at odds with a monastic community with an aristocratic or royal patron' (Tester *et al* 2014, 219ff, 386ff). Like Northampton, Flixborough was also reinter-preted by John Blair as being a minster site (2011), a contributory part of his argument being the presence there of over twenty metal styli for writing on wax, by far the largest such assemblage from England; evidence for such a degree of literacy might be most expected on a monastic site, but Tim Pestell has underlined their potential use for accounting and managing estates (2004, 40) although it must be admitted that they are singularly absent from demonstrably commercial sites. When examined closely, the Northampton finds assemblage is notable mostly for its paucity of high-status objects; a single shrine mount does not make a minster nor does a single stylus, possibly two, evidence a *scriptorium*[1].

---

[1] John Blair quotes two more styli associated with the Northampton complex (1996) but this is subsequently amend-ed (2015, 208); one of these styli came from the site of the

In any case, however, the debate at Northampton is not in respect of whether or not there was a minster but whether the great timber and stone halls were part of the minster. In respect of excavated sites Northampton's meagre finds profile is most nearly paralleled by those at the majority of great hall complexes (McBride 2020, 50). Given the variety of evidence before us there is clearly a danger, in seeking to define whether high-status sites of the period were secular or monastic, of developing increasingly circular arguments when based solely or largely on the presence or absence of rich finds' assemblages.

Understanding Northampton's middle Anglo-Saxon status: some thoughts on context

Throughout the period we have been considering Northampton is not mentioned in documentary sources but are we able to deduce anything from the later documentary record? Prior to the 12th century the place-name for Northampton was *Hamtun*. In *The Place-Names of Northamptonshire* we find that 'it is on the whole probable that the Old English *hamtun* generally carried something of the sense of the modern "home farm," or, in more general terms, of a central residence contrasted with outlying and dependent holdings. ... It suggests a time when something anticipatory of later manorial development had begun to appear – the 8th rather than the 6th century. Where all must be conjecture, it may be surmised that the original Northampton was a royal residence and estate, at which were rendered the dues payable by the men of the folk – the *provincia* or *regio* settled around it.' (Gover *et al* 1975, xvii). Kenneth Cameron has 'translated' *hāmtūn* as 'home farm' but he suggested that the compound has a precise meaning beyond its literal sense which is presently unknown (1996, 58, 142, 148). James Campbell argued that while *tūn* can have a variety of meanings it would appear that it was importantly, and from an early date, used to designate a royal vill (Campbell 1979, 50; cf Sawyer 1983, 283).

Although there were no associated burials, it seems reasonable to assume that the stone building that seems to have extended under the present St Peter's church was a precursor of it. There also appears to be little doubt that St Peter's church had minster status, Kingsthorpe and Upton churches once being dependent chapelries of St Peter's. Yet both were royal manors in Domesday Book and subsequently the hundredal manors for the hundreds of Spelhoe and Nobottle Grove. While John Blair suggests that this may merely reflect an ecclesiastical relationship (1996, 107) it seems reasonable to postulate that the ecclesiastical dependency reflected secular organisation and that we are looking at a former substantial royal estate. Indeed the *thorp* element, which represents a secondary settlement, a dependent outlying farmstead or hamlet, supports

this thesis. Richard Jones notes that a large number of early Uptons were associated with royal and major ecclesiastical holdings in the 8th to 10th century and were a normal part of elite Anglo-Saxon estate organisations (2012, 305, 312).

The legend of St Ragener should also be considered in the context of the relationship of minsters and administrative centres. Ragener, a nephew of St Edmund, king and martyr, died in the same year that Edmund was killed, namely 869. The Chronicle of Hugh Candidus, completed in or after 1155, lists 'Et in Hamtune sanctus Ragaher rex' in a list of saints' resting places, and his memory lingered on, for the 'fraternytye of Seynt Reginary in the church of Seynt Peter' is recorded as late as the 16th century (Williams 1984, 126). Alan Thacker has stressed how in pre-Viking Mercia it was quite common for the Mercian royalty generally to foster cults and royal cults were frequently associated with royal administrative centres and in particular with minsters established in these locations. Such a minster often had a large parish or *parochia* covering the same area as that dependent on the royal *tun*, with the minster's spiritual renders paralleling the secular dues owed at the *tun*. The close relationship of royal *tun* and minster is underlined (Thacker 1985, 1f). It was tempting, although without any further foundation, to wonder whether East Anglian influence could have spread westwards into Mercia for a brief flowering before the Danish invasions of the later 9th century, with Ragener even being the last pre-Viking lord to hold *Hamtun* (Williams 1984, 126). Bob Meeson has recently suggested that the relics of St Editha were taken to Tamworth, possibly by Aethelflaed, perhaps to keep them safe but perhaps also to protect the burh (2015, 36); in the same vein, and again entirely speculatively, might her brother Edward the Elder have done the same for Northampton by bringing Ragener's remains there, but if that were the case might not a saint associated with Mercia or Wessex have been favoured? To the south-west of Northampton, St Rumwold, a lesser known Mercian royal saint, was associated with a number of locations that Alan Thacker considers may originally have been the interconnected ecclesiastical centres of a large royal estate (1985, 6).

Understanding Northampton's middle Anglo-Saxon status: some conclusions

Is then Anglo-Saxon England so totally different to Carolingian Europe? Are minsters the sole drivers of continuity in terms of administrative, economic and indeed architectural matters? It would seem, rather, that there are a number of interlocking arguments that need to be disentangled.

Throughout the Anglo-Saxon period we can see the consolidation of royal power and the establishment of the kingdom of England as a unified state, yet one decentralised geographically as a result of a mobile, peripatetic kingship and localised estate management. While it may well be that some rural royal administrative sites moved, mirroring a general middle Anglo-Saxon settlement shift (cf Taylor 1983 passim; Hamerow 1991), and witans were generally held at royal residences in the countryside

Northampton Greyfriars, some 600 metres to the north-east of the palaces site (Oakley *et al* 1978, 148–9) and although it is of possibly 8th- or 9th-century date a stylus would not be out of place on a medieval monastic site. The third possible stylus was found on the site of the castle in the late 19th century (Sharp 1881–2, pl 4, 7) a little to the north-west of the hall complex.

(Sawyer 1983, 277), there would seem to be justification for considering that some former Roman towns such as Canterbury, Lincoln, York and London were continuing centres through which royal authority was exercised on an ongoing basis (Blair 2005, 271ff,) and other similar but undocumented permanent or semi-permanent centres are to be expected. Martin Biddle believes that there was a very significant stone hall in the centre of Winchester from the mid-7th century, and that it was royal power established within the former Roman town that led to the construction of the first phase of the Old Minster, with major north Italian influence in respect of foundation techniques and more generally (Martin Biddle pers comm). Many Mercian assemblies were held at Tamworth (Sawyer 1983, 286), which certainly by the 780s or 790s had become a stable royal centre and would be a further excellent candidate location for the finding of another stone hall. In Wessex, however, it would appear that, away from Winchester, it was not until the early 9th century that Tamworth-style bases and shire centres emerged: Kingston-on-Thames and Wilton by 838, Southampton by 840, Wantage by 849, Chippenham by 853, Amesbury by 858 and Somerton by 860 (Blair 2005, 325; 2018 107). Even where royal administrative centres moved it should perhaps not be unexpected to find a stone hall, at least on some sites. And why were many bishoprics established which then continued to function in what had been Roman seats of government? Surely not all administrative centres exercising royal authority lacked permanence?

Are we also to accept that, while kings and other secular lords were happy to donate estates and monies for the glorification of god and the creation of permanent architectural manifestations of their devotion and munificence, they would have been, in contrast, parsimonious in terms of their own residences? Rather it would seem perfectly reasonable to expect the royal image to be projected in and ambitions to be reflected in prestigious stone buildings on high-status secular sites in Anglo-Saxon England. Indeed the presence of mortar mixers at Bamburgh and Dunbar would appear to point us in this direction (Kirton and Young, 2012; Perry 2006, 63; cf also Shapland 2015, 495). Again, although downplayed by John Blair (2018, 85), Asser, in his life of King Alfred talks about buildings decorated with gold and silver on Alfred's instructions, halls and chambers marvellously constructed by him in stone and timber and royal vills, also built in stone, moved to more suitable locations (*Quid loquar ... <de> aedificiis aureis et argenteis incomparabiliter, illo edocente, fabricatis? De aulis et cambris regalibus, lapideis et ligneis suo iusso mirabiliter constructis? De villis regalibus lapideis antiqua positione motatis et in decentioribus locis regali imperio decentissime constructis?* (Stevenson 1904, 76, section 91).

In seeking to provide a secular architectural setting appropriate for a royal or aristocratic administrative centre it is important not to separate the secular from the ecclesiastical dynamic. While some minsters truly developed their own momentum one must remember the close relationship between royal administrative centres and ancient minsters founded at such centres. Surely a more pluralist approach should be followed which recognises the interconnectedness of the church and royal authority?

The Northampton halls will undoubtedly continue to generate debate. To date they are unique in their succession of timber and stone halls, the scale of the stone hall, and their location within what was or would become a major urban centre. Perhaps there are Anglo-Saxon stone halls waiting to be uncovered elsewhere, although presently eluding us, in both secular and ecclesiastical contexts. John Blair, without adducing any certain parallel on a contemporary English minster site, defers to his expectations of what he argues one might reasonably expect to find in such a location at this time as a result of Carolingian influence. On the other hand, looking to continental parallels and in the absence of firm evidence to the contrary, the interpretation of the Northampton hall as having secular, perhaps royal, but certainly high-status, associations would also seem eminently reasonable (cf for example Gem 1993, 39).

Northampton *c*.875–1100

The documentary background

In 913 we have the first historical reference to Northampton. The Anglo-Saxon Chronicle records that 'the army from Northampton rode out after Easter and broke the peace, and killed many men at Hook Norton and round about there'. In 914 'Earl Thurcetel came and accepted him [King Edward] as his lord, and so did all the earls and the principal men who belonged to Bedford, and also many of those who belonged to Northampton'. In 917 'the army from Northampton and Leicester and north of these places broke the peace, and went to Towcester, and fought all day against the borough, intending to take it by storm, but yet the people who were inside defended it until more help came to them, and the enemy then left the borough and went away. And then very quickly after that, they again went out with a marauding band by night, and came upon unprepared men, and captured no small number of men and cattle between Bernwood Forest and Aylesbury.' 'In the autumn of the same year King Edward went with the army of the West Saxons to Passenham, and stayed there while the borough of Towcester was provided with a stone wall. And Earl Thurferth and the *holds* submitted to him, and so did all the army which belonged to Northampton, as far north as the Welland, and sought to have him as their lord and protector'. On 30th November 1010 'the Danes came to Northampton and at once burnt that town and as much about it as they pleased...' (*ASC*, 62–6, 90).

We can thus see that at the beginning of the 10th century Northampton was in the hands of the Danish army, under the leadership of one of their earls who each held territory around one of their strongholds. It was very much on the front line, and it held control over a substantial area that perhaps extended from Towcester as far north as the river Welland. It is not referred to as a borough nor are we told whether it was fortified or not, and we are not given any indication as to its size. Documentary sources are similarly uninformative about other centres of the Danelaw with places such as Leicester, Derby, Stamford and Bedford only really emerging as strongholds of the various earls and their armies during the campaigns of Edward the Elder from 913 onwards. Furthermore, in the absence of significant archaeological data, we can only speculate about the size and character of these settlements (Hall 1989; 2001). In terms of more temporary camps, the defended area at Repton, Derbyshire, where the Viking army wintered in 873–4, enclosed an area of just under 1.5 hectares (Biddle and Kjølbye-Biddle 2001); it has been suggested that the spread of finds extending over some 55 hectares represents the encampment of the *micel here* at Torksey the previous year (Hadley and Richards 2016, 26).

The archaeological evidence

For the size and character of Northampton at the beginning of the 10th century we have to turn to archaeology (Fig 27). A good general indicator in providing a framework for its topographical development is provided by pottery, which is now present in considerably increased quantities (Figs 28–29, 39; see Appendix 1). The early-middle Anglo-Saxon hand-made wares are replaced by the wheel-thrown shelly St Neots-type ware and sandy Northampton ware (Williams 1974). While St Neots-type ware has been recognised as continuing from the mid-9th to the 12th century, Northampton ware has been considered to have been restricted to the 10th century, possibly even the first half of it (cf. Denham 1985b, 55). Perhaps, however, undue caution has been exercised in the past with regard to the dating of the introduction of Northampton ware, influenced by the thinking at the time regarding the start date for production of other wheel-thrown sandy wares, such as Stamford ware. Gareth Perry, while rejecting Paul Blinkhorn's ideas for the widespread introduction of wheel-thrown pottery within the area that became the Danelaw prior to the Scandinavian settlement, has recently suggested that production of Stamford, Ipswich-Thetford, Leicester, Thetford, Stafford and Torksey wares commenced in the last quarter of the 9th century (2013; 2016, 101ff; see also Dodd *et al* 2014, 85–93, 101). A strong case can thus be made for bringing the start of Northampton ware production back into the last quarter of the 9th century. Taken with the coin evidence this has significant implications for the chronology of settlement development in the area at the west end of Northampton.

We can note that both Northampton ware and St Neots-type ware are well represented on the sites around St Peter's Street and Chalk Lane (Figs 28–29, 39) but they are also common further to the east, indicating an expansion of settlement into these areas. Indeed, small quantities of both these fabrics have been found on outlying sites beyond, in areas where there is presently no clear evidence for settlement until after the Norman Conquest (see below). Since it is generally difficult to refine the chronology of individual sites between the end of the 9th and the first half of the 11th century, this for the most part is not attempted when describing the various sites, but some more specific observations are made at the end of this section.

The structural evidence mirrors the picture of expansion provided by the pottery but it also witnesses a radical change in the character of the settlement. The stone hall appears to have fallen out of use by sometime in the first half of the 10th century, based on the pottery assemblage in the robber trenches of its walls and also from a sunken-featured building set within its former interior. We cannot be sure whether it continued in use as a building or a shell during the Danish occupation, and here one can note how the church at Repton was incorporated into the defensive circuit of the Viking camp of 873–4 (Biddle and Kjølbye-Biddle 2001), or whether it was already in the process of being pulled down. Was material from the stone hall used for construction or reconstruction work on St Peter's church or for building defences around the settlement, and, if so, at what date? – during or after the Danish occupation? Immediately to the south-west of the site of the hall were the remains of several fragmentary timber posthole buildings, somewhat irregularly disposed, associated with a metalled area; the complex was perhaps entered by a gate. The deposits relating to one of these posthole buildings were overlain by a 'thin yellow-green' layer, interpreted as a floor. There were few signs of walling although much of the area was disturbed by later pits and it is possible that this was a surface-built structure, evidence for which is rare in late Saxon Northampton. Other timber buildings lay to the north and south and sunken-featured buildings to the east and south. Silver-, copper-alloy- and iron-working and also antler-working and small-scale skin processing were undertaken. Two St Edmund Memorial pennies were associated with the metalworking and a further example was found in later deposits a little to the east (Williams J H 1979, 140; Williams *et al* 1985, 43).

In Chalk Lane a structure *c*.10m by 3m was defined by six substantial post-pits, 1.3m to 1.9m in diameter, three down each side. The evidence is not entirely clear as no post-pipes could be made out but a building of two bays, each *c*.5.0m long and *c*.3.0–3.5m wide, is suggested. There was an internal cellar, about 3.0m square and 1.0m deep, and immediately to the north was a sunken-featured building *c*.4.0m by 3.3m by 1.0m. deep. Postholes to the west might define further buildings or alternatively fence lines within a yard. The main building was replaced by a hall in excess of 7m long by 4m wide and, but this time constructed with lines of posts set in shallow postholes. Outside was a yard and cultivated area and also an area of pits for the disposal of rubbish (Figs 30–32). Associated with these buildings were evidence for iron-, silver- and copper-working, weaving and bone-working, three St Edmund Memorial pennies, one securely stratified on the floor of the cellar, and a copper-alloy Urnes-style animal-head terminal. The impression was given of an isolated property rather than a building belonging to an intensively built-up complex (Williams and Shaw 1981, 96ff).

Within the limited area available for investigation on the Marefair site further possible evidence for timber buildings was noted, with the postholes aligned north-west to south-east and north-east to south-west. Crucible fragments again attested silver-working and there were also indications of copper-alloy- and iron-working. Does the rare evidence for silver-working at this date here and on the 'palaces' site and Chalk Lane witness the presence of a mint in this area? There was a further St Edmund

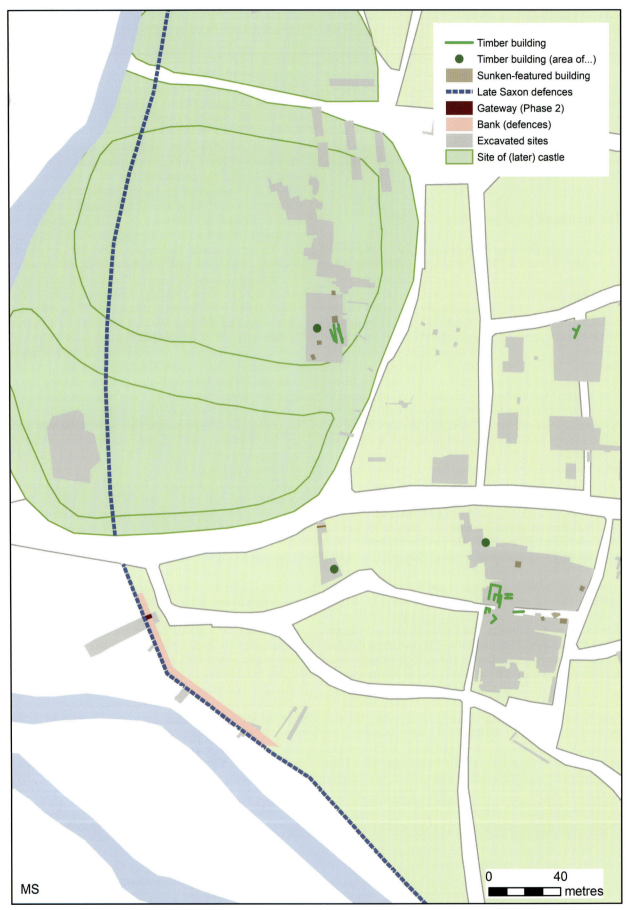

Legend:
- Timber building
- Timber building (area of...)
- Sunken-featured building
- Late Saxon defences
- Gateway (Phase 2)
- Bank (defences)
- Excavated sites
- Site of (later) castle

0 — 40 metres

MS

Fig 27a: Late Saxon Northampton *c*.875–1066, west

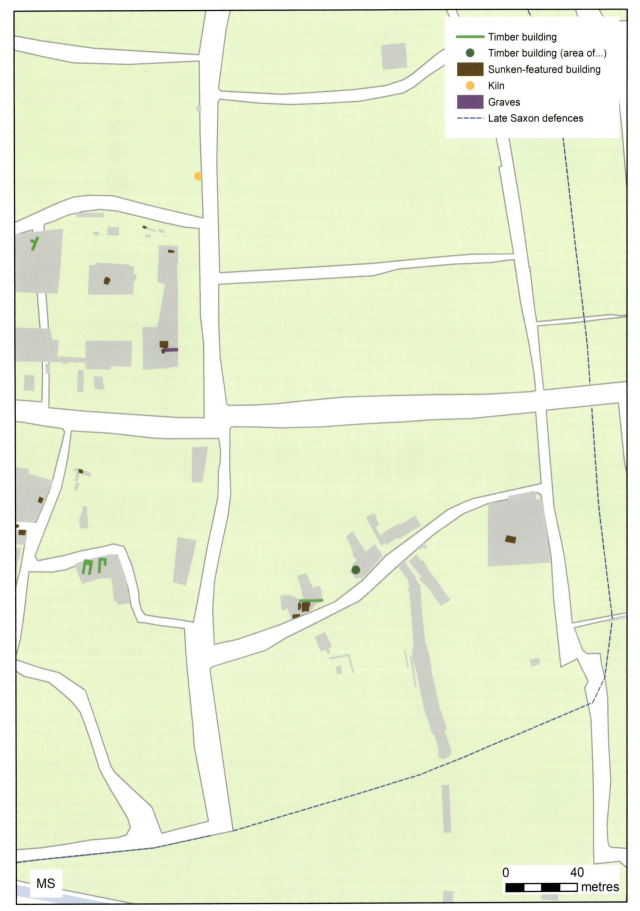

MS

0   40 metres

Fig 27b: Late Saxon Northampton *c*.875–1066, east

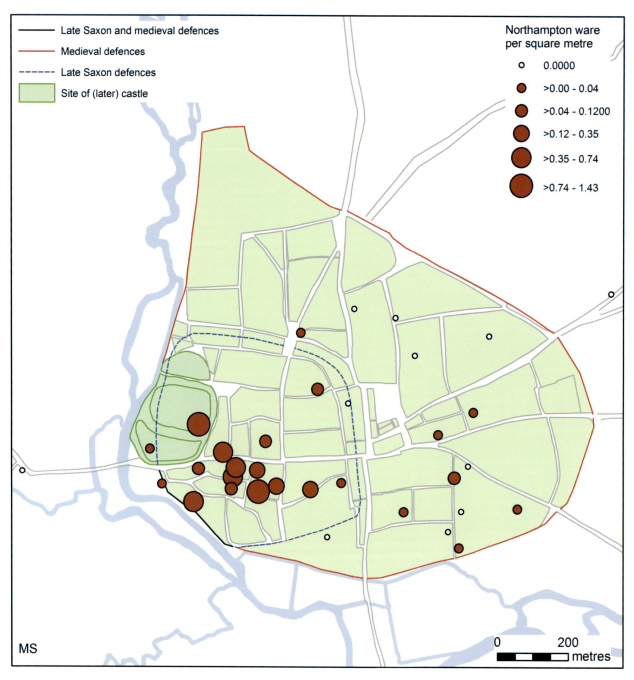

Fig 28: Northampton ware distribution

Memorial penny and possibly a fragment of another, both in later contexts (Williams F 1979, 46; Archibald 1979; Bayley 1979a and b).

The evidence for late Saxon activity on the Sol Central site, immediately to the east, was surprisingly limited and patchy but this may well have been due to the mitigation strategy adopted in advance of development, with some areas of potentially undisturbed deposits remaining unexcavated (Miller and Watson 2005, 1). Five sunken-featured buildings of various sizes were noted, mainly in the east part of the site, and there were traces also of a single timber-framed building aligned north-east to south-west. The areas around the buildings appear to have been unenclosed but were dotted with pits, postholes

and the occasional ditch. Before the end of the 10th century the south-east corner of the site began to receive human burials and this use continued into the 11th and 12th centuries (Miller and Wilson 2005, 7ff). A little to the north lay a site where Northampton ware was produced (Williams 1974).

Black Lion Hill saw increased activity in the 11th century; postholes at the south of the site witness one or more buildings but no plan could be established (Shaw 1985). Excavations at Northampton Station, at the low-lying western end of the outer bailey of the castle, have indicated that pre-Conquest structures were absent in this area (Chapman 2021c, this volume 79–127) but it should be noted that three St Edmund Memorial pennies

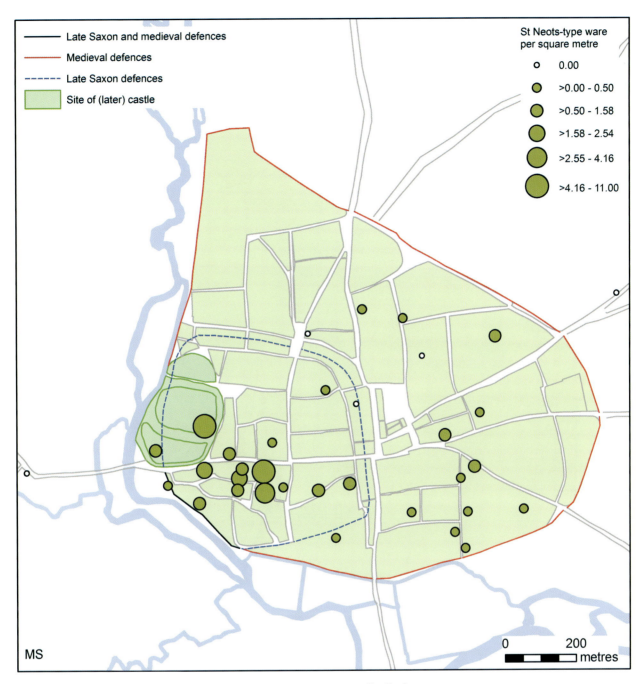

Fig 29: St Neots-type ware distribution

were found during the destruction of the castle for the railway in the late 19th century (Sharpe 1881–2, 246; Rigold 1959).

Moving eastwards from St Peter's we can see on Gregory Street two rectangular timber buildings, set parallel to each other and aligned north-south, associated with a metalled surface (Figs 33–34). The first was at least 10m long by c.4.5m wide. It had been rebuilt several times and burnt floor levels survived. Slag and hammer-scale suggest metalworking (Williams 1982a, 24; RCHM 1985, microfiche 388–9).

In Woolmonger Street were the remains of further posthole structures and cellars. The best preserved of the cellars, which measured 4.5m long by 4.2m wide

and 1.0m deep, lay within the western bay of a posthole building at least 11.8m long by 6.4m wide (Fig 35). Although a complete ground plan did not survive, it is possible that two bays, each 5.6m square, were separated by a central passage 0.8m wide (Soden 1998–9, 76). The building is particularly interesting in that its east-west alignment respects that of Marefair and Gold Street, and indeed buildings on St Peter's Street and Gregory Street, rather than the sinuous line of Woolmonger Street itself, which it partly underlies.

Marefair/Gold Street may have preserved the line of a Roman road running from the Romano-British small town at Duston, c.1.5km to the west, along the Nene valley to the Romano-British settlement at Irchester. If this were

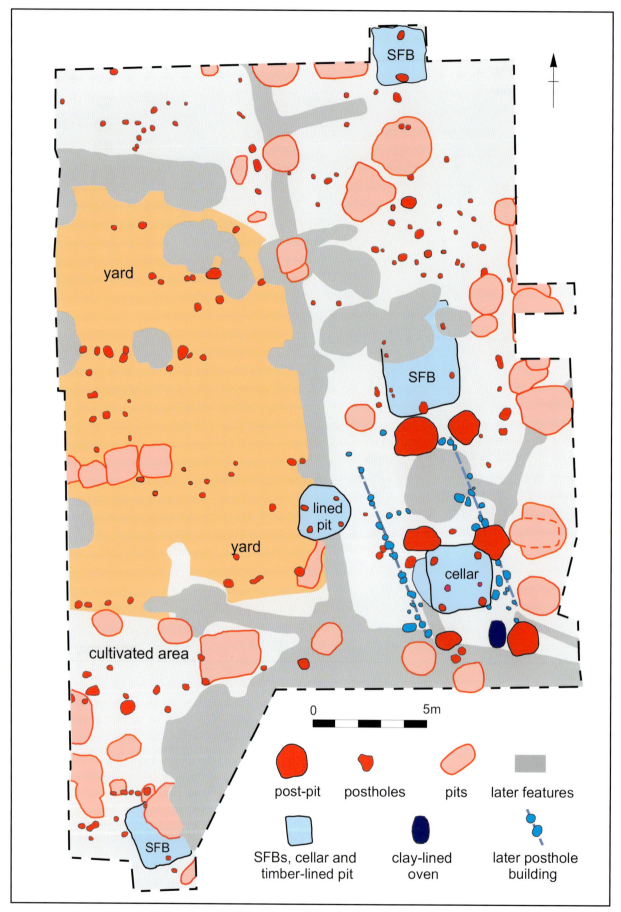

0   5m

post-pit   postholes   pits   later features

SFBs, cellar and   clay-lined   later posthole
timber-lined pit   oven   building

Fig 30: Successive late Saxon structures in Chalk Lane, with associated features

Fig 31: (left) Chalk Lane; the earlier late Saxon building, which contains a square cellar, is defined by two lines of large post pits, and there is a sunken-featured structure beyond (see Fig 32). The posthole bases of the west wall of a later timber building are visible to the left

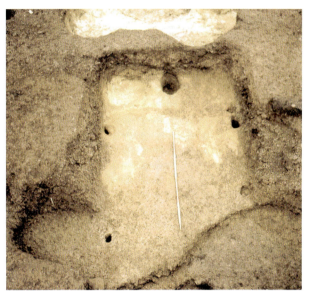

Fig 32: Chalk Lane, the sunken-featured structure to the north of the posthole building, looking south

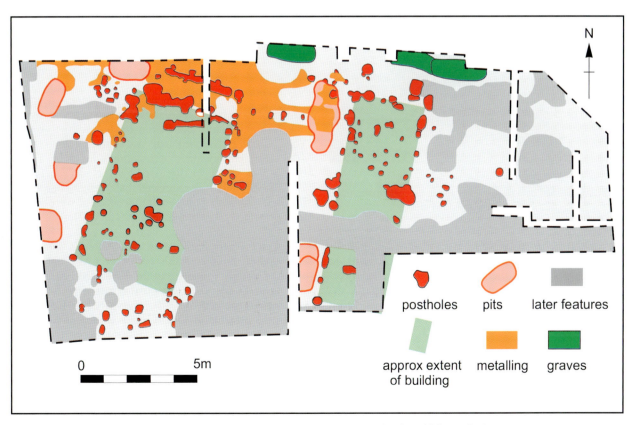

Fig 33: Late Saxon timber buildings in Gregory Street; note also the middle Anglo-Saxon graves

Fig 34: The late Saxon timber buildings in Gregory Street, from the east

Fig 35: Woolmonger Street, showing the north wall of a timber building, defined by a row of posts and in the foreground part of a deep cellar within the building

the case the road may well have influenced the alignment of later development but there is little here or on other sites to support the idea of an early gridded street pattern (cf Soden 1998–9, 113; see also below). To the south, in St James' Square, there was further late Saxon activity, which possibly included flax retting (Williams and Farwell 1983). At the east end of Woolmonger Street, adjoining Kingswell Street, a late Saxon cellared building measuring 5.0m by 3.5m by 1.16m deep was aligned west-north-west to east-south-east, and there were also postholes and three pits. The small quantity of Northampton ware and the developed nature of the associ-

ated dominant St Neots-type ware perhaps indicate that this occupation was 11th- rather than 10th-century in date (Brown 2008, 185, 195). A few sherds of St Neots-type ware and Northampton ware from the limited investigations on the Moat House Hotel site point to probable 10th-century activity in the area (Chapman 2001, 100), and a little further north just four pre-Conquest sherds were found among a much larger ceramic assemblage (McCarthy 1976, 142).

A number of late Saxon cellars and sunken-featured buildings have been noted above; they are a widespread phenomenon within late Saxon towns such as Oxford, York, Chester, Thetford and Wallingford (Dodd 2003, 40–1). Similar structures at London, admittedly a little later in date, have been discussed by Horsman *et al* (1988, 70, 108–9) where it is suggested that the more deeply cut features, such as those at Woolmonger Street, were cellars, used principally for storage, and that they belonged to the shops of craftsmen and merchants.

St Peter's and presumably St Gregory's continued as churches throughout this period and All Saints' was almost certainly founded before 1086 (see below). The origins of St Mary's, close to the castle, probably lay sometime in the 11th or 12th century (RCHM 1985, fiche 379). It is possible that there was a church in the north-east quadrant of settlement, dedicated to St Catherine, but this is somewhat speculative (Williams 1982c, 82). It has been postulated that the cemetery on the Sol Central site (see above) belonged to the chapel of St Martin, the original location of St Andrew's priory (Miller *et al* 2005, 68).

The topographical framework

As long ago as the early 1950s Alderman Frank Lee, in a perceptive paper ahead of its time, analysed the street pattern of Northampton and argued that it was possible to see an early defensive line defined by two concentric sets of streets: the outer ring, represented by Scarletwell Street, Bearward Street, the Drapery and Bridge Street, would have once lain outside the defences, while Bath Street, Silver Street, College Street and Kingswell Street would have been just inside the defences (1954; cf Figs 1–2). The west and south parts of the circuit would have followed the edge of the higher ground overlooking the streams of the river. Marefair and Gold Street would have constituted a main east-west axial street with Horsemarket and Horseshoe Street as the north-south axis, the inhabited area thus being divided roughly into quadrants. From the east gate, just to the west of the present All Saints' church, roads would have radiated out along what are today Abington Street, St Giles Street and Derngate, in the directions of Kettering, Wellingborough and Bedford. Similarly, at the north gate at the Mayorhold there was a bifurcation of routes, northwards to Leicester and north-eastwards across Northampton Heath towards Kettering. Glenn Foard has noted how the route across the heath respects the furlong boundaries of the medieval field system (Foard 1995, 113; see also Williams 1982c, map opposite 79). This important observation would seem to underline the antiquity of both the route layout and also the field system. In terms of further documentary confirmation, we can observe that the church of All Saints, standing just outside the postulated east gate, is mentioned alongside St Peter's church in an entry in Domesday Book which can now justifiably be seen to relate to Northampton (Williams 2014, 53, 180).

The area of late Saxon occupation seems to have been bounded on the south and west by the river Nene and one of its tributaries, and to have been largely confined within the Lee line to the east and north. As already noted, limited quantities of Northampton ware have been found to the east of All Saints', particularly in the St Giles' Street excavations, but nowhere in association with any structural remains, even though the areas excavated have in some cases been quite extensive (cf Fig 28). It seems reasonable to regard this pottery as following the normal pattern of discard to be found around a village or town although it is possible that there are extra-mural settlement sites waiting to be discovered. Similarly, only small amounts of St Neots-type ware have been recovered from sites outside the late Saxon defences except at the St Giles' Street site where it formed a reasonably large proportion of the assemblage (Fig 29). This may indicate occupation along a road leading out from the east gate, which would not be surprising. Given, however, that St Neots-type ware continued in production into the 12th century and that much of the St Neots-type ware on the St Giles' Street site was in what is considered to be in its more developed fabric, this need not have taken place in the late Saxon period, although All Saints and Mayorhold may well have been the locations for extra-mural markets at a fairly early date.

The fossilisation of an early defence-line by parallel rings of streets is well demonstrated elsewhere, for example at the pre-Conquest burh at Nottingham (Barley and Straw 1969) and the Norman town at Bristol (Lobel and Carus-Wilson 1975, 4b, Map 2). At Rothenburg ob dem Tauber in Germany not only do former intramural and extramural streets continue to define the 12th-century defensive enceinte preserved within the expanded later medieval town but one can still pass through two of the gates set within this line. Thomas Welsh has challenged Frank Lee's conclusions (1996–97; 2002), looking to medieval and later traditions and explanations for various elements of the street pattern, but analysis of the distribution of late Saxon and medieval pottery, as demonstrated in this paper, and the topographical evidence for the defensive enceinte itself, taken in conjunction with the behaviour of roads approaching the postulated gates, are most compelling. It is unfortunate, however, that archaeological investigations have yet to confirm the Lee line, the very few sites along the proposed circuit where any observations were possible having suffered from below ground disturbance from cellarage and pit digging.

Remains of late Saxon defences have, however, been located at Green Street to the south-west of the town (Fig 36; Chapman 1999 and Chapman 2021 b, this volume 129–136). The defences followed a curved alignment from Black Lion Hill round towards the bottom of Horseshoe Street, protecting the area of raised ground to the north-east where settlement was located. Two phases of 'late Saxon' defences were recognised. Constructed above an occupation soil that produced Maxey ware (Fig 36, a), in the first phase an earthen bank about 6m wide had a timber revetment and was fronted by a ditch, probably at least 8m wide and over 2m deep (Fig 36, b). Sometime before the 12th century the defences were refurbished and the timber revetment was replaced by a stone one at least 0.6m wide (Fig 36, c) and a gateway with a metalled road surface was made through the defences. We do not know the dimensions of the gateway but it seems to have been too close to where one would expect Northampton's main west gate to have been, on Black Lion Hill, for it to have been either another main gate into the burh or some sort of postern, unless perhaps it was providing access to a wharf alongside a then navigable river. This entrance had been blocked before the post-Conquest construction of a wall surmounting the existing bank (Fig 36, d).

These two phases of defences appear to resemble most clearly those associated with Edward the Elder, for example at Oxford (Dodd 2003, 21–3). The beginning of the 12th century probably saw the construction of the medieval town wall over the existing defences and Civil War defences followed the same course, although by the time of Speed's map of 1610 there would appear to have been little or nothing on the ground left to map.

The north-south and east-west axial streets within the line of the defences have already been noted and a number of other streets, such as St Katherine's Street and Castle Street seem to respect the east-west axial alignment. On Woolmonger Street some timber structures follow this alignment rather than that of the present street (Soden 1998–9, 112). More generally several post-built structures across the settled area are similarly orientated (see Fig 27), but, overall, buildings are somewhat irregularly disposed, with post-built structures and sunken-featured buildings

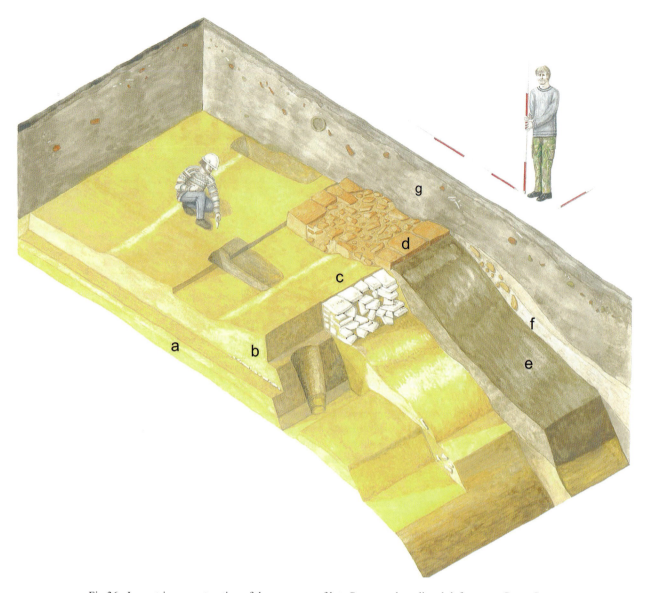

Fig 36: Isometric reconstruction of the sequence of late Saxon and medieval defences at Green Street

intermixed. The street frontages of closely packed houses, characteristic of the later medieval town, are very much missing and it would certainly be speculative to argue for a regular grid pattern of streets within the town at this time, although this may have been the case, as in other late Saxon towns (cf Biddle and Hill 1971).

A chronology for the development of the late Saxon settlement

Can we then refine the late Saxon town's development further? St Edmund Memorial pennies were struck by the Scandinavian rulers of the southern Danelaw between c.895 and c.917/8 and did not continue in circulation beyond c.920. Many of the coins would have been struck in East Anglia but it is probable that there were mints in the East Midlands and Stewart Lyon has suggested that Northampton and Stamford may have been among the mints for the coinage, based on the subsequent history

of some of the moneyers named on the coins (Blackburn 2001, 132; Blunt et al 1989, 100; Lyon, S 2001, 72–4). Seven, possibly eight, examples were found during excavations in the areas around St Peter's church. Together with the three 19th-century finds from the site of the castle, they are sufficiently numerous to suggest that at least some of the structural evidence associated with them belongs to the period of the Danish occupation of Northampton. Indeed, it can be noted that there are rather more St Edmund Memorial pennies from the excavations discussed in this paper than pennies from the rest of the late Saxon period up to the Norman Conquest. There are also two objects decorated in Anglo-Scandinavian style, the sword pommel with Borre style decoration from the area of the stone hall and the copper alloy terminal in the form of an Urnes-style animal head from Chalk Lane, although the former could date from later in the 10th century and the latter is probably later still (Williams et al 1985, 41; Goodall 1985, 66; Goodall and Webster 1981, 122). If the beginnings of Northampton ware are brought back into the later 9th century (see above and Appendix 1) the case for the earliest late Saxon deposits belonging to the period of Danish occupation is further strengthened. The structures most likely to be associated with this phase would be some of the irregularly disposed posthole structures at the west end of St Peter's Street and, in Chalk Lane, the earlier rectangular post-built structure with a cellar and the relatively deep sunken-featured building immediately north of it. The absence of St Edmund Memorial pennies from sites not in the immediate vicinity of St Peter's church might suggest that any Danish occupation was concentrated in this area, although we must recognise that we are dealing with a relatively small number of coins. Does the earlier phase of late Saxon defences revealed at Green Street relate to Danish occupation? Whether or not that is the case the restricted area of clearly Danish occupation might suggest that any associated defensive circuit enclosed an area somewhat less than that enclosed by the 'Lee line' defences.

There are further implications for the development of Northampton from the time of its capture by Edward the Elder in 917 through to the Norman Conquest. Although settlement activity was present on sites across the whole of the area within the Lee defence line there is no extended structural sequence for this period on individual sites and one has therefore to question the intensity of development and just how early Northampton became truly urban. Loveluck has commented on, for example, the relatively sparse occupation along street frontages at Oxford and Stafford, with there being significant open or cultivated areas within Hereford and Worcester (2013, 346), although the late 9th-century agreement made between Ealdorman Æthelred, his wife Æthelflæd and the Church of Worcester, referring to market rights and profits from land rents and the proceeds of justice suggests some form of urban society (Baker and Holt 2004, 133). Blair suggests that evidence for formal urban development as opposed to gradually intensifying occupation clusters within what later became recognisably towns generally does not seem to appear until the second half of the 10th century (2018, 339ff). Are we then looking at the burh established by Edward in 917, presumably with its defensive enceinte following the Lee line, as initially very much providing adequate space as a refuge in troubled times, with it only gradually developing its more commercial, urban functions (cf Thomas and Boucher 2002, 187–8)?

Domesday Book and beyond

At the time of the Norman Conquest Northampton was a middling shire town. Domesday Book shows it having just over 300 houses with the town rendering £30.10s to the king. If Portland was also part of the town a further £12 was due, giving a total of £42.10s (*Domesday Book* B, 1,5; Williams 2014, 17, 179). On this basis the town was significantly less prosperous than London, York and Lincoln and would have ranked between twentieth and thirtieth in the land, similar to towns such as Chichester, Derby, Guildford, Ipswich, Nottingham and Worcester.

In 1130 the farm was considerably raised, to £100, a figure then exceeded only by London and Lincoln. It had important royal connections, with Waltheof, the Saxon earl of Northampton, marrying the Countess Judith, the niece of William the Conqueror, only for him to be executed for treason in 1076. Their daughter Maud married Simon de Senlis I, who came from a powerful French family and probably became earl of Northampton in 1089. Northampton's medieval defences enclosed an area of about 100 hectares, an intramural area only exceeded in this country at London and Norwich. According to tradition Simon de Senlis constructed the walls, but we have no firm evidence for this. He is similarly attributed with commencing the building of the castle, although the first documentary record of the castle relates to 1130 and the known earthworks excavated to date clearly belong to the early 12th century and were probably a creation of King Henry I (Chapman 2021d, this volume 163–4). Simon certainly founded St Andrew's priory in the late 11th century and St James' abbey was established by William Peverel in the western suburbs in the early 12th century (Chapman *et al* forthcoming). The churches dedicated to St Giles and the Holy Sepulchre were probably in existence by the second quarter of the 12th century.

What is clear is that Northampton was expanding dramatically outside its Saxon defences and certainly by the 1170s, based on tallages and aids rendered to the Crown, it was among the foremost towns of England (Williams 2014, 17–23). The distribution of post-Conquest shelly wares (Figs 37 & 39) clearly shows settlement expanding over the whole of the area within the medieval walls and beyond. The next century saw the town at its height, only for it to recede to become a middling county town until fairly recent times.

Conclusion

Northampton's rich history may not be as readily appreciated as that of some of the cathedral cities of England or towns where medieval town walls and fine contemporary buildings have survived, but its importance during the last two thousand years must not be forgotten. The dramatic development of Northampton in the Anglo-Saxon and medieval periods has been much illuminated by archaeological investigations and historical research over the last fifty years which have revealed a clearer picture than that so far obtained for many English towns. A large number of questions, however, remain unanswered and it is important to build on the results already achieved and ensure that any future development is accompanied by an appropriate archaeological response suitably designed to clarify the outstanding issues relating its origins and growth.

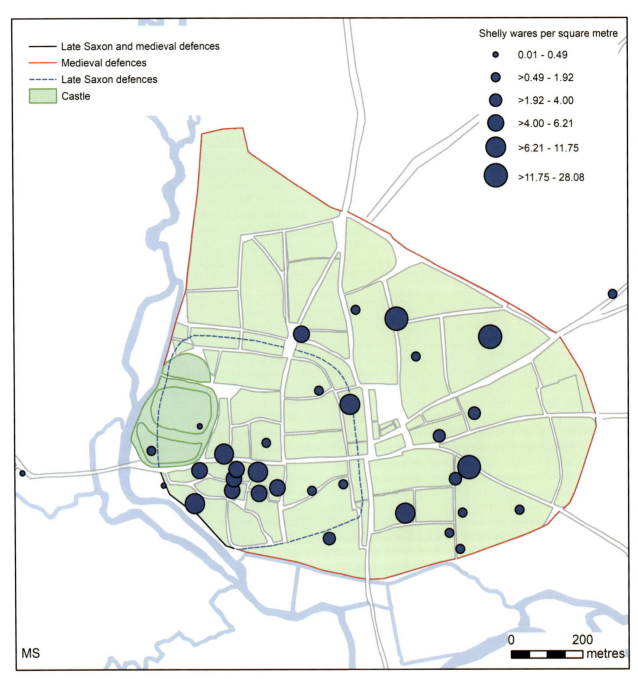

Fig 37: Distribution of medieval shelly wares

Appendix 1: Using Ceramic Evidence to Analyse the Origins and Growth of Early Northampton

Michael Shaw

Introduction

This appendix presents a summary of a piece of research undertaken as part of my doctoral thesis on 'Approaches to the analysis of the topography, origins, growth and development of English medieval towns' (Shaw 2020). It uses the distribution of the most common types of pottery (Indicator Pottery Types) found in Northampton to delineate the areas of settlement at various stages of its history.

Methodology

This work has been possible because virtually all the pottery analysis carried out in the town has used the Northampton Pottery Type Series (NTS) or its successor, the Northamptonshire County Type Series (CTS). The one exception has been in respect of the MoLAS excavations at Sol Central, Marefair, where the Bedfordshire County Type Series was employed, but a correlation table gave the NTS and CTS equivalents (Slowikowski 2005).

The plotting and analysis were undertaken using Esri's ArcGIS mapping software. A shapefile with associated database was created recording the number of sherds of each of the major pottery types recovered from excavations in the town since 1973[2]. Figure 2 shows the sites used in the analysis. Pottery from watching briefs was not included as it normally amounted to only a small number of sherds and the sites were not subject to detailed investigation. Where there have been several interventions in the same area, particularly where evaluation has been followed by set-piece excavation, the pottery quantities have been amalgamated. These comprised: Woolmonger Street, St James' Place and St James' End; Angel Street and St John's Street; separate pieces of work on the Northampton High School for Girls, Derngate by Northamptonshire Archaeology and Oxford Archaeology; adjacent excavations at The Riding carried out by Northampton Development Corporation in 1981–2 and by AOC Archaeology in 1999; and work at Sol Central, Marefair (the site of the former Barclaycard House), where an evaluation by Northamptonshire Archaeology in 1998 preceded further work by MoLAS between 1998

and 2002. The adjoining sites in the St Peter's area – St Peter's Street, St Peter's Gardens (the 'Saxon palaces site') and The Green – have not been combined as each was a large-scale excavation with a differing research design. Table 2 is an extract from the shapefile database showing the pottery sites, their area in square metres, the number of sherds of each indicator pottery type from each site and references to the original pottery reports.

All sherds of the major pottery types were counted including those found as a residual element in features from a later period. This was considered acceptable as there was no evidence from any of the sites that material had been brought in from elsewhere so that the pottery as a residual element was likely to have come from contexts close by, a common phenomenon at complex urban sites with intercutting features. Not to have done so would have risked missing information. For instance at the Sol Central Marefair a reasonably large number of early-middle Saxon and middle Saxon sherds were recovered from residual contexts (36 and 24 sherds respectively) although no features of this date were discovered during the excavations. The excavation strategy adopted at this site, however, was to excavate deposits down to the formation level of the proposed development rather than down to the natural subsoil (Miller and Wilson 2005, 1). Accordingly, I would consider that the earlier sherds found as a residual element indicate activity of these periods on or adjacent to the site which were not uncovered due to the excavation strategy. Greater confidence in this assertion is provided by the results from the Marefair excavation site 60m to the west which was excavated down to the natural subsoil and where features of early/middle Anglo-Saxon date were discovered (Williams F 1979, 43–46).

It is worth emphasising the value of using a single type series. This has enabled pottery from a succession of excavations, carried out by a variety of organisations and studied by a number of different specialists over a period of more than 40 years, to be analysed in an integrated manner. The NTS was established at the time of major investigations in the town in the 1970s (McCarthy 1979, 153–65). It was used, with amendments and modifications as further evidence presented itself, by all subsequent ceramic specialists until 1997 when it was incorporated into the County Type Series (CTS). This involved a change of prefix and code but otherwise it has been subject only to further refinements rather than wholesale restructuring, a testament to the rigour with which the original type series

---

2   A simple count of the number of sherds was used as this figure was recorded for all of the sites whereas figures for estimated vessel equivalent (EVE) or weight are only recorded for a selection of the later sites

Table 2: Extract from Pottery Database showing the number of sherds of each indicator pottery type from each site and references to original pottery reports

Site Name	Area (m²)	Pottery types (by sherd count)						References
		EMS	Maxey	N'pton	St Neots	Shelly	Total	
46–50 Sheep St	400	0	0	0	4	524	528	Blinkhorn 2006
Angel Street & St John's St	1467	1	0	2	73	15564	15640	Blinkhorn 2021a; Blinkhorn 1993
Black Lion Hill	194	34	1	14	492	966	1507	Denham 1985a
Chalk Lane	900	1265	77	1285	7213	9	9849	Gryspeerdt 1981
College Street	20	0	0	0	0	235	235	Gryspeerdt 1982
Commercial St	20	0	0	0	1	80	81	In archive
Cow Lane	293	0	0	0	5	260	265	Blinkhorn 2021
Derngate B	8	0	0	0	8	150	158	Shaw & Denham 1984
Freeschool St	22	1	0	4	242	257	504	Shaw & O'Hara 1990
Green Street	460	0	15	17	9	51	92	Blinkhorn & Soden 1999
Gregory Street	401	0	9	390	1668	2348	4415	In archive
Greyfriars	1617	0	0	0	0	2274	2274	Gryspeerdt 1978
Horseshoe St. A	126	0	0	43	43	554	640	In archive
Kingswell Street	1186	0	0	29	1783	1555	3367	Blinkhorn 2008
Marefair	290	43	3	213	181	2357	2797	Gryspeerdt 1979
Mayorhold	190	0	0	2	0	873	875	McCarthy 1976
Moat House Hotel	182	0	0	12	30	150	192	Blinkhorn 2001
Newlands	60	0	0	0	2	1031	1033	In archive
Northampton High School combined	897	1	0	2	5	1094	1102	Shaw 1991; Shaw *et al* 1992; Blinkhorn 2002
Northampton Station	855	1	2	19	502	1061	1585	Blinkhorn 2021b
Sol Central Marefair (MOLA/ NA combined)	3337	36	24	388	1563	2734	4745	Blinkhorn 1998; Slowikowski 2005
St Edmund's End (Kettering Road)	92	1	0	0	0	176	177	Williams E & Shaw 1997
St Giles' Street (Guildhall)	180	0	0	2	233	449	684	Denham 1997
St James' End	96	0	0	0	0	47	47	Blinkhorn 1996
St John's Car Park 2012	489	0	0	0	2	522	524	McSloy 2017
St Peter's Gardens	900	273	10	531	2100	4165	7079	Denham 1985b
St Peter's Street	1425	148	83	722	985	6407	8345	McCarthy 1979
St Peter's Way	15	0	0	8	8	124	140	In archive
Swan St North (Derngate A)	12	0	0	1	5	44	50	Shaw & Denham 1984
Swan St South	330	0	0	5	29	622	656	Denham & Shaw 1994
The Convent	25	2	0	0	25	702	729	In archive
The Green	1135	5	0	132	1796	7048	8981	Denham 2021
The Riding combined	252	0	0	2	23	879	904	Denham 1984; Blinkhorn 2005
Woolmonger Street combined	1845	101	3	395	2668	2568	5735	Denham 1983; Blinkhorn 1995; Soden 1999

Abbreviations: EMS = Early-middle Saxon wares; Maxey = Maxey-type ware; N'ton = Northampton Ware; St Neots = St Neot's-type ware; Shelly = Shelly wares

was established. Where there have been refinements this is discussed under the individual pottery types.

Michael Shaw would like to thank Andy Chapman and Northamptonshire Archaeology/MOLA Northampton for providing copies of unpublished excavation and ceramic reports, Andy Heald of AOC Archaeology for supplying a copy of the pottery report on their excavations at The Ridings, and his thesis supervisors, Roger White and Henry Chapman, and Eleanor Ramsey for her GIS advice.

Indicator Pottery Types

The indicator pottery types are described below with their common name (eg Maxey-type ware) and approximate date range, followed by their NTS and CTS codes. The NTS codes are used as the primary code in the discussion as these are the codes used in most of the previous detailed discussions of the pottery from Northampton, and they encompass the various later divisions and refinements.

Early-middle Saxon wares (*c*.400–900) NTS S1–2[3]

All early-middle Saxon wares. S1 has a 'black, gritty' fabric, of which there are many sub-divisions, while S2 comprises grass-tempered wares. These wares are not given a separate number in the CTS but are described individually. It is unfortunate that these fabrics cannot be more precisely dated but their recovery from features with early Anglo-Saxon radiocarbon dates and the presence of non-ceramic finds of this date from a number of the sites indicate that many must date to earlier within the period.

Maxey-type ware (*c*.650–850) NTS S3 CTS 97

Calcareous pottery with affinities to Maxey-type III wares but are thought to be local. Although not common, S3 is a valuable indicator as it encompasses the period of the middle Anglo-Saxon settlement.

Northampton ware (*c*.875–1000) NTS W1[4] CTS 130

Quartz-tempered pottery, commonly wheel-thrown, but there are also hand-made examples or hand-made bases with wheel-turned rims. A kiln site was discovered during development in Horsemarket, Northampton in

1971 (Williams 1974). This ware has affinities to other late Saxon wheel-thrown pottery often found at centres within the Danelaw, such as Thetford, Stafford, and, especially, Stamford. There has been much discussion as to whether these wares were introduced during the period of Danish incursions in the later 9th century, or whether their origins were earlier still (Hurst 1976, 314, 318; Perry 2016, 101–8; Blinkhorn 2013; Dodd *et al* 2014, 85–94, 100–03). In the case of Northampton it has been possible to recognise a Northampton ware horizon within the wider late Saxon period, often associated with St Edmund Memorial pennies. Denham (1985, 55) considered the issue and tentatively suggested a date of *c*.900 – *c*.975 for the *floruit* of Northampton ware. Since then, however, the period of usage of the St Edmund Memorial coinage has been refined and it would appear to be largely restricted to the period *c*.895 – 917–8 (see above). Hence the beginning of Northampton ware may be put back to the end of the 9th century, the time when the settlement was in the hands of the Danes. An end date for its production is less easy to determine but, given that it forms a distinct early sub-phase within the late Saxon period, it is likely to have ceased production within the 10th century.

St Neots-type ware (*c*.850–1100/1200) NTS T1 (subsequently divided into T1(1) and T1(2)[5]); CTS 100 (=T1(1)); 200 (=T1(2))

A calcareous pottery, common in Northampton and across the region. Sub-divisions have been suggested (Denham 1985, 53–4). The most important one is between T1(1), a predominantly black-grey sub-type, and T1(2) which is mainly red-reddish brown (Denham 1985, 28–29). These are the most common varieties and there may be chronological implications, for T1(1) is thought to date to 900–1100, while T1(2) is ascribed a date range of 1000–1200. For the current analysis T1 has been treated as a single fabric since pottery reports prior to 1985 did not record the sub-division. The implication of the sub-division as recorded on the sites excavated after 1985 is, however, considered in the discussion.

Shelly wares (*c*.1100–1400) T2/330 shelly coarseware (1100–1400); T2(2)/319 Lyveden/ Stanion A ware (1150–1400), 320 Lyveden/ Stanion B ware (1225–1400)

Shelly wares are the dominant post-Conquest pottery type in Northampton and hence form a valuable indicator of settlement areas in the broad 1100 – 1400 period. Later pottery reports have distinguished Lyveden/Stanion wares from the general pottery type but as these were not differentiated in earlier reports they have been included in the totals for this type as a whole.

---

3 'Early-middle Saxon wares' has been retained here for pottery, as being an established term for pottery in Northamptonshire, although archaeologists and historians now most commonly refer to the periods 410–650 and 650–850 as early and middle Anglo-Saxon respectively and this practice is followed elsewhere in this paper.

4 The NTS distinguished two related fabrics (W32, W34; see Denham 1985, 54)) which are not included in the sherd count. They are a minor part of the assemblage and hence their non-inclusion does not materially affect the distribution pattern.

---

5 Also sub-types T1(3) and T1(4) which form a minor part of the T1 assemblage (see Denham 1985, 30).

The pottery analysis

Much consideration was given as to the best way of showing the results of the pottery analysis graphically. The advantage of using a computerised database, such as that available within ArcGIS, is that once the data have been entered, it is possible to make an almost infinite number of calculations and to present them in a wide variety of ways.

Two approaches were tested:

- to divide the number of sherds of pottery of each indicator type recovered from each site by the size of the area excavated in square metres. Hence at Black Lion Hill 492 sherds of St Neots-type Ware came from an area of 194m^2, an average of 2.54 sherds from each square metre.

- to calculate, using sherd count, the percentage of each fabric out of the total of indicator pottery types as a whole. Hence the 492 sherds of St Neots-type ware from Black Lion Hill represent 32.65% of the total number of indicator pottery sherds recovered from the site.

Both approaches have their merits and their drawbacks. The former suffers from the fact that the sites differ in the depth and type of deposits and the amount of sampling of features; ideally we would use cubic metres excavated but this data is not available for the majority of sites. The latter perhaps provides a truer reflection of the intensity of excavation at each site but gives a higher percentage figure for the later pottery types at those sites which do not have early occupation.

The two methods were tested as part of the broader research project and in general the results were similar, but the number of sherds per square metre was preferred as this gives greater comparability between sites with early occupation and those without. Accordingly, for the present paper an initial illustration (Fig 38) shows the percentage of each indicator pottery type from each excavation and also gives an indication of the size of the site[6]. This provides a useful introduction to the range of pottery types found and the location of the areas excavated, while a second figure (Fig 39) presents the percentage per square metre of each indicator pottery type on each site. It reproduces at a reduced scale the figures relating to each indicator pottery type contained in the main text (Figs 4, 25, 28, 29, 37). It enables the differences between the five distributions to be readily compared, but the reader is referred to the larger individual illustrations in the main text for the detail.

Figure 38 demonstrates that there is a concentration of data within the south-west quarter of the medieval walled area of Northampton, both in terms of the number of sites excavated and also in the size of sites (eight of the eleven sites with excavated areas in excess of 500m^2 (see footnote 6), lie in this area). There is a reasonable spread

of sites to the east but little information for the northern part of the town. This reflects the lack of opportunity for excavation in this area rather than any deliberate policy.

The early-middle Saxon wares

If we turn to the individual pottery distributions early-middle Saxon wares can be seen to be largely restricted to the south-west quarter between Chalk Lane to the west and Woolmonger Street to the east (Figs 4 & 39A); radiocarbon dates from the former and non-ceramic finds from the latter suggest early Anglo-Saxon activity at these sites so we can be reasonably sure that this distribution does encompass the early Anglo-Saxon period. The small number of sherds found on sites to the east of the Lee line for the location of the defences, only one or two per site, may not be sufficient to suggest actual settlement. Given, however, the ubiquity of early-middle Anglo-Saxon sites in Northamptonshire, including around Northampton itself, there is at least the possibility that some may do so (Shaw 1993–4; Parry 2006, 91–4, 271).

Maxey-type ware

The incidence of Maxey-type ware is important as the life of this pottery type is broadly the same as that of the middle Anglo-Saxon settlement (Figs 25 and 39B). It is not, however, present in great numbers in Northampton, so its occurrence should be treated with care – the largest number of sherds from a single site is 83 from St Peter's Street. The need to analyse the data with caution is further illustrated by the assemblage from Green Street, where of 15 sherds recovered from a small excavation; fourteen were from a single vessel, giving a spurious high incidence. This problem could have been overcome by using a count of the maximum number of vessels but these figures were not estimated for the earlier site investigations. If we disregard this 'false' reading, high percentages of Maxey-type ware are restricted to the St Peter's Street/Marefair/Chalk Lane/Gregory Street area, and we may be seeing here a true reflection of the extent of the high-status settlement of this period, although we can note the small number of sherds from the Northampton Station site (two sherds) to the west and Woolmonger Street (three sherds) to the east. This restricted distribution also has implications for the theory that the Lee line represents a middle Anglo-Saxon rather than a late Saxon defensive line (see main text) for the few sherds from Woolmonger Street are the only ones to have been found east of the line of Horsemarket/ Horseshoe Street.

In looking at the incidence of pottery from the middle Anglo-Saxon period we should be aware also that a proportion of the early-middle Saxon wares belong to this period. Nevertheless, pottery does not appear in any great quantities on the Northampton sites at this period, nor in fact do other finds, a feature which it shares with a number of high-status sites of this period elsewhere. Hamerow (2015, 343) suggests that this may be due to the erosion of occupation layers, as well as early medieval patterns of deposition and waste disposal. Certainly on

---

6   There are five different sizes of 'pie': Size 1: 0–100m^2; Size 2: 101–200m^2; Size 3: 201–500m^2; Size 4: 501–1000m^2; Size 5: >1000m^2.

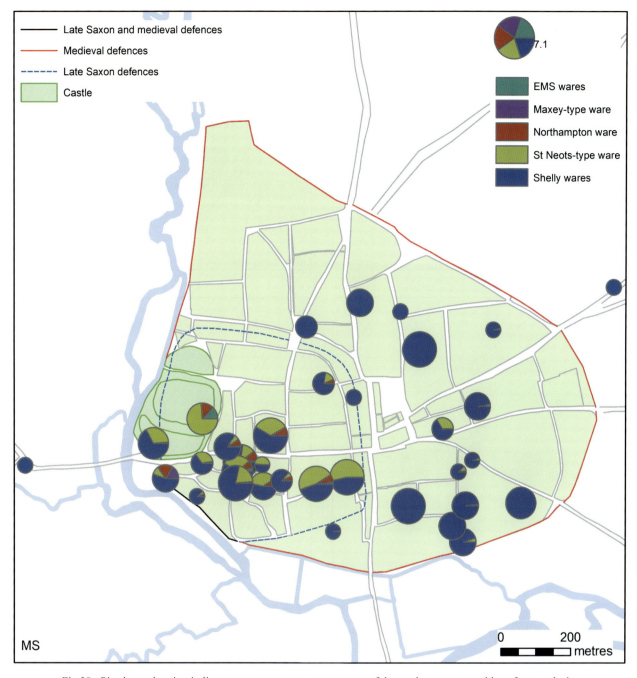

Fig 38: Pie charts showing indicator pottery types as percentages of the total pottery assemblage from each site

the 'palaces' site the middle Anglo-Saxon levels include neither sunken-featured buildings nor rubbish pits, from which so much of the pottery from the earlier and later periods was recovered.

It is worth remarking also on the virtually total absence of middle Saxon Ipswich ware from Northampton sites, with only one definite sherd having been recovered, from Chalk Lane (Gryspeerdt 1981, 110). The production period of this pottery type is now thought to be between around 720–850, a similar date to that of the Anglo-Saxon 'palaces', and it has often been seen as an indicator of a high-status site, although this is not exclusively the case (Blinkhorn 1998, 8–9; 2012, 1, 90). Why then is there such a dearth of Ipswich ware from Northampton? Blinkhorn

(2012, 70) has plotted its distribution showing that it is most common, unsurprisingly, in a 'Primary Zone' covering East Anglia, but also occurs in lesser quantities in a 'Secondary Zone' on sites in the Midlands, the North-East and the South-East, including Northamptonshire. He has also suggested that pottery was used as a cultural identifier in Anglo-Saxon England, so that Ipswich ware was part of the 'social kit' of the inhabitants of East Anglia in the middle Anglo-Saxon period (Blinkhorn 2013, 158–9); hence it could be speculated that Northampton lay within a Maxey-type ware rather than an Ipswich ware zone. Ipswich ware is, however, found at other sites in Mercia; accordingly its non-appearance at Northampton remains, for the moment, a conundrum.

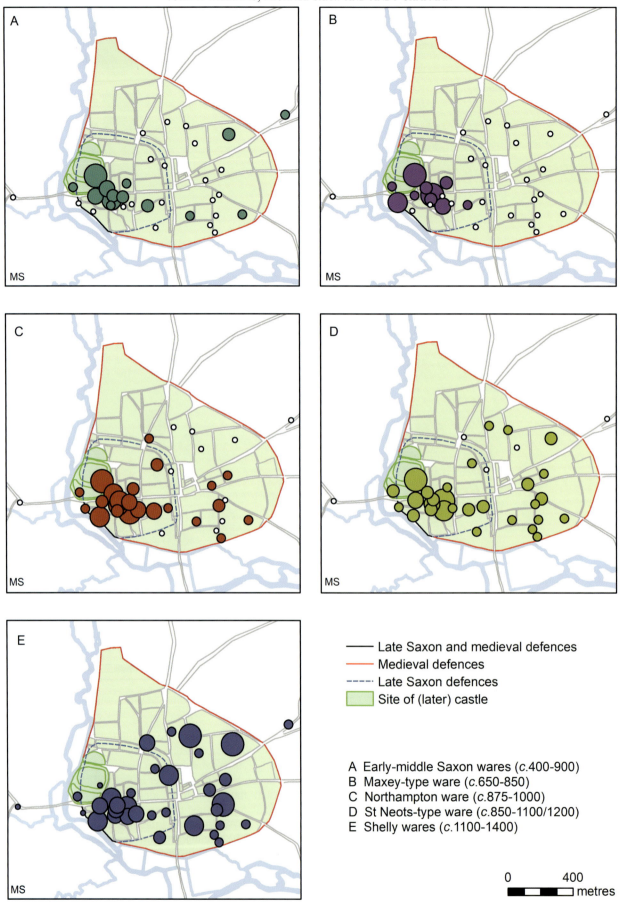

Late Saxon and medieval defences
Medieval defences
Late Saxon defences
Site of (later) castle

A Early-middle Saxon wares (*c*.400-900)
B Maxey-type ware (*c*.650-850)
C Northampton ware (*c*.875-1000)
D St Neots-type ware (*c*.850-1100/1200)
E Shelly wares (*c*.1100-1400)

0   400
metres

Fig 39: Comparative distributions of indicator pottery types
(See Figs 4, 25, 28, 29, 37 for the individual distributions and quantifications)

Late Saxon wares

If we turn to the late Saxon period, Northampton ware may broadly indicate the extent of occupation in the late 9th and 10th centuries (Figs 28, 39C). All sites within Lee's defensive line contain pottery of this type apart from the small-scale excavations at College Street, so we can suggest that settlement had spread to this line during the time when Northampton ware was being produced. There is a small incidence of this pottery beyond the Lee line. While it is tempting to suggest that the two sherds from the Mayorhold, outside the north gate, could represent expansion of occupation into this area and the two each from the excavations at St Giles' Street and The Riding could indicate activity along the road east out of the late Saxon settlement, there are also small numbers of sherds from excavations in the south-east of the medieval walled area (Swan Street South five sherds; Angel Street/ St John's Street two sherds; Northampton High School for Girls sites two sherds; Swan Street North one sherd) in areas away from the main routes out of the town; accordingly, we may be seeing no more than sherds discarded away from the settlement area.

St Neots-type ware largely spans the late Saxon period, but sub-divisions (notably NTS T1(2)/CTS 200) continue into the 12th century (Figs 29, 39D). There is again a high incidence and widespread distribution within Lee's defensive line but with a greater penetration to the east outside the late Saxon defences, particularly on the St Giles' Street site which lies on a main route out of the town. Where, however, the sub-divisions of this ware have been recorded, the pottery recovered from the sites to the east has been mainly of the later variant, so we may be seeing largely 12th-century rather than earlier expansion.

Medieval shelly wares

Although it falls outside the period covered in this paper, the incidence of shelly wares of the 12th–15th century is included to show the dramatic expansion of settlement in the medieval period (Figs 37, 39E). Pottery of this date is present in quantity on every site (apart from Chalk Lane which was by this time sealed by the bailey bank of Northampton Castle), including the suburbs to the west (St James' End) and east (St Edmund's End).

A research model for Northampton

The research presented above provides a model for the origins and early development of Northampton which supplements the story told by the excavated structural evidence and the historical sources. It furnishes a relatively objective view, and one which can be refined and extended as further excavation data becomes available.

A number of caveats, however, need to be entered. As discussed, the sites were not chosen to give a spread across the town but were a result of development pressure, which was concentrated in the south-west quarter. Work here has provided nationally, and even internationally, important information about middle Anglo-Saxon and late Saxon settlement. Ideally, however, we might wish for a number of substantial excavations on the major routes out of the late Saxon town. The balance has been rectified a little recently with large-scale work at Angel Street (Brown 2021) although this is in a back-street area, so settlement here is likely to have begun later than on the main streets and routes out of the town.

In addition, the investigations were undertaken by a number of different organisations and individuals over a period of more than 40 years. Fortunately, however, there has been a large element of continuity and general agreement over their purpose – to recover the story of the origins, growth and development of the town of Northampton, though the limiting of some excavations, such as the MOLAS work at Sol Central, to areas and levels directly affected by development proposals, has contributed to a rather 'bitty' story in these cases.

The differing size of the excavations should also be borne in mind. The results from St Peter's Street where an area of 1425 m^2 was investigated over a period of three years have a great deal more validity than those of Derngate Trench B where an area of 8 m^2 was dug in a single day. It would be possible to remove the smaller sites from the analysis and if, say, sites less than 100m^2 were omitted the results would arguably have a greater validity. The spread of sites would be considerably reduced, however, and the results would not be significantly different.[7]

In addition, we would wish for greater precision in the dating of the pottery types. Hopefully future work, with greater access to more precise independent dating techniques may go a long way to achieving this.

---

7   Ten of the 34 sites would be removed – see Fig 37, size 1 sites.

Appendix 2: The Radiocarbon Dates

Andy Chapman

The radiocarbon dates from the excavations in the 1970s and 1980s

The excavations at Northampton St Peter's Street, St Peter's Gardens, Chalk Lane, Gregory Street and Black Lion Hill in the 1970s to early 1980s, all produced bone and some charcoal suitable for radiocarbon dating, although in some instances it had been necessary to combine samples in order to obtain sufficient weight to enable analysis. A total of 25 dates were listed in the 'palaces' report (Walker and Otlet 1985, 64–66, table 15), and these are relisted here with modern calibrations (Table 3). In order to simplify description and discussion through this text, the dates in Table 3 have been allocated reference numbers, and in discussion of the original dates reference is to the calibrated dates derived from Stuiver (1982) as published in 1985 (Williams *et al*).

These radiocarbon dates helped to provide a chronological framework for both the development of the timber and stone hall complex and its potential relationship to other sites nearby, even though the interpretation of these results was faced with several difficulties, as discussed below, and did not appear to support the initial assumption that the timber hall most probably had an origin in the 7th century.

A fundamental problem was that the radiometric radiocarbon analysis available at the time required large sample sizes, and even then there was a significant error range. As a result the Northampton samples, where it was often a struggle to meet the minimum sample size, inevitably produced conventional dates with large error values, typically ± 60 to 80 years (the most extreme value of ± 120 years has been omitted from the tabulated dates as being too broad to be of any practical value). Given the large error values in the conventional dates (BP), the calibrated date ranges are similarly broad, quoted at the time as a 'central' date ± a standard error typically 50 to 80 years.

This would have been less problematic if the groups of dates derived from the structure of the timber hall and from the mortar mixers and associated levels, had shown greater internal consistency. The samples from the timber hall included two from the filling of the construction trench, considered to relate to the construction of the hall, while a further three came from posthole fills, and therefore potentially derived from material contemporary with the dismantling of the timber hall and the construction of the stone hall or later. However, no such sequence is evident within the radiocarbon results, which can only be described as widely spread across a broad span of time.

In an attempt to produce a closer dating for the timber hall, 'average' dates were created by taking the weighted mean and standard error for the group of all seven dates associated with the structure (Walker and Otlet 1985, table 15), comprising dates 6–11 and the date omitted here at ± 120 years, and two smaller subsets of six and five dates (Table 3: dates 6–11 and dates 7–11), where the dates at the extremes of the range were progressively excluded.

A similar process was undertaken for the group of four dates related to the mortar mixers and a layer associated with the probable minster (Table 3: dates 12–15), and a smaller subset of three dates (dates 12–14).

The derived mean date for the timber hall phase from a subset of five dates was cal AD 850±70, and from a subset of three dates from the mixer spread and mixer 2 the derived date was cal AD 810±70 (Walker and Otlet 1985, 64–66, table 15). The mean date for the later phase of activity was thus slightly earlier than that for the timber building, although statistically they cannot be separated. The successive halls had therefore produced nearly identical mean dates, with that for the timber hall phase being much later than the expected date in the 7th century.

The integrity of the radiocarbon dates

Taking the mean of a group of disparate dates so widely spread that it seems unlikely that they could have derived from a single event merely provides an average of those disparate dates, and the derived mean cannot define any significant or meaningful point in time. With the dates available this was done twice: for the samples associated with the timber hall and then for deposits associated with the mortar mixers and thus the construction of the stone hall, as described above. That the two groups produced nearly identical mean values serves to demonstrate that within both stratigraphic groups there are issues of intrusion and/or residuality, as the only alternative is that a significant proportion of the radiocarbon dates are themselves subject to error.

As the two groups should span the lifetime of the timber hall and the construction of the overlying stone hall, it can be suggested that there was perhaps more disturbance of the earlier deposits, such as the fills of the timber hall construction trench, than had been recognised during excavation and, consequently, both contamination of the early deposits by later material and the introduction of residual material into the later deposits.

There is, however, a particular problem in respect to the dates from the construction trench of the timber hall. Apart from material within the postholes, which might relate to the end of the life of the hall, the samples came from the base of a construction trench that was over 1m deep when dug, although it had been subsequently truncated in many places by later disturbance; the trench had been infilled at the time the hall was built with a compact mixture of weathered ironstone around timber posts set at intervals of about 0.6m. It is difficult to explain how extraneous material could have arrived within the trench away from the postholes, although animal action cannot be totally ruled out. Contamination is a far more reasonable possibility with the mortar spreads, where the deposits were relatively thin and directly overlain by later layers. However, great care was taken at the time of excavation to minimise the risk of samples not relating to the horizon to which they were assigned.

Given the relationship between the timber and stone halls, with the latter almost directly superimposed on the former, a strong case can be made for the stone hall having been a direct and immediate replacement of the former and thus close contemporaneity of samples from posthole fills and mortar spreads is not a major issue.

The alternative to accepting that intrusion or residuality of material had occurred would be to view the radiocarbon dates themselves as having such a wide scatter, even when derived from single events, that they become essentially almost meaningless. However, there are two instances in which single deposits were dated through the submission of two separate samples, and in both instances the derived dates are closely consistent, indicating that the original dating process, within the error limits then obtainable, would appear to have been reliable. One context with consistent dates is SFB D86 at Chalk Lane (Table 3, date 3), where the original conventional dates (HAR-3688 at 1510±70BP and HAR-3689 at 1450 ± 70 BP) were close enough to be combined to give a conventional date of 1475±55 BP. Similarly, the two dates for the mortar mixer spread F56 (Table 3, dates 12 and 13), HAR-1245 at 1310±90 and Har-1246 at 1300±60 could also have been combined to give a single date.

While small pieces of animal bone within a deposit may be either residual or intrusive, there is a single charcoal sample related to the timber hall (Table 3, date 6). This sample came from layer 766.1 within the western annex (Williams *et al* 1985, loose plan Trench AA: Phase 1). It was considered to be a possible floor layer: 'yellowish red (Munsell colour) burnt sand, with ironstone fragments, some ash and charcoal flecks' (Williams *et al* 1985, microfiche 67). The layer had partly been preserved where it had subsided into the top of an underlying foundation trench, 766.2 (Williams *et al* 1985, fig 7, Section Z-Z[1]). This is the best candidate for a reliable sample as it comprised charcoal most likely to be contemporary with the layer from which it came. The result from this sample will be considered below.

Recalibrating the radiocarbon dates

In the years since the publication of the 'palaces' report (Williams *et al* 1985) there has been much progress in developing the calibration curve to enable conventional radiocarbon dates to be recalibrated to calendar years, and for this reason alone providing modern calibrations for the existing radiocarbon dates is clearly worthwhile, despite the error factors. This also puts them in a form in which they can be directly compared to more recently obtained dates, expressed as date ranges with specified probability levels of confidence, rather than as mean dates with error values. The event being dated should be viewed as falling within the specified date range to the given level of confidence, rather than a central value that inevitably tends to be seen and quoted as the most likely date, an approach that is statistically incorrect.

The dates catalogued in the original report (Williams *et al* 1985, table 15) have been calibrated using IntCal13 (Table 3), and are also plotted using OxCal v4.2.4 (Fig 40). They are tabulated at the 68.2% confidence level, showing the individual levels of confidence when there is more than one date range, and at the 95.4% level of confidence. Where the 95.4% confidence level includes extreme isolated date ranges at a very low level of confidence these have been omitted from the tabulation, and only the date ranges with high confidence levels are quoted, with the percentages rounded to the nearest integer.

A national recalibration of funded radiocarbon dates resulting from analyses conducted before 1981 has been published by English Heritage, and it includes some of the dates listed in Table 3 (dates 1–3 and 12–20) (Jordan *et al* 1991, 122–124). These were calibrated using the curves available in 1986, and the results tally with the present recalibration to between 0–10 years, showing that recent changes to the calibration curves are too minor to make any difference to historical interpretations.

The seven dates specifically relating to the timber hall (Table 3, dates 6–11, omitting the date with a 120 year error value), have also been recalibrated more recently by Austin (2017, 59–60, table 2.4) for his study of Anglo-Saxon great hall complexes. These recalibrations were based on IntCal13, the same calibration used in the present study.

The recalibrated dates as listed in Table 3 are used elsewhere in this paper.

The origin and use of the timber hall

If the conclusion is that the issues with the available radiocarbon dates are largely ones of intrusion and residuality, and not one of erratically scattered dates that would negate any attempt at reinterpretation, how can we use the available data to say anything useful about the likely date for the origin and use of the timber hall?

While it may be considered simplistic and lacking in statistical rigour, one simple solution is to view the block of dates related to the timber hall and mortar mixer *en masse* in a search for consistency and grouping, irrespective of stratigraphic groupings. Considering the dates at the 68% confidence level also enables a tighter time frame to be postulated, although the level of confidence is consequently also reduced.

When the dates from the timber hall and the mortar mixers are viewed in this way (Table 3: dates 6–15), four of the ten (dates 6, 7, 12 and 13) have closely comparable ranges that overlap between cal AD *c.*660–770 at 68% confidence, the later 7th to the later 8th century. We may also note that one of these dates is the charcoal sample (date 6) from the possible floor layer, which is considered the sample most likely not to have been subject to contamination.

It can therefore be suggested that rather than the date of AD *c.*750 suggested in the 'palaces' report, it is more likely that the use of the timber hall complex at Northampton lay between the later 7th and later 8th century, cal AD *c.*660–770. A date of construction within the final four decades of the 7th century is therefore within the range of possibilities.

Duration of use of the hall complex

Using the same grouping approach, there are a couple of dates at 68% confidence spanning the late 8th to late 9th century (dates 8 and 15), *c.* cal AD 765–875. It can be tentatively suggested that this range might cover the demise of the timber hall in the later 8th century and the construction and use of the stone hall through to the late 9th century, and the advent of Danish control.

The demise of the stone hall

There are three dates (Table 3: dates 9–10 and 14) centred on the late 9th to early 11th century, *c.* cal AD 870–1020, which may relate to the demise of the stone hall and the development of settlement through the period of Danish control and the century following the Saxon re-conquest of the early 10th century. In respect of dates 9–10 this means suggesting that bone became deposited within the fills of the timber hall construction trench long after its demolition, but on a densely occupied urban site is such disturbance beyond the realms of the possible?

The samples from gully A759 at St Peter's Street can also be considered here. It was argued in the excavation report that the late date for these gullies (Table 3: dates 16–17), cal AD 865–1015 and cal AD 940–1050, both at 68% confidence, should be seen as dating the final filling of these features, and not their origin. So they might join the dates considered above that span the period of Danish control and the Saxon re-conquest.

The probable minster church

The date relating to the probable minster church (date 15), does not necessarily have to follow the same chronology as the halls, but unfortunately the high error value of ± 80 years provides a calibrated date range of cal AD 655–905 at 88%, too broad to be of use, and at 68% confidence there are early, cal AD 685–780, and later options, cal AD

790–875, at similarly low confidence levels of 37% and 31%. So in this instance all options remain open.

St Gregory's church

In respect of the burials close to the site of St Gregory's church, if we ignore the broad date with the ±100 years error value (date 21), the earliest date is cal AD 670–780 at 53% confidence (date 22) indicating that burial may have been taking place here as early as the 7th century while the third dated burial (Table 3: date 23) indicates that there were burials here between the later 9th century and the beginning of the 11th century, the period following the Saxon re-conquest. The early date for a burial near St Gregory's church provides supporting evidence for a potential late 7th-century origin for the timber hall.

Late Saxon occupation

The earlier phase of SFB 2 (2B) on St Peter's Street has given a date of cal AD 580–770 at 68% confidence (Table 3: date 18), which is an acceptable early-middle Anglo-Saxon date. Interestingly, the overall pottery assemblage from SFB 2 contained 15 sherds of early-middle Saxon pottery, as well as a brooch of the late 5th-early 6th century, among a predominantly later ceramic assemblage (Williams 1979, 94). The other two radiocarbon dates from the SFBs (Table 3: dates 19–20), are cal AD 1026–1262 and cal AD 1205–1410. While again there may be problems with contamination from later activity, particularly with date 20, it could be that the Phase 4 activity at St Peter's extended beyond the Norman Conquest.

Conclusion

The difficulties relating to the radiocarbon dates associated with the major timber and stone hall complexes to the east of St Peter's church were recognised in the original publication, where it was concluded that 'taken with the other evidence [they] perhaps suggest that the [timber] hall was constructed in the middle of the 8th century' (Williams *et al* 1985, 39).

The process that produced a date in the mid-8th century for the origin of the timber hall has been shown to be unsound, and the present re-assessment, looking at the grouping of dates, has drawn attention to a cluster of four dates that together span the late 7th to late 8th century, cal AD *c.*660–770 at 68% confidence. This cluster can be seen as defining a period of increased activity on the site that seems most likely to relate to the origin and use of the timber hall, with the possibility that the timber hall may have been constructed in the later 7th century or soon after. It is also likely that the origin of St Gregory's church was broadly contemporary, given the earliest dated burial.

Unless material suitable for radiocarbon dating remains in the site archive, there is no further possibility of resolving this issue from existing material. A future excavation of the site of the church of St Gregory at

Table 3: Radiocarbon determinations for Northampton

No	Site Context	Sample type	Laboratory reference	Conventional Radiocarbon Age BP	cal AD 68% confidence 95% confidence
1	St Peter's Gardens AA441 SFB?	charcoal	HAR-5557	1590±60	*410–540* 340–600
2	Chalk Lane D86 SFB	bone	HAR-3688/89	1475±55	*545–640* 525–655 (79%)
3	A141 SFB	charcoal	HAR-3935	1320±70	*650–770* 600–880
4	Black Lion Hill A110/167 Building	bone	HAR-5560	1340±80	*625–770* 560–880
5	C15 ditch	bone	HAR-5561	1180±70	*770–900 (56%)* 685–985
6	St Peter's Gardens AA766.1 Charcoal layer (hall floor?)	charcoal	Har-5556	1300±80	*650–775 (63%)* 600–895 (94%)
7	St Peter's Gardens: *The timber hall* AA479.17 PH in CT	bone	Har-5558	1310±70	*650–770* 610–885
8	AA479.11 PH in CT	bone	Har-5553	1220±70	*765–885 (54%)* 685–905 (86%)
9	AA926/479 CT	bone	Har-5551	1100±80	*865–1020 (63%)* 765–1050 (89%)
10	AA926.11 PH in CT	bone	Har-5552	1070±80	*870–1040 (67%)* 770–1155
11	AA465 CT	bone	Har-5555	1010±70	*970–1050 (41%)/ 1080–1150 (27%)* 885–1190
12	St Peter's Street *The mortar mixers* F56Mixer spread	bone	Har-1245	1310±90	*640–780 (58%)* 565–900 (94%)
13	F56Mixer spread	bone	Har-1246	1300±60	*660–770* 640–880
14	F293Mixer 2	bone	Har-1452	1080±80	*870–1030 (66%)* 770–1060
15	Layer associated with minster	Bone	Har-1720	1240±80	*685–780 (37%) 790–875 (31%)* 655–905 (88%)
16	St Peter's Street Gully A759	bone	Har-1244	1110±80	*865–1015 (62%)* 760–1045 (90%)
17	Gully A759	bone	Har-1454	1030±80	*940–1050 (44%)* 855–1185 (91%)
18	St Peter's Street-SFBs K172 SFB 2B	charcoal	Har-1225	1190±70	*765–900 (55%)* 680–980
19	K171 SFB 3	bone	Har-1431	880±70	*1045–1095 (23%) 1120–1220 (46%)* 1026–1262
20	K177 SFB 2A	bone	Har-1437	700±70	*1255–1320 (45%) 1350–1390 (23%)* 1205–1410
21	Gregory St C315 Grave	human bone	Har-4390	1360±100	*580–770* 530–890 (91%)
22	C410 Grave	human bone	Har-4810	1260±70	*670–780 (53%)* 650–900 (93%)
23	C408 Grave	human bone	Har-4809	1140±70	*860–980 (50%)* 765–1020 (91%)

Laboratory: Har=Harwell; Calibration: Intcal13; plot OxCal v4.2.4
PH=posthole; CT=construction trench; SFB=sunken-featured building

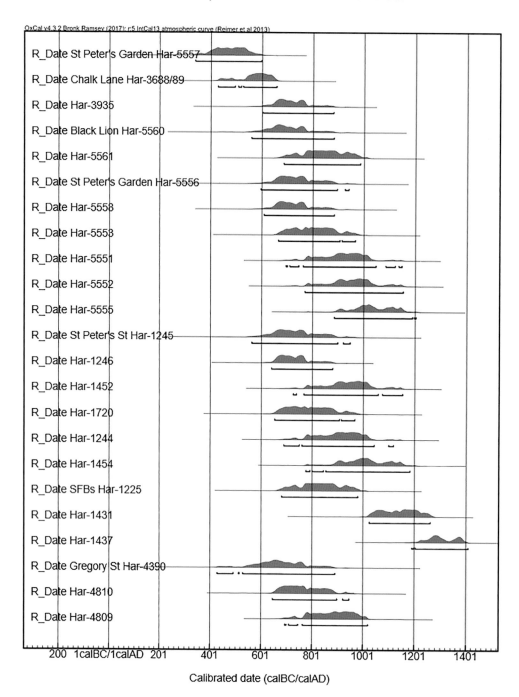

Fig 40: plot of radiocarbon dates (from OxCal v4.3.2)

the eastern end of the complex, with the application of modern radiocarbon dating to early burials and the church itself might hopefully produce a parallel chronology that can be related to the existing knowledge of the form and development of this middle Anglo-Saxon hall and church complex.

Appendix 3: Mortar Mixers

John H Williams

In 1973 three mortar mixers were excavated on St Peter's Street. Although a number of 'mortar discs' had been previously recorded, the Northampton examples were the first to have been recognised as mixers when they were published (Williams J H 1979, 118–34). Daniel Gutscher excavated a 'mortar disc' at Zurich Münsterhof in 1977, drawing attention at the same time to other examples from continental Europe, and independently interpreted them as mechanical mortar mixers (1981). Two further mixers associated with the stone hall complex at Northampton were published in 1985, referencing at the same time Gutscher's work (Williams *et al* 1985, 21–6, 36–7).

Since then evidence for mixers has continued to be revealed and in 2011 Sophie Hüglin was able to assemble a corpus of 65 examples from 37 locations in Britain, Belgium, France, Germany, Italy, Poland and Switzerland (2011). The list contained in Table 4 updates Hüglin's list, omitting three examples and including some further examples from this country (Bamburgh, Dunbar, Wallingford, Winchester and possibly London) and Italy (Brina, Miranduolo, Monterotondo, San Salvatore a Vaiano, Vetricella). The vast majority of mixers clearly date to the period between the 8th and the 11th century. There is an occasional example that might be a little later, although sometimes the dating evidence is a little inconclusive.

The essential features of the mixers as found comprised a circular basin, perhaps cut into the ground to a depth of about 0.3m, a substantial central posthole dug down below the bottom of the basin, and often evidence for wattle-work lining the periphery of the basin (Figs 19–24). The mixers were normally between 2m and 2.5m in diameter but with a few bigger examples, the largest being 4m across. Mortar residues were frequently found within the bowls, in many cases with concentric curved striations in their surface related to the centre point of the mixer. In Northampton mortar mixer 3, a line of voids followed a straight line across the mixer through its centre and were interpreted as representing paddle positions (Figs 21–22; and see below).

Approaches to mortar mixer reconstruction

On the basis of the archaeological evidence of the first three mixers found at Northampton a theoretical reconstruction was attempted (Fig 41). It was suggested that a fixed central post supported a beam from which were suspended a number of paddles, with the beam being rotated around the central post on some sort of bearing and the paddles mixing the mortar. A fairly robust structure was proposed, which could withstand the pressures of rough usage. It was calculated that, with a mix depth of 0.35m, between two and four men would have been required to power the mixer (Wapples 1979). It is interesting to note that Brian Hope-Taylor recorded hoof marks around the mixer at Bamburgh, which he argued indicated the use of animal power for what he referred to as his 'gin gang' (Kirton and Young 2012, 253).

Fig 41: Mortar mixer reconstruction based on Northampton mixers 1–3 (from Williams 1979, 118)

Gutscher, on the basis of two postholes found on the Zurich Münsterhof site outside the mixer and set at 90° to each other in relation to the central post, suggested in his reconstructions a framed superstructure, which would have provided the machine with increased stability (Fig 42), the mixer otherwise working on the same principles as the Northampton mixer (Gutscher type A). With the Zurich Münsterhof and one of the Lindenhof examples, rather than there being a central posthole, there was instead a large central opening which Gutscher interpreted as being for a stone on which an upright post would have sat and rotated (Gutscher type B). No certain further examples of Type B are known. Detailed plans of mixers and the area immediately around them have rarely

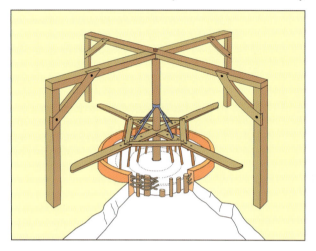

Fig 42: Daniel Gutscher's mortar mixer reconstruction
(after Gutscher 1981)

been published but the author has not been able to find any further examples with postholes suitably located for supporting a superstructure and yet Gutscher's framed superstructure continues to be adopted in a number of German and Swiss publications. Indeed, it is interesting, but perhaps not surprising, to note how English publications tend to refer to the Northampton reconstruction while German and Swiss publications look to Gutscher's models.

Recent years have seen a spate of discoveries of mortar mixers in Tuscany. This has inspired a programme of experimental archaeology at the Rocca di San Silvestro involving both the burning of lime and the subsequent mixing of mortar (Fichera 2011 and pers. comm. Alessandro Fichera). The mixer that has been built, with a diameter of about 2m, follows the same basic principles as the Northampton and Gutscher reconstructions but it is a much more lightweight construction (Fig 43).

The essential differences to the Northampton reconstruction are:

1. a much lighter cross-beam, not dissimilar in size to a round fence post.
2. a metal bearing comprising a vertical rod fixed to the top of the central post, with a hollow pipe, to engage around the rod, driven through the cross beam; rotation is smooth without the need for grease (Figs 44–45).
3. a narrow horizontal strip of metal linking the bottoms of the paddles (Fig 46). No such strips are recorded as having been found during archaeological investigations but without them, with the paddles just comprising upright sticks, the lime and sand fail to

Fig 43: Alessandro Fichera's mortar mixer reconstruction in action

get mixed properly. The strips act in a similar way to the metal strips found within modern mortar mixers and plasterers' pan type turbo mixers and considerably aid the mixing process. It was noticeable, when I visited Rocca San Silvestro in 2018 and saw (and indeed operated) Alessandro Fichera's reconstructed mixer, how the metal strips resulted in a build-up of mortar immediately in front of the strips as the mixer was rotated (Figs 47); the less fluid the mixture within the mixer the more prominent was the ridge created and the greater the time that was needed, after stopping mixing, for the mortar in front of and behind the paddles to sink back down to the general level of the mix. In support of such strips it can be noted, with Northampton mixer 3, that there is a continuous ridge across the mixer along the line of the paddle holes rather than a heightening of the mortar around each of the paddle holes, as might be expected if there had been no strips (cf Fig 21; see also Williams J H 1979, plates 36–39 and fig 70). If the metal strips of the reconstruction had, in the original mixers, been of organic materials such as leather or wood any archaeological survival would have been somewhat fortuitous. The vertical paddles themselves could leave concentric trails in the surface of the mix such as have been noted in a number of mixers (Fig 48).

The lightweight construction and a restriction of depth of mix to 0.20m–0.25m has reduced the power necessary to drive the mixer and it can easily be rotated by one or two persons, as I personally experienced. It can be operated continuously and has proved able to mix considerably greater quantities of mortar much more effectively and more quickly than a larger team of workers mixing by hand. The paddles in particular might seem to be vulnerable, but they have lasted remarkably well; the cross beam has been subject to cracking. Nonetheless, while creaking musically during its operation, the mixer has proved to

Fig 46: Alessandro Fichera's mortar mixer reconstruction: the narrow horizontal strip of metal linking the bottoms of the paddles

Fig 44: Alessandro Fichera's mortar mixer reconstruction: the top of the central post with a vertical rod forming the spindle around which the cross-beam holding the paddles rotates

Fig 47: Alessandro Fichera's mortar mixer reconstruction in action, showing the build-up of less fluid mortar in front of the metal strips as the mixer was rotated

Fig 45: Alessandro Fichera's mortar mixer reconstruction: the cross-beam of the mixer with the pipe which fits over the spindle of the central post

Fig 48: Alessandro Fichera's mortar mixer reconstruction in action, showing the concentric trails left in the surface of a fluid mix

Table 4: List of mortar mixers known to 2020

Site (Quantity)	Reference	Site (Quantity)	Reference
Britain (14+1?)		**Italy (15)**	
Bamburgh	Kirton and Young 2012	Brina	Baldassarri and Parodi 2011
Dunbar	Perry 2000, 62–4, 73	Donoratico (3)	Bianchi et al 2011
Duxford	Lyons 2011, 103–5	Miranduolo	Causarano, M-A 2011
Eynsham (2)	Hardy et al 2003, 73–6, 487–9	Rocca di Montemassi	Causarano, M-A 2011, 58–60
London (?)	Howell et al 2017, 154	Monterotondo	Russo 2011
Northampton (5)	Williams J H 1979, 118–34; Williams et al 1985, 21–6, 36–7	Sabiona	Bierbrauer and Nothdurfter 2015, Beilage 3
Wallingford	Soden 2018, 21 & 70, figs 4.8–4.10	San Salvatore al Monte Amiata	Causarano, M-A 2011, 56ff; Bianchi 2011, 11
Wearmouth (2)	Cramp 2005, 1–2, 93–6, 101–3, 110	San Salvatore a Vaiano (2)	Bianchi 2011, 12
Winchester	Kjølbye-Biddle and Biddle in press	San Vincenzo al Volturno (2)	Riddler 1993, 206–8; Hodges et al 2011, 153–4
Belgium (3)		Vetricella (2)	pers comm G Bianchi
Thier d'Olne (2)	Witvrouw 2006	**Poland (5)**	
Wellin	Archéologia 129 (1979), 82	Poznań (4)	Józefowiczówna 1967, 32–39; Gutscher 1981, 184
France (1)		Wišliza	Józefowiczówna 1967, 39–42; Gutscher 1981, 184–6
Grenoble	Baucheron 1998	**Switzerland (25)**	
Germany (9)		Aesch-Saalbünten	Marti 2000, 176–9, Tafel 25
Aulendorf	Schmidt 1995	Basle	Hüglin 2011, 193–5
Bärenthal	Klug-Treppe 2010	Dissentis (3)	Scheidegger 1990, 250–1
Burg Wittelsbach	Gutscher 1981, 188	Dornach	Nold 2004, 9–11
Herrieden	Steeger 2005	Embrach (5)	Matter, A 1994
Kirchheim/Teck	Schäfer 1987	Lenzburg	Weber 2004
Mönchengladbach	Borger 1958, 51–2, 210; Gutscher 1981, 182–4	Müstair (5)	Sennhauser 1995; Hüglin 2011, 206
Reichenau (2)	Zettler 1988, 191–2, Abb.50–1; Schmidt-Thomé 2007	Sissach	Burnell 1998, 36–47; Marti 2000, 162–6, Tafel 264
Schuttern	Gutscher 1981, 182	Üetliberg (3)	Windler 1991
Numbers in brackets in site column indicate multiple examples of mixers from the same location		Zurich, Münsterhof	Gutscher 1981, 178–80
		Zurich, Lindenhof (3)	Vogt 1948, 64–6;

For the revision of the Italian examples vis à vis Hüglin's list, see Bianchi 2011, 12ff. Grove Priory in England has also been omitted. Although it may have been a device for the mixing of mortar it was not of the standard circular form. A possible example from London, while displaying convincing characteristics of a mortar mixer, is late (by radiocarbon dating) and although found beneath a mason's yard it had little or no mortar directly associated.

be stable and there would appear to be little justification for some of the elaborate superstructures that have been proposed. With the mixer being able to be built in a day and with the only 'technical' parts being the bearing and the strips across the bottom of the paddles, the technology would have been readily transportable by a master craftsman skilled in lime and mortar production, and paddles and the transverse beam were easily replaceable – an example recalling the modern disposable society.

Bibliography

Anderton, M, (ed) 1999 *Anglo-Saxon Trading Centres: Beyond the Emporia,* Sheffield Archaeol Monog

ASC: *The Anglo-Saxon Chronicle, A revised translation,* D Whitelock with D C Douglas and S J Tucke (eds), 1965, Eyre and Spottiswoode

Archibald, M M, 1979 The coins and counters, *in* F Williams 1979, 69

Archibald, M M, Metcalf, D M, and Rigold, S E, 1979 The coins, counters and a token, *in* J H Williams 1979, 243–6

Archibald, M M, and Metcalf, D M, 1985 The coins, *in* Williams *et al* 1985, 64

Austin, M H, 2017 *Anglo-Saxon 'Great Hall Complexes', Elite Residences and Landscapes of Power in Early England, c. AD 550–700* (University of Reading PhD thesis)

Baker, N, and Holt, R, 2004 *Urban Growth and the Medieval Church: Gloucester and Worcester,* Routledge

Baldassarri, M, and Parodi, L, 2011 Cantieri e technice costruttive tra X e XI secolo: il caso del Castello della Brina (SP), *Archeologia dell'Architettura,* **16**, 70–85

Bamford, H M, The worked flint, *in* J H Williams and M Shaw 1981, 126–130

Barley, M W, and Straw, I F, 1969 Nottingham, *in* Lobel 1969

Bassett, S, 2007 Divide and rule? The military infrastructure of eighth- and ninth-century Mercia, *Early Medieval Europe,* **15**, 53–85

Baucheron, F, Gabayet, F, and de Montjoie, A, 1998 Autour du groupe épiscopal de Grenoble. Deux millénaires d'histoire, *Documents d'archéologie en Rhône-Alpes,* **16**, 127–9

Bauer, I, Frascoli, L, Pantli, H, Siegfried, A, Weidmann, T, and Windler, R, 1991 Üetliberg, Uto-Kulm, Ausgrabungen 1980–1989, A: Textband

Bayley, J, 1979a The crucible fragments, *in* F Williams 1979, 69

Bayley, J, 1979b The non-ferrous slag, *in* F Williams 1979, 73

Bayley, J, 1988 Crucibles and moulds, *in* Daniels 1988 184–7

Bede *Lives of the abbots,* in *Bede Historical Works* **II** (Loeb Edition (1930)), 392–445

Bianchi, G, 2011 Miscelare la calce tra lavoro manuale e meccanico. Organizzazione del cantiere e possibili tematismi di ricerca, *Archeologia dell'Architettura,* **16**, 9–18

Bianchi, G, Chiarelli, N, Crisci, G M, Fichera and Miriello, D, 2011 Archeologia di un cantiere curtense: il caso del Castello di Donoratico (LI) tra IX e X secolo. Sequenze stratigrafiche e analisi archeometriche, *Archeologia dell'Architettura,* **16**, 34–50

Biddle, M, and Hill, D, 1971 Late Saxon Planned Towns, *Antiq J,* **51**, 70–85

Biddle, M, and Kjølbye-Biddle, B, 2001 Repton and the 'great heathen army', 873–4, *in* Graham-Campbell *et al* 2001, 45–96

Bierbrauer, V, and Nothdurfter, H, 2015 *Die Ausgrabungen in spätantik-frühmittelalterlichen Bischopssitz Sabiona–Säben in Südtirol I (Frühmittelalterliche Kirche und Gräberfeld)*

Blackburn, M, 2001 Expansion and control: aspects of Anglo-Saxon minting, *in* Graham-Campbell *et al* 2001, 125–142

Blair, J, 1992 Anglo-Saxon minsters: A topographical review, *in* Blair and Sharpe (eds) 1992, 226–66

Blair, J, 1996 Palaces or minsters? Northampton and Cheddar reconsidered, *Anglo-Saxon England,* **25**, 97–121

Blair, J, 2005 *The Church in Anglo-Saxon Society,* Oxford University Press

Blair, J, 2011 Flixborough revisited, *Anglo-Saxon Studies in Archaeology and History,* **17**, 101–7

Blair, J, 2015 The making of the English house: Domestic planning, 900–1150, *Anglo-Saxon Studies in Archaeology and History,* **19**, 184–206

Blair, J, 2018 *Building Anglo-Saxon England,* Princeton University Press

Blair, J, and Sharpe, R, (eds) 1992 *Pastoral Care Before the Parish* (Studies in the Early History of Britain), Continuum International Publishing

Blinkhorn, P, 1993 The pottery, *in* Shaw 1993, 19–21

Blinkhorn, P, 1995 *Woolmonger Street Pottery: Assessment Report,* Unpublished Northamptonshire Archaeology Archive Report

Blinkhorn, P, 1996 The pottery, *in* Shaw and Soden 1996, 9–10, table 2

Blinkhorn, P, 1998 Appendix A: Pottery, *in* Soden 1998

Blinkhorn, P, 1999 Of cabbages and kings: production, trade and consumption in middle Saxon England, *in* Anderton 1979, 4–23

Blinkhorn, P, 2001 The Saxon and medieval pottery, *in* Chapman 2001, 99

Blinkhorn, P, 2002 The pottery, *in* Hiller *et al* 2002, 46–50

Blinkhorn, P, 2005 *Pottery from the Riding, Northampton,* Unpublished AOC Archaeology Archive Report

Blinkhorn, P, 2006 Saxon, medieval and post-medieval pottery, *in* Brown 2006, 114–7

Blinkhorn, P, 2008 The pottery, *in* Brown 2008, 194–99

Blinkhorn, P, 2012 *The Ipswich Ware Project: Ceramics, Trade and Society in Middle Saxon England,* Medieval Pottery Res Group Occ Paper, **7**

Blinkhorn, P, 2013 No pots please, we're Vikings: pottery in the southern Danelaw, 850–1000, *in* Hadley and ten Harkel 2013, 157–71

Blinkhorn, P, 2021a Pottery, in Brown 2021, 152–191

Blinkhorn, P, 2021b The early medieval pottery from Northampton Station, *in* Chapman 2021c, 100–104

Blinkhorn, P, 2021c The medieval and post-medieval pottery, *in* Finn 2021, 373–377

Blinkhorn, P, and Soden, I, 1998–9 The pottery, *in* Chapman 1999, 55–8

Blunt, C E, Stewart, B H I H, and Lyon, C S S, 1989 *Coinage in Tenth-century England, From Edward the Elder to Edgar's Reform,* Oxford University Press

Borger, H, 1958 *Das Münster S. Vitus zu Mönchen-Gladbach. Die Kunstdenkmäler des Rheinlands,* **6**

Bradley, J, (ed) 1988 *Settlement and Society in Medieval Ireland,* Irish Studies, Boethius Press

Brennan, N, and Hamerow, H, 2015 An Anglo-Saxon great hall complex at Sutton Courtenay/Drayton, Oxfordshire: A royal centre of early Wessex? *Archaeol J,* **172.2**, 325–50

Brown, J, 2006 The archaeology at 46–50 Sheep Street, Northampton, *Northamptonshire Archaeol,* **34**, 103–23

Brown, J, 2008 Archaeological excavation at the corner of Kingswell Street and Woolmonger Street, Northampton, *Northamptonshire Archaeol,* **35**, 173–214

Brown, J, 2021 *Living opposite the Hospital of St John: Excavations in medieval Northampton 2014,* Archaeopress Archaeology

Bruce-Mitford, R, (ed) 1975 *Recent Archaeological Excavations in Europe,* Routledge

Burnell, S, 1998 *Die reformierte Kirche von Sissach BL, Mittelalterliche Kirchenbauten und merowingerzeitliche „Stiftergräber"*

Callebaut, D, 1994 Résidences fortifiées et centres administratifs dans la vallée de l'Escaut (IXᵉ- XIᵉ siècle), *in* Demolon *et al* 1994, 93–114

Cameron, K, 1996 *English Place Names,* Batsford

Campbell, J, 1979 Bede's words for places, *in* Sawyer 1979, 34–51

Campbell, J, (ed) 1991 *The Anglo-Saxons,* Penguin

Carlyle, S, Gebber, J, and Armitage, P L, 2017 Medieval and later activity in the former precinct of St John's Hospital, Northampton, *Northamptonshire Archaeol,* **39**, 181–96

Carver, M, 2010 *The Birth of a Borough, An Archaeological Study of Anglo-Saxon Stafford*, Boydell Press

Causarano, M-A, 2011 I Miscelatore di malta di Miranduolo (Chiusdino, SI) e il cantiere tra X ed inizio XI secolo. Confronto con i casi del territorio interno Maremmano e Senese, *Archeologia dell'Architettura*, **16**, 51–61

CCSL: Corpus Christianorum Series Latina 119A: *Bedae Venerabilis Opera, Pars II, Opera Exegetica 2A: De Tabernaculo; De Templo; In Ezram et Neemiam,* ed D Hurst 1969

Chapman, A, 1999 Excavation of the town defences at Green Street, Northampton 1995–6 *Northamptonshire Archaeol*, **28**, 25–60

Chapman, A, 2001 Excavations at the Moat House Hotel, Northampton, 1998 *Northamptonshire Archaeol*, **29**, 93–103

Chapman, A, 2021a Prehistoric Northampton: A circular ring ditch and a flint scatter, *Northamptonshire Archaeol*, **41**, 17–24

Chapman, A, 2021b The late Saxon town defences at Green Street, Northampton: a review of the evidence and a radiocarbon date, *Northamptonshire Archaeol*, **41**, 129–136

Chapman, A, 2021c Late Saxon and Saxo-Norman occupation beneath the Outer Bailey of Northampton Castle, *Northamptonshire Archaeol*, **41**, 79–127

Chapman, A, 2021d Northampton Castle, Part 1: Introduction, pre-castle archaeology and the history and topography of the castle, *Northamptonshire Archaeol*, **41**, 137–189

Chapman, A, Chapman, P, and Anderson, T, forthcoming The Augustinian Abbey of St James, Northampton, and its cemetery: Excavations 1999–2001, *Northamptonshire Archaeology*

Cleere, H F, 1979 The metallurgical remains, *in* J H Williams 1979, 278–9

Cleere, H F, 1985 The iron-working slag, *in* Williams *et al* 1985, 70

Cleere, H F, and Oakley, G, 1979 The slag, *in* F Williams 1979, 71

Cowie, R, and Blackmore, L, 2008 *Early and Middle Saxon Rural Settlement in the London Region*, MoLAS Monog, **36**

Cramp, R, 1988 Decorated moulds, *in* Daniels 1988, 187–90

Cramp, R, 2005 *Wearmouth and Jarrow Monastic Sites*, **1**, English Heritage

Cramp, R, 2006 *Wearmouth and Jarrow Monastic Sites*, **2**, English Heritage

Cramp, R, Cherry J, and Lowther, P, 2006 Copper alloy and silver, *in* Cramp 2006, 230–81

Cubitt, C, (ed) 2003 *Court Culture in the Early Middle Ages*, Studies in the Early Middle Ages (Book 3), Brepols

Daniels, R, 1988 The Anglo-Saxon monastery at Church Close, Hartlepool, Cleveland, *Archaeol J*, **145**, 158–210

DeGregorio, S, 2006 *Bede On Ezra and Nehemiah*, (Translated with an introduction and notes), Translated Texts for Historians, **47**, Liverpool University Press

Demolon, P, Galinié, H, and Verhaeghe, F, 1994 *Archéologie des villes dans le Nord-Ouest de l'Europe (VIIᵉ – XIIIᵉ siècle)*, Actes du IVᵉ Congrès International d'Archéologie Médiévale (Douai, 1991)

Denham, V, 1983 The pottery, *in* Williams and Farwell 1983, 146–50

Denham, V, 1984 The pottery, *in* Williams and Farwell 1984, 93–100

Denham, V, 1985a The pottery, *in* Shaw 1985, 123–32

Denham, V, 1985b The pottery, *in* Williams *et al* 1985, 46–63

Denham, V, 2021, The pottery, in Shaw 2021b, 276–287

Denham, V, and Shaw, M, 1994 The pottery, *in* Shaw and Steadman 1994, 143–47

Denham, V, and Shaw, M, 1997 The pottery, *in* Shaw 1997, 111–5

Dodd, A, (ed) 2003 *Oxford Before the University: The Late Saxon and Norman Archaeology of the Thames Crossing, the Defences and the Town*, Thames Valley Landscapes Monog, Oxford Archaeology

Dodd, A, Goodwin, J, Griffiths, S, Norton, A, Poole, C, and Teague, S, 2014 Excavations at Tipping Street, Stafford, 2009–10, *Staffordshire Archaeol Hist Soc Trans*, **47**

Dodd, A, and Hardy, A, 2003 The Anglo-Saxon sequence, *in* Hardy *et al* 2003, 463–92

Domesday Book: Domesday Northamptonshire, Thorn, F, and Thorn, C, (eds) 1979, Phillimore

Dornier, A, (ed) 1977 *Mercian Studies*, Leicester University

Early, R, 2003 Methodology and systems of analysis: The château at Mayenne, *in* Vila *et al* 2003, 61–81

Fichera, G, 2011 Archeologia sperimentale alla Rocca di San Silvestro (LI). Dal ciclo di produzione della calce alla costruzione di una casa *Archeologia dell'Architettura*, **16**, 86–95

Finn, C, 2021 From medieval quarry pits to a 19th century foundry at Cow Lane (Swan Street), Northampton, *Northamptonshire Archaeol*, **41**, 361–385

Foard, G, 1995 The early topography of Northampton and its suburbs, *Northamptonshire Archaeol*, **26**, 109–22

Gai, S, 2001 Nouvelles données sur le palais de Charlemagne et de ses successeurs à Paderborn (Allemagne), *in* Renoux 2001, 201–12

Gem, R, 1993 Architecture of the Anglo-Saxon church, 735 to 870: from Archbishop Ecgberht to Archbishop Ceolnoth, *J Brit Archaeol Assoc*, **146**, 29–66

Goodall, A, 1985 The non-ferrous objects, *in* Williams *et al* 1985, 66

Goodall, A, and Webster, L, 1981 objects of copper alloy, *in* Williams and Shaw 1981, 122

Gover, J E B, Mawer, A, and Stenton, F M, 1975 *The Place-names of Northamptonshire*, English Place-Name Soc, **10**

Graham-Campbell, J, Hall, R, Jesch, J, and Parson, D N, (ed) 2001 *Vikings and the Danelaw, Select Papers from the Proceedings of the Thirteenth Viking Congress*, Oxbow Books

Gryspeerdt, M, 1978 The pottery, *in* Williams 1978, 133–47

Gryspeerdt, M, 1979 The pottery, *in* Williams F 1979, 57–67

Gryspeerdt, M, 1981 The pottery, *in* Williams and Shaw 1981, 108–21

Gryspeerdt, M, 1982 The pottery, *in* Williams 1982b, 69–73

Gutscher, D, 1981 Mechanische Mörtelmischer *Zeitschrift für schweizerische Archäologie und Kunstgeschicte*, **38**, 178–88

Hadley, D M, and ten Harkel, L, (eds) 2013 *Everyday Life in Viking-age Towns: Social Approaches to Towns in England and Ireland*, Oxbow Books

Hadley, D M, and Richards, J D, 2016 The winter camp of the Viking great army, AD 872–3, Torksey, Lincolnshire, *Antiq J* **96**, 23–68

Hall, R, 1989 The five boroughs of the Danelaw: a review of present knowledge, *Anglo-Saxon England*, **18**, 149–206

Hall, R, 2001 Anglo-Scandinavian urban developments in the East Midlands, *in* Graham-Campbell *et al* 2001, 143–55

Hamerow, H F, 1991 Settlement mobility and the 'middle Saxon shift': rural settlements and settlement patterns in Anglo-Saxon England, *Anglo-Saxon England*, **20**, 1–17

Hamerow, H, 1993 *Excavations at Mucking 2: The Anglo-Saxon Settlement*, English Heritage

Hamerow, H, 2015 Discussion, *in* Brennan and Hamerow 2015, 343–6

Hardy, A, Dodd, A, and Keevill, D, 2003 *Aelfric's Abbey, Excavations at Eynsham Abbey, Oxfordshire, 1989–92*, Oxford Archaeology, Thames Valley Landscapes Monog, **16**

Haslam, J, 1987 Market and fortress in England in the reign of Offa, *World Archaeol*, **19.1** (Urbanization), 76–93

Haupt, A, 1916 Die spanische-westgotische Halle zu Naranco und die nordischen Königshallen, *Monatshefte für die Kunstwissenshafte,* **9**, 242–63

Hen, Y, 2009 Liturgy and religious culture in late Anglo-Saxon England, *Early Medieval Europe*, **17**, 329–42

Hicks, A, 2015 *Destined to Serve: Use of the Outer Grounds of St Augustine's Abbey, Canterbury, Before, During and After the Time of the Monks. Canterbury Christ Church University Excavations 1983–2007,* Canterbury Archaeological Trust, Occasional Paper

Higham, N J, and Hill, D H, (eds) 2001 *Edward the Elder, 899–924,* Routledge

Hiller, J, Hardy, A, and Blinkhorn, P, 2002 Excavations at Derngate, Northampton, 1997–2000, *Northamptonshire Archaeol*, **30**, 31–62

Hodges, R, (ed) 1993 *San Vincenzo al Volturno 1: The 1980–86 excavations part 1,* Archaeol Monog Brit School Rome, **7**

Hodges, R, Leppard, S, and Mitchell, J, 2011 *San Vincenzo Maggiore and its workshops,* Archaeol Monog Brit School Rome, **17**

Hope-Taylor, B, 1977 *Yeavering: an Anglo-British Centre of Early Northumbria,* English Heritage Archaeological Monog

Horsman, V, Milne, C, and Milne, G, 1988 *Aspects of Anglo-Norman London: 1. Building and Street Development,* London: London & Middlesex Archaeological Society, Special paper, **11**

Howell, I, Bowsher, D, Dyson, T, and Holder, N, 2007 *The London Guildhall: an Archaeological History of a Neighbourhood from Early Medieval Times, Part 1,* MOLAS Monog, **36**

Hüglin, S, 2011 Medieval mortar mixers revisited, Basle and beyond, *Zeitschrift für Archäologie des Mittelalters*, **39**, 189–212

Hugot, L, 1965 Die Königshalle Karls des Grossen in Aachen *Aachen Kunstblätter*, **30**, 38–48

Hunter, J, and Oakley, G, 1979 The glass, *in* Williams F 1979, 74–6

Hurst, J G, 1976 The pottery, *in* Wilson 1976, 283–348

Hylton, T, 1998–9 Small finds, *in* Soden 1998–9, 97–101

Jones, R, 2012 Hunting for the meaning of the place name Upton, *in* Jones and Semple (eds) 2012, 301–15

Jones, R, and Semple, S, 2012 *Sense of Place in Anglo-Saxon England*, Paul Watkins Publishing

Jordan, D, Haddon-Reece, D and Bayliss, A, 1994 *Radiocarbon Dates from Samples Funded by English Heritage and Dated before 1981,* English Heritage

Józefowiczówna, K 1967 Uwagi w spornej sprawie „baptysteriów" w wolsce X i XI wieku, *Slavia Antiqua* **14**, 31–129

Kirton, J, and Young, G, 2012 An Anglo-Saxon mortar-mixer at Bamburgh Castle, *Archaeol Aeliana*, **41**, 251–8

Kjølbye-Biddle, B, and Biddle, M, in press *The Anglo-Saxon Minsters of Winchester,* Winchester Studies, **4.i**

Klug-Treppe, J, 2010 Bärenthal, Kreis Tuttlingen, Neue Erkentnisse zu Kirche, Siedlung und frühmittelalterlichem Friedhof, *Archäologische Ausgrabungen in Baden-Württemberg 2010,* 198–203

Lee, F, 1954 A new theory of the origins and early growth of Northampton, *Archaeol J*, **110**, 164–74

Lobbedy, U 2003 Carolingian royal palaces: The state of research from an architectural historian's viewpoint, *in* Cubitt (ed) 2003, 129–54

Lobel, M D 1969 *Historic Towns,* **1**, Lovell Johns-Cook, Hammond & Kell Organisation

Lobel, M D and Carus-Wilson E M 1975 Bristol, *in* Lobel and Johns 1975

Lobel, M D and Johns W H 1975 *The Atlas of Historic Towns*, **2**, London Scolar Press in conjunction with The Historic Towns Trust

Loveluck, C, 2007 *Rural Settlement, Lifestyles and Social Change in the Later First Millenium AD: Anglo-Saxon Flixborough in its Wider Context. Excavations at Flixborough,* **4**, Oxford, Oxbow Books

Loveluck, C, 2013 *Northwest Europe in the Early Middle Ages: c AD 600–1100, a Comparative Archaeology,* Cambridge University Press

Loyn, H R, and Percival, J, 1975 *The Reign of Charlemagne, Documents of Medieval History,* Hodder & Stoughton

Lyon, S, 2001 The coinage of Edward the Elder, *in* Higham and Hill 2001, 67–78

Lyons, A, 2011 *Life and Afterlife at Duxford, Cambridgeshire,* East Anglian Archaeol, **141**

Marti, R, 2000 *Zwischen Römerzeit und Mittelalter, Forschungen zur frühmittelalterlichen Siedlungsgeschicte der Nordweschweiz (4–10 Jahrhundert),* Archäologie und Museum, **41**

Matter, A, 1994 Frühgebäude und fünf Mörtelmischwerke südöstlich des ehemaligen Chorherrenstifts in Embrach (Kanton Zürich), *Zeitschrift für Archäologie und Kunstgeschichte,* **51**, 45–76

McBride, A, 2020 *The Role of Anglo-Saxon Great Hall Complexes in Kingdom Formation, in Comparison and in Context AD 500–750,* Archaeopress Archaeology

McCarthy, M, 1976 The pottery, *in* Mynard 1976, 137–42

McCarthy, M, 1979 The pottery, *in* Williams J H 1979, 151–229

McSloy, E R, 2017 The medieval and later pottery, *in* Carlyle *et al* 2017, 187–89

Meeson, R A, 2015 The Origins and Early Development of St Editha's Church, Tamworth *Staffordshire Archaeol Hist Soc Trans,* **48**, 15–40.

Miller, P, and Wilson, T, with Harward, C, 2005 *Saxon, Medieval and Post-medieval Settlement at Sol Central, Marefair, Northampton, Archaeological Excavations 1998–2002,* Mus London Archaeol Service Monog, **27**

Millett, M, with James, S, 1983 Excavations at Cowdery's Down Basingstoke, Hampshire, 1978–81, *Archaeol J*, **140**, 151–279

Minter, F, Plouviez and Scull, C 2016 *Rendlesham Survey 2008–2014,* Suffolk County Council

Mynard, D, 1976 Excavation on the Mayorhold, Northampton, 1971, *Northamptonshire Archaeol*, **11**, 134–50

Nold, A, 2004 Ein Herren- oder Meierhof am Kohliberg in Dornach? *Archäologie und Denkmalpflege im Kanton Solothurn* **9**, 7–46

Oakley, G E,, with Goodall, I H, and Rigold, S E, 1978 The copper alloy objects, *in* Williams 1978, 147–52

Oakley, G, and Webster, L E, with Bayley, H, 1979 The copper alloy objects, *in* Williams 1981, 248–67

Parry, S, 2006 *Rounds Area Survey: An archaeological study of the landscape of Raunds, Northamptonshire, 1985–94,* Oxbow Books

Perry, D, A 2000 *Castle Park, Dunbar: 2000 Years on a Fortified Headland,* Soc Antiq Scotland Monog **16**

Perry, G J, 2016 Pottery production in Anglo-Scandinavian Torksey (Lincolnshire): reconstructing and contextualising the *chaîne opératoire, Medieval Archaeol*, **60.1**, 72–114

Pestell, T, 2004 *Landscapes of Monastic Foundation, The Establishment of Religious Houses in East Anglia c 650–1200,* Boydell Press

Plumier, J, and Regnard Maude (eds) 2006 *Voies d'eau, commerce et artisanat en Gaule mérovingienne,* Études et Documents Archéologie, **10**

Poulik, J, 1975 Mikulčice: capital of the lords of Greater Moravia, *in* Bruce-Mitford 1975, 1–31

Rauch, C, 1976 *Die Ausgrabungen in der Königspfalz Ingelheim 1909–1914*

RCHM 1985 *An Inventory of the Historical Monuments in the County of Northampton, V: Archaeological Sites and Churches in Northampton,* Royal Commission on Historical Monuments (England)

Renoux, A, (ed) 2001 *"Aux marches du palais", Qu'est-ce-qu'un palais médieval?* Actes su VIIe congrés international d'archéologie médieval Le Mans – Mayenne 9–11 septembre 1999

Riddler, I, 1993 The garden court, *in* Hodges 1993, 191–209

Rigold, S, 1959 Finds of St. Edmund Memorial and other Anglo-Saxon coins from excavations at Thetford, *Brit Numismatic J,* **29**, 189–90

Russo, L, 2011 Il miscelatore da malta del cantiere edilizio altomedievale di Monterotondo Marittimo (GR), *Archeologia dell'Architettura,* **16**, 62–9

Ryan, M, 1988 Fine metalworking and early Irish monasteries: the archaeological evidence, *in* Bradley 1988, 33–48

St Joseph, J K, 1975 Air Reconnaissance: Recent Results, 39, *Antiquity,* **49**, 293–5

St Joseph, J K, 1982 Sprouston, Roxburghshire: an Anglo-Saxon settlement discovered by air reconnaissance, *Anglo-Saxon England,* **10**, 191–9

Sanchez-Pardo, J, and Shapland, M, (eds) 2015 *Churches and Social Power in Early Medieval Europe,* Studies in the Early Middle Ages, **42**, Brepols

Sawyer, P, (ed) 1979 *Names, Words and Graves: early medieval settlement,* University of Leeds

Sawyer, P, 1983 The royal *tun* in pre-Conquest England, *in* Wormald *et al* 1983, 273–99

Schäfer, H, 1987 Stadtarchäologische Untersuchungen, *in* Kirchheim/Teck, Kreis Esslingen *Archäologische Ausgrabungen in Baden-Württemberg 1986,* 270–4

Scheidegger, F, 1990 *Aus der Geschichte der Bautechnik, Band 1: Grundlagen*

Schmidt, E, 1995 Bauarchäologische Beobachtungen im Schloß Aulendorf im Kreis Ravensburg *Archäologische Ausgrabungen in Baden-Württemberg 1994,* 241–5

Schmidt-Thomé, P, 2007 Ausgrabung im ehemaligen Mönchsfriedhof des Klosters Reichenau-Mittelzell, Kreis Konstanz, *Archäologische Ausgrabungen in Baden-Württemberg 2006,* 227–9

Semple, S, 2013 *Perceptions of the Prehistoric in Anglo-Saxon England (Medieval History and Archaeology),* Oxford University Press

Sennhauser, H R, 1995 Müstair, Ausgrabung und Bauuntersuchung Kloster St. Johann, Bericht über das Arbeitsjahr 1995 *Jahrbuch 1995 der Historichen Gesellschaft von Graubunden,* 62–9

Shapland, M, 2015 Palaces, churches and the practice of Anglo-Saxon kingship, *in* Sanchez-Pardo and Shapland 2015, 495–522

Sharpe, S, 1881–2 Description of antiquities found on the site of the castle at Northampton *Associated Archit Socs Rep and Papers,* **16**, 243–51

Shaw, M, 1984 Medieval period excavations in Derngate, Northampton, *Northamptonshire Archaeol,* **19**, 63–82

Shaw, M, 1985 Excavations on a Saxon and medieval site at Black Lion Hill, *Northamptonshire Archaeol,* **20**, 113–38

Shaw, M, 1991 *Northampton High School for Girls, Derngate, Northampton. Archaeological Assessment: Stage 1,* Northamptonshire Archaeology report

Shaw, M, 1993 *Archaeological Evaluation at St John's Street, Northampton, 1990,* Northamptonshire Archaeology report

Shaw, M, 1994 The discovery of Saxon sites below fieldwalking scatters: settlement evidence at Brixworth and Upton, *Northamptonshire Archaeol,* **25**, 77–92

Shaw, M, 1997 Recent work in medieval Northampton: archaeological excavations on St Giles' Street, 1990, and St Edmund's End, 1988, *Northamptonshire Archaeol,* **27**, 101–41

Shaw, M, 2021a *Approaches to the analysis of the topography, origins, growth and development of English medieval towns: case studies of selected towns and their wider applicability,* University of Birmingham PhD thesis (http://etheses.bham.ac.uk/id/eprint/11081)

Shaw, M, 2021b Excavations at The Green, Northampton, 1983: the Anglo-Saxon and medieval phases, *Northamptonshire Archaeol,* **41**, 257–304

Shaw, M, and Denham, V, 1984 The Pottery, *in* Shaw 1984, 70–1, 73, 76–9

Shaw, M, and Denham, V, 1994. The Pottery, *in* Shaw 1994, 143–47

Shaw, M, and O'Hara, P, 1990 *Archaeological Evaluation at Freeschool Street/Gregory Street, Northampton,* Northamptonshire Archaeology report

Shaw, M, and Soden, I, 1996 *Archaeological Evaluation of the former Travis Perkins Site, St James' End, Northampton,* Northamptonshire Archaeology report

Shaw, M, and Steadman, S, 1994 Life on a medieval backstreet. Archaeological excavations at Swan Street, Northampton, *Northamptonshire Archaeol,* **25**, 143–47

Shaw, M, Steadman, S, and Webster, M, 1992 *Northampton High School for Girls, Derngate. Archaeological Evaluation: Stage 2,* Northamptonshire Archaeology report

Slowikowski, A, 2005 The pottery, *in* Miller *et al* 2005, CD4–12

Soden, I, 1998 *Archaeological Evaluation at Barclaycard, Marefair, Northampton Stage 2: Trial Excavation,* Northamptonshire Archaeology report

Soden, I, 1999 A story of urban regeneration: excavation in advance of development off St Peter's Walk, Northampton 1994–7, *Northamptonshire Archaeol,* **28**, 61–128

Soden, I, 2018 *Excavation of the Late Saxon and medieval churchyard of St Martin's, Wallingford, Oxfordshire,* Archaeopress Archaeology

Stamm, O, 1955 Zur karolingischen Königspfalz in Frankfurt am Main, *Germania* **33**, 391–401

Steeger, W, 2005 Ausgrabungen an den Westtürmen der ehemaligen Stiftskirche St Vitus und St Deocar in Herrieden. Landkreis Ansbach, Mittelfranken, *Das archäologische Jahr in Bayern 2004,* 146–149

Stevenson, W H, (ed) 1904 *Asser's Life of King Alfred,* Oxford, Clarendon Press

Story, J, 2003 *Carolingian Connections: Anglo-Saxon England and Carolingian Francia, c. 750–870,* Routledge

Taylor, C, 1983 *Village and Farmstead: A History of Rural Settlement in England,* George Phillip 1960, reprinted 1983 Sheridan House /Littlehampton Book Services

Tester, A, Anderson, S, Riddler, I, and Carr, R, 2014 *Staunch Meadow, Brandon, Suffolk: A High Status Middle Saxon Settlement on the Fen Edge,* East Anglian Archaeol, **151**

Thacker, A, 1985 Kings, saints, and monasteries in pre-Viking Mercia, *Midland Hist,* **10**, 1–25

Thomas, A, and Boucher, A, 2002 *Hereford City Excavations: Further Sites and Evolving Interpretations 1976–1990,* **4**

Thomas, G, 2017 Monasteries and places of power in pre-Viking England: trajectories, relationships amd interactions, *in* Thomas and Knox 2017, 97–116

Thomas, G, 2018 Mead-halls of the *Oiscingas*: A new Kentish perspective on the Anglo-Saxon great hall complexes, *Medieval Archaeol,* **62,** 262–303

Thomas, G, and Knox, A, 2017 *Early Monasticism in the North Sea Zone,* Anglo-Saxon Studies in Archaeology and History, **20**

Thordeman, B 1979 Die karolingische Palastanlage zu Aachen, *Acta Archaeologica* **35**, 171–87

Vila, X M A, Rotea, R B, and Borrazás, P M, (eds) *Archaeotecture, archaeology of architecture.* Brit Archaeol Rep, International Ser, **1175**

Vogt, E, 1948 *Der Lindehof in Zürich*

Walker, A J, and Otlet R L, with Williams, J H, 1985 The carbon-14 measurements, *in* Williams *et al* 1985, 64–6

Wapples, C, 1979 Calculation of motive power required to drive mixers, *in* Williams J H 1979, 129

Weber, E, 2004 Neueste Grabunsserkenntnisse aus dem Landstädtchen Lenzburg, *Argovia*, **116**, 121–44

Webster, L, 1991 Various contributions, *in* Webster and Backhouse 1991

Webster, L, and Backhouse, J, 1991 *The Making of England, Anglo-Saxon Art and Culture AD 600–900,* British Museum

Weise, G, 1923 *Zwei fränckische Königspfalzen*

Welsh, T, 1996–97 Northampton alternatives: conjecture and counter conjecture, N*orthamptonshire Archaeol*, **27**, 166–76

Welsh, T C, 2002 The double streets and the Norman town, *Northamptonshire Archaeol,* **30**, 119–26

White, R, and Young, J, 2020 Frogmore Hall, Atcham, Shropshire – Excavations June 2017, *Trans Shropshire Archaeol Hist Soc, 95, 103–32*

Williams, E, and Shaw, M, 1997 The pottery, *in* Shaw 1997, 130–3

Williams, F, 1979 Excavations on Marefair, Northampton, 1977, *Northamptonshire Archaeol*, **14**, 38–79

Williams, J H, 1974 A Saxo-Norman kiln group from Northampton, *Northamptonshire Archaeol,* **9**, 46–56

Williams, J H, 1977 The early development of the town of Northampton, *in* Dornier 1977, 131–52

Williams, J H, 1978 Excavations at Greyfriars 1972, *Northamptonshire Archaeol,* **13**, 96–160

Williams, J H, 1979 *St Peter's Street, Northampton, Excavations 1973–1976,* Northampton Development Corporation, Archaeol Monog, **2**

Williams, J H, 1982a *Saxon and Medieval Northampton,* Northampton Development Corporation

Williams, J H, 1982b Four small excavations on Northampton's medieval defences and elsewhere, *Northamptonshire Archaeol*, **17**, 60–73

Williams, J H, 1982c Northampton's medieval parishes, *Northamptonshire Archaeol*, **17**, 74–84

Williams, J H, 1984 From 'palace' to 'town': Northampton and urban origins, *Anglo-Saxon England,* **13**, 113–36

Williams, J H, 2014 *Town and Crown: the Governance of Later Thirteenth-Century Northampton,* Northamptonshire Rec Soc, **XLVII**

Williams, J H, 2021 Brave New World: Northampton Development Corporation and archaeology 1970–85, *Northamptonshire Archaeol,* **41**, 5–15

Williams, J H, and Farwell, C, 1984, Excavations in The Riding, Northampton, 1981–82, *Northamptonshire Archaeol,* **19**, 83–106

Williams, J H, and Farwell, D, 1983 Excavations of a Saxon site in St James' Square, Northampton, 1981, *Northamptonshire Archaeol,* **18**, 141–52

Williams, J H and Shaw, M, 1981 Excavations in Chalk Lane, Northampton, 1975–1978, *Northamptonshire Archaeol,* **16**, 87–135

Williams, J H, Shaw, M, and Denham, V, 1985 *Middle Saxon Palaces at Northampton,* Northampton Development Corporation Archaeol Monog, **4**

Wilson, D M, (ed) 1976 *The Archaeology of Anglo-Saxon England,* Methuen/ Cambridge University Press New edition 1981

Windler, R, 1991 Mittelalter, *in* Bauer *et al* 1991, 55–64

Winkelman, W, 1972 Est locus insignis quo Patra et Lippa fluentant, *Chateau Gaillard*, **5**, 203–16

Witrouw, J, 2006 Le centre domanial du haut moyen âge du Thier d'Olne à Engis, *in* Plumier and Regnard 2006, 269–86

Wormald, P, 1982 The Age of Bede and Aethelbald, *in* Campbell 1991, 70–100

Wormald, P, (ed) with Bullough, D, and Collins 1983, R, *Ideal and Reality in Frankish and Anglo-Saxon Society,* Wiley–Blackwell

Zettler, A, 1988 *Die frühen Klosterbauten der Reichenau. Ausgrabungen, Schriftquellen,* St. Gallen Klosterplan (Archäologie und Geschicte)

Northamptonshire Archaeology, **41**, 2021, 79–127

Late Saxon and Saxo-Norman occupation beneath the Outer Bailey of Northampton Castle

by

Andy Chapman

with contributions from Paul Blinkhorn, Pat Chapman, Tora Hylton, Philip L Armitage, Anne Davis, Michael J Allen and Richard I Macphail

Summary

In 2013 the forecourt of Northampton Station was subject to open area excavation in advance of the construction of a new station. Beneath the medieval levels within the Outer Bailey of Northampton Castle (which are reported separately) there was a sequence of late Saxon to Saxo-Norman ditches, pits and wells. The primary fill of a well has been radiocarbon dated to the 10th century, suggesting the presence of nearby occupation at this time. Late Saxon curvilinear boundary ditches, which ended in a seasonally damp area adjacent to the river, are dated to the 11th century, as are several pits. By the later 11th century there was a new rectilinear ditch system, perhaps marking a change in land divisions following the Norman Conquest. The pre-castle features and the contemporary buried soil produced quantities of animal bone, indicating that the area had been a dumping ground for butchery and craft waste through the 11th century. The site produced no evidence of pre-Conquest town defences. Either the excavated area lay outside the defences, with a defensive bank on the higher ground to the immediate east, or the river had provided a sufficient defence in this area, as it did later for the castle. Clearance to enable construction of the Outer Bailey of Northampton Castle occurred between AD1100–1150, perhaps around AD1120 during the reign of Henry I.

Introduction

Northamptonshire Archaeology (now MOLA Northampton) was commissioned by West Northamptonshire Development Corporation (WNDC), on behalf of Network Rail and London Midland, with funding support from Northamptonshire County Council, to excavate a trial trench within the short-term car park and taxi rank in front of the main entrance to the then Northampton Station; the footprint of the proposed new station (NGR SP 7477 6043; Fig 1). The evaluation, carried out 22–24 October 2012 (Chapman 2012), established that intact deposits, including a pre-Conquest pit and a length of medieval stone wall dating to the early

use of Northampton Castle, survived beneath more recent levels.

Given the positive results from the evaluation, there was a requirement to excavate the footprint of the new station building prior to construction. The excavation was carried out between March and June 2013, a total of 11 weeks. The site was opened to its full extent in three stages due to problems with arranging muck-away and the consequent initial need to retain space for spoil dumping, and also to enable the southernmost road to be retained for taxi access for as long as was feasible. The excavated area measured 37.5m north-south and from 21.7m to 28.3m east-west, a total area of 804m²(0.08ha). During 2013 a watching brief was carried out during the digging out of the buried foundations of the Victorian station to the immediate west of the excavated area, and in 2015 during the digging out of the concrete floor slab of the 1960s station building to the north of the excavated area.

Following the completion of the watching brief in 2015, an assessment report was prepared (Chapman 2016). The full report on the excavations was issued in 2018 (Chapman). The current report deals with the deposits and finds pre-dating the construction of Northampton Castle, with the residual flints, and the castle and later deposits reported separately (Chapman this volume 17–24 and 191–255). All of these reports utilise the results and illustrations presented in the client report of 2018.

Acknowledgements

Thanks are due to the staff of the principal contractor, The Buckingham Group, particularly Andy Latham, Paul Morrant and Lee Whiter, for their co-operation in making the excavation possible, including the provision of plant, site accommodation, safety fencing and muck-away. Thanks are also due to the Station Master, Den Law, for his co-operation with site visits and press access, and his interest in the excavation. Andy Chapman was project manager and site director for Northamptonshire Archaeology (latterly MOLA Northampton), with Tim Upson-Smith as site supervisor. The main fieldwork team was Kirsty Beecham, Rob Bailey, Garreth Davey, Anne Foard, Tom Garside, Erhan Raymon and Tim Sharman, supplemented by brief appearances from Rob Smith, James Burke, Gemma Hewitt and Lou Huscroft. The office-based finds supervision was by Pat Chapman. Specialist reports have been provided by Paul Blinkhorn, Pat Chapman, Tora Hylton, Philip L Armitage, Anne Davis, Michael J Allen and Richard I Macphail. Pottery illustrations are by Amir Bassir, and other illustrations are by Andy Chapman. Thanks must also go to Northampton Museums & Art Gallery and Northamptonshire Libraries who hold the finds and records relating to antiquarian and archaeological work at the castle from the 19th and 20th centuries, and also to Brian Giggins, Graham Cadman and James Edgar who have supplied information and copies of original drawings, plans and photographs, including material from Northampton Borough Council planning department.

Location, geology, topography and survival of archaeological deposits

The development area lies west of the town centre of Northampton, within the parish of St Peter, bounded by Black Lion Hill and the approach to West Bridge to the south, the railway lines to the west and the then current station building to the north. To the east there is a revetment wall with the car parking further east raised with respect to the development area (Fig 2).

The station forecourt comprised access roads for taxis, buses and cars, and contained parking bays for the disabled and short-term car parking. Below ground disturbance in this area had comprised shallow electrical cables and also deeper drainage runs. The drainage was associated with over a century of use as the forecourt to both the Victorian station and its successor of the mid-20th century.

A major sewer believed to run to the east of the footprint of the new station was fortuitously located during the archaeological excavations, having been constructed by tunneling between vertical shafts, showing it to lie beneath part of the footprint of the new station. This timely discovery enabled the foundations of the new station to be suitably modified to protect the underlying sewer.

The geology of the area is mapped as alluvium at the west of the site with Upper Lias clay and Northampton Sand and Ironstone to the east, across the main public car park.

Archaeological deposits and soil layers had survived in this location as it was the lowest lying part of the former castle complex. The old ground levels rose steadily to both the east and the north, so that while stratified medieval deposits survived across the southern half of the excavated area, across the northern half recent deposits came down directly onto the natural. Further north, beneath the previous station, truncated natural was seen beneath the modern formation deposits for the concrete floor slab.

To the east, the natural also rose and, given the presence of the revetment wall and the raised area of car parking

to the east, ground levels contemporary with castle and pre-castle deposits might still survive across at least parts of the western half of the raised car park.

To the south-east, the old station access road rose to meet the rising approach to the modern West Bridge (Fig 2). Deposits related to the Outer Bailey bank had survived immediately adjacent to the steep slope along the southern side of the site, as seen in watching brief. This indicates that the approach to the West Bridge had been raised well above the level of medieval deposits, which may still lie sealed beneath. It is therefore possible that any early roads approaching earlier bridges may survive at some depth beneath the present carriageway. However, it is unlikely that there will be any opportunity in the foreseeable future where this area could become available for investigation.

The issues of the site topography, the early soils and the depth of burial of medieval deposits are discussed below by Evans and McPhail in greater detail.

Archaeological background

The excavations in the 1960s demonstrated that the Inner Bailey bank on the eastern side of the castle had been constructed over deposits and features of late Saxon date, forming part of the late Saxon town (Chapman 2020b, this volume) (Fig 2). More extensive excavations to the immediate south of this area, currently the Chalk Lane car park, examined in detail another area of late Saxon deposits that had been sealed beneath the Inner Bailey bank (Williams and Shaw 1981).

During the levelling of the castle in the late 19th century, quantities of pottery and other finds recovered from the underlying soils were described as Roman, since Saxon pottery forms and fabrics had not then been recognised (Kennett 1968 and 1969). So it has long been evident that much of the footprint of Northampton Castle stood on land previously occupied and forming the north-western quarter of the late Saxon town.

A modern overview of the pre-Conquest evidence has been provided by John Williams, the head of the Northampton Development Corporation Archaeological Unit during the 1970s to mid-1980s (Williams *et al* this volume, 25–77).

Summary of the late Saxon to Saxo-Norman chronology

The excavation has produced features from the period when the area was part of the late Saxon town and continuing into the post-Conquest period, dated by the pottery assemblages and radiocarbon dating to the 10th, 11th and early 12th centuries. These deposits were associated with a thick soil horizon. Above and cut into the soil horizon were features and deposits that relate to the early life of the castle, through the early to late 12th century (Table 1).

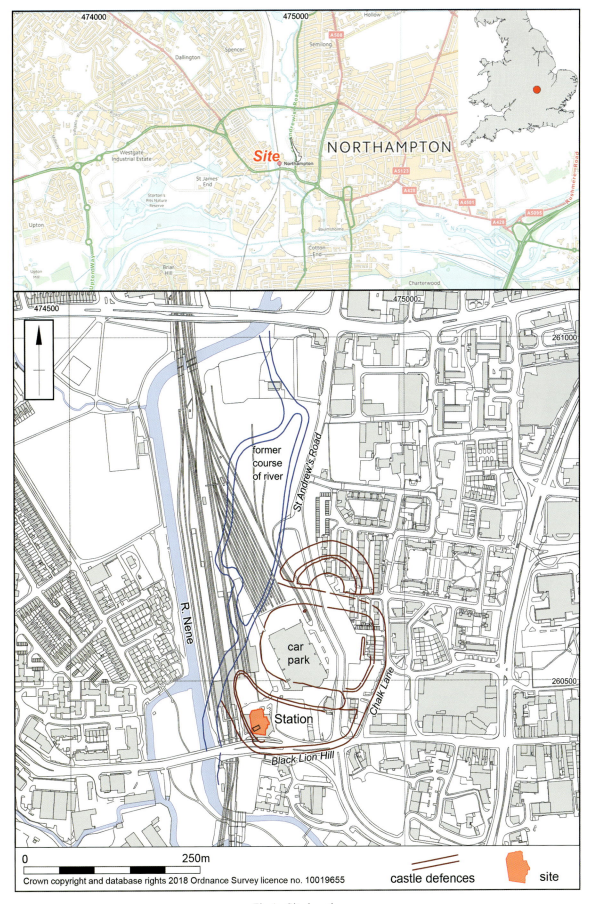

Fig 1: Site location

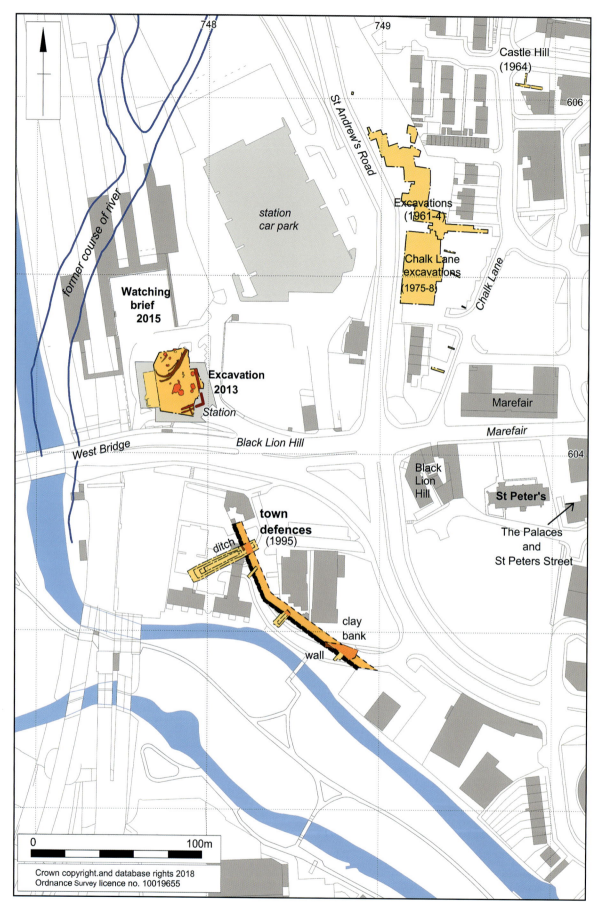

Fig 2: The late Saxon features in relation to the town defences and other sites

Table 1: Summary of chronological sequence and historical context to AD1200

Period/Date	New archaeological evidence	Late Saxon town and Northampton Castle
Late Saxon town (pre–AD1000)	AD950–1000 Well shaft (radiocarbon date from primary fills) Some pottery	Late Saxon town: Construction of town defences?
Late Saxon and Norman town (AD1000–c.1120)	AD1000–1100 (CP LSAX 2) Boundary ditch systems and pits (possible cellared structure). Deposition of animal bone at the margin of the town, dumping of butchery and craft workshop waste AD1100–1150 (CP M1) New boundary ditch system, continued bone deposition	Growth of the Late Saxon town: timber buildings, timber-lined cellars and material indicating craft trades, such as bone and metalworking, including silver smithing. Coins minted in Hamtun. Norman town: Reorganisation following the Conquest Early castle of Simon de Senlis?
Norman castle (AD c.1120–1200) Norman and Angevin kings	AD1100–1150 (CP M1) Creation of Outer Bailey Construction of stone building AD 1150–1200 (CP M2) Final use of building and demolition Pit and gully cutting through building remains	Construction of Royal Castle by Henry I Main buildings within Inner Bailey Castle flourishes through reign of Henry II King John makes frequent visits

The Late Saxon and Saxo-Norman town (AD 900–c.1120)

The excavated area lay at the westernmost end of the late Saxon town, probably with a contemporary bridge crossing to the immediate south-west. To the south, the contemporary town defences have been excavated (Chapman 1999 and Chapman this volume 129–136), and other nearby sites that have produced late Saxon deposits comprise the excavations on the north-east side of the castle and west of Chalk Lane in the 1960s (Chapman this volume, 154–162) and 1970s (Williams and Shaw 1981), as well as on Black Lion Hill (Shaw 1985), St Peter's Street (Williams 1979) and the Palaces (Williams *et al* 1985) east of St Peter's Church, and on the north side of Marefair (F Williams 1979). Further east, parts of an extensive area were excavated before the construction of Sol Central, also on the north side of Marefair (Miller *et al* 2005). These sites are also discussed in the overview of late Saxon Northampton (Williams *et al* this volume, 44–55).

The excavated features at the station comprised successive boundary ditch systems, scattered pits, including a possible cellared structure; a yard area of hard surfacing and an associated buried soil. To the west the ground dropped away onto seasonally wet river margins, and for much of this period the area had been utilised as a convenient dump for animal bone waste from butchery and craft workshops (Fig 3). Given the site topography and the projected line of the defences from the south (Fig 2), any contemporary town defences could only have lain on the higher ground to the east, which would have left the excavated features outside the defended town. These issues are considered in greater detail in the discussion.

The 10th century

In the excavated area, a few contexts produced only single sherds of either the earlier St Neots ware, type T1(1) or Northampton ware and may, therefore, date to the 10th century (CP1, AD900–1000). However, while there are no features that contain a significant assemblage of purely 10th-century pottery, quantities were present as residual finds in later groups, so it seems likely that a focus of 10th-century activity did lie nearby. Preserved waterlogged seeds from the primary fill of well 277 (Fig 3), near the eastern margin of the site, gave a radiocarbon date spanning the late 9th to late 10th centuries (Table 2), indicating that the origin of this feature lay in the 10th century, perhaps at the western margin of domestic activity. The fill of the subsidence hollow, (276), produced 63 sherds of pottery, weighing 438g, dated to the early 12th century (AD1100–1150: CP M1). While there is only a sparse presence of 10th-century pottery within the excavated area, the southern pit group, which was only recognized once the soil horizon had been fully removed, comprised a hearth and a shallow pit, perhaps dating to the 10th into 11th centuries. Both were heavily truncated and were perhaps the surviving remnants of an early phase of activity contemporary with the early well.

The 11th century

The majority of the pottery assemblage from the ditches, pits and wells is dated to the 11th century (Ceramic phase LSAX2, AD1000–1100) as defined by the presence of the later St Neots ware, type T1 (2).

The curving western ditch system might have had an origin in the 10th century, but there was little or no pottery from the primary fills to confirm this. It certainly formed a boundary through much of the 11th century, being

Table 2: Radiocarbon date from a late Saxon well

Site Context	Sample	Laboratory reference	Conventional Radiocarbon Age BP	Calibrated date Intercept *68% confidence* *95% confidence*
Primary fill (323) well 277 Pre-castle	seeds	Beta-460426 NCS13/323	1120+/-30	**Cal AD 900/925/945** *Cal AD 890–975* **Cal AD 880–990 (92%)**

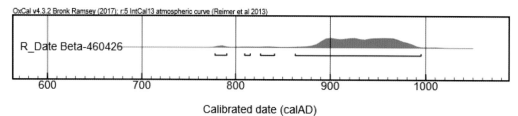

OxCal v4.3.2 Bronk Ramsey (2017); r:5 IntCal13 atmospheric curve (Reimer et al 2013)

R_Date Beta-460426

600   700   800   900   1000

Calibrated date (calAD)

Laboratory: Beta Analytic, Miami, Florida, USA; Calibration: Intcal13; Plot: OxCal v4.3.2

replaced by a rectilinear ditch system to the east in the later 11th century, probably as part of a reorganisation following the Norman Conquest.

The early 12th century

The subsidence fills over the western ditch system and some of the central pits, and the recut ditches of the eastern and southern ditch systems, produced pottery dated to the early 12th century (CP M1: AD1100–1150). This indicates that the final phase of the eastern and southern boundary ditches were still open and functioning as boundaries into the early decades of the 12th century. The creation of the Outer Bailey of the castle, where there are layers and structures dated to the same ceramic phase, must therefore have occurred between AD1100–1150, a date around 1120, during the reign of Henry I, would seem most likely.

Note that the calibrated dates presented here, which are rounded to the nearest five years, differ slighlty from those in the client report (Chapman 2018, Table 2.2), as they have been revised according to the most recently released radiocarbon calibration, Intcal 20, but this has made no significant difference to the interpretation.

At 68% confidence, the new calibration offers alternative dates of Cal AD 890–935, essentially spanning the period of Danish control of the town, and cal AD 940–975 following the Saxon re-conquest, but as they have equal confidence values, at 34%, there are no grounds for any preference. All we can say is that deposition of organics into the disused well occurred at some time between the later 9th century and the end of the 10th century, although the sparse presence of 10th century pottery in this area may favour a date in the later 10th century, and therefore relating to the period of Danish control.

The natural and depth of burial

The site natural typically comprised compact orange to red-brown sands, with a gritty texture due to the presence of small inclusions of ironstone. This is actually a remnant early subsoil horizon overlying the Northamptonshire sands deposits. Only a limited area of this subsoil was excavated by hand, but the overlying soil horizon and both late Saxon and medieval features produced a small group of 46 struck flint, with the majority, 34, coming from the late Saxon soil horizon and cut features. This assemblage is described in a separate paper (Chapman this volume 20–21).

On the slope to the west the natural contained much clay, probably through earthworm action as a result of the deposition of clayey silts above it during seasonal wet periods. In the south-western corner of the site there was also infiltration of clays from the overlying Outer Bailey bank, which made it impossible to define layer boundaries in this area with any precision as they were all clay-rich.

At the southern end of the site the natural was recorded at 60.15m aOD, but this was probably truncated a little during machine stripping, with a true level at around 60.20–60.25m aOD (Fig 3). Here the natural lay 1.55m below modern ground level, overlain by the late Saxon soil horizon, medieval building and yard deposits, late medieval/post-medieval soils, and modern deposits relating to the railway station.

To the south-east and east, the modern ground level rose considerably, as the station access road in the south-east corner of the station forecourt had to rise to meet the rising approach to the modern West Bridge (Fig 4, S.79). As a result, the natural here lay up to 1.95m below ground level, with the upper 0.80m of deposits dating to the mid-19th century onward. The modern deposits overlay post-medieval buried topsoil, 343, and a soil horizon, 334, marking the period of long-term stability and minimal ground disturbance from the abandonment of the medieval road, perhaps from the early 13th century onward.

In the sunken area to the west, sloping down towards the river, the level of the natural dropped to 59.60m aOD and still deepening.

The level of the natural at the northern end of the site was 60.75m aOD, 0.55m higher than at the southern end of the site. Across all of the northern part of the site, excluding the western margins, the natural was directly overlain by

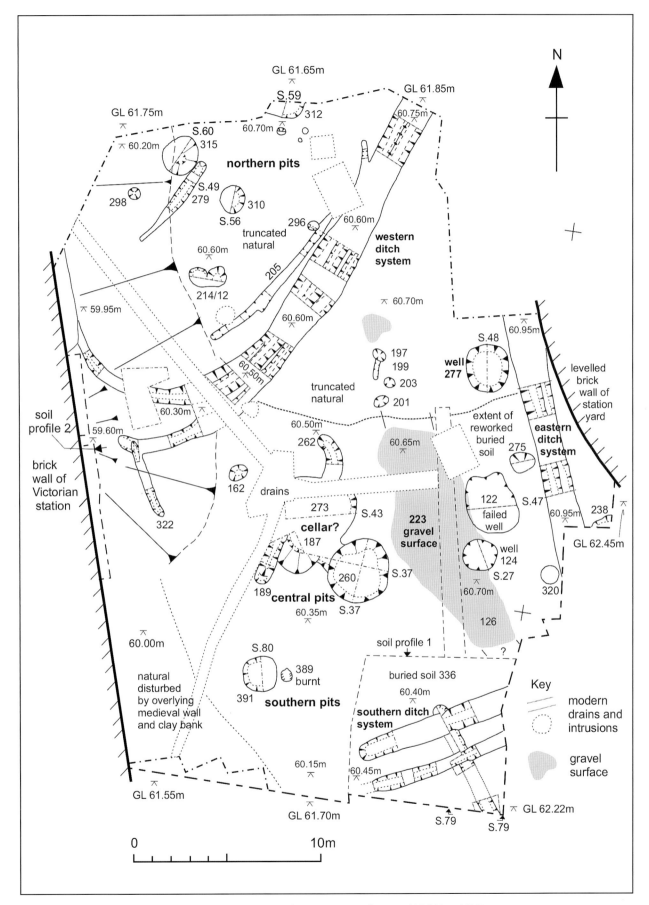

Fig 3: The late Saxon and post-Conquest features (AD900–*c*.1120)

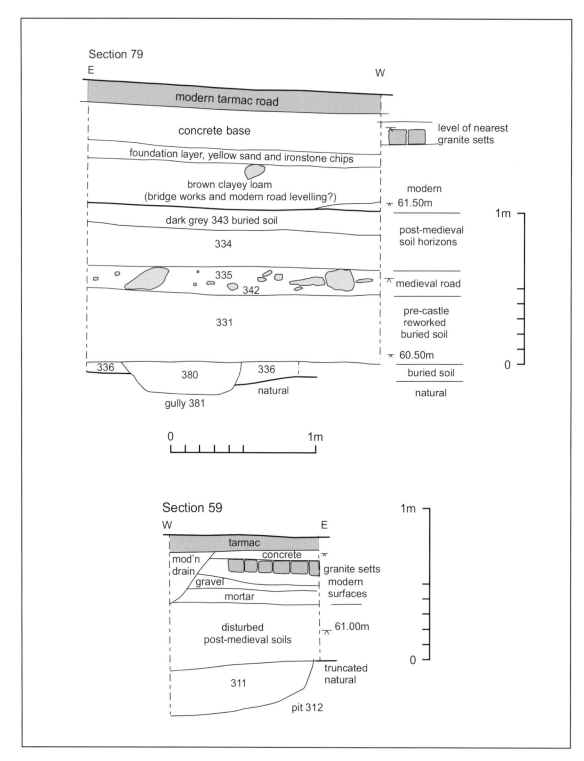

Fig 4: Trench edges to the south-east, S.79, and north, S.59, showing varying depths of burial

recent soils and was only 0.90m below modern ground level (Figs 3 and 4, S.59). All late Saxon and medieval deposits had been lost, but cut features still survived, although truncated.

The late Saxon/post-Conquest soil horizon

Following excavation of the medieval deposits, what remained across the southern half of the site was an apparently homogeneous soil horizon, up to 0.45m thick, with cut features sealed beneath it.

It was necessary to remove this soil horizon, but as the whole of the site was not available for excavation at the same time, which would have permitted progress in a strictly chronological sequence, different areas were excavated at different times with different methodologies for the removal of the buried soil. This had a significant effect on developing an understanding of this deposit (Table 3).

As hand removal had been specified in the brief issued by the planning archaeologist, the late Saxon soil horizon above and east of the group of central pits was removed by hand by the full excavation team using a combination of spades and mattocks in a vigorous fashion. This was clearly not conducive to recognising fine distinctions in stratification, but was the only effective means of removing such a quantity of material within a reasonable time scale. The result was that the soils were taken down to clean natural, where there was a clear colour and soil difference, and where the early features became clearly visible. However, it was noticed during this process that the ironstone yard surface (223) stood proud of the natural, indicating the presence of a lower buried soil on which the metalled surface had been laid, but which had not been distinguished from the upper buried soil during the hand digging.

Examination of an exposed section by geo-archaeologist Mike Evans, also identified a distinction between a basal layer, up to 100mm thick, and the bulk of the deposit above this (see soil geoarchaeology report; Fig 27, soil profile 1).

Subsequently, the south-east corner of the site was stripped by machine with careful use of a toothless bucket, working down in horizontal spits (331), in a way not possible with collective hand digging. Using this methodology, the southern ditch system was seen to cut the lower buried soil (336/345). So in this instance careful machine stripping was the more effective technique for recognising fine distinctions in stratigraphy, rather than the inevitably messy process of bulk soil removal using hand tools. The major advantage is that the machine bucket exposes extensive areas of freshly cleaned surface in each sweep of the bucket, effectively acting as a giant trowel, making both changes in colour or texture more readily evident and also the presence of features cutting this lower soil horizon.

Given the excavation of the early soil horizon in different areas by different methodologies, numerous context numbers were given on site, and these are correlated in Table 3.

The buried soil

The buried soil (336) as exposed in plan by machine stripping in the south-eastern corner of the site, showed the southern ditch system cutting through it. This buried soil horizon was up to 100mm thick, comprising grey-brown, slightly clayey loam, containing scattered small pieces of ironstone and limestone (Figs 3 and 4, S.79). The base of this buried soil (345) and the top of the natural was ironpanned, indicating seasonal waterlogging at the interface with the natural, which as discussed above, was actually just an earlier buried soil.

Some animal bone was embedded in the ironpanning, and animal bone was present throughout layer (336), with a concentration of smaller stones at the interface between this and the overlying soil horizon (331), which contained few stones.

This buried soil is described by geo archaeologist Mike Evans as, "probably representing a relict portion of a truncated lower soil profile (bB) of a former soil", while from examination of the soil micromorphology, Richard I Macphail concluded that this was, "a strongly biologically worked and homogenised, with very fine to coarse occupation debris", including "charcoal, coprolitic bone and examples of burned eggshell, for example, which with coatings and infills of very abundant iron-phosphate-stained faecal waste, are suggestive of intensive middening and occupation.

The reworked soil horizon

The bulk of the soil horizon pre-dating the castle deposits was a homogeneous soil comprising a grey-brown clayey loam, with some people seeing a greenish tinge to it. It was firm to compact, generally 100–300mm thick but up

Table 3: The late Saxon soil horizon contexts

Location	Under Outer Bailey Bank	Hollow to West	Under medieval building	East of medieval building	SE corner	East of yard 223
Methodology	Machine Excavated (heavily contaminated with clay from above)	Mixed hand & machine excavation to natural	Machine excavated to natural	Hand excavated to natural & surface 223	Machine excavated to top of 336 then hand excavated	Machine excavated
Castle deposits	Castle	Castle deposits 106 (merging) 106	Castle deposits	Castle deposits	Castle deposits	Castle deposits
Upper reworked soil	369		387/173	256/206	331	120/125/ 249
Lower buried soil		157 (mottled)			336/345	
Natural	Natural	Natural	Natural	Natural	Natural	Natural

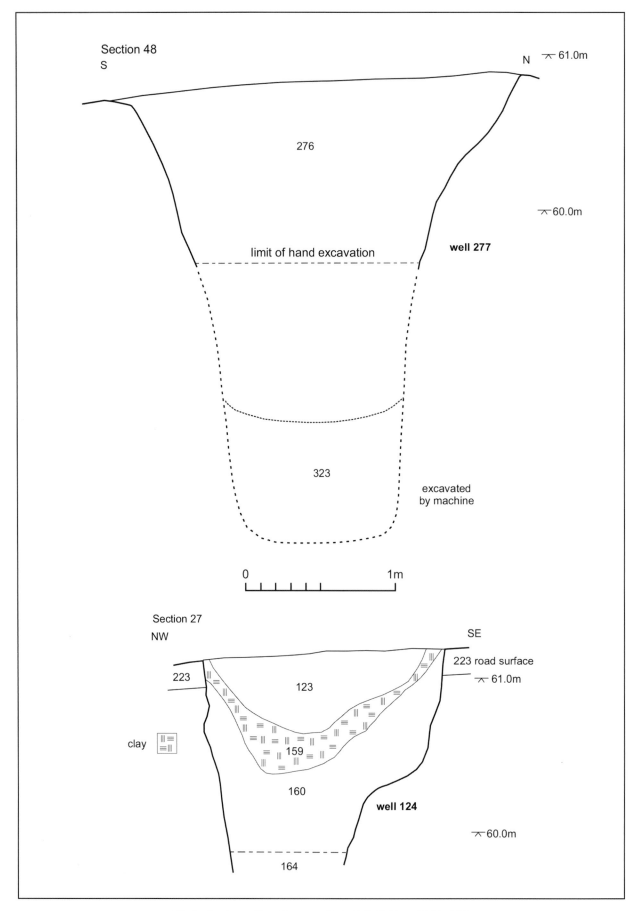

Fig 5: Sections of late Saxon well pits 277, S.48, and 124, S.27

to 450mm thick in the south-east corner of the site (Fig 4, S.79, 331).

It produced some pottery, with the latest material dated to the early 12th century (CP M1: AD1100–1150). It also contained substantial quantities of animal bone broadly similar to the material from the late Saxon ditches and pits.

While the cut features could only be seen beneath this soil horizon, the geo archaeologist, Mike Evans, describes this layer as the body of the pre-castle soil horizon with subsequent reworking, so that contemporary cut features were only visible towards the base of the deposit, where the soils had not been reworked. From examination of the soil micromorphology, Richard I Macphail concluded that, "the dark earth (331) was a homogeneous, humic sandy loam soil, very poorly sorted", and, "characterised by rare strongly burned mineral material, occasional coprolitic bone, charcoal and faecal waste".

Complementing the results of the soil geo archaeology, the analysis of the animal bone by Philip L Armitage indicated that it was, "derived from slaughtering, butchery, craft and domestic waste, indicating that at times the area was unoccupied waste ground", perhaps to such an extent that it became a foraging ground for wild animals, which might account for the presence of bone from a badger.

The bone assemblage is dominated by cattle and sheep, but also includes quantities of pig, domestic fowl, some geese and rare bones of red and roe deer. However, there are also quantities of non-food animals; including horse, dog and cat (see Table 9). Some of the debris derives from horn working and there are also several examples of long bones abandoned in the process of manufacturing ice skates, with a single surviving complete example (see Fig 25).

The river margins

The hollow on the western side of the site was filled with up to 0.60m of fairly homogeneous, but heavily mottled, red-brown clayey loam (157). The rich red colour was a product of iron minerals in the soils, which were probably seasonally, rather than permanently wet or waterlogged. The layer contained few stones, apart from occasional pieces towards the bottom, just above the natural. The layer contained some pottery, dated to the 11th century (CP LSAX2), and much animal bone. The mottled deposits were present up to and a little beyond the top edge of the hollow. The upper late Saxon fill (106) was less mottled and merged with both the broader late Saxon soil horizon to the east and with the castle soil horizons above.

By the time the castle was constructed, the hollow would have been little more than a gentle slope. The south-west corner of the Outer Bailey bank therefore sat on ground comprising a substantial depth of water deposited and clayey silts across a formerly lower-lying river margin.

The eastern wells and pits

Towards the eastern margin of the excavated area there were two well shafts and a failed well (Fig 3). The waterlogged primary fill of well 277, which contained a rich assemblage of charred cereal and weed seeds and preserved fruit stones, has been radiocarbon dated to the 10th century (Table 2), although the fills of the subsidence hollow at the top of the well contained pottery dated to the early 12th century. This is therefore the earliest dated feature on the site. Well 124 contained pottery dating to the 11th century.

The wells pre-dated the eastern boundary ditch, and may have served properties to the east through the 10th to mid-11th centuries, but if so those properties must have lain outside the projected northward continuation of the town defences, if the defences were present in this area.

Well pit 277

This lay just beyond the northern limit of the preserved soil horizon (Fig 3). At the surface, the shaft was slightly oval, measuring 2.70m north-south by 2.25m. The upper edges were slightly eroded, but below this were near vertical, with the main shaft 1.5m in diameter (Fig 5, S.48). It was excavated by hand to a depth of 1.2m, with a homogeneous upper fill (276) of soft dark brown clayey silt, containing a quantity of pottery and animal bone (Fig 6). Below this, the shaft was sectioned by mechanical excavator. To a total depth of 2.3m the fill showed little stratification or differentiation from the upper fill, suggesting that it had been deliberately backfilled. There was no indication of any former lining, certainly not in stone and there were no evident decayed timbers. The total depth of the shaft was c.3.0m, and the bottom 0.80m of the fill (323) comprised blue-grey clayey waterlogged silts. An 80litre soil sample from this layer produced a wide range of waterlogged plant remains, including cereals, weed seeds and fruit stones, plus a small amount of charred plant remains. The presence of this material indicates that the disused well had been used for rubbish disposal, or at least had been open with debris accumulating within it, for some time before it was backfilled.

A failed well 122

To the south of well 277 and immediately north of well 124 there was an irregular pit that appears to have been an attempt to excavate a well shaft. It had failed at an unknown depth due to the collapse of the sides during excavation (Fig 3).

Fig 6: The homogeneous upper fills of the partially excavated well pit 277, looking west (Scale 2m)

The pit was sub-rectangular in plan, 3.1m long by 2.6m wide. During the original excavation the pit side had collapsed inwards, blocking the shaft with an irregular block of natural ironstone in clay. The upper fill of grey silty sand (280) both surrounded and overlay the collapsed natural. No further excavation was attempted. The uppermost fill (121) contained some pottery dated to the 11th century (CP LSAX2).

Well pit 124

In contrast to the failed well 122, almost immediately adjacent there was a successful shaft 124, which cut through the adjacent gravel surface (126/223) (Figs 3; 5, S.27 and 7). The shaft was circular, 2.6m diameter, but narrowing to 1.2m diameter at a depth of 0.9m. It was excavated by hand to a depth of 1.3m and below this by machine to a depth of c.2.5m, where the top of an underlying tunneled Victorian brick sewer was encountered, so the bottom of the well had been lost.

The lowest fill excavated (164) was grey clay with blue-green mottling, seasonally wet rather than waterlogged. Above this there was a dumped layer of orange-brown clay (160), containing some charcoal, pottery and animal bone. A soil sample produced a small assemblage of charred cereal and arable weeds. Above this there was a distinctive sealing layer of tenacious blue-grey clay (159), which had been laid at the contemporary ground level, where it was 0.1m thick. It had subsequently slumped by up to 0.5m due to consolidation of the underlying fills. The fill of the subsidence cone (123) contained both pottery and much animal bone. All fills containing pottery (160 and 123) are dated to the 11th century (CP LSAX2).

Pits 275 and 320

Close to the well shafts and alongside the eastern ditch system there were two small pits (Fig 3). Pit 275 was 1.3m in diameter by 0.56m deep, with a cone-shape profile and a fill (274) of grey silty loam with frequent charcoal and some animal bone. Pit 320, to the south, was of similar size, 0.9m diameter, but was not excavated as it was lost to the damage caused by remedial works on the Victorian sewer disturbed when sectioning well 124.

Fig 7: Partially excavated well pit 124, looking east (Scale 2m)

Pit 238

In the small area exposed to the east of the eastern ditch system, there was a pit 238 in the south-eastern corner of the area. This was over 1.0m in diameter and in excess of 0.30m deep, with steep sides.

The western boundary ditch system

In the ditch system east of the hollow the sequence of cuts all had fills of homogeneous clayey-silts, similar in colour and lacking in stone inclusions, making it difficult to determine the sequence of recutting. Based on all the recorded sections and the presence of a subsidence fill over the final ditch fills in some sections, and the overall plan form, a sequence of development has been established.

The western ditch system began as a single ditch with a shallower slot or gully to the west, perhaps holding a timber fence (Fig 8, Phase 1a/b). It was replaced by a single ditch, later recut on much the same line, which turned sharply westward then northwards as it descended the slope of the hollow to the west (Fig 8, Phase 2). An origin in the 10th century is possible, although there is insufficient pottery from the early fills to confirm this, but it was in use through the early to mid-11th century, probably being replaced by the eastern and southern ditch systems sometime after the Norman Conquest but before the end of the 11th century.

Phase 1a

The earliest form of the ditch system comprised both the easternmost ditch 288/234/191/230/406 and the shallow slot to the west 319/294/205/232, with the two elements 2.8m apart to the south but converging towards the north, where they may have been only 0.5m apart. It is unclear whether the early eastern ditch had been totally removed by the Phase 2 ditches further north, or whether it may have terminated in line with the northern terminal of the slot to the west (Fig 8).

To the north the Phase 1 ditch, 288, was c.0.6m wide by 0.25m deep, with a bowl-shaped profile, but it was broader and deeper further south, 191, c.1.0m wide by 0.4m deep (Fig 9, S.51 and S.21). These ditches appeared to be of a single phase, but to the south, near the top of the hollow a clear recut, 218 cutting 406, (Fig 9, S27) suggests that the broader ditches to the north may have had two unresolved phases, perhaps having been narrower and more slot-like when originally cut. The early, Phase 1a, ditch to the south, 406, was a U-shaped slot, 0.30m wide and 0.16m deep, with a recut 218 of similar dimensions but with a more eroded, V-shaped profile (Fig 9, S.27). The early cut may have terminated just below the top edge of the sunken area, immediately south-west of Section 27, with the terminal defining the east side of an opening or entrance, 2.5m wide, between this ditch and a length of early slot 322, in the base of the hollow. The isolated length of linear slot 322, aligned north-south, was 4.2m long by 0.5m wide and 0.35m deep, with steep sides, a flat base and rounded terminals (Figs 8 and 9, S.36). The fill (321) was stiff dark grey-brown silty clay, with orange mottling as a result of water action, and was generally similar to,

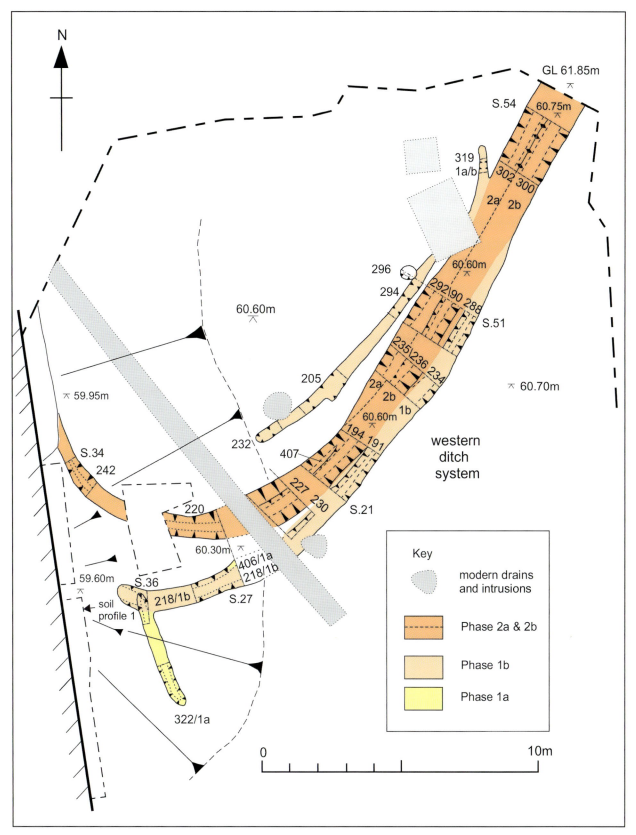

Fig 8: The development of the western ditch system

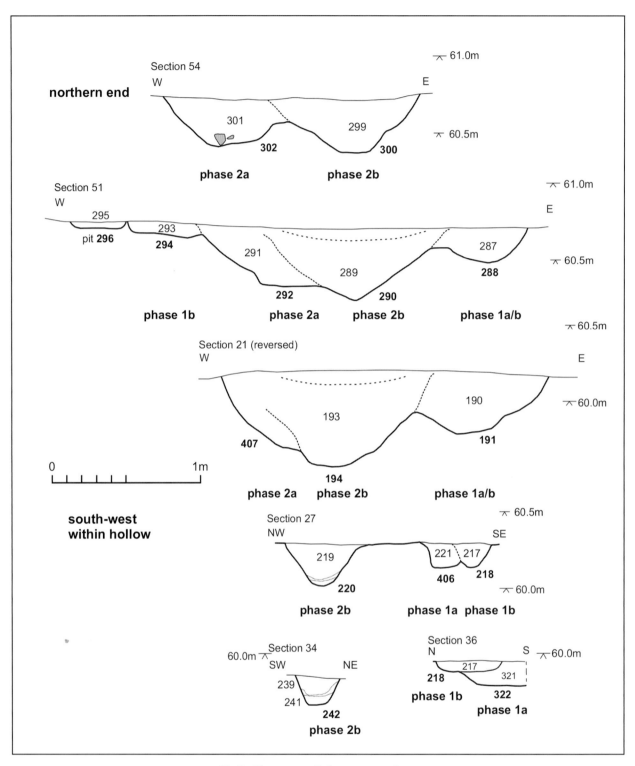

Fig 9: The western ditch system, sections

but much darker than the orange-brown mottled natural clay, and more closely similar to the mottled clayey silts filling the hollow (157). The fill contained a few sherds of 11th-century pottery and a quantity of animal bone.

Phase 1b

While the original ditch to the south-west 406 terminated, the recut, 218, continued down the slope and cut the early slot 322 at right angles (Figs 8 and 9, S.36). To the west it became shallower and disappeared, with no evident terminal, suggesting that it had once continued further westward but subsequent active erosion of the base of the hollow had removed the terminal.

The narrow slot or gully forming the western component of the early ditch system 232/205/294/319 was 13.1m long (Fig 8). At the southern terminal 232, on the top edge of the hollow, the slot was 0.40m wide by 0.24m deep, with a narrow, U-shaped profile. However, north of an abrupt widening of the cut, it was 0.65m wide by 0.35m deep, with steep sides and a broad flat base. This may suggest that, like the contemporary ditch to its east, there were two phases of development. This profile was maintained further north, 294, but it became progressively shallower as result of progressive truncation of the natural by later activity (Fig 9, S.51). At the northern terminal 319 it barely survived, at only 0.02m deep. The fill was of brown-grey clayey loam, with few inclusions, with orange mottles towards the upper edge of the hollow.

It is suggested that the western slot likely held a timber fence set to the west of a contemporary boundary ditch, but this too, although deeper, also had a U-shaped, slot-like profile for much of its length. It is therefore possible that the Phase 1 form comprised a pair of timber-fenced boundaries, with the eastern element the more substantial and deeply founded of the two.

Phase 2

The original ditch and slot was replaced by a single ditch, running between the two earlier features (Fig 8 and Figs 10–11). It was generally both broader and deeper than its predecessors, with the recut the deepest element of the system.

To the north, on a truncated surface, the ditch 302 had moderately steep sides, showing signs of erosion, and a flat base, 1.04m wide by 0.31m deep, and the recut along the eastern side 300, was broadly similar but deeper, at 0.36m (Fig 9, S.54). To the south, where the surface was less truncated, the initial cut, 292 and 407, reached a maximum depth of 0.50m, with the recut, 290 and 194, up to 0.63 deep and c.1.4m wide (Fig 9, S.51 and S.21).

The fills were similar to those of the earlier ditch, also becoming more clayey and mottled towards the top edge of the hollow, containing few stones but quantities of both pottery and animal bone. Along the deepest length of the ditch there was a shallow subsidence hollow, which produced some pottery of the early 12th century.

To the west, on the slope of the hollow, there was only a single cut, 220 and 242. The sudden narrowing of the ditch here may suggest it had originally terminated on the top edge of the slope, Phase 2a. Downslope, the ditch curved northwards, turning back on itself, where it was cut away by the foundations for the Victorian station. At the bottom of the hollow, it was a steep-sided, U-shaped slot, 0.50m wide by 0.40m deep, with a fill of grey-brown silty clay (Fig 9, S.34).

An early southern ditch

A length of early ditch in the south-eastern corner of the site, 347/381, may have been contemporary with the western ditch system (Figs 12, 13 and 15). It was aligned north-west to south-east and comprised a narrow,

Fig 10: The western boundary ditches, looking south-west, showing ditches 288/290/292 in foreground (Scale 2m)

Fig 11: The western boundary ditches within the hollow, looking east (Scale 2m)

U-shaped slot, 0.80m wide by 0.20m deep, with a terminal at its northern end (Figs 4, S79 and 13, S.65). The fills (346/380) produced a few sherds of pottery dated to the 11th century (CP LSAX2: AD1000–1100).

The eastern and southern ditch systems

To the east and south, there were lengths of linear ditch that may have formed parts of a rectilinear boundary system (Fig 12). Pottery from the fills of the original ditches is dated to the 11th century (CP: LSAX2), and this ditch system was probably created in the later 11th century, replacing the western ditch system, perhaps as a result of reforms to land holding within the town in the decades following the Norman Conquest. The pottery from the later cut is dated to the first half of the 12th century (CP: M1).

The eastern ditch system

This ditch was recorded for a length of 13.5m along the eastern margin of the site. The composite ditch system

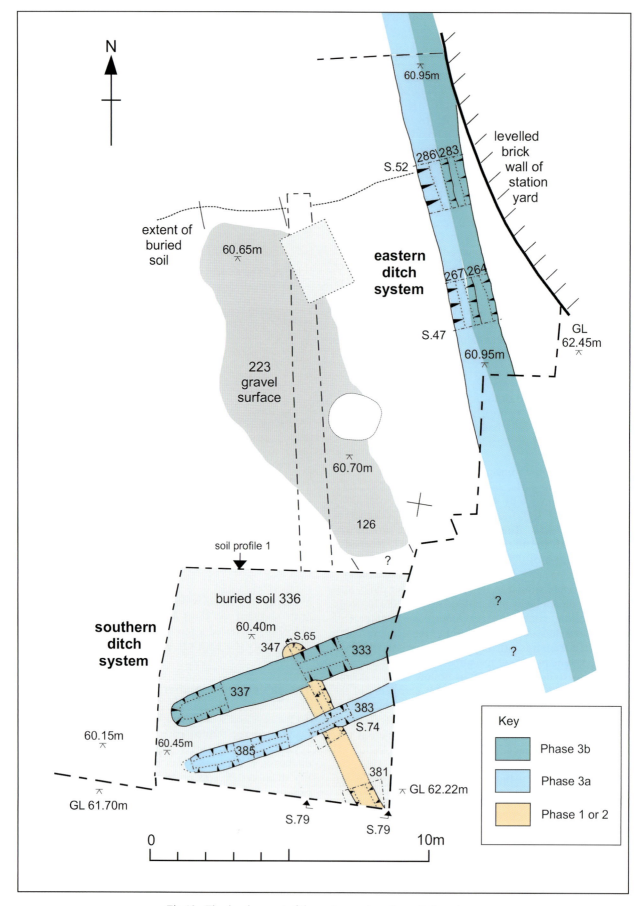

N

levelled
brick
wall of
station
yard

60.95m

S.52

286 283

eastern
ditch
system

267 264

S.47

60.95m

GL
62.45m

extent of
buried
soil

60.65m

223
gravel
surface

60.70m

126

?

soil profile 1

buried soil 336

?

southern
ditch
system

60.40m

S.65

347

333

?

337

383

S.74

60.15m

60.45m

385

381

GL 62.22m

GL 61.70m

S.79

S.79

0   10m

Key

Phase 3b

Phase 3a

Phase 1 or 2

Fig 12: The development of the eastern and southern ditch systems

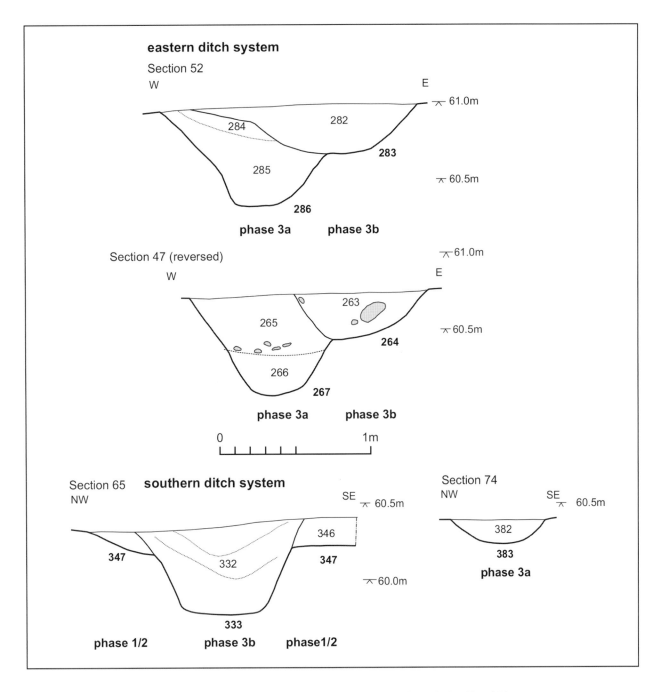

Fig 13: The eastern and southern ditch systems, Sections 52, 47, 65 and 74

was 1.5–1.9m wide, with the original ditch, 286 and 267, having a steep-sided, U-shaped profile, 1.3m wide by 0.65m deep, with some erosion of the upper edges (Figs 13, S.47 and 14). The recut along the eastern edge, 283 and 264, also had a broad flat base with eroded edges, but was much shallower, at 0.32m deep (Figs 13, S.47 and 14). The primary fill (266) was a grey-brown silty clay loam, while the upper fill (265) was grey-brown sandy clay with some orange mottling, containing some small ironstone. To the north the fills (285) were sealed by redeposited natural clay (284), probably backfilling and consolidation prior to the cutting of the new ditch 264/283. The fill of the recut (263/282) had a similar matrix but contained

fewer small stones, and also contained some pottery dated to the early 12th century.

The southern ditch system

In the south-east corner of the site, the southern ditch system comprised a pair of parallel ditches (Fig 12). A small group of pottery from the shallower southern ditch is dated to the 11th century, while the later ditch, to the north, produced a larger pottery assemblage, including parts of three cresset lamps from the western terminal, 337, which are dated to the early 12th century (CP: M1).

The southern ditch, 383 and 385, was 0.65m wide by 0.15m deep, with a broad flat base and a fill (382/384)

Fig 14: The eastern boundary, looking south, showing ditch 267 and the shallower recut, ditch 264 (left), Section 47 (Scale 2m)

of grey-brown silty clay with orange mottling from the natural (Fig 13, S.74).

The northern ditch, 333, had a steep-sided, U-shaped profile and at its western terminal, 337, it was 1.03m wide by 0.71m deep, with a complex sequence of fills (Fig 13, S.65 and Fig 15). The primary fill was a grey-brown sandy loam, almost stone free, while secondary fill had orange mottles of redeposited natural and chips of ironstone (332), these deposits, excavated as one, produced a small group of cresset lamp fragments deposited at the terminal in the primary fill. They suggest that a contemporary building lay close by. There was also an upper fill of homogeneous grey-brown sandy clay.

The gravel surface

A length of ironstone gravel surface (126/223), aligned south-east to north-west, was up to 4.3m wide, but was generally around 3.0m wide, and was traced over a total length of 18.5m (Figs 3 and 12). The eastern margin of the surface was cut by well pit 124, which is dated to the 11th century, while to the south the southern ditch system cuts across its path. It is suggested that the yard surface was in use during the 11th century but probably fell out of use with the reorganisation of the boundary system in the later 11th century. To the north, it survived to the northern limit of the preserved late Saxon soil horizon, and north of this was largely lost, although a former continuation was indicated by an irregular remnant of surviving surface

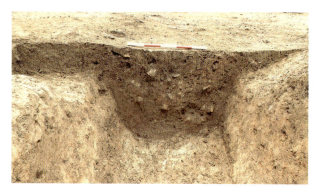

Fig 15: The southern boundary, showing the shallow early ditch 347, cut by ditch 333 (Fig 13, S.65) (Scale 0.5m)

north of a cluster of small features, 197/199/201/203 (Fig 3). To the south-east, it continued beneath later deposits that were removed during emergency remedial works on the modern sewer, so it was not possible to establish whether the surface had once continued further south or its relationship to the southern ditch system.

The surface lay within a shallow hollow in the lower buried soil (336), bottoming slightly into the natural. As the buried soil was largely removed with the upper soil horizon during hand excavation, as previously discussed, the surface was generally left standing slightly proud of the natural. It comprised a compacted, partly iron-panned spread, 100–200mm thick, of clean ironstone chips in orange-brown sand. This is the natural shattered ironstone

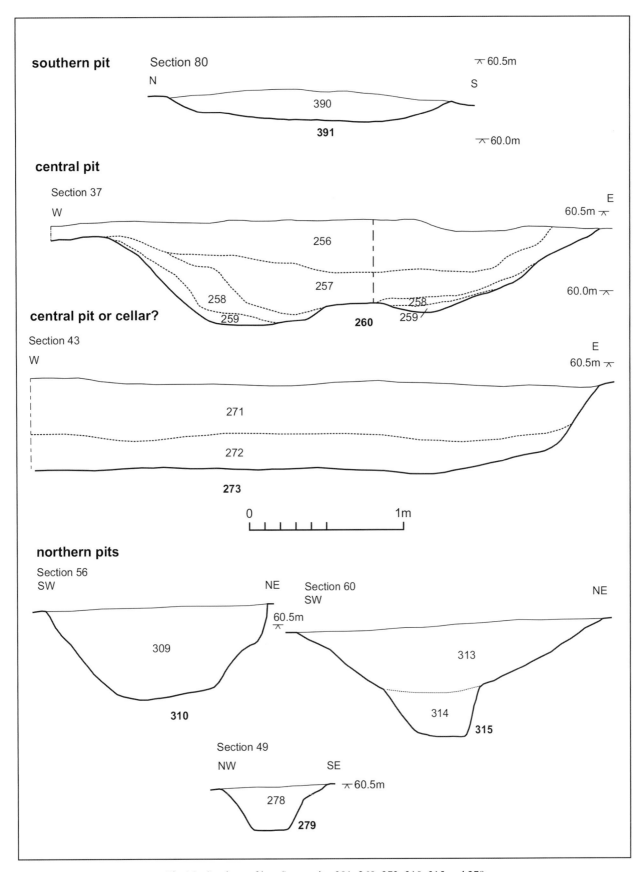

Fig 16: Sections of late Saxon pits, 291, 260, 273, 310, 315 and 279

in sand that occurs across much of the town, dug up and redeposited to form the surface. There were pieces of animal bone and some pottery within the matrix, and also an iron knife blade.

The southern pits

In the southern part of the site, directly beneath the medieval building, and therefore seen only at the final phase of excavation, when the buried soil beneath the building was removed by machine, there were two heavily truncated features 389 and 391 that may belong to an early phase of activity in the 10th century, perhaps contemporary to well 277 (Fig 3).

Hearth 389 comprised a shallow oval pit, 0.65m long by 0.55m wide and 0.05m deep (Fig 17). The natural along the sides, but not the bottom, had been scorched red and black, indicating burning *in-situ*. The fill (388) was a fine black silty loam, with white ashy material against the scorched sides of the pit. This fill produced a piece of lead, and an associated remnant of buried soil (393) produced four reasonably large sherds of early St Neots ware and Northampton ware, indicating a date in the 10th century.

Pit 391, immediately to the west of the hearth 389, was a shallow sub-square pit, 1.80m wide by 0.20m deep, with a broad flat base (Fig 3; Fig 16, S.80). The fill (390) was of orange-brown sandy clay, contained much redeposited natural clay but no burnt debris. There was some animal bone and a little pottery, dated to the 11th century.

The central pit group

Near the centre of the excavated area there was a cluster of large pits, 260, 187 and 273, all with moderately steep sides and broad slightly concave bases (Figs 3 and 19). The upper fills were similar to the general soil horizon and produced some pottery, a few domestic objects and quantities of dumped animal bone similar in character to the animal bone from the reworked soil horizon.

Fig 17: Hearth 389, looking west, showing scorched natural beneath (Scales 0.5m)

To the west of the central pit group, an isolated small pit 162, which had first been located during the trial trenching (Chapman 2012, 10, pit 13), was oval, 1.1m long by 0.80m wide and 0.20m deep, with a bowl-shaped profile. The fill (12) was of dark grey-brown slightly clayey loam, containing frequent flecks of charcoal, and sparse small stones, some burnt. A copper alloy brooch (SF2) was recovered from the interface between the pit fills and the overlying reworked soil horizon.

The only large pit fully excavated, 260, was 3.1–3.4m diameter by 0.90m deep with moderately steep to steep sides and an undulating base, with the shallow hollows filled with clean silts and sands (259) (Fig 16, S.37). The primary fill appeared to be largely eroded natural (258), while the bulk of the lower fill (257), up to 0.35m deep, comprised dark grey clayey loam, with some charcoal and sparse small stones, and also pottery, bone, two lead objects (SF39 & 40) and a bone ring (SF41). The upper fill (256) was up to 0.55m deep and comprised greenish-grey clayey loam, similar to the soil horizon, and contained pottery and animal bone. The pottery assemblage is dated to the 11th century (CP LSAX2).

To the immediate north, another pit, 273, was investigated in a single partial section, due to the presence of modern drains to the north and west (Fig 16, S.43 and Fig 18). This pit had moderately steep sides and a flat base, 0.55m deep. The lower fill (272), up to 0.20m deep, was of yellow-brown silty clay loam containing charcoal, a small quantity of pottery dated to the 11th century, and animal bone. The upper fill (271), up to 0.35m deep, comprised dark grey-brown clayey loam with quantities of pottery and animal bone. The pottery assemblage is dated to the early 12th century (CP M1) because it incorporated material filling a shallow subsidence hollow overlying the main fills. To the south-west a single quadrant was excavated of this or another pit, 187, which showed the same sequence as pit 273: a darker lower fill (186) and an upper fill (185) similar to the reworked soil horizon. It is possible that 273 and 187 may have been the northern and southern ends of a single large sub-rectangular pit, 5.5m long by *c*.4.0m wide and 0.55m deep, comparable to the cellared structures seen at other contemporary sites in Northampton (see Discussion).

The interpretation of this feature as a cellared structure would also be consistent with the recovery of domestic items, such as the bone ring from pit 260, to the immediate east, and a copper alloy brooch from pit 162, a little to the west. Soil samples from pits 260 and 273 produced small quantities of charred cereal grains and chaff, some weed seeds and the occasional charred fragments of hazelnut shell and a probable horse bean.

A broad curving gully, 262, extended north from the pit group for 2.0m and a similar gully, 189, extended south of the pit group for 1.5m. The relationship of gullies to pits was not established, as the fills were closely similar, and they may have been contemporary and associated. The northern gully 262 was 1.0m wide by 0.50m deep with a U-shaped profile and a fill of brown silty clay loam. Gully 189 was 0.95m wide by 0.56m deep with a U-shaped profile. Both were almost the same depth at the pits. Pottery of early 12th century date came from both gullies, in contrast to the 11th-century pottery from the pits, so the gullies appear to be a later addition.

Between the northern end of the gravel surface and an outlying patch of gravel, there was a cluster of small pits (Fig 3). Pit 197 was 0.46m in diameter by 0.14m deep, with moderately steep sides and a rounded base. The fill (196) of dark grey-brown loam contained animal bone, charcoal and an iron object (SF16). A narrow slot 199, 0.26m wide by 0.07m deep, with a U-shaped profile extended 1.03m south from pit 197, and had a similar fill (198). To the south there were a further two similar pits 201 and 203, 0.70m diameter by 90mm deep and 0.60m diameter by 50mm deep, with dark fills similar to those of pit 197. None contained any pottery, but there was a horseshoe (SF18) from pit 201.

The northern pit group

Across the area to the west of the western ditch system, there was a scatter of small pits, postholes and a length of linear gully (Fig 3). These features produced small

Fig 18: Central pit, 273, looking north, with modern drainage sump, left (Scale 2m)

quantities of pottery dated to either the 11th century or the early 12th century. As the reworked soil horizon did not survive in this area, the two features dated to the early 12th century, pit 310 and gully 279, could be contemporary with either the final phase of pre-castle occupation or the earliest use of the castle, but they are described here for convenience.

Features dated to the 11th century

Pit 315 was near circular, 1.80–2.00m diameter by 0.73m deep, with a central steep-sided base, 0.60m diameter by 0.30m deep, and shallowly sloping upper edges, which could be interpreted as deriving from the digging out of a deeply-set post (Fig 16, S.60). The fill of the possible posthole (314) was red-grey to orange-brown sandy clay, while the upper cone had a fill (313) of mid grey-brown clayey loam. To the south-west, 3.0m centre-to-centre, there was another possible post-pit 298, 0.64m diameter by 0.39m deep, with near vertical sides and a rounded base, and a fill (297) of dark grey-brown silty clay. This lay on the slope into the hollow, with its base at around the same level as pit 315, suggesting that they may have been a pair of post-pits.

At the northern edge of the site, there was a sub-circular pit 312, lying partly beyond the excavated area. It was at least 2.0m diameter by 0.30m deep, with near vertical sides and a flat base, but was disturbed by a modern drain. The fill (311) was dark grey silty loam, with charcoal, pottery and animal bone.

To the immediate south of pit 312 there was a cluster of three small postholes, from 0.25m to 0.45m in diameter and all around 0.22m deep, with steep sides and fills of grey-brown silty sand.

Fig 19: The central pit group during excavation, showing pit 260, right of centre

To the south there was a pair of shallow irregular pits 212 and 214, each 0.50m in diameter by 0.20m and 0.25m deep, with fills of light grey-brown loam with orange mottles

To the east, the western slot of the ditch system was cut by a shallow pit 296, 0.48m diameter by 0.04m deep, with a flat base, and a fill (295) of yellow-brown silty sand (Fig 9, S.51)

Features dated to the early 12th century

A linear slot 279, aligned north-east to south-west, was 5.3m long by 0.68m wide and 0.90m deep (Fig 16, S.49). It had steep sides and a flat base, perhaps suggesting that it may have held a short length of wooden fence. The fill (278) was dark grey-brown silty clay, and the assemblage of 27 sherds of pottery dated to the early 12th century (CP M1) was by far the largest from any of the features in this area. To the west, it cut the water-deposited clayey silts (157) filling the hollow, indicating that it was late in the sequence of activity.

To the east, circular pit 310 was 1.40m diameter by 0.60m deep, with moderately steep sides and a rounded base (Fig 16, S.56). The fill (309) was of homogeneous dark brown-grey silty clay loam, with occasional small stones. The pottery and animal bone largely comprised small and eroded pieces, not primary deposition.

The early medieval pottery from Northampton Station
Paul Blinkhorn

The early medieval pottery assemblage from the station, comprising 559 sherds weighing 5.1kg, was quantified using the chronology and coding system of the Northamptonshire County Ceramic Type-Series (CTS) (Table 4). The range of fabric types is typical for Northampton (McCarthy 1979).

The following, not included in the Northamptonshire type-series, were also noted:

F1: Early/middle Anglo-Saxon Granite-tempered ware, c.AD450–850. Sparse to moderate angular granite up to 2mm, many free quartz grains and mica platelets. 1 sherd, 15g, EVE = 0

F370: Lead-Glazed whiteware, 11th-12th century? Hard, smooth white fabric with few visible inclusions. Crackled internal green glaze. 1 sherd, 27g, EVE = 0

The sherd of fabric F370 is unidentified, but is potentially foreign *exotica*. It is from the foot-ring base of a bowl with a thick internal glaze and patches of glaze on the outer surface. It does not appear to be of Western European origin, and is of 11th-12th century date. Its source is unknown, but it has similarities to some Byzantine Green-glazed white wares (Dark 2001, 60), although other eastern sources are possible. The fabric is very hard, either high-fired earthenware or a low-fired stoneware. Glazed stonewares are known from Germany, but date to the 15th to16th centuries (Gaimster 1997), and are generally closed forms such as mugs.

Chronological and Qualitative Analysis

Each context-specific assemblage was given a ceramic phase-date based on the range of ware-types present (Table 5), along with the occurrence by number and weight of sherds and EVE, and the mean sherd weight for the phase.

The presence of a sherd of hand-built Anglo-Saxon pottery and two sherds of middle Anglo-Saxon Maxey-type ware is perhaps no surprise given the proximity of early/middle Saxon settlement at Chalk Lane and Green Street (Williams and Shaw 1981; Chapman 1999).

Otherwise, the range of fabric types present and the pottery occurrence per ceramic phase (Table 6) indicate that the main episode of activity began in the 11th century (Ceramic Phase (CP) LSAX2). Just ten sherds of pottery could be given a phase date of LSAX1, and most occurred as groups of one or two small sherds. However, Northampton ware makes up over a quarter of this small group, and thus the groups could represent low-level activity dating to the 10th century, when such pottery peaked in use. Overall, however, Northampton ware is scarce, which supports an 11th-century start date for the main phase of activity.

The occurrence of vessel types by ceramic phase (Table 7) shows that the Saxo-Norman LSAX2 assemblage is dominated by jars, along with smaller numbers of bowls.

Table 4: Quantification of the early medieval pottery

Fabric code	Fabric name (date range)	Sherds	Weight (g)	EVE
F1001	Romano-British	1	4	0.00
F97	Northampton-type Maxey ware (AD650–850)	2	16	0.0
F100	T1(1) type St Neots ware (AD850–1100)	107	720	1.93
F130	Northampton ware (c.AD900–late 10th century)	19	185	0.50
F200	T1 (2) type St Neots ware AD1000–1200	395	3,832	3.30
F205	Stamford ware (AD850–1250)	35	311	0.32
F209	South Lincs Oolitic ware (AD1100–1300)	1	21	0.00
Total		**559**	**5085**	**6.05**

Table 5: Ceramic phase definition and pottery occurrence per ceramic phase

Ceramic Phase	Date range	Defining wares	Sherds	Weight (g)	Mean sherd (g)	EVE
LSAX1	AD900–1000	F100, F130, F205	10	97	9.7	0.27
LSAX2	AD1000–1100	F200	239	2,176	9.1	2.35
M1	AD1100–1150	F330, F360	893	17,514	19.6	10.77

M1 fabrics F330=shelly coarsewares & F360=Misc. sandy coarsewares, are quantified in report on medieval pottery, Blinkhorn in Chapman this volume xx-xx, table x.. These fabrics, as well as Fabrics F200, F205 & F209, quantified in Table 4, all span the period AD1100–1150, the transition from town to castle, and it is not possible to provide separate phased quantifications.

Table 6: Pottery occurrence per ceramic phase by fabric type, by weight, expressed as a percentage of the phase assemblage

Fabric/ Ceramic Phase	F100	F130	F205	F200	F330	F319	F346	F324	F322	Total weight (g)
LSAX1	72.2%	27.8%	0	–	–	–	–	–	–	97
LSAX2	15.1%	2.3%	5.4%	75.4%	–	–	–	–	–	2,176
M1	1.5%	0.3%	0.6%	9.9%	84.1%	–	–	–	–	17,514

Shaded cells = residual

Table 7: Vessel occurrence per ceramic phase, by EVE, expressed as a percentage of the phase assemblage

Ceramic Phase	Jars	Bowls	Jugs	Lamps	Total EVE
LSAX1	0.22	0.05	0	0	0.27
LSAX2	1.49	0.86	0	0	2.35
M1	8.00	0.83	1.19	0.75	10.77

This is entirely typical for the period in the region (eg Slowikowski 2005, 13). Stamford ware jugs are entirely absent from the rim assemblage, although some glazed body sherds are present that are from such vessels.

Pottery from late Saxon/Saxo-Norman deposits

The pre-castle assemblages, mainly due to the limited range of vessel types in use at the time and the fact that most of the groups are fairly small, have little to offer in terms of understanding the site other than in the areas of chronology and, in a few instances, taphonomy.

Perhaps the most striking feature of the pottery is the relative paucity of Northampton ware, linked with the fact that there are few features which produced only T1(1) type St Neots ware, with most also producing sherds of the later Saxo-Norman T1(2) types, suggesting that there was little late Saxon activity here before the 11th century.

Just 19 sherds of Northampton ware occurred, compared with 502 sherds of St Neots ware. This is a very different ratio to that at other sites in the town. For example, at St Peter's Gardens, 254 sherds of Northampton ware occurred, along with 677 sherds of St Neots ware

(Denham 1985, table 2). McCarthy (1979, 227) noted that the occurrence of Northampton ware at the St Peter's Street and Chalk Lane sites suggested very strongly that the material peaked in use during the mid-late 10th century, the so-called "W1 horizon" (ibid). By the 11th century, the amount of Northampton ware present had dropped dramatically.

A similar pattern was more recently noted at the excavations at Sol Central in Northampton, where c.1000 sherds of the earlier types of St Neots ware were noted along with 352 sherds of Northampton ware (Slowikowski 2005, table 11). In the Saxo-Norman deposits, just over 450 sherds of T1(2) St Neots ware were noted, along with 54 sherds of Stamford ware (ibid), which is a similar ratio to that noted here.

Thus, the low occurrence of Northampton ware at this site is in keeping with the general pattern of early activity being largely confined to the 11th century. As noted above, the small groups of pottery that can be dated to Ceramic Phase (CP) LSAX1 have, on average, 25% Northampton ware, which is far more like the proportions expected in the W1 horizon, and indicates that there was only low-level activity at this site in the 10th century. As Northampton ware is not present as residual material in later features, this shows that the dearth of features with a ceramic date in the 10th century was not due to them being disturbed or destroyed by later activity. It may be noted, however, that the primary fill of well 277 has been radiocarbon dated to the 10th century, indicating that there was nearby occupation in the 10th century, but with cut features perhaps largely located to the east of the excavated area.

It is also perhaps worthy of note that the Stamford ware assemblage, which is larger than that of Northampton ware, is almost completely 11th-12th century in date, consisting of glazed jars and pitchers in late fabrics. Denham (1985,

56) noted that the Stamford ware at the St Peter's Gardens site seemed to generally post-date the W1 horizon, and the bulk of the Stamford ware from St Peter's Street was of 12th to early 13th-century type (McCarthy 1979, 164). Furthermore, Red-painted wares, which are either early Stamford ware or continental imports of the late 9th to early/mid-10th century, were entirely absent at this site, despite occurring at both St Peter's Street (ibid 165) and St Peter's Gardens (Denham 1985, 56), where there was fairly extensive activity in the 9th and 10th centuries.

The latest pottery from this pre-castle phase is medieval Shelly Coarseware (F330), usually in fairly small quantities and often in the upper fills of features. Lyveden 'A' ware (F319) is entirely absent, despite occurring in later phases of activity, which suggests very strongly that the pre-castle phase came to an end sometime in the first half of the 12th century, when many of the earth-cut features appear to have been deliberately back-filled during a phase of consolidation and re-organization.

No cross-fits were noted, but sherds of what appeared to be the same vessels occurred in entirely different features, such as fragments of a Stamford ware glazed jug in wells 124 and 277. The general lack both of vessels that could be reconstructed and of cross- and re-fits from the pre-castle features, and the generally low mean sherd weight for LSAX2 features (9.1g) suggests the most of the material was the product of secondary deposition, and thus it seems probable that many of the features from the phase were backfilled with material removed for landscaping, and at broadly the same time.

Western boundary ditches

The pottery from this feature group (61 sherds, 835g, EVE=0.75) is dominated by Saxo-Norman groups largely comprising T1(2) type St Neots ware (47 sherds, 741g, EVE=0.64), suggesting a largely 11th-century date for the backfill. The rest of the assemblage comprises a few sherds of T1(1) type St Neots ware and a single sherd of Stamford ware. These earlier sherds are all very small and most likely residual. Certainly, the sherd of Stamford ware, which weighs only 2g, is in Kilmurry's fabric D, which is generally of 10th century date (ibid 135). A small amount of medieval material (CP M1) was noted in the subsidence fills.

The stratified St Neots ware consists of a mixture of jars (EVE = 0.45) and inturned-rim bowls (EVE=0.19) which is entirely typical of the tradition. No cross-fits were noted, and few re-fits, indicating that the assemblages are the result of secondary deposition.

Central and Southern pit groups

These groups produced 51 sherds with a total weight of 926g. The bulk of the pottery from these features are jars and inverted rim bowls in T1(2) St Neots ware, indicating a date in the 11th-12th centuries. The fill (388) of a small pit 389, containing burnt debris, and a remnant of early buried soil (393), both produced earlier pottery, in the form of a few reasonably large sherds of T1(1) St Neots

ware and Northampton ware. This pit and layer are likely to date to the 10th century.

Eastern boundary ditches

This feature group produced just 21 sherds of pottery weighing 342g. Most are small and worn sherds of Saxo-Norman St Neots ware, but three sherds of Shelly Coarseware were present in the latest re-cut, including a large and fresh rim sherd from a fairly large jar (Fig 20, 1). This indicates that the final backfilling of the re-cut ditch occurred in the early 12th century

Southern boundary ditches

These only produced a fairly small pottery assemblage, 31 sherds weighing 630g. The two earliest ditches contained small assemblages of 11th century date, with a residual sherd of Maxey ware also present in fill (384) of gully 385. The latest ditch produced an assemblage dating to the 12th century, consisting mainly of shelly coarseware, including large fragments from three lamps at the ditch terminal (Figs 20, 2 & 3 and Fig 21), along with single sherds of sandy coarseware and Stamford ware.

Catalogue of Illustrated pottery (Fig 20)

1: Rim and upper body from a fairly large jar, rim diameter 300mm. Grey with orange surfaces (shelly coarseware, fabric F330). Fill 282, ditch 283
2: Lamp bowl, with thick sooting around the inside of the rim. Grey with orange surfaces (fabric F330). Fill 340, ditch 337 (see also Fig 21)
3: Base and stem of pedestal lamp. Grey with pale orange surfaces (fabric F330). Fill 340, ditch 337

The yard surface

The yard surface included a small pottery assemblage of 11 sherds, weighing 77g, which is entirely late Saxon/Saxo-Norman in date. It mostly consists of St Neots ware, but a fairly large rimsherd of Northampton ware is also present. The feature appears to date to the 11th century.

Wells

The well fills produced a fairly large assemblage of 126 sherds weighing 1216g, with much of the material, 63 sherds weighing 438g, in well 277. This largely comprised St Neots ware of both types, along with five sherds of Stamford ware, all from a green-glazed vessel in a fairly coarse fabric, and a few sherds of shelly coarseware, indicating that the upper fill dates to the early years of the 12th century. The primary fill has been radiocarbon dated to the 10th century.

The other wells produced assemblages which consisted entirely of St Neots wares along with a few sherds of

Stamford ware. The upper fills of well 124 produced a large sherd of a green-glazed Stamford ware jug which is very similar to the sherds from the upper fill of well 277, although cross-fits could not be made. This suggests that both features were backfilled with material from a single source, albeit with a gap of anything up to a century between the two actions.

The north-western pits

The pits to the north-west of the western boundary ditches, showed a similar pattern to other features belonging to the pre-castle phase. They produced a small assemblage, 48 sherds weighing 456g, of St Neots ware, mostly T1(2) types, and shelly coarseware from gully 279 and pit 310. Two sherds of Northampton ware and a single sherd of residual early/middle Saxon ware, from pit 310, were also noted.

The late Saxon soil horizon

The thick soil horizon contained 193 sherds of pottery weighing 2,261g. The assemblages, like those from the cut features from the pre-castle period, are dominated by T1(2) St Neots ware (119 sherds, 1,194g), along with

shelly coarseware (34 sherds, 760g). T1(1) St Neots ware (30 sherds, 182g) is also present, along with five sherds of Northampton ware and two of Stamford ware.

Single sherds of residual Romano-British and Maxey ware pottery were also noted, along with what appears to be a fragment of imported *exotica*, possibly of eastern Mediterranean origin (Fig 22, a & b). A sherd, of glazed whiteware (fabric F370), from the late Saxon soil horizon (331), has some parallels with Byzantine wares of the time (see Dark 2001, 60). Assuming it is reliably stratified, the date, fabric and quality of the glaze suggest that it is from a similarly exotic source. At the time of writing, it remains unprovenanced.

The mean sherd weight for the T1(1) St Neots ware, 6.1g, is far lower than that for the T1(2) types (10.0g), suggesting much, if not all of the former is residual, and that much of the T1(2) ware dates to the 12th century, as T1(1) generally fell from use at the end of the 11th century. The complete lack of Lyveden 'A' ware again indicates that this deposit dates to no later than the first half of the 12th century.

Some of the sherds of the shelly coarseware are fairly large and fresh, making it very unlikely that they are intrusive or residual. The fact that most of the 11th-century material is small and abraded whilst that of the 12th century is larger and fresher would fit with such a scenario, with the earlier material having been subject to distur-

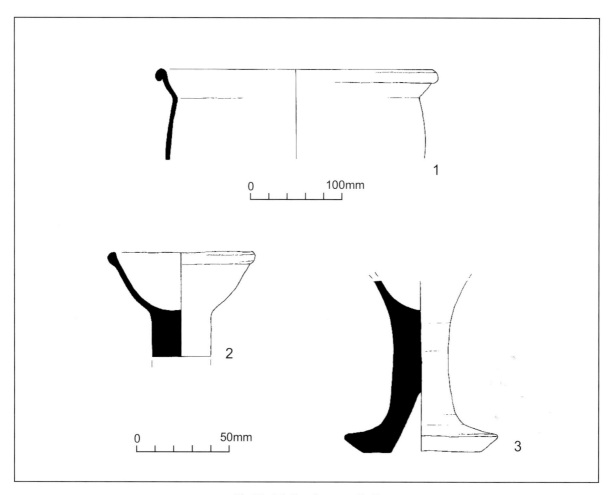

Fig 20: Medieval pottery (1–3)

Fig 21: Pottery lamps from the southern boundary ditch
(lamp bowl 80mm in diameter)

bance and attrition for longer. No cross-fits were noted, suggesting it is all the product of secondary deposition.

The overall assemblage suggests that it is all the product of secondary deposition, and that much of it was disturbed during landscaping and re-organization of the area. It is entirely conceivable from the physical condition of the pottery that this soil horizon had been reworked as a result of landscaping at more or less the same time as latest the pre-castle features were backfilled and consolidated.

Pottery bibliography

Blinkhorn, P, 2010 The Saxon and medieval pottery, 259–333, *in* A Chapman, *West Cotton, Rounds: a study of medieval settlement dynamics AD450–1450. Excavation of a deserted medieval hamlet in Northamptonshire, 1985–89,* Oxbow Books

Blinkhorn, P, 1999 Middle and Late Saxon Pottery, *in* A Chapman, 1999, 55–7

Blinkhorn, P, 2021 The medieval and post-medieval pottery, *in* A Chapman 2021 Excavation within the Outer Bailey of Northampton Castle, 2013–15, *Northamptonshire Archaeol,* **41**, 225–233

Chapman, A, 1999 Excavation of the Town Defences at Green Street, Northampton, 1995–6, *Northamptonshire Archaeol,* **28**, 25–60

Dark, K, 2001 *Byzantine Pottery,* Tempus

Denham, V, 1985 The Pottery, *in* J H Williams, M Shaw and V Denham, *Middle Saxon Palaces at Northampton,* Northampton Development Corporation Archaeol Monog, **4**, 46–64

Gaimster, D, 1997 *German Stoneware,* British Museum Publications

Kilmurry, K, 1980 *The Pottery Industry of Stamford, Lincs. c.AD850–1250,* British Archaeology Rep British Ser, **84**

McCarthy, M, 1979 The Pottery, *in* J H Williams, *St Peter's St, Northampton: Excavations 1973–76,* Northampton Development Corporation Archaeol Monog, **2**, 151–242

McCarthy, M, and Brooks, C M, 1988 *Medieval Pottery in Britain, AD 900–1600,* Leicester: Leicester University

Mellor, M, 1994 Oxford Pottery: A Synthesis of middle and late Saxon, medieval and early post-medieval pottery in the Oxford Region, *Oxoniensia,* **59**, 17–217

Slowikowski, A, 2005 Pottery Production and Use, *in* P Millar and T Wilson with C Harward, *Saxon, medieval and post-medieval settlement at Sol Central, Marefair, Northampton,* MoLAS Monog, **27**, 62– 4

Williams, J H, and Shaw, M, 1981 Excavations in Chalk Lane, Northampton, *Northamptonshire Archaeol,* **16**, 87–135

Young, J, and Vince, A, with Nailor, V, 2005   *A Corpus of Anglo-Saxon and Medieval Pottery from Lincoln,* Lincoln Archaeological Studies, **7**

a   b

Fig 22: Base of bowl, with a) uniform buff fabric, glossy and crackled apple-green glaze on inner surface and b) footring base. Lead-glazed whiteware, import (fabric F370), layer (331), pre-castle soil horizon (scale 10mm)

Late Saxon and post-Conquest finds from Northampton Station
Tora Hylton
with contributions
by Andy Chapman and Paul Clements

The excavations produced a single Roman coin and 24 finds from deposits pre-dating the construction of the castle. There is evidence of craft manufacturing to produce recreational items from bone and antler, together with lead working debris. This is in contrast to the finds from castle deposits which are associated with trade and hunting/warfare, and relate to higher-status activities taking place in and around the castle (see Hylton, 234–240, in Chapman this volume 191–255).

Acknowledgements

The iron objects, excluding nails and small fragments, were submitted for X-ray, which was undertaken by Dr Graham Morgan of CGM Conservators. This provided a permanent record and in some cases it enabled identification and revealed technical details not previously visible.

Roman coin by Paul Clements

From the fill (190) of ditch 191 on the late Saxon western ditch system, there is a contemporary copy of a Roman copper-alloy *nummus* of the 4th century AD (SF15). The coin is 9mmm in diameter, the obverse depicts a diademed bust facing right with the partial legend D N CON, indicating that it is a copy of a coin from the Constantinian dynasty, AD305–361.

Late Saxon and post-Conquest finds

Twenty-four artefacts were recovered from late Saxon/post-Conquest deposits (Table 8). The majority were recovered from the southern half of the site, a small number from pits 197, 260, 273 and 399 and also the southern boundary ditches, but the largest concentration were from the extensive reworked soil horizon (113, 157, 173 and 206), which covered much of the southern half of the site and pre-dated the construction of the Outer Bailey.

Although the number and range of finds is small, the assemblage provides an insight into some of the activities taking place at that time. There is evidence for bone and antler working, to produce skates and gaming pieces; textile working, sewing; and the presence of fragments of lead waste and offcuts suggest the working and utilisation of lead. In addition, there are personal items relating to dress and recreation, a small group of tools, an iron shackle and also horse furniture.

Personal possessions

This category comprises small portable items which would have been worn as jewellery, or held by an individual for

Table 8: Quantification of late Saxon and post-Conquest finds

Object type	Number
Personal possessions	
Costume and jewellery	2
Recreation (skates)	6
Equipment and furnishings	
Locks (shackle)	1
Nails	2
Tools	
Knives	1
Whetstone	1
Textile working	1
Horse equipment	
Horseshoes	2
Miscellaneous and unidentified	
Copper alloy	2
Iron	2
Lead (waste and off cuts)	4
Total	**24**

recreational use. The assemblage includes a copper alloy brooch, a bone/antler finger ring and six bone skates.

Jewellery

An unusual copper alloy disc brooch, SF2, decorated with a deeply-incised motif, was recovered from a small pit 162, at the north end of the original trial trench. The brooch is small, 23mm in diameter and 2mm thick (Fig 23). The front is decorated with a geometric design: a roughly incised circle is divided into six equal triangular sectors by three finely-incised diameter lines, and an inner incised circle divides each sector in two. In the outer part of each sector there is a rectangular slot and in the inner triangular sections small triangular recesses. Remains of a black fill, presumably enamel, can be seen within some of the recesses when examined under a microscope. The edge of the brooch is bevelled and decorated with short closely-spaced incised lines, which radiate from the outer edge of the incised circle. The underside of the brooch is flat but there are diametrically opposed patches of irregular corrosion, presumably indicating where the loop and catch-plate, both now missing, were once positioned.

Although small disc brooches are not uncommon, a brooch decorated with a similar motif has not been found, although it has been identified as representing a type that dates to the later 9th and 10th centuries (Kevin Leahy pers comm). Although it was not possible to locate a parallel, Dr Leahy feels that there are enough similarities with some of the examples illustrated in Rosie Weetch's recent thesis catalogue (unpublished) to establish a link.

Part of a lathe turned bone/antler finger ring, SF41, was recovered from pit 260. The hoop is plain and well-worn with a D-shaped cross-section, 4mm wide and 5mm deep. The internal diameter of 18mm suggests that it would

Fig 23: Late Saxon copper alloy disc brooch, SF2
(Scale: 10mm)

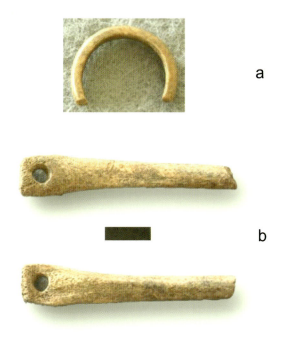

Fig 24: a) Late Saxon bone ring, SF41, b) bone needle, SF43
(Scale 10mm)

have been suitable for an adult (Fig 24a). Similar plain finger rings manufactured from bone and antler have been recorded at Coppergate, York (Macgregor 1999 *et al*, fig 903, 7699) and Winchester (Biddle 1990, fig 369, 4390) where they were recovered from deposits dated to the *c.*10th to11th centuries.

Tools

The tools comprise a needle, presumably for textile working, part of a whittle-tang knife and a whetstone.

Bone needle, SF43, up to 48mm long with the lower end missing (Fig 24b), was found within the mottled silts, 157, filling the base of the wet hollow on the western margin of the site. It is made from the distal end of a pig fibula (Rebecca Gordon pers com). The end has been modified to form a slightly spatulate head, 8mm wide, with a flat apex and a knife-cut circular perforation. The shaft has an oval section and the surface displays signs of moderate polishing. Typologically this needle displays similarities to Group 3, pig fibula pins from York (MacGregor *et al* 1999, fig 910, 6884), where the heads have been heavily modified to form a narrow profile. They were probably used as needles.

A knife, SF34, was recovered from the late Saxon yard surface (126). It is incomplete, just the junction of the blade and tang survive, making it impossible to determine the original shape of the blade. However, its small proportions suggest it would have been for domestic/personal use rather than industrial.

A whetstone, SF25, was recovered from pre-castle soil horizon (206). It is made from micaceous schist (Norwegian Ragstone), a type of metamorphic rock, suited to the sharpening of ferrous metal knives and tools, which was exported from Norway to Great Britain from the 9th century onwards. The whetstone has been deliberately fashioned into a smooth-faced elongated, tapering rod, and although incomplete (the upper end is missing), the surviving dimensions, 86mm long, 13–16mm wide and 7–10mm thick, suggest that it was originally a personal hone probably perforated at the lost upper end so it could be suspended from a belt.

Recreation: ice skates

Two bone ice skates and four modified bones, probably intended to be skates but discarded before completion, were identified during analysis of the animal bone assemblage by Philip L Armitage: the individual bones are more fully described within the animal bone report. The skates were all recovered from late Saxon deposits, one from the fill (289) of ditch 290, on the western ditch system and five from the buried soil horizon: one from layer (173) and four from layer (387).

Two skates had been manufactured from horse metacarpus III bones and four from cattle leg/foot bones: a radius, a metacarpus and two metatarsus bones. Characteristically, the distal and proximal ends have been modified. Two examples display "upswept" toes and heels, while others have been more crudely worked, but the modifications suggest that they too were intended to be used as skates.

Two of the skates had been used, with their anterior surfaces worn and polished. These comprise a horse metacarpus (Fig 25) and a cattle radius. None of the skates have holes for attaching a strap to secure the skate to the foot, so they all appear to be skates that would not have been secured to the foot during use. The foot would have rested on the skate and a pole with a sharp metal spike would have been used to push the skater forward and propel them across the ice. Bone skates of this type are typically recovered from late Saxon and Saxo-Norman deposits.

On the complete horse metacarpus, Armitage records that: "the distal (toe) and proximal (heel) ends of the bone have been modified/shaped (upswept). There is no pointed toe or strap holes which are present in many bone skates from other Saxon/medieval sites; for example those from Norwich dated to the 12th and 13th centuries (Margeson

Fig 25: Bone skate worked on a horse metacarpus (Scale 10mm)

1993, 218, figs 166–7), but the anterior surface exhibits the degree of polishing/wear consistent with contact with the ice surface as found in other examples (see MacGregor 1975 & 1985, 141–144). As explained by MacGregor (1975, 387), experienced adult skaters probably had no need to lash their bone skates to their shoes/boots and thus the absence of perforations is not unexpected in certain bone skates."

Bones skates from late Saxon and Saxo-Norman contexts, broadly 9th to 12th centuries, have been recovered at other sites in the town, including three examples from St Peter's Street (Oakley 1979, 315 & fig 140), five from Chalk Lane (Gryspeerdt *et al* 1987, 130–132), one from the fill of the charnel house at Horseshoe Street (N74, M123, SF198) (unpublished) and a partly finished example from the Palaces site (Harman and Shaw 1985, 75).

Horse furniture

Two incomplete horseshoes were recovered from the pre-castle soil horizon (206). One is difficult to identify with certainty and may be an ox shoe, SF24, but the other represents an early type of horseshoe, often referred to as a 'Norman' horseshoe, dating to the 11th-12th centuries, SF23. Typologically it equates to Clark's Type 2a horseshoe (1995, 86) with rectangular or ovoid countersinkings and a circular nail hole. The terminal of the horseshoe is thickened (a calkin), a feature which helped to prevent the horse from slipping in wet conditions.

An iron shackle

Of interest is an iron shackle or fetter, SF26, recovered from the extensive buried soil (206). It is corroded, but X-ray analysis has revealed details of its form (Fig 26 a & b). It comprises a U-shaped shackle, 90mm internal diameter, formed from circular-sectioned bar, 10mm diameter, with expanded terminal loops/eyes, 26mm

a)

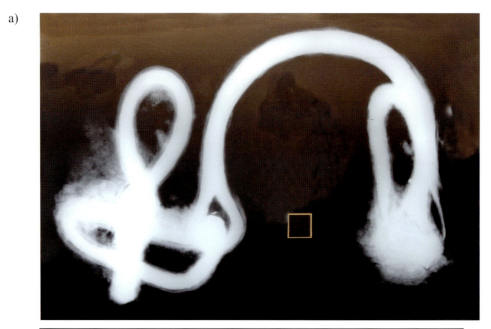

b)

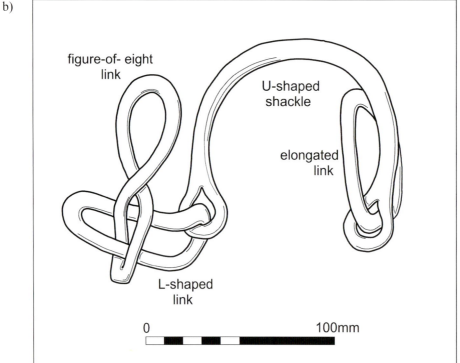

figure-of- eight
link

U-shaped
shackle

elongated
link

L-shaped
link

0   100mm

Fig 26: a) X-ray of iron shackle with attached links, SF26 (Scale 10mm) and
b) interpretative drawing based on the object and the X-ray

wide. Attached to the eyes are variously shaped interlocking links, also formed from circular-sectioned rod.
On one side there is a single elongated link, *c.*85mm long
by 30mm wide (damaged), which would have closed
across the end of the shackle. Attached to the other eye
are two links which would have connected the shackle to
the padlock, which is now missing. The X-ray and visual
examination suggests that these comprise an elongated

link bent into an L-shape, 80mm long, set in the eye of the
shackle and attached to a figure-of-eight link, *c.*108mm
long, twisted through a right angle at the mid-point.

Shackles would have been used to secure the limbs of
animals or humans. This example resembles part of a pair
of shackles from the Old Minster, Winchester, dated to
the late 10th to 11th centuries, which also has curving
L-shaped links (Goodall 1990, fig 314).

Worked stone by Andy Chapman

From the fill (380) of late Saxon gully 381, there is a fragment from a small block of ironstone, heavily blackened and reddened through burning (SF57). It measures 110mm by 90mm and is 130mm thick, with one face gently undulating while the opposed face has been chisel-cut flat. It is difficult to explain the presence of a cut block of stone in a pre-Conquest context, unless it relates to the nearby St Peter's church, where there had been both churches and a stone hall from the 8th-9th centuries.

Metalworking debris by Andy Chapman

A total of 1.67kg of slag was recovered. The majority of this material, 83.5%, came from the pre-castle buried soil, 53.2%, and ditch and pit fills, 30.3%. Only 275g (16.5%) of slag came from castle deposits, and it is most likely that all of the slag recovered came from pre-castle activity, with a small amount residual in castle deposits.

From the pre-castle buried soil (106), there is a roughly plano-convex oval 'cake' of ferrous slag, 90mm long by 70mm wide and up to 30mm thick, possibly a smithing hearth bottom. The rest of the material from the buried soil comprises small pieces of ferrous slag, some with quite fluid and/or glassy surfaces, and fuel ash slag, also sometimes with glassy surfaces. The largest single group, from layer (157) includes fragments of ferrous slag up to 50mm diameter.

From the pre-castle gravel surface (126) there are several small pieces of ferrous slag, up to 30mm diameter, to a total weight of 350g, and including a single larger piece, up to 75mm long but broken, with a smooth convex base and an uneven surface, which may be another smithing hearth bottom.

Also of interest is a piece of hearth slag from the fill (276) of well 277, which has a distinct curvature indicating that it had come from the circular wall of a smithing hearth, although the curvature is too irregular to reliably indicate the overall size of the hearth.

This small group of material is indicative of iron smithing being carried out nearby in the 11th to early 12th centuries, prior to the clearance of occupation to make way for the castle.

Bibliography: other finds

Biddle, M, (ed) 1990 *Object and Economy in medieval Winchester*, Winchester Studies, **7**

Biddle, M, 1990 Unidentified Bone Objects, *in* Biddle 1990, 1129–1145

Clark, J, 1995 *The Medieval Horse and its Equipment c.1150–c.1450; Medieval Finds from excavations in London*, **5**

Egan, G E, 2005 *Material Culture in London in an age of transition: Tudor and Stuart period finds c1450–c1700 from excavations at riverside sites in Southwark*, MoLAS Monog, **19**

Goodall, I H, 1990b Locks and Keys, *in* M Biddle 1990, 1001–1036

Gryspeerdt, M, Harman, M, and Williams, J H, 1981 The worked bone, *in* J H Williams and M Shaw 1981, 130–132

Harman, M, and Shaw, M, 1985 The worked bone and antler, *in* J Williams *et al*, 1985, 75

Hinton, D A, 1990 Fitting from Reliquaries and other Fines Caskets, *in* M Biddle 1990, 762–81

Hinton, D A, 1990 Harness Pendants and Swivels, *in* M Biddle 1990, 1047–1053

Hylton, T, 2021 Medieval finds from the castle, *in* Chapman 2021 Excavation within the Outer Bailey of Northampton Castle, 2013–15, *Northamptonshire Archaeol*, **28**, 25–60

Jessop, O, 1996 A New Artefact Typology for the study of Medieval Arrowheads, *Medieval Archaeol*, **XI**, 192–205

MacGregor, A, 1975 Problems in the interpretation of microscopic wear patterns: the evidence from bone skates, *Journal of Archaeological Science*, **2**, 385–390

MacGregor, A, Mainman, A J, and Rogers, N S H, 1999 *Craft Industry and Everyday Life: Bone, Antler, Ivory and Horn from Anglo-Scandinavian and Medieval York*, The Archaeol of York, The Small Finds, **17/12**

Margeson, S, 1993 Norwich Households. Medieval and Post-Medieval Finds from Norwich Survey Excavations 1971–78, *East Anglian Archaeol Report*, **58**

Oakley, G E, 1979 The Copper Alloy Objects, *in* J H Williams 1979, 248–264

Oakley, G E, 1979 The Worked Bone, *in* J H Williams 1979, 308–18

Oswald, A, 1975 *Clay pipes for the Archaeologist*, British Archaeol Rep, **14**

Ward-Perkins, J B, 1940 (reprinted 1993) *London Museum Medieval Catalogue 1940*, Anglia publishing

Williams, J H, 1979 *St Peter's Street, Northampton: Excavations 1973–1976*, Northampton Development Corporation Monog, **2**

Williams, J, Shaw, M, and Denham, V, 1985 *Middle Saxon Palaces at Northampton*, Northampton Development Corporation Monog, **4**

The mammal, bird, fish and amphibian bones from pre-castle deposits
Philip L Armitage

This report summarizes the results of the study conducted on hand-collected and sieved animal bone elements and fragments that were identified and analysed following standard zooarchaeological methodological procedures and criteria (see Armitage 1999, 102–103).

For the purposes of the animal bone study, the submitted material was divided into two main periods, based on the dating from finds and the structural and stratigraphic relationships, as follows:

Pre-castle: the late Saxon/Saxo-Norman town (11th century to early 12th century)

Medieval castle (early 12th century to late 12th/early 13th century)

By far the largest proportion of the assemblage (79%) is derived from the late Saxon/Saxo-Norman town contexts, most particularly from the pre-castle soil horizon, and is considered below (Table 9). Of these 2,567 bone elements/fragments, 2,528 (98.5%) are from thirteen mammalian species, 27 (1.05%) from four bird species, seven (0.25%) from three amphibian species, and five (0.2%) from

Table 9: The identified animal bone elements/fragments (NISP) from late Saxon deposits

Species	Late Saxon/ Saxo-Norman (hand)	(sieve)	Totals
Mammals:			
cattle *Bos* (domestic)	1180	6	1186
sheep *Ovis* (domestic)	955	20	975
goat *Capra* (domestic)	5	–	5
pig *Sus* (domestic)	100	8	108
horse *Equus caballus* (domestic)	129	–	129
dog *Canis* (domestic)	82	1	83
cat *Felis* (domestic)	31	–	31
red deer *Cervus elaphus*	1	–	1
roe deer *Capreolus capreolus*	2	–	2
fallow deer *Dama dama*	–	–	–
badger *Meles meles*	5	–	5
brown hare Lepus cf. capensis	–	–	0
weasel *Mustela nivalis*	–	1	1
house mouse *Mus musculus*	–		2
Subtotals	**2490**	**38**	**2528**
Birds:			
domestic fowl *Gallus gallus* (domestic)	15	4	19
grey-lag/domestic goose *Anser anser*/domestic	5	1	6
rock dove/domestic pigeon *Columba livia*/domestic	1	–	1
carrion crow *Corvus corone*	–	–	–
Corvid cf. raven *Corvus corax*	1		1
Subtotals	**22**	**5**	**27**
Amphibians:	–	–	–
common toad *Bufo bufo*	–	1	1
common frog *Rana temporaria*	–	5	5
frog/toad	–	1	1
Subtotals	**0**	**7**	**7**
Fish:			
cod *Gadus morhua*	–	–	–
herring *Clupea harengus*	–	1	1
plaice *Pleuronectes platessa*	–	–	–
freshwater eel *Anguilla anguilla*	–	4	4
Subtotals	**0**	**5**	**5**
Totals	**2512**	**55**	**2567**
Percentages	***97.86%***	***2.14%***	

two fish species (Table 9). Omitted from analysis were quantities of highly fragmented animal bones that remain unidentified owing to the absence of surviving diagnostic features; further such fragments had also been discarded during excavation.

The small assemblage relating to the medieval castle is presented separately, and comparative quantifications between the periods are included with the material from the castle (Armitage this volume ***-***).

Anatomical distributions (body-part representations) of the main domesticates from these contexts are summarised in Table 11 and similar data for domestic fowl and goose presented in Table 12.

The tabulated data presented comprises: calculated withers heights of the cattle, sheep, horses and dogs (Table 13), ageing of sheep & horse dentition (Tables 14 & 15) and condensed summaries of the major associated bone groups (ABGs) (Table 16).

In the discussion of the medieval assemblage, comparisons are made to other late Saxon to Norman assemblages from Northampton (see Armitage this volume, table x)

Metrical data on the major species form an appendix at the end of the client report (Armitage 2018, tables 7.10 – 7.14) and these are not repeated here.

Condition

For both periods, the preservation overall is assessed as fair to good with relatively few specimens exhibiting effects from weathering, erosion, leaching or biological degradation (1.1% late Saxon/Saxo-Norman town and 0.8% medieval castle); suggesting most of the bone was disposed of and buried in a comparatively short time. There is a relatively low incidence of dog gnawed bone in the two assemblages (Table 10) with no apparent discernible spatial pattern. Likewise, the incidence of burnt bone is exceptionally low (a total of two cattle and one sheep). Bones from several late Saxon/Saxo-Norman deposits include specimens encrusted with silt and/or patches of orange-brown earthy/clayey material, and these derive from the lower lying areas that were at least seasonal wet.

Post-depositional disturbance/attritional damage to skulls and jawbones among the bone material dumped in the late Saxon/Saxo-Norman period is indicated by the high incidence of isolated/loose cattle, sheep, pig and horse teeth (Table 11). The buried soil yielded the highest frequencies of cattle and sheep teeth (combined 56%); the major groups of loose horse teeth were from this soil horizon and the western ditch system.

Table 10: Number of dog gnawed bones

Period	Cattle	Sheep	Pig	Horse
Late Saxon/ Saxo-Norman	12	2	1	1
Medieval Castle	2	2	–	–
Totals	**14**	**4**	**1**	**1**

Table 11: Late Saxon/Saxo-Norman bone: anatomical distribution for main domesticates

Anatomy	Cattle	Sheep	Goat	Pig	Horse
Horn Core	19	50	4	–	–
Horn Core & Skull	7	11	–	–	–
Skull	15	21	–	4	–
Premaxilla	4	3	–	–	–
Maxilla	5	5	–	5	4
Mandible	60	83	–	9	6
Incisor	5	6	–	7	12
Canine	–	–	–	8	3
Upper Cheek teeth	47	54	–	–	10
Lower Cheek teeth	46	104	–	7	9
Indet.Tooth frag	–	5	–	3	–
Hyoid	3	–	–	–	–
Indet.Vert. frag	24	2	–	–	–
Atlas	4	2	–	–	1
Axis	–	6	–	–	3
Cervical	4	3	–	–	11
Thoracic	22	6	–	1	11
Lumbar	19	4	–	1	–
Caudal	6	–	–	–	–
Rib	265	93	–	4	15
Scapula	40	21	–	7	2
Humerus	44	46	–	10	1
Radius & Ulna	1	–	–	–	2
Radius	39	70	–	8	2
Ulna	10	10	–	3	–
Carpal	1	–	–	–	–
Metacarpus	32	58	–	–	6
Innominate	33	28	–	5	4
Femur	18	8	–	2	1
Tibia	34	89	–	13	4
Fibula		–	–	1	–
Calcaneum	20	6	–	3	1
Astragalus	14	1	–	–	3
Os Centrotarsale	1	–	–	–	1
Metatarsus	45	73	–	1	6
Metapodial	1	–	–	3	1
Phalanx I	21	8	–	–	5
Phalanx II	3	3	–	1	1
Phalanx III	2	–	–	–	4
Long Bone Shaft frag	272	96	–	2	–
Totals	**1186**	**975**	**5**	**108**	**129**
Percentages	*49.4%*	*40.6%*	*0.2%*	*4.5%*	*5.4%*

Hand collected and sieved bone combined

Table 12: Late Saxon/Saxo-Norman bone: anatomical distribution for domestic fowl and goose

Anatomy	Domestic fowl	Goose
Scapula	2	1
Coracoid	3	2
Humerus	3	1
Radius	1	–
Ulna	4	1
Femur	2	–
Tibiotarsus	2	–
Synsacrum	1	–
Rib	1	–
Furculum	–	1
Totals	**19**	**6**

Hand collected and sieved bone combined

Butchery (primary, secondary and tertiary)

Among the cattle, sheep and pig bone from the late Saxon/ Saxo-Norman town deposits there is a combined total of 89 (3.9%) displaying evidence of chopping/knife cuts. (For the medieval castle contexts, eleven cattle, sheep and pig bones (2.3%) have similar butchery marks.)

A major component of the quantities of cattle and sheep long bone shaft pieces (some exhibiting spiral fracturing) recovered from the late Saxon/Saxo-Norman deposits are meat bones that had been smashed open to extract the marrow. Noteworthy are high frequencies of parts of cattle ribs (including chopped shafts) from the pre-castle soil horizon (106, 173, 296 & 256) and fills (257), (271) and (261) of pits 260 and 273, and associated gully 262. Fill (271) of pit 273 also yielded 11 sheep rib pieces, seven of which had been chopped through the shaft.

Evidence of chopping associated with the removal of cattle and sheep horn cores for the purposes of horn working is documented below, together with data on horse, cattle and pig bones used in bone working (see below, craft waste).

The animals

Cattle

Reconstructed withers heights (Table 13), show that for both periods all animals were of similar stature to other contemporary late Saxon/Saxo-Norman and medieval cattle throughout Britain, including both small individuals reminiscent of the unimproved stock of the Iron Age and

Table 13: Calculated withers/shoulder height (m) for horse, cattle, sheep, horse and dog

Species	Mean	Min	Max	No
Cattle:				
Late Saxon/Saxo-Norman	1.131	1.048	1.226	15
Medieval castle	1.134	1.085	1.171	5
Sheep:				
Late Saxon/Saxo-Norman	0.593	0.557	0.657	15
Medieval castle	–	0.601	0.668	2
Horse:				
Late Saxon/Saxo-Norman	1.371	1.268	1.463	6
Medieval castle	–	–	1.311	1
Dog:				
Late Saxon/Saxo-Norman	0.592	0.522	0.662	3
Medieval castle, pit 360, female dog ABG	–	–	0.628	1

Notes

Cattle: method of Matolcsi 1970 & Fock 1966 (von den Driesch & Boessneck 1974)

Sheep: method of Teichert (von den Driesch & Boessneck 1974)

Horse: method of Kieswalter 1888 (von den Driesch & Boessneck 1974)

Dog: method of Harcourt 1974

larger beasts (see Armitage 1982, 53; O'Connor 1982, 21). Among the recovered cattle horn cores three types are recognised (classification of Armitage and Clutton-Brock 1976): three short horned females and one medium horned castrate from the late Saxon/Saxo-Norman contexts; one small horned female, one short horned female, one medium horned male and two medium horned castrates from the medieval castle contexts.

Eighteen (18) animals represented by jawbones/lower cheek teeth in the late Saxon/Saxo-Norman assemblage are aged on their dental eruption and wear (criteria of Bond & O'Connor 1999, 546; age range after Halstead 1985) as follows: the majority, thirteen were adults (5 to 8 years); four sub adults (18 to 30 months) and one immature (c.18 months). Attempts to sex the metacarpal bones applying the method/indices of Howard (1963) provide few definitive determinations: two cows and five cows/steers from the late Saxon/Saxo-Norman assemblage; one bull (?) and four cows/steers from the medieval castle contexts.

Sheep

Horned sheep in the late Saxon/Saxo-Norman material are represented by horn cores from 33 rams, four rams/ castrates and a single female: all adult/young adult animals. In addition, there is a "stumpy" horn core similar to that of a two-year old Soay ram from Hirta (St Kilda) in the Natural History Museum London (Armitage in Clutton-Brock *et al* 1990, 10). The assemblage also includes two crania with scurs (small knob-like, rudimentary horn cores) and a polled (naturally hornless) cranium (possibly from a ewe). There are no four-horned sheep such as those identified by Harmon (1979, 328) in late Saxon deposits from St Peter's Street. Similar polled and scurred sheep, however, were recorded from St Peter's Street (ibid), as well as from the excavations on Woolmonger Street (Armitage 1998–9, 105) and at the corner of Kingswell Street and Woolmonger Street (Armitage 2008, 207).

Of special interest among the male horn cores are several very large/"massive" types with a more markedly triangular cross-sectional shape and greater degree of torsion, producing a spiral-like configuration. Horn cores of this distinctive form have previously been recovered from late Saxon/medieval features at North Elmham Park (Noddle 1980, 397) and pre-Norman/12th-century deposits at Flaxengate, Lincoln (O'Connor 1982, 29–30).

Determinations of the ages at death in 58 sheep from the late Saxon/Saxo-Norman deposits and seven from the medieval castle, are based on dental eruption and wear in the lower cheek teeth (method of Payne 1973) (Table 14).

Calculated withers heights (Table 13) show that for both periods, all animals were of comparable size to other contemporary late Saxon/medieval sheep throughout Britain. Two pathologies are recorded in the late Saxon/ Saxo-Norman sheep: 1) the effects of periodontal disease is noted in the region of the first molar tooth in a jawbone from (121), pit 122; 2) a right horn core of an adult ewe, pre-castle soil horizon (173), has a lesion (slight "thumb-print" impression) on the medial surface arising from a metabolic bone disease possibly due to malnutrition during pregnancy and lactation (Clutton-Brock *et al* 1990, 6–9; Albarella1995; Bartosiewicz 2013, 160–161).

Table 14: Ageing of the late Saxon/Saxo-Norman and medieval sheep dentition

Age class	Suggested age range	Late Saxon/ Saxo-Norman	Medieval Castle
A	0 to 2 months	–	–
B	2 to 6 months	–	–
C	6 to 12 months	2	–
D	1 to 2 years	5	–
E	2 to 3 years	18	3
F	3 to 4 years	14	3
G	4 to 6 years	14	1
H	6 to 8 years	1	–
I	8 to 10 years	4	–
	Totals	**58**	**7**

Method of Payne 1973

Goats

Apart from a single metacarpal bone from the pre-castle soil horizon (206), goat is represented entirely by horn cores: two males and two females (late Saxon/ Saxo-Norman contexts) and a single male (medieval castle context). All other *ovicaprine* bones examined are ascribed to sheep (applying the criteria of Boessneck *et al* 1964).

Pigs

All the pig material derives from domestic animals. The ages of slaughter documented for these pigs fits well into the pattern recorded at other late Saxon-medieval sites; characterised by the dominance of juvenile, immature and sub-adult animals. Based on the sexing of eleven lower canine teeth (tusks) (method of Mayer and Brisbin 1988) the animals represented are recognised almost exclusively as males: ten male teeth and a solitary female specimen.

Horses

The late Saxon/Saxo-Norman equid dentition shows an age range from *c.*6 to *c.*17 years (Table 15). From length measurements taken on selected bones, the calculated withers heights of the living animals for both periods (Table 13) compares with the size ranges documented for other contemporary late Saxon/Saxo-Norman and medieval equids throughout Britain; and included one small individual (1.27m) only slightly taller in stature than the modern New Forest pony in the collections of the Natural History Museum London (reg.no.H37) whose withers height was 1.22m.

Horse pathologies

The fill (271) of late Saxon/Saxo-Norman pit 273 yielded bones from the right hind leg of an adult horse in which the tarsal bones (central tarsal, T1/2 & T3) of the hock joint are fused to the proximal articular surface of metatarsus III. This pathological condition is known as "spavin" (Bartosiewicz 2013, 124) and is believed to be a side effect of inflammation or concussion. Faulty shoeing,

Table 15: Ageing of late Saxon/Saxo-Norman horse dentition

Age range	No
6 to 7 years	1
8 to 9 years	2
9 to 10 years	2
11 to 14 years	3
14 to 15 years	1
16 to 17 years	1

Method of Levine 1982

heavy draught work or working on hard surfaces could have brought about such a condition, which may have resulted in a degree of lameness (Baker and Brothwell 1980, 118), rendering the animal generally unfit for heavy working and possibly the reason for putting it down. However, as there is no evidence of the advanced chronic stages of the condition (known as "Jack spavin") – whereby fusion occurs between the proximal metatarsus, small tarsal bones and the astragalus, accompanied by exostoses (Bartosiewicz 2013, 124–125, figs 102 & 103) – the animal may therefore still have been available for light working, in which case another explanation for its death would apply.

A second pathological condition among the late Saxon/ Saxo-Norman assemblage is apparent in the jawbone of a male horse (aged 9 to 10 years) from fill (380) of gully 381, the early phase ditch cut by the southern ditch system, where the second premolar exhibits considerable oblique wear of the occulusal surface extending as far back as the third cusp resulting in a marked overall reduction in the crown height. This condition probably arose from trauma caused by frequently bridling of the animal. Such bit wear has been recorded in over 90% of frequently bridled horses by Brown & Anthony (1998, 331; referenced by Bartosiewicz 2013, 134).

Minor species

Roe deer

Two bones were recovered from late Saxon/Saxo-Norman contexts: one radius from pre-castle soil horizon (206) and one metatarsus from fill (257) of pit 260.

Dogs

Among the late Saxon/Saxo-Norman dog bones two occurrences of pathologies are noted. From the pre-castle soil horizon (173) there is a right ulna of a small adult dog with evidence of an old fracture that despite having healed had resulted in the formation of a fistula abscess. In an adult skull from fill (185) of pit 187, the first upper left molar tooth had been lost ante-mortem with closure & healing over of the alveolus (result of trauma and/or inflammation); the upper right first molar tooth, however, was unaffected.

Cats

Part skeletons of two adult cats (Table 16) are from the fill (282) of ditch 283 and the fill (340) of ditch 337, both part of the latest pre-castle boundary ditch system, dating to the early 12th century. As is common with cats from other contemporary Saxon and medieval sites, the Northampton animals are much smaller and more gracile compared with modern domestic cats.

Badger

Skeletal remains of an adult badger (Table 16) came from pre-castle soil horizon (206). There is no indication of how this animal died. No butchery or skinning (knife cut) marks are evident on the surviving bones and no traumatic injury or pathology could be detected.

Weasel

Pieces of a skull of an adult animal were recovered from fill (388) (soil sample 14), pit/hearth 389, late Saxon/Saxo-Norman period.

House mice

Two sieved soil samples produced evidence for the presence of these rodent vermin during the late Saxon/Saxo-Norman period: one humerus from fill (160) (sample 4), well 124 and one innominate bone from fill 272 (sample 3), pit 273. Pits and wells acting as "pit-fall" traps may account for the presence in the fills of the small wild fauna (mice and weasel).

Birds

Rock dove/domestic pigeon

A coracoid from the late Saxon/Saxo-Norman period, fill (276) of well 277, is either from a wild caught dove or from a domestic pigeon.

Corvids

Based on metrical analysis, a tibiotarsus from the late Saxon/Saxo-Norman period, fill (384) of ditch 385, is believed to be from a raven (criteria of Tomek and Bocheński 2000).

Amphibians

Amphibian remains came from late Saxon/Saxo-Norman sieved samples: a toad sacrum and immature frog tibio-fibula, fill (160) of well 124 (Sample 4); one immature frog vertebra, fill (311) of pit 312 (Sample 9); and three dorsal vertebrae from the same frog came from fill (323) of well 277 (Sample 10).

Fish

There are scant bones of sea fish from the site. From the late Saxon/Saxo-Norman period, there is one herring vertebra, fill (311) of pit 312 (Sample 9).

Butchery and food waste, diet and status in the late Saxon/Saxo-Norman town

The assemblage of food bones from the late Saxon/Saxo-Norman town display similarities in composition to those from Woolmonger Street and Kingswell Street previously studied by Armitage (1998–9 and 2008); with the anatomical distributions of the cattle, sheep and pig bones indicating the presence of waste from all stages of slaughter, primary and secondary butchering, intermingled with refuse from kitchen and table (Table 17).

Table 16: Major articulated/associated bone groups (ABGs) from pre-castle deposits

Group/Context	Feature	Species	NISP	Age	Anatomy/bone elements present
SAX.SOIL 206	Layer	Badger	5	Adult	left jawbone & bones of fore and hind legs: right radius & humerus and R & L femur
SAX.SOIL 206	Layer	Horse	2	Adult	lower right leg: metarsal bones III & IV
E.DITCH 282	Ditch 283	Cat	8	Adult	skull, jawbones & limb bones: cranium frag, R & L mandibles, radius, ulna, innominate bone and R & L tibia
S.PITS 271	Pit 273	Horse	[4]	Adult	lower hind leg bones: calcaneum, astragalus, os centrotarsale, metatarsus III (with fused metarsarsal bones II & IV)
					Pathology: spavin NISP omits fused T1+2, T3 and navicular
S.PITS 272	Pit 273	Dog (Mni = 2)	8	2 Adults	leg bones from 2 dogs: 2 humerus; 2 tibia & 4 metapodial bones
W.DITCH 299	Ditch 300	Horse	27	Adult	backbone & ribs: 1 atlas; 1 axis; 5 cervical; 10 thoracic & 10 ribs
S.DITCH 340	Ditch 337	Cat	23	Adult	backbone, ribs, pelvis & leg bones: 6 lumbar vert.; 1 sacrum; 5 ribs; 2 humerus; 1 radius; 2 ulna; 2 innominates; 2 femur; 2 tibia; 1 calcaneum

Table 17: Relative proportional frequencies of main domesticates (based on NISP): Comparison of late Saxon/ Saxo-Norman assemblages from Northampton

Site Period	cattle	sheep/goat	pig	No
Northampton Castle Station, 2013				
Late Saxon/Saxo-Norman town (11th to early 12th century)	52.2%	43.1%	4.7%	2274
Medieval Castle (early 12th to late 12th century)	43.0%	46.3%	10.7%	488
Woolmonger Street, 1993–7				
Late Saxon (900 to 1000)	39.2%	51.5%	9.3%	904
Saxo-Norman (1000 to 1250)	44.8%	48.5%	6.7%	2875
Corner of Kingswell St and Woolmonger St, 2005				
Saxo-Norman to 11th to 12th centuries	32.3%	56.7%	11.0%	430
St Peter's Street 1973–6				
Group 2 (850/900 to c.1100)	43.4%	39.5%	17.1%	2442

Sources: (a) Armitage this report; (b) Armitage 1998–9; (c) Armitage 2008; (d) Harmon 1979
No = Total cattle + sheep/goat + pig bones

The diet of the inhabitants appears to have been heavily dependent on the meat of domestic livestock, predominantly cattle and sheep, with a lesser contribution made by pig (Table 11), supplemented with the flesh of domestic fowl and geese. The consumption of fish appears paltry; somewhat surprising in the case of freshwater species (apart from freshwater eel) given the proximity of the River Nene. There is a similar paucity of evidence of game animals in the diet, which is limited to the occasional roe deer and red deer.

The age at death data for the cattle indicate that many of the animals supplied to feed the town had previously been kept principally for working as draught animals, or in the case of cows, for breeding and milk production; and only slaughtered when they were no longer fit for working or had become barren.

Although there were prime meat animals among the sheep contributing to the food supply of the town (Table 16; age categories C to E) many others had probably been kept primarily for their wool and/or for breeding and milk yield; and as in the case of the older cattle, only sent for slaughter when no longer productive.

Craft manufacturing

Horn working debris

Out of the 37 male/castrate sheep horn cores from the late Saxon/Saxo-Norman contexts, fourteen had been chopped through the horn core base or just below it (the latter leaving a small portion of cranium attached). In this way, the horn was detached from the head for the purposes of horn working.

Further evidence of this procedure is seen in two crania from horned sheep, one from pit 273 and the other from ditch 283, where the horn in each case has been chopped off. Exactly the same method of horn detachment from the skull is evident in five of the cattle horn cores. Although the five goat horn cores lack evidence of chopping these probably also derive from horn working activity in the area.

It is believed the sheep, goat and cattle horn sheaths would have been pulled off the core after a period of prolonged soaking/softening following immersion in water. Whilst it seems the usual practice was to pull off the intact horn sheaths from the cores, occasionally the solid tip of the sheath was cut off in advance, perhaps for making handles or buttons (MacGregor 1989, 137). It is therefore of interest that one of the sheep horn cores, from the soil horizon (387), and one of those of cattle, from another part of the soil horizon (256), have had their tips removed.

Bone working debris

Evidence for the manufacture and/or use of bone ice skates is provided by several worked horse and cattle long bones. These are fully described below. The most complete example, from pre-castle soil horizon (173), is also discussed and illustrated in the finds report (Fig 15).

Worked horse metacarpus III, made into and used as an ice skate
Pre-castle soil horizon (173)
In this example of a bone skate, the distal (toe) and proximal (heel) ends of the bone have been modified/ shaped (upswept). There is no pointed toe or strap holes which are present in many bone skates from other Saxon/ medieval sites; see for example those from 12th to 13th-century Norwich (Margeson 1993, 218, figs 166–7) but the anterior surface exhibits the degree of polishing/ wear consistent with contact with the ice surface as found in other examples (see MacGregor 1975 & 1985,141–144). As explained by MacGregor (1975, 387) experienced adult skaters probably had no need to lash their bone skates to their shoes/boots and thus the absence of perforations is not unexpected in certain bone skates.

Worked cattle right radius, possibly a bone skate
Pre-castle soil horizon (387, 1)
This incomplete/distally broken radius shows evidence of smoothing and wear on the anterior surface. Examples of

bone skates fashioned from cattle/horse radii have been recovered from Saxon/medieval sites but these are less frequently encountered compared with the more common skates made from horse/cattle metacarpal and metatarsal bones (MacGregor 1985, 142). A similar example however was recovered from St Peter's Street (Cat.ref.WB76) (see Oakley 1979, 315–316, fig140 WB76).

Worked cattle metacarpus, modified as an ice skate but never used?
Pre-castle soil horizon (387, 2)
Distal and proximal ends have been worked in the same manner as found in examples of bone skates but the toe end is not pointed and there is no surface polishing wear (anterior side). There seems to be a knife cut mark centrally on the anterior surface (evidence of skinning?).

Worked cattle metatarsus, modified as an ice skate but never used?
Pre-castle soil horizon (387, 3)
Distal and proximal ends have been worked in the same manner as found in examples of bone skates but the toe end is not pointed and there is no surface polishing/ wear (anterior surface).

Worked cattle metatarsus, intended as a bone skate but not finished?
Pre-castle soil horizon (387.4)
Somewhat crude shaping attempts of the distal and proximal ends (chopping marks) are in evidence but otherwise there is no clear indication as to whether or not this bone was going to be fashioned into a bone skate or used for another purpose.

Worked horse metacarpus III, possibly an unfinished (rejected/unused) ice skate
Fill (289) of late Saxon ditch 290
Although exhibiting the "classic" modifications (pointed upswept toe and upswept heel end) of bone skates, this horse metacarpus III does not show evidence of polishing/ wear on the anterior surface (in contrast with the example from 173, above).

Disposal of horse and dog carcasses

The isolated equid teeth and bone found scattered throughout the site, in pits, gullies, wells and soil layers, provide no clues as to procedures that may have been adopted by the inhabitants of the late Saxon/Saxo-Norman town for disposing of horse carcasses in a manner and at specific locations in order to prevent these remains becoming an obnoxious nuisance. Disposal of some larger parts of horse carcasses in pits and ditches is indicated, however, by the presence of articulated remains of a lower hind leg in pit 273 and parts of the spine and ribs of another horse thrown into ditch 300, on the western ditch system. A similar absence of any recognisable, specific spatial distribution/locations of the dog remains at the site prevents an understanding of whether or not any formal/ regulated arrangement existed for the disposing of dead dogs.

Perhaps the lack of evidence of care in disposing of deceased non-food animals is not surprising for, even in the later medieval period (15th century), town dwellers apparently were only too ready to dispose of dead horses, dogs and cats in any open space that they considered to be waste ground; despite ordinances against such a practice (Salusbury 1948, 77–78). Temptation also seems to have existed in disposing of slaughter-yard/butchery offal and domestic food waste in a similar manner. Inhabitants of the late Saxon/Saxo-Norman town apparently exploited an open unoccupied area closely adjacent to the settlement as a convenient dumping site for such a purpose, which had the unforeseen consequence of attracting animal scavengers (as discussed below).

Site environment and urban scavengers in the late Saxon/Saxo-Norman town

The presence of skeletal remains of a badger at an urban site deserves special attention. A first interpretation is that this animal had been hunted in the wild for its fur (as was suggested for the badger mandible from a late 11th to 12th-century context at Castle Mall, Norwich despite the absence of any evidence of knife cutting (Albrarella *et al* 1997, 46). It is worth noting that even up to the Victorian/Edwardian period, badger-skin waistcoats were highly prized items of apparel (as featured in the tale "Red spider" by Baring-Gould 1909, 8–9). Secondly, the Northampton badger may have been exploited for its fat and meat as well as for its fur (see Fairnell 2003, 40). This latter interpretation for the occasional use of badgers for human food seems to be supported by the discovery of a butchered badger humerus of late Saxon date from excavations in Winchester (Strid 2011, 22). However, careful examination of the Northampton remains failed to detect either butchery or skinning (knife cut) marks.

Perhaps a third possible interpretation needs to be considered: namely, that this animal was foraging in the area when it met its demise (killed by a dog(s): though there is no sign of traumatic injury on any of the surviving bones). Although the preferred territory/habitat of badgers is deciduous woodland, hedgerows and scrub where there is adequate cover and little disturbance by man or other animals (Neal 1977, 361), modern studies reveal the presence of solitary badgers foraging in suburban parks, gardens and derelict/disused areas (Clinging 1984, 8; Cresswell and Harris 1988).

The location where the badger remains were found would have in some respects offered a somewhat similar environment in the late Saxon period: a low lying marginal area, which was seasonally wet and generally damp, the ideal foraging territory for a badger seeking its primary, preferred source of food: earthworms. As omnivores, badgers will also eat grubs, beetles, amphibians and even mice (Neal 1977, 363) and given that the area was clearly used for dumping butchery and food waste, conditions would have been ideal for attracting and sustaining high population densities of such prey species (see O'Connor 2000).

The presence of dumped fresh organic waste matter would also have served as a perfect breeding ground for flies, which in turn attracted frogs (ibid, 17). Other scavengers identified among the animal bones from the site include *Corvids* (carrion crow & raven), birds highly successful in exploiting the urban environment; as indicated by the frequency of their remains at other late Saxon and later medieval urban sites throughout Britain (O'Connor 1993, 159).

The presence of a weasel at this site is also no surprise given this animal was a well-known predator in towns up to the Elizabethan period (Armitage 1985, 69). It is unclear whether the cats represented by the part skeletons from ditches 283 and 337 were feral animals roaming the area predating mice and rats, or burials of household pets from human habitation close by.

Animal bone bibliography

Albarella, U, Beech, M, and Mulville, J, 1997 *The Saxon, Medieval and Post-Medieval Mammal and Bird Bones Excavated 1989–91 from Castle Mall, Norwich, Norfolk*, English Heritage AML Report, **72/97**

Albarella, U, 1995 Depressions on sheep horncores, *Journal of Archaeological Science, 22*, 699–704

Armitage, P L, 1977 *The Mammalian Remains from the Tudor Site of Baynard's Castle, London: A Biometrical and Historical Analysis*, PhD Thesis, Royal Holloway College & British Museum (Natural History)

Armitage, P L, 1980 A preliminary description of British cattle from the late twelfth to early sixteenth century, *The Ark,* **VII (12)**, 405–413

Armitage, P L, 1982 Developments in British cattle husbandry from the Romano-British period to early modern times, *The Ark, IX (2)*, 50–54

Armitage, P L, 1985 Small mammal faunas in later medieval towns: A preliminary study in British urban biogeography, *Biologist Journal of the Institute of Biology, 32 (2)*, 65–71

Armitage, P L, 1990 Growth, form and inheritance of the horns and horn cores,10–18, *in* J Clutton-Brock *et al* 1990, 1–56

Armitage, P L, 1999 Faunal remains, *in* I Soden 1999, 102–106

Armitage, P L, 2008 Mammal, bird and fish bones, *in* J Brown 2008, 206–208

Armitage, P L, 2021 The mammal, bird, fish and amphibian bones from medieval deposits, *in* A Chapman 2021 Excavation within the Outer Bailey of Northampton Castle, 2013–15, *Northamptonshire Archaeol*, 41, 240–244

Armitage, P L, and Clutton-Brock, J, 1976 A system for classification and description of the horn cores of cattle from archaeological sites, *Journal of Archaeol Science, 3*, 329–348

Armitage, P L, and West, B, 1985 Faunal evidence from a late medieval garden well of the Greyfriars, London, *Transactions of the London and Middlesex Archaeol Soc, 36*, 107–136

Baker, J, and Brothwell, D, 1980 *Animal Diseases in Archaeology*, London: Academic Press

Baring-Gould, S, 1909 *Red Spider*, London: Collins Clear-Type Press

Bartosiewicz, L, 2013 *Shuffling Nags, Lame Ducks. The Archaeology of Animal Disease*, Oxbow Books

Boessneck, J, Müller, H-H, & Teichert, M, 1964 Osteologische Unterscheidungmerkmale zwischen Schaf (*Ovis aries* Linné) und Ziege (*Capra hircus* Linné, Kühn-Archiv, Bd **78**, H1–2

Bond, J M, and O'Connor, T P, 1999 *Bones from Medieval Deposits at 16–22 Coppergate and Other Sites in York*, The Archaeology of York, 15/5, York Archaeol Trust & CBA

Bourdillon, J, and Coy, J, 1980 Statistical Appendix: MS Faunal Remains Project, University of Southampton, *to accom-*

pany J Bourdillon and J Coy The Animal bone, 79–120, *in* P Holdsworth *Excavations at Melbourne Street, Southampton, 1971–76*, Southampton Archaeological Research Committee Council, British Archaeol Research Rep, **33**

Brown, D, and Anthony, D, 1998 Bit wear, horseback riding and the Botai site in Kazakstan, *Journal of Archaeological Science, 25*, 331–347

Brown, J, 2008 Excavations at the corner of Kingswell Street and Woolmonger Street, Northampton, *Northamptonshire Archaeol, 35*, 173–214

Clinging, V, 1984 Sheffield Mammal Report 1980–1983, *The Sorby Record, 22*, 3–10

Clutton-Brock, J, Dennis-Bryan, K, Armitage, P L, & Jewell, P A, 1990 Osteology of the Soay sheep, *Bulletin British Museum (Natural History) Zoology Series,* **56 (1)**, 1–56

Corbet, G B, and Southern, H N, (eds) 1977 *The Handbook of British Mammals*, Blackwell Scientific Publications (for The Mammal Society) (Second Edition)

Cresswell, W J, and Harris, S, 1988 Foraging behaviour and home-range utilization in a suburban Badger (*Meles meles*) population, *Mammal Review, 18 (1)*, 37–49

von den Driesch, A, 1976 *A Guide to the Measurement of Animal Bones from Archaeological Sites*, Peabody Museum Bulletin, **1**

von den Driesch, A, and Boessneck, J, 1974 Kritische Anmerkungen zue Widerristhöhenberechnung aus Langenmassen vor-und frühgeschichlicher Tierknochen, *Saugetierkundliche Mitteilungen, 22*, 325–348

Fairnell, E H, 2003 *The Utilisation of Fur-bearing animals in the British Isles. A Zooarchaeological Hunt for Data*, Unpublished MSc Thesis, University of York.

Halstead, P, 1985 A study of mandibular teeth from Romano-British contexts at Maxey, *in* F Pryor, Archaeology and Environment in the Lower Welland Valley, *East Anglian Archaeol, 27*, 219–24

Harcourt, R A, 1974 The dog in Prehistoric and early historic Britain, *Journal of Archaeol Science, 1*, 151–175

Harmon, M, 1979 The mammalian bones, *in* J H Williams 1979, 328–332

Howard, M, 1963 The metrical determination of the metapodials and skulls of cattle, 91–100, *in* A E Murant & F E Zeuner (eds) *Man and Cattle*, Royal Anthropological Institute of Great Britain and Ireland

Hylton, T, 1999 Small finds, *in* I Soden 1999, 97–101

Hylton, T, 2008 Other finds, *in* J Brown 2008, 200–206

King, C M, 1977 Weasel *Mustela nivalis*, *in* G B Corbet and H N Southern (eds) 1977, 338–345

Lawson, G, and Margeson, S, 1993 Diversions, *in* S Margeson 1993, 211–215

Lemppenau, U, 1964 *Geschlechts- und Gattungsunterschiede am Becken mitteleuropäischer Wiederkäuer*, PhD Thesis, Universität München

MacGregor, A, 1975 Problems in the interpretation of microscopic wear patterns: the evidence from bone skates, *Journal of Archaeological Science, 2*, 385–390

MacGregor, A, 1985 *Bone, Antler, Ivory & Horn: The Technology of Skeletal Materials since the Roman Period*, London: Croom Helm

MacGregor, A, 1989 Bone, antler and horn industries in the urban context, 107–128, *in* D Serjeantson and T Waldron (eds) *Diet and Crafts in Towns. The Evidence of Animal Remains from the Roman to the Post-Medieval Periods*, BAR British Series, **199**

Margeson, S, 1993 *Norwich Households. Medieval and Post-medieval Finds from Norwich Survey Excavations 1971–78*, East Anglian Archaeol Rep, **58**

Mayer, J J, and Brisbin, I L, 1988 Sex identification of *Sus scrofa* based on canine morphology, *Journal of Mammalogy,* **69 (2)**, 408–412

Neal, E J, 1977 Badger *Meles meles*, *in* G B Corbet and H N Southern (eds) 1977, 357–366

Noddle, B, 1980 The animal bones, 375–412, *in* P Wade Martin, *Excavations at North Elmham Park 1967–72*, East Anglian Archaeol, **9 (2)**

Oakley, G E, 1979 The worked bones, *in* J H Williams 1979, 308–318

O'Connor, T, 1982 *Animal Bones from Flaxengate, Lincoln c 870–1500*, Lincoln Archaeol Trust, The Archaeol of Lincoln, **18–1**, Council for British Archaeol

O'Connor, T P, 1993 Birds and the scavenger niche, *Archaeofauna*, **2**, 155–162

O'Connor, T P, 2000 Human refuse as a major ecological factor in medieval urban vertebrate communities, *in* G Bailey, R Charles and N Winder (eds) *Human Ecodynamics*, 15–20, Oxbow Books

Payne, S, 1973 Kill-off patterns in sheep and goats: the mandibles from Aşvan Kale, *Anatolian Studies*, **23**, 281–303

Salusbury, G T, 1948 *Street Life in Medieval England*, Oxford: Pen-in-Hand Publishing

Soden, I, 1999 A story of urban regeneration: excavations in advance of development off St Peter's Walk, Northampton, 1994–7, *Northamptonshire Archaeol*, **28**, 61–127

Strid, L, 2011 Section 11: Mammal and Bird Bones, *in* B Ford & S Teague 2011 *Winchester a City in the Making: Archaeological excavations between 2002–2007 on the sites of Northgate House, Staple Gardens and the former Winchester Library, Jewry St* https://library.thehumanjourney.net/663/.../Animal_Bone_Report.pdfA.p... [Accessed 17/08/2015]

The, T L, and Trouth, C O, 1976 Sexual dimorphism in the basilar part of the occipital bone of the dog (*Canis familiaris*), *Acta anat*, **95**, 565–571

Tomek, T, and Bocheński, Z M, 2000 *The Comparative Osteology of European Corvids (Aves: Corvidae), with a Key to the Identification of Their Skeletal Elements*, Polska Akademia Nauk: Kraków

West, B A, 1982 Spur development: recognising caponised fowl in archaeological material, 255–261, *in* B Wilson, C Grigson and S Payne (eds) 1982 *Ageing and Sexing Animal Bones from Archaeological Sites*, British Archaeol Rep, British Series, **109**

Williams, J H, 1979 *St Peter's Street, Northampton: Excavations 1973–1976*, Northampton Development Corporation Monog, **2**

The charred and waterlogged plant remains from pre-castle deposits
Anne Davis

Bulk environmental soil samples were processed by flotation and submitted for assessment of the plant remains. Four samples from pre-castle deposits were taken on to full analysis: from the fills of two wells and two pits (Tables 18–22).

Sample 10 from the base of a late Saxon well 277 contained organic plant material, whose abundance was estimated on the following scale: + up to 10 items, ++ 11 to 50, +++ 51 to approx. 250, ++++ over 250 (many hundreds) (Tables 18–19). The flots were scanned using a low-powered binocular microscope, and charred plant remains sorted, identified and counted (Tables 20–22). Results were recorded on the MOLA Oracle database, and full species lists with abundance of plant remains recovered from each sample are shown in the tables.

The northern well, 277

Large assemblages of plant remains both waterlogged (Tables 18–19) and charred (Tables 20–21) were recovered from sample 10, fill (323), a machine bucket scoop from the base of well 277.

The well sample contained the only uncharred plant remains found on the site (Tables 18–19). They included a large number of fruit stones, mainly from sloe but also several from plum/bullace (*Prunus domestica*) and cherry (*P. avium/cerasus*). Other food remains, found in smaller quantities, were apple pips and endocarp (from the core) (*Malus domestica/sylvestris*), blackberry/raspberry pips (*Rubus fruticosus/idaeus*) and hazelnut shell (*Corylus avellana*). A number of fruits from beet (*Beta vulgaris*) may have come from plants cultivated as green vegetables, though the seeds themselves would not have been eaten.

While fruit stones and apple cores may have been discarded directly into the disused well, it is likely that some of the food remains, such as the blackberry pips, arrived in human faeces. Evidence for this is seen in the many fragments of corn cockle seeds (*Agrostemma githago*), from a plant which was a frequent weed of cereal crops in the past, and whose seeds were thus incorporated in bread, and are a very common component of cesspit assemblages. Occasional seeds of flax/linseed (*Linum usitatissimum*) and hemp (*Cannabis sativa*), both oily, nutritious seeds, may also have been used as food, or could be waste from the processing of their plant stems for use in textiles.

Numerous seeds of wild plants came mainly from ubiquitous plants of waste and other disturbed-ground habitats, such as common chickweed (*Stellaria media*), fat hen (*Chenopodium album*), stinging nettle (*Urtica dioica*) and black nightshade (*Solanum nigrum*), but a significant number of characteristic arable weeds, including stinking mayweed (*Anthemis cotula*), black bindweed (*Fallopia convolvulus*), thorow-wax (*Bupleurum rotundifolium*) and sun spurge (*Euphorbia helioscopia*) were also present, suggesting the presence of cultivated land in the vicinity. Seeds from several grassland plants, such as lesser stitchwort (*Stellaria graminea*), self-heal (*Prunella vulgaris*), field scabious (*Knautia arvensis*) and hawkbit (*Leontodon autumnalis/hispidus*) may have come from local meadows and pasture.

Altogether the evidence suggests that seeds from several sources found their way into the well, probably by dispersal as well as by deliberate discarding of waste.

Almost 200 charred cereal grains consisted of equal numbers of free-threshing wheat (*Triticum aestivum/turgidum*) and oats (*Avena* sp.), with smaller quantities of rye (*Secale cereale*) and barley (*Hordeum vulgare*) (Table 20). Several rachis fragments from bread wheat (*Triticum* cf. *aestivum* s.l.) suggest that the wheat grains are also likely to come from this species, but no oat florets were found to indicate whether those grains came from cultivated oats or a wild species.

Charred weed seeds were not particularly numerous, and several were from large-seeded species such as wild radish (*Raphanus raphanistrum*), cleavers (*Galium aparine*) and

Table 18: Waterlogged wild plant remains from fill 323 of late Saxon well 277

Wild plants	part	presence
Bryophyta indet. (mosses)	–	+
Ranunculus acris/repens/bulbosus (buttercups)	–	+
Thalictrum cf. *flavum* (common meadow rue)	–	+
Papaver sp. (poppy)	–	++
Brassica/Sinapis sp. (wild cabbage, mustard etc)	–	+
Thlaspi arvense L. (field penny-cress)	–	+
cf. *Barbarea* sp. (winter-cresses)	–	+
Silene sp. (campion)	–	+
Agrostemma githago L. (corn cockle)	–	+++
Stellaria media (L.) Vill. (common chickweed)	–	++++
Stellaria graminea L. (lesser stitchwort)	–	++
Chenopodium album L. (fat hen)	–	++
Atriplex spp. (orache)	–	+++
Malva sp. (mallow)	FR	+
Euphorbia helioscopia L. (sun spurge)	–	++
Aethusa cynapium L. (fool's parsley)	–	+
Bupleurum rotundifolium L. (thorow-wax)	–	+
Heracleum sphondylium L. (hogweed)	–	+
Polygonum aviculare agg. (knotgrass)	–	++
Persicaria maculosa Gray (redshank)	–	+
Fallopia convolvulus (L.) A. Love (black bindweed)	–	+
Rumex spp. (docks)		+++
Urtica urens L. (small nettle)	–	++
Urtica dioica L. (stinging nettle)	–	++
Salix sp. (willow)	FR	+
Hyoscyamus niger L. (henbane)	–	+
Solanum nigrum L. (black nightshade)	–	++
Prunella vulgaris L. (self-heal)	–	+
Stachys sp. (woundworts)	–	+
Galeopsis sp. (hemp-nettle)	–	+
Marrubium vulgare L. (white horehound)	–	++
Lamium sp. (dead-nettles)	–	+
Sambucus nigra L. (elder)	–	++
Knautia arvensis (L.) Coulter (field scabious)	–	+
Anthemis cotula L. (stinking mayweed)	–	++
Carduus/Cirsium spp. (thistles)	–	++
Onopordum acanthium L. (Scotch thistle)	–	+
Lapsana communis L. (nipplewort)	–	++
Leontodon autumnalis/hispidus (hawkbit)	–	+

Key: + up to 10 items, ++ 11 to 50, +++ 51 to approx. 250, ++++ over 250 (many hundreds). FR – fruit; – seed

brome grass (*Bromus* sp.) suggesting that the assemblage may represent a semi-cleaned crop or crops, requiring final hand sorting to remove the larger seeds (Table 21). Alternatively, as the disused well was obviously used for refuse disposal, a mixture of grains burnt accidentally during food preparation may have become mixed after deposition with weeds and a little chaff sieved from grains during an earlier stage of processing, and perhaps subsequently used as fuel. A single charred sloe stone (*Prunus spinosa*) and two unidentified fragments of pulses (*Vicia/Lathyrus/Pisum* sp.), possibly beans or peas, were the only other food remains preserved in this way (Table 22).

The southern well, 124

Sample 4, from fill (160) produced a smallish assemblage of about 60 charred cereal grains with almost half of the identified specimens coming from oats (*Avena* sp.) (Tables 20 & 22). Wheat (*Triticum* sp.) and barley (*Hordeum vulgare*) were less abundant and only a very small number of rye (*Secale cereale*) grains were seen. A number of charred weed seeds, the majority from stinking mayweed (*Anthemis cotula*), were again typical of the arable weeds found in charred cereal assemblages.

Pits 273 and 260

Charred cereal remains were recovered in sample 5 from fill (272) of pit 273 and sample 7 from fill (257) of pit 260, with 300 grains counted in sample 5 and approximately half that number in sample 7 (Tables 20–22). Sample 5 produced a fairly clean assemblage, consisting mainly of wheat grains (*Triticum* sp.) with just a few chaff fragments in the form of wheat and barley (*Hordeum vulgare*) rachis nodes and relatively few weed seeds, suggesting that

Table 19: Waterlogged food plant remains from late Saxon well 277

Food and other useful plants	part	presence
Beta vulgaris L. (beet fruit)	FR	++
Linum usitatissimum L. (cultivated flax)	–	+
Rubus fruticosus/idaeus (blackberry/raspberry)	–	++
Rosa sp. (rose)	–	+
Prunus spinosa L. (sloe)	–	+++
Prunus domestica L. (plum/bullace)	–	++
Prunus avium/cerasus (cherry)	–	+
Malus domestica/sylvestris (apple)	–	+
Malus domestica/sylvestris (apple)	EC	+
Cannabis sativa L. (hemp)	–	+
Corylus avellana L. (hazelnut shell)	–	+

Key: + up to 10 items, ++ 11 to 50, +++ 51 to approx. 250, ++++ over 250 (many hundreds). FR – fruit; EC – Endocarp (core)

it had been quite thoroughly cleaned and was perhaps accidentally burnt during food preparation.

Sample 7 contained roughly equal numbers of wheat grains and oat grains (*Avena* sp.), with weed seeds numbering roughly the same as the grains. This assemblage may consist of a single, part-cleaned crop, needing a final sieving before use, or it could be a mixture of accidentally burnt grains with the final cleanings sieved from this or another crop, and used as fuel.

Apart from the cereals, plant food remains from these two pits were limited to occasional charred fragments of hazelnut shell (*Corylus avellana*), and a single cotyledon of probable horse bean (*Vicia faba*) in sample 7.

Discussion

While all four of the common cereal grains were present in all of the four analysed samples, from the pre-castle deposits there was a clear predominance of free-threshing wheat and oat grains, with the total numbers of wheat grains slightly exceeding that of oats. Barley and rye were present in all samples but in significantly smaller numbers. The same two cereals were also clearly the most numerous in three of the five assessed samples from this period which were not studied in detail, suggesting that wheat and oats may well have been the most widely used cereals on the site at this time. The presence of a few fragments of chaff from hexaploid bread wheat in sample 10 may indicate the use of this species, but chaff from tetraploid rivet wheat as well as bread wheat has been found in late Saxon samples from West Cotton, Raunds, Northamptonshire (Campbell 1994) and Higham Ferrers (Moffett 2001), and too few rachis fragments were recovered here to be sure which wheats were in use. Despite the relative abundance of oat grains no florets from this cereal survived, so it is not possible to say whether the grains came from cultivated oats or from a wild species, perhaps growing as a weed in the wheat crop.

Documentary evidence shows wheat to have been the preferred cereal, particularly for bread-making (Hagen 1995, 18), and oats may have been ground to flour and included in bread, or used as meal. Beer could also be made from oats, though barley was the preferred grain for brewing.

Table 20: Charred cereal plant remains from pre-castle deposits

Feature:		Well 124	Well 277	Pit 273	Pit 260
Fill:		160	323	272	257
Sample:		4	10	5	7
Scientific name (common name)	part				
Cereal grains					
Triticum aestivum/turgidum (free-threshing wheat)	S	5	42	147	12
Triticum sp. (wheat)	S	5	4	3	3
cf. *Triticum* sp. (wheat)	S	2	10	14	3
Triticum/Secale sp. (wheat/rye)	S	1	9	6	2
Secale cereale L. (rye)	S	3	17	12	8
cf. *Secale cereal* (rye)	S	-	5	11	5
Hordeum vulgare L. (6–row barley (hulled))	S	8	14	5	6
cf. *Hordeum vulgare* (6–row barley (hulled))	S	2	4	6	2
Avena sp. (oat)	S	10	40	17	16
cf. *Avena* sp. (oat)	S	9	16	9	6
Cerealia (indet. cereal (est))	S	15	20	–	20
Cereal chaff					
Triticum cf. *aestivum* s.l. (bread wheat)	R	–	10	–	–
Triticum aestivum/turgidum (free-threshing wheat)	R	–	–	4	–
Secale cereale L. (rye)	R	–	1	–	–
Hordeum vulgare L. (barley)	R	1	–	4	1
cf. *Hordeum vulgare* (barley)	R	–	1	–	1
Cerealia (indet. Cereal)	R	–	–	–	–
Cerealia (indet. Cereal)	CN	–	10	–	4
cf. Cerealia (indet. Cereal)	RT	–	+	–	–

Key to plant parts: S – seed; CN – culm node; FR – fruit; HD – seed head;
NS – nutshell; R – rachis fragment; RT – root; WD – wood

Table 21: Charred wild plant remains from pre-castle deposits

Feature:		Well 124	Well 277	Pit 273	Pit 260
Fill:		160	323	272	257
Sample:		4	10	5	7
Wild plants	**part**				
Ranunculus acris/repens/ Bulbosus (buttercup)	S	–	–	–	–
Raphanus raphanistrum L. (wild radish)	FR	–	–	–	1
Agrostemma githago L. (corn cockle)	S	–	5	1	3
Chenopodium album L. (fat hen)	S	3	–	–	–
Chenopodium sp. (goosefoot)	S	2	–	6	6
Atriplex sp. (orache)	S	–	–	2	-
Chenopodium/Atriplex spp. (goosefoot/orache)	S	-	–	–	–
Hypericum sp. (St John's wort)	S	1	–	–	–
Silene sp. (campions)	S	–	–	–	–
cf. *Silene* sp. (campions)	S	–	–	–	–
Malva sp. (mallow)	FR	–	–	–	2
Vicia/Lathyrus sp. (vetch/wild pea)	S	1	1	2	2
Fallopia convolvulus (L.) A. Love (black bindweed)	S	–	-	1	–
Rumex spp. (dock)	S	3	1	7	2
Urtica urens L. (small nettle)	S	–	–	–	8
Quercus sp. (oak)	FR	–	–	–	–
Prunella vulgaris L. (self-heal)	S	–	–	–	1
Plantago lanceolata L. (ribwort)	S	–	1	1	2
Galium aparine L. (cleavers)	S	–	1	–	–
Galium cf. *aparine* (cleavers)	S	–	–	–	–
Galium sp. (bedstraws)	S	–	–	–	2
Anthemis cotula L. (stinking mayweed)	S	13	3	24	17
Anthemis cotula L. (stinking mayweed)	HD	-	1	–	–
Tripleurospermum inodorum L. (scentless mayweed)	S	–	–	–	3
Centaurea sp. (knapweed)	S	–	–	–	1
Picris hieracioides (hawkweed ox-tongue)	S	–	–	1	–
Asteraceae indet.(-)	S	2	–	–	–
Luzula sp. DC (woodrush)	S		–	–	–
Eleocharis palustris/uniglumis (spike-rush)	S	–	–	–	–
Carex spp. (sedges)	S				
Bromus sp. (bromes)	S	2	7	4	6
cf. *Bromus* sp. (bromes)	S	–	–	2	–
Avena/Bromus sp. (oat/brome)	S	–	6	5	2
Poaceae indet. (grasses)	S	6	2	6	15

Key to plant parts: S – seed; FR – fruit; HD – seed head; WD – wood

The proportions of charred grains, chaff and seeds in samples can be used to interpret crop related activities such as stages of crop processing (cf. Hillman 1981; 1984). Very little chaff was found in these samples, and weed seeds were also relatively scarce, ranging from 13% of total charred items in sample 10 to 46% in sample 7, indicating that the early stages of crop processing and cleaning, to separate the grain from straw, chaff and weeds, had been completed elsewhere. As all the samples came from refuse contexts, however, each may have included more than one waste product so each assemblage may have derived either from a single semi-cleaned cereal product, burnt accidentally during drying or subsequent food preparation, or from mixtures of cleaned grain with sieving from the final stages of crop-processing used as fuel.

The preservation of organic remains in the northern well fill provides useful information about the plant-based diet

Table 22: Charred food plant remains from pre–castle deposits

Feature:		Well 124	Well 277	Pit 273	Pit 260
Fill:		160	323	272	257
Sample:		4	10	5	7
Food plants	**part**				
cf. *Vicia faba* (horsebean)	seed	–	–	–	–
Vicia/Lathyrus/Pisum sp. (vetch/wild pea/garden pea)	seed	1	2	1	1
Prunus spinosa L. (sloe)	seed	–	1	–	–
Corylus avellana L. (hazel)	nut shell	–	–	+	+

of the site's inhabitants. Fruits and nuts such as blackberry (*Rubus fruticosus*), elderberry (*Sambucus nigra*), sloe (*Prunus spinosa*), crab-apple (*Malus domestica/sylvestris*), and hazelnut (*Corylus avellana*) would have been widely available from trees and bushes growing wild, though it is possible that cultivated varieties of some, such as plums and apples, may also have been available. Finds of fruits from beet (*Beta vulgaris*) suggest that the leaves and/or roots of this plant were used as vegetables, and some evidence was found of charred legumes, although none could be identified as cultivated species but only as vetch/pea (*Vicia/Lathyrus/Pisum* sp.).

Occasional seeds of both flax (*Linum usitatissimum*) and hemp (*Cannabis sativa*) may indicate the use of seeds from both plants as food, or as sources of oil, but it is likely that the main use of these plants was as fibre crops for the manufacture of cloth, ropes etc from their fibrous stems.

Plant remains bibliography

Campbell, G, 1994 The preliminary archaeobotanical results from Anglo-Saxon West Cotton and Raunds, *in* J Rackham (ed), *Environment and economy in Anglo-Saxon England: a review of recent work on the environmental archaeology of rural and urban Anglo-Saxon settlements in England*, CBA Res Rep, **89**, London, 65–82

Hagen, A, 1995 *A second handbook of Anglo-Saxon food and drink: production and distribution*, Frithgarth

Hillman, G, 1981, Reconstructing Crop Husbandry Practices from Charred Remains of Crops, *in* R Mercer 1981 *Farming Practice in British Prehistory*, Edinburgh, 123–62

Hillman, G, 1984 Interpretation of archaeological plant remains: The application of ethnographic models from Turkey, *in* W van Zeist and W A Casparie (eds) 1984 *Plants and Ancient Man*, Rotterdam, 1–41

Moffett, L C, 2001 *Crops and other plant remains from Higham Ferrers, Kings Meadow Lane*, Draft Ancient Monuments Laboratory Report, London: English Heritage

Wilson, C A, 1973 *Food and drink in Britain, From the Stone Age to Recent Times*, Harmondsworth

Soil geoarchaeology
Michael J Allen with Richard I Macphail

The site was visited by Mike Allen, on 2 May 2013, in particular to examine the basal buried soils sealed by dark earth and occupation deposits. The aims of the exami-nation and analyses was to identify and characterise the buried soil and overlying deposits and determine the nature of the human activity associated with these deposits and their burial. In view of the proximity to the River Nene the identification of any flooding and alluvia-tion was also important.

Two exposed profiles were examined; both of which had a clear and distinct basal horizon approximately 100mm thick. Both profiles were cleaned in the field and described following standard sedimentological notation (Hodgson 1976) and munsell colours recorded moist. An undisturbed kubiena sample (K1) was taken from the base of Profile 1 and soil micromprohological examination was undertaken by Richard Macphail.

Profile 1: late Saxon/Saxo-Norman occupation

Profile 1 was taken on a north-facing temporary baulk, south of the main late Saxon pit group (see Fig 3), which retained a full profile from just below ground level to the natural (Table 23). The nearest comparison section lay in the south-east corner of the excavated area (see Fig 4, Section 79).

Below 0.5m of occupation deposit or 'dark' earth (331) with coarse blocky structure, was a 100mm thick clear stone-free humic fine sandy loam probably representing a relict portion of a truncated lower soil profile (bB) of a former soil possibly contemporary with the nearby late Saxon pits (336). This profile was described in the field and the basal portion sampled in 120mm x 80mm foil kubiena tin (K1) (Fig 27).

The buried soil may be cut by Saxon features from higher in the profile but with the cuts latterly obliterated by biotic activity. This may be the basal (bB) of the soil contemporary with the Saxon features.

Soil micromorphology by Richard I Macphail

A single 150mm long thin section (manufactured by *Earthslides*) taken through the buried soil and dark earth at Profile 1 was studied employing soil micromorphology (Courty *et al* 1989; Goldberg and Macphail 2006) (Table 24).

The thin section was analysed using a petrological microscope under plane polarised light (PPL), crossed polarised light (XPL), oblique incident light (OIL) and using fluorescence microscopy (blue light – BL), at magnifications ranging from x1 to x200/400. Thin sections

Fig 27: Soil Profile 1, showing basal truncated buried soil and kubiena sample K1

were described, ascribed soil microfabric types (MFTs) and microfacies types (MFTs), and counted according to established methods (Bullock *et al* 1985; Courty 2001; Courty *et al* 1989; Macphail and Cruise 2001; Stoops 2003; Stoops *et al* 2010). Sixteen characteristics were identified and counted from the two layers in the single thin section analysed.

The dark earth, (331) was a homogeneous, humic sandy loam soil, very poorly sorted with common stones including quartzite pebble and ironstone (max 17mm) and 3mm-size sandy subsoil clast. The layer was character-

ised by rare strongly burned mineral material, occasional coprolitic bone, charcoal and faecal waste, with rare examples of weathered earthworm granule and other biogenic calcite. Quantities of animal bone within this deposit were derived from slaughtering, butchery, craft and domestic waste, indicating that at times the area was unoccupied waste ground, and at the interface with the buried soil, the bone was often iron stained (Chapman pers comm).

Pedofeatures are composed of occasional iron staining and iron-phosphate impregnated soil, very abundant broad and very broad burrows, and very abundant broad organo-mineral excrements with working down into buried soil below.

The base of the dark earth was stony with much bioworking; again probably by earthworms. Much ironstone was concentrated here, alongside examples of burned mineral material, charcoal, and faecal waste, but in much less quantity compared to the buried soil. This interface also included a weathered example of an earthworm granule, which may record a period of stasis and dark earth soil formation. Weathering *in situ* then led to minor decalcification of the earthworm granule and other calcareous material.

The buried soil (336) was a heterogeneous sandy loam with very dominant humic and fine charcoal-rich soil, and with frequent burrow-infilled humic, but less fine charcoal-rich, soil. There were few ironstone and ferruginous oolitic sandstone gravels (max 5mm). There were traces of shell, burned eggshell, occasional charcoal (max 0.5–1.5mm) and coprolitic bird bone (yellow stained often, max 1.2mm), very abundant faecal waste

Table 23: Soil Profile 1

Depth (mm)	Soil unit (context)	Sample	Description
post-medieval medieval			Sharp contact with pits and scoops cutting deposit below
0–490 Late Saxon	(331) occupation soil/ 'dark' earth	K1	Dark greyish brown stone-free fine sandy loam to silty clay loam with weak coarse moderate blocky structure, rare small and medium stones, occasional large stones (masonry), abrupt wavy boundary
490–640 Late Saxon	(336) relict former soil bB 'Buried soil'		Brown to strong brown (7.5YR 4/4–4/6) firm essentially stone-free, but poorly sorted humic fine sandy loam with weak medium blocky structure, rare fine charcoal pieces
640+	Parent material		Medium gravels in a strong brown sandy loam matrix with some strong brown to reddish-brown distinct mottles and iron stains

Table 24: Profile K1 at base of Soil Profile 1

Depth (mm)	Soil unit (context)	Sample	Description
0–80 Late Saxon	(331) Occupation soil/ 'dark' earth	20mm 40mm 60mm	Dark brown stone-free fine sandy loam, weak medium blocky structure, abrupt boundary
80–140 Late Saxon	(336) Relict former soil bB 'Buried soil'	80mm 100mm 120mm	Brown to strong (7.5YR 4/4–4/6) fine sandy loam, from, rare fine charcoal pieces, stone-free
140–150	Parent material	140mm	As above, some strong brown to reddish-brown distinct mottles and Fe stains

infills and staining (humic, probable iron-phosphate, which sometimes included articulated phytoliths and plant tissues. There are many opaque impure clay void coatings (~100 µm) in the lower part, with abundant matrix infills and silt loam fills of very broad burrows, many moderate iron impregnations with rare fan-like ferrihydrite/iron-phosphate infills, and very abundant probable amorphous iron-phosphate void hypocoatings and infills associated with faecal waste, very abundant broad (1–3mm) and abundant very broad (3–5+mm) burrows, and very abundant broad organo-mineral excrements embedded in matrix – partial total biological fabric.

In summary, this is a strongly biologically worked and homogenised humic sandy loam soil composed of the local sandy loam soil and very fine to coarse occupation debris. The latter includes charcoal, coprolitic bone and examples of burned eggshell, for example, which with coatings and infills of very abundant iron-phosphate-stained faecal waste, suggestive of intensive middening and occupation, similar to enclosed sites such as Pevensey Castle, Late Roman to early medieval phases (Macphail 2011). Later bioworking and wash from the above dark earth' levels also occurred.

Soil Profile 2: Western section

The section on the western edge of the excavations, adjacent to the brick wall of the former station, was on the river side of the site on a slope dropping towards the river (see Fig 3). The baulk contained a gleyed alluvial occupation deposit with good blocky structure and many mottles indicating local groundwater gleying (157). A basal deposit, again c.100mm thick, was evident over the natural gravels (Fig 28). The basal deposit was a firm massive silty loam with clear interped coatings (hand lens). This is probably an illuviated 'dark earth' deposit largely resulting from the downward movement of silt and clay washed from the overlying occupation deposit under higher groundwater conditions (Table 25).

Here, both the occupation deposit and the basal deposit

Fig 28: Soil Profile 2, showing the occupation soil (106) sealing a basal silty horizon (157) (with the brick wall of the Victorian station in thebackground)

contained animal bone, typically mineralised and iron stained.

Soil Profile 2 is subject to ground water gley, possible alluviation, and illuviation. The basal deposit, layer (157) is a soil similar to that seen in Profile 1 (331/336), but here subject to localised illuvial silt and *in situ* post-depositional alteration as a result of alluviation.

Note: illuvium is material displaced across a soil profile, from one layer to another one, by the action of water.

Discussion

The buried soil has the background character of a sandy loam soil probably formed on river terrace sediments (River Nene) and Jurassic ironstone-rich drift. The soil is, however, essentially an anthropogenic soil with very high quantities of faecal waste present. This is similar to the late Saxon occupation soils at Bedford Castle (Macphail and Crowther 2009). The high concentrations of faecal material more closely resemble Saxon to medieval dark earth at Pevensey Castle, East Sussex (Macphail 2011), where within-wall middening was intensive, and concentrations of faecal matter were recorded in the bulk chemistry and by microprobe studies.

The overlying dark earth has a similar, but faecal matter-rich, character, with examples of hearth waste in the form of ashed mineral material also present. In addition, the dark earth at Profile 1, appears to record a period of stasis and more intensive bioworking by earthworms compared to the probably gradually accumulated buried soil. This stasis or period of dark earth soil formation led to minor soil decalcification and weathering of biogenic calcite, such as earthworm granules. This has also been recorded at a number of dark earth sequences, for example at Winchester and Canterbury; this occurred at these examples before late Roman-early medieval middening was renewed (see Macphail, 2010).

Conclusions

The soil shows evidence of intensive early activity, transforming a sandy soil developed on the river gravels to an anthropogenic one created by tramping and the addition of occupation debris and faeces; typical of high levels of occupation and human and animal thoroughfare. This anthropogenic soil was enveloped in a central midden and the discard of occupation debris including general waste, animal faecal waste and egg shells; and also the deposition of bulk animal bone, as a mixture of waste from slaughtering, butchery, as well as craft and domestic waste. This soil developed with humic occupation, but was not continual; as stasis and worm working occurred indicating periods when stable horizons existed.

The buried soil and dark earth were extensive within this area; and deposits on the lower slope nearer the river showed effects of higher local groundwater conditions, and of possible flooding or at least water and silt input. The high level of bioturbation (trampling, mixing, worm-working etc) of the soils may have led to the eradication of features cut through the soils, and which were

Table 25: Soil Profile 2

Depth (mm)	Soil unit (context)	Description
0–380 Post-medieval	(105)	Firm dark greyish-brown sandy silt loam, moderate medium blocky structure, rare medium and large stones, rare fine fibrous roots, common fine charcoal, common small and medium moderate very strong brown to dark reddish-brown mottles, clear wavy boundary
380–640 medieval	(106)	As above, but lighter brown/greyish-brown weaker and larger structure
640–740 Late Saxon	(157)	Massive brown silty loam, stone-free, mottles as above, stronger locally, clear inter-ped coatings of silt/clay (hand lens) – illuviated soil, abrupt wavy boundary
740+	Parent material	Medium gravels in a sandy loam

only largely archaeologically recognisable where they cut the basal buried soil or the gravels.

Geoarchaeology bibliography

Bullock, P, Fedoroff, N, Jongerius, A, Stoops, G, and Tursina, T, 1985 *Handbook for Soil Thin Section Description*, Wolverhampton: Waine Research Publications

Courty, M A, 2001 Microfacies analysis assisting archaeological stratigraphy, 205–23, *in* P Goldberg, V T Holliday and C R Ferring (eds) *Earth Sciences and Archaeol*, **9**, New York: Kluwer Academic/Plenum Publishers

Courty, M A, Goldberg, P, and Macphail, R I, 1989 *Soils and Micromorphology in Archaeology* (1st Edition), Cambridge University Press, Cambridge Manuals in Archaeol

Goldberg, P, and Macphail, R I, 2006, *Practical and Theoretical Geoarchaeology*, Oxford: Blackwell Publishing

Hodgson, J M, 1976 *Soil Survey Field Handbook,* Harpenden: Soil Survey Tech Monog, **5**

Macphail, R I, 2010 Dark earth and insights into changing land use of urban areas, 145–165, *in* G Speed and D Sami (eds) 2010 *Debating Urbanism: Within and Beyond the Walls c.AD 300 to c.AD 700 (Conference Proceedings Leicester University Nov 15th 2008)*, Leicester Archaeol Monog, **17**

Macphail, R I, 2011 Soil micromorphology, 109–201, *in* M Fulford and S Rippon (eds) 2011 *Pevensey Castle, Sussex. Excavations in the Roman fort and Medieval keep, 1993–95*, Salisbury: Wessex Archaeol Rep, **26**

Macphail, R I, and Crowther, J, 2009 *Castle Lane, Bedford: Soil micromorphology, chemistry and magnetic susceptibility*, Unpublished report for Albion Archaeol

Macphail, R I, and Cruise, G M, 2001 The soil micromorphologist as team player: a multianalytical approach to the study of European microstratigraphy, 241–267, *in* P Goldberg, V Holliday and R Ferring (eds) 2001 *Earth Science and Archaeology*, New York: Kluwer Academic/Plenum Publishers

Stoops, G, 2003 *Guidelines for Analysis and Description of Soil and Regolith Thin Sections*, Madison Wisconsin: Soil Science Society of America

Stoops, G, Marcelino, V, and Mees, F, 2010 *Interpretation of Micromorphological Features of Soils and Regoliths*, Amsterdam: Elsevie

Discussion

Site activities and the deposition of animal bone

In the late Saxon period, the excavated area was low-lying with the ground dropping to seasonally wet river margins at the western edge of the excavated area. To the south there was probably a road approach to a timber bridge spanning the river. To the east there must have been a scarp onto higher ground, perhaps utilised by the town defences, as discussed below. The excavated area was, therefore, a small piece of marginal land beside a road, and perhaps between a town gate to the east and a bridge to the west.

The general usage of this piece of marginal land is best illustrated by a combination of the geo archaeology and the animal bone assemblage. The buried soil horizon was, "strongly biologically worked and homogenised, with very fine to coarse occupation debris", including "charcoal, coprolitic bone and examples of burned eggshell, for example, which with coatings and infills of very abundant iron-phosphate-stained faecal waste, are suggestive of intensive middening and occupation. This might suggest that at times this ground was used for corralling live animals probably awaiting slaughter, which may explain the presence of an iron shackle. The animal bone adds to this picture, as it was "derived from slaughtering, butchery, craft and domestic waste, indicating that at times the area was unoccupied waste ground", and the presence of bones from a badger suggest it may have been a foraging ground for wild animals.

Whilst an unpromising plot of land, the animal bone also tells a story of nearby activities, as some of the bone debris was derived from horn working and several cattle and horse long bones had been abandoned in the process of manufacturing ice skates. The general scatter of bone also comprised a mixture of waste from butchering and general food waste. So we know that people were living and carrying out trades near enough for this piece of land to be a convenient waste tip. There was also a small group of other domestic finds from a cluster of pits.

Standing as waste ground may have been the fate of this area through much of the 11th century, but the ditches and pits do suggest it was not totally waste throughout this period. The earliest dated feature is a well pit, where the primary fill deposited following its disuse has given a broad radiocarbon date spanning much of the 10th century.

This waterlogged deposit also produced a rich assemblage of preserved plant material from a wide range of foodstuffs. Contemporary pottery is sparsely represented, but the southern pits, one of which was a shallow hearth base, were both heavily truncated and evidently part of an early phase of activity. They were perhaps contemporary with the northern well, and the hearth base may even denote the presence of a small timber structure otherwise removed by later activity.

By the 11th century, and perhaps with an earlier origin, there was a curvilinear boundary ditch system to the north. Initially, this may have comprised a fence line set in a narrow slot to the north of a parallel ditch, but later it comprised just a ditch, with the longevity of the boundary indicated by the multiple recuts. Some of the sparse datable features to the north of this boundary date to the early 12th century, and are either contemporary with the later boundary ditch or the early use of the castle. There is therefore only demonstrable contemporary occupation to the south of this boundary.

In the 11th century, to the east a failed well and a second well pit indicate a continuing need for a water supply. The southern well also cut a laid surface of ironstone gravel forming a yard surface to the immediate east of a group of large but relatively shallow pits. The northernmost pit(s) was disturbed by modern drainage and was not fully excavated, but at 5.5m long by 4.0m wide and 0.55m deep, with steep sides and a flat base, it may have been a single sub-rectangular pit. The overall dimensions are similar to the cellared structures seen at Chalk Lane, pit 70, 3.0m square by 1.0m deep and building B79, 4.8m long by 3.3m wide and 0.95m deep (Williams and Shaw 1981, 96–100); at Woolmonger Street, Cellar 1, 4.5m square and 1.0m deep (Soden 1999, 77–79) and Kingswell Street, Building A, 5.0m long by 3.5m wide and 1.16m deep (Brown 2008, 185–186). This speculation is unconfirmed, and this may seem an unlikely setting for an occupied structure, but it would provide an on-site context for the provision of a well.

The deposition of the quantities of animal bone had either preceded or were, perhaps, partly contemporary with the central pit group within the 11th century. The fills of the fully excavated pit contained c.8kg of animal bone, while the partially excavated pit/cellar produced nearly 3kg. The subsidence fills of the early well produced a further 2kg and the other well 2.5kg of animal bone. The three northernmost sections across the curvilinear boundary system each produced between 1–2kg of animal bone.

It may have been just the vagaries of deposition, given the 98kg of bone deposited across the entire area, with a proportion bound to end up redeposited in later or contemporary cut features, but the assemblage from the fills of the pit/cellar did contain some items of particular interest, including bones related to horn working, part of the articulated lower leg of a horse, and a pig bone with a bored perforation. This may suggest that the central pit group was related to some ongoing activities connected with the usage and deposition of waste animal bone, although all the examples of horse and cattle bone partially worked as skates came from the general soil horizon, suggesting the manufactory lay elsewhere. It may be that the larger pit and the pit/cellar were in use during a brief period when this area was utilised for something other than waste dumping.

The deposition of animal bone may have come to a halt during the later 11th century, perhaps following the Norman Conquest, as the two sections across the late rectilinear boundary to the east, in use late 11th to early 12th centuries, produced much less bone, 0.45kg and 0.7kg, with similar quantities from the southern ditch, which may just be low-levelled residual re-deposition. The rectilinear eastern and southern boundaries mark the provision of new boundaries following the Norman Conquest, and in use up to the time the area was levelled to make way for the Outer Bailey of the castle. The southern boundary may lie parallel to a road approaching the West Bridge, while the eastern boundary may lie parallel to the line of the town defences sitting on higher ground to the east.

The late Saxon town defences

In the overview of Anglo-Saxon Northampton, it has been assumed that the line of the defences, as excavated at Green Street continued northward, across the site of the future castle, to complete a full circuit (Fig 2; Williams *et al* this volume, 46, fig 27a; and Chapman this volume 129–136). The projected line lies a little to the east of the excavated area.

To the east there is now a raised car park, with a high retaining wall, a few metres to the east of the end of the new station. However, it should be noted that the current retaining wall lies several metres east of its Victorian predecessor, with the uncovered curving foundations of that earlier wall forming the eastern limit of the excavated area (see Fig 3), While it is likely that the western end of the raised car park had itself been raised to create an area level with the naturally higher ground further east, it may still reflect the late Saxon topography, with a scarp descending onto the low lying ground of the excavated area, itself only a little above the wet riverside zone.

Such a scarp may have been only part of the natural riverside topography, but it would also have provided a suitable location for a defensive bank, set at the top edge of the scarp, and perhaps similar to the bank to the south at Green Street, some 6m wide, initially fronted by a timber revetment and later by a stone revetment (Chapman this volume, 133, Fig 3).

The presence of contemporary features within the excavated area, and in particular the rectilinear eastern boundary ditch, would suggest that there was no substantial defensive ditch, probably because the nearby river channels provided sufficient protection on the west side of the Anglo-Saxon town, as they did later did for the castle itself.

Future archaeological potential

If the Saxon defensive bank does lie to the east of the excavated area, it may still be at least paertially preserved beneath the west end of the raised car park. However, as the original Victorian revetment wall, which probably more closely respected the earlier topography, was later relocated eastwards to provide a broader approach to the station forecourt, evidence may have been lost at that time. During the excavations of 2013 there was no opportunity to examine the area immediately in front of the current revetment wall, as it was in continuous use for access. However, use for access continued through the construction works, so the underlying levels have probably not been extensively truncated by recent works. So, both the area at the base of the revetment wall as well as the whole of the raised car park to the east, offer the potential to examine both the Saxon defences and an extensive area within the Outer Bailey of the castle.

The construction of the Outer Bailey of Northampton Castle

An important conclusion emerging from the well-stratified pottery assemblages is that pottery of the early 12th century (Ceramic phase M1, dated AD1100–1150) was deposited in features sealed beneath the castle deposits and also in features relating to the early use of the Outer Bailey of the castle. This indicates that the Outer Bailey was constructed sometime within the period AD1100–1150, and a date of *c*.1120, within the reign of Henry I, has been suggested. This would imply that the Inner Bailey was also in existence by around AD1120, but how much earlier it may have been constructed cannot be determined from the excavations at the station. This will be considered in greater detail in the account of the castle deposits and in the overview of the castle and the excavations of the 1960s (Chapman this volume, 191–255 & 164–164)

General bibliography

Chapman, A, 1999 Excavation of the town defences at Green Street, Northampton, 1995–6, *Northamptonshire Archaeol*, 28, 25–60

Chapman, A, 2012 *Archaeological evaluation of the concourse at Northampton Castle Station*, Northamptonshire Archaeol report, **12/188**

Chapman A, 2016 *Excavation at Northampton Station within the Outer Bailey of Northampton Castle, 2013–2015: Assessment report*, MOLA Northampton report, **16/02**

Chapman A, 2018 *Excavation and watching brief within the Outer Bailey of Northampton Castle, 2013–2015*, MOLA Northampton **18/117**

Chapman, A, 2021 Prehistoric Northampton: A circular ring ditch and flint scatters, *Northamptonshire Archaeol*, **41**, 17–24

Chapman, A, 2021 The late Saxon town defences at Green Street, Northampton: a review of the evidence and a radiocarbon date, *Northamptonshire Archaeol*, **41**, 129–136

Chapman, A, 2021 Northampton Castle, Part 1: Introduction, pre-castle archaeology, and the history and topography of the castle, 137–189

Chapman, A, 2021 Excavation within the Outer Bailey at Northampton Castle, 2013–15, *Northamptonshire Archaeol*, **41**, 191–255

Kennett, D H, 1968 Early medieval pottery in the Nene Valley, *Northampton County Borough Museums and Art Gallery J*, **3**, 3–14

Kennett, D H, 1969 Socketed bowls from Northampton Castle, *Northampton County Borough Museums and Art Gallery J*, **6**, 50

Knight, D, Vyner, B, and Allen, C, 2012 *East Midlands Heritage; An updated Research Agenda and Strategy for the Historic Environment of the East Midlands*, Nottingham Archaeological Monog, **6**, York Archaeol Trust

Miller, P, Wilson, T, with Harward, C, 2005 *Saxon, medieval and post-medieval settlement at Sol Central, Marefair, Northampton: Archaeological excavations 1998–2002*, Museum of London Archaeol Service (MoLAS) Monog, **27**

Shaw, M, 1985 Excavations on a Saxon and medieval site at Black Lion Hill, Northampton, *Northamptonshire Archaeol*, **20**, 113–138

Soden, I, 1999 A story of urban regeneration: Excavations in advance of development work of St Peter's Walk, Northampton, 1994–7, *Northamptonshire Archaeol*, **28**

Williams, F, 1979 Excavations on Marefair, Northampton, 1977, *Northamptonshire Archaeol*, 14, 38–79

Williams, J H, 1979 *St Peter's Street, Northampton: Excavations 1973–1976*, Northampton Development Corporation Monog, **2**

Williams, J H, and Shaw, M, 1981 Excavations in Chalk Lane, Northampton, 1975–1978, *Northamptonshire Archaeol*, **16**, 87–135

Williams, J, Shaw, M, and Denham, V, 1985 *Middle Saxon Palaces at Northampton*, Northampton Development Corporation Monog, **4**

Williams, J H, Shaw, M, and Chapman, A, 2021 Anglo-Saxon Northampton Revisited, *Northamptonshire Archaeol*, **41**, 25–77

Northamptonshire Archaeology, **41**, 2021, 129–136

The late Saxon town defences at Green Street, Northampton: a review of the evidence and a radiocarbon date

by

Andy Chapman

Summary

Excavation of a length of the town defences at Green Street in the mid-1990s is reviewed. A sample of animal bone from beneath the defensive bank has been radiocarbon dated, giving a broad date spanning the 9th century AD. As a result, from the archaeological evidence the question of whether the excavated defences had an origin during the Danish occupation of the late 9th to early 10th centuries or in the early to mid-10th century following the Saxon re-conquest is still unproven either way. The presence of Northampton Ware pottery, dated to the 10th century, within the clay bank, still supports a date in the 10th century, as part of the reorganization of the eastern region, the Danelaw, with the creation of burhs as safe places for the promotion of trade and manufacturing following the re-conquest by Edward the Elder, son of Alfred, in AD 917.

Introduction

A length of the late Saxon and medieval town defences of Northampton was excavated in 1995–96 at Green Street, in advance of a housing development, Emerald Court: the site lay to the south of Black Lion Hill and the site of Northampton Castle (Chapman 1999) (Fig 1: NGR SP 74826034). A full sequence of development for the defences was recovered. The dating of the sequence, based on small quantities of stratified pottery was, however, insufficiently precise to determine whether the origin of the defences lay in the later 9th to early 10th centuries, during the Danish occupation, or the early to mid-10th century, in the decades following the Saxon re-conquest of AD 917.

No datable pottery or material suitable for radiocarbon dating was recovered from the fills of the original timber slot, but there was much animal bone in the soil horizon buried beneath the original clay bank, and this bone had the potential to provide a *terminus-post-quem* for the construction of the bank through radiocarbon dating. The layer had also contained a small pottery assemblage, 14 sherds all from a single Raunds-type Maxey Ware bar-lug vessel of middle Saxon date (AD 800–900).

The only dating evidence for the construction of the clay bank was from:

"the appearance of Northampton Ware, with its finely potted vessels reminiscent of Stamford products, [which] marks a watershed in local ceramic traditions. This distinctive Northampton Ware horizon is found throughout the area of the Saxon town; it was first identified at St. Peters Gardens where it was dated to c.900–975 AD (Denham 1985, 55). It is the Northampton Ware associated with the construction of the bank which dates the original defences to the tenth century." (Blinkhorn & Soden1999, 57)

From examination of the finds in the site archive held by Northampton Museums and Art Gallery, bone samples were extracted for dating on the basis that small and intact bones, showing a fresh appearance, might be less likely to have been a product of secondary deposition than fragmented and abraded bone.

Acknowledgements

Thanks are due to Louise Hannam-Jones of Northampton Museums & Art Gallery for arranging access to the Green Street site archive in order that the material could be assessed, and to the Museum Service for providing permission to remove a sample for radiocarbon dating. The radiocarbon dating was carried out by Beta Analytic, Miami, USA, and was jointly funded by Andy Chapman and Northamptonshire Archaeological Society. Line Illustrations are by Alex Thompson from the original publication (Chapman 1999). Figure 1 and photographs are by Andy Chapman.

The town defences at Green Street

The excavation of the town defences at Green Street provided a full sequence of development, particularly so in trench 1 of the three main trenches, as summarised below (Figs 3–6).

The prehistoric soil horizon

Soil horizons of prehistoric and Middle Saxon date were preserved beneath the late Saxon clay bank.

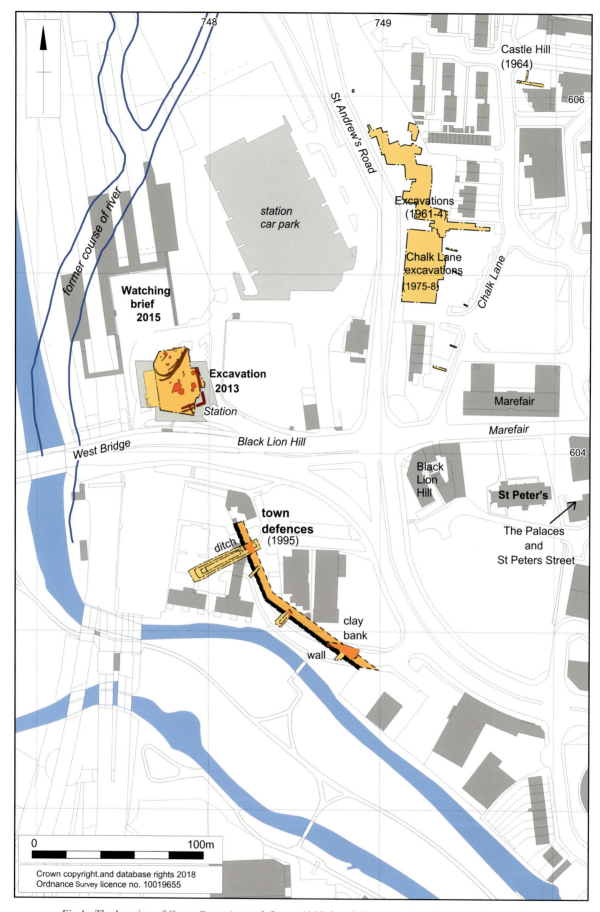

Fig 1: The location of Green Street (town defences 1995) in relation to nearby elements of the late Saxon town

Fig 2: General view of trench 1 in December 1995, looking south-west, after overnight snow, showing the top of the clay bank, foreground, and the medieval town wall, centre, with the town ditch beyond

"Evidence of Neolithic to early Bronze Age activity comprises a scatter of worked flint, including a leaf-shaped arrowhead, recovered from a soil horizon directly overlying the natural in trench 1; a V-shaped ditch may also be contemporary. This is consistent with the recovery of quantities of worked flint and some prehistoric features at other excavations in this area of the town." (Chapman 1999, 33: Chapman this volume 17–24).

"Layers and features preserved beneath the defensive bank were investigated...a total area of 6m² was exposed and 4m² was excavated to the natural. In trench 1 the natural was overlain by a uniform soil horizon of light brown to light yellow-brown gritty silty sand, up to 220mm thick (69/129, [Fig 4])". *"A total of 21 struck flints was recovered, 11 came from the prehistoric soil horizon ...and 3 were residual in the fills of the adjacent late Saxon slot, F97 [Fig 4]."* (Chapman 1999, 41)

The Middle Saxon soil horizon

"A soil horizon overlying the prehistoric level and sealed by the defensive bank in trench 1 contained middle Saxon pottery associated with a few small postholes; a nearby deep pit may also be contemporary. This evidence for domestic occupation extends the known limits of the middle Saxon town to the lower slopes immediately above the river. The recovery of Maxey-type ware but the lack of Ipswich ware, as at other nearby sites, may suggest that this activity dates to after c.800 AD." (Chapman 1999, 33)

"In trench 1 the upper pre-bank soil horizon was exposed and fully excavated (100/128, [Fig 4]... The general layer comprised a light brown to light grey-brown sandy loam moderately flecked with comminuted charcoal, it was up to 200mm thick and contained occasional chips or small pieces of ironstone and some large sherds of middle Saxon Maxey Ware. (Chapman 1999, 42)

The clay bank with a timber revetment (10th century)

The original defences comprised a clay bank, 6m wide, fronted by a timber revetment, which was set within a continuous slot with post-pits for larger uprights at intervals (Fig 3, Late Saxon I). The only dating for this event was provided by the presence of Northampton ware, which is broadly dated to the 10th century, in the clay forming the bank. The pottery dating is, however, insufficiently precise to determine whether the origin of the defences lay in the later 9th to early 10th centuries, during the Danish occupation, or the early to mid-10th century, in the decades following the Saxon re-conquest.

"The bank was 6.0m wide in trench 1 and had a maximum height of 650mm towards its outer face [Fig 4]; in trench 2 the bank stood 900mm high... In all three trenches the bank comprised a homogeneous clean light yellow-brown tenacious clay, virtually devoid of stones; it contained only the very occasional chip of ironstone no more than 50mm in length. At the front of the bank in trench 1 it was possible to discern three levels of make-up, with the upper and lower clays separated by a layer or lens of mixed clays with yellow and orange-brown sand (Fig [4], S13, layer 109). Over the inner half of the bank, which stood 250–400mm high, only a single layer could be identified. It is possible...that additional material was added later against the rear of the bank, where there was a darker deposit of sticky brown clayey loam with some charcoal flecking [Fig 4, S13, 127]." (Chapman 1999, 45)

"A 2.3m length of linear slot...was 380–480mm deep, cutting through the pre-bank soil horizons and 50–100mm into the natural. The inner edge was steeply inclined and could be followed upward against the face of the bank for 250mm. The outer edge survived to a height of only 150–300mm as a result of a later lowering of the ground level. It was more gently inclined, at 45⁰, but it is uncertain whether this is original, perhaps serving to aid the insertion of the timbers, or whether it was a result of the dismantling of the revetment, when digging out along the front of the slot would have aided the removal of the timbers. The flat bottom of the slot was 220mm wide. Three post-pits were set along the inner edge of the slot at 0.70m intervals centre-to-centre [Fig 3, late Saxon I]. They were only identified following the excavation of the bulk of the slot fill...They had circular to oval bases, c.150mm in diameter and c.100mm deeper than the slot." (Chapman 1999, 42)

The stone revetment and gateway (11th century)

In the second phase the timber revetment was dismantled, and it was replaced by a limestone wall set on top of the filled in construction slot. At Green Street this coincided with the removal of a length of the bank to form a gateway,

a postern gate perhaps, with a metalled road surface. Two post-pits cut into the adjacent bank might have held the uprights of a timbered gatehouse (Fig 3, Late Saxon II). It cannot be determined whether this occurred before or after the Norman Conquest.

"There were few finds directly associated with this phase. The gateway is likely to have been in use through the 11th century, but whether the introduction of the stone wall and gateway occurred only in the earlier 11th century or was perhaps a much earlier feature, introduced in the 10th century, cannot be determined. A stone wall was added to the Saxon defences at Hereford in the early to mid-10th century, while the Anglo-Saxon Chronicle records the addition of a stone wall to the defences at Towcester in 917 AD...The absence of any direct evidence for timbers indicates that the timber revetment had been systematically dismantled. The slot was backfilled and the ground surface had been raised with dumped clay prior to the construction of a stone revetment wall. This was built largely in flat-laid but unmortared limestone. Only the inner part abutting the clay bank had survived, but scattered pieces of limestone associated with patches of possible lime mortar may suggest that its outer face and/or its upper levels had been mortared.

The discovery of a west gate through the early town defences raises fundamental questions about the provision of access to and from the late Saxon town as a whole, and the arrangement of the early street pattern. Does it represent merely an additional, and perhaps subsidiary, west gate? Or, does it denote the location of the river crossing and the primary western access route within the late Saxon town?" (Chapman 1995, 36)

Restoration of the bank and the medieval wall (12th century)

In the third phase of development, probably in the early to mid-12th century, and perhaps close in date to the appearance of a stone wall along the front of the outer bailey bank of the castle (see Chapman this volume, 197–207), a broader wall in ironstone was constructed on top of the bank, at the front.

"In the third major phase of defensive works, the gateway was taken out of use when a substantial new wall was constructed on top of ...the existing bank. The wall ran right across the gateway and the bank was reinstated behind it. The new town wall was 1.85m wide and was built largely in ironstone, with good courses of roughly squared facing stones and a rubble core bonded with clay. At less than 2.0m wide this length of the town wall did not form a formidable barrier but...this is not likely to be typical of the remainder of the medieval defensive circuit. The late Saxon ditch was replaced by a ditch up to 25m wide, but as only the upper fills were investigated it

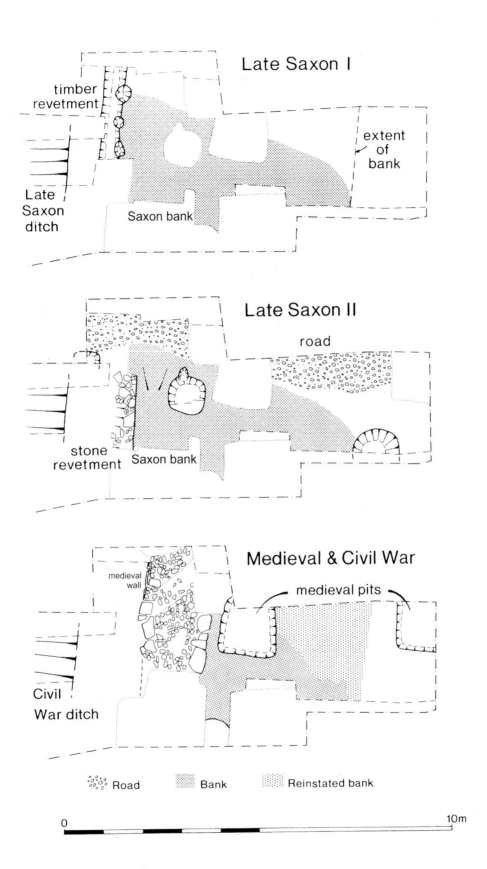

Fig 3: The development sequence of the town defences (Chapman 1999, fig 4)

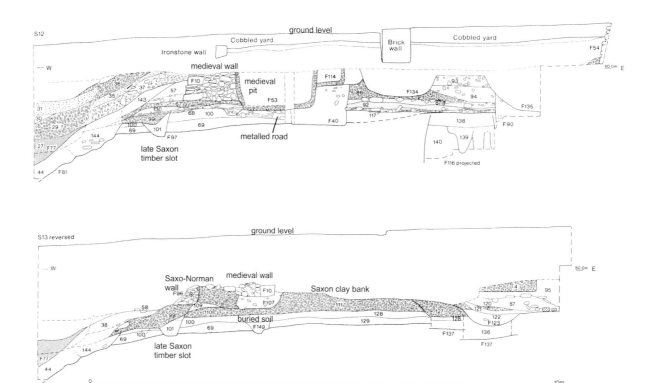

Fig 4: Sections showing the clay bank, 111, overlying the buried soil horizon, 100, the late Saxon timber slot, the later stone wall and the medieval wall, with the ditch to the south-west (Chapman 1999, fig 10)

is impossible to tell whether this represents a single massive ditch or was a result of recutting. To the south this ditch presumably opened into the river channel flanking the southern defences." (Chapman 1995, 36–38)

A reconstructed projection of this sequence (also by Alex Thompson) appears in the overview of late Saxon Northampton (Williams *et al* this volume, 54, fig 36).

A radiocarbon date from beneath the late Saxon bank at Green Street

No datable material, either charcoal or bone, had been recovered from the fills of the original timber slot, but there was much animal bone in the soil horizon, layer 100, buried beneath the original bank. Permission was obtained from Northampton Museums and Art Gallery to access the site archive and to remove a sample on animal bone suitable for radiocarbon dating (Table 1).

The resulting date spans the entire 9th century, 770–900 Cal AD at 87.5% confidence or 800–890 Cal AD at 56.5%.

Conclusions

It had been hoped that, lacking suitable material from other significant contexts, a radiocarbon date from the underlying soil horizon, might provide a meaningful *terminus post quem* (tpq) for the construction of the defensive clay bank. The result has provided a *tpq*, but given both how early the date is and its broad span, we can only say that the construction of the clay bank certainly occurred no earlier *c*.AD800, which is not a great help, and could have occurred at any time after AD890–900. This is equally not a great help, as the presence of Northampton Ware pottery (dated to the 10th century) within the clay bank, had already provided support for a date in the 10th century.

While both options remain technically possible: firstly, that the defences were constructed in the later 9th to early 10th centuries, within the period of Danish occupation, or secondly, in the early to mid-10th century following the re-conquest under Edward the Elder in AD 917, the available evidence still favours the later date. The author also favours this conclusion, with the defences created as part of the reorganization of the town and the region, with the burh of *Hamtun* becoming a safe, or at least safer, place for the promotion of trade and production following the re-conquest by Edward the Elder in AD 917.

It seems we must await a future investigation of the defences to back up this preference with less equivocal dating evidence, although given the inherent limitations on pottery dating and radiocarbon dating, the required precision to a few decades either way may remain elusive.

Fig 5: Section showing the late Saxon revetment slot, bottom left, sealed by the Saxo-Norman limestone road surface, and above this the medieval ironstone wall, truncated by a medieval clay-lined pit, right (Scale 2m)

Fig 6: The worn metalled road surface, mainly limestone, towards the inner end of the gateway opening, looking north, clay bank to south (Scale 2m)

Table 1: Radiocarbon date from Green Street, Northampton

Laboratory & Sample No. Description	Sample	C13/C12 d15N	Conventional Radiocarbon date BP	Calibrated date *68% confidence* 95% confidence
Beta-482207 GS95/100 Soil horizon beneath bank	Animal bone (cattle)	−22.6 7.43	1180+/-30	*780–790 (11.7%)* *800–890 (56.5%)* **730–740 (0.7%)** **770–900 (87.5%)** **920–950 (7.2%)**

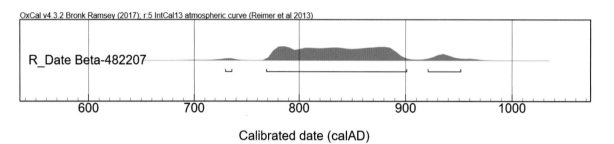

OxCal v4.3.2 Bronk Ramsey (2017); r:5 IntCal13 atmospheric curve (Reimer et al 2013)

R_Date Beta-482207

600   700   800   900   1000

Calibrated date (calAD)

Laboratory: Beta Analytic, Miami, Florida, USA; Calibration: INTCAL 13; Plot: OxCal v4.3.2

Bibliography

Blinkhorn, P, and Soden, I, 1999 The pottery, *in* A Chapman 1999, 55–58

Chapman, A, 1999 Excavation of the town defences at Green Street, Northampton, 1995–6, *Northamptonshire Archaeol*, **28**, 25–60

Denham 1985 The Pottery, *in* J H Williams et al, 1985, 46–62

Williams, J H, Shaw, M, and Denham, V, 1985 *Middle Saxon Palaces at Northampton*, Northampton Development Corporation Monog, **4**

Wiiliams, J H, Shaw, M, and Chapman, A, 2021 Saxon Northampton Revisited, *Northamptonshire Archaeol*, **41**, 25–77

Northamptonshire Archaeology, **41**, 2021, 137–189

Northampton Castle
Part 1: Introduction, pre-castle archaeology, and the history and topography of the castle

by

Andy Chapman

Summary

Northampton Castle was a major royal castle through the 12th and 13th centuries but thereafter it declined in importance. Through the 15th and 16th centuries it was the site of the county gaol and sessions house, but became fully derelict once these functions transferred to the town following the destructive town fire of 1675. The castle then stood as a scenic ruin, but encroachment of housing onto the Inner Bailey defences began in the early 19th century. In the mid-19th century the building of a new rectory, followed by the first railway and a straightened approach to the new West Bridge affected parts of the Outer Bailey. By this time there was antiquarian interest, particularly from Sir Henry Dryden and local architect E F Law and family, who together provided plans and photographs of the castle as it then survived. Further recording was carried out in 1879–80 when much of the Inner Bailey was swept away in the construction of a new railway. Eighty years later, the small portion of the north-east corner of the Inner Bailey that had survived and the nearby Castle Hill mound were subject to excavation in the early 1960s. This included examination of the castle bank and ditch, as well as royal apartments and a kitchen range. It was demonstrated that the Castle Hill mound had been constructed in the mid-17th century during the Civil War, and was not an early motte. It is also suggested that a medieval building beneath Castle Hill, previously interpreted as a church with an apsidal end, may have been part of a gatehouse at the eastern end of an elongated and otherwise lost barbican protecting the north gate. These previously unpublished excavations are the main focus of this report, although the earlier records are used to provide the broader picture of the whole castle. In Part 1, a broad overview of the context of the 1960s excavations is followed by an account of the pre-castle archaeology seen through the antiquarian records and the 1960s excavations. A concise history of the castle is followed by an account of the various works from the 19th century onward that have recorded elements of the castle archaeology enabling an overall, although incomplete, plan of the castle to be produced. Part 1 ends with a consideration of the topography of the castle and its relationship to the medieval town. Part 2 will deal with the detailed archaeological record for the castle defences, the buildings of the Inner Bailey, and the Castle Hill mound. Excavations within the Outer Bailey of the castle in 2013 in advance of building the present station are published separately in the same volume.

Introduction

"Neare unto the towne there is an ancient Castle ruynous" Norden 1593

Northampton Castle, a major royal castle through the 12th and 13th centuries, stood at the west end of the medieval town, lying to the north of the approach to the west gate and bridge, modern Black Lion Hill (Figs 1 & 2, centre NGR SP 7485 6055). It occupied what had been part of the north-western quarter of the early medieval town, whose buildings in this area had been levelled prior to the construction of the castle. The majority of the castle ruins were lost in the clearance of the area in the late 19th century to make way for a new railway station and goods yard.

The genesis of this report

The principal objective behind this report is to provide a first published account of the excavations conducted by Dr John Alexander of Cambridge University in 1961–64 on the surviving part of the Inner Bailey and the adjacent castle defences, and the nearby Castle Hill mound. The detailed account of the results of these excavations will form Part 2 of this study, while Part 1 will provide a broader account of the castle drawn from the documentary and antiquarian record, the background to the excavations of 1961–64 and an account of the pre-castle archaeology (see Table 1).

Together, Parts 1 and 2 will form the largest published compendium of plans, photographs and descriptive text relating to the recorded structure of Northampton Castle, taking in both previously published and much unpublished material.

As described in more detail below, following the excavations of 1961–64 Dr Alexander completed a draft text for a report (1968), but no finds analysis or reporting was completed and no illustrations were prepared. From the mid-1970s to the mid-1980s the Northampton Development Corporation (NDC) Archaeological Unit did much to bring the finds and records together, and had

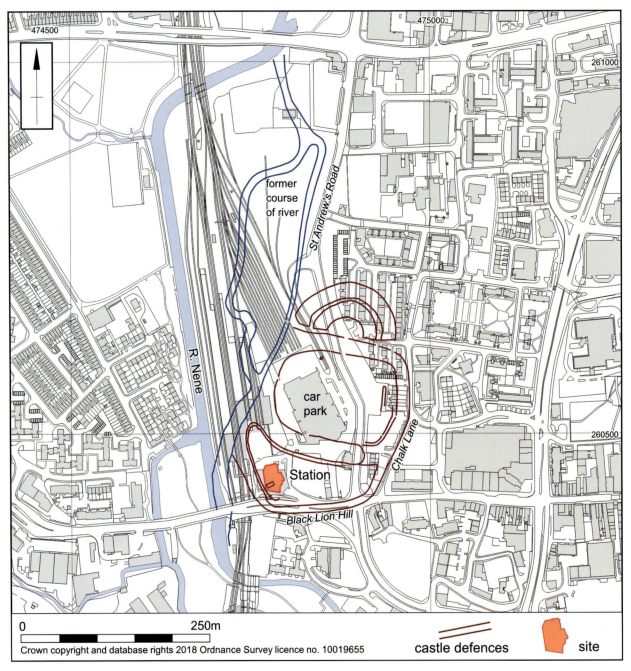

Fig 1: The location of Northampton Castle within the modern townscape, and showing the excavation site of 2013

begun a re-analysis of the site records. When the NDC closed down in the mid-1980s the Northamptonshire Archaeology Unit, within the County Council, inherited the work in progress, which then fell to the present author. With the aid of a backlog grant from English Heritage, finds reports (for those finds that had been located and recovered) were commissioned and a draft publication report was prepared along with a series of plans and sections. Unfortunately, a majority of the planned finds reports did not come to completion and a report was not published at the time.

In retirement, the author has returned to the report he drafted in the mid-1980s, and the related paperwork on the broader history of the castle that was collected at that

time, to finally bring together an account of the 1960s excavations set within the broader story of Northampton Castle as a major royal castle through the reigns of Henry I to Edward I, and its subsequent decline in importance in the later medieval period.

Some known unknowns of Northampton Castle

Despite the catalogue of investigation to be presented, it must be remembered that there is much that we' do not know and can now never know about Northampton Castle, given the loss of so much without record in the late 19th century: the unknowable unknowns. There is,

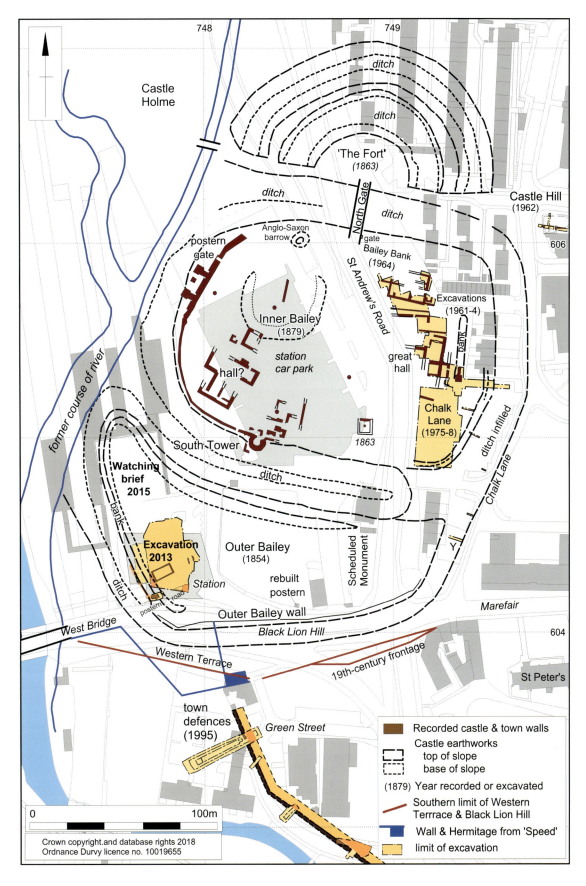

Fig 2: Northampton Castle and the town defences, showing the accumulated topographical and archaeological records over the modern townscape

however, some remaining potential within the limited buried remains that are likely to still survive, and these are listed below for reference, before we delve more deeply into the known knowns of the castle.

In particular, there is the likelihood of surviving archaeological deposits within the raised station car park fronting onto Black Lion Hill, including the small raised area of the Scheduled Monument to the east (where the ground level remains as it was in the late 19th century). These two areas occupy the central and eastern parts of the Outer Bailey.

Also, to the east of St Andrew's Road there is the 'raised' garden area and further north the extensive grass verge, with the road cutting across what was the north-east corner of the interior of the Inner Bailey, the northern arm of the Inner Bailey ditch, including part of the inner gateway, and the defences to the north, known as The Fort, probably last refurbished for the Civil War in the mid-17th century (Fig 2). Modern boreholes have also shown that at least the lower levels of the southern arm of the Inner Bailey ditch, separating the Inner and Outer Baileys, still survive beneath the railway station car park.

It is also suggested in this study that further remains of a north-eastern outer gateway may survive beneath the remnant of the Castle Hill mound and the road to the north of it, lying to the immediate north-east of the Inner Bailey. This might be the only survival of once extensive stone-built barbican defences protecting the approach to the north gate, an interpretation not previously presented.

The recent excavations in the Outer Bailey in 2013, in advance of the new station, are reported separately in this volume (Chapman 2021b 79–127 and 2021d, 191–255), where it is noted that beneath the raised approach to the modern west bridge there is probably an intact sequence of deposits from the early medieval town onward. This may include an early bridge and its approach road, and also the very south-western corner of the castle's Outer Bailey defences. However, access to investigate such a resource is unlikely to be realised at any time in the near future as it would entail the long-term closure of the west bridge crossing, a major part of the local road system.

Acknowledgements

Thanks must go to Northampton Museums and Art Gallery, Northamptonshire Libraries and the Northamptonshire Record Office (now the Archives and Heritage Service, West Northamptonshire Council), who between them hold finds, records and photographs relating to antiquarian and archaeological work at the castle from the 19th and 20th centuries. Given that my copies of many of these records were collected in the 1980s, while others have been obtained second hand from other researchers, it is now not possible to assign every record to a specific source. Thanks are also due to English Heritage (now Historic England) who funded the preparation of the draft report in the mid-1980s.

Graham Cadman, formerly of Northamptonshire Heritage, NCC, and James Edgar (2013), independent researcher, are thanked for supplying information and copies of original drawings, plans and photographs, including material from Northampton Borough Council planning department. Thanks must also go to Brian Giggins, who had access to my first draft from the 1980s when he was preparing his MA thesis on *Northampton's Forgotten Castle* (1999). In his studies he has taken background research much further, particularly with regard to post-medieval events in the environs of the castle, and he has kindly provided a draft of his more recent work (2017), then still in progress, to inform my current reporting.

Some posts to the Facebook site *Northampton Past* have also provided useful information, in particular several posts, and also the public lectures, by local historian Ruth Thomas. I must also reference the website of Friends of Northampton Castle, an organisation that has done much to raise the public profile of Northampton Castle, even though their website material contains some weak or unsupported assumptions and demonstrable errors.

Thanks must also go to the staff of the former Northampton Development Corporation Archaeological Unit, and in particular to Helen Bamford who carried out an extensive analysis of the site records from the 1960s which provided a base for the current report, and who proof read and commented on the first draft of my report in the mid-1980s. Glenn Foard, formerly with the Northamptonshire Archaeology Unit/Northamptonshire Heritage in the country council, must be thanked for his comments at the time on the first draft, and for his publications, particularly in relation to the castle during the Civil War (Foard 1995). The general plan of the castle and the other line drawings illustrating the excavations of the 1960s appearing in Part 2 were prepared by the late Ken Connor, illustrator for the NDC Archaeological Unit. These have been digitised and edited by Andy Chapman. Part 2 will also include reports on animal bone by Mary Harman and medieval window glass by Louise Monk, both of which were prepared in the 1980s.

We must also thank Sir Henry Dryden and E F Law and family for their plans and photographs through the second half of the 19th century. Without their work the only available base plans would be those recorded on the 19th-century town maps. There is also Rev R M Serjeantson, and his excellent study of the history and structure of the castle (1907–8), which has provided most of the material for the history presented in this paper, while there is a more concise summary of the castle and its buildings in *The History of the Kings Works* (Brown, Colvin & Taylor 1963, 750–753).

Finally, we must also thank all those who have carried out the actual physical work of demolishing/excavating at the castle, as they have also made this report possible. They are represented here by the digging teams from 1879–80, who demolished the western wall and cleared much of the interior; from the 1960s excavations on the eastern defences; and my own team from the excavations in 2013 within the Outer Bailey (Fig 3).

The structure of the report

For reference, the contents of the report for Parts 1 and 2 are listed below (Table 1).

Northampton and its castle: a brief introduction

This brief introduction to the history and structure of the castle is provided to set the scene for those unfamiliar

with Northampton and its castle. All aspects mentioned here will either be considered in greater detail in subsequent sections or in associated papers within the same volume (as referenced), while the detail of the archaeo-

1879-80: the demolition team, with their shovels and picks, after exposing the western curtain wall, including the postern gate later to be reconstructed on Black Lion Hill

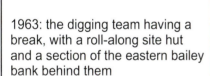

1963: the digging team having a break, with a roll-along site hut and a section of the eastern bailey bank behind them

2013: the digging team, wearing Network Rail approved safety wear, standing in a pit dating to the late 12th century, during excavations in the outer bailey prior to the building of the new station

Fig 3: Three generations of excavators at Northampton Castle: a) the demolition team in 1879-80, b) the excavation team in 1961 and c) the excavation team at the new station 2013

logical remains for the Inner Bailey and Castle Hill will be presented in Part 2, due to appear in *Northamptonshire Archaeology*, **42**, 2022.

The early medieval town

The origins of the town lay in the early Anglo-Saxon period, with archaeological evidence for an initial low level of occupation, no more than a small settlement. However, the appearance of the St Peter's church complex in the later 7th-early 8th centuries AD, comprising churches to either side of a large timber hall, must have heralded a parallel growth in the size and status of the surrounding town to service such an important and high status group of buildings, whether or not it was an ecclesiastical centre (a minster complex), or a secular hall with attendant churches (Williams *et al* 1985; Williams *et al* 2021, this volume, 25–77).

The replacement of the timber hall with an even larger stone hall marked the continuing importance of the town as a regional centre towards the eastern edges of the then dominant kingdom of Mercia. Through the period of Danish control and the decline of Mercia, in the 9th century, and the subsequent re-conquest of eastern England by Edward the Elder of Wessex in the early to middle 10th century, it remained an important regional centre, and had certainly acquired a defensive circuit, comprising a clay bank fronted by a timber revetment and a ditch, by the mid-10th century (Chapman 1999; Chapman 2021c, this volume, 129–136). Excavations at the new railway station in 2013 suggest there may have been some rearrangement of property boundaries, at least within the area of the town later occupied by the Outer Bailey, between the Norman Conquest and the construction of the Outer Bailey in the

early 12th century (Chapman 2021b & d, this volume, 79–127 & 191–255).

A medieval royal castle

This large royal castle may have had an origin in a motte created by Simon de Senlis I, earl of Northampton in the late 11th to early 12th centuries, but there is no reliable documentary or archaeological evidence to support this popular local supposition.

The form of the castle as it survived into the late 19th century should be attributed to Henry I, who was certainly in possession of the castle from the early 12th century. The castle was probably under construction in 1106, when Henry is recorded as meeting his brother, Robert, Duke of Normandy, in Northampton. The absence of court rolls for this crucial period at the beginning of the 12th century leaves the details of when and how the castle became a royal possession unconfirmed by reliable documentary evidence, but in 1122 Henry kept Easter in the castle 'in great state', indicating that it contained halls and apartments suitable for such a royal visitation. In 1130 Henry paid the monks of St Andrew's for land to enable a further extension of the castle, where is unknown, but perhaps either the defences around the north gate or even the addition of the Outer Bailey to the south.

As a royal castle, it was to enjoy a position of considerable importance through the 12th and 13th centuries as a central location for parliaments and other state occasions that gathered the royalty and nobility in one place. But through the 14th century royal visits became less frequent, and when the last Northampton parliament was held in 1380, during the reign of Richard II, the meetings took place in St Andrew's Abbey and not the castle, denoting its poor physical state at this time. Thereafter, the castle

Table 1: The structure of the report

Part 1: Introduction, pre-castle archaeology, and the history and topography of the castle

Introduction
Northampton and its castle: a brief introduction (an abbreviated summary to set the scene)
The excavation programme of 1961-64 (the objectives, progress and the long path to reporting)
Prehistoric and Roman activity on the site of Northampton Castle (as seen in all the records)
Anglo-Saxon settlement on the site of Northampton Castle (largely as recorded in 1961-64)
A concise history of Northampton Castle (largely drawn from Serjeantson 1907-8)
Town maps and antiquarian interest (the 19th century sources of information)
Excavations and survey from 1961 (the 20th- & 21st-century sources of information)
The general plan of Northampton Castle (the records used in creating a modern general plan)
The topography of Northampton Castle and its environs (the castle location in relation to the town)
The castle and its relationship to the contemporary town (speculations on the town development)

Part 2: The archaeology of the Inner Bailey and Castle Hill

Introduction
The castle and its buildings: The documentary evidence
The castle defences: the antiquarian and archaeological evidence
Possible early town defences, the northern defences and the lost barbican
The buildings of the Inner Bailey
The Outer Bailey
The Castle Hill mound and the underlying medieval building
Finds from the excavations of 1961-64
Conclusions and Northampton Castle today

was in decline and neglected, although some buildings were maintained to function as the court house for sessions of the justices and as the county gaol, although it was to remain a royal property until the reign of Charles II in the 17th century.

The Civil War, mid-17th century

In the mid-16th century John Leland, poet and antiquary, wrote, *"The Castle standeth hard by the West Gate and hath a large kepe. The Area of the Residue is very large and bullewarkes of yerth be made afore the Castelle Gate"*, while in the early 17th century it was described by the historian John Norden (1593) more concisely, *"Neare unto the towne there is an ancient Castle ruynous"*. Our only visual depiction of the castle, set within the broader context of the medieval walled town, was provided by

John Speed in 1610 as a corner insert on his county map, although it was likely already more 'ruynous' than he depicted it to be (Fig 4).

The defences around the north gate were refurbished in the mid-17th century during the Civil War (1642–51) and soils from partially digging out the ditches was used to construct the Castle Hill mound, presumably as a gun emplacement to protect the approach to the north gate.

Following the restoration of the monarchy in 1660 both the castle and the town walls were slighted, since Northampton had supported the Parliamentarian cause. Following a major town fire in 1675 and the consequent need to rebuild much of the town, the sessions house and gaol were moved into the town (Bassir 2021, this volume 387–402). It is likely that a proportion of the stone used in the rebuilding came from the convenient stone quarry of the then derelict castle walls and buildings, which probably explains why, by the mid-19th century, the walls

A	St Andrews mill	G	Marhold	N	The Hermutage	T	The Towre
B	S Andrews Abbey	H	Graye Friers	O	S. Iames end	V	Darngate
C	North Gate	I	The Drapery	P	Bridge stret	W	St Thomas well
D	St Sepulchres	K	S Kathrens	Q	St Iohns	X	St Gylles
E	sheepe market	L	The Checker	R	Alhallowes	Y	Free Schole
F	S.Edmonds end	M	The Castell	S	St Peters	Z	The Mill

Reprinted and enlarged 1971 for Northampton Public Libraries from the 1610 original by John Speed

Fig 4: Plan of Northampton by John Speed 1610

most accessible to the townsfolk on the northern and eastern sides had gone, while those to the south and, in particular, the west survived to be recorded in the 19th century.

A scenic ruin, 18th century

Through the 18th century to the early/mid-19th century the castle survived as a grassed over scenic ruin, with orchards in both the Inner and Outer Baileys, while the ditches became partially silted and grassed hollows, although given the original width and depth of these ditches they were still hollows some metres deep. However, in the early to mid-19th century the process of steady attrition began, and piece by piece the castle was to succumb to the growth of the Victorian industrial shoe-town of Northampton, with its need for more housing and access to the most modern transport, the railway.

New housing and the coming of the railway, 19th century

Fortunately, the gradual destruction of the castle did not pass without record. From 1854 onward surveys by the well-known local historian and antiquarian, Sir Henry Dryden of Canons Ashby, and the surveys and photographs compiled by local architect E F Law, along with his brother and sons, enable us to provide an accurate general base plan along with some elements of detail, such as the form of the western defences, and also parts of the internal layout, with a group of buildings in the southern part of the Inner Bailey recorded in the late 19th century, most probably those that had remained in use longest to serve as the sessions house and the gaol into the 17th century.

The finally stages of this process of survey and record occurred in 1879–80, when the building of the second much enlarged railway, with a new station and an extensive goods yard, with the newly built St Andrew's Road forming the boundary to the east, resulted in the destruction of the greater part of the castle, and a drastic change in the local topography. The levelled area for the new station and the goods yard was created by terracing into the hillside, taking most of the castle remains away in the process.

This is most clearly evident today in the high brick revetment wall along the eastern side of St Andrew's Road at its southern end, with the north-eastern corner of the Inner Bailey surviving above this, and a truncated length of the bailey bank standing behind houses fronting onto Chalk Lane. Chalk Lane and its northernmost end, Castle Terrace, follow the line of the long buried ditch around the eastern side of the castle's Outer and Inner Baileys, and it is the only element of the modern townscape that directly respects the plan of the now lost royal castle (Fig 2).

The excavations of 1961–64

By the beginning of the 1960s the surviving part of the Inner Bailey was itself under threat from a new road scheme, and Dr John Alexander of Cambridge University directed four seasons of excavation, 1961–64, which examined the castle defences and two main building ranges within the north-east corner of the Inner Bailey, along with trial trenches into the Castle Hill mound to test the supposition that it may have been an early motte. The road scheme was later cancelled, so this area still survives largely as it was in the 1960s although with some newer housing within the footprint of the castle. The details of this excavation programme are recorded in detail below, with the pre-castle archaeology considered in Part 1 while the castle archaeology forms much of Part 2.

Excavation at Chalk Lane 1975–8

Further clearance of buildings along the west side of Chalk Lane enabled an area beneath the levelled bailey bank to be excavated in 1975–8 by the Northampton Development Corporation Archaeological Unit, where there was a well-preserved sequence of pre-castle occupation within the early medieval town, while the line of the south-eastern corner of the Inner Bailey ditch was also identified (Williams and Shaw 1981).

Excavation prior to the new Station 2013

In 2013 the building of a new railway station provided a first opportunity to excavate to the south, within the Outer Bailey. Here there was a well-preserved sequence of pre-castle occupation, and a small stone building dating to the 12th century within the south-western corner of the Outer Bailey. The foundation of a stone revetment wall along the outer face of the Outer Bailey bank was also identified, along with a possible postern gate providing access to the west bridge. This work is published separately as accounts of the pre-castle archaeology (Chapman 2021b, this volume 79–127) and the castle archaeology (Chapman 2021d, this volume, 191–255).

Minor works

Other minor pieces of work are detailed within the catalogue of sources for the production of a general plan

The excavation programme of 1961–64

What survived of the castle in 1961 was the north-east corner of the interior of the Inner Bailey, lying to the east of St Andrew's Road and flanked by a short length of the inner face of the bailey bank, which was truncated to the east by properties fronting onto Chalk Lane. To the north, a length of the bailey bank and the partially infilled castle ditch lay within the grounds of the late Victorian rectory, which fronted onto Fitzroy Street (formerly Castle Lane). Beyond the castle to the north-east, a slightly raised area, extensively built over, marked the site of the Castle Hill mound, in the angle of Castle Terrace and Castle Street (Fig 2; Figs 5 & 6; with the location the main features of the lost castle added in red lettering).

By the 1950s the post-war redevelopment of Northampton was in hand, and the Chalk Lane area, which had been built up from the early 19th century, was seen to be in need of extensive clearance. There were also plans at the beginning of the 1960s to create a new road, running north-eastwards from St Andrew's Road, which would have cut a broad swath across an extensive area of the Victorian industrial housing to the north of the town centre.

During the 80 years between the creation of the new railway station and goods yard in 1879–80 and the excavations of 1961–64, remarkably little had changed across the castle site as a whole. In the Chalk Lane area this can be illustrated through the respective maps of the Ordnance Survey 1:500 scale map of 1885 and the Borough Surveyors map of 1956 produced in preparation for the redevelopment (Figs 5 & 6).

The only significant change had been the removal of the terraces of houses from the earlier 19th-century built over the levelled parts of the eastern bailey bank and the infilled castle ditch, and a partial replacement with sparser new housing at the north end of Chalk Lane. Behind these properties lay 1–2 Castle Grounds, railway cottages built between 1880 and 1890, with the houses and their gardens occupying the remaining part of the interior of the Inner Bailey, which were cleared a little later. These clearances provided access to the interior of the Inner Bailey and the levelled defences for the excavations that began in 1961.

In addition, the Castle Hill mound, already impinged upon in the 19th century, was to be further truncated by roadworks at the abruptly angled junction of Castle Terrace and Castle Street, with houses already cleared from the junction to enable the widening and realignment of the roads. The late Victorian rectory and its gardens, as well as 19th-century houses on the corner of Castle Terrace, were also to be cleared, and this area was examined in the final stages of the excavations in 1964. Finally, the clearance of 19th-century housing to the north of Fitzroy Street, across the earthworks beyond the north gate, provided an opportunity to cut a section across the ditch that had been surveyed by Sir Henry Dryden in 1863, immediately prior to the building of those houses.

On the initiative of the Inspectorate of Ancient Monuments of the then Ministry of Public Buildings and Works, and with the co-operation of the Borough Council, excavations were conducted on these areas from 1961 to 1964 under the direction of Dr John Alexander of Cambridge University.

There were three main objectives:

Section the two surviving lengths of the bailey bank and locate and section the infilled bailey ditch;

Excavate a trial trench within the Inner Bailey to see if any building remains survived;

Section the Castle Hill mound in an attempt to locate the edges of the presumed motte and its ditch, and also to examine any deposits beneath the mound.

The progress of the excavations

In 1961, 17 April to 27 May, two initial trenches above St Andrew's Road and west of Chalk Lane examined the bailey bank, the castle ditch and the underlying pre-castle occupation. A third trench was opened to examine more of a building abutting the inner face of the bailey bank. In his interim report Dr Alexander (1961) noted that "*between 9 and 12 men worked on the site supplied by Chowns Ltd and Henry Martin Ltd. Mrs G[wen] Brown was my assistant and volunteers came from Northampton and neighbourhood*". The hired labourers were there to do the heavy digging, removing the bulk deposits above walls and evident stratified deposits.

We may note that among the volunteers working at the castle there were a number of memorable names from later years of archaeology in the county: including Dennis Jackson, who went on to be a founding member of NAS and excavator of numerous sites, particularly within the quarries along the Nene valley and the ironstone quarries around Corby, with a particular interest in the Iron Age; Mary Traxton, a founder member in the 1960s and still the driving force today behind The Wellingborough and District Archaeological Society; and a young Robert Moore, who was to be part of the Northampton Museum and Art Gallery service at Guildhall Road for many years, and also a recent contributor to this journal.

We should also note that Harold Frost, local architect, was responsible for the majority of the site photography throughout the four years, and it would be impossible to make any meaningful interpretation of the excavations without his excellent photographs. The photographic record comprises high quality black and white negative images on glass quarter-plates (4.25" x 3.25"/108 x 83mm), held by Northampton Museum and Art Gallery, which are supplemented by a relatively early use of colour 35mm transparencies, Kodachrome. He also went to extreme lengths to capture views from the best angles, as here in 1961 during the excavation of a section of the bailey bank, the underlying late Saxon deposits and castle ditch to the west of Chalk (Fig 7a), and now within the Chalk Lane car park (Fig 7b).

An additional piece of work in 1961, was the opportunity to excavate a trench to the north of the castle, where two new blocks of flats were then under construction between Bath Street and Scarletwell Street, two streets at the north-western end of the double street pattern that had been proposed as fossilising the line of the defensive circuit of the late Saxon town. The ground was heavily disturbed but there was an early deeper feature that may have been part of an early ditch or quarry pit, but the records are too incomplete and uncertain to reach a definitive conclusion. This work is not published in this study.

In 1962, excavation was carried out for two weeks in June, with six narrow but deep trenches excavated into the Castle Hill mound, which demonstrated that this was not an early motte (Alexander 1962) (Fig 8).

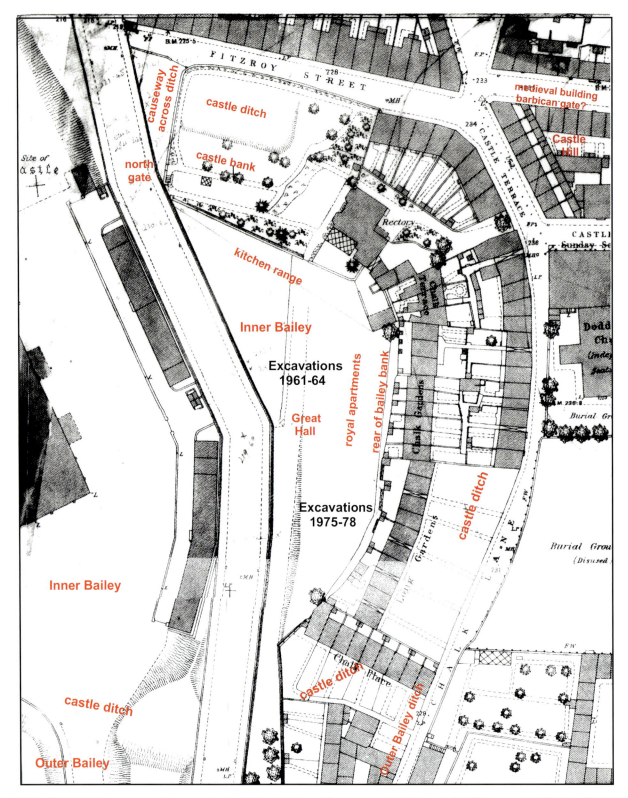

Fig 5: The Chalk Lane area as shown on the 1st Edition Ordnance Survey map (original scale 1:500, surveyed 1883-84 published 1885), with elements of the castle labelled in red

The initial objectives were largely fulfilled in the first two years. In 1963–64 excavations continued with work on site supervised by Harold Frost and Gwen Brown, with the support of the Archaeology Section of the Northamptonshire Natural History Society. Dr Alexander remained the overall

director but was less often on site, and numerous letters survive from Harold Frost to John Alexander reporting the weekly progress of the excavations.

In 1963 the excavation of trench III within the Inner Bailey was completed, and further trenches were opened

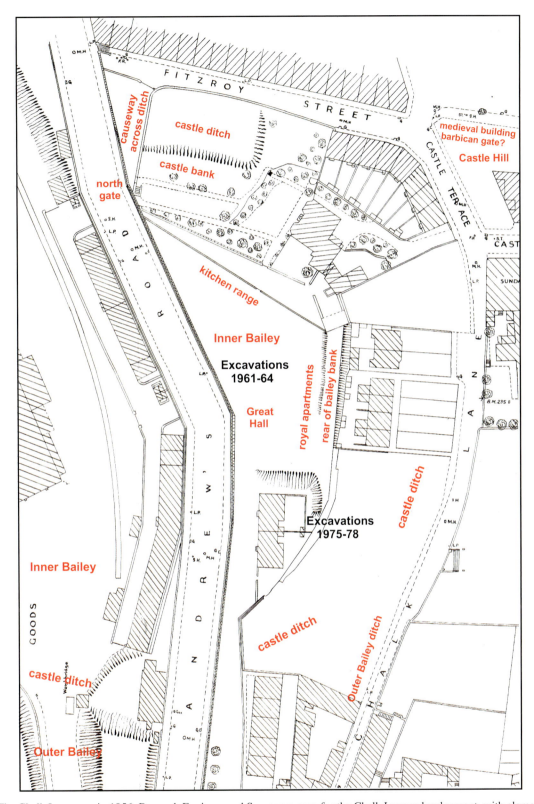

Fig 6: The Chalk Lane area in 1956, Borough Engineer and Surveyors map for the Chalk Lane redevelopment, with elements of the castle labelled in red (original scale 1:500)

to the north, across a former allotment garden, which exposed parts of a building range against the northern defences, which at least in its later use formed a large kitchen range (Fig 9a & b). This area is now a garden with plaques recording the former presence of the castle (Fig 9c).

Within the excavation paperwork there is a record of the expenses for 1963, with a total expenditure of around £1000.00, including the wages for the labourers and the

Fig 7a: Photographer Harold Frost improvises a high-level viewing point in 1961 using a single ladder and putting much faith in four slender retaining ropes

Fig 7b: A similar view to Fig 7a, showing the gable end of the same house on Chalk Lane, now at the northern end of the present car park, with the truncated bailey bank to the left (Photo: Andy Chapman 17 October 2021)

Fig 8: The surviving north-west corner of the Castle Hill mound in 1962, showing the truncated mound still standing above the surrounding street levels, looking south-west with houses on Castle Terrace in the background

cost of machine hire (Fig 10). The compensation for lost produce refers to the allotment that had occupied the northern part of the Inner Bailey area, whose presence had prevented excavation there in 1961.

The final formal excavation took place over two weeks in June 1964. There was further work to complete the excavation of the trenches within the Inner Bailey, while in the north-eastern corner of the defences the demolition

of the rectory and the levelling of its gardens enabled a number of pieces of additional work to be undertaken. A trench was excavated into the bailey bank at a possible location of an early motte, as indicated by an early ditch found in 1963, but this failed to find any evidence for a motte beneath the bailey bank. The northern building range within the Inner Bailey continued into the rectory gardens, and a further three trenches were excavated, locating the rear wall abutting the bailey bank. In addition, a small trench excavated close to St Andrew's Street confirmed the survival of part of the north gate of the castle, as seen and recorded in the 19th century.

The final stages of work took place later in the year. Between October and November 1964 the bailey bank within the rectory garden was removed by machine excavation during the redevelopment, but through the work of Harold Frost and the Northamptonshire Natural History Society it was possible to obtain a section across the bank. Also, as the area of the rectory garden was levelled to the natural bedrock and the foundation trenches for six blocks or housing were laid out, it was possible to trace the inner and outer edges of the castle ditch and inside the line of the ditch pits pre-dating the castle were exposed and partly excavated (see Figs 19–21). At around the same time, the clearance of Victorian housing across the defences beyond the north gate, north of Fitzroy Street, known as The Fort, had enabled sections behind the cellars of the levelled buildings to be examined, and in November when construction contractors excavated further trenches into the ditch, Harold Frost photographed and drew the section of the outermost ditch. With these final episodes of rescue archaeology as redevelopment began, the excavations came to an end.

The road development which had threatened the area of the Inner Bailey examined by Dr Alexander was eventually cancelled. The excavated trenches were left open for some considerable time and evidently became a local playground and rubbish dump, with complaints about the state of the site appearing in the local press. Eventually, they were backfilled and the area was grassed over, to create the much the same state as exists to this day.

a) July 1963

b) August 1963

Fig 9a & b: Views looking north-west across the surviving part of the Inner Bailey, with St Andrew's Road and the station goods yard in the background, showing the area: a) at the commencement of excavation in July 1963 on the former allotment, and b) at the end of excavation in August 1963, with labelled trench numbers

Fig 9c: A summer evening tour of the castle site for NAS members, looking from the north-east corner of the Inner Bailey south-westwards over St Andrew's road, across the station raised car park, the Inner Bailey, and towards the new station, the west end of the Outer Bailey (Photo Pat Chapman, June 2017)

Excavations at Site of Northampton Castle

Summer 1963

List of Expenses paid to 10th October, 1963

	£	s.	d.
Wages	563	12	5
Photographs	73	14	6
Machine Excavations	194	7	6
Equipment	27	4	-
Compensation re loss of produce	22	8	-
Travelling, subsistence	15	19	9
Honorarium to Mrs. G. Brown	50	-	-
Insurance	2	10	-
Petty cash payments	13	15	11
	£963	12	1

There is a known outstanding commitment for fencing costing £80 or thereabouts.

Borough Treasurer's Office,
Northampton.
15th October, 1963. RC/MH

Fig 10: The expenses record for the castle excavations in 1963

Reporting on the excavations of 1961–64

Each year Dr Alexander produced an annual interim report for the Ministry of Public Buildings and Works (Alexander, 1961, 1962, 1963 and 1964) and two short notes were published in the annual summaries in *Medieval Archaeology*, the journal for the Medieval Society (1962–3, **6–7**, 322–3 & 1964, **8**, 250, 257–8). During the course of the excavations there had been much local interest, and the site archive contains numerous local newspaper cuttings through the four years (Fig 11).

Subsequently, other commitments prevented Dr Alexander from publishing the excavations in full. A first draft for such a report was prepared in the late 1960s (Alexander 1968), although no drawings or finds reports were ever prepared. The finds from the excavations, for which there are many site finds lists, have had an unhappy history. It would appear that while some finds, including all the architectural stone, went to Northampton Museum, other material was apparently sent off to various specialists, but neither the finds themselves nor reports were ever forthcoming.

Fig 11: A collage of some of the many newspaper reports covering the excavations of 1961–64

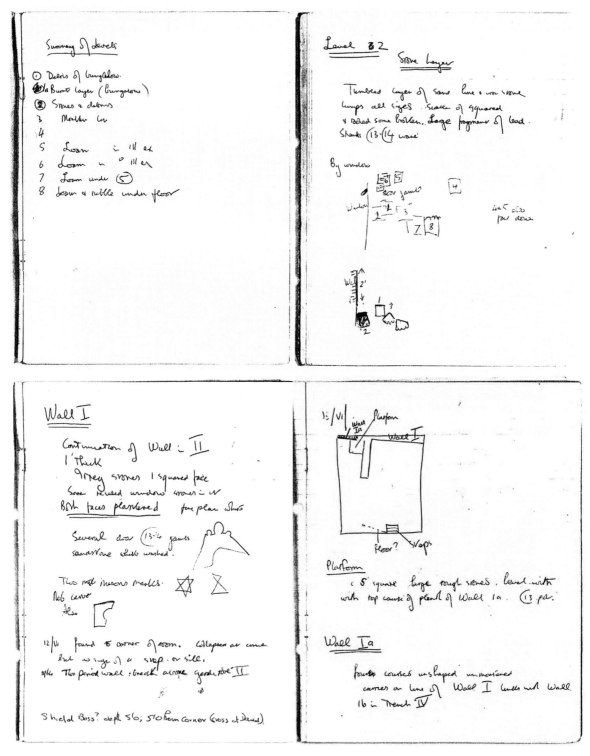

The site records themselves comprise a series of note books, mainly those Woolworths red notebooks that on the back cover carried tables of highest mountains and longest rivers and similar useful information (for those of us of a certain age who would remember using these). While a context numbering system of sorts was in use, the notebooks would not be recognised by anyone who has worked in archaeology since the 1970s as a context

recording system, let alone a single context record (Fig 12). Numbers start at 1 for each trench, and might start as 1 again within a trench extension, as in Trench I and Trenches 1a-1e. Beyond numbered features such as pits or walls, where numbers are allocated to a specific entity, numbered soil deposits cannot be taken to be necessarily discrete stratigraphic elements, as it is evident that single context numbers were often allocated to the

Fig 12: Sample pages from the site notebook for Trench III, recording the collapsed building stone and rubble from the royal apartments

152

bulk removal of soils that might encompass, for instance, a major soil deposit(s) along with the fills of wall robber trenches, which do not appear to have been recognised during bulk soil removal, and were certainly not recorded in plan, although they can be seen in sections both drawn and photographed. Site plans and sections were drawn in pencil on graph paper to imperial scales.

All of the original primary site record, notebooks and drawings on paper, as brought together by the NDC and Northamptonshire Archaeology, were deposited with Northampton Museum and Art Gallery in the mid-1980s, along with the glass-plate negatives.

In the 1970s a reassessment of the site records and finds was initiated by the NDC Archaeological Unit. The pottery assemblage was examined by Mike McCarthy, and this work formed the basis for the creation of the Northampton medieval pottery type-series that became the base for work on pottery from excavations conducted by the NDC in the 1970s and 80s. It has now been absorbed in the County Pottery Type Series (CTS) as established by the Northamptonshire Archaeology Unit, within the county council. Many of the vessels from the castle excavations were drawn in the 1970s, and this material forms part of the site archive generated by the NDC, but a formal pottery report on the castle assemblage was not produced.

The analysis of the site records was carried out by Dr Helen Bamford, who copied and annotated the sections and, given the inadequate context numbering of the original record, a new comprehensive numbering system was created, with context descriptions recorded on a card index system. Ink on drafting film copies of the paper plans and sections generated by Helen Bamford for the NDC and photocopies of the original site notebooks were retained by Northamptonshire Archaeology, and the notebooks have since been scanned to pdf format to create a digital record. This work had not been completed when the NDC was closed down, and the records were handed over to Northamptonshire Archaeology Unit at the end of 1984. The current author took over the task, having previously worked for the NDC and with Helen Bamford.

A project design for continuing the work was submitted to English Heritage and a grant was awarded from the backlog publication budget. An attempt was made to recover more of the missing finds, and visits to both Dr Alexander at Cambridge and Gwen Brown at Wellingborough did produce some additional material, while following up on a letter sent to the Victoria and Albert Museum in the 1960s resulted in the return of the painted window glass, which had sat in a suitcase in their basement for some 20 years.

The original grant proposal included the analysis of the pottery and the publication of a pottery report, but while analysis and the quantification of data got underway, for various reasons this report was never completed. Similarly, a report on the architectural stonework, housed in Northampton Museum, was commissioned but was also never completed. A small group of finds, mainly comprising iron and lead building fittings from the collapsed rubble in trenches II and III, over the royal apartments, was also commissioned, but, unfortunately, the relevant specialist died before completing the work.

Given these difficulties, it was decided that a report on the 1960s excavations alone would be of less value than a more general presentation of those results within a review of all the evidence for the structure of Northampton Castle, which is why the original report became a more summary account of the 1960s excavations set within a general review of the existing understanding of the history and archaeology of the castle as a whole. Publication drawings were produced at the time, by Ken Connor, but the report was never finalised for publication.

Returning to the report in 2020–21, it has become possible to include more illustrations and photographs than would have been possible in the 1980s, in the days before the many benefits of digital report compilation and publication had become available. The report presented in Parts 1 and 2 of this study is therefore a heavily revised and extended version of the draft report from the 1980s, much enhanced with additional plans and images, and also benefitting from further research carried out subsequently by others, such as Brian Giggins. All original material from the excavation archive and the analysis of the 1980s that remain in the possession of the author will be submitted to archive following the full publication of this report.

The presentation of the accumulated evidence begins with the pre-castle archaeology, as presented below.

Prehistoric and Roman activity on the site of Northampton Castle

All of the excavations conducted within and around the site of the castle have produced evidence for earlier activity. This ranges in date from the Mesolithic to the late Saxon/Saxo-Norman occupation of the early medieval town that preceded the construction of the castle itself.

Prehistoric flint scatters

Excavations in the vicinity of the castle have all produced some quantity of worked flint, including Mesolithic types and Neolithic/early Bronze Age material. The Chalk Lane excavations (Williams and Shaw 1981) have provided the largest assemblage of worked flint, as beneath the bailey bank the earlier deposits had not been as disturbed as is usually the case, and these preserved buried soils were also sampled quite extensively.

It was the favourable circumstances for the survival of the early buried soils at Chalk Lane, and the excavation of much of the available deposit, that created a disparity in numbers of recovered flint between Chalk Lane and the nearby more disturbed sites, and there is no basis to the simplistic claim that Chalk Lane was "where Northampton began", as made in the opening chapter of a recent history of the town (Ingram 2020, 4, fig 1).

Within the worked flints there is a high proportion of Mesolithic types as well as Neolithic/early Bronze Age material, and some were possibly associated with a series of pits and hollows cut into the subsoil, rather than merely residual in soil horizons or later features (Bamford 1981).

While there is no clear evidence for Earlier Neolithic activity in the castle area, flint implements, pottery and some excavated features on the Chalk Lane, Marefair and St Peter's Street sites do attest to a Late Neolithic/ Early Bronze Age presence. The flint assemblages and their possible significance, and a possibly round barrow ring ditch at St Peter's Street, are discussed further by Chapman (2021a, this volume, 17–24).

Worked flints recovered from the 1960s excavations in the pre-castle deposits beneath the bailey bank and in the buried soil beneath Castle Hill, were summarised by Alexander (1969, 4):

"At Castle Hill…in trenches A1 and A3 four micro-lithic blades, a microlithic core and 20 struck flakes came from the top 1m of the soft weathered sand overlying the sandstone. They were fresh and unpatinated and were scattered through the layer…At Chalk Lane twelve more struck flakes, two with retouching and four with signs of utilisation also came from the top 60cm of the weathered sandstone in Trenches 1a, 1b, 1c and 1d and ten more from the original ground surface. All are of general Mesolithic type and suggest some activity here sometime before the 3rd millennium BC."

Note: Given the usage of small nodules of flint derived from the local gravels, Neolithic and Bronze Age flakes from Northamptonshire are typically much smaller than contemporary worked flint from sites on or close to Chalk geology, so small undiagnostic flakes may have been Neolithic or Bronze Age in date rather than, as assumed by Alexander, a Mesolithic date for all the material, both recognised types and struck flakes.

The Iron Age is represented by only a few sherds of pottery, possibly associated with a feature, from the Chalk Lane site. No features of prehistoric date were located during the excavations of the 1960s, but then none of the trenches were excavated fully enough to have exposed a sufficiently large area of natural subsoil to permit the recognition of such features, even if present.

Roman activity

No features of Roman date have been located in the vicinity of the castle; but pottery, building materials, and some coins dating to the 2nd-4th centuries AD, have occurred as residual finds.

Some Roman pottery was recovered during the 19th-century excavations (see Fig 13, 2), but at the time the late Saxon/Saxo-Norman pottery was also considered to be of Roman date, giving the spurious impression that there was extensive Roman settlement beneath the castle.

Like the flints, Roman pottery was generally concentrated in pre-castle deposits, although also present in later contexts. This applies to the excavations of the 1960s and to those by the NDC Archaeological Unit in the 1970s. In the former instance most of the Roman sherds came from the Anglo-Saxon deposits beneath the bailey bank on the east side of the castle and also to the north-east, while only a few were from medieval contexts within the Inner Bailey.

Anglo-Saxon settlement on the site of Northampton Castle

Investigations in the late 19th century

Early Anglo-Saxon

It is recorded that in the investigation of a small mound to the west of the north gate (see Fig 2), a human skeleton was found along with and a portion of a heavy sword, tentatively identified as a scramasax, which would suggest that this feature was a burial mound of early Anglo-Saxon date.

"…a small mound, which appeared on removal to be of the same date as the earthwork, as the soil was similar. It had apparently been formed as a sepulchral tumulus, as under it were found the remains of a human skeleton, and a portion of a heavy sword with a wooden hilt, which however crumbled when exposed to the air. The sword is now in the Northampton Museum." (Scriven 1880, 204)

"I have had an opportunity of sending the weapon to Mr A Franks, the Curator of the Department of British Antiquities at the British Museum, whose opinion is as follows :- Mr. Franks thinks it is a 'scramma sax', or rather a half one, a type of weapon rare in England, but common on the Continent." (Scriven 1882, 71)

If recovered and excavated today, this would be a site of major significance to the early archaeological record of the town. As it is, it is difficult to assess its veracity with nothing more than the available written account to go on. A modern assessment of the supposed *scramasax* might be informative, and if any of the human bone was retained (which often it wasn't in those days) there would at least be the potential for radiocarbon dating.

Late Saxon

During the levelling of the castle in the late 19th century, pits and wells of late Saxon date were recorded both within the Inner Bailey and beneath the bailey bank (Scriven 1880 and Sharp 1882, 245–47).

"The original surface of the ground had apparently been occupied for many years by human habitations, and contained many curious relics which will, when they are arranged, throw some light on the history of Northampton from an early period. The soil was filled from one end to the other with bones of the domestic animals, and the subsoil was honey-combed with pits and hollows of various depths, containing pottery, implements of bone and iron, and personal ornaments…All that it is necessary to say about them here…is that a great part of the antiquities found below the original surface are undoubtedly Saxon, and the [castle] earthwork is, therefore, not earlier than that period. To make this perfectly clear, it should be added that the same kind of remains were found below the original surface under the embankment, and in particular that a Saxon coin was found in a well which was afterwards covered over by the embankment, as shewn at f in the section [see Fig 36a]. This well was one of several deep pits of the early period which reached the water bearing stratum, and which were distinguished from the later wells described by Mr Law, by their being unwalled, and by the nature of their contents. In this one were found, besides the coin mentioned above, two

fragments of iron spearheads, and a quantity of clippings of leather." (Scriven 1880, 205)

Sharp provided an overview of the animal bone assemblage pre-dating the castle and then continued with the finds:

"The other Saxon antiquities consist of numerous spear and arrow heads, two very barbed spear-heads (perhaps fish spears), Knives and what appear to be tools (four socketted for handles), all in iron; many small stone hones, each with a hole for slinging (probably from a girdle) which may have been used for sharpening spears, arrows, etc. Of bone, a long well-made needle, an instrument well worked and sharpened at both ends (perhaps a knitting needle), three scoops...two with characteristic incised ornamentation, bronze tweezers, very Roman in pattern, but more ornamental, and having lettering along one limb – another smaller and plainer; whorls – one annular, well made and symmetrical; others dome-shaped and flat-bottomed, one ornamented with an incised pattern, all of stone, others of the same shape, but made of the rounded parts of bone joints, doubtless used for some game.

Coins – Eadweard the Elder (ad 901–924)...moneyer, "AEDIRAED". 6 others (adhering) of the same type, moneyer's name illegible; Eadgar (959–975)...moneyer, "MANIA"; 3 St Edmund (Abbey of St. Edmundsbury, tenth century); Edward the Confessor (1042–1066).,,moneyer "LEOFWINE-ON-WILY" (Wilton); same reign, small size (halfpenny'?)...moneyer "LEOFWIG-ON-LYND" (London). The Saxon coin found in the well under the earthwork, near the south-west corner of the Castle, is very imperfect, but I believe it to be of the reign of Edward the Confessor, and I fancy...belonging to the latter half of the reign." (Sharp 1882, 245–47)

While finds of metalwork and bone were correctly identified as Saxon, the late Saxon/Saxo-Norman pottery, as already noted, was then considered to be of Roman date (Fig 13, 1 & 3–5). In 1882 the systematic study of early medieval pottery was still some decades away, with the most significant advances from the 1950s onward. However, the early pottery from the castle was reassessed and republished by David Kennett (1968).

"Northampton was the first place from which early medieval pottery was published. The first series of excavations on Northampton Castle were published as long ago as 1882, but the pottery was then considered Roman. Since Sharp wrote his paper groups of early medieval pottery have been published from Oxford [in Oxoniensia 1939 onward] and Cambridge [Hurst 1956], and a large series of excavations from Bedford [Kennet in Bedfordshire Archaeological Journal, 4 (1968)]. Further excavation in Northampton itself has added to the known range and it is to be hoped that Dr Alexander's excavations will received a fairly speedy publication." (Kennett 1968, 3)

Occupation beneath the eastern bailey bank

The excavations of the 1960s included the investigation of pre-castle levels sealed beneath the bailey bank in an area immediately to the north of, and in part later overlapped by the Chalk Lane site of the 1970s (Fig 14).

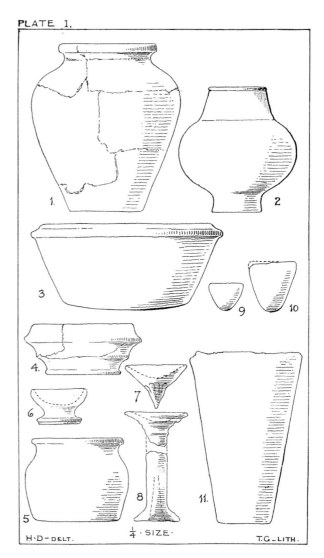

PLATE 1.

H·D–DELT.   ¼ · SIZE ·   T.G–LITH.

Fig 13: Illustration from Sharp 1882 showing 2, Roman pottery; and characteristic late Saxon pottery: 1, Stamford ware jar, 3–4 inturned rim bowls; 7–8 cresset lamps, and 9–10 metalworking crucibles

Trench I was excavated in 1961 to locate the castle ditch, with stratified late Saxon deposits surviving at the west end of the trench. In 1964 more of the bailey bank to the west was removed to expose a more extensive area of the underlying late Saxon deposits, Trenches Ia-Ie, actually a single area but subdivided by narrow baulks (Fig 15).

While up to 0.9m of stratified deposits had survived, the excavation of the Trench I extensions (Ia-Ie) in 1964 ran for only two weeks, which was clearly insufficient to deal with such a deep and complex sequence, where one section shows 10 layers of soil deposition. Comparison of the original section drawings to the photographic evidence indicated the presence of some errors in the recorded sequence, but for cut features that did not appear in section the proposed phasing cannot now be interrogated. What is presented, therefore, reflects the original proposed sequence, conflated to two phase plans, but it

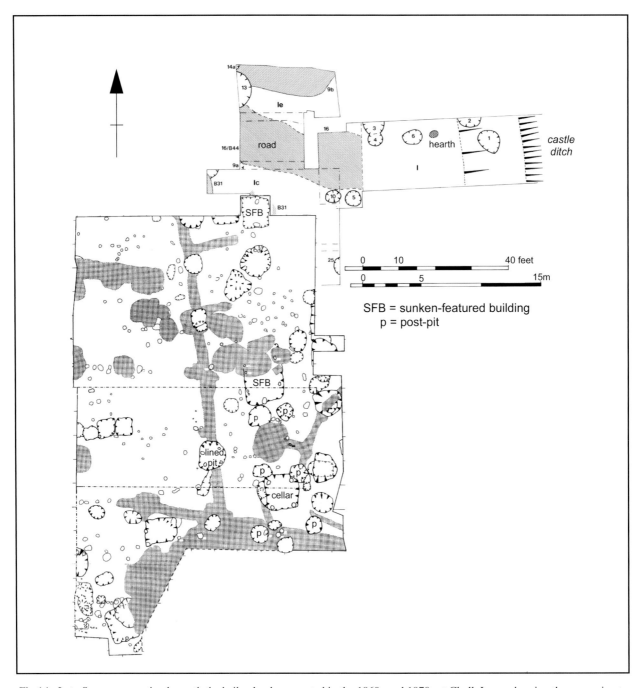

Fig 14: Late Saxon occupation beneath the bailey bank excavated in the 1960s and 1970s at Chalk Lane, showing the approximate juxtaposition of the two sites: the phasing is not necessarily in parallel

must be recognised that this may contain errors (Fig 15: phases 1B-1C and phases 2–4).

A site plan was only drawn once the area had been taken down to natural, and some features in Trench Ie were only ever recorded on a sketch plan. Original site numbers, allocated from 1 within each trench and sub-trench (ie 1a/1, 1b/1 etc), are occasionally supplemented with additional context numbers, with a B suffix, to allow for omissions in the site records. (These are from the renumbering introduced by Helen Bamford in the 1980s.)

Most of the pottery from these deposits was not available for study in the 1980s. It was examined during the

1960s, and the notes made then suggest that the bulk of it was of shelly wares in forms dating to the mid-10th to late 11th centuries (St Neots-type wares), but including some glazed wares [Stamford wares?] of the 11th-12th centuries (Alexander 1961, 2). No early/middle Saxon pottery was found (or recognised) within the recovered material.

Phase 1A

Within the more fully excavated trenches, Ia and Ib, the earliest level was a relict early subsoil of weathered ironstone in red sand, from which came several struck

E. Defences: Pre-castle Occupation

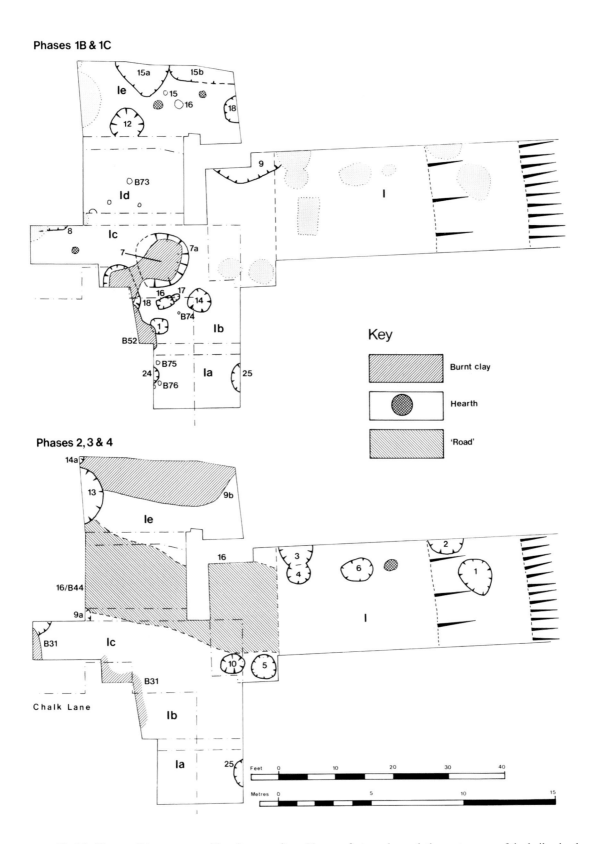

Fig 15: The possible sequence of late Saxon to Saxo-Norman features beneath the eastern arm of the bailey bank recorded in 1961 and 1964

157

flints, as noted above, and as also seen beneath the Castle Hill mound.

Phases 1B and 1C

Above the early subsoil two successive general soil horizons, of stony brown loam and grey-brown loam pre-dated the earliest features. To the south, in trench Ic, a deep circular pit, 7a, lay to the north-east of a sunken-featured building (SFB),18, which was re-excavated during the Chalk Lane excavations in the 1970s (Fig 14, SFB from Williams and Shaw 1981, 98, figs 6 and 7, feature B14). To the east of the SFB there was a cluster of shallow pits and postholes, 1, 17 and B74. These features were all partly sealed by a thin spread of small ironstone fragments in yellow-brown sand, possibly laid to form as an extensive overlying yard surface, only surviving where it had subsided into the underlying pits.

The subsequent deposits would appear to relate to industrial activity, probably metalworking, which would parallel the focus on metalworking seen in the late Saxon deposits to the south in the 1970s escavation. A layer of dark grey loam with much charcoal produced half a crucible and material described as 'bronze dross'. Above this, an extensive layer of sandy clay with a heavily burnt surface, Ic/7 & B52 (Fig 15), was interpreted by the excavator as a hearth complex, and was sealed by a layer of dark grey, charcoal-rich, loam. Two pits to the east, 14 & 16, may have been contemporary with this upper surface, as the pits fills contained quantities of burnt clay.

While the stratigraphic sequence to the south, in Trenches Ia–Ic, cannot be tied with certainty to the sequence to the north, Trenches Id and Ie, it is possible that some early postholes in Id, B73 etc, and several broad but generally shallow pits in Trench Ie, 12, 15a, 15b and 18, and a similar pit, 9, to the east in Trench I, were all broadly contemporary with the hearth complex.

Phases 2 and 3

A compact deposit of ironstone fragments, including thin loamy lenses, 0.3–0.4m thick, were interpreted by the excavator as a metalled road some 5m wide, running west-east, 16/B44 in Trench Id, and 16 across the west end of Trench I. (Further east both the bailey bank and the underlying pre-castle stratigraphy had been removed by later activity.) A dark grey loam, 9, containing pottery and animal bone, covered both the possible road surface and also much of the areas to the north, 11 in Trench Ie, and south, 9 in trenches Ia and Ib.

Along the southern and northern margins of the road, deep pits cut through both the loam and the road surface. To the south this comprised pits 9a in Trench Ic, and pit 10 and well 5 in Trench I. To the north this comprised pit 13 in Trench Ie and probably similarly deep pits cut into natural in Trench I, pits 1, 2 , 3, 4 and 6 (Figs 16 & 17), which suggest that the road had continued further eastward. The dimensions and fill descriptions for the pits, as recorded in site notebook, are listed in Table 2.

The well, pit 5, was 4ft 6in (1.37m) diameter. It was excavated to a depth of 15ft (4.57m) and was probed to a depth of 20ft (6.1m), where it was wet, probably bottoming on or into the natural Lias clays. It was interpreted as having been open up to the time that the bailey bank was created, as while the lower fills were of fine silts, the upper 9ft (2.74m) of the fill had been "thrown in immediately before the bank was raised, and a hollow [void] 2ft 6in [0.76m] deep formed in the shaft through consolidation of this fill" (Alexander 1961).

Table 2: The dimensions and fills of late Saxon pits in Trench 1

Pit	Diameter ft in (m)	Depth ft in (m)	Fills
1	4' 6" (1.37m)	3' 8" (1.12m)	Brown loam, no ash, pottery and bone (11th-12th centuries)
2	4' 6" (1.37m)	–	Brown loam, red ash layer in bottom, pottery (10th–11th centuries)
3	5' (1.52m)	3' 6" (1.07m)	Black soil layer and brown loam, pottery (10th–11th centuries)
4	4' (1.22m)	3' 6" (1.07m)	Pottery (10th–11th centuries)
6	4' 6" (1.37m)	7' 6" (2.28m)	Much bone and pot
10	4' (1.22m)	6' (1.83m)	–

Fig 16: Late Saxon deposits beneath the bailey bank in trench I, 1961, pits 1 and 2 near the west edge of the castle ditch, looking north-west

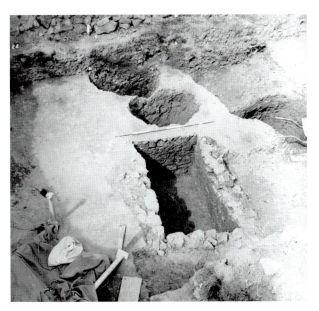

Fig 18: Fig 18: Burnt clay surface (Ie/9b) beneath the bailey bank, Trench Ie, 1964, looking east

Fig 17: Late Saxon deposits beneath the bailey bank in trench I, 1961, pits 3 and 4, looking north, with a Victorian stone-lined cess pit in the foreground

Phase 4: Industrial activity or site clearance

In Trench Ie, to the north, a final episode of burning comprised an extensive spread of sandy clay, 9b, with a heavily burnt surface, including areas of intense reddening interpreted as hearths (Figs 15 and 18). A similar layer to the south was seen only in section in Trenches Ib and Ic, B31. These burnt surfaces and also the fills of the latest pits, lay directly beneath the bailey bank of the castle.

In the excavations of 1961 the metalled surface was described as having "been burnt by a fierce fire" (Alexander 1961, 2). A further description paints a more vivid image as: "over some 200 sq ft [18.6 m^2] the ground was covered with wood ash and charcoal; in places it was reddened and in others large fragments of wood (the largest 2ft by 1ft by 5in [0.6m by 0.3m by 125mm]) lay where they had burnt." (Alexander 1964, 4)

Given that these deposits lay directly beneath the first rubble layers of the bailey bank, it would seem more likely that they were in fact the debris from fires that were part of the clearance and burning of timber structures to clear the ground for the construction of the castle defences, and that construction began by heaping material directly onto the burnt debris of the levelled buildings of the late Saxon/ Saxo-Norman town.

Conclusions

It would seem that the sequence excavated in the 1960s was broadly contemporary with Phases 3A-3C on the adjacent Chalk Lane site of the 1970s (Williams and Shaw 1981); the late Saxon cellared building and its smaller post-built successor (Fig 14). While metalworking debris came from the Chalk Lane excavations, no hearth structures were found, so the possible hearth complex in Trench Ic, Phase 1C, might provide a possible source for that metalworking debris.

If the interpretation of the metalled road running east-west is correct, it may imply some degree of more formal town planning coming into operation either within the late Saxon period or perhaps the post-Conquest prior to the construction of the castle, as has been suggested with the boundary ditch systems to the south beneath the Outer Bailey (Chapman 2021b, this volume, 93–96).

The Rectory gardens: pits beneath the bailey bank to the north-east

On the north-eastern side of the castle, a length of the bailey bank in the rectory garden was levelled in 1964 to make way for a group of six residential blocks (Figs 19–21, D1–D6). These residential blocks lay largely across the castle ditch, but in two, D4 and D6, late Saxon pits, I–IX, and a modern well, were observed and partially excavated in the sides of the excavated foundation trenches. These features were described by Harold Frost in a letter to John Alexander, dated 5 November 1964:

"There are five deep pits on D6 [I-V], possibly four or five shallower pits of quite different character on D4, and one doubtful pit on D2…All five pits [on D6] produced pottery, three in fair quantity, III, IV and V. Most of the pottery is dark red to black shell tempered, wheel turned with a large variety of rim sections which are well formed [these will be St Neots type wares, and a sketch in the site notebook indicates that the group from pit IV included a distinctive inturned rim bowl], and in addition four pits, I, III, IV and V, have produced green glazed sherds with a cream or pinky-cream hard body [Stamford ware/ Northampton ware]. Pit I produced a small fragment of dark blue glass and Pit V part of a bronze pin with an ornamental [head] and a bronze ring with a small gap… Three at least of the D6 pits, I, II and V are much deeper than they are wide (V is 8' 9" [2.7m] deep from the top of the ironstone)…Only one of the pits on D4 goes down to the footing level. The fill of these pits is mainly fairly soft ash in many thin well defined strata and unlike the D6 pits, do not obviously promise many sherds or bones, although [Dennis] Jackson did in fact find three sherds of the shell tempered ware similar to the others…These pits tend to be wide shallow saucer shaped depressions."

The site note book contains detailed sketches of Blocks D6 and D4 showing the pits. In Block D6 pit IV, which was cut into ironstone natural, was 5ft 6in (1.7m) deep,

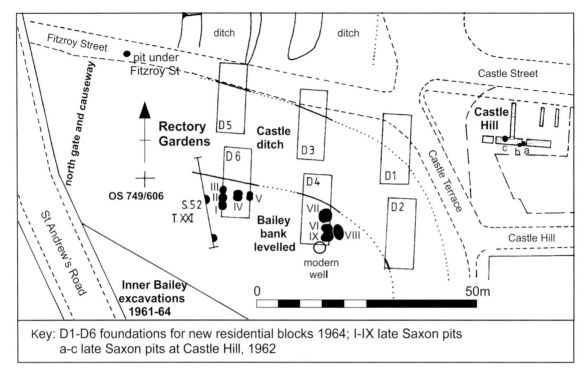

Fig 19: Late Saxon pits beneath the north-eastern arm of the bailey bank; seen 1964 in the foundation trenches for six new residential blocks, D1-D6

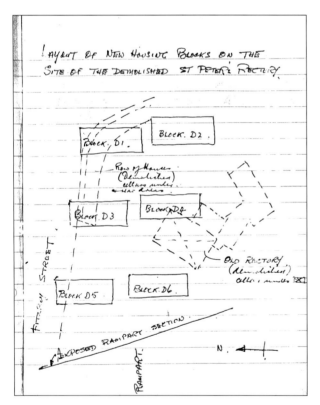

Fig 20: Sketch by Harold Frost showing the pits and the north-eastern arm of the castle

while pit III was 6ft (1.8m) deep and pit V was a pair of intercutting pits, with a combined diameter of 6ft (1.8m). The pits in Block D4 were typically of larger diameter,

but shallower, with Pit VIII spanning some 10ft (3.0m) although not necessarily a single cut. The fill of pit VII was of "*dark brown loam containing stones, pottery, bone, charcoal etc, without any clearly defined stratification, except for a continuous thin black layer just above the bottom, and scattered thin black patches throughout. There was very little pottery or bone in the bottom 12in (0.3m)*" (Fig 21).

To the west, the late Saxon ground surface was exposed but not investigated, although at the base of the section across the bailey bank in the Rectory gardens, a further two pits were visible in the section (Figs 19–21, S.52).

A further pit was seen in the side of a sewer trench beneath Fitzroy Street, to the west of block D5, when the road was being removed to make way for the new development. The pit was oval, 2ft 6in by 3ft 6in (0.76m by 1.1m) diameter and 2ft (0.6m) deep, with steep sides and a flat base (Fig 22).

Given the rescue, if not salvage, archaeology context of the work in the Rectory gardens, it must be remembered that the pits that were seen and recorded by virtue of being disturbed by the construction trenches for the new buildings, would have been only a fraction of the pits likely to have existed across this area, along with many other smaller pits and postholes of which no traces would have been visible in the circumstances.

It is also possible that in the intervening areas between the six blocks of housing further late Saxon features may well survive in places and, of course, the lower parts of the castle ditch will certainly survive beneath the housing. This area could therefore repay archaeological examination if these buildings were ever to be levelled and replaced.

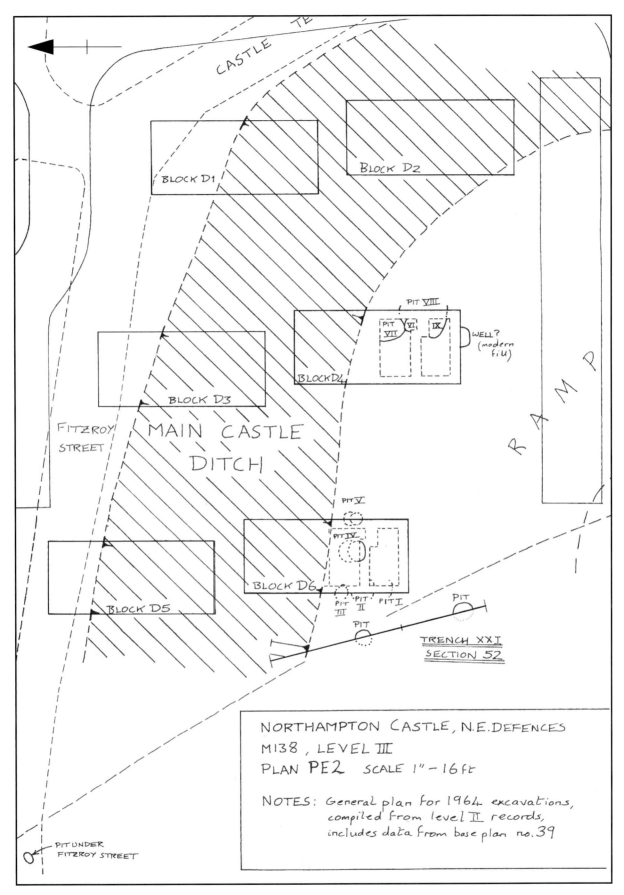

Fig 21: Extract from 1980s archive plan, compiling details of late Saxon pits and the castle ditch as recorded in the 1960s site plans and notebooks

161

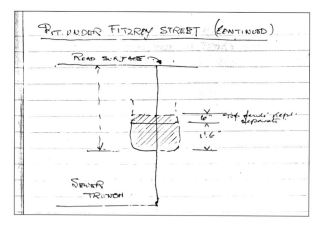

Fig 22: Sketch by Harold Frost showing the pit
beneath Fitzroy Street in 1964

Late Saxon pits beneath the Castle Hill mound are described in Part 2, within the section on Castle Hill and its archaeology.

Other Anglo-Saxon settlement in the environs of the castle

The primary objective of the excavations carried out in the vicinity of the castle during the 1970s and early 1980s was to examine as fully as possible evidence for the development of the town during the Anglo-Saxon period, and the archaeological evidence for the early medieval town is reviewed in this volume (Williams *et al* 2021, 25–77).

Most significantly, excavation of the St. Peter's Street area revealed a major middle Anglo-Saxon timber hall, dating to the late 7th to early 8th centuries, later replaced by a stone-built hall, and flanked to the west and east by the churches of St Peter and St Gregory, denoting that Northampton had become a town of regional importance.

The best preserved sequence of domestic occupation was found on the Chalk Lane site, where the bailey bank had sealed and protected the pre-castle levels from later disturbance. Two phases of early/middle Saxon occupation were identified, followed by three phases of late Saxon occupation: with a substantial post-built structure with a cellar, and other structures; a general soil horizon; and a final phase with a smaller post-built structure and numerous pits (Williams and Shaw 1981: Fig 14). During the late Saxon period various industrial activities had been practised in this area, including silver and (probably) copper alloy working. Numerous crucible fragments were found, as well as ferrous slag and hearth lining material. Tools and debris from textile manufacture and bone working were also found.

A further area of late Saxon occupation lay beneath the low lying south-west corner of the Outer Bailey excavated in 2013 (Chapman 2021b, this volume, 79–127). This area probably lay on the slopes immediately outside the town defences, and while there were boundary ditches, pits, two wells, there were no certain timber buildings to indicate direct occupation. Meanwhile, the substantial bone assemblage containing butchery and craft waste, and including bones from a badger, probably scavenging

on the dumped meat bones, indicate that for much of the 11th into 12th centuries this area was low lying close to the western river crossing, and suitable and convenient for the dumping of such noisome material as butchers waste.

Conclusion

The available evidence from excavated deposits beneath the castle, as fragmentary and as scattered as they are, leaves no doubt that dense late Saxon occupation had covered pretty much the entire extent of the castle area, with the 1970s excavation at Chalk Lane (Williams and Shaw 1981) and the 2013 excavation within the Outer Bailey (Chapman 2021b, this volume, 191–255) providing two more detailed 'snap shots' of small parts of the pre-Conquest town that was lost beneath the castle. The construction of the castle had therefore entailed the destruction of a substantial area of domestic settlement comprising timber houses, small workshops, pits, yards and cultivated areas, set within a network of ditched boundaries and gravelled roads.

This was all swept away with the construction of the castle.

A concise history of Northampton Castle

Having been a royal possession for the greater part of the medieval period there is a wealth of documentary evidence relating to the castle and events that took place within it. A concise summary of the castle's historical role is required to illustrate both its importance as a royal residence, a stronghold and the setting for events of national importance, including parliaments and trials, and also to provide a context for the physical structure of the castle and the story of the growth and decline of that structure that will be presented in Part 2.

The primary source for the historical summary presented here is the well documented study of the castle's history compiled in the early 20th century by the Rev R M Serjeantson (1907–8), who also made similar documentary studies for the religious institutions of medieval Northampton. This has been supplemented where necessary by reference to *The History of the Kings Works* (Brown *et al* 1963, **2**, 750f), the Victoria County History (Page (ed) 1930, **3**, 33f), and the Royal Commission volume on Northampton (RCHME 1985, 50 and M332f).

The history does, however, begin with two issues where the archaeological evidence is of relevance: firstly whether there was a pre-Conquest fortification on the site (as opposed to the presence of pre-Conquest town defences), and secondly who began the construction of the castle, and when.

A pre-Conquest fortification?

It has been stated that *"it is more than likely there was some sort of Saxon or Danish fortification in place on the site prior to the building of the Castle"* (Friends of

Northampton Castle website, *A Castle for Northampton*, viewed 9 March 2021).

The archaeological evidence for pre-castle occupation that we have, as discussed above, from around the north-eastern corner of the castle and also to the south from beneath the western end of the Outer Bailey, all relates to domestic occupation, so there is no archaeological evidence for the presence of a specific pre-Conquest fortification on the site. However, it must be recognised that for much of the area we have no evidence beyond the recovered finds and the noted presence of numerous pits when much of the castle was levelled for building in the late 19th century.

For the pre-Conquest town defences, the line established by the excavations at Green Street can be projected northwards, and this coincides with the line of the wall and the adjacent hermitage, as shown on Speed's map of 1610 (see Fig 2, in blue), which ran north to meet the revetment wall along the south side of the Outer Bailey. This coincidence lends support to the idea that the early town defences probably did continue along the western side of the town, along a line that would run across the western half of both the Outer Bailey and the Inner Bailey. In the modern topography, this is most closely marked by the western end of the raised station car park next to Black Lion Hill, although the modern revetment wall at the western end lies east of the original revetment wall of the late 19th century, when the first station was built.

The present vertical drop from the raised car park down to the forecourt in front of the new station might reflect a pre-existing slope in the natural ground level, and such a break of slope would have been the obvious location for a late Saxon bank, which would have enhanced the difference in height, with the ground dropping away to the west onto wet river margins, as demonstrated in the excavations of 2013 beneath the new station (Chapman 2021b, this volume, 129–136). The presence of the nearby river indicates that there was no need for an accompanying ditch, and this is supported by the presence of late Saxon domestic features on that low lying land, as recorded in 2013, which would have lain outside the late Saxon defensive bank.

In any future development, both the western end of the raised car park and the ground at the foot of this revetment up to the north wall of the new station should be a priority area for establishing whether the late Saxon town defences did originally continue northwards across what became the site of the castle. The walkway to the east between the new station and the revetment wall was never available for investigation in 2013, as it provided the main route onto the site throughout the excavation and the subsequent construction works, but there is no indication that the ground here was deeply disturbed during those works, so it remains an area of archaeological interest.

The building of a castle at Northampton, Simon de Senlis I or Henry I

Both historically and archaeologically the origin of the castle remains uncertain, although you might not

believe so given the frequent confident attributions not just to Simon de Senlis I, but also to the exact year. Wikipedia tells us it was 1084 (referencing *A Castle for Northampton*, Friends of Northampton Castle (FoNC), viewed in September 2019). Similarly, YouTube videos produced by FoNC tell us that *"in the late 11th century Simon de Senlis, earl of Northampton, was ordered to build a castle by William the Conqueror"*. (eg YouTube: Northampton Castle-Virtual tour, posted July 22, 2014).

This attribution to an order from William the Conqueror is particularly problematic, as there is no reference to a castle in the Domesday Survey, which was completed in 1086, and it seems special pleading to argue that it does not appear as the castle had not then been completed. Also, William the Conqueror died in 1087 and it is generally argued, although not documented, that Simon de Senlis was probably granted the earldom by William Rufus in around 1089.

We do know that immediately after the Norman Conquest the Earldom of Northampton was held by the Saxon Waltheof, who married King William's niece, the Countess Judith. Waltheof was executed for treason in 1076 and Maud, the daughter of Waltheof and Judith, subsequently married Simon de Senlis.

What we can state, is that there is no primary documentary evidence to tell us either when or by whom the construction of a castle at Northampton began. It is a great pity that there are no relevant court rolls for this period, as these might have established the advent of royal possession and expenditure. The earliest surviving Pipe Roll, which were maintained by the Exchequer to record the auditing of the sheriffs' accounts, dates from 1129–30, and there is a continuous series only from 1155–56. They do, however, provide much information about the nature and costs of works at Northampton Castle through the later 12th to 14th centuries.

The *Vita et Passio Waldevi Comitis'* (The life and passion of Count Waltheof) does credit Simon, the successor to Waltheof, with the construction of the castle, *"Qui primo construxit castrum de Northamptonia et abbatiam Sancti Andreae"* (who first constructed the castle at Northampton and the abbey of St Andrew) (Giles 1854, 18), which would imply a date around 1100. However, such biographical portraits, hagiography (lives-of-the-saints), cannot be relied on to contain only factual documentary evidence, as truth was always liable to be embroidered to enhance the story and the standing of the subject, so this is not a reliable primary document.

The first documentary reference to Henry I at Northampton is in 1106, when he is recorded as meeting his brother, Robert, Duke of Normandy, in an ill-fated attempt to settle their differences. The castle is not specifically mentioned, but it is generally assumed that this was the probable location for the meeting, which would imply that by then it contained buildings suitable for such a meeting. It therefore seems most likely that in 1106 the castle was a royal possession although perhaps still under construction at the time.

Following Simon's death, sometime between 1111 and 1113, the town reverted to the King, and it is recorded that in 1122 Henry I kept Easter at the castle in great state, indicating that it was then a royal possession (Serjeantson

1907–8, 2). The first reference to royal expenditure on the castle in the Pipe Rolls occurs slightly later, in 1130 when the Sheriff was ordered to pay the monks of St Andrew's an annual rent of 3s 8d for land which the King had taken into his castle (Pipe R. 31 Henry I, 135).

We must also ask the question, if Simon de Senlis I did start building a castle at Northampton, what was it that he might have built: a castle to the plan as we now know it or something much smaller, such as a motte and bailey castle largely in earth and timber? As we will see later, at its full extent Northampton Castle was large, a size fit for a king and most likely too large to be the work of an earl? Unfortunately, there is no unequivocal evidence for an earlier structure later taken into or removed by a larger royal castle.

It has recently been argued by Ingram (2020, 273–4) that the Castle Hill mound is that early motte, "hidden in plain sight", but this ignores the evidence from the excavations of the 1960s that the Castle Hill mound was created during the Civil War refurbishment of the approach to the north gate of the castle, and also that it overlay a medieval building. While the archaeological evidence is being published in this article in detail for the first time, there was much local publicity on the results of the excavations at the time (see Fig 11, lower right newspaper cutting, "*Archaeologist has solved the mystery of Northampton Castle Mound*").

A length of ditch was found in the 1960s beneath the buildings in the north-eastern corner of the Outer Bailey and at the time this was considered as possibly encircling a motte (Alexander 1963), but in 1964 excavations further to the north-east in the rectory gardens, where a length of the bailey bank was levelled, failed to produce any supporting evidence for this theory. As noted at the time, "*the motte is still unconfirmed*" (Alexander 1964, 5), but it is still a possibility that this ditch was related to some unfinished early castle construction.

The excavations within the Outer Bailey in 2013 have provided a more specific date range for that element of the castle. Pottery sealed beneath the castle deposits is dated to 1100–1150, and cereal grains from a hearth in a stone building within the Outer Bailey have been radiocarbon dated to 1120–1220 cal AD (60% confidence, Beta-410140, 890+/-30BP) (Chapman 2021c, this volume, 197, table 2). As a result, it is suggested that construction of the Outer Bailey was probably ongoing through the 1120s within the reign of Henry I. Brian Giggins (pers comm) has suggested that the land taken in from the monks of St Andrew's in 1130 may have been the land occupied by the Outer Bailey, which is possible but unproven, and it could perhaps equally have been land to the north of the Inner Bailey used to create a more secure and extensive barbican to protect the north gate.

In conclusion, we can suggest that Simon de Senlis I may have begun construction of a castle at Northampton in the late 11th century, but if so, it was probably swept aside in a much larger scheme of works initiated by Henry I, probably soon after 1100, with the Inner Bailey perhaps substantially complete by the time of his meeting with his brother in 1106. When Henry spent Christmas at the castle in 1122, the Outer Bailey may have been under construction, while the taking in of further land in

1130 was probably the final work to complete the castle, possibly related to works beyond the north gate that may have included the provision of a strengthened barbican. The newly suggested interpretation that the building beneath the Civil War Castle Hill mound was perhaps a gate house at the eastern end of an elongated barbican can be seen as part of such a strengthened barbican, with a gate that faced directly into the town to provide an imposing front to the medieval townsfolk approaching along the length of medieval Castle Lane, which ran to the original main north-south thoroughfare of Northampton, the Horsemarket.

The mid- to later 12th century: Stephen, Henry II and Richard I

King Stephen paid several visits to Northampton during his troubled reign (1135–1154). For his support of the King, Simon de Senlis II was granted the earldom and the town in 1138. Throughout that period Simon held the castle securely and loyally for the king through the troubled times of the Anarchy. He died in 1153 when, with his son being under age, the town reverted to the King. When Simon de Senlis III acquired the earldom in 1159 the town remained a royal borough.

After the accession of Henry II in 1154, the castle and town became a regular focus for events of national importance. No doubt the location of Northampton was a major factor in this, providing as it did a convenient central meeting place to gather the barons and the clergy. In 1157 a great council was held there to settle an ecclesiastical dispute.

In October 1164 the castle was to be the setting for the first documented treason trial, that of Thomas Becket, the Archbishop of Canterbury, perhaps the most dramatic single event in the history of the castle. The King was in residence at the castle and Becket at the Priory of St. Andrew's. The proceedings took place partly in the Great Hall and came to an end with the escape of Becket through the north gate of the town on his way to temporary exile in France, and subsequent death at Canterbury Cathedral following his return to England in 1170. There will be further mention of this trial within the description of the castle buildings in Part 2, as the contemporary accounts make mention of several buildings within the castle.

During the rebellion of 1173–1174 Northampton supported the King and in a short visit to England Henry II rallied his followers at Northampton, although in May 1174 the burgesses were defeated in battle before the walls of the town. Following his return to England in July of that year, Henry came to Northampton again, to receive the captured William the Lion, King of Scots and, five days later, the submission of the leading rebels. As part of the process of restoring order, a great council was held at the castle in 1176 at which the Assize of Northampton was passed. Another great council was held there in January of the following year.

In the reign of Richard I (1189–1199) Papal delegates came to Northampton in 1191 to settle a dispute between the Bishop of Durham and the Archbishop of Canterbury, the King's half-brother. Three years later a great council was held at the castle when Richard spent Easter there, after his return from captivity. Given the small amount of time that Richard spent in England during his reign, visits to Northampton Castle were also necessarily infrequent.

The 13th century, John, Henry III and Edward I

The reigns of John (1199–1216) and Henry III (1216–1272) seem to have marked the high point of the castle's history. When John succeeded his brother Richard, but before he came to England to assume the throne, it was to Northampton that the barons were summoned to swear their allegiance before his representatives. John himself visited the town at least thirty times during his short reign. In 1205 a great council was held at the castle, and in 1211 it was the scene of the meeting between the King and the papal legates Pandulph and Durandus, in their unsuccessful attempt to settle his dispute with the Pope and the Archbishop of Canterbury, Stephen Langton.

Northampton was heavily involved in the civil war of 1215. The town was seized by the rebel barons but, lacking siege engines, they failed to take the castle and withdrew after a fifteen day blockade. When the King finally agreed to the demands of the barons at Runnymead, Northampton was one of the four royal castles which John surrendered as a guarantee. When war broke out again only three months later, the castle was again held for the King and a second siege was raised by John's army of mercenaries.

Henry III, who was only nine years old when he succeeded his father, visited the castle in 1218 and again in 1222; but when in 1223 the Pope declared him of age, Faulkes de Breaute, the constable of Northampton, was one of those who refused to surrender custody of their castles. The rebel constables planned to meet at Northampton at Christmas, but were forestalled by Henry, who announced his own intention of keeping the feast there. Under threat of excommunication by the Archbishop of Canterbury the confederates came to the King to surrender, all except de Breaute himself, who was subsequently found guilty of appropriating other men's lands and exiled to France.

The castle continued to be favoured as a royal residence, and the Liberate Rolls between 1248 and 1252, as well as a survey commissioned in 1253, record in some detail a series of additions and improvements to the King's houses there, as well as repairs to the defences.

The importance of Northampton and its castle as a stronghold is underlined by the fact that in 1264–1265, during the civil war between the King and rebel barons led by Simon de Montfort, the town was attacked and changed hands three times, returning to the King finally after the death of de Montfort at the battle of Evesham in 1265.

The King and Queen spent Christmas of that year at the castle, and two parliaments were held there, in January and October of the following year, and another two years later in 1268.

During the reign of Edward I (1272–1307) the castle saw less activity. But the continuing importance of Northampton may be gauged by the fact that when David, Prince of Wales, was hung, drawn and quartered in 1283,

Northampton was one of the four towns in England to which the quarters were sent, the others being York, Winchester and Bristol, while the head went to London. Prior to that, in the same year, the parliament summoned to provide funds for the King's wars in Wales was held partly in Northampton.

The 14th century, Edward II, Edward III and Richard II

Arrangements for the funeral of Edward I and for the coronation and marriage of his son, Edward II, in 1308 were made at a parliament in Northampton, and the new King stayed at the castle. Further parliaments were held there in 1309, 1318 and 1320.

The detailed accounts rendered by Nicholas de Segrave, constable from 1307 to 1315, provide a picture of the daily functioning of the castle at this time. Expenses included the salary of the deputy constable and the wages of a watchman and porter, as well as an extra eight archers and four crossbowmen maintained for the defence of the castle during a time of tension within the realm. Receipts included sums for the payment of the castle guards and for the guarding of prisoners committed by the sheriff, as well as the rents due for herbage (grazing rights) in the castle ditches and the castle meadow, and rents from a fishery.

By the reign of Edward III (1327–1377) the role of the castle as a centre for affairs of state was diminishing. Parliaments met there in 1328, when the first Statute of Northampton was passed and the King laid formal claim to the throne of France, and in 1338, when the future Black Prince, then aged eight years, presided over the assembly to raise funds for the war with France.

The King visited in 1342, when a tournament was held, but between that date and 1380, when the last Northampton parliament was held, under Richard II, the only extant records relate to people committed to the castle gaol. This shift of emphasis in the second half of the 14th century is seen also in an order from Richard II in 1385 for the making of a house for the King's gaoler. In 1391 the constableship of the castle reverted to the sheriff of the county, further emphasising the decline in the importance of the castle as a royal residence and fortress.

The 15th and 16th centuries: the Justices' hall and the gaol

By the beginning of the 15th century, with the castle having ceased to be of any great importance as a royal possession, the only buildings maintained then and subsequently were the gaol and the Justices' hall used for sessions of the courts. In 1451 the various rents due to the castle and thus to the Crown, were granted by Henry VI to a Robert Caldecote. This practice continued until 1629 when Charles I sold the fee of the property to Gilbert North Esq, of Westminster, and the castle ceased finally to be the property of the Crown.

The 17th century and the Civil War

During the Civil War of 1642–1651 the castle played a minor role. The town supported the Parliamentarian cause and both the town and the castle defences were renovated to some extent. The archaeological record indicates that the Castle Hill mound was constructed as part of these works, and it would have provided a raised platform on high ground on which to mount ordnance to cover the approach to the north gate. However, the only active use of the castle through the war was as a gaol for prisoners.

In 1662, after the restoration of the Monarchy, Charles II ordered the slighting of the town defences to ensure that they could not be used again and, according to a contemporary account, some part of the castle walls was pulled down (Serjeantson 1907–8, 48).

The courthouse and prison buildings were in use until 1671, but following the Northampton fire of 1675 even these functions were finally moved to new buildings within the town. With this event the castle ceased to have any practical function and became an unoccupied ruin, and no doubt a convenient stone-quarry for the rebuilding of the town.

Town maps and antiquarian interest

In this section we look at the broad base of the physical evidence through time that defines the overall plan of the castle. Once that general plan has been established, in Part 2 we will look at the more detailed evidence for individual elements of the castle plan and its buildings.

Following its final minor role in the story of the Civil War in the mid-17th century, the history of the castle can be followed at a broad brush level through the successive town maps, with the later maps running parallel to the beginnings of antiquarian interest from the mid-19th century. The antiquarian records show a growing urgency through decades of gradual encroachment, as the Victorian shoe town expanded, and even more so through the final destructive act, as the construction of the new railway and St Andrew's Road removed the greater part of the then surviving remains in 1879–80.

Town maps

The plan of Northampton in 1610 by John Speed contains the only pictorial representation of the castle prior to the slighting of its defences (Fig 23a). Another early plan by a French artist, dated c.1650, was most probably only a debased version of Speed's map (Serjeantson 1907–8, 23). The portrayal of the castle by Speed is in broad agreement with later plans, as well as providing some supplementary information, if of uncertain reliability. It shows the circuit of the Inner Bailey wall with the gate house to the north and towers to the west, south and east. The schematic nature of the drawing is indicated by its depiction of a rectangular tower to the south, which is known to have been round, serving as the prison in the 17th century (Serjeantson 1907–8, 56). The single building in the south-west corner of the Inner Bailey must

be the Justices' hall, which remained in use until the later 17th century, although a more complex pattern of building walls were recorded in this area in the late 19th century during the levelling of the Inner Bailey, see below. While Speed may have omitted some partially standing ruins, it would seem that other buildings within the Inner Bailey had been levelled by this time. To the south, the Outer Bailey wall and earthworks are also shown, along with the hermitage and a length of town wall running across what is now Black Lion Hill, and then uphill to meet the Outer Bailey wall, a further wall and two buildings lay between the hermitage and the southern end of West Bridge.

The slighting of the castle defences in 1662, following the reformation of the monarchy, was followed by the fire of 1675, which destroyed much of the town and led to the building of a new sessions house within the town. The abandoned castle ruin, as previously noted, was probably used as a stone quarry during the rebuilding of the town.

By 1680 the majority of the castle site had been bought by the Hazelrigg family, and a survey of the property in 1743 provided the first measured plan of the castle site (Fig 23b; Serjeantson 1907–8, 54). The castle was then in much the condition in which it was to remain until the early 19th century. The earthwork of the ditch around the north-eastern and eastern sides of the Inner Bailey (the Upper Roundabout) by then partially silted up and grassed over; the western defences (the Nether Roundabout); while both the Inner and Outer Baileys had become orchards also serving as pasture. The main access to the Inner Bailey was still from the north, on the site of the medieval gate. The earthworks to the north, last refurbished during the Civil War, stood on a roughly triangular area of open ground, called The Fort in 1680 and later known as Castle Ground (Page (ed) VCH, **3**, 35; Serjeantson 1907–8, 54).

The only significant innovation between 1610 and 1743 lay to the south-east, where there was a cluster of buildings in and beyond the eastern corner of the Outer Bailey. There was also a walled garden and a wall running northwards to meet the south-east corner of the Inner Bailey, cutting off the eastern arm of the Inner Bailey ditch from the southern arm. These features are not as fully shown on the later maps (Fig 23c-d & Fig 24e) but appear in much the same form on Henry Dryden's survey of 1854, where all the walls at the eastern end of the Outer Bailey are noted as modern (Fig 24f & Fig 31). It would seem therefore that the medieval wall at the eastern end of the Outer Bailey had definitely been lost by 1854, and it may have gone as early as the middle of the 18th century.

In addition to the town maps of 1746, 1807 and 1847 (Fig 23c-d & Fig 24e), a schematic sketch plan and views of the castle ruins accompanied the first antiquarian description of the site, published in the Gentleman's Magazine in 1800 (Serjeantson 1907–8, 57 and Giggins 1999, 22, fig 3.3). This sketch plan tells us that in 1800 the eastern ditch was still an open earthwork with a terminal to the east, as both the map evidence and the documentary evidence tells us that by the early 19th century the eastern arm of the castle ditch had been fully infilled and built over, with two rows of small terraced houses and the rectory at the north-east corner (Fig 24e & f).

The line of the original wall at the eastern end of the Outer Bailey is unknown. It may have coincided with the

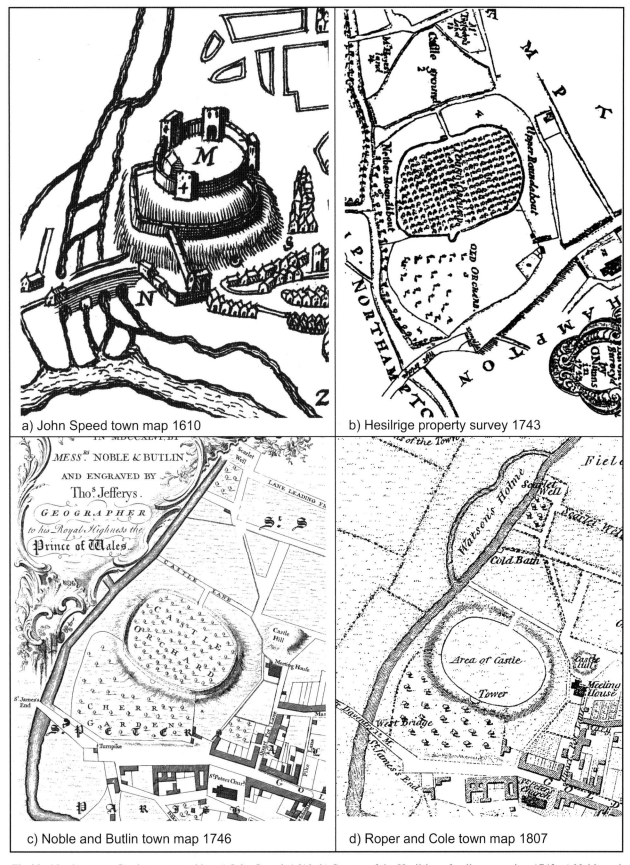

a) John Speed town map 1610

b) Hesilrige property survey 1743

c) Noble and Butlin town map 1746

d) Roper and Cole town map 1807

Fig 23: Northampton Castle as mapped by: a) John Speed, 1610; b) Survey of the Hesilrigge family properties, 1743; c) Noble and Butlin town map, 1746; d) Roper and Cole town map, 1807

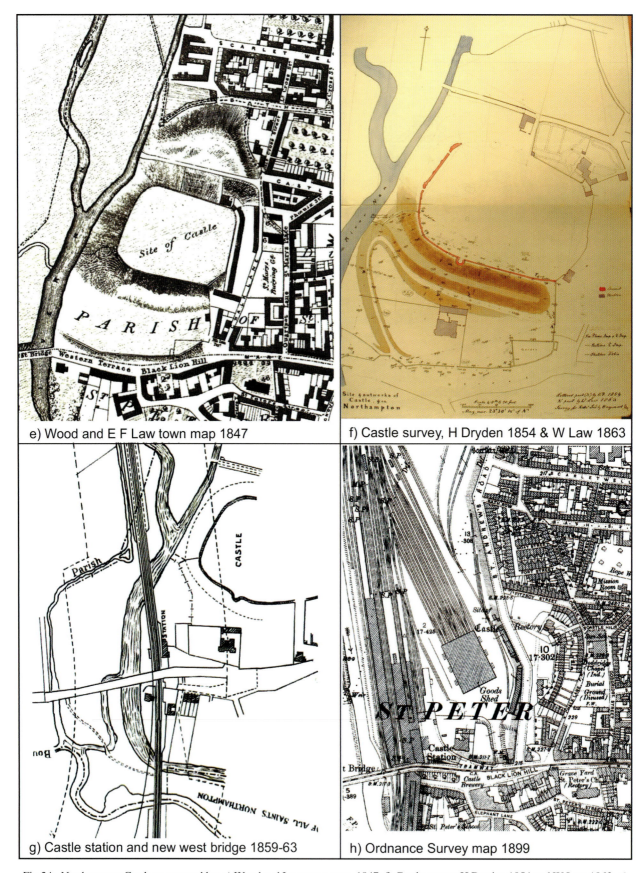

e) Wood and E F Law town map 1847

f) Castle survey, H Dryden 1854 & W Law 1863

g) Castle station and new west bridge 1859-63

h) Ordnance Survey map 1899

Fig 24: Northampton Castle as mapped by: e) Wood and Law town map, 1847; f) Castle survey H Dryden 1854 and W Law 1863: g) Castle station and new west bridge 1859–63; h) Ordnance Survey map 1899, showing the new station and the new St Andrew's Road

later boundary wall or it may have lain a little further to the east. Speed in 1610 shows the eastern Outer Bailey wall running to the wall of the Inner Bailey, so we must assume that either the wall ran down into the southern arm of the Inner Bailey ditch and up the other side or that there was an early causeway here, with the later boundary wall, as recorded by Dryden, running across the level ground either on a pre-existing causeway or on ground where a continuous castle ditch had been infilled to create a causeway.

This is of significance as Brian Giggins has argued for the presence of a causeway at the south-east corner of the Inner Bailey throughout the medieval period (Giggins 1999, 89, 93, 95 & 97, figs 6.7–6.10), and has also postulated the presence of a gate at the south-east corner of the Outer Bailey to provide direct access from the Inner Bailey and the Outer Bailey onto Black Lion Hill (ibid, fig 6.7, 27 Gate?).

There is no indication on any of the maps of any opening or gateway at the south-east corner of the inner or Outer Baileys, and there is no reason why the eastern terminal of the southern ditch of the Inner Bailey was not merely a product of the infilling of the eastern arms of the Inner and Outer Bailey ditches, which had been completed shortly after 1800. This is also implied by the results of the excavations at Chalk Lane in the 1970s, which recorded the inner edge of the castle ditch running almost up to the 19th-century terminal at the east end of the southern arm (see Part 2). We must conclude, therefore, that there is no evidence to indicate that the causeway at the south-east corner of the Inner Bailey was an original feature, or that there were eastern gateways providing access from the Inner Bailey to the Outer Bailey and onto Black Lion Hill.

It can also be suggested that the supposed gateways to the south-east are rendered unnecessary by known posterns in the Inner and Outer Bailey curtain walls, which would have provided direct access to the west bridge. The 19th-century records show a postern gate to the west of the south tower providing access between the Inner and Outer Baileys, while the excavations in the Outer Bailey in 2013 indicate that there was probably a postern gate at the south-west corner of the Outer Bailey (Chapman 2021d, this volume, figs 9, 11 & 12), which coincides with an opening at the western end of the Outer Bailey wall recorded by Dryden in 1854 (Fig 24f & 31).

The town maps of 1746 and 1807 also show the Castle Hill mound, although it did not appear on Speed's map of 1610. This artificial mound lay immediately outside the north-east corner of the Inner Bailey and the idea that it might have been an early motte has been recently resurrected, as previously noted. The archaeological evidence to show it was a Civil War construction will be presented and discussed in Part 2.

Antiquarian interest and the coming of the railway

The major period of active destruction of the castle took place during the 19th century, and this process was well documented in the local press, while in 1859 the Illustrated London News carried a short description of the ruins and a view of the south tower. This material has been summarised previously by Scriven (1879–80, 204–10) and Serjeantson (1907–8, 54–5).

In the early part of the 19th century the Castle Hill mound to the north-east of the castle was largely levelled and built over (Fig 24e), with the material probably contributing to the infilling the eastern arm of the castle ditch, along with material from parts of the eastern bailey bank that must have also been levelled at this time to create space for the new houses. This is described in more detail in Part 2, within the account of the excavations at Castle Hill.

It is from the mid-19th century that antiquarian and local interest is supplemented by the first true archaeological survey and recording.

The first railway and the new West Bridge

In response to plans drawn up in 1853 to rebuild the West Bridge as part of the construction of a railway line, in 1854 Sir Henry Dryden compiled a plan of the earthworks (Fig 24f) and elevations of the revetment wall along the south side of the Outer Bailey, as these were to be destroyed to enable the straightening of the approach to the new West Bridge. There is a description and illustrations of the southern Outer Bailey wall as recorded by Dryden in the report on the excavations of 2013 in the Outer Bailey (Chapman 2021d, this volume, 199–200, figs 6–8).

By the time of this survey there was already a large house within the Outer Bailey, a new rectory for St Peter's church (Figs 24f and 25).

A council meeting, as reported in the *Mercury* on 16 April 1853, had considered the proposal to build a new West Bridge, with the Council and Earl Spencer to contribute £1,000 each, with the work being done by the London and North Western Railway Company, who would also meet most of the cost (Goodfellow 1980, 152).

The Mercury reported on 13 September 1856 that, *"Operations have commenced for the formation of the railway which is to connect this town with Market Harborough. A temporary bridge of wood has been constructed with great celerity across the River Nene parallel with the West Bridge and a little north of it. The venerable West Bridge itself will soon be demolished. Parts of the structure are believed to be of very remote antiquity"*. (from Goodfellow 1980, 152)

The new bridge, opened in December 1857, was 30ft (9.1m) wide compared to the 18ft (5.5m) of the old bridge and stood much higher. This required a new raised approach, and the old approach along Western Terrace became a cu-de-sac to the south of the higher and wider approach to the new bridge, which to the north overlay the south-western corner of the Outer Bailey wall and part of

Fig 25: Photograph of the old west bridge in 1853, looking north-east, with the new rectory in the background, the first new building, a rectory, within the Outer Bailey of the castle

a possible postern gate, with the bailey wall further east removed in the straightening of Black Lion Hill.

While only indirectly relevant to the castle, we include a view of the old west bridge in 1853 (Fig 25). As noted by local historian Ruth Thomas, this is certainly one of the earliest, if not the earliest, photograph of Northampton. In the background can be seen the recently built and rather fine rectory for St Peter's, with its corner turret, sitting near the centre of the Outer Bailey. A newspaper article in the Northampton Mercury, dated 19 February 1859 commented, *"the lover of the picturesque will miss the old bridge which retained some of its earliest features and was an attractive object from the meadows with its many*

arches of varied form and its huge dissimilar buttresses. It had seen Northampton through many changing fortunes for when it was demolished the traces of its drawbridge were discovered."

The new railway was considered to be noisy and intrusive, so the rectory was converted to a school and a house, Castle Cottage, built over the north-east corner of the Inner Bailey earlier in the century, was purchased as the new rectory. The house/school in the Outer Bailey was sold to the new railway company in 1879, and later became Warner's Hotel (Serjeantson 1907–8, 54 footnote). The rectory to the north-east was demolished in the early

Fig 26: Sketch of the castle from the west by Henry Dryden in 1854, with the western and southern arms of the curtain wall coloured brown, centre-left, and the wall fronting the Outer Bailey bank above Black Lion Hill, right, and also showing the new rectory within the Outer Bailey, right

Fig 27: The south-eastern corner of the curtain wall, looking east towards the southern circular bastion, hidden in the trees, and the earthwork of the castle ditch, with the Outer Bailey out of view to the right

1960s prior to the archaeological excavations and a new wave of rebuilding (see Figs 5 & 6).

Before the intrusion of the first railway, Dryden had also taken the opportunity to sketch the view of the castle from the west using a "camera", to project an image onto a screen that he could then trace (Fig 26). He coloured the castle walls for emphasis. To the far left is the western wall, with the postern gate and the scars of the supporting buttresses. It is only to the far right that we can see the wall along the south side of the Outer Bailey, along with another view of the new rectory built within the Outer Bailey. While this scene was to undergo the first stage of its transformation in the 1850s, we must remember that while the view from the west was then still picturesque, as we have already seen through the town maps that the north-eastern corner of the Inner Bailey defences had already been levelled and built over some decades earlier, with just remnants of the bailey bank surviving behind the houses and in the garden of Castle Cottage, later the new rectory.

The first excavation 1863

The Hazlerigg family had been selling parts the castle grounds from the earlier 19th century, and the final portions were sold in June 1861, some 12 acres comprising: the Inner Bailey; the castle ground (the Fort) to the north; the Castle Holme island to the north-west; and the Nether Roundabout, the slopes down to the moat and river on the north and west sides of the Inner Bailey. This was all sold to Samuel Walker and in March 1863 he undertook the first recorded digging on the site. A considerable amount of good stone was unearthed, but the only addition to an understanding of the site was the discovery in the south-east corner of the Inner Bailey of a vaulted chamber with a circular central column base, which will

be described in Part 2 in the account of the castle buildings. These remains were photographed by W Law, and in the same year he also surveyed the Inner Bailey. It was this plan to which Dryden added his earlier plan of the Outer Bailey (see Fig 24f and 31). He also surveyed the concentric ditches of the Fort, encircling the north gate of the castle, before they were levelled and built over, and this survey was added to the plan of the castle published by E F Law in 1879 (see Fig 32). The earliest photographs of the castle were taken in the same year by C Law (Figs 27 & 28a).

The first station and its railway line, which ran across the south-western corner of the Outer Bailey, had left the Inner Bailey largely unaffected (Fig 24g). In this quiet interlude there was a last opportunity to record more picturesque views of the undisturbed parts of the castle, such as the crumbling castle wall along the south side of the Inner Bailey (Fig 27) and views of the western defences standing above the river (Fig 28a & b).

The destruction of the Inner Bailey 1879–80

While the eastern defences and the Outer Bailey had been encroached upon during the first half of the 19th century, the interior of the Inner Bailey remained intact until 1879, when the building of a new railway, a new station, a large goods shed and sidings, as well as the creation of St Andrew's Road along the eastern margin of the railway site, resulted in the total destruction of all but the north-eastern corner of the interior of the Inner Bailey.

To the west, the river channel that had formed part of the western defences was infilled, and the flow was diverted westward into a new straight canalised course. To the east, the creation of the extensive levelled area required for the railway works involved the lowering of the ground

Fig 28: Even after the appearance of the first railway the western side of the Inner Bailey still formed a picturesque ruin suitable for both photography a), with boys fishing in the river, and b) oil painting, as here by E Law in 1878, the year before work began on the demolition of the castle

surface by several metres, and thus the removal of all building remains.

As a result, the entire topography of the area was completely altered in a single year. While the team of workmen progressively dismantled the remains of the

Fig 29: The demolition of the castle ruins in 1879, showing a horse drawn wagon on rails inside the western curtain wall, including the postern gate, with soil removed to the level of the wall foundations

castle and terraced into the hillside, local architect E F Law drew plans and elevations of the exposed walls and also photographed some of them (Law 1879–80 and Serjeantson 1907–8). The castle earthworks and numerous pits and wells, mainly late Saxon in date, were described by R G Scriven (1879–80 and 1881–82), and the collections of recovered finds were studied by S Sharp (1881–82) and deposited in Northampton Museum. A single find from this time, a stylised chess piece, appears within an overview of medieval chess pieces from Northampton (Chapman 2021e, this volume 403–409, fig 4).

The major features examined and recorded at this time were: the western wall of the Inner Bailey with its postern gate (Fig 29), which had been rebuilt from ground level after the original wall set on top of the bailey bank had collapsed in 1266; the south tower and associated lengths of the southern curtain wall (Fig 27); and the remnants of buildings across the south-west quarter of the Inner Bailey, which will all be described in detail in Part 2.

Excavations and survey from 1961

The Inner Bailey and Castle Hill 1961–64

The context of these excavations, which lie at the centre of this study, lay in the proposed post-war clearance and rebuilding around the junction of Castle Terrace and Fitzroy Street at the northern end of Chalk Lane, and the threat of a new road running eastwards from St Andrew's Road through the surviving north-eastern corner of the interior of the Inner Bailey, as outlined previously (see Figs 5 & 6). These threats provided the opportunity to investigate the north-east corner of the interior of the Inner Bailey, which had not been built over (see Fig 9), along with lengths of the bailey bank and ditch to the east, and the Castle Hill mound to the north-east (see Fig 8).

Following the excavations of the early 1960s, the trenches in the north-east corner of the Inner Bailey were eventually backfilled, and as the road scheme that was to cut across this area was cancelled, the area was grassed over and survives in that state today, backed by a truncated remnant of the bailey bank behind the houses fronting onto Chalk Lane. The mound between this area and the Chalk Lane car park is a spoil heap from the excavations in 1963–64.

The corner at the junction of Castle Terrace and Castle Street, where trenches were cut into the Castle Hill mound in 1962 is still undeveloped, but now largely enclosed as a fenced garden (see Figs 8 and 38a). Neighbouring properties to the east that also overlay the mound, particularly The Golden Lion public house, have been redeveloped, apparently without any requirement for relevant pre-emptive archaeological work. Given the depth of the significant deposits, neither test pits or a watching brief would have been likely to produce any useful results, but on the positive side, unless deep cellars were part of the new development, the base of the mound and anything beneath may lie deep enough to have escaped extensive damage, although it will now be inaccessible for the foreseeable future.

The northern arm of the castle ditch still lies beneath the six blocks of low rise housing that were built in the 1960s across the area once occupied by the Victorian rectory and its gardens, and as has already been noted with respect to the late Saxon deposits, only the uppermost fills of the castle ditch will have been disturbed (Figs 19–21). So this site still retains archaeological potential in terms of both the castle ditch and late Saxon features under the former bailey bank, although being shallower these would have been liable to rather more disturbance. The former area of the defences around the north gate, The Fort, has also been built over again, although it also partly lies beneath the broad grass verge alongside St Andrew's Road.

Excavations and recording 1970s and 1980s

Watching brief 1971

In 1971 the retaining wall along the east side of St Andrew's Road adjacent to the area excavated by Dr Alexander, was lowered and the ground behind battered back. A watching brief was maintained during this work by the Northampton Development Corporation archaeologist Dennis Mynard. The truncated western ends of several walls were located, most but not all of which could be equated with walls recorded by Dr Alexander, including part of the north gate. The results were summarised in *South Midlands Archaeology*, **2**, 1972, 19:

"NORTHAMPTON CASTLE

During January and February 1971 a watching brief was kept on the lowering of the St Andrew's Road wall and the battering back of the area behind it. Only where the wall runs through the site of the Inner Bailey of the castle were features of archaeological interest revealed, and these largely confirmed the results of Alexander's excavation in 1961, 1963 and 1964.

In all, the footings and/or lower courses of eleven walls were uncovered and recorded. Three were parts or continuations of Alexander's walls while four could be associated with buildings excavated by him, and one was part of the north gate. The other three were not related to hitherto known structures.

Two patches of burning between the walls could have been hearths but had no associated finds, and the top of a well noted by Alexander was partially demolished in the course of the work.

Four small collections of pottery were recovered. A St Neots rim came from the old soil level below one wall, 12th-13th century sherds occurred in the rubble filling of another, and sherds of a 13th-14th-century Potterspury jug in the destruction layer of a third. Finally, late-19th-century pieces were found in the rubble fill behind the St Andrew's Road wall, erected c.1880."

The features exposed were more fully described in a set of archive notes prepared by Dennis Mynard, 12 February 1971. These were accompanied by an annotated plan (No A50/M.18/1), which the author has not seen.

Chalk Lane excavation 1975–78

Extensive excavations within the bounds of the castle were undertaken by the Northampton Development Corporation Archaeological Unit, 1975–78, along the west side of Chalk Lane and immediately south of the 1960s trenches, currently the Chalk Lane car park (Williams and Shaw 1981). The objective of this excavation was to examine pre-castle levels formerly protected by the bailey bank, which here had been levelled in the 19th century. However, there was also a robber trench of a length of medieval wall at right angles to the bailey bank, which was probably situated at or beyond the southern end of

the great hall and royal apartments, and was perhaps even part of the boundary around the royal court. The south-eastern corner of the Inner Bailey ditch was also located and trial trenches to the east located what is probably the northern end of the eastern arm of the Outer Bailey ditch (see Fig 35, and see Part 2 for details and illustrations).

Watching brief 1988

In 1988 Mike Shaw and Alan Williams of the Northamptonshire Archaeology Unit maintained a watching brief during groundworks for the construction of a car park in the area of the former railway goods-shed to the north-east of the station. An island of preserved deposits was located on the west side of St Andrew's Road around the northern arm of the castle ditch where a new access road, still in use today, was being created, as reported in *South Midlands Archaeology*, **19**, 1989, 29–30.

"Northampton, Castle Station (SP 74856064)

The construction of an exit-road from the new car park on to St Andrew's Road at the north involved cutting approximately 1m off the edge of a bank of earth which ran parallel with the main road and was c.2m high. It was assumed to be a recent dump, but at its southern end the bailey ditch of the castle survived to a width of 16m. As exposed, the upper filling was entirely of nineteenth-century material which had been dumped from the construction of the railway-extension, but otherwise the ditch was observed to survive below the level of the car park which effectively seals the earlier deposits. A series of late Saxon deposits was present in the bank-section to the north of the bailey ditch. They comprised a separate ditch, 4m wide and 1m deep, which was filled with grey-brown clay, in addition to overlying layers. A hearth overlay the north side of the ditch and a shallow ?trench occurred at the south. The late Saxon levels did not survive at the level of the car park to the west, but a 10–20m wide bank of earth between the exit-road and St Andrew's Road can be expected to contain contemporary deposits."

As this summary notes, a surviving bank of earth between the exit road and St Andrew's Road *"can be expected to contain contemporary deposits"*, but much of this area is probably that now occupied by a more recent overflow car, so much of that mound would may have been levelled for the creation of this small car park without further investigation.

The new railway station 2012–15

With plans for the building of a new station moving forward, Northamptonshire Archaeology was commissioned by the West Northamptonshire Development Corporation, on behalf of Network Rail, to conduct a desk-based assessment of land at the station, which took in much of the former extent of Northampton Castle (Walker *et al* 2011). A number of areas where medieval deposits or features might survive were identified, but given the known levelling of the castle in 1879–80 and the low level of the forecourt in the front of the station, it was considered unlikely that any formerly above ground deposits could have survived in this area, although deeper cut features might have.

The assessment of 2011 was demonstrated to be false in October 2012, when Northamptonshire Archaeology was commissioned to excavate a single trial trench within the forecourt car park in front of the then station. There was a one week timetable with the condition that the minimum number of parking spaces should be taken out of commission while the rest of the car park remained in use. The location chosen was later seen to have lain within the footprint of the former cast-iron and glass awning in front of the Victorian station, under which horse-drawn carriages could stop under cover, and the pits that had held the cast iron upright stanchions supporting the awning were found in the subsequent open area excavations (see Chapman, 2021d, this volume, fig 53).

Beneath the cobbles of the Victorian station forecourt there was a depth of brown soils and beneath that a length of stone wall was surrounded by deposits containing pottery dating to the 12th century, contemporary with the first century of the use of the castle. A deeper sondage at one end of the trench also located a small late Saxon pit under a buried soil horizon.

Having demonstrated the presence of significant archaeology beneath the car park, an open area excavation was undertaken from March to June 2013, exposing the remains of a small stone building within the Outer Bailey of the castle and abutting the bailey bank, with a nearby metalled road surface running south-westwards (Fig 30). Below the castle deposits there were also late Saxon ditches and pits and a soil horizon containing a significant animal bone deposit from butchery and craft activities.

The details of the trial trenching of 2012 are available in Chapman 2012, while for the excavation of 2013 there is an initial assessment report, Chapman 2016, and a full client report, Chapman 2018, which also includes results from the watching brief during the levelling of the old station in 2014–15. The results are also published within this volume as follows: the residual flints (Chapman 2021a, 17–24), the pre-castle deposits (Chapman 2021b, 79–127), and the features pertaining to the Outer Bailey of the castle (Chapman 2021d, 191–255), all drawn from the client reports.

It also needs recording that the impetus that led towards the commissioning of the trial trench which demonstrated the presence of significant castle remains, may not have

Fig 30: General view of the excavations in May 2013, looking north, showing a medieval building under excavation and the 1960s railway station

happened without pressure from various local individuals and particularly from the Friends of Northampton Castle (FoNC).

Recent surveys and a test pit 2017–19

The most recent work at the castle comprises topographic and geophysical surveys by MOLA (Museum of London Archaeology) Northampton (formerly Northamptonshire Archaeology) on behalf of Northampton Borough Council in 2017–18, to assess the below ground survival of deposits relating to the castle along the eastern side of St Andrew's Road; encompassing the surviving raised ground within the north-east corner of the Inner Bailey, and the sloping and lower lying ground to the north across the northern defences, and around the north gate (Walford and Chapman 2017 and Walford 2018).

In 2019, following on from those earlier surveys, a small test pit was excavated within the north-east corner of the Inner Bailey, where it was demonstrated that the east wall of the undercroft and royal apartments abutting the bailey bank, as exposed in the excavations of 1961–4, was still surviving *in-situ* (Shipley 2019).

The general plan of Northampton Castle

Surveys contributing to a plan of Northampton Castle

In the mid-1980s when the author inherited the task of producing a report on the excavations of the early 1960s, an immediate issue was the lack of a modern general plan of the castle related to the Ordnance Survey map base and the National Grid. Such a plan was necessary to enable the castle plan to be related to the modern topography of the town so the trenches excavated in the 1960s could be added to the base plan, as well as serving as the base plan for any future work: little thinking at the time that I might contribute some of that future work by excavating in the Outer Bailey in advance of the new station building in the 2010s.

Copies of all the surveys available were transcribed by hand onto drafting film at a common scale of 1:500, so they could be overlaid and compared, and these were all tied to the National Grid using the First edition OS plan of 1885, also at a scale of 1:500, by matching common points of the street pattern, boundary walls and buildings.

The contributing plans included the survey of the Outer Bailey by Sir Henry Dryden in 1854, which had been tied to W Law's earlier survey of the Inner Bailey (Fig 31). The unpublished master plan of the Inner Bailey produced by E F Law and sons was not available at the time, but the published version of that plan was, and this included the internal buildings recorded in 1879 (Fig 32). There was also a small sheet with a standalone survey from 1863 of the earthworks beyond the north gate. Other plans used included the Survey of the Hesilrige Property from 1743 (Fig 33), as transcribed by Rev R M Serjeantson for his study of the castle (1907–8); and the fold-out plan of the

castle from the same volume based on the Law's plan but with the addition of the then current topography from the Ordnance Survey, showing St Andrew's Road along with the original Castle Station, with its platforms and the good shed, and the new canalised and straightened river course (Fig 34).

Using these sources a single master plan was created by the author at 1:500 on drafting film. In compiling the master plan the close consistency between the various contributing plans was striking, but perhaps not surprisingly as, apart from the survey of 1743, they were all ultimately derived from the surveys of E F Law and sons and Sir Henry Dryden, who were all evidently competent surveyors.

Around the north-east corner of the Inner Bailey, which had already been largely levelled before the mid-19th century, the line of the castle ditch was established from work carried out in the 1960s, as previously described (see Figs 19–21). Adjacent to Chalk Lane the line of the ditch was established from a combination of work in the 1960s, particularly the section across the castle ditch, and from the 1970s excavations at Chalk Lane at the south-east corner of the Inner Bailey, where the additional trial trenches (eg Fig 2, Y) helped to establish the presence of an Outer Bailey ditch that continued southwards from this corner.

Ironically, the more difficult task was establishing the location of the 1960s trenches within the Inner Bailey, as the only general plan was both incomplete, in not including the trenches excavated in 1964, and was not tied to enough fixed points in the surrounding topography. It was necessary to establish a best fit for the original trenches in relation to the line of St Andrew's Road, the houses fronting onto Chalk Lane, and the known slight overlap with the northern end of the Chalk Lane excavations from the 1970s, a task also undertaken by Brian Giggins in his study (1999, fig A1.1).

The 1:500 master plan was redrawn for publication at a reduced scale by the late Ken Connor (Fig 35, with some amended and additional labelling). This plan was subsequently digitised by staff at the Historic Environment Record to form part of the digital HER records (see Fig 2).

The general plan of Northampton Castle

Northampton Castle occupied a total area of some 5.25 hectares (13 acres), measuring a total of 320m north-south by 210m east-west, and comprised three main elements (Fig 35):

A sub-rectangular Inner Bailey lay on the highest ground, with its gateway facing north. At *c*.3.0 hectares (7.4 acres), the Inner Bailey and its defences account for more than a half of the total area of the castle. Within the curtain wall it measured *c*.150m east-west by *c*.105m north-south, an area of 1.4 hectares (3.5 acres). The Inner Bailey contained the major buildings, including royal apartments set against the bailey bank to the east and a great hall to the immediate west of those apartments, as partially excavated in the early 1960s. The buildings recorded in the south-west quadrant of the Inner Bailey in the 19th century were probably those in use as the

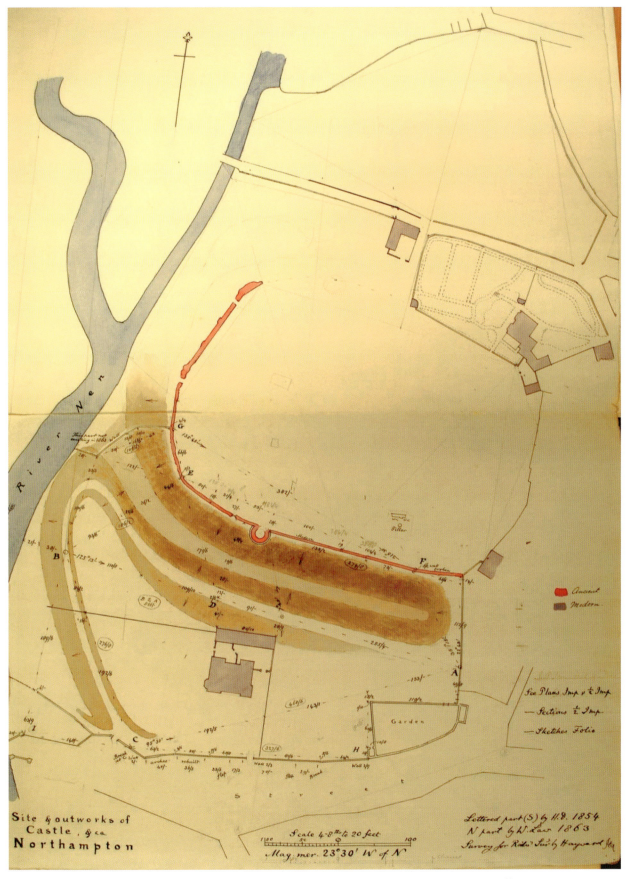

Fig 31 General plan of Northampton Castle by Henry Dryden 1854 and W Law 1863

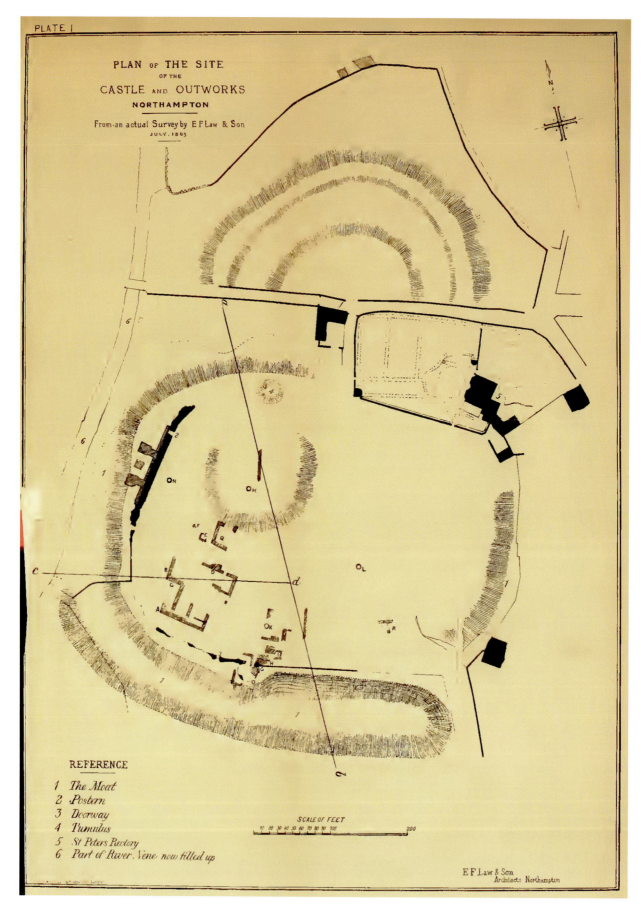

Fig 32: Plan of Northampton Castle (from E F Law 1880)

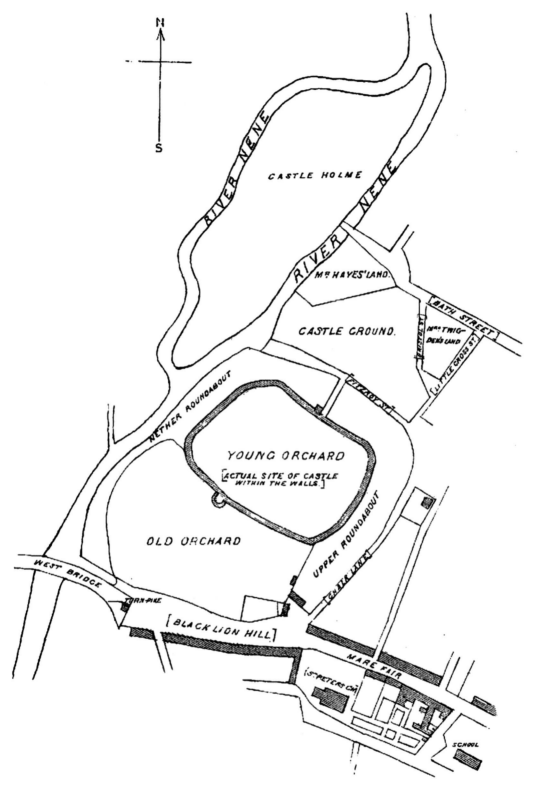

Survey of the Hesilrige Property 1743.

From the original Kindly lent by A.Walker Esq.

Fig 33: Transcription of the survey of the Hesilrige Castle Property 1743
(from Serjeantson 1907-8, 55)

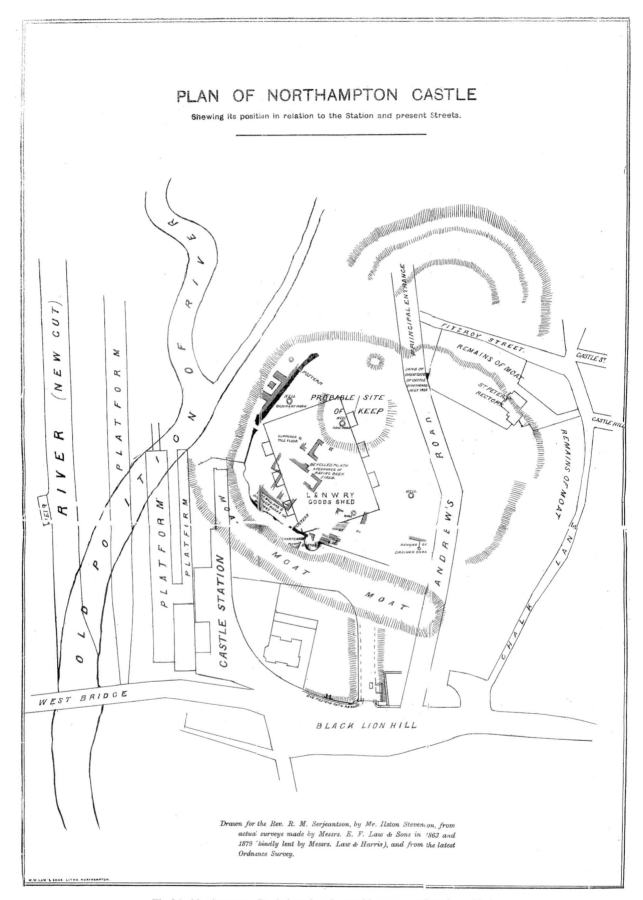

Fig 34: Northampton Castle based on Law with streets and station added
(fold-out plan from Serjeantson 1907–8)

Northampton Castle

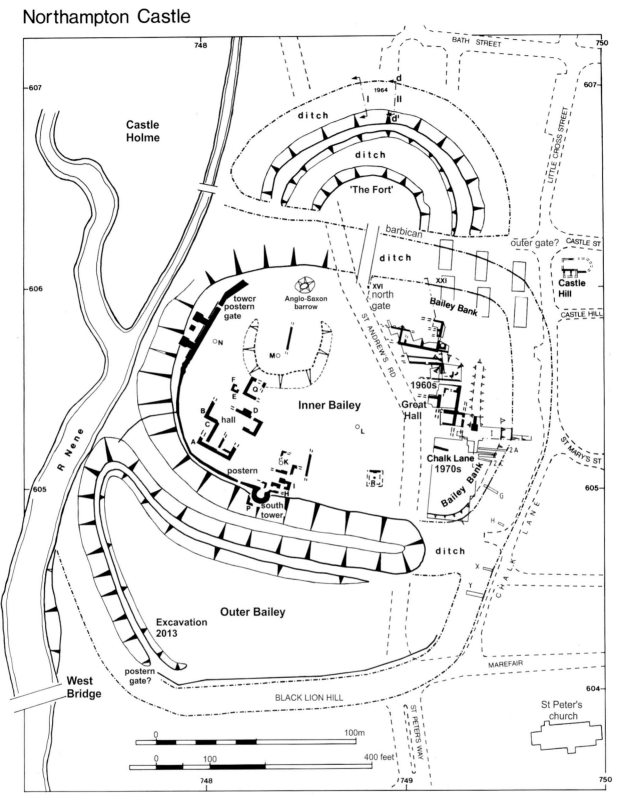

Fig 35: Plan of Northampton Castle (after Chapman 1985, with additions)

sessions hall and the gaol up to the fire of 1675. There are known postern gates at the north end of the western wall, probably with a tower to its immediate north, and to the west of the south tower, presumably with a timber bridge to provide access to the Outer Bailey. We must note that there is no archaeological evidence for the presence of a tower keep within the Inner Bailey, and there is equally no archaeological evidence for the presence of a tower on the western curtain wall, as postulated by Giggins (1999, 90 & fig 6.7).

The Outer Bailey lay to the south. Excluding the defences, it extended c.165m east-west by up to c.55mm north-south, with a long narrow tongue running north-westwards around the rounded south-west corner of the Inner Bailey. The usable area measured c.0.76ha (c.1.9 acres). A small building in the south-west corner, excavated in 2013, was in use only through the 12th century, and a road to the south of this building led to a probable postern gate, which would have provided direct access to the West Bridge.

To the north the concentric ditches surrounding the north gate, The Fort/Castle Ground, either derive from or were at least extensively modified during the partial refortification of the castle during the Civil War of the mid-17th century. However, it might be expected that there would have been a stone-built barbican to protect the approach to the north gate, and it is suggested that perhaps the medieval building found beneath the Civil War Castle Hill mound in the excavation in 1962, was an outer gateway at the end of such a barbican. It would have provided a very visible and imposing first impression of the castle for those approaching from the east along Castle Lane (modern Castle Street is cut off from the dual-carriageway of the modern Horsemarket).

The topography of Northampton Castle and its environs

Having summarised the basic plan form of the castle we must now add the third dimension of its three-dimensional topography, but this only makes sense if placed within the broader topography of the medieval town.

The topography of the medieval town

The topography across the medieval town shows a ridge of higher ground aligned north-east to south-west, ending at the castle set above river channels to its south and, most closely, to its west (see Shaw 2021, fig 5.5). The high point on the medieval town defences lay on the modern Mounts, at a little above 90m aOD. Along the medieval defences to the south-east the ground dropped away to around 85m at the medieval east gate, Abington Street/Abington Square leading to the junction of the Kettering and Wellingborough Roads, and also dropped away to the north-west, to around 78-79m at the medieval north gate, Broad Street/Sheep Street to Regent Square and Barrack Road, with the round church of the Holy Sepulchre nearby on Sheep Street. Across the southern and western parts of the medieval town the ground slopped down towards the respective rivers courses, falling below 60m aOD on the descent down Bridge Street to the South Bridge, and slightly higher, at around 60m aOD, at the West Bridge, below the castle.

The castle topography

The topography of the castle site has been drastically altered since the mid-19th century, but the surveys by Dryden and the Laws, modern Ordnance Survey maps and levels taken during recent excavations provide enough data to make a general description possible. The destruction caused by the Victorian quarrying to create the level area on which the present station car park stands, can be gauged by the level of St. Andrew's Road where it crosses the eastern side of the Inner Bailey. Here the road level, at c.67m OD, is some 4m lower than the ground level within the surviving corner of the Inner Bailey.

The river closely flanking the west side of the castle is the northern, Brampton, branch of the river Nene. In the medieval period there were numerous smaller channels running across a broad stretch of marshy ground, as depicted by Speed in 1610 (Fig 4), with much of this system having been lost by the earlier 19th century, when a much simpler channel system lay west of the castle, although the island of Castle Holme still survived to the north. To the south, the main branch of the river diverged away from the castle below the West Bridge, and did not contribute directly to the castle defences.

The Inner Bailey straddled the western end of the ridge of higher ground that ran diagonally across the medieval town. The highest point of the castle site lay around its north-east corner, at around 70-71m aOD, where it has been suggested that there was an outer gate at the west end of Castle Lane that controlled the access to the north gate of the castle, which lay a little lower, as the ground began to fall away towards the river to the west. Beyond the north gate, across concentric ditches of The Fort, the ground dropped away by some 5-6m, to around 65.5m aOD. The outer ditch of the concentric ditches was excavated in the 1960s and was bottomed at 58.5m aOD, with the river level to west at around 60m aOD, indicating that this would have been a permanently wet ditch when fully open.

The eastern side of the Inner Bailey, the location of the royal apartments and the great hall, was on the highest ground, with the preserved ground level beneath the bailey bank at between 70-71m aOD. The bottom of the adjacent ditch was at 61m aOD. This is a little above river level, but as the ditch was cut into the Lias Clays that underlie the pervious Ironstone geology, ground water would still have been channelled into the ditch keeping it damp and at least seasonal wet.

The ground within the Inner Bailey fell away to the west, as shown in the partial section across the western half of the bailey created by Scriven (Fig 36a, section c-d). Beyond the western wall, there was a scarp some 5-6m high above the river, as shown in the 19th-century views of the western wall (Fig 28a & b). This indicates a total fall of some 5m across the width of the Inner Bailey.

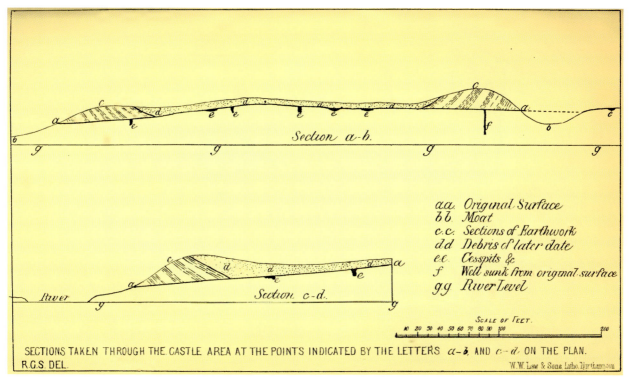

Fig 36a: Sections across the Inner Bailey of Northampton Castle from Scriven 1880, section lines a-b & c-d shown on Fig 32)

Fig 36b: Fig 36b: Sections across the Outer Bailey of Northampton Castle
(from survey by Henry Dryden, for location points E-B & D see Fig 34)

To the south the Outer Bailey was also across lower lying ground, as shown in the profiles recorded by Henry Dryden (Fig 36b). The lowest point of the Outer Bailey, and of the entire castle, lay in the south-west corner, the area excavated in 2013. It was being the lowest lying part of the castle that had led to the survival of stratified medieval deposits, including a stone building, and even across the northern half of the excavated area all medieval stratified deposits had been lost (Chapman 2021b, this volume, fig 4). The modern ground level within the station car park lay at 61.70m aOD, while the floor surface within the excavated building lay a metre deeper at 60.70m aOD

(Chapman 2021d, this volume, fig 19). The south-west corner of the Outer Bailey therefore lay some 10m (33 feet) lower than the north-eastern corner of the Inner Bailey and the approach to the north gate.

The comparative size of Northampton Castle

This was one of the largest castles in England, although the defended bailey at the Tower of London is larger than the Inner Bailey at Northampton (Fig 37 & Table 3). The overall dimensions of Northampton Castle

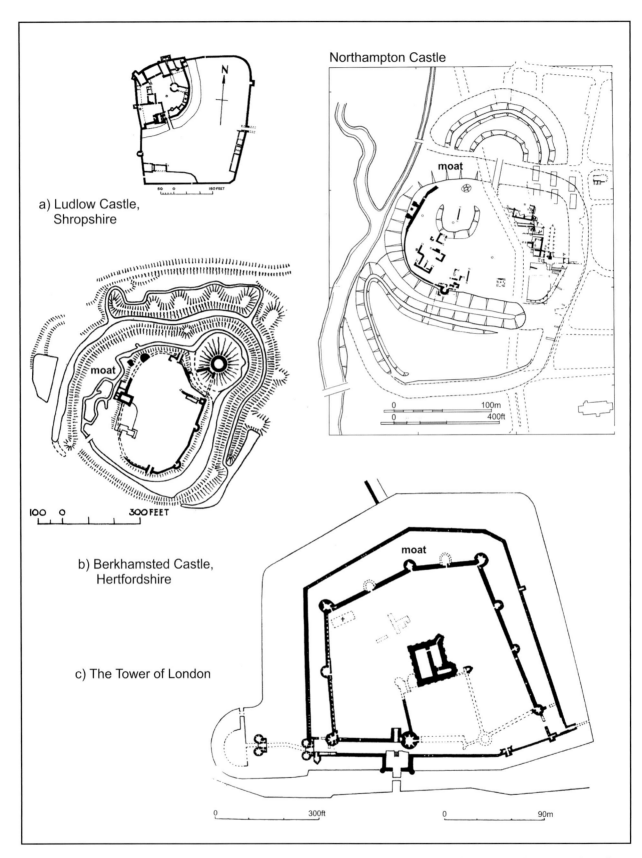

Fig 37: Northampton Castle in comparison to some other English castles: a) Ludlow; b) Berkhamsted and c) Tower of London

slightly exceed the total size of Castle Rising, Norfolk, which was built in the mid-12th century by William d'Aubigny II, who had risen to become Earl of Arundel and constructed Castle Rising with his new wealth. Northampton was also larger than Kenilworth Castle, Warwickshire, founded in the early 1120s by Geoffrey de Clinton, Lord Chamberlain and treasurer to Henry I, and made sheriff of Warwickshire by the king to counter-balance the power of his nearby rival Roger de Beaumont Earl of Warwick, and owner of Warwick Castle. In the later 12th century Kenilworth was garrisoned by Henry II›s forces, and was subsequently taken fully into royal possession. The castle was significantly enlarged by King John at the beginning of the 13th century, with the help of the huge water defences it was able to withstand the six-month-long siege of Kenilworth in 1266, thought to be the longest siege in Medieval English history.

Northampton Castle was therefore, comparable in size and status to some of the major castles that still survive as ruins, and founded by either the king or members of his leading nobility.

It dwarfs many other castles: the whole of Ludlow Castle, Shropshire, built in the late 11th century probably by Walter de Lacy, and one of the earliest stone castles in England, would fit within the Inner Bailey at Northampton, as would the whole of the motte and bailey at Berkhamsted, Hertfordshire. This was a Norman castle held by Robert of Mortain, William the Conqueror's half-brother, and granted by subsequent kings to their chancellors. It was substantially expanded in the mid-12th century, probably by Thomas Becket. Edward III, who further developed the castle in the 14th century, gave it to his son, Edward, the Black Prince (Fig 37a & b). Pembroke Castle, Wales, is another smaller castle easily encompassed by Northampton Castle (Table 3).

Table 3: Comparative sizes of castles

Name	Overall dimensions
Northampton Castle	320m × 210m
Castle Rising, Norfolk	270m × 190m
Kenilworth, Warwickshire	270m × 170m
Tower of London	240m × 220m
Pembroke Castle, Wales	150m × 120m
Berkhamsted Castle, Herts	130m × 100m

The castle and its relationship to the contemporary town

The direct approach to the north gate of the medieval castle was east to west along Castle Lane from the Horsemarket, a high-level route leading to the highest point of the castle site. The Horsemarket is believed to have been the main north-south road of the Anglo-Saxon town (although modern Castle Street is cut off from the dual-carriageway of the modern Horsemarket), providing access to the north gate of the late Saxon town and the important market centre of the Mayorhold (Figs 38 & 39).

Fig 38a: Looking east and slightly uphill along Castle Street from the north-east corner of the Outer Bailey, with the surviving rise of the Castle Hill mound to the right, now partially enclosed within a fenced garden. The postulated outer gateway to the castle barbican would have spanned the road from the trees on the right to the tree on the left (Photograph: Andy Chapman, 17 October 2021)

Fig 38b: Looking west and slightly downhill along Castle Street, with the postulated outer gate to the barbican lying at the end of the blocks of buildings left and right, while the white building in the background lies across the former approach to the north gate (Photograph: Andy Chapman, 17 October 2021)

From east to west the ground dropped from around 74m aOD at the Horsemarket to around 70m aOD at the north-east corner of the castle, adjacent to Castle Hill, where it has been suggested that the medieval building that lay beneath the Castle Hill mound may have been an outer gateway to an extended barbican protecting the north gate of the castle. A gateway in this location would have provided a very visible and imposing first impression of the castle for those perhaps entering through the Mayorhold and the north gate before approaching the castle from the east along Castle Lane, possibly the route followed by Thomas Becket on his way from St Andrew's Priory to trial within the castle in 1164 (Figs 38 & 39).

The east-west axis of the medieval town, from All Saints Church, along Gold Street and Marefair to the castle, although also forming an axis of the late Saxon town, was perhaps then of lesser importance. This might explain why the only known gateway linking the castle to this axis was the postern gate at the south-west corner of the Outer Bailey, partially excavated in 2013, which gave direct access to the West Bridge (Chapman 2021d, this volume 191–255).

Possibly as a result of assuming a greater importance for this route in the Norman period, Giggins (1999, 89, fig 6.7, 27 gate?) suggested that there may have been a gate at the south-east corner of the Outer Bailey to provide direct access onto Black Lion Hill and Marefair, although there is no archaeological evidence to support this. We now suggest that the interpretation by Giggins was a result of seeing the castle within the context of the high medieval town, and in this context the north gate of the castle appears, in effect, to be turning its back on the major medieval thoroughfare of Black Lion Hill/Marefair/Gold Street, but this argument does not apply if at the time the Horsemarket and the Mayorhold were still perhaps the most important focal points for trade within the Norman town.

The transition from the Anglo-Saxon to the medieval town

Michael Shaw in his recent study (2021, 172–173), notes that the process *"undertaken by the Normans at other major urban centres…was the insertion of a castle into the late Saxon town [as] a visible demonstration of the power and control of the new overlords. Another was a huge expansion of the town and a diminution of the status of the earlier settlement, with the chief focus of activity moving to the area outside the late Saxon settlement"*. However, he also notes that at *"other major centres such as Bristol, Norwich and Hereford… the role of the late Saxon town is downplayed by the founding of Norman quarters of a similar size…Northampton can perhaps be seen as an extreme case where the Norman town grew to entirely dwarf the earlier settlement"*.

While Northampton may have been an extreme example of Norman expansion, given the huge disparity in size between the area within the double street pattern and the known defences of the medieval town, an alternative possibility is that there is something missing in our current understanding of the development of the town in the post-Conquest period.

If we were to argue that the known medieval defences actually had a later, post-Norman origin, as has been suggested by Thomas Welsh (1997), and we accept the double street pattern as defining the extent of the late Saxon town, then we are perhaps losing sight of what was a more modest Norman expansion beyond the late Saxon town as this was later lost within a larger expansion that only reached completion in the mid-12th century, perhaps as a result of Northampton then being a favoured town of the Plantagenet kings, particularly Henry II, John and Henry III, and at its peak as a venue for royal visits and state events.

Perhaps it has been all too easy to see Speeds map of the town as a visualisation of the medieval town from shortly after the Conquest, rather than what it actually is, a record of the town as it stood at and beyond the end of the medieval period, with the processes of evolution no longer visible within that plan, beyond that of the double street pattern.

The southern river crossing

It was long ago noted by Robert Moore (1973) that to the south of the town the most likely early river crossing (west of the medieval South Bridge) was at the mill, which lay at the southern end of Tanner Street/Narrow Toe Lane (Fig 39). These streets ran northwards to end at St Peter's Street to the south of Marefair, while north of Marefair this line continued northwards as Quart Pot Lane and terminated to the north at Castle Lane (now Street), a whole block south of the northern arm of the double street pattern. Marefair/Gold Street, leading to the West Bridge, provided the east-west axis, as it still does today.

Moore's idea was later revived by Thomas Welsh to suggest that this line may have been the north-south axis of a much smaller late Saxon town, with the continuation of the axial road to a river crossing south of the town supported by the reported discovery of a paved causeway on this line in the late 19th century (Welsh 1997, 173).

However, it has been argued by Michael Shaw that this north-south axis owed it origin to the Middle Saxon 'elite centre' comprising St Peter's church, the sequence of timber and stone halls, 'The Palaces', and St Gregory's church to the east (Shaw 2021, fig 5.38; Williams *et al* 2021, this volume 25–77). This arrangement places the 'elite centre' at the very heart of a Middle Saxon town that may have comprised roughly four blocks of land extending from the slopes above the river to the west and south and ending to the east at Horseshoe Lane/Horsemarket and to the north along Castle Lane.

It may also be noted that the central north-south road of the double street pattern, Horseshoe Lane has no evident southwards continuation to a new river crossing. As mapped by Speed in 1610, at its southern end Horseshoe Lane turned westwards and ran to the postulated earlier river crossing at the mill, suggesting that the original Middle Anglo-Saxon river crossing was retained within the late Saxon town.

However, at the postulated south-eastern corner of the late Saxon town, Kingswell Street lies outside the defences and is set at an angle, converging with Bridge Street, the medieval and present approach to the South Bridge. Attention has been drawn to his misalignment by Thomas Welsh (2002, fig 1) in his critique of the double street pattern theory, but here we may suggest that it would make sense as a new road either leading from a newly created gateway in the south-east corner of the late Saxon town defences or even created following the levelling of the existing defences, to provide access to a newly established river crossing serving the expanded Norman town, with the early river crossing subsequently abandoned.

Documentary evidence for the later origins of the medieval walled town

As with the castle, tradition had attributed the building of the known medieval town walls to Simon de Senlis I, so the entire creation of the medieval town plan, with the castle and the circuit of the medieval defences was seen to occur within the 40 years or so immediately following the Conquest of 1066. What we are suggesting here is that the

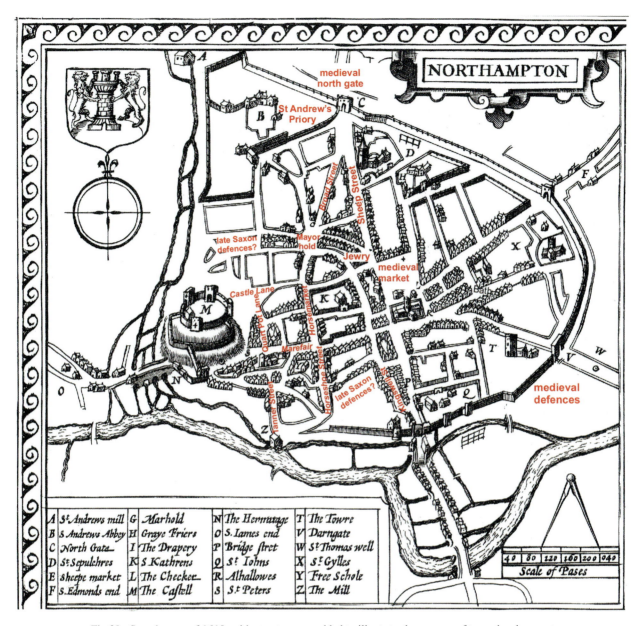

Fig 39: Speeds map of 1610, with street names added to illustrate the process of town development

entire process may actually have taken nearer to a century, with the castle being a product of the early to mid-12th century and the construction of the town defence perhaps overlapping with the construction of the castle but perhaps only completed around the mid-12th century.

We have already proposed that the castle as we know it was built for Henry 1 in the earlier 12th century. In relation to the medieval defences there are documents relating to Simon de Senlis in the later 11th century that do refer to a "*fossam burgi*" (town or burh ditches), however, these could be references to retained defences of the Anglo-Saxon town (RCHME 1985 microfiche 327–330). This is also consistent with one of the earliest unambiguous documentary references to the town walls in Richard 1's charter to Northampton in 1189, and the earliest murage grant, for work on the town walls in 1224 (RCHME 1985, microfiche 327–330).

Between 1138 and 1154, during the reign of King Stephen, Earl Simon de Senlis II granted St Andrew's Priory 16s and 14d rent in exchange for rents lost because of the wall and bailey by which the vill [town] is enclosed, "*propter murum et ballium quibus villa clauditur*", which is the earliest reference to a wall (*murus*). These grants also parallel the earlier payment to St Andrew's in 1130 for land taken into the castle. So here we may be seeing land being taken in both for the final stage of castle construction from 1130 and perhaps the commencement or an early stage in the construction of the town defences in 1138. There are also documentary references to an Eastgate before 1166, although it is not certain that this relates to new medieval defences.

In his arguments that the known medieval defences were of a later date, and not the *Nova Burgus*, the new borough, mentioned in 1086, Welsh has cited the recorded development of the market and Newlands at the centre of

187

the town (Welsh 1997, 168). In 1235 there was a decree in the Close Rolls against fairs and markets being held in the Churchyard of All Saint church, at the centre of the new medieval town, and that they should move to the "waste place to the north", the present market square (Welsh 1997, 168). So, as argued by Welsh, it was only into the 13th century that the focal point of the medieval town had fully shifted to All Saints Church and to a new market place to its north. In addition, the Newlands or "*Terra Nova*" to the east of the market were a further response and expansion of growth around this new market centre, and not to be confused with the "*novus burgus*", the Norman new borough recorded in 1086.

We may also note that while the Northampton Jewry was close to the medieval market north of All Saints church, it also had direct access to the Mayorhold along Bearwood Street, where there were a number of Jewish owned houses that lay beyond the core of the Jewry. As Marcus Roberts has argued that medieval Jewry's were always placed close to the centres of trade (Roberts 2021, this volume, 305 in this case the location of the Jewry was ideal to serve both the early, and perhaps still significant focus of the Mayorhold, at the old north gate of the town, and also the now more important medieval market place (Fig 39). It may also be significant that the Jewry lay on land within the double street pattern, land that would have only become available for development following the levelling of the old town defences in the decades following the Conquest.

The continuing importance of the Mayorhold following the Conquest may also be indicated by the presence of a diagonal road, Broad Street, that lies diagonally to an otherwise rectilinear street pattern, linking the old north gate and the Mayorhold to the new north gate, with Sheep Street linking the new market to the north gate: suggesting that the Mayorhold remained of sufficient importance to warrant a direct link to the new medieval north gate.

Much of the above is speculation based on map regression, and it is difficult to confirm any of the arguments from archaeological evidence or through available documents, which are themselves often ambiguous or lacking in detail and open to varying interpretations. It is a discussion that also illustrates how, despite Northampton being well served with documentary evidence and archaeological investigation, there are still large gaps in our understanding of the development and structure of the medieval town.

However, a model in which the influence of the late Saxon town plan was still dominant well into the 12th century may explain why the castle was provided with a north gate and not a south gate, in addition to the topographic argument that the north gate lay at the end of the high level approach, rather than having direct access from a low level approach from the south.

It was perhaps only with the full development of the high medieval town wall towards the middle of the 12th century, and the later refocussing of the centre of trade and business away from the Mayorhold and onto the new market square to the north of All Saints church, that the castle with its north gate became perhaps a little detached from the economic life of the town, although it did still

connect directly with St Andrew's Priory, as the major religious institution within the town.

Conclusions

In Part 1, we have looked at our knowledge of the castle from the documentary record of its history to the antiquarian record of its form and structure. We have also examined the evidence for pre-castle archaeology, and particularly that derived from the excavations in the 1960s. Finally, we have used the various sources to provide a general plan based purely on the recorded evidence through survey and excavation, the known knowns, and have pointed to areas that still have the potential to contain further below ground deposits, the known unknowns.

The castle plan has been set within the topography and plan of the medieval town, and there has been some speculation that the medieval plan of town defences and the central market place, as later mapped by John Speed, may only have emerged from the mid-12th century, and does not provide a model for the Norman New Borough, the *Nova Burgus*.

Achieving this has involved using antiquarian and archaeological records spanning some 170 years from the 1850s to 2020, although there are still many gaps in the record, particularly in relation to the arrangement of the interior and changes to those arrangements through time, which can never now be filled, the unknowable unknowns.

In Part 2 the survey and archaeological record for the defences and buildings of the Inner Bailey and for the structure of the Castle Hill mound and the medieval building beneath it will be examined and illustrated in detail.

Bibliography

Alexander, J, 1961 *Northampton Castle 1961*, unpublished MSS

Alexander, J, 1962 *Interim report: The Excavations at Northampton (Castle Hill) 1962*, unpublished MSS

Alexander, J, 1962–3 Northampton Castle, *Medieval Archaeol*, **6–7**, 322–3

Alexander, J, 1963 *Northampton Castle 1963*, unpublished MSS

Alexander, J, 1964 Northampton and Northampton Castle, *Medieval Archaeol*, **8**, 250 & 257–8

Alexander, J, 1964 *Northampton Castle 1964*, unpublished MSS

Alexander, J, 1968 *Early Northampton: with Special Reference to the Castle: A Report on the Excavations carried out in 1961–5*, unpublished MSS

Bailey, B, Pevsner, N, and Cherry, B, 2013 *The Buildings Of England: Northamptonshire*, Yale

Bamford, H, 1981 The worked flints, *in* Williams and Shaw 1981, 126–30

Bassir, A, 2021 The history and development of the Northampton County Gaol and Northampton Museum and Art Gallery, *Northamptonshire Archaeol*, **41**, 387–402

Bridges, J, 1791 *The History and Antiquities of Northamptonshire*

Brown, J, 2008 Excavations at the corner of Kingswell Street and Woolmonger Street, Northampton, *Northamptonshire Archaeol*, **35**, 173–214

Brown, R A, Colvin, H M, & Taylor, A J, 1963 *The History of The Kings' Works. Volume II: The Middle Ages*, 750–753

Chapman, A, 1984 *Northampton Castle: A review of the archaeological evidence*, Northamptonshire Archaeology Unit, unpublished draft MSS

Chapman, A, 1999 Excavation of the Town Defences at Green Street, Northampton, 1995–6, *Northamptonshire Archaeol*, **28**, 25–60

Chapman, A, 2001 Excavation at the Moat House Hotel, Northampton, 1998, *Northamptonshire Archaeol*, **29**, 93–101

Chapman, A, 2004 *Archaeological desk-based assessment of land at Castle Station, Northampton*, 2004, Northamptonshire Archaeology report

Chapman, A, 2012 *Archaeological evaluation of the concourse at Northampton Castle Station*, Northamptonshire Archaeology report, **12/188**

Chapman A, 2016 *Excavation at Northampton Station within the outer bailey of Northampton Castle, 2013–2015: Assessment report*, MOLA Northampton report, **16/02**

Chapman, A, 2018 *Excavation and watching brief within the Outer Bailey of Northampton Castle 2013–2015*, MOLA Northampton report **18/117**

Chapman, A, 2021a Prehistoric Northampton: A circular ring ditch and flint scatters, *Northamptonshire Archaeol*, **41**, 17–24

Chapman, A, 2021b Late Saxon and Saxo-Norman occupation beneath the Outer Bailey of Northampton Castle, *Northamptonshire Archaeol*, **41**, 79–127

Chapman, A, 2021c The late Saxon town defences at Green Street, Northampton: a review of the evidence and a radiocarbon date, *Northamptonshire Archaeol*, **41**, 129–136

Chapman, A, 2021d Excavation within the Outer Bailey of Northampton Castle, 2013–15, *Northamptonshire Archaeol*, **41**, 191–255

Chapman, A, 2021e Medieval chess pieces from Northampton, *Northamptonshire Archaeol*, **41**, 403–409

Deacon, M, 1980 *Philip Dodderidge of Northampton, 1702–51*, Northamptonshire Libraries

Dryden, H, 1896 Northampton Castle, *Northamptonshire Notes and Queries*, **6**, 818

Eastman, P M, 1879 An Hour among the Echoes of Northampton Castle, *Lectures on the History & Literature of Northamptonshire*

Edgar, J, 2013 *Northampton Heritage Gateway: Statement of Significance: Gazetteer: 1 Northampton Castle (site of)*, draft document prepared for The Churches Conservation Trust and Northamptonshire County Council

Foard, G, 1994–95 The Civil War Defences of Northampton, *Northamptonshire Past and Present*, **9.1**, 4–44

Giggins, B, 1999 *Northampton's Forgotten Castle*, MA thesis, School of Archaeological Studies, University of Leicester (digital copy online)

Giggins, B, 2017 *Northampton Castle: A review/retrospective/reconsidered*, MSS of work in progress

Giles, J A, 1854 Vita et Passio Waldevi Comitas, in *Vita Quorundum Anglo-Saxonum: Original Lives of the Anglo-Saxons and others who lived before the Conquest*, Caxton Society, 1–30

Goodfellow, A V, 1980 The bridges of Northampton, *Northamptonshire Archaeol*, **15**, 138–155

Hartshorne, C H, 1848 *Historical Memorials of Northampton: taken chiefly from unprinted records* (available as modern scanned legacy reprint)

Ingram, M, 2020 *Northampton: 5,000 Years of History*, Northampton Tours

Kennett, D H, 1968 Early Medieval Pottery in the Nene Valley, Journal of the Northampton Museums and Art Gallery, **3**, 3–14

Law, E F, 1880 The Ruins at the Old Castle, Northampton, *Association of Architectural Societies Reports and Papers*, **15**, 198–203

Moore, R, 1973 Late Saxon/Danish defences, *Northamptonshire Archaeol*, **8**, 18–19

Page, W, (ed) 1930 *The Victoria History of the Counties of England: Northamptonshire*, 33–34

Reynolds, T C, 1800 *The Gentleman's Magazine*, **70**, 928–9

RCHME 1985 *An Inventory of the Historical Monuments in The County of Northampton, Volume 5; Archaeological Sites and Churches in Northampton*, Royal Commission on the Historical Monuments of England

Roberts, M, 2021 The Topography and Archaeology of the Medieval Synagogue and Jewry, Northampton, *Northamptonshire Archaeol*, **41**, 305–333

Scriven, R G, 1880 The Earthwork on the site of the Castle at Northampton, *Associated Architectural Societies Reports and Papers*, **15**, 204–10

Scriven, R G, 1882 Some additional Notes on the Earthwork on the Site of the Castle at Northampton, *Associated Architectural Societies Reports and Papers*, **16**, 71–72

Serjeantson, R M, 1907–8 The Castle of Northampton, *Journal of Northants Nat History Soc & Field Club*

Sharp, S, 1882 Description of the Antiquities found on the site of the Castle at Northampton, *Associated Architectural Societies Reports and Papers*, **16**, 243–251

Shaw, M, 2021 *Approaches to the analysis of the topography, origins, growth and development of English medieval towns: case studies of selected towns and their wider applicability*, University of Birmingham PhD thesis

Shipley, A, 2019 *Archaeological investigation and recording on land at the site of Northampton Castle, St Andrew's Road, Northampton: October 2019*, MOLA Northampton report, **19/115**

Soden, I, 1999 A story of urban regeneration: Excavations in advance of Development off St Peter's Walk, Northampton, 1994–7, *Northamptonshire Archaeology*, **28**, 61–127

Walford, J, 2018 *Topographic survey on the site of Northampton Castle, St Andrew's Road, Northampton, January 2018*, MOLA Northampton report, **18/52**

Walford, J, and Chapman, A, 2017 *Archaeological geophysical survey on the site of Northampton Castle, St Andrew's Road, Northampton, May 2017*, MOLA Northampton report **17/72**

Walker, C, Chapman, A, and Simmonds, C, 2011 *Archaeological desk-based assessment of land at Castle Station, Northampton*, Northamptonshire Archaeology report, **11/155**

Williams, J H, 1979 *St Peter's Street, Northampton Excavations 1973–1976*, Northampton Development Corporation Monog, **2**

Williams, J H, 1979 *Northampton – the first 6000 years*, Northampton Development Corporation

Williams, J H, 1982 *Saxon and Medieval Northampton*, Northampton Development Corporation

Williams, J H, and Shaw, M, 1981 Excavations in Chalk Lane, Northampton, 1975–1978, *Northamptonshire Archaeol*, **16**, 87–135

Williams, J H, Shaw, M, and Denham, V, 1985 *Middle Saxon Palaces at Northampton*, Northampton Development Corporation Monog, **4**

Williams, J H, Shaw, M, and Chapman, A, 2021 Anglo-Saxon Northampton Revisited, *Northamptonshire Archaeol*, **41**, 25–77

Welsh, T, 1997 Northampton Alternatives: Conjecture and Counter-Conjecture, *Northamptonshire Archaeol*, **27**, 166–176

Welsh, T, 2002 Northampton: the double streets and the Norman Town, *Northamptonshire Archaeol*, **30**, 119–126

Welsh, T, 2011 *Notes on Northampton Castle*, unpublished notes

Welsh, T, 2012 *Document Search: former St Mary's Parish (west of Horsemarket)*, unpublished notes

Northamptonshire Archaeology, **41**, 2021, 191–255

Excavation within the Outer Bailey of Northampton Castle, 2013–15

by

Andy Chapman

with contributions from Philip L Armitage, Paul Blinkhorn, Pat Chapman, Steve Critchley, Anne Davis and Tora Hylton

Abstract

In 2013 the forecourt of Northampton Station was subject to open area excavation in advance of construction of a new station. This work was followed by a watching brief during the digging out of the buried foundations of the adjacent Victorian station. In 2015 there was an intermittent watching brief during the demolition of the 1960s station building. The late Saxon and Saxo-Norman deposits pre-dating the castle are reported separately. Clearance to enable construction of the Outer Bailey of Northampton Castle had probably occurred by around AD1120, during the reign of Henry I. A watching brief adjacent to the excavated area located the mortared ironstone foundations of a revetment wall along the front of the 7.5m wide, Outer Bailey bank. There was also a probable postern gate providing direct access between the Outer Bailey and the West Bridge river crossing. A small building within the Outer Bailey was 11.0m long by 5.6m wide, with unmortared stone walls, a wide doorway towards the eastern end of the north wall, and a succession of four large hearths occupying much of the western end of the building. The deeply founded west wall abutted the inner face of the bailey bank, while the other walls were ground laid. Remnants of other walls further east were probably parts of another building, with small areas of scorched soils suggesting a connection with cooking, and perhaps brewing, to feed the castle garrison. The pottery largely comprises utilitarian cooking pots. Other finds were sparse: two arrowheads and a scabbard chape attest to its military role, and gilded mounts for use on horses and on caskets or boxes attest to its status and wealth, while a group of horseshoes came from the road. The buildings had a short lifetime, as they had been levelled by the end of the 12th century or shortly after. Thereafter, there was no further building within this part of the Outer Bailey, and no disturbance until the appearance of the railway stations and a rectory in the mid to late 19th century.

Background

Northamptonshire Archaeology (now MOLA Northampton) was commissioned by West Northamptonshire Development Corporation (WNDC), on behalf of Network Rail and London Midland, with funding support from Northamptonshire County Council, to excavate a trial trench within the short-term car park and taxi rank in front of the main entrance to the then Northampton Station; the footprint of the proposed new station building (NGR SP 7477 6043; Fig 1). The evaluation, carried out 22–24 October 2012 (Chapman 2012), established that intact deposits, including a length of medieval stone wall and a pit pre-dating the building of the castle, survived beneath more recent levels (Fig 2).

Given the positive results from the evaluation, there was a requirement to excavate the footprint of the new station building prior to construction. The excavation was carried out between March and June 2013, a total of 11 weeks (Fig 3). The site was opened to its full extent in three stages due to problems with arranging muck-away and the consequent initial need to retain space on site for spoil dumping, and also to enable the eastern, southern and western roads around the former car parking area to be retained for taxi access for as long as was feasible. The full excavation area measured 37.5m north-south and from 21.7m to 28.3m east-west, a total area of 804m^2 (0.08ha). During July 2013 a watching brief was carried out during the digging out of the buried foundations of the Victorian station to the immediate west of the excavated area. The area to the east between the excavated area and the revetment wall to the raised car park was retained as a site access road and for materials storage through much of 2013, so there was no opportunity for archaeological investigation of this zone. In 2015 there was a final watching brief during the digging out of the concrete floor slab of the 1960s station building to the north of the excavated area.

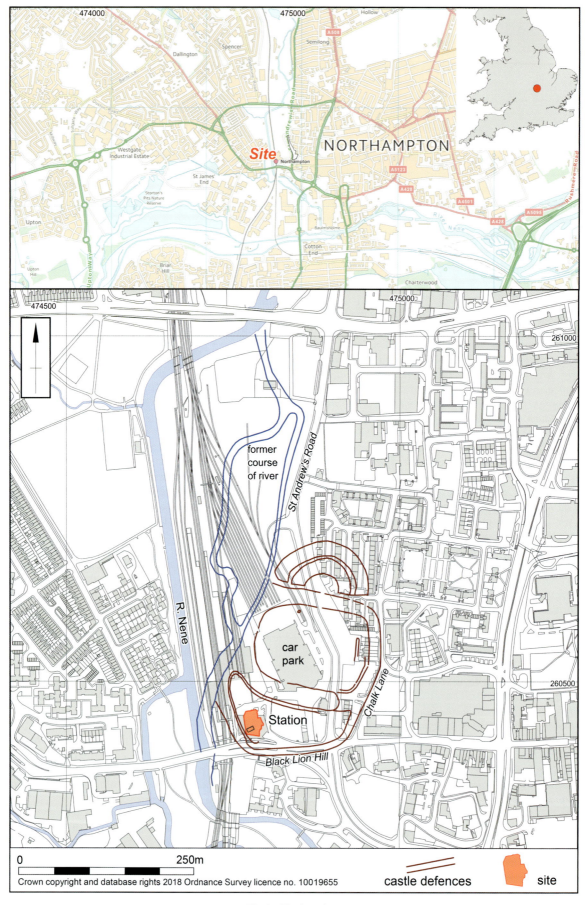

Fig 1: Site location

Following the completion of the watching brief in 2015, an assessment report was prepared (Chapman 2016), and the full client report on the excavations and finds was issued in 2018 (Chapman 2018).

The current report deals with the deposits and finds within the Outer Bailey of Northampton Castle, with the pre-Castle deposits reported separately (Chapman this volume 79–127). Both of these reports utilise the results and illustrations presented in the client report of 2018. An overview of the history and structure of the castle and an account of the excavations of the early 1960s are provided in a separate report (Chapman this volume 137–189).

Acknowledgements

Thanks are due to the staff of the principal contractor, The Buckingham Group, particularly Andy Latham, Paul Morrant and Lee Whiter, for their co-operation in making the excavation possible, including the provision of plant, site accommodation, safety fencing and, eventually, muck-away. Thanks are also due to then Station Master, Den Law, for his co-operation with site visits and press access, and his personal interest in the excavation. For Northamptonshire Archaeology (latterly MOLA Northampton), Andy Chapman was project manager and site director, with Tim Upson-Smith as site supervisor. The main fieldwork team was Kirsty Beecham, Rob Bailey, Garreth Davey, Anne Foard, Tom Garside, Erhan Raymon and Tim Sharman, supplemented by brief appear-

Fig 2: North wall of medieval building as seen in the trial trench in 2012

Fig 3: Breaking the tarmac in March 2013, looking north towards the footbridge and station

ances from Rob Smith, James Burke, Gemma Hewitt and Lou Huscroft. The office-based finds supervision was by Pat Chapman. Specialist reports have been provided by Philip L Armitage, Paul Blinkhorn, Pat Chapman, Steve Critchley, Anne Davis and Tora Hylton. Thanks must also go to Northampton Museums and Art Gallery and Northamptonshire Libraries who hold the finds and the records relating to antiquarian and archaeological work at the castle from the 19th century and 20th centuries, and also to Brian Giggins, Graham Cadman and James Edgar who have supplied information and copies of original drawings, plans and photographs, including material from Northampton Borough Council planning department. Posts to the Facebook site *Northampton Past* have also provided useful information, in particular several posts by local historian Ruth Thomas.

Location, geology and topography

The development area lies to the west of Northampton town centre, within the parish of St Peter. It is bounded by Black Lion Hill and the approach to West Bridge to the south, the railway lines to the west and the then current station building to the north. To the east there is a revetment wall with the car parking to the east on a raised level with respect to the development area (Fig 4).

The station forecourt comprised access roads for taxis, buses and cars surrounding parking bays for the disabled and short-term car parking. Below ground disturbance comprised shallow electrical cables and multiple deeper drainage runs associated with over a century of use of the forecourt in providing access to the Victorian station and its successor of the mid-20th century.

A major town sewer that was believed to run to the east of the footprint of the new station was fortuitously located during the archaeological excavations, showing it to lie beneath part of the footprint of the new station. This timely discovery enabled the foundations of the new station to be suitably modified to protect the underlying sewer.

The geology of the area is mapped as alluvium at the west of the site with Upper Lias clay and Northampton Sand and Ironstone to the east, across the main public car park.

The survival of intact archaeological deposits derives from this location occupying the lowest lying part of the former castle complex. The ground levels rise steadily to both the east and the north, so that while stratified medieval deposits survived across the southern half of the excavated area, across the northern half recent deposits came down directly onto natural. Further north, beneath the old station, truncated natural was seen beneath the modern formation deposits for the concrete floor slab.

To the east, the natural also rises, but given the presence of the revetment wall and the raised area of car parking to the east, ground level contemporary with the castle might still survive across parts of the raised car park.

To the south-east, the old station access road rises to meet the rising approach to the modern West Bridge (Fig 4). Deposits related to the Outer Bailey bank had survived immediately adjacent to the steep slope along the southern side of the site, as seen in the watching brief. This indicates

that the approach to the West Bridge has been raised well above the level of medieval deposits, which may still lie sealed beneath. It is therefore possible that any early road approaching an early bridge may survive at some depth beneath the present carriageway. However, it is unlikely that there will be any opportunity in the foreseeable future where this area could become available for investigation.

There are further details about the depth of burial of deposits in the report on the pre-Castle deposits (Chapman this volume 84–87).

Historical and Archaeological context

A broad overview of the history and structure of the castle is provided in a separate report (Chapman this volume 137–189), and only a brief overview and material relating to the area occupied by the Outer Bailey appears below.

The Victorian station, the 1960s station and the new station building all lie within a small area at the western end of the Outer Bailey, and at the south-western corner of the much larger area once occupied by Northampton Castle (Fig 4).

The origins of the castle remain unclear due to a lack of reliable documentary evidence. It is possible that Simon de Senlis I may have begun to build a castle in the later 11th century, but this would likely have been on a much smaller scale.

The castle as recorded in plan before its destruction seems most likely to date to the reign of Henry I (1100–1135). In 1106 a meeting was held at Northampton between Henry I and his brother, Robert, Duke of Normandy, and while the castle is not specifically mentioned this would seem the most likely venue for such a meeting. So the Inner Bailey might date from around 1100 onward. In 1122 it is recorded that Henry I kept Easter at the castle in great state (Serjeantson 1908, 2), and the results of the present excavation suggest that the Outer Bailey was perhaps in place or at least under construction at around this time, as the latest pre-castle deposits contained pottery dated 1100–1150, while the deposits associated with the building within the Inner Bailey also produced the same pottery type, indicating a construction date somewhere between 1100 and 1150.

The royal castle had probably reached its full physical extent by the mid-12th century, and it continued to be a major royal castle through the 13th and 14th centuries. Thereafter, it declined in importance and by the later 17th century, following the Civil War and the Fire of Northampton, it was largely derelict and ruined, and a convenient source of building stone (see Chapman this volume, 165–166).

From the mid-19th century onward parts of the castle earthworks and surviving walls were the subject of antiquarian record, and they were also recorded on a series of town maps. There was a first stage of railway works and the building of a new West Bridge in the mid-19th century, which impinged on the western and southern sides of the Outer Bailey, with the new line and station opening in 1859.

The majority of the surviving ruins and earthworks were demolished and quarried to make way for the larger

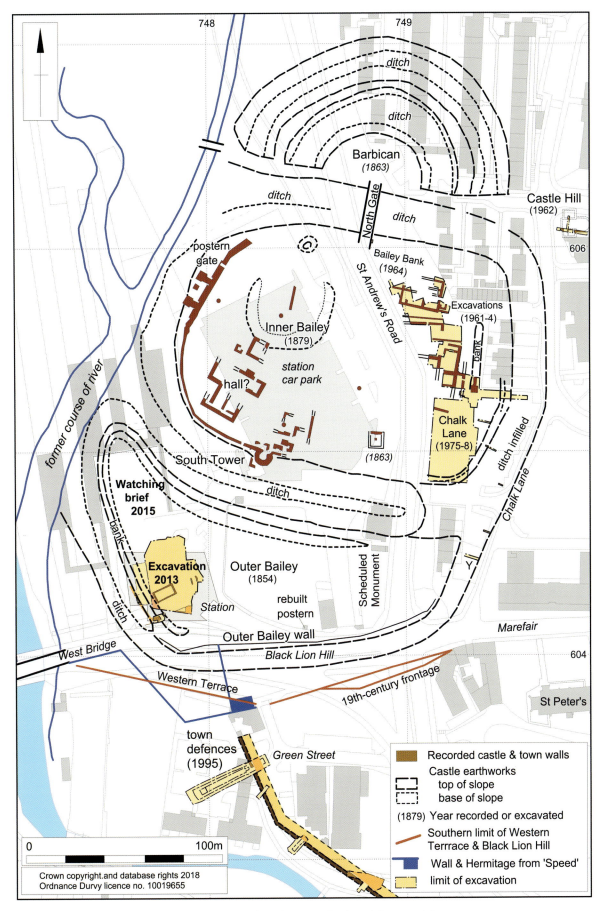

748 749

ditch

ditch

Barbican
(1863)

Castle Hill
(1962)

606

ditch

North Gate

ditch

postern
gate

Bailey Bank
(1964)

St Andrew's Road

Excavations
(1961-4)

Inner Bailey
(1879)

bank

*station
car park*

hall?

**Chalk
Lane**
(1975-8)

ditch infilled

(1863)

South Tower

ditch

Chalk Lane

former course of river

**Watching
brief
2015**

bank

**Excavation
2013**

Outer Bailey
(1854)

Scheduled Monument

Y

ditch

Station

rebuilt
postern

Marefair

Outer Bailey wall

604

West Bridge

Black Lion Hill

Western Terrace

19th-century frontage

St Peter's

town
defences
(1995)

Green Street

	Recorded castle & town walls
Castle earthworks	
	top of slope
	base of slope
(1879)	Year recorded or excavated
	Southern limit of Western Terrrace & Black Lion Hill
	Wall & Hermitage from 'Speed'
	limit of excavation

0 100m

Crown copyright.and database rights 2018
Ordnance Durvy licence no. 10019655

Fig 4: General plan of Northampton Castle and the town defences

railway station and an extensive goods yard (now the car park) in the late 19th century, 1879–80, with the goods shed built in 1880 and the new station opening in 1881. The eastern boundary was formed by the new St Andrew's Road, with only the easternmost side of the interior and defences of the Inner Bailey surviving to the east of St Andrew's Road, with Chalk Lane following the line of the castle ditch.

Records were made during the levelling of the site (Law 1880 and Scriven 1880; 1882), with a quantity of finds also being recovered (Sharp 1882). More recent excavations have taken place in the 1960s and 1970s to the east of St Andrew's Road, along with some minor investigations alongside St Andrew's Road carried out more recently.

A small area at the junction of Black Lion Hill and St Andrew's Road is a Scheduled Monument (SM No 89), forming a tree covered 'mound' at its original ground level and standing above the surrounding ground which has been lowered. This area would have lain at the eastern end of the Outer Bailey.

Summary of site chronology

The pre-castle soil horizon and the latest phase of the pre-castle activity are dated to the early 12th century (Ceramic Phase (CP) M1, AD1100–1150), as are the earlier layers and deposits associated with use of the excavated medieval building within the Outer Bailey (Table 1). This indicates that pottery was still being deposited into some of the pre-castle ditches in the early decades of the 12th century, so the creation of at least the Outer Bailey of the castle must have occurred after AD1100 but well before AD1150, perhaps at around 1120, during the reign of Henry I.

The excavated building and the other features are all dated to the 12th century. The building was probably out of use and levelled by the end of the century (CP: M2), with only a small proportion of the pottery dated to the late 12th to early 13th century (CP: M3), indicating that some activity continued into the early 13th century, most probably usage of the metalled road.

There are no structures or finds dating to the life of the castle through the 13th-15th centuries or in the immediate post-medieval period. The presence of a considerable depth of developed and undisturbed soils above the 12th-century deposits supports the pottery evidence in indicating that through the 13th to 15th centuries there were no activities that had caused any significant below ground disturbance, at least at this western end of the Outer Bailey. The depth of the overlying homogeneous and largely stone-free soils, 0.30m, indicates a long period of stability, with at least this area of the Outer Bailey apparently under grass, despite the possible continued presence of a postern gate providing direct access to the West Bridge.

The picture is one of intensive use of this area through the 12th century, with the excavated building and other

Table 1: Summary of the medieval chronology and historical context

Period/Date	New archaeological evidence	Late Saxon town, Northampton Castle and Railway station
Late Saxon town (pre–AD1000)	AD900–1000 Well shaft (radiocarbon date from primary fills) Some pottery	Late Saxon town: Construction of town defences?
Late Saxon and Norman town (AD1000–c.1120)	AD1000–1100 (CP LSAX 2) Boundary ditch systems and pits, with possible cellared structure. Deposition of animal bone at the margin of the town, dumping of butchery and craft workshop waste	Growth of the Late Saxon town: timber buildings, timber-lined cellars and material indicating craft trades, such as bone and metalworking, including silver smithing. Coins minted in Hamtun.
	AD1100–1150 (CP M1) New boundary ditch system, continued bone deposition	Norman town: Reorganisation following the Conquest Early castle of Simon de Senlis?
Norman castle (ADc.1120–1200) Norman and Angevin kings	AD1100–1150 (CP M1) Creation of Outer Bailey, with a revetment wall fronting a bank. Construction of stone building AD 1150–1200 (CP M2) Final use of building and demolition Pit and gully cutting through building remains	Construction of Royal Castle by Henry I Main buildings within Inner Bailey Castle flourishes through reign of Henry II King John makes frequent visits
High medieval castle (AD1200–1500) The Plantagenet kings	AD1200 onward Postern gate probably still in use, but road disused Soil horizons developing No below ground features	Castle flourishes, Henry III improves royal apartments Second Baron's wars (1263–64) Castle declines from late 13th into 14th centuries Last Parliament, Richard II, 1380

features, perhaps including a second building, all connected with feeding men presumably garrisoned at the castle and living within the Outer Bailey. In contrast, from the early 13th century onward there is apparent total inactivity, with the building levelled and even the metalled road falling out of use a few decades later and becoming grassed over. How far this one corner is indicative of a decline in usage of the Outer Bailey as a whole is unclear, but whatever was happening, it was not resulting in significant below ground disturbance.

To the west of the excavated area, the foundations of the Victorian station were partly dug out without archaeological supervision, but a subsequent visit identified the presence of the mortared wall foundations for a revetment wall at the front of the Outer Bailey bank.

The radiocarbon date

A sample of charred barley grain from charcoal-rich soils associated with the hearths in the medieval building within the Outer Bailey was submitted for radiocarbon dating to help define the site chronology (Table 2). The calibrated dates presented here, which are rounded to nearest five years, differ slightly from the results presented in the client report (Chapman 2018, table 2.2) as they have been derived from the most recently released new calibration, Intcal 20, and the accompanying text has been revised accordingly. The new calibration strengthens the interpretation that the date for the use of the hearth most likely lies within the 100 year period 1120–1220, and more specifically probably within the later 12th century, as also indicated by the pottery assemblage.

The Outer Bailey defences as recorded by Henry Dryden

The internal space of the Outer Bailey, excluding the defences, extended c.165m east-west by up to c.55mm north-south, with a long narrow tongue extending north-westwards around the rounded south-west corner of the Inner Bailey. The usable area measured c.0.76ha (c.1.9 acres) (Fig 4).

The surviving earthworks and walls of the defences were surveyed by Henry Dryden in 1854, shortly after the construction of a building, initially a rectory, within the Outer Bailey, and before the first railway encroachment (Figs 6 & 7) (Dryden 1896). The process of encroachment onto the Outer Bailey through the second half of the 19th century is described in more detail following the account of the excavations; for the moment we are only concerned with the information the 19th century records provide for the form and structure of Outer Bailey defences.

The bailey bank and its revetment

Dryden records a counterscarp bank along the north side of the Outer Bailey, flanking the southern arm of the massive Inner Bailey ditch. To the west this bank turned abruptly southward, flanking the western side of the Outer Bailey (Fig 7). It is the southern end of this bank that was recorded in the excavation of 2013. No wall was recorded by Dryden, so the medieval wall on a mortared ironstone foundation recorded fronting this length of bank during the watching brief, as described below, had evidently been levelled before this time. This might have occurred as late as the early 19th century, perhaps sometime between Roper and Cole's map of 1807, which shows a wall around the western end of the Outer Bailey, and Wood and Law's map of 1847, which shows the west end of the Outer Bailey open to the river.

The eastern terminal to the Inner Bailey ditch is believed to be a product of the infilling of the eastern arm of the Inner Bailey ditch at an earlier date, and not an original feature. This is discussed further in the overview of the history and structure of the castle (Chapman this volume, 169).

Along the south side of the Outer Bailey, Dryden recorded a wall in both plan and elevation (Figs 6–8). There were no associated earthworks recorded, but

Table 2: Radiocarbon dates

Site Context	Sample	Laboratory Reference (sample)	Conventional Radiocarbon Age BP	Calibrated date *68% confidence* **95% confidence**
Hearth within building Outer Bailey of Castle	Charred grain (Barley)	Beta-410140 (NCS13/362)	890+/-30	*Cal AD 1055–1075 (13%)* *Cal AD 1155–1215 (55%)* **Cal AD 1045–1085 (23%)** **Cal AD 1120–1220 (70%)**

OxCal v4.4.2 Bronk Ramsey (2020); r.5 Atmospheric data from Reimer et al (2020)

R_Date Beta-410140

800   900   1000   1100   1200   1300

Calibrated date (calAD)

Laboratory: Beta=Beta Analytic. Calibration: Intcal20, plotting OxCal v4.4.2

Fig 5: The excavated area, with the northern half of the medieval building in the foreground and the previously excavated area behind, with the wall of the Victorian railway station, to the left, forming the western limit of excavated area, looking north-west

Table 3: *Summary of the post-medieval chronology and historical context*

Period/Date	New archaeological evidence	Northampton Castle / Northampton Railway station
Post-medieval (16th–18th centuries)	Soil horizons developing Disturbed by tree holes	Court and gaol at castle Castle sold by Henry VIII Buildings of court and goal within Inner Bailey until late 17th century Civil War (1642–51): Refurbishment of castle defences Fire of Northampton (1675): followed by stone robbing Earthwork remains with interior under grass and orchards.
Modern 19th century	Inner and Outer Bailey under orchards Victorian station: Granite setts of station yard. Drains cutting earlier deposits	North-east corner of Inner Bailey ditch infilled Inner and Outer Bailey under orchards Mid-19th century, building within Outer Bailey and S wall of Outer Bailey levelled prior to straightening road, a new West Bridge and the first railway incursion. Late 19th century, most castle earthworks levelled to make way for new larger railway station and goods yard 1960s tarmac laid over setts
20th century	Tarmac car park and modern services Excavations on east side of Inner Bailey in 1960s and 1970s	Victorian station demolished New station built
2013–2015	Archaeological excavation of forecourt. Digging out of Victorian station foundations	Construction of new station Levelling of old station

Dryden (1896) did note that the surface inside the Outer Bailey was "much higher inside the wall than outside", so it is likely that soil had accumulated to a sufficient depth on the inside to have levelled off the inner slope of the Outer Bailey bank along this southern arm. Dryden also noted that prior to his survey a gradual downslope on the south side of the wall had been cut back to a near vertical face, to widen the road along Black Lion Hill, with this leaving the face of the wall exposed along the top of the cut back, with the base of the wall to the east standing at least 4 feet (1.2m) above the road (Fig 8, right). There are contemporary drawings that also show this.

Dryden (1896) describes this wall as being in red ironstone. On the higher ground to the east, the foundation courses, below a chamfered offset, were c.4 feet deep (c.1.2m). The wall thickness above the offset was 2 feet 3 inches (0.69m). The foundations were of coarse stonework, while above the offset it was of better coursed squared blocks including some ashlar, perhaps reused. In some places the wall had clearly been rebuilt quite recently.

On the lower ground to the west, the foundations were up to c.7 feet (2.1m) deep, and there was a row of stone arches, each less than 1.0m wide (Figs 7 and 8), perhaps to strengthen the wall on this low lying area or to allow water flow in times of flood, or perhaps a combination of both. The arched length of the southern wall lay at an angle to the remainder and immediately to the west of a cross wall running north from the hermitage, as recorded by Speed in 1610, which blocked and controlled access into the town, but was long gone by the time of Dryden.

West of the arched length, the wall angled back towards the north-west and there was a narrow gateway between this wall and a further length of the wall that continued westwards, and then bifurcated, with a pair of walls diverging to the west towards the river (Fig 9). These walls ignored the line of the western bank, indicating that the wall fronting the western bank of the outer bailey, as found in excavation, had been levelled before this time.

A later plan by Henry Dryden (1896) is useful in showing the line of the demolished southern Outer Bailey wall projected on the road arrangement as it was by the late 19th century (Fig 10). The gateway, as shown on the original survey (Figs 6 and 9) coincides with the offset to the south of the new station (H) (Fig 10). It was in this location that there may have been a medieval postern gate, as partially seen during a watching brief in 2013. From within the outer bailey this was approached along a metalled road, as located in the south-east corner of the excavated area.

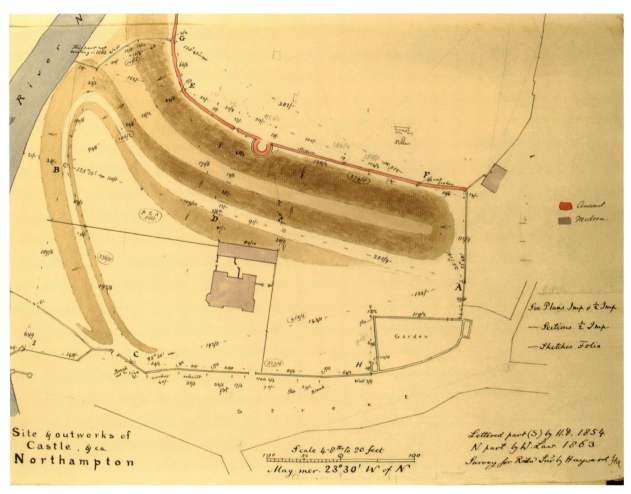

Fig 6: The Outer Bailey, as surveyed by H Dryden in 1854, with the southern arm of the Inner Bailey and its curtain wall, as surveyed by W Law in 1863

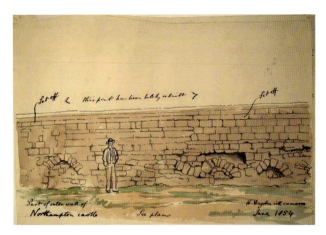
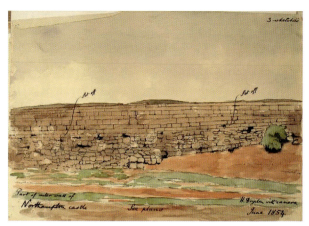

Fig 7: The wall on the south side of the Outer Bailey, drawn by H Dryden using a 'camera' in 1854

Fig 8: The western length of the Outer Bailey wall with arches, as shown on Dryden's
original survey drawing of 1854

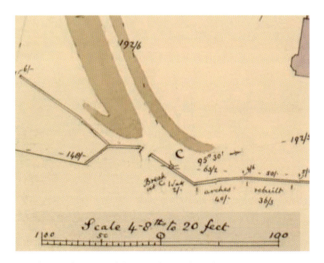

Fig 9: Close up of the Dryden's plan of 1854 to show the
opening at the western end of the southern outer bailey wall

of the trial trenches excavated in the 1970s beyond the south-east corner of the Chalk Lane excavations and west of Chalk Lane did record a ditch continuing southward, which could be the very northern end of an Outer Bailey ditch on the east side of the castle, just south of a junction with the south-east corner of the Inner Bailey ditch (Fig 4, trench Y).

This ditch appears to have been infilled long before any modern mapping and perhaps even before Speed's map of 1610. The filling in of such a ditch would have helped create the broad, dog-legged, approach of Black Lion Hill, between the western end of Marefair and the West Bridge. The line of the old southern frontages of Black Lion Hill and West Terrace (Figs 4 and 11) (mapped from a combination of John Speed's map of 1610 and the Ordnance Survey maps predating the construction of St Peters Way, when the line of the Black Lion Hill frontage was finally lost), lay 22–30m south of the wall along the southern side of the Outer Bailey, with perhaps approaching half of this width, c.10–12m, once taken up by an Outer Bailey ditch.

An Outer Bailey ditch

It is assumed that in its original form the Outer Bailey bank would have been flanked by a ditch to the west, south and east, although probably not on the scale of the recorded ditch on the eastern side of the Inner Bailey. One

The interior of the Outer Bailey

There are no antiquarian records or maps to indicate that any medieval buildings within this area had survived into even the early 17th century, when recorded on Speed's map of 1610, and by the mid-18th century it was shown as

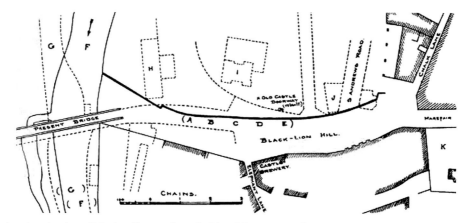

Fig 10: Plan showing the demolished wall around south side of the Outer Bailey (A-E) in comparison to the realigned and new roads (dashed lines), with the river course realigned (from F to G), and the station (H) serving the new railway of the late 19th century (from Dryden 1896)

the Old Orchard on the Survey of the Hesilrige Property of 1743 and a Cherry Garden on the Noble and Butlin map of 1746. The small building in the south-western corner of the Outer Bailey, as excavated in 2013, had been levelled around the end of the 12th century, and there was no further significant below ground disturbance of this area within the lifetime of the castle.

Excavation of the Outer Bailey defences

The Outer Bailey bank

The inner face of the Outer Bailey bank lay in the south-western corner of the excavated area, and the foundations of a mortared ironstone revetment wall along the outer face of the bank was seen to the west in a watching brief following the partial digging out of the brick walls of the Victorian station (Fig 11). Unfortunately, the brick foundations of much of the Victorian station were dug out without prior notification, making it difficult to determine what had been lost during the unobserved works. A deep cellar under the northern end of the station cut deeply into natural and would have destroyed all archaeological deposits in that area (Fig 11). Further south, the station levels had been dug out to around the level of the natural. However, in the south-west corner of this area, the foundations of a mortared wall partially survived (Figs 11–13).

The inner edge of the Outer Bailey bank was effectively defined by the deeply founded western wall of the building abutting the bank, and there was no general revetment of the inner face, indicating that it sloped down to meet the ground surface within the interior. The Outer Bailey bank at this point was 7.5m wide between the revetment wall and the west wall of the internal building. Given a slope of 45° on the inner face, the bank could have been as high as 6–7m, but a slope of around 30° would have been more stable and would suggest a height of around 4.0–4.5m.

The south-western corner of the excavation was extensively disturbed by modern drains and several shallow modern pits, but between these the ground comprised tenacious pale yellow clay (325) at a level of 61.00 to 61.05m aOD (Fig 19). This was clean Lias clay presumably cast up from an adjacent ditch to form the base of the Outer Bailey bank. This layer may have been up to 300mm thick, but it was impossible to establish a clear interface between the bank and the underlying natural, as clay had infiltrated the sandy and gritty ironstone natural, probably as a result of long term water action (illuviation), so that the two layers merged over a broad boundary. To the south of the building the bank spread outwards to the east, but its exact extent was only broadly definable due to the leaching of clay into the soils both below and beyond the bank.

At some stage the front edge of the bank was overlain by a distinctive but disturbed layer (348) of medium brown gritty to sandy loam containing charcoal flecks and scattered pieces of ironstone and limestone, 50–120mm long (Fig 19). This deposit extended southwards from the south-west corner of the building for at least 3.5m, but had been much disturbed by the Victorian drains in this area.

The outer revetment wall

The foundations of the outer revetment wall, 400, were seen at an oblique angle in a section provided by a temporary limit of excavation during the digging out of the Victorian station walls. The construction trench was 0.50m deep, with a vertical side and an undulating flat bottom (Fig 13, S.81 and Fig 14). It was cut through a pre-castle soil horizon (403) of medium brown sandy loam with some red-brown mottles, free of stones, and bottomed within this soil just above natural (402) of coarse orange-brown sand containing some pieces of ironstone.

The wall foundation (400) comprised ironstone and some limestone rubble, with stones measuring 150–250mm, set in a matrix of pale yellow-brown sandy lime mortar, mixed with some of the pre-castle soil. Above the buried soil, the basal 200mm of the clay bank survived (404), a light brown hard and tenacious clay, with a vertical face against the wall footings, which comprised closely-set and steeply-pitched ironstone, 150–200mm long, set in

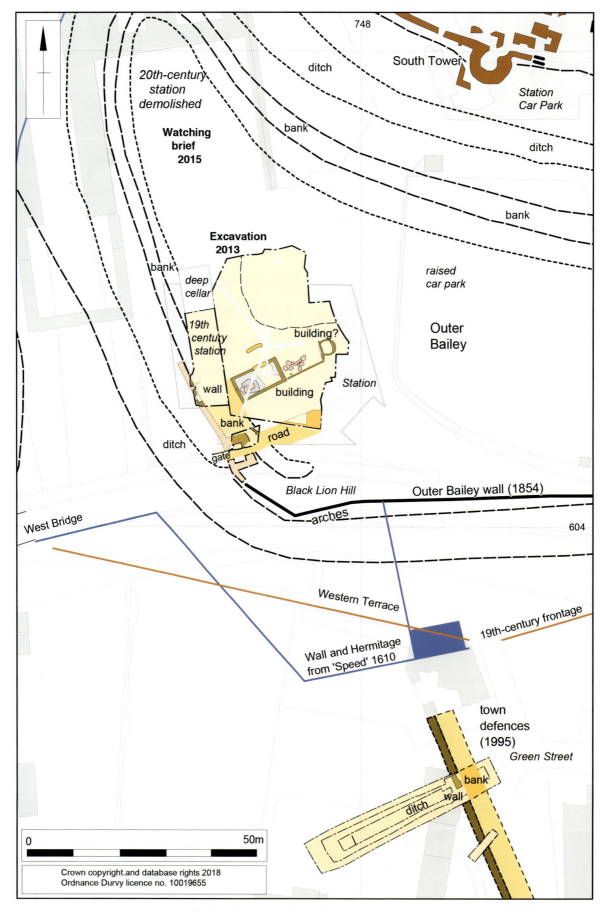

Fig 11: The Outer Bailey of Northampton Castle

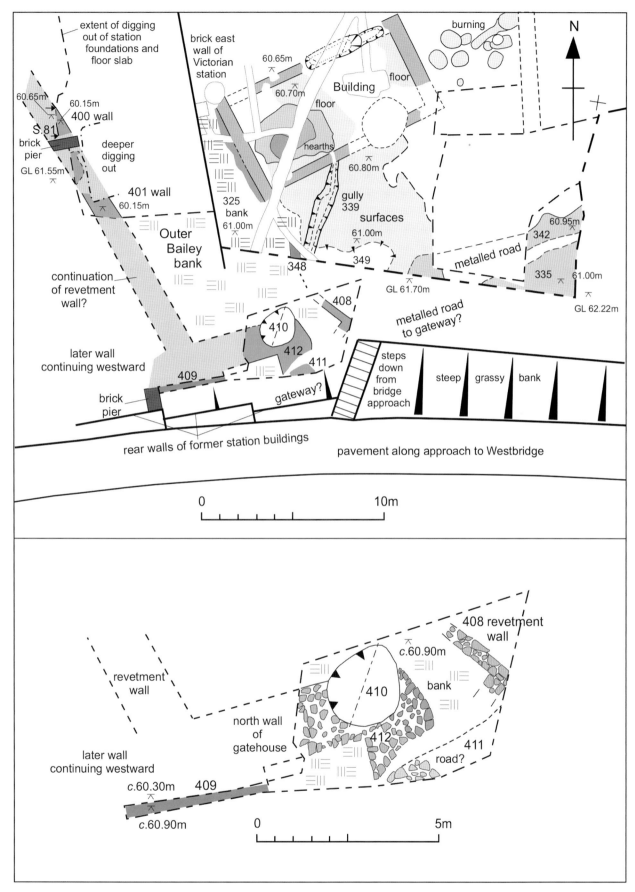

Fig 12: The revetment wall, the Outer Bailey bank and the possible postern gate

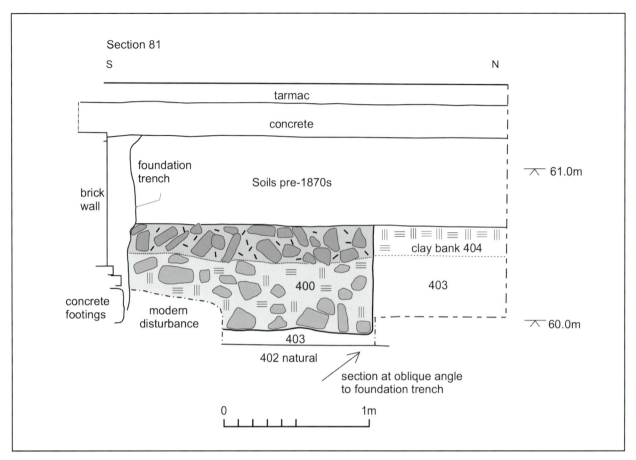

Fig 13: The foundations of the Outer Bailey bank revetment wall, 400, Section 81

Fig 14: The foundations of the Outer Bailey bank revetment wall, 400, seen obliquely in section, looking west (Section 81)

Fig 15: The foundations of the Outer Bailey bank revetment wall, seen in section, 400, (right of brick pier) and in section and plan 401 (left corner), as exposed when digging out the old station foundations, looking south-west

clean pale yellow lime mortar, although this upper stonework had been much disturbed and disordered.

Further south, the wall was again seen in section with a short length of the basal foundations surviving in plan 401 (Figs 12 and 15). Both to the south of the brick pier and further south, wall 401, the outer edge of the foundations was recorded, giving a width of 1.20m.

The possible postern gate

The digging out of the southern end of the Victorian station walls up to the modern revetment wall retaining the rising approach to the West Bridge was also carried out without prior notification. The area south of the observed Outer Bailey revetment wall, 400/401, had already been dug over and backfilled, while to the south the exposed level was below the castle horizons. What was left was a section at the foot of the approach to West Bridge and a small island of intact castle deposits to the south of the main excavation (Fig 11).

In the section to the south, the foundations of an ironstone wall, c.0.5–0.6m deep, with disordered ironstone in the overlying soils, was visible for a length of c.4m, but at an oblique angle that made estimating its original width or alignment impossible (Fig 16). It was also not possible to

obtain levels given the salvage natural of the work, but the base of these foundations is estimated at c.60.3m aOD and the top at c.60.9m aOD.

It is suggested that wall 409 is likely to be the foundations of the wall shown on Dryden's survey of 1854 (Figs 6, 9 & 10), which continued directly westward to the river, and was constructed after the revetment wall along the front of the Outer Bailey bank had been levelled. It is likely that the eastern end of the later wall would have lain in the area of the western end of the postulated gatehouse, but no attempt is made to reconstruct the walls in this area as there is too little evidence.

The island of intact but disturbed archaeological deposits to the east contained two lengths of wall (Figs 12 and 17) which make no sense in terms of a continuation of the pattern seen to the north, with the Outer Bailey bank fronted by a revetment wall, and a more complex interpretation of the disturbed and fragmentary remains is required.

To the north-east was a narrow L-shaped wall, 408, in ironstone with some limestone (Figs 12, 17 and 18). The northern arm survived for a length of c.2.0m and the wall was 0.45m wide with a single course surviving. The larger facing stones met at the centre of the wall. At the eastern end there was a short surviving length of a southwards continuation at a right angle, which was 0.55m wide. This

Fig 16: The south wall of the Outer Bailey 409, in section, looking south-east towards the bridge approach

wall was directly overlain by modern deposits related to the concrete base for the flight of steps leading up to the South Bridge approach. It is suggested that this narrow L-shaped wall was a revetment around the low inner tail of the Outer Bailey bank on the northern side of an opening through the bank leading to a postern gate.

To the west there was a remnant of a more substantial wall, 412 (Figs 11 & 17). The eastern face, of larger ironstone slabs, was slightly curved and there was an infill of smaller ironstone rubble. The western face had a right-angled corner, although there were few good facing stones. Within the angle of the walls there was a surface of hard pale clay, possibly a clay-floor. The northern wall face had largely been removed by a large but shallow oval pit, 410, filled with disordered ironstone rubble, but a disturbed remnant of the northern face of the wall survived to the west. The northern arm of wall 412 was c.1.8m wide and the eastern arm was up to 2.0m wide. The eastern arm had a robbed end to the south, where there was a deeper disturbance that extended eastwards, passing to the south of wall 408. To the west this deeper area contained a scatter of large slabs of limestone (411). It is possible that this deeper disturbed area marked the northern edge of the metalled road, continuing westward from where it was recorded in the south-east corner of the main excavation.

It is suggested that this L-shaped length of wall, c.2m wide, formed the north-eastern corner of a square or rectangular gatehouse protecting a postern gate that provided direct access from the Outer Bailey to the medieval West Bridge, and occupied much the same location as the gateway shown on Dryden's survey of 1854 (Fig 10).

The width of the building might have been c.7.5m (c.24 feet) assuming that the front was in line with the revetment wall. It the plan was square, with walls 2.0m thick this would have provided an internal space within the gatehouse c.3.5m square (c.12 feet square), sufficient for a narrow access and space to either side for small guard chambers.

The building abutting the Outer Bailey bank

Pre-building layer

Beneath the southern half of the building, and continuing southwards under the yard surface, there was a layer (344) of un-weathered angular ironstone chips measuring 20–80mm, which contained a small quantity of pottery dated to AD1100–1150 (Ceramic phase M1) and directly overlay the thick late Saxon soil horizon (Figs 19 & 20).

Fig 17: Stone walls, 412 (top left) and 408 (right), associated with the possible postern gate, looking north-west

Under the western end of the southern wall, 328, the layer was only 40mm thick, but at the surviving eastern end of the wall it was 80–90mm thick. It continued across the interior of the building, although it had been lost to later disturbance in the south-east corner and had been cut through for the construction of the hearth bases. It was not present under the northern wall or the eastern wall, although what may be the same deposit had survived immediately outside the southern end of the eastern wall (Fig 20, layer 138).

The layer extended to the south of the building as a continuous deposit for 5m and continued, more disturbed and truncated, for a further 3m, underlying the margins of the road. To the south-east, the basal layer of the road (342) was also very similar, but with scattered larger fragments of ironstone, although these may have come in from later mixing and disturbance of the road levels.

To the west, layer (344) lapped over the eastern margins of the clays (325) forming the bailey bank. This area was disturbed by modern drains, but there was a remnant of a narrow band of brown charcoal-flecked loam (348) containing frequent fragments of ironstone and some limestone, 50–120mm across, possibly part of a once more extensive layer of soil and stone lying against the face of the bank, perhaps comprising debris from the construction of the building.

Layer (344) therefore appears to have been an exten-sive levelling and consolidation layer pre-dating both the building and road construction, probably to provide a stable and quick drying surface when the underlying soil horizon would have been clayey and sticky when wet.

The building

This rectangular building measured 11.0m by 5.6m enclosing a single room, 9.5m long by 4.5m wide, an internal area of 42.75m^2 (Figs 20–22). A broad doorway founded in a deeper slot, 140, within the eastern half of the northern wall, 110, had been dug out when the building was demolished and levelled. Four metres to the north, a length of slightly curving steep-sided slot, 115, may have held timbers forming an outer screen to this doorway or perhaps even the outer end of a timbered porch. A sandy clay floor, 135, partly survived against the eastern wall, 132, and to the west of the doorway, with both areas containing a patch of scorching. The south-western corner of the building contained a sequence of three hearths surrounded by charcoal-rich hearth debris.

The floor levels had been sealed beneath demolition debris, but the interior of the building had been much disturbed by drains and stanchion bases related to the construction and use of the Victorian railway station, as briefly catalogued below.

Fig 18: Wall 408, possibly a revetment wall flanking the corner of the bailey bank inside a postern gate, looking south-west

In the descriptive texts that follow, for simplicity the building is assumed to have a west-east alignment.

The western wall

The western wall, 327, which abutted the tail of the Outer Bailey bank, was the only wall provided with foundations, 330, of significant depth. These were set in a deep construction trench, 0.90m wide by 0.70 deep, with vertical sides and a flat base 386 (Figs 20 & 23, S78). The footings, 330, filled the trench and comprised four courses of large ironstone blocks and slabs, up to 0.45m long and up to 0.25, thick, with some infilling with smaller stones (Fig 24 a-d).

The standing wall, 327, was 0.7m wide with the inner face slightly overhanging the inner edge of the foundations leaving a broad step, 0.2m wide, between the outer face of the standing wall and the outer edge of the foundations. This step was overlain by bank material 325. There also appeared to be a remnant of bank material against the inner wall face, indicating that the foundation trench had cut through the tail of the pre-existing bank. The wall had been levelled to a height of 0.30m, typically four courses of flat-laid ironstone, with a core of small ironstone, with the contemporary floor level with the top of the second course.

At either end of the building the west wall ran a little beyond the width of the building itself. The junction with the southern wall had been removed by a drain while no wall had survived at the west end of the northern wall, where there may have been a corner doorway, see below.

The southern and eastern walls

These were ground laid with the floor and external surfaces abutting the lowest course. There was no use of mortar, so presumably they were either fully drystone or clay/earth bonded.

The southern wall, 328/139, was 0.55–0.60m wide, significantly narrower than both the western and eastern walls (Figs 23, S.77 and 25 a-b). The western end of the southern wall was particularly well preserved, at 0.36m high with three or four courses surviving. The foundation course was of larger roughly-squared blocks of ironstone, 200–260mm thick and 300–350m deep, meeting at the centre of the wall. The two to three courses above this were of smaller ironstone, 40–110mm thick and up to 200m deep, with a core of small ironstone rubble.

The eastern wall, 132, was 0.75–0.80m wide, comparable to the western wall, surviving to 0.20–0.25m high, typically as two courses of roughly-squared ironstone slabs and blocks, but varying between one and three courses depending on the thickness of the stone, which ranged from 50–250mm thick (Figs 23, S.30 and 25, c). The facing stones had a depth of 0.30–0.35m and there was core of smaller rubble.

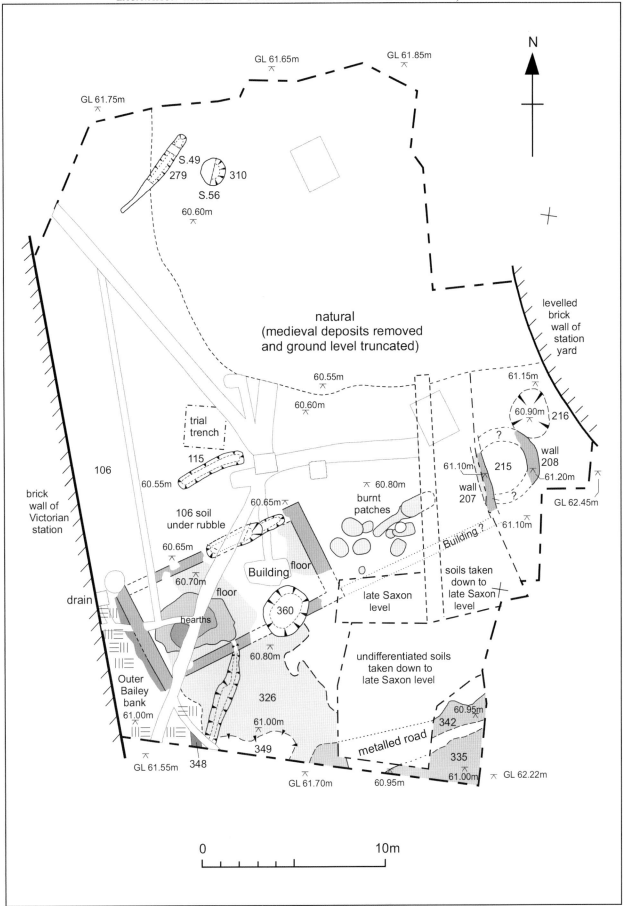

N

GL 61.65m

GL 61.85m

GL 61.75m

S.49
279

310

S.56

60.60m

natural
(medieval deposits removed
and ground level truncated)

levelled
brick
wall of
station
yard

60.55m

61.15m

60.60m

60.90m

216

trial
trench

115

60.55m

wall
208

61.10m

215

106

brick
wall of
Victorian
station

60.55m

61.20m

GL 62.45m

60.65m

60.80m

burnt
patches

wall
207

61.10m

Building ?

106 soil
under rubble

60.65m

60.65m

60.70m

Building

floor

floor

drain

hearths

360

late Saxon
level

soils taken
down to
late Saxon
level

60.80m

undifferentiated soils
taken down to
late Saxon level

Outer
Bailey
bank

326

60.95m

342

61.00m

61.00m

metalled road

335

349

61.00m

GL 61.55m

348

GL 61.70m

60.95m

GL 62.22m

0

10m

Fig 19: The medieval Outer Bailey (AD1120–1200)

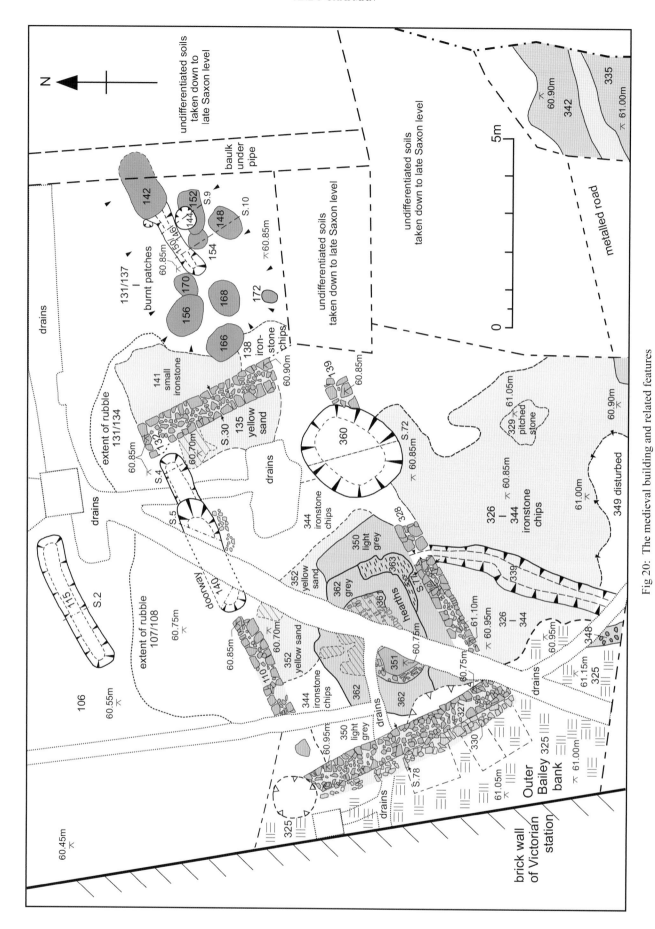

Fig 20: The medieval building and related features

Fig 21: The northern half of the medieval building, looking north, showing the eastern wall 132 (right), the end of the southern wall 139 (left), and the northern wall, background, with the interior disturbed by Victorian drains and stanchion pits (centre) largely unexcavated

Fig 22: General view of the medieval building, looking north, showing the western wall 327 (left) and the southern wall 328 (foreground), with floor levels and hearths exposed and modern drains partially excavated

The northern wall and the doorways

The northern wall was of the same width and build as the southern wall, with the western end surviving to the same height (Fig 26, a & b). To the west the wall ended where it was truncated by a modern drain, and in the space between the drain and the western wall no wall stone survived although there was a single irregular slab of ironstone at the appropriate level to be part of a stone threshold. This suggests that there was probably a corner doorway c.1.25m wide.

However, the main doorway occupied much of the eastern half of the north wall, although all that survived was a length of steep-sided slot, 140, 3.25m long by 0.90m wide and 0.33m deep, partly removed by a modern drain (Fig 23, S.5). A shallower robber trench continued to the east wall (Fig 23, S.4). The fill (133) of the slot was dark grey-brown friable loam containing the occasional small fragment of ironstone up to 100mm long. The evidence suggests that a door surround had probably been removed for reuse when the building had been levelled. However, the sparse stone content within the slot backfill suggests that what was removed was probably a timber door surround, perhaps founded on a ground plate set in the slot. Part of a cooking pot was recovered, with further sherds coming from nearby floor levels (see Fig 35, 7).

If the surround had comprised timbers, these could have been up to c.300mm (1 foot) square, with the doorway structure c.2.75m (c.9 feet) wide and the opening c.2.15m (c.7 feet) wide.

The northern slot 115

Four metres (c.13 feet) to the north of the doorway, centre of slot to centre of slot, there was a slightly curving length of steep-sided, flat-bottomed slot, 115, 3.8m long by 0.60m wide and 0.30m deep (Fig 23, S.2,).

This slot appears to be related to the doorway to its south, and the simplest explanation would be to suggest that this slot held a timber screen, while the more complex interpretation is to suggest that perhaps there was a direct physical link, with timbers from the doorway to the slot forming a timber fore-structure in front of the doorway, perhaps a roofed space. This could also explain why the outer slot was longer than the doorway slot, and why the robbing had extended to the very eastern end of the north wall. If slot 115 had held a timber screen c.3.4m (c.11 feet) long a more shallowly-founded wall could run from the eastern end of the slot to the shallow slot between the doorway slot 140 and the east end of the building. This suggests the presence of an L-shaped timber screen in front of the doorway, perhaps roofed as a lean-to structure, with access to the doorway from the western side only. This would have provided an additional enclosed and perhaps roofed space measuring 3.0m wide by c.3.5m long, a floor area of 10.5m², adding another 25% to the floor area of the main building, and even more in terms of usable space as around 20% of the main building was occupied by the hearth complex.

The fill (114) of slot 115 was dark grey-brown friable loam containing charcoal, and some small pieces of ironstone and limestone, some heat reddened. The fill also produced pottery, including the rim and upper body of a large jar and a jug handle (Fig 35, 8 & 9).

Despite the small size of this feature there was also a rich assemblage of animal bone and charred seeds. The animal bone assemblage made a significant addition to the other contemporary material in showing that use of the building was associated with a high status diet, with the slot containing choicer cuts of beef and mutton, as the two staple meats, but in additional there was also part of the pelvis and lower leg of an adult red deer, a foot bone from a young red deer, an ulna from a hare, an unspurred tarso-metatarsal bone from a hen and a humerus from a young chick, perhaps indicative of backyard poultry keeping, and a vertebrae from a plaice, then a relatively expensive marine fish.

The charred seed assemblage was the largest from the site, dominated by cereal grains, mainly free-threshing wheat, and some chaff, but also including bread wheat, rye and barley, with the low proportion of weeds indicating that the cereals had been cleaned ready for consumption before they were accidently burnt. The sample also included hazelnut shell and a range of legumes including probable horse beans (*Vicia faba*) and possible cultivated peas.

The floor levels

Across the eastern half of the building a floor level only survived against the eastern wall, while a more extensive area of floor and the hearth complex survived in the western half of the building (Fig 20). The area inside the northern doorway had been both truncated and disturbed by a combination of Victorian drains and a stanchion pit.

Above the pre-building levelling layer of ironstone chips (344), there had probably been a general sub-floor or floor of clean yellow-brown sandy clay, 50–60mm thick. This survived to the east (135), against wall 132, and to the west (352) around the northern and eastern margins of the hearth complex and abutting the northern wall. To either side of the northern door, there were irregular patches of reddened, scorched floor, similar to but not as intense as those to the east of this building, but of comparable size. Above the sub-floor to the east there was a patchy survival of an earthen floor/occupation layer of medium brown sandy loam (130). This layer produced a number of domestic finds, including an intact perforated whetstone (Fig 42), and numerous refitting pottery sherds found both in this occupation deposit and the rubble over and around the building, including much a shellyware globular jar (Fig 35, 6), suggesting that much pottery had probably been discarded when the building fell out of use. This may also be true of the vessels that ended up in the later pit, 360.

The hearth complex

The south-western corner of the building contained a sequence of probably four successive overlapping hearths, all disturbed by later drains (Figs 20, 27 and 28). The full complexity of the sequence was only evident once most of the surrounding deposits of hearth debris had been removed to expose the scorched areas beneath the early hearths (Fig 27).

The probable first hearth, 375, only survived to the north of hearth 351 and west of hearths 374 and 361, as an irregular and disturbed patch of reddened scorching

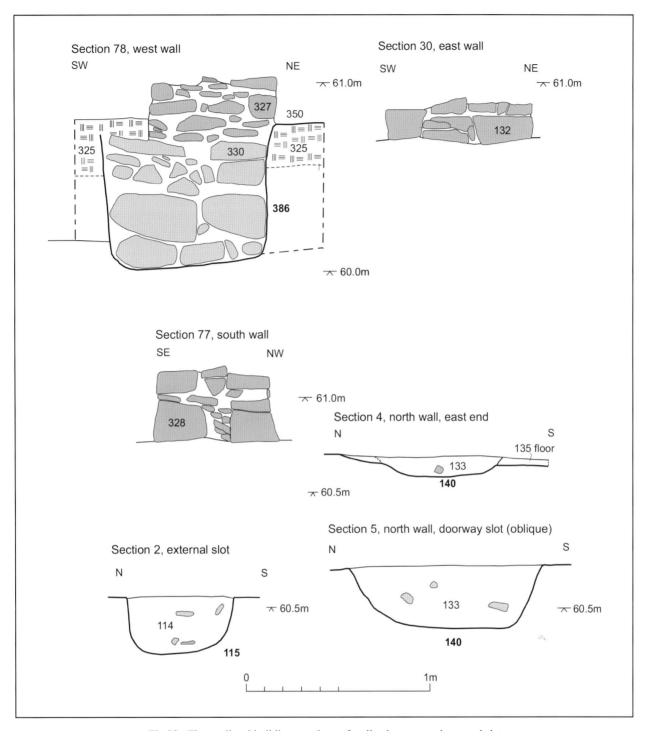

Fig 23: The medieval building: sections of walls, doorway and external slot

around a central area of blackened surface over reddened scorching. This blackened area would have lain beneath a hearth stone, removed when the hearth was decommissioned and replaced. Any former continuation eastwards and southwards had been removed by the later hearths.

The second hearth 374 was defined by a rectangular area of heat reddening, c.1.8m long by 1.4m wide, and a partially surviving central area of blackening over the reddened surface. Both the reddening and the overlying blackened surface was also visible in the section provided

by the modern drain (Figs 27, S.70 & 28, b), where the scorched ground 373, underlay the unburnt base of the final hearth 361. This surviving hearth base would have been overlain by an upper surface of hearth stones that had been removed prior to the construction of the third hearth.

The area of most intense charcoal (363), surviving to the east of the final hearth 361 and its debris (362) (Fig 20), was probably contemporary with the second hearth. The deposit was only 5–20mm thick, described as 'compressed charcoal', possibly all derived from a single board of

Fig 24: The west wall, 327/330: a) in plan looking north, showing the standing wall, 327; b) after further excavation, showing the standing wall and the partially exposed broader foundation, 330 (left); c) the wall and foundations in section, S78, and d)The exposed face of the western wall foundation, looking north-east

wood, since the wood grain on all the charcoal across the scatter shared a common grain alignment of south-west to north-east. Much of this deposit was probably removed in the construction of the final hearth 361.

The end of the third hearth lay to the south-west, comprising a single massive slab of limestone, 351, perhaps 1.0m long and 0.8m wide by 90–100mm thick, and a narrow surround of pitched ironstone, burnt red to purple (Fig 27, S.67). The surface of the slab was grey,

powdery and friable, and the entire slab was laminating and fragmenting as a result of intense and repeated heating, with the ground beneath scorched red (Fig 28, c). This hearth may have been rectangular, like its predecessor and successor, with the southern half of the scorching beneath the final hearth, which penetrated deeper into the ground, belonging to this hearth, but with any superstructure removed. This would indicate a rectangular form, c.1.8m long by 1.4m wide.

Fig 25: The south wall 328: a) in plan looking east; b) wall 328 in section, S77, looking west, and c) the east wall 132, and yellow sandy clay floor with scorching (left), looking east

The fourth and final hearth, 361, was another rectangular setting, at least 1.4m long by 1.2m wide, comprising small pieces of pitched ironstone set in a matrix of brown clayey loam, which had remained unburnt. A partial fired clay surface survived, burnt red to purple, with only the tops of the pitched stones burnt. Unburnt stones along the surviving eastern edge of the hearth suggest that an original kerb of some form, possibly just a raised clay kerb or a second upper layer of pitched stones, had been lost. This final hearth may have had a relatively short period of use, as the scorching had not even penetrated to the base of the pitched stones and its clay matrix, especially when viewed in contrast to the intense burning associated with its predecessor, 351.

The hearth complex was surrounded by an extensive spread of charcoal-rich hearth debris, extending 3.4m east–west by 2.5m north-south. Immediately around the eastern half of the final hearth 361 there was a zone 0.50–0.80m wide, comprising dark-grey sandy loam with moderate charcoal flecking (362). This post-dated the narrow band of intense charcoal (363), contemporary with the second hearth 374 and partially removed in the construction of the later hearths, as discussed above.

An outer zone (350), which abutted the southern wall of the room and extended eastwards to the centre of the building, comprised fine light grey silty loam with frequent charcoal flecks. It may have been part of the broader occupation horizon (130) that overly the floor levels to the north and east, but darker and containing more charcoal through lying close to the hearths, and containing fewer domestic finds.

A soil sample from the charcoal-rich soils (362) around the final hearth produced a lower level of cereals than slot 115, north of the building, but they were similarly mainly of free-threshing wheat, although almost 20% were oats, with some rye and barley. There was little chaff, but weed

Fig 26: The north wall: a) in plan, looking north-east; b) in plan, looking south-west, with doorway slot disturbed by modern drain, foreground, and c) the external slot 115

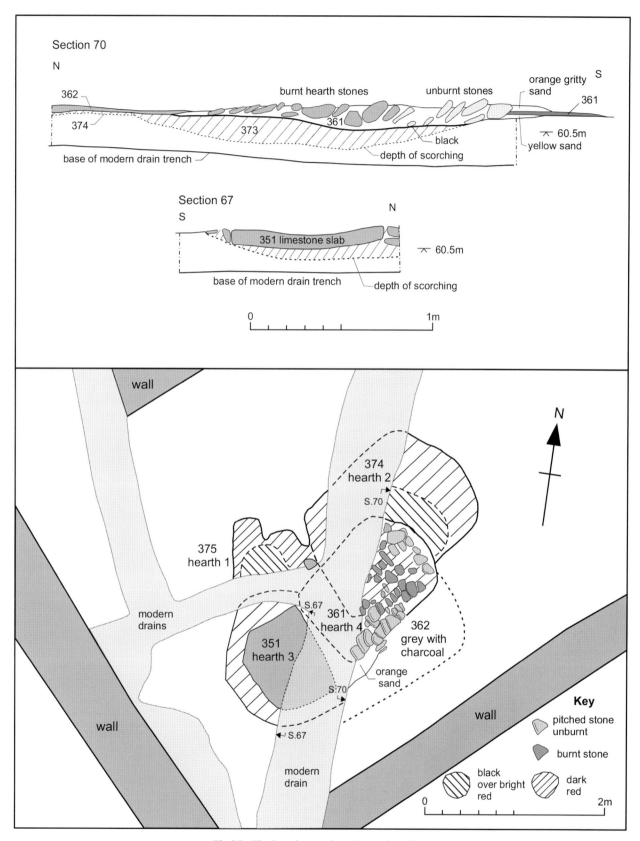

Fig 27: The hearth complex, plan and sections

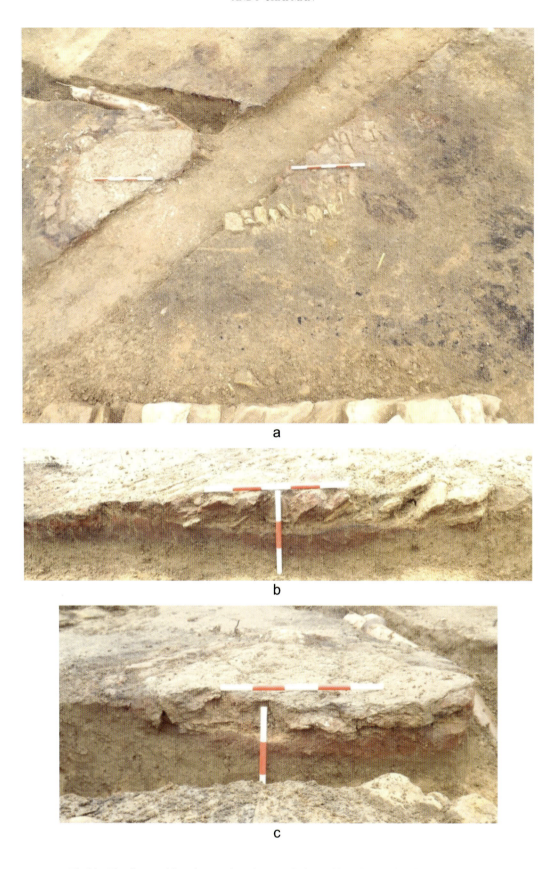

Fig 28: The floor and hearth complex: a) general view of hearth complex, looking north;
b) hearth 361, in section, looking east and c) hearth stone 351, in section, looking west

seeds were numerous, with species such as dock (*Rumex* spp.), stinking mayweed (*Anthemis cotula*) and wild grasses (Poaceae) especially common. The deposit therefore comprised either grain not fully cleaned or perhaps a mixture of cleaned grain along with weed debris from the sieving of a different crop, which had been discarded in the hearth.

The size of these hearths, at up to 1.8m long by 1.4m wide places them a magnitude above the simple central open hearths within a medieval domestic kitchen, where the hearth stones and surround would typically measure no more than *c*.1.0m in diameter (Chapman 2010, 232–236 & Fig 7.86). If the hearths in this building were being used for cooking, then they were cooking on a larger scale, probably for a significantly greater number of people. This is especially so if the additional areas of scorched floor and the multiple areas of scorching to the east of the building, as discussed below, were also all part of a single larger process of providing food and drink to people working and perhaps garrisoned within the Outer Bailey of the castle.

External surfaces south of the building

To the south of the building, the ironstone 'gravel' of the pre-building levelling layer (344) and the remnant layer of stone-rich material (348) against the sloping face of the clay bank, as described previously, was overlain by an extensive soil horizon (326) of medium brown slightly clayey loam, containing a sparse scatter of small fragments of ironstone and some limestone and a little pottery and bone (Fig 20). The pottery is all dated to the earlier 12th century (CP: M1, AD1100–1150), suggesting that the soil horizon accumulated early in the life of the building and probably contained much residual pottery.

Soil horizon (326) accumulated against the lower face of the southern wall of the building to a depth of 200mm, and its presence might suggest that there was little associated activity to the immediate south of the building, as there was no southern doorway, and therefore no reason to provide an adjacent metalled surface.

However, 3.0m to the south of the building, soil horizon (326) was overlain by a small patch of surviving metalled surface (329) comprising steeply-pitched fragments of ironstone, often burnt, and aligned parallel to the south wall of the building (Fig 20). This suggests that there had once been a more extensive and well-laid surface of pitched ironstone that had been largely lost to later disturbance. Whether this was part of a surface that extended northwards and was associated with the building or extending southward and associated with the use of the road seen in the south-east corner of the excavated area, cannot be determined. Pottery from this remnant upper surface is dated to the late 12th to early 13th century (CP: M3) indicating that it was still in use some decades after the building was levelled.

Towards the limit of excavation in the south, both soil horizon (326) and the underlying ironstone surface (344) had been truncated leaving a hollow filled with a mixed layer of medium brown loam (349), which produced the only medieval coin from the site, a silver penny dating to

the reign of Stephen, probably issued sometime between AD1130–1145. The pottery from this deposit is dated to the mid- to late 12th century (CP: M2), broadly contemporary with the adjacent building. The disturbance is likely to be associated with usage of the adjacent road, with a small remnant of detached ironstone road surface surviving to the east of the disturbed area, where it overlay the pre-building ironstone surface (344).

Burning east of the building

The east wall of the building was abutted by a rough surface (141) of flat-laid ironstone and limestone in a matrix of brown sandy loam. This was overlain by a soil horizon (131) that had accumulated in a hollow along the wall face, where it contained pottery, and up to the top of the levelled wall courses. Around and over the north-east corner of the building the uppermost deposit was the demolition rubble 134, but further south and east the ground was more truncated and no demolition rubble survived, with deposits contemporary with the use of the building lying directly beneath later soil horizons, which were removed by machine.

To the east of the building a shallow sub-rectangular hollow, *c*.3.0m wide by *c*.6.0m long, contained eight patches of scorched ground with a linear gully extending westwards from the largest scorched area (Figs 20 and Figs 29–30). The westernmost scorched patch 166 lay above a layer (138) of small ironstone chips, which was probably the easternmost appearance of the extensive layer (344) that underlay the southern half of the building and the yard to the south (Fig 20). The hollow was bounded to the west by surface (141). Above the burnt patches the hollow was filled with worn small pieces of limestone, 100–120mm diameter, in a matrix of brown loam (137).

The areas of scorching were typically brick red across the centre and dark purple around the edges with the occasional blackened patch and the occasional ironstone fragment or small cobble within the soil also burnt purple-red. They were all typically oval with the three smallest, 156, 170 and 172, 0.50–0.60m long by 0.35–0.55m wide and the five medium-sized patches, 148, 152, 156, 166 and 168, 0.90–1.30m long by 0.65–0.85m wide (Table 4). Each patch was sectioned, and the scorching was seen to penetrate from 50–100mm into the ground (Fig 30, S.10 and S.9).

The largest area of scorching, 142, at the north-east limit of the group, was sub-rectangular, *c*.1.80m long by 1.0mm wide. Extending from the western end was a shallow gully 146/150, 2.0m long, 0.50m wide and up to 100mm deep, with a rounded profile (Fig 30, S.10). The fill of the gully was distinct from the scorched areas in containing a darker mix of burnt soils with quantities of grey-black soil with some charcoal, and it also produced a quantity of pottery, including a full profile of an Oxford Ware jar (see Fig 39, 18), and an iron knife, SF13 (see Fig 41b).

The purple-red colour and the occasional blackening of each scorched area indicates that there was prolonged and intense heating of the ground from a source standing just above this level, in a similar fashion to the scorching

Table 4: Dimensions of scorched areas east of the building

Fill/'cut'	Length (m)	Width (m)	Depth of scorching (mm)
141/142	c.1.80	1.00	100
147/148	1.00	0.85	90
151/152	1.30	0.80	100
153/154	0.60	0.50	30
155/156	0.90	0.65	110
165/166	1.15	0.85	70
167/168	1.15	0.85	70
169/170	0.60	0.55	60
171/172	0.50	0.35	50

seen beneath the hearth stone within the main building, and it should also be noted that there were two patches of scorched floor within that building.

In this instance there was no indication that stones had stood above these scorched areas. Although such stones may have been removed, it is possible that each scotched area had been created by a portable structure, such as a brazier stand, which had stood in one position for a period of time before being relocated. However, metal braziers would normally stand on legs well above the ground, to allow air flow, and could only create a scorched patch if hot ashes fell through the base and accumulated in a still-burning heap directly on the ground. An alternative would a metal fire basket set close to ground, to be used in cooking rather than heating.

The oval plan of the scorched patches also indicates that whatever caused them was itself elongated, either oval or sub-rectangular. There appears to have been two sizes, creating small scorched patches 0.5–0.6m long and larger patches 0.9–1.4m long. The largest patch, 142, may mark the position of a more permanent structure, with the associated gully perhaps acting as a flue to provide an increased air flow to raise the temperature. In two instances burnt patches are partially overlain by a later burnt patch, indicating that the area was in use for some time.

No industrial residues were recovered in association with these scorched patches, so the favoured interpretation is that they are the locations of free standing fire-baskets used in cooking to supply food in bulk to men living and/or working within the Outer Bailey of the castle. They may have supplemented usage of the large hearth within the building, perhaps at times when the castle was holding additional men, such as during a royal visit. The large numbers of plain cooking pots associated with the building and also from the pit that cut the levelled south wall of the building are the sort of vessels that would have been utilised during the preparation of food in and around this building.

This area might also have been under cover. To the east a remnant of truncated wall 207, described below, may have been the eastern wall of a structure that perhaps extended as far west as to abut the surviving building and

to enclose the areas of scorching (see Fig 29, Building?). If so, it must have been a later addition, with more shallowly founded walls, perhaps an insubstantial shelter shed open to the north. The truncation of the scorched areas and the subsequent filling of the hollow above them may have been associated with the levelling of such a structure.

The only feature not directly related to the episode of burning, was a small circular pit 144, 0.60m diameter and 0.40m deep, with near vertical sides and a flat base, which cut an area of scorching. The homogeneous fill of grey-brown clayey loam with some ironstone fragments also contained some burnt soil and stones derived from the burnt patch 152 that it cut through, and the bone assemblage included both hare and carrion crow.

A possible eastern building

A small focus of activity lay to the east of the scorched areas, with c.2.0m of the intervening space comprising only homogenous soils, which were taken down by machine. When a stone wall, 207, was seen in the exposed section, the area to the east was taken down to the level of the new wall, and a further wall remnant 208, lay a little further to the east (Fig 19).

Wall 207 was a straight wall, 0.80m wide with a single surviving course comprising irregular flat-laid slabs of ironstone up to 0.45mm long (Figs 19 & 31). To the east of wall 207 a layer of grey-brown loam containing small pieces of ironstone, 215, may have been a levelled layer filling a hollow resulting from subsidence related to the underlying ditch system of the early 12th century. Set into this layer there was a remnant of a curving wall 208, 0.70m wide and comprising one or two courses with larger facing stones and smaller rubble infill (Fig 31).

Both walls survived to lengths of c.3.2m, with each truncated at both the northern and southern end, indicating that they had once extended to greater lengths, but no trace of such continuations had survived. Both lengths of wall had probably survived as they lay within a slightly sunken area over an earlier ditch system.

It seems likely that wall 207 was the eastern wall of an otherwise lost rectangular building or open-sided shed, as already noted above in respect to the cluster of scorched areas to the west. The distance between wall 207 and the end wall of the western building is 10m, although wall 207 was aligned at a slight angle to the other building, comparable to the 11m-length of the surviving building. It is, therefore, possible that wall 207 was the sole surviving wall of a second building, which may even have abutted the east end of the main building. If so, then the areas of scorching might have been fire-basket locations or even truncated hearth bases under a structure perhaps open-fronted for ease of access and use.

If it is assumed that wall 208 had once continued its circular course, then it would have enclosed an area c.2.7m in diameter, abutting the face of wall 207, where the wall faces were 2.2m apart, with an outer circumference of c.4.0m.

Similar D-shaped spaces, around 2.0m in diameter, with a circular wall abutting a straight wall have been seen in medieval village buildings at Raunds, where such a struc-

Fig 29: The scorched areas, gully 150 (left) and pit 144 (centre background), looking north-east, after excavation

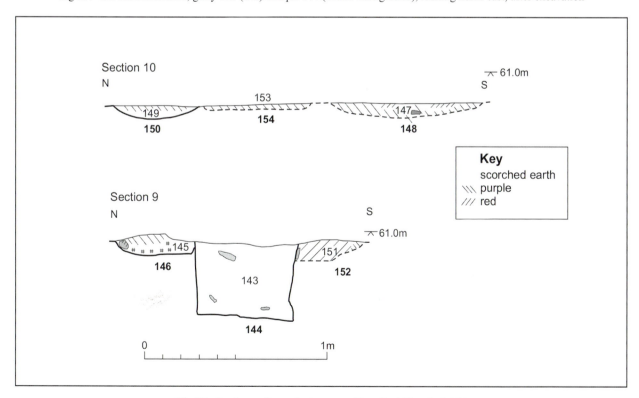

Fig 30: Sections of scorched areas, with gully 150 and pit 144

ture lay at the end of a 13th-century malt house at West Cotton (Chapman 2010, figs 7.74 and 7.75) and at the end of a late medieval combined malt house and bakehouse/ kitchen at Furnells manor (Audouy and Chapman 2008, figs 5.45 and 5.46). In these instances it was suggested that the circular space was to hold a large wooden vat, a tun perhaps, in which to steep barley to encourage sprouting as the first stage of producing malted barley for brewing. This interpretation would be in keeping with the presence of the hearths in the main building and the area between, perhaps at least partially enclosed, containing successive burnt patches perhaps from temporary fire baskets,.

Putting these three elements together: the building containing a large hearth, the succession of temporary fire baskets/hearths, perhaps at least partially enclosed, and a D-shaped structure perhaps associated with preparing barley for malting, we have a building complex set in the south-west corner of the Outer Bailey all aimed at providing food and drink to men garrisoning the castle, with use of this complex running through much of the 12th century.

To the north of the curving wall 208 there was an ill-defined shallow hollow, 216, up to 2.5m in diameter that contained a mixed fill (222) including much ironstone building stone, probably derived from the demolition of the adjacent walls (Fig 19). Within this fill were bones from two or three chickens.

The medieval road

In the south-east corner of the excavated area, there was a disturbed sequence of road surfaces with a total thickness of 160mm (Figs 19, 20 & 32). The road was in excess of 2.0m wide, with the southern edge lying beyond the excavated area. While the northern side of the road was not sharply defined, it was evidently aligned north-east to south-west and heading towards the south-west corner of the Outer Bailey, where it has been postulated that there was a postern gate.

In the south-east corner of the excavated area the earliest surface (342), direct overlay the pre-castle soil horizon and comprised ironstone chips and small fragments of ironstone, with a single horseshoe in this deposit. The composition of the layer was similar to the pre-building levelling layer of ironstone chips (344), but with some larger pieces of ironstone, and both layers may have been part of a single formation process providing consolidated surfaces prior to construction of both building and road.

Above this there was a mix of disordered soil and stones containing pottery, part of a semi-articulated animal carcass and six horseshoes (335). The mixed soils only produced seven sherds of pottery, all residual from the underlying soil horizon. Patchy areas of intact road surface did survive and comprised flat-laid ironstone, 200–300mm across, with worn surfaces and smoothly rounded edges, often cracked *in-situ* (Fig 32).

If the postern gate remained open throughout the medieval period, as seems likely given the presence of a gateway in the same position in the mid-19th century,

Fig 31: Curving wall 208 and wall 207, background, looking west

Fig 32: Disturbed road surface, 335, of worn and cracked ironstone, looking west

passage through it must have been light enough or infrequent enough for it not to require a metalled road. This would suggest that access was only to and from the Outer Bailey, with no provision for direct access to the Inner Bailey, with usage of the Outer Bailey declining sharply during the late 12th to early 13th centuries, and remaining at a low level throughout the later use of the castle.

The demolition of the building

Towards the end of the 12th century, the building was levelled. The walls were all lowered to a height of 0.20–0.35m high, three or four average width courses. The interior of the building was filled with demolition rubble (324), comprising a medium brown slightly clayey loam containing small and medium fragments of ironstone wall stones scattered through the matrix, but with large wall stones clustered against the wall faces, indicating that the lower courses had simply been pushed over into the interior. There was little pottery or animal bone in this deposit, reflecting its rapid deposition.

The base of the demolition rubble that extended up to 3m to the north (108) and north-east (134) of the building

were a little more mixed and above the densest rubble there were mixed deposits of rubble in a soil matrix (107) and (131) that produced substantial assemblages of both pottery and animal bone, with these deposits combined producing 2.5kg of animal bone and 6.6kg of pottery, the major part of the castle assemblage, only matched by the 4.4kg of pottery from the late pit 360.

There was no rubble around the south-east corner of the building, but this area had the most extensive later disturbance, which had removed the south-east corner of the building itself and the internal floors at this corner. It is uncertain when this occurred, but it might have coincided with the digging of the large pit, 360, which must have occurred only shortly after demolition.

However, there was also no rubble beyond the western half of the southern wall of the building, where survival was better, and this might suggest that this area had been deliberately kept clear of rubble, perhaps because of the continued use of the road to the south of the building.

The only part of the building that was fully robbed at this time was the eastern half of the northern wall where the door surround had been removed to the base of its deep construction slot, 140, along with the adjacent lengths of stone wall. It seems likely that this was to recover the door surround intact for reuse in another building; although the paucity of stone in the construction slot fill might indicate that this was a timber rather than a stone surround.

It is likely that following demolition the building would have formed a raised platform, from the south wall northwards, which perhaps became quite rapidly grassed over.

Pit 360

A short length of the eastern end of the southern wall, 139, with partially displaced stones, lay on the edge of a large oval pit, 360, which had removed 2.0m of the wall (Fig 20). The pit measured 2.6m by 2.2m and was 1.0m deep with a flat base and consistently steep sides, suggesting that it was filled quite rapidly with little time for the upper edges to show any signs of additional collapse or erosion (Fig 33–34).

The primary fill (379), which had been deposited from the northern edge, was of loose dark grey-brown silty sand. It contained 4.4kg of pottery as large sherds which comprised most of four large shelly coarseware jars with sooted bases (see Figs 35–38). These are broadly contemporary with the pottery in use within the building, and it is

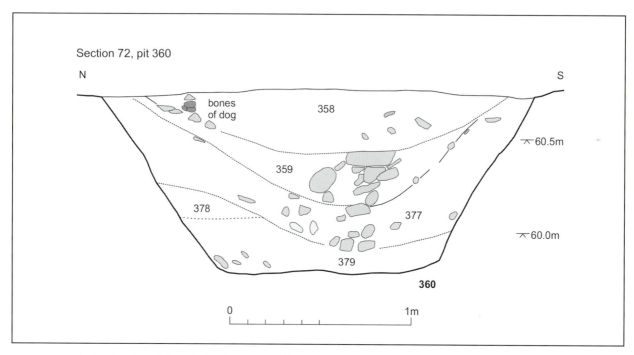

Fig 33: Section of pit 360, showing stone rubble within the secondary fills and dog bones in the upper fill

Fig 34: Pit 360, looking east

possible that they came from dumped pottery left within the building at abandonment and levelling, similar to the material from the occupation layer (130).

The pit fills above this (377, 359 and 358) contained little pottery and had probably been dumped in rapid succession, comprising grey-brown sandy loams containing quantities of ironstone building rubble, probably from the levelled building, with the larger stones rolling towards the centre of the pit due to the steep tip angles against the pit sides. Against the northern upper edge of the pit, where layers 377, 359 and 358 merged, there was a cluster of animal bone that included much of one dog, and parts from others. A scatter of larger stone rubble across the top of the pit at surface level, removed before the section was cut; was probably a final consolidation of the pit fills after the deposition of the dogs, perhaps as partial carcasses.

Drain/gully 339

Following the levelling of the building, a curving length of gully, 339, cut through the southern wall of the building and continued southwards for at least 5m, deepening to the south (Fig 20). Its relationship to the later roadway was not established. This probable drain was up to 0.8m wide by 0.2m deep. It cut through the building wall at right angles, but if it did continue through the internal demolition rubble this was not recognised during excavation. The fill (338) was loose dark grey-brown clayey silt, containing pottery and animal bone, but a soil sample produced little, probably reflecting the declining use of this area at the time.

The medieval and post-medieval pottery
Paul Blinkhorn

The pottery assemblage dating to the 11th century and later comprises 1,531 sherds with a total weight of 27.73kg. The estimated vessel equivalent (EVE) by summation of surviving rimsherd circumference is 17.34. The assemblage was quantified using the chronology and coding system of the Northamptonshire County Ceramic Type-Series (CTS) (Table 5).

The pottery occurrence by number and weight of sherds per context by fabric type is shown in Table 6. The range of fabric types is typical of Saxo-Norman and medieval sites in the town (McCarthy 1979), although it is striking that usually common 13th-century wares, such as Lyveden/Stanion 'B' Ware (fabric F320), Brill/Boarstall Ware (fabric F324) and Potterspury Ware (fabric F329) are almost entirely absent. This suggests very strongly that after the early years of the 13th century there was very little activity in this area that resulted in below ground pottery deposition.

Chronological and Qualitative Analysis

Each context-specific assemblage was given a ceramic phase-date base on the range of ware-types present (Table 6), along with the occurrence by number and weight of sherds and EVE, and the mean sherd weight for the phase.

The range of fabric types present and the pottery occurrence per ceramic phase (Table 7) indicate that the main episode of activity, which had begun in the late Saxon

Table 5: Quantification of the medieval and post-medieval pottery

Fabric code	Fabric name (date range)	Sherds	Weight (g)	EVE
F200	T1 (2) type St Neots Ware (AD1000–1200)	395	3,832	3.30
F205	Stamford ware (AD850–1250)	35	311	0.32
F330	Shelly Coarseware (AD1100–1400)	1,021	21,482	12.31
F319	Lyveden/Stanion 'A' ware (AD1150–1400)	41	946	0.70
F346	Bourne 'A' Ware (late 12th-14th century)	21	508	0.18
F360	Miscellaneous Sandy Coarsewares (AD1100–1400)	8	39	0.00
F324	Brill/Boarstall Ware (AD1200–1600)	1	7	0.15
F209	South Lincs Oolitic ware (AD1100–1300),	1	21	0.00
F345	Oxford Ware (mid/late 11th-14th century)	3	518	0.27
F371	Early Brill/Boarstall Ware, late 12th-13th century	1	43	0.11
F403	Midland Purple ware (AD1450–1600)	2	12	0.00
F1000	Miscellaneous 19th- and 20th-century wares	2	11	0.00
Total		**1,531**	**27,730**	**17.34**

Ware quantified above not included in the Northamptonshire type-series:

F371	Early Brill/Boarstall Ware, Oxfordshire fabric OXAW (Mellor 1994, 111).

Fabrics F200, F205 & F209 span the period AD1100–1150, the transition from town to castle, and it is not possible to provide separate phased quantifications.

Table 6: Ceramic phase definition and pottery occurrence per ceramic phase

Ceramic Phase	Date range	Defining Wares	Sherds	Weight (g)	Mean sherd (g)	EVE
M1	AD1100–1150	F330, F360	893	17,514	19.6	10.77
M2	mid-late 12th century	F319	147	1,857	12.6	1.88
M3	late 12th to early 13th century	F346, F371	347	6,793	19.6	4.27
M4	early-mid 13th century	F320, F324	22	267	12.1	0.23
M5	mid-13th to 14th century	F329	0	0	0	0
M6	15th to mid-15th century	F322, F365, F405	0	0	0	0
M7	mid-15th to mid-16th century	F369, F403, F404	2	12	6.0	0
MOD	19th to 20th century	F1000	2	11	5.5	0
		Totals	**1,662**	**28,727**	**17.3**	**19.77**

Table 7: Pottery occurrence per ceramic phase by fabric type, by weight, as a percentage of the phase assemblage

Fabric/ Ceramic Phase	F100	F130	F205	F200	F330	F319	F346	F324	F322	Total weight (g)
M1	1.5%	0.3%	0.6%	9.9%	84.1%	–	–	–	–	17,514
M2	0.8%	1.6%	1.6%	1.6%	85.2%	7.8%	–	–	–	1,857
M3	1.5%	0.3%	0.8%	6.1%	73.2%	11.8%	5.8%	–	–	6,793
M4	0.4%	0	3.0%	0	58.1%	0	32.2%	2.6%	–	267

Shaded cells = residual

town of the 11th century (Ceramic Phase (CP) LSAX2, see Blinkhorn this volume ***-***), continued into the early life of the castle, until the late 12th century/early 13th century (CP M3).

The end date for the main phase of activity is supported by the almost total absence of wares very common in the early to mid-13th century. The latest medieval pottery, the two sherds of Midland Purple Ware aside, is a single sherd of a Brill/Boarstall Ware jug, Other than Stamford Ware, the only other glazed pottery from the site are sherds of a large glazed Bourne 'A' Ware vessel (F346) which is generally dated to the 13th to 14th centuries. However, such pottery is known from late 12th to early 13th century contexts in Lincoln (Young and Vince 2005, 171). There are a number of typological factors which support this end-date. For example, all the Lyveden/Stanion 'A' Ware rimsherds are forms which date to the mid-12th to early 13th centuries, with later types entirely absent. It would appear therefore that the main period of pottery disposal generally ceased in the earlier decades of the 13th century at the absolute latest. This is discussed in more detail below.

The medieval (M1–M3) assemblage is fairly well-preserved, and a number of vessels associated with the excavated building, and in particular pit 260 perhaps associated with the levelling and clearance of the building, could be reconstructed to a full profile.

The presence of residual pottery is very low, with no more than 4% of the pottery in any of the main phases being redeposited material (Table 7). The mean sherd weight (Table 6) is also large, at up to 17.3g. The rimsherd occurrence shows that the medieval groups are

overwhelmingly dominated by jars, along with a small number of bowls and jugs (Table 8). This is again typical of contemporary assemblages in the region.

The Castle

The pottery from the Castle levels, particularly the bailey bank and the building, suggest that this phase of activity started very soon after the backfilling of the latest pre-castle features, and ended in the first decade or two of the 13th century, as indicated by the absence of common glazed wares of the 13th to 14th centuries, other than a single sherd of the Brill/Boarstall Ware.

The only glazed ware present, other than Stamford Ware, are fragments of a single, highly-decorated Bourne 'A' Ware pitcher (Fig 36, 11a-b). Such pottery is traditionally dated to the 13th-14th centuries (see McCarthy and Brooks 1988, 259). However, the kilns were excavated in the 1960s and have never been fully published, and the material appears to have been dated largely on typological

Table 8: Vessel occurrence per ceramic phase, by EVE, as a percentage of the phase assemblage

Ceramic Phase	Jars	Bowls	Jugs	Lamps	Total EVE
M1	8.00	0.83	1.19	0.75	10.77
M2	1.69	0	0.19	0	1.88
M3	3.89	0.23	0.15	0	4.27

grounds. More recently, this material has been shown to occur in Lincoln in horizons dated to *c.*AD 1170–1210 (Young and Vince 2005, 171).

Some of the pottery from this phase is very well preserved, and includes a number of near-complete Shelly Coarseware jars, particularly in the demolition rubble of the building. This suggests that there was a domestic midden associated with the building and, given the number of vessels that showed signs of being heated, cooking seems likely to have taken place there.

The Outer Bailey bank
The clay remnants of the Outer Bailey bank, which were much disturbed by later activity, produced only a small assemblage of pottery (15 sherds, 273g) comprising a mixture of small Saxo-Norman sherds, which are almost certainly residual, and a handful of larger fresher sherds all from individual vessels that date to the first half of the 12th century (CP M1). The assemblage includes the rim of a Shelly Coarseware jug (fabric F330), a typical product of the pottery tradition of the 12th century.

The bank also produced a sherd of Bourne 'A' ware (fabric F346), from layer (325), a disturbed area. It is probably from the base of a vessel found within the building demolition.

The building
The features associated with the building produced a very large group of pottery comprising 683 sherds, weighing 12,835g (EVE = 7.82), with many large sherds and vessels that could be partly reconstructed (eg Fig 35, 4–9). The bulk of it comprises Shelly Coarseware (fabric F330), with 601 sherds weighing 11,023g (EVE = 6.50). There were numerous cross-fits from either an earthen floor or occupation layer (130) to the overlying rubble (107, 109, 131, 133 & 134). This suggests that the pottery was probably originally from a midden associated with the use of this building, and was incorporated into the rubble during the demolition and levelling of the structure. There was very little residual material, with just six small late Saxon sherds present.

Twenty-six sherds (826g) of Lyveden/Stanion 'A' Ware are mainly from a single jar (Fig 35, 4). The vessel is in a very coarse fabric with an everted, triangular rim-form with internal finger-tipping and also with faint incised wavy lines on the shoulder. This is a typical product of the industry in the mid-12th to early 13th centuries (Blinkhorn 2010, 287). The later vessels of this type, in the 13th to 15th centuries, usually have very distinctive plain, double-beaded rims, a finer fabric and lack any sort of incised decoration (ibid).

The vessel occurrence profile also indicates a 12th century date. The bulk of the rims are from jars (EVE = 7.16), along with four bowl rims (EVE = 0.24) and two from jugs (EVE = 0.42). A single largely complete lamp-stem in Shelly Coarseware (fabric F330) was also noted, as was a single large fragment of a vessel with thumbed applied strips and a handle terminal, probably from a large jug or storage jar. The rest of the Shelly Ware jars appear to be fairly large, globular vessels with simple everted rims (Fig 35, 5–7). Slot 115, which is associated with the building, produced pottery of a similar date and

range, such as fragments of Shelly Ware jugs, with strap handles (Fig 35, 9) and a jar with a thumbed "piecrust" rim (Fig 35, 8).

Illustrated pottery (Fig 35)
4: Full profile of jar, rim diameter 270mm, height *c.*190m. Uniform dark grey fabric, brown patches and light sooting on the outer surface. Lyveden/Stanion A ware (fabric F319). Rubble (131), Building
5: Rim and upper body from large jar, rim diameter 285mm. Pale orange fabric with a grey core. Shelly Coarseware (fabric F330). Rubble (131 & 134), Building
6: Rim and body from globular jar, rim diameter 210mm. Orange fabric with a grey core, some sooting on outer surface (fabric F330). Occupation layer/floor (130/135), Building
7: Full profile of jar, rim diameter 250mm, height *c.*250mm. Grey fabric with greyish-orange surfaces (fabric F330). Even sooting on the outer surface of the lower body and base, lime-scale on the inner base. Occupation layer/floor (130/135) and fill (133) of doorway robber trench 140, Building
8: Rim and upper body of jar, with pie-crust rim, rim diameter 260mm. Uniform orange fabric (fabric F330). Fill (114) of slot 115, Building
9: Jug handle. Uniform pale orange-brown fabric with a grey core (fabric F330). Fill (111) of slot 115, Building

Fragments of the Bourne 'A' Ware highly-decorated glazed vessel (Fig 36, 11a-b) were mainly in rubble layer (134), but with cross-fits to the fill (133) of the doorway robber trench 140 and a stony deposit (222) within the hollow 216, north of the curving wall to the east 208. Another large but non-joining sherd from the base of a handle was noted in a remnant of late yard surface (329), to the south of the building (Fig 36, 12), and a fragment of the base was in a disturbed area of the adjacent Outer Bailey bank, layer (325). The only other glazed wares are ten sherds of Stamford Ware, mostly later products of the industry, dating to the 12th century. One very distinctive sherd had part of a large area of applied strip decoration (Fig 36, 13), a style of decoration which is generally late 12th century in date, and very similar to a vessel from Stamford Castle (Kilmurry 1980, fig 78.1).

Illustrated pottery (Fig 36)
11: Glazed jug, orange fabric with a grey core. Same as 12? Dull green glaze on the outer surface, Bourne 'A' (fabric F346). Rubble (134) Building and stony fill (222) of hollow 216
12: Glazed jug, handle terminal from highly decorated glazed jug. Same as 11? Orange fabric with a grey core. Dull green glaze on the outer surface, Bourne 'A' (fabric F346). Late yard surface (329)
13: Pale buff fabric with a pale grey core. Glossy green-ish-yellow glaze on outer surface, Stamford ware (fabric F205). Rubble (134), Building

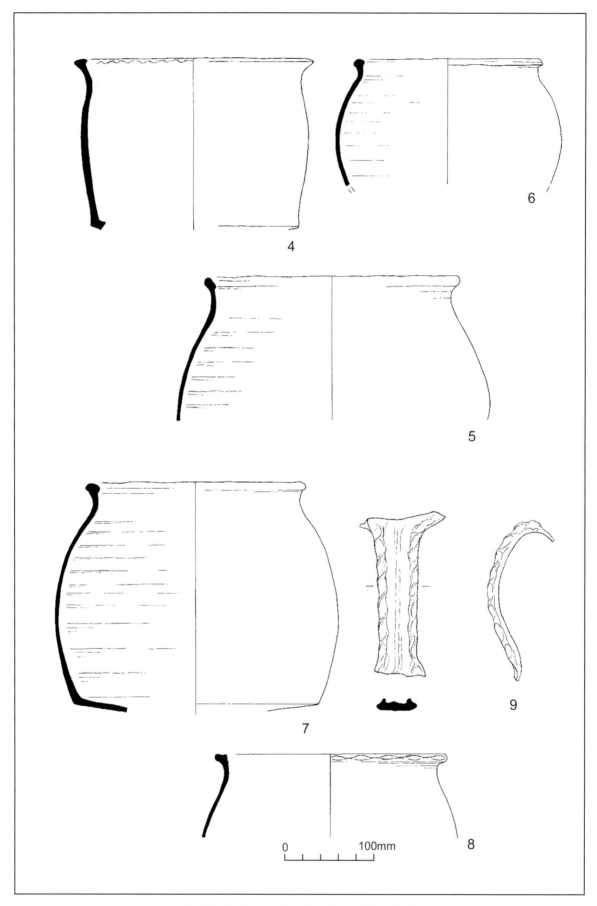

Fig 35: Medieval pottery from the building (4–9)

11a

11b

12

13

Fig 36: Medieval pottery (11–13) (scale 10mm)

The yard

The yard surface (326) south of the main building produced an assemblage of 76 sherds weighing 1142g, mostly comprising Shelly Coarseware and Lyveden 'A' vessels. A single rimsherd from a glazed Bourne 'A' Ware jar was also present and, given the lack of other glazed wares, this strongly suggests a date in the late 12th to 13th centuries. Also present are a handle and a number of rouletted bodysherds from Shelly Coarseware jugs, along with a sherd of Stamford Ware with a late glaze and fabric. All these are typical of the 12th to early 13th centuries. The few refits suggest that most of the pottery is the result of secondary deposition.

Pit 360

Pit 360 cut through the south wall of the levelled building, but the pottery appears no later in date, with no definite evidence that any of it is dated beyond the second half of

the 12th century. The group comprises 62 sherds, weighing 4443g, with the bulk of the assemblage consisting of Shelly Coarsewares (54 sherds, 4362g). The rest of the material consists of a few sherds each of F205, F200 and F319, suggesting a date in the second half of the 12th century. The assemblage is generally in good condition, and mainly comprises a small group of Shelly Coarseware jars, which can be partially reconstructed (Figs 37 & 38, 14–16; Fig 39, 17), all of which are quite large. One of them has the terminal of a thumbed applied strip present (Fig 39, 17), indicating it was a storage jar or possibly a large jug. Such vessels are fairly typically of the 12th century. Another jar (Figs 37 & 38, 14) is evidently a waster that was both fired and utilised, as indicated by the sooted base; despite the distorted rim where the upper body had sagged, probably before firing.

One of the sherds of Stamford Ware is from a jar rim with an everted rim and glossy pale green glaze on both surfaces, and incised horizontal cordons on the outer body. It pre-dates the late 11th century (Kilmurry 1980, 130). The small rim assemblage comprises entirely jars, other than a single Shelly Coarseware jug rim. As noted above, this is very typical of the 12th century.

The whole assemblage was checked for cross-fits with the pottery from the building, but none were made, so it cannot be stated with any confidence that the material from this pit came from the same source, despite being broadly the same date and in a condition which suggests it has been subject to very little transportation or reposition. Given the nature of the assemblage, which is very similar in composition and the range of vessel forms, the pottery clearly must have been introduced as fill from a disused midden or similar, possibly from a different source to that used in the levelling of the building.

Illustrated pottery (Figs 37–39)

14: Full profile of a jar, rim diameter 195mm, height 210mm. Pale orange-brown fabric with a grey core. Shelly Coarseware (fabric F330). Outer surface of lower body is lightly sooted. Distorted in firing but still utilised, Primary fill (379), pit 360

15: Full profile of a jar, rim diameter 275mm, height *c.*255mm. Pale orange-red fabric with a grey core (fabric F330). Outer surface of lower body is lightly sooted. Primary fill (379), pit 360

16: Full profile of a jar, rim diameter 270mm, height *c.*275mm. Pale orange fabric with a grey core (fabric F330). Outer surface of lower body is lightly sooted. Primary fill (379), pit 360

17: Lower body and base of a storage jar or jug. Orange-red fabric with a grey core (fabric F330). Outer surface of lower body is lightly sooted. Primary fill (379), pit 360

Areas of scorched soil and a gully east of the building

Shallow gully 150 produced only two sherds of pottery, but one of them is a full profile of an Oxford Ware jar (Fig 39, 18). Such vessels are generally date to the 11th to 14th centuries. This example is hand-made and wheel-finished rather than thrown, so it probably dates to the earlier part of the tradition, which is in keeping with the general pattern of pottery deposition at the site. The presence of a small sherd of Shelly Coarseware in the same feature indicates that this pot is most likely of 12th century date. A single small, non-joining bodysherd from the same pot occurred in fill (143) of pit 144.

The rest of the pottery from areas of scorched soils consisted of small groups of small sherds, suggesting that all of the pottery was a product of secondary deposition, most likely residual material in the underlying soils.

The eastern road

This feature produced a small pottery assemblage, 29 sherds weighing 276g, but it is one of the very few features from the site which shows activity continuing into the 13th century. The evidence comes in the form of a small rimsherd from a Brill/Boarstall jug, the only pottery of this type from the entire site. There was also a large fragment of a Bourne 'A' glazed jug, which is almost certainly from the same vessel as those from the rubble around the building (Fig 36, 12). Both of these come from the upper surface of the road (329). It is of note that all the pottery from the lower surface of the road (335) is late Saxon and Saxo-Norman, probably residual from earlier soils that here were perhaps utilised or disturbed in the formation of the basal layers of the road.

The eastern walls

The eastern walls 207 and 208 produced a small assemblage of small abraded sherds of Saxo-Norman material, probably all residual.

Two groups of pottery occurred in the stony soil layer (215) between the two walls. A total of 115 sherds, weighing 1884g, appear to be of early–mid 12th century date. A fairly large portion of the material comprises refitting sherds forming the full profile of a large Shelly Ware jar (Fig 39, 19). Most of the other sherds are fairly large and in reasonably good condition and it seems likely that this material, given its good state of preservation, may be the partial remains of a midden associated with this eastern building. This group was checked against the pottery from the main building and pit 360, but no cross-fits were noted, suggesting that this was not the source of the material used in the backfill and consolidation of those features.

The disturbed soils (209) left following machine stripping over walls 207 and 208 contained 26 sherds, weighing 366g (EVE = 0.46). Most of the pottery is Shelly Coarseware, along with a few sherds of Lyveden 'A' Ware, but also present is a fairly large and fresh rimsherd from an early Brill/Boarstall coarseware jar. This indicates a date between the late 12th to early 13th centuries for the deposit, suggesting that final activity in this area did extend into the early 13th century.

Illustrated pottery (Fig 39)

18: Full profile of jar, rim diameter 245mm, height *c.*240mm. Dark grey fabric with a greyish-orange outer surface, evenly sooted below the waist and on the edge of the rim. Oxford ware (fabric F345). Fill (149), gully 150.

19: Shelly coarseware (fabric F330). Full profile of large jar, rim diameter 300mm, height 245mm. Grey fabric with pale orange surfaces. Outer surface evenly sooted below the shoulder, lime-scale and scorch-mark on inner surface of the base-pad. Soil layer (215), below and between eastern walls 207 and 208

Bibliography: pottery

Blinkhorn, P, 2010 The Saxon and medieval pottery, 259–333, *in* A Chapman, *West Cotton, Raunds: a study of medieval settlement dynamics AD450–1450. Excavation of a deserted medieval hamlet in Northamptonshire, 1985–89,* Oxbow Books

Blinkhorn, P, 1999 Middle and Late Saxon Pottery, *in* A Chapman, 1999, 55–7

Blinkhorn, P, 2021 The early medieval pottery from Northampton Station, in A Chapman 2021 Late Saxon and Saxo-Norman occupation beneath the Outer Bailey of Northampton Castle, *Northamptonshire Archaeol*, **41**, 100–104

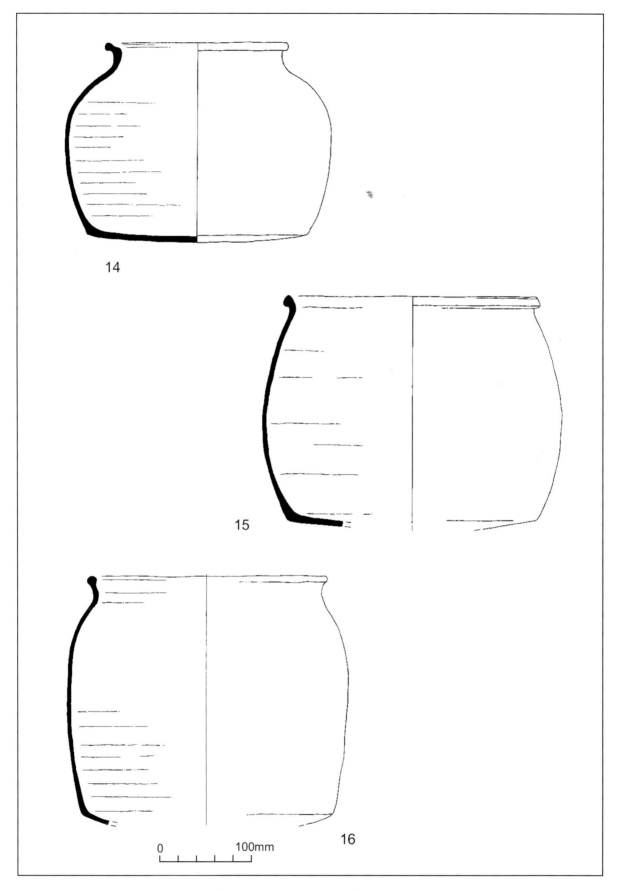

Fig 37: Medieval pottery from pit 360 (14–16)

14   15

16

Fig 38: Medieval pottery from pit 360, showing the sooted bases of the cooking pots (Scale 50mm)

Chapman, A, 1999 Excavation of the Town Defences at Green Street, Northampton, 1995–6, *Northamptonshire Archaeol,* **28**, 25–60

Dark, K, 2001   *Byzantine Pottery,* Tempus

Denham, V, 1985 The Pottery, *in* J H Williams, M Shaw and V Denham, *Middle Saxon Palaces at Northampton,* Northampton Development Corporation Archaeol Monog, **4**, 46–64

Gaimster, D, 1997*German Stoneware,* British Museum Publications

Kilmurry, K, 1980 *The Pottery Industry of Stamford, Lincs. c.AD850–1250,* British Archaeol Rep British Ser, **84**

McCarthy, M, 1979 The Pottery, *in* J H Williams, *St Peter's St, Northampton: Excavations 1973–76,* Northampton Development Corporation Archaeol Monog, **2**, 151–242

McCarthy, M, and Brooks, C M, 1988 *Medieval Pottery in Britain, AD 900–1600,* Leicester: Leicester University

Mellor, M, 1994 Oxford Pottery: A Synthesis of middle and late Saxon, medieval and early post-medieval pottery in the Oxford Region, *Oxoniensia,* **59**, 17–217

Slowikowski, A, 2005   Pottery Production and Use, *in* P Millar and T Wilson with C Harward, *Saxon, medieval and post-medieval settlement at Sol Central, Marefair, Northampton,* MoLAS Monog, **27**, 62– 4

Williams, J H, and Shaw, M, 1981 Excavations in Chalk Lane, Northampton, *Northamptonshire Archaeol,* **16**, 87–135

Young, J, and Vince, A, with Nailor, V, 2005   *A Corpus of Anglo-Saxon and Medieval Pottery from Lincoln,* Lincoln Archaeol Studies, **7**

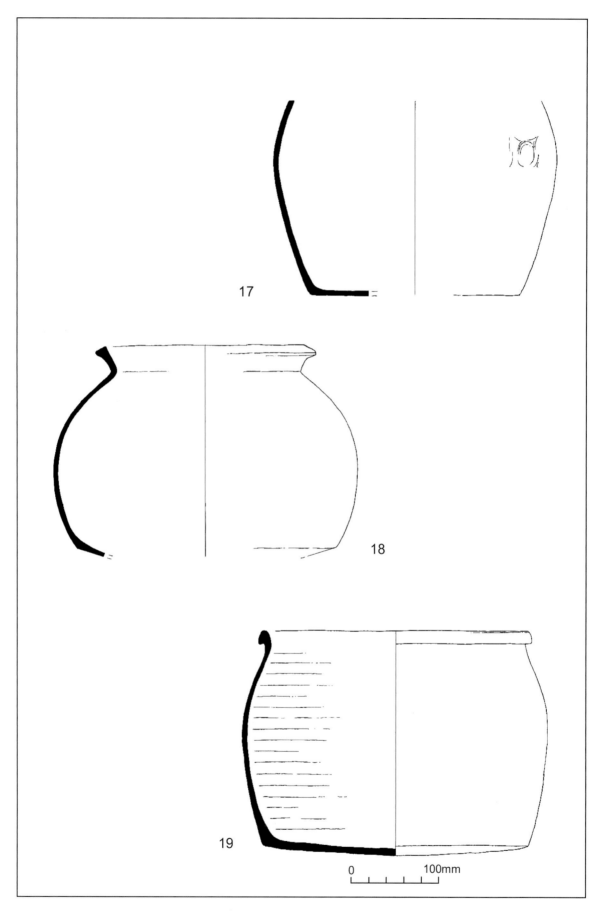

Fig 39: Medieval pottery (17–19)

Medieval finds from the castle
Tora Hylton
with Andy Chapman, Pat Chapman and Steve Critchley

The excavations produced 35 portable finds from deposits relating to the medieval building and the adjacent road surface within the Outer Bailey of the castle. In addition, there is a small group of architectural stone and ceramic roof tile. There are a few post-medieval finds, but only those relating to the medieval and later stratigraphy are included. Finds from pre-castle deposits are reported separately (Hylton this volume 105–109).

The iron objects, excluding nails and small fragments, were submitted for X-ray, undertaken by Dr Graham Morgan of CGM Conservators. This provided a permanent record and in some cases it enabled identification and revealed technical details not previously visible.

One group of artefacts was associated with the medieval building, coming from rubble deposits 109, 134 and 183; a soil layer 130 immediately above the intact floor surface, and also a small group of pits, 170 and 201, and a gully 150 adjacent to the eastern wall of the building. Another group was recovered from the remains of road surfaces 335 and 342 in the south-east corner of the site.

The assemblage is small but, as would be expected, the range represented is significantly different from the pre-castle material (Table 9). Manufacturing activities

are not represented and the finds reflect higher status activities including: trade; the use of weapons, either for hunting or warfare; and there is greater evidence for the presence of horses. The presence of gilded mounts, both for use on horses and for ornamenting caskets and boxes attest to greater wealth.

Equipment and furnishings

Two copper alloy mounts would have been used to enhance items like chests, boxes and caskets.

From rubble layer 131 beyond the north-east corner of the medieval building, there is a copper alloy strip (SF11), 47mm long (incomplete, broken at one end) by 6mm wide with a rounded terminal, with spots of gilding

Table 9: Quantification of finds from the medieval castle (12th century)

Object type	Number
Equipment and furnishings	
Decorative mounts	2
Nails	4
Tools	
Knives	1
Hones and sharpeners	1
Horse equipment	
Horseshoes	13
Pendant	1
Weapons	
Arrowheads	2
Scabbard chape	1
Trade	
Coins	1
Scales (Balance fork)	1
Weight	1
Miscellaneous and unidentified	
Copper alloy	2
Iron	2
Lead (waste)	3
Total	**35**

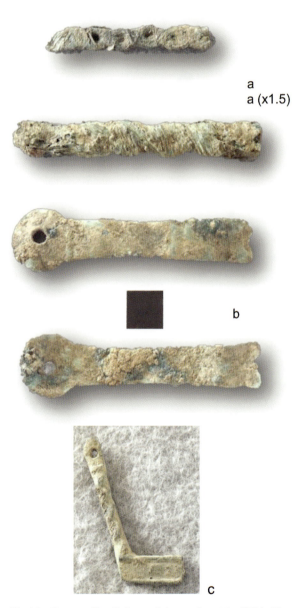

a
a (x1.5)

b

c

Fig 40: Copper alloy fittings: a) decorative strip. SF11; b) decorative strip with rounded terminal, SF49 and c) scabbard chape, incomplete, SF6 (Scale 10mm)

evident on the upper surface (Fig 40, a). The decorative motif, formed by punched depressions and scalloping on both edges, forms a two-strand interlace. However, this is partly obscured by the mineralised remains of organic material that had been tightly wrapped around the mount. This is particularly evident on the plain back (Fig 40, shown at x1.5 for clarity). There is a similar example from Winchester (Hinton 1990, fig 222, 2368, 2376), recovered from a 14th to 15th-century deposit.

From the clay of the Outer Bailey bank, 325, there is part of a gilded hinge-strap (SF49), from a small box or casket (cf Hinton 1990, fig 223, 2383). The fitting is 68mm long, incomplete, broken at a probable attachment perforation. The strip is 10–12mm wide, with the sides slightly concave, and the terminal is 18mm in diameter. A pronounced ridge separates the strip from the rounded terminal, which is slightly domed, with a central attachment perforation from which linear mouldings radiate (Fig 40, b). There are traces of gilding on the strip and the terminal.

Weapons

Objects derived from weaponry comprise: a chape, the protective fitting from the end of a sword scabbard, and an arrowhead for military or hunting use.

Scabbard chape

Part of a cast copper alloy scabbard chape (SF6) was recovered from rubble deposits (109) abutting the north wall of the medieval building, dating to the 12th century. Only half the chape survives, 42mm high and 28mm wide (incomplete). Originally it would have comprised two angled arms at either end of a plain horizontal band with marginal raised ridges; the right hand arm and the end of the horizontal band are lost (Fig 40, c). The surviving arm has a D-shaped section; the inner face is flat and the convex outer surface is ornamented with oblique mouldings giving a twisted-rope effect. The chape would have been secured to the scabbard by a rivet through each of the perforated terminal lugs. This is an early sword chape of the 11th-12th centuries, of simple form, less ornate than those of the high medieval period. An example of similar form and decoration from Gravely, Cambridgeshire is recorded on the Portable Antiquities Database (Unique ID: BH-297687; https://finds.org.uk/database/search/results/q/BH-297687; Accessed 02/03/2018).

Arrowheads

There are two socketed arrowheads from medieval contexts. An almost complete example (SF46) (Fig 41, a), was recovered from a soil horizon (334) above the medieval road surfaces in the south-east corner of the site. Arrowheads of this type are distinctive; they have a circular socket and a square cross-section narrowing to a long thin point, which is missing. The arrowhead is 96mm long, with the pointed end missing. The end of the socket is 10mm in diameter and it is c.50mm long, with the blade beyond the socket 5mm square, tapering to 4mm at the break. There is an incomplete socket fragment (SF21) from the demolition rubble (134).

The arrowhead may be equated to Museum of London Medieval Catalogue Type 7 (Ward-Perkins 1940, fig 16) and Jessop's Type M7 (1996, fig 1). Characteristically, weapons of this type would have been shot from a cross bow or longbow and their slender profile ensures that they are ideal for penetrating heavy cloth, leather or mail, and even shields or armour. Similar examples have been recorded from castle sites elsewhere in England (cf ibid 1996, 198) dating from the 11th to 14th centuries.

Tools

A whittle-tang knife (SF13) was recovered from a gully 150, east of the medieval building. Whittle-tang knives terminate in a tapered prong (tang) on to which an organic handle of wood, horn or bone would have been hafted. With the exception of the tip of the tang, the knife is complete and the X-ray reveals that the tang is central to the blade with a sloping shoulder and that the back of the blade and the cutting edge are horizontal with a curving taper to the tip (Fig 41 b). The knife is relatively short measuring just c.93mm long, with the blade 73mm long and up to 15mm wide, and the tang 20mm long, but incomplete.

A micaceous schist whetstone (SF8) was recovered from the occupation level (130) above the floor in the medieval building. This is a complete example of a large personal hone, 130mm long, up to 17mm wide and 13mm thick, worn smooth, with the broader upper end drilled to hold a thong for suspension from a belt (Fig 42).

Coins and trade

Evidence for commercial activity is represented by a worn hammered silver coin, a fragment from a balance and a possible lead weight.

Medieval coin by Steve Critchley

There is a single medieval coin (SF47) a silver penny, from disturbed deposits (349) to the south of the building on the margins of the metalled road. The coin is in a poor condition, with the obverse design lost, so there is no indication of the monarch. The reverse has a Cross Moline in the centre, and while the surrounding lettering is illegible, the cross itself suggests that this is an issue of Stephen c.1135–1154, either the Watford type issue 1136–1145 or an irregular Civil War issue, c.1130– c.1145.

Balance

Balances are used for the accurate weighing of precious commodities. A small fragment of a 'stirrup' or balance fork (SF31), just 19mm long, was recovered from the general medieval soil horizon (106). Although incomplete, the fragment represents the lower half of a balance fork-arm which has fractured through the small circular hole at the base. The hole would have connected the "pointer" and balance arm by means of a spindle. Balances

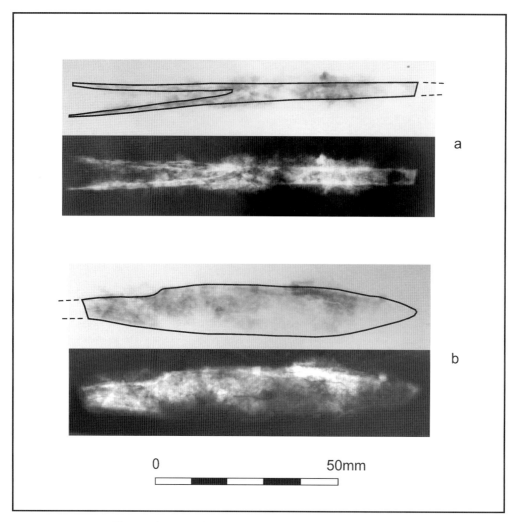

Fig 41: a) Socketed iron arrowhead, SF46; b) iron knife, SF13

are not uncommon in Saxon and medieval deposits, they are generally assumed to have been the property of merchants and craftsmen and therefore their constituent parts are often recovered from urban contexts. Evidence for the use of balances has been recovered elsewhere in Northampton, including a complete balance arm with pointer and balance fork from St Peter's Street (Oakley 1979, fig 111, 91).

A possible lead weight (SF10) was recovered in the evaluation from a layer of small ironstone (27) beyond the north wall of the medieval building and sealed by the demolition rubble (108). The weight is sub-spherical, recessed at the top, perforated and weighs 38.9g equivalent to 1.37ounces.

Horse furniture

Horseshoes
Thirteen horseshoes, one complete and 12 incomplete, were recovered from medieval deposits. Seven of the horseshoes were recovered from the south-east corner of the site on a worn surface (335) and an ironstone surface

(342), the remains of a roadway. Smaller numbers were recovered from the fills of pits and other soil layers (Table 10).

Three types of horseshoe were identified, based on shoe shape, counter sinking and the shape of the nail hole (cf. Clark 1995).

Type 1: the earliest type represented (SF53 and SF56) (Fig 43, a). The shoe is broad, the outer edge is rounded (but may be slightly wavy), it has a wide web with rectangular counter sinkings and circular nail holes. Type 1 dates to the 10th to 11th centuries.

Type 2: the predominant type, with nine examples: (SF1, 9, 12, 14, 50–52, 54 and 55) (Fig 43 b & c). Five horseshoes were recovered from the worn road surface 335, two from a medieval layer (131) over the burnt areas east of the building, one from gully 170, and one from soil horizon (17) over the medieval building. This type of horseshoe is often referred to as a "Norman" horseshoe. The outer edge displays varying degrees of waviness, created during the punching of the counter-sunk depressions, they have rectangular or ovoid counter sinkings with circular (Type 2a) or rectangular (Type 2b) nail holes. There are three nail holes on each branch and

236

Fig 42: Whetstone in micaceous Schist (Norwegian Ragstone), SF8 (Scale 10mm)

Table 10: Classification of horseshoe types

Context/ type	Horseshoe type
17, Soil over building	Type 2 – Incomplete, branch only, SF1
131, rubble beyond building	Type 2a – Incomplete, branch only, thickened calkin, SF9
	Type 2a – Incomplete, branch only, thickened calkin, SF12
	Type 3 – Incomplete, toe section only, SF18
Fill 169, gully 170	Type 2a – Incomplete, branch only, SF14
215, E under wall 208	Unidentifiable-Incomplete, heel only, thickened calkin, SF29
335, SE worn surface	Type 2a – Incomplete, branch only, SF50
	Type 2a – Incomplete, terminals/heels missing, SF51
	Type 2b – Complete (L: 110mm, W: 95mm), thickened calkin, SF52
	Type 1 – Incomplete, terminal of branches missing, SF53
	Type 2a – Incomplete, branch only, SF54
	Type 1, Incomplete, terminals of branches missing, SF56
342, SE ironstone surface	Type 2a – almost complete (L:108mm, W: 92mm, one heel missing, SF55

the heel is tapered. Horseshoes of this type date to the 11th-12th centuries.

Type 3: the latest horseshoe type present, typologically it equates to Clark's Type 4. There is just one example (SF18), and it was recovered from layer (131), rubble abutting the external face of the eastern wall 132 of the medieval building, together with two examples of Type 2a horseshoes. From the 13th century changes occur in the method of production, resulting in squared nail holes with no countersinking. This type has a broad web, which tapers towards the heel and it dates to the mid-13th to 14th centuries.

Five horseshoes are furnished with calkins, a feature on the underside of the heels which helps to prevent the horse from slipping on soft ground. Only one type of calkin is represented, thickened calkins, Museum of London Type A (Clark 1995, 81) and they only occur on Type 2 shoes. The calkins measure up to 13mm deep and extend from 9–15mm from the heel of the shoe.

Horse harness pendant

A complete horse harness pendant (SF3) was recovered from a medieval/post-medieval soil layer (102), above the levelled medieval building. The pendant is cast, annular in form, 21mm diameter, with an integral suspension loop, 30mm long. The pendant has a D-shaped cross-section and decorative mouldings, which give a 'segmented' appearance; and patches of gilding are evident on the upper surface. This example is not dissimilar to a plain annular pendant from Winchester which dates to the mid-13th century (Biddle 1990, fig 337, 3929).

Worked stone by Andy Chapman

From the demolition rubble (324) within the medieval building, there is a pillar of ironstone from a window or door surround (SF48). It stands 300mm (12in high) and is 155mm (6in) wide by 130mm deep. It comprises a three-quarter round moulding, with the back left roughly flattened while the curving face retains vertical chiselling lines. The top and bottom have also been chisel cut. Part

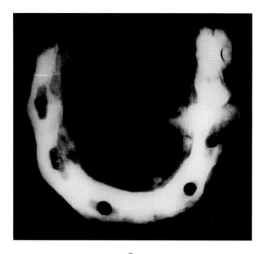

a

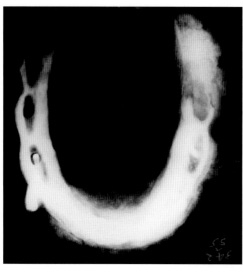

b

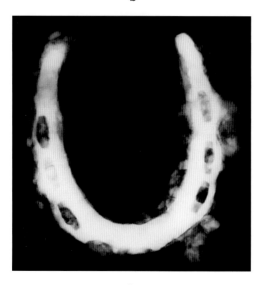

c

Fig 43: Horseshoes: a) Type 1, 10th-11th century, SF56; b) & c) Type 2, "Norman" horseshoes, 11th-12th century: SF55 and SF52 (not to scale)

of the right hand face has been chisel-cut flat and 100mm from the top there is an additional cut back a further 15mm deep (Fig 44, SF48). This pillar may have been part of either the door surround that had been removed from the north wall of the building when it was demolished or part of a window surround within this same building. No traces of mortar survive on the stone.

From soils (215) associated with the eastern walls there is a damaged block of ironstone (SF37). It has a rectangular face, 170mm (6.5in) high by 195mm (7.75in) wide, with diagonal chisel lines. At either end there are remnants of the faced sides, both of which cut back at a little more than a right angle (Fig 44, SF37). These also show diagonal chiselling, as do the top and bottom of the block. The shape of this piece suggests it was from decorative stonework associated with a door or window surround.

While only two fragments of faced building stone were recovered amongst the quantities of disordered irregular building rubble, they are perhaps sufficient to indicate that buildings in this part of the Outer Bailey were at least provided with cut stonework for the window and door surrounds. With the early demise of the buildings in this area, which were levelled at around the end of the 12th century or early in the 13th century, it is likely that cut stone was largely taken away for reuse elsewhere within the castle.

Ceramic tile by Pat Chapman

Shouldered roof tile

From the robber trench, 140, of the doorway to the main building, there is a large sherd, weighing 320g, from the top left corner of a roof tile. The outward sweep of the edge from below the peg hole indicates that this was a shouldered roof tile. The tile is 20mm thick, in a hard reddish-brown fine sandy clay fabric with very occasional small calcareous inclusions up to 4mm long. There are small areas of blackening on the surface and very fragmentary traces of lime mortar adhering to the top surface adjacent to a peg hole, 8mm in diameter.

A large number of shouldered tiles had been reused to line graves and other features at St James' Abbey, Northampton (A Chapman forthcoming). The tile from the castle is very similar to a short tile from grave 3236 at the abbey, with a curve rather than the more usual straight drop to the shoulder (P Chapman forthcoming). The peg hole is slightly smaller than the 10mm diameter of the peg hole on the tile from St James' Abbey, but the same diameter as on shouldered tiles recovered from excavations at Angel Street, Northampton, in the heart of the medieval town. At Angel Street an assemblage of 57 sherds from shouldered roof tiles were recovered (P Chapman in J Brown 2021, 192–5, figs 3.13–3.16).

In London the shouldered peg tile roofing system fell out of use towards the end of the 12th century or during the early 13th century (Smith 1998–99; Armitage et al 1981; Betts in Schofield et al 1990) to be superseded by smaller and thinner rectangular peg tiles, used throughout the rest of the medieval and post-medieval periods. The use of shouldered tiles at Northampton Castle in the

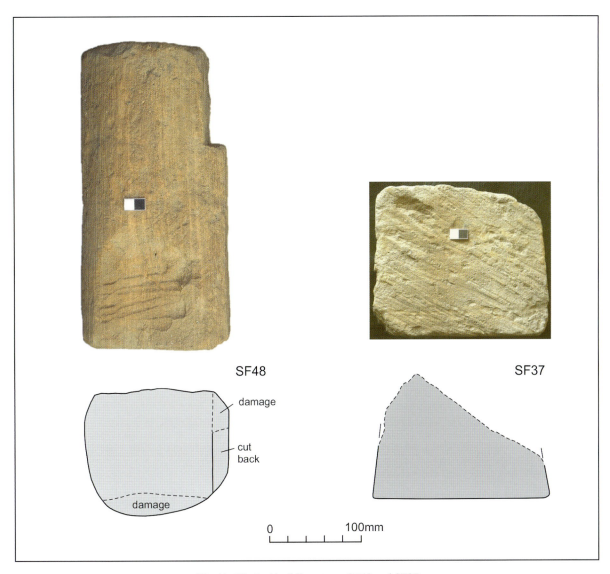

Fig 44: Worked building stone, SF48 and SF37

12th century is consistent with the dates from London. St James' Abbey was built in the 12th century, and the original buildings were probably roofed with shouldered tiles that were subsequently removed with some being stockpiled for use to line graves and also a drainage sump, probably in the 13th century, although the individual graves are not precisely dated. At Angel Street the tile sherds were also coming from deposits dating to the 12th and 13th centuries.

With both the abbey and the castle we are evidently looking at high status sites, and the presence of shouldered tile at Angel Street would suggest the presence of a nearby stone building there also of some status, perhaps the nearby Hospital of St John.

Other roof tile

A small roof tile sherd, weighing just 50g, came from gully 339, which post-dated the levelling of the main building. The sherd is 15mm thick in a fine hard fabric of orange-brown silty clay with some calcareous and burnt stone inclusions of up to 8mm. This sherd comes from a standard peg or nib roof tile of the type used from the 13th century with little variation until the arrival of machine-made tiles from the late 18th century onwards.

Post-medieval finds

A button of the mid-17th century was recovered from a disturbed area (325) on the Outer Bailey bank. It is an undecorated solid button, plano-convex in shape with the corroded remains of the iron loop on the underside (cf. Egan 2005, fig 33, 209).

A small bulbous clay tobacco-pipe bowl is decorated with a thin band of rouletting just below the rim: typologically it equates to Oswalds Type G4, which dates to *c.*1600–40 (1975, 37–41). It was from soil horizon (334) above the medieval road surfaces and below buried topsoil (343), in the south-east corner of the site.

Other finds: Bibliography

Armitage, K H, Pearce, J E, and Vince, A, 1981 Early medieval roof tiles from London, Exhibits at Ballots, *The Antiquaries J*, **61(ii)**, 359–362

Betts, I M, 1990 Appendix 3: Building materials, *in* J Schofield *et al* 1990, 220–229

Biddle, M, (ed) 1990 *Object and Economy in Medieval Winchester*, Winchester Studies, **7**

Biddle, M, 1990 Unidentified Bone Objects, *in* M Biddle 1990, 1129–1145

Brown, J, 2021 *Living opposite to the Hospital of St John: Excavations in medieval Northampton 2014*, Archaeopress Archaeol

Chapman, A, Chapman, P, and Anderson, T, forthcoming The cemetery and buildings of St James' Abbey, Northampton, *Northamptonshire Archaeol*

Chapman, P, 2021 Building material, *in* J Brown, 192–197

Chapman, P, forthcoming Medieval roof tile, *in* A Chapman *et al* forthcoming

Clark, J, 1995 *The Medieval Horse and its Equipment c.1150– c.1450; Medieval Finds from excavations in London*, **5**

Egan, G E, 2005 *Material Culture in London in an age of transition: Tudor and Stuart period finds c1450–c1700 from excavations at riverside sites in Southwark*, MoLAS Monog, **19**

Goodall, I H, 1990b Locks and Keys, *in* M Biddle 1990, 1001–1036

Gryspeerdt, M, Harman, M, and Williams, J H, 1981 The worked bone, *in* J H Williams and M Shaw 1981, 130–132

Harman, M, and Shaw, M, 1985 The worked bone and antler, *in* J Williams *et al*, 1985, 75

Hinton, D A, 1990 Fitting from Reliquaries and other Fines Caskets, *in* M Biddle 1990, 762–81

Hinton, D A, 1990 Harness Pendants and Swivels, *in* M Biddle 1990, 1047–1053

Hylton, T, 2021 Late Saxon and post-Conquest finds from Northampton Station, *in* A Chapman 2021 Late Saxon and Saxo-Norman occupation beneath the Outer Bailey of Northampton Castle, *Northamptonshire Archaeol*, **41**, 105–109

Jessop, O, 1996 A New Artefact Typology for the study of Medieval Arrowheads, *Medieval Archaeol*, **XI**, 192–205

MacGregor, A, 1975 Problems in the interpretation of microscopic wear patterns: the evidence from bone skates, *Journal of Archaeol Science*, **2**, 385–390

MacGregor, A, Mainman, A J, and Rogers, N S H, 1999 *Craft Industry and Everyday Life: Bone, Antler, Ivory and Horn from Anglo-Scandinavian and Medieval York*, The Archaeol of York, The Small Finds, **17/12**

Margeson, S, 1993 *Norwich Households. Medieval and Post-medieval Finds from Norwich Survey Excavations 1971–78*, East Anglian Archaeol Rep, **58**

Oakley, G E, 1979 The Copper Alloy Objects, *in* J H Williams 1979, 248–264

Oakley, G E, 1979 The Worked Bone, *in* J H Williams 1979, 308–18

Oswald, A, 1975 *Clay pipes for the Archaeologist*, British Archaeol Report, **14**

Schofield, J, Allen, P, and Vince, A, 1990 Medieval Buildings and Property Development in the Area of Cheapside, *Trans London Middlesex Archaeol Soc*, **41**, 39–238

Smith, T P, 1998–1999 London's earliest medieval roofing tiles: a comparative study, *Medieval Ceramics*, **22–23**, 66–71

Ward-Perkins, J B, 1940 (reprinted 1993) *London Museum Medieval Catalogue 1940*, Anglia publishing

Williams, J H, 1979 *St Peter's Street, Northampton: Excavations 1973–1976*, Northampton Development Corporation Archaeol Monog, **2**

Williams, J H, and Shaw, M, 1981 Excavations in Chalk Lane, Northampton, 1975–1978, *Northamptonshire Archaeology*, **16**, 87–135

Williams, J, Shaw, M, and Denham, V, 1985 *Middle Saxon Palaces at Northampton*, Northampton Development Corporation Archaeol Monog, **4**

The mammal, bird, fish and amphibian bones from medieval deposits
Philip L Armitage

Introduction

This report summarises the results of the study conducted on hand-collected and sieved animal bone elements and fragments that were identified and analysed following standard zooarchaeological methodological procedures and criteria (see Armitage 1999, 102–103).

For the purposes of the animal bone study, the material is divided into two main periods, based on the dating from finds and the structural and stratigraphic relationships, as follows:

Late Saxon/Saxo-Norman town (11th – early 12th centuries)

Medieval castle (early 12th – late 12th century/ early 13th century)

By far the largest proportion of the assemblage (79%) was derived from the late Saxon/Saxo-Norman contexts, which is considered separately (Armitage this volume 109–118). This report considers the smaller assemblage from medieval deposits within the Outer Bailey of Northampton Castle (Table 10).

Condition

For both periods, the preservation overall is assessed as fair to good with relatively few specimens exhibiting effects from weathering, erosion, leaching or biological degradation (1.1% late Saxon/Saxo-Norman town and 0.8% medieval castle); suggesting most of the bone was disposed of and buried in a comparatively short time. There is a relatively low incidence of dog gnawed bone in the two assemblages (see Armitage this volume, 110, table 10) with no apparent discernible spatial pattern. Likewise, the incidence of burnt bone is exceptionally low (a total of two cattle and one sheep).

The animals

The major domesticates are present in relatively small numbers in comparison to the pre-castle deposits, and the tabulated data for withers height and age by dentition in the medieval assemblage are not repeated here (see Armitage this volume, tables 13 & 14).

Table 10: The identified animal bone elements/fragments (NISP) from medieval castle deposits

Species	Other deposits		pit 360	
	(hand)	(sieve)	(hand)	Totals
Mammals:				
cattle *Bos* (domestic)	210	–	–	210
sheep *Ovis* (domestic)	225	–	–	225
goat *Capra* (domestic)	1	–	–	1
pig *Sus* (domestic)	52	–	–	52
horse *Equus caballus* (domestic)	37	–	–	37
dog *Canis* (domestic)	30	–	66	96
cat *Felis* (domestic)	1	–	–	1
red deer *Cervus elaphus*	8	–	–	8
roe deer *Capreolus capreolus*	–	–	–	–
fallow deer *Dama dama*	2	–	–	2
badger *Meles meles*	–	–	–	5
brown hare Lepus cf. capensis	7	–	–	7
weasel *Mustela nivalis*	–	–	–	1
house mouse *Mus musculus*	–	–	–	2
Subtotals	**573**	**0**	**66**	**3167**
Birds:				
domestic fowl *Gallus gallus* (domestic)	28	–	–	47
grey-lag/domestic goose *Anser anser*/domestic	8	–	–	14
rock dove/domestic pigeon *Columba livia*/domestic	–	–	–	1
carrion crow *Corvus corone*	1	–	–	1
Corvid cf. raven *Corvus corax*		–	–	1
Subtotals	**37**	**0**	**0**	**64**
Amphibians:	–	–	–	
common toad *Bufo bufo*	–	–	–	1
common frog *Rana temporaria*	–	–	–	5
frog/toad	–	–	–	1
Subtotals	**0**	**0**	**0**	**7**
Fish:				
cod *Gadus morhua*	1	–	–	1
herring *Clupea harengus*	–	–	–	1
plaice *Pleuronectes platessa*	–	1	–	1
freshwater eel *Anguilla anguilla*	–	–	–	4
Subtotals	**1**	**1**	**0**	**7**
Totals	**611**	**1**	**66**	**3245**
Percentages	***18.8***	***0.03***	***2.03***	

Cattle

Reconstructed withers heights have shown that for both periods all animals were of similar stature to other contemporary late Saxon/Saxo-Norman and medieval cattle throughout Britain, including both small individuals reminiscent of the unimproved stock of the Iron Age and larger beasts (see Armitage 1982, 53; O'Connor 1982, 21).

Sheep

Reconstructed withers heights have shown that for both periods all animals were of similar stature to other contemporary late Saxon/Saxo-Norman and medieval cattle throughout Britain.

Goats

Goat is represented by a horn core from a single male. All other *ovicaprine* bones examined are ascribed to sheep (applying the criteria of Boessneck *et al* 1964).

Pigs

All the pig material derives from domestic animals. The ages of slaughter documented for these pigs fits well into the pattern recorded at other late Saxon-medieval sites; characterised by the dominance of juvenile, immature and sub-adult animals.

Horses

The late Saxon/Saxo-Norman equid dentition show an age range from *c.*6 to *c.*17 years (Armitage this volume 113, table 15). Length measurements on selected bones also show that the calculated withers heights of the living animals for both periods compares with the size ranges documented for other contemporary late Saxon/Saxo-Norman and medieval equids throughout Britain (Armitage this volume, 112, table 13).

Part of the spine and ribs of a young adult horse were recovered from mixed soils associated within the road surface, 335, along with several horseshoes (Table 11).

Minor species:
Red deer

There are parts of two animals from the medieval deposits. Bones from the left hind quarters of an adult animal were recovered from fill (114) of slot 115 (Table 11).

Morphological features of the innominate bone (criteria of Lemppenau 1964, 20) and metrical comparison of the metatarsal bone with those of modern red deer of known sex (collections of the Natural History Museum London: documented by Armitage 1977, 219) identify the animal as female. Based on the greatest length in the metatarsal bone the withers height in the living animal is calculated to have been 1.022m (method of Godynicki 1965; referenced by von den Driesch & Boessneck 1974).

A younger red deer (sex indeterminate) is represented by a metatarsal bone (with unfused distal epiphysis) from fill (111) of slot 115.

Fallow deer

Medieval castle gully 339 produced two bones: one complete metacarpus and one fragment of proximal epiphysis (caput) of a femur.

Dogs

The fill (359) of pit 360, dated late 12th-early 13th century, contained the part-skeleton (including skull & jawbones) of an adult dog identified as a female (criteria of The and Trouth 1976), whose shoulder height in the living animal is estimated to have been 0.63m (method of Harcourt 1974) (Table 11).

The dog from pit 360 is slightly larger than a dog from Phase 2b (*c.*1000/1074–1250) deposit, Woolmonger Street, Northampton, which had a calculated shoulder height of 0.57m (Armitage 1998–1999, 104). Both of these Northampton dogs compare well with the medium to larger-sized dogs from Flaxengate, Lincoln (contexts dated 900–1200AD) documented by O'Connor (1982, 37) and fall within the upper height range of Anglo-Saxon dogs documented by Harcourt (1974): 0.30–0.71m.

Hare

Seven hare bones came from medieval castle deposits (and none from pre-castle deposits): one ulna, fill (114), slot 115; one femur, fill (143), pit 144; one radius, layer (183) associated with wall 207; one scapula, road layer (222); one ulna, building rubble (108) and one rib and one innominate bone, building rubble (134).

Table 11: Major articulated/associated bone groups (ABGs) from the medieval castle

Group/ Context	Feature	Species	NISP	Age	Anatomy/bone elements present
Building 114	Slot 115	Red Deer	5	Adult Female	pelvis & lower left hind leg: 1 innominate bone; 1 calcaneum; 1 metatarsus; 1 os centrotarsale; 1 first phalanx
E.Road 335	Surface	Horse	20	Young Adult	part spine with ribs: 15 thoracic vertebrae & 5 ribs
Pit 360 359	Pit 360	Female Dog	57	Adult	skull, jawbones, backbone, ribs & leg bones: 1 skull; 2 mandibles; 1 axis; 5 cervical; 12 thoracic; 6 lumbar; 1 sacrum; 16 ribs; 2 scapula; 2 humerus; 2 radius; 1 ulna; 2 metacarpals; 2 innominate bones; 1 femur; 1 first phalanx

Birds:
Domestic fowl

Medieval deposits associated with the excavated building; including the slot 115 and soils (107) above the levelled building rubble, produced a larger group than that from the pre-castle deposits (28 to 19 bones). Measurements taken on selected bones (Table 12) reveal the majority of these birds would have been similar in size to, or just slightly larger than, modern bantams; probably somewhat scrawny to the modern eye. Metrical data for the femora from the castle assemblage reveals these birds to have been of comparative sizes to those of middle Saxon Southampton documented by Bourdillon & Coy (1980, statistical appendix): indicating no improvement had been made in the stock of domestic fowl between the 8th to 10th centuries through to the 12th century.

Layer (107) over building rubble (108) associated with the medieval building yielded a tibiotarsus, which had exostoses (bony outgrowths) on the lateral side of the distal epiphysis; an example of an arthropathy (osteoarthritis).

An unspurred tarsometatarsal bone from the fill (114) of slot 115 is identified as a hen (criteria of West 1982) and together with a humerus from a young chick this perhaps indicates backyard poultry keeping was taking place in the locality; as documented at the Kingswell Street and Woolmonger Street site (Armitage 2008, 207).

Geese

It is difficult to say whether the majority of the bones belonged to wild grey-lag geese or domestic geese. Based on the distal width (Bd = 20.1mm) of the incomplete tarsometatarsus from the castle period, layer (215) associated with walls 207 and 208, this individual probably was a domestic goose, comparing with the largest measurable tarsometatarsus from medieval King's Lynn (Bd = 20.5mm) identified by Bramwell (1977, 401) as a domestic goose. Two immature bones (one humerus & one tarsometatarsus) came from building rubble (131). All other goose bones from both periods are from adult birds.

Fish

From the medieval castle there is a plaice caudal vertebra from fill (111) of slot 115 (Sample 2), associated with the building. The richest deposit comprises four freshwater eel vertebrae from fill (338) of gully 339, a late feature cutting the medieval yard and the south wall of the building, with the only hand-collected specimen a cod articular from the same deposit (Sample 14).

Butchery, food waste, diet and status

Analysis of the food waste reveals the continued important contribution to the diet provided by cattle, sheep and to a lesser extent pigs (Table 10). Wild game features more prominently during the castle period, in contrast to the noticeably meagre inclusion of hunted wild game animals in the late Saxon/Saxo-Norman diet,

This is especially apparent in the food refuse from slot 115, associated with the building, which provides evidence for the consumption of hare and red deer. Viewed in isolation, the presence of the immature red deer metatarsus found in slot 115 could be interpreted as raw material intended for bone working: the long straight shaft of this essentially "meat-poor" bone made it ideal for this purpose. Such bones often were imported into towns in skins destined for tawyers who subsequently passed (sold) these to the bone worker. However, the discovery of remains of a part complete hind leg of red deer in the same deposit that included the metatarsus (see Table 11), lends support to the suggestion made by Strid (2011, 33) that metapodials were included in portions of venison supplied by medieval butchers: but usually such meat was only available to the wealthier/privileged members of medieval society.

The presence of plaice, what for those times was a relatively expensive marine fish, in the sieved soil sample from slot 115, also reflects the purchasing power of the inhabitants. Still further supporting evidence that the food refuse from slot 115 signifies a high status diet is in the quality of the two staple meats. There is a good selection of the choicer cuts of beef and mutton: 25% of the cattle

Table 12: Summary of measurements taken on selected domestic fowl bones

Anatomy	Measurement (mm)	No	Min	Max	Mean
Late Saxon/Saxo-Norman					
Ulna	GL = greatest length	3	70.9	73.6	72.13
Medieval Castle					
Ulna	GL = greatest length	2	56.7	61.2	--
Femur	GL = greatest length	4	69.3	75.8	72.2
	Lm = medial length	4	65.4	70.1	67.9
	Bp = proximal breadth (width)	4	13.6	15.3	14.4
	Dp = proximal depth	4	9.3	10.5	9.8
	SC = smallest breadth (width)	4	6.0	6.4	6.2
	Bd = distal breadth (width)	4	13.5	14.6	13.9
	Dd = distal depth	4	11.5	12.1	11.1

bones represent high value meat; 54.5% medium meat value; 20.5% lowest food value (tail bones & feet); 11.5% of the sheep bones represent high value meat; 82.3% medium meat value; 5.9% lowest food value (tail bones and feet).

Based on the NISP data (Table 10) proportionately more chickens appear to have been eaten in the medieval castle period (28 to 19 in pre-castle deposits). However, the higher value for the castle assemblage may be inflated by over half (54%) of the domestic fowl bones deriving from a single deposit, the mixed and disturbed fills (215) of an irregular hollow, 216, adjacent to the curved wall, 208, which are probably the remains of two to three birds. Of interest are two domestic fowl bones from slot 115; comprising an unspurred tarsometatarsal bone identified as a hen (criteria of West 1982) and a humerus from a young chick, which together perhaps suggest backyard poultry keeping was taking place in the locality; as documented at the Kingswell Street and Woolmonger Street site (Armitage 2008, 207).

Bibliography: animal bone

The full bibliography is available in the report on the pre-castle animal bones assemblage:

Armitage, P L, 2021 The mammal, bird, fish and amphibian bones from pre-castle deposits, *in* A Chapman 2021 Late Saxon and Saxo-Norman occupation beneath the Outer Bailey of Northampton Castle, *Northamptonshire Archaeol*, **41**, 109–117

The charred and waterlogged plant remains from medieval deposits
Anne Davis

Introduction and methods

Two bulk environmental soil samples, from fills of a slot and a hearth associated with the building within the Outer Bailey, were processed by flotation and submitted for assessment of the plant remains, with both taken on to full analysis (Tables 13–15). Material from the underlying late Saxon/Saxo-Norman deposits has been considered separately (Davis this volume, 118–122).

The flots were scanned using a low-powered binocular microscope, and charred plant remains sorted, identified and counted. Sample 13, from the hearth deposits within the building, contained too many small weed seeds (<1mm) for these to be fully separated and quantified. The numbers of seeds from these taxa are marked with an asterisk in Table 13, and are almost certainly underestimated.

Slot 115, north of doorway

The largest assemblage of charred plant remains from the site (including the pre-castle deposits), comprising almost 600 items, came from sample 2, fill 111 of slot 115 (Tables 13–15). Cereal grains made up the majority of these remains, many fragmented and unidentifiable, with almost 90% of those identified from free-threshing wheat (*Triticum aestivum/turgidum*). A number of chaff fragments also came mainly from wheat, with some identifiable as rachis nodes and internodes of bread wheat (*Triticum* cf. *aestivum* s.l.), though many were too fragmentary to identify to species. Several rachis fragments from rye (*Secale cereale*) were also present. Weed seeds made up only 10% of the assemblage, suggesting that the wheat had been fully cleaned, ready for consumption or milling, before it was accidentally burnt, perhaps during parching prior to milling.

Several hazelnut shell fragments (*Corylus avellana*) and charred legumes were also present in this sample. Five large legumes in sample were identified as probable

Table 13: Charred cereal plant remains from medieval deposits

Feature:		Slot 115	Hearth 351
Fill:		111	362
Sample:		2	13
Scientific name (common name)	**Plant part**		
Cereal grains			
Triticum aestivum/turgidum (free–threshing wheat)	–	230	72
Triticum sp. (wheat)	–	16	9
cf. *Triticum* sp. (wheat)	–	38	16
Triticum/Secale sp. (wheat/rye)	–	16	5
Secale cereale L. (rye)	–	10	4
cf. *Secale cereal* (rye)	–	6	4
Hordeum vulgare L. (6–row barley (hulled))	–	4	4
cf. *Hordeum vulgare* (6–row barley (hulled))	–	3	1
Avena sp. (oat)	–	14	17
cf. *Avena* sp. (oat)	–	7	8
Cerealia (indet. cereal (est))	–	100	30
Cereal chaff			
Triticum cf. *aestivum* s.l. (bread wheat)	R	15	–
Triticum aestivum/turgidum (free–threshing wheat)	R	45	3
Secale cereale L. (rye)	R	10	–
Hordeum vulgare L. (barley)	R	1	–
cf. *Hordeum vulgare* (barley)	R	–	1
Cerealia (indet. Cereal)	R	5	–
Cerealia (indet. Cereal)	CN	10	4

Key to plant parts: – seed; CN – culm node; FR – fruit; HD – seed head; NS – nutshell; R – rachis fragment; RT – root; WD – wood

Table 14: Charred wild plant remains from medieval deposits

Feature:		Slot 115	Hearth 351
Fill:		111	362
Sample:		2	13
Wild plants	Plant part		
Ranunculus acris/repens/ Bulbosus (buttercup)	–	2	1
Raphanus raphanistrum L. (wild radish)	FR	1	1
Agrostemma githago L. (corn cockle)	–	–	1
Chenopodium/Atriplex spp. (goosefoot/orache)	–	–	8*
Silene sp. (campions)	–	–	12*
cf. Silene sp. (campions)	–	–	8*
Malva sp. (mallow)	FR	1	–
Vicia/Lathyrus sp. (vetch/wild pea)	–	15	10
Rumex spp. (dock)	–	6	14*
Quercus sp. (oak)	FR	–	1
Plantago lanceolata L. (ribwort)	–	–	1
Galium cf. aparine (cleavers)	–	–	1
Anthemis cotula L. (stinking mayweed)	–	23	28*
Luzula sp. DC (woodrush)	–	–	1
Eleocharis palustris/uniglumis (spike–rush)	–	–	12*
Carex spp. (sedges)	–	1	–
Bromus sp. (bromes)	–	2	3
Avena/Bromus sp. (oat/brome)	–	4	3
Poaceae indet. (grasses)	–	6	25*
Indeterminate	–	–	4
Indeterminate	WD	+++	++++

Table 15: Charred food plant remains from medieval deposits

Feature:		Slot 112	Hearth 351
Fill:		111	362
Sample:		2	13
Food plants	part		
cf. Vicia faba (horsebean)	–	5	–
Vicia/Lathyrus/Pisum sp. (vetch/wild pea/garden pea)	–	10	5
Prunus spinosa L. (sloe)	–	–	–
Corylus avellana L. (hazel)	NS	+	++

horse beans (*Vicia faba*), though none possessed the hilum necessary for definite identification. A number of smaller legumes, identified as vetch/pea (*Vicia/ Lathyrus/ Pisum* sp.) were of a comparable size to cultivated peas or vetches though identification was not possible.

Hearth 351, Building

Cereal grains recovered from sample 13, layer 362, dark charcoal-rich soils around the hearths within the building, were less numerous than those from slot 115, but were similarly composed mainly of free-threshing wheat (*Triticum aestivum/turgidum*), though in this case almost 20% were oats (*Avena* sp.). Very little chaff was seen but, unlike the other samples from this site, small weed seeds were very numerous, with species such as (*Silene* sp.), docks (*Rumex* spp.), stinking mayweed (*Anthemis cotula*) and wild grasses (Poaceae) especially common. This suggests either that the burnt grain had not been fully cleaned, and was yet to undergo a final sieving to remove the weed seeds, or that the assemblage contained a mixture of cleaned grains with weed seeds removed by sieving (probably from a different crop) and discarded in the hearth.

Discussion of the medieval samples

Wheat was clearly the dominant cereal species represented in the two medieval samples, and while the results from only two samples cannot be taken as representative of the site, wheat was the favoured grain for bread-making, as it produces a lighter and tastier loaf than other cereals, so might be expected in a high status situation such as a castle. Rye and barley each made up a very small proportion of the grains in both samples, with oats only a little more abundant in sample 13, from the hearth. As in the late Saxon samples, the oats could not be identified to species as no florets survived, so these may have been either cultivated or wild oat grains.

As organic remains were not preserved in these samples, the only non-cereal foods represented were hazelnut shell fragments and a number of large charred legumes, several of which from slot 115 were identified as probable horse beans. Peas and beans were widely grown during this period, and would have been a valuable food source, particularly for days when meat was not allowed. They have a long storage life when dried and could be eaten whole or ground to flour. They were frequently added to pottage, the thick cereal-based soups which were widely eaten throughout the medieval period by all social classes (Wilson 1973, 183).

Plant remains: Bibliography

Davis 2021 The charred and waterlogged plant remains from pre-castle deposits, *in* Chapman 2021, Late Saxon and Saxo-Norman occupation beneath the Outer Bailey of Northampton Castle, *Northamptonshire Archaeology*, **41**, 118–122

Wilson, C A, 1973 *Food and drink in Britain, From the Stone Age to Recent Times*, Harmondsworth

Post-medieval soil horizons and the coming of the railway

As a postscript to the account of the medieval archaeology and related finds, this final section accounts for the physical changes from post-medieval to modern times that impacted on the Outer Bailey of the castle, to leave an island of stratified medieval deposits in the low-lying south-western corner.

Post-medieval soil horizons

Around the south-eastern corner of the excavated area the modern ground level rose as the access road to the station forecourt had to meet the rising approach to the new West Bridge, constructed in the mid-19th century along with the first railway. As a result, the natural here lay up to 1.95m below ground level with the sequence of medieval and post-medieval soil deposition surviving beneath modern deposits (see Chapman this volume 86, fig 4).

The medieval road of the 12th to early 13th centuries was overlain by a homogeneous and largely stone free soil horizon (334), *c*.0.25m thick, and this was sealed by a buried turf line of dark grey soils (343), *c*.0.125m thick. Soil horizon (343) produced a sherd of post-medieval window glass and an early clay tobacco-pipe bowl dated to the early 17th century.

This depth of soil build-up spans a prolonged period from the early 13th century through to the 19th century in which there was minimal below ground disturbance in this area, and the same was probably true for much of the interior of the Outer Bailey, as the earliest maps all depict the area as open ground containing an orchard. In one temporary section there were a number of pits at regular intervals that can be interpreted as probable tree-planting pits, but the majority of these post-medieval soils were machine excavated.

The upper 0.80m of deposits date from the mid-19th century onward, and comprise 0.3m of dumped clayey soils capped by the foundation layers beneath the tarmac of the road rising to meet the approach to the West Bridge.

In contrast, at the northern end of the site modern soils lay immediately on top of truncated natural, with both the late Saxon and medieval stratigraphy lost, so that only deeper cut features survived (see Chapman this volume 86, fig 4).

The Victorian railway station and its drains

The mid-19th century station

The sequence of development and destruction across the Outer Bailey was catalogued by Henry Dryden in the late 19th century, as discussed previously in relation to the description of the Outer Bailey defences (see Figs 6–10).

The process is also well catalogued through the recorded

history of the railway lines (Gough 1984), and online through *Wikipedia: Northampton railway station.* (https://en.wikipedia.org/wiki/Northampton_railway_station: accessed 29/10/2018).

A proposal made by the London and North Western Railway (L&NWR) for a railway line from Market Harborough to Northampton received Parliamentary approval in 1853. The line's terminus in Northampton was to be on part of the old orchard occupying the Outer Bailey. This had been purchased in 1852 by the absentee Rector of the Parish of St Peter as the site of a new rectory (Gough 1984, 30). The L&NWR agreed to purchase the land for £5,250, and also undertook to complete the parsonage and to rent it back to the Reverend, which explains the presence of both the station and the rectory so close together (Fig 45).

The rectory lay near the centre of the Outer Bailey and would certainly have been at least partly cellared, which would have removed underlying deposits. It later became a school and subsequently Warner's Hotel (see Chapman this volume, 170, figs 25 & 26), as it was considered far too noisy to have a rectory so close to a railway station. The subsequent rectory lay across the north-eastern corner of the Inner Bailey, and was demolished in the Chalk Lane improvement scheme that led to the excavations in the early 1960s (Fig 46).

The new railway cut across the south-west corner of the Outer Bailey but largely occupied the triangular area between the bridge approach, the old river course and the Outer Bailey bank, although to the south the Outer Bailey

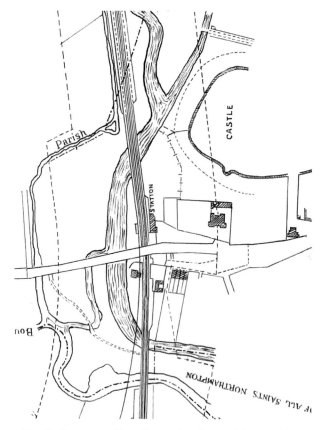

Fig 45: The new railway line and station, and the new West Bridge 1850s, with the south wall of the Outer Bailey removed

bank and wall were levelled to allow for a straighter approach to the West Bridge and for the access to the new station (Fig 45).

The late 19th century clearance

It was only towards the end of the century, 1879–80, that the proposed new railway station and extensive associated sidings and large goods shed, along with the construction of St Andrew's Road, forming the eastern boundary to the station area, resulted in the levelling of much of the surviving earthworks and buildings within the Inner Bailey, and the straightening of the river course and its relocation further to the west (Fig 46 and see Fig 4).

The newly formed Great Northern and London and North Western Joint Railway wished to access the coalfields of Nottinghamshire and Yorkshire, and in 1875, the L&NWR obtained powers to quadruple the main line to the north and to form a new line, the Northampton Loop, through Northampton (Gough 1984, 76).

Additional land was needed at Castle Station to allow for expanded passenger and goods facilities, but owing to the adjacent branch of the River Nene, the only way to expand was eastwards onto the Inner Bailey of the castle. In December 1876, the L&NWR purchased the site from William Walker and subsequently demolished the remains of the castle, following a local debate between the virtues

of retaining the town's heritage and promoting the development and economy of the town, following much the same lines as it would today. The single concession, following a local petition, was the dismantling of the postern gate on the western wall of the Inner Bailey and its reconstruction in the boundary wall of the approach to the new station, where it remains to this day. The rebuilt station opened north to Rugby in December 1881 and south to Roade in April 1882.

This development effectively removed the castle from the visible topography of the townscape (Fig 46). All that then remained lay to the east of St Andrew's Road; with the curve of Chalk Lane marking the eastern edge of the Outer Bailey ditch, while the developed plots to the west of Chalk Lane lay over the levelled bank and the infilled ditch. Hidden behind these houses there was a truncated remnant of the Inner Bailey bank and the undisturbed north-eastern corner of the interior of the Inner Bailey, which was to be excavated by Dr John Alexander in the 1960s (Chapman this volume 137–189).

The Victorian station building and its forecourt

The new station building was a two-storey structure comprising a central block with a low-pitched hipped roof, and two cross-wings with gable roofs (Figs 47 and 48). The surviving foundations of the east wall of the

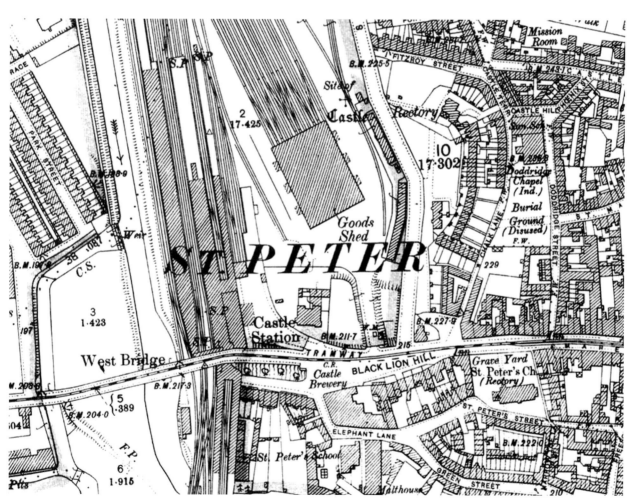

Fig 46: The railway station, Ordnance Survey 1st edition, 1890

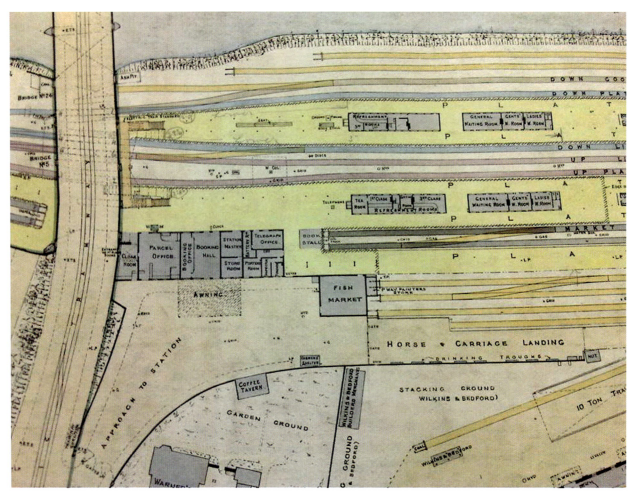

Fig 47: Plan of the Victorian station showing the approach to the station, with a cast iron and glass canopy (awning) spanning the entrance (north to right)

Fig 48: Victorian postcard showing the station forecourt with the glass canopy providing shelter for passengers arriving in horse-drawn carriages

248

Fig 49: The brick foundations of the east wall of the Victorian station, forming the western edge of the excavated area

Fig 50: Survival of granite setts across the station forecourt, with the backfilled trial trench to the left, looking north

building formed the western boundary of the excavated area. It was a plain brick wall with the bottom two courses offset and standing on mortared brick-rubble foundations down to the level of the natural subsoil (Fig 49).

The northern wing of the new station stood over a deep cellar, which was exposed during the digging out of the station foundations in 2013. The cellar contained a large furnace that had provided heating for the building. Within this area all archaeological deposits would have been destroyed, as the cellar cut deep into the underlying natural.

The granite setts of the station forecourt survived intact across the greater part of the excavated area. They had been set in a matrix of sand and cement, and had only been removed in places where some modern traffic islands had been inserted and by the evaluation trench excavated in 2012 (Figs 50 and 51). The modern drainage and electric cables were all too shallow to have had a significant impact on the granite setts.

The paving of granite setts was sealed beneath tarmac in the early 1960s (Fig 52). The cast iron and glass canopy, provided for the convenience of horse-drawn carriages had also become redundant. It was dismantled and replaced by a narrow glass canopy running the full length of the station above the pavement along the frontage. The western edge of the granite setts ended in line with this pavement, and on demolition the modern pavement was lifted but not the granite setts (Fig 51).

The cast iron canopy and the drains

Below the granite setts of the forecourt, the system of ceramic drains along the frontage of the Victorian station was largely intact. These were recorded where they impacted on medieval deposits, but to the north and east some of the system lay above the medieval levels and were removed without record (Fig 53).

Features that had caused particular damage to the medieval deposits associated with the intact building comprised a row of four stanchion pits (Fig 53, S) that had held the cast iron uprights supporting the cast iron

Fig 51: The western edge of the granite setts in front of the Victorian station, with the backfilled trial trench to the right, looking north

and glass canopy at the front of the station, enabling those arriving in carriages to enter the station without exposure to the elements (Fig 48). The canopy was c.15m long (50ft) by 9.75m wide (32ft), divided into three bays. There was also an associated system of drainage. A deep sump lay immediately beyond the stanchion on the south side of the central bay, with shallow drains running along the entire frontage of the canopy. In addition, two larger angled drains came from either end of the main station building with another coming from the east side of the forecourt.

There was also a drain running along the pavement along the station frontage, and a drain coming from a downpipe on the station itself, linked into these drains, with the construction trenched breaking through the west wall of the medieval building. In the south-western corner of the excavation, a curving drain ran alongside the curving footpath that approached the south end of the station (see Figs 47 & 48).

Fig 52: The station in the early to mid-1960s, shortly before demolition, showing the tarmac surface and a narrow canopy running the length of the building

The Victorian sewer

The official service plans indicated that a main sewer lay immediately to the east of the proposed new station, with the station footprint designed to avoid passing above the sewer. However, it had been shown during investigations to the south in the 1980s and 90s around Green Street that the course of the sewer there did not agree with the official plans. A trial trench excavated in 1987 unexpectedly encountered the sewer, within a broad construction trench, some way east of its official position (Chapman 1999, fig 2). In the 1990s, permission to excavate one trench across the medieval defences was initially denied on the basis that the sewer lay there, and in order to enable the trench to be excavated it was necessary to use the results from the 1980s trial trenching to demonstrate that this was not the case.

There was evidently a similar error in the service plans for the station area. With the stripping of the site two modern rectangular "pits" were encountered, each 2.4m (8ft) long by 1.8m (6ft) wide (Fig 53). Little attention was given to these evidently modern pits until towards the end of the excavation, when a deep machine cut pit was excavated to obtain soils samples from the base of a late Saxon well shaft. At a depth of over 3m the top of a brick-built structure was encountered, and it became evident that this could only be the top of a brick-lined sewer. In contrast to the area to the south of Black Lion Hill where the sewer was built within an open trench, here

the sewer had been bored below ground between a series of vertical access shafts. The two extant examples were 12.5m apart (*c*.15m/50ft centre to centre). The scale of the sewer can be appreciated by the fact that internal sewer inspections are carried out by workmen paddling canoes along its length.

The accidental and fortuitous discovery of the sewer during the archaeological works, enabled the foundations of the station to be redesigned, so that the load above the sewer could be carried on a concrete raft

The 1960s station

The Northampton to Peterborough railway line, served by a station on Bridge Street, was closed to passenger traffic in 1964. This left Northampton Castle station as the only station serving the town so it was renamed simply Northampton Station in April 1966; a controversial issue with some locals, with a recent unsuccessful attempt made to have the new station reassigned the name Castle Station.

As part of the improvements along the line that accompanied electrification, some outbuildings were demolished and the ends of the two non-through lines were filled in to make additional space for the construction of a new station across the northern side of the station forecourt, enabling the Victorian station to stay in use while the new building was under construction. The new station was constructed through 1966.

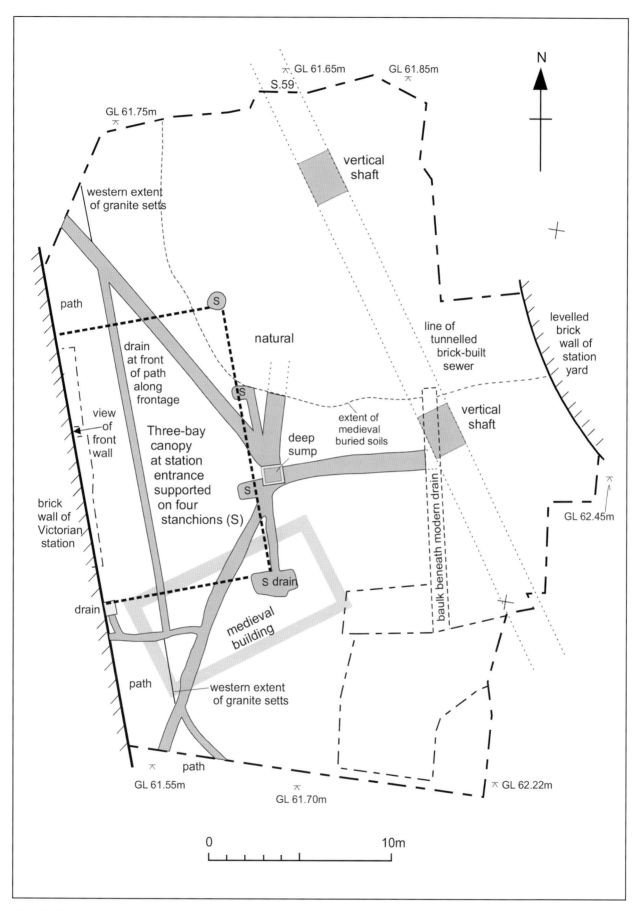

N

GL 61.65m
S.59

GL 61.85m

GL 61.75m

vertical
shaft

western extent
of granite setts

path

S

drain
at front
of path
along
frontage

natural

line of
tunnelled
brick-built
sewer

levelled
brick
wall of
station
yard

view
of
front
wall

Three-bay
canopy
at station
entrance
supported
on four
stanchions (S)

S

deep
sump

extent of
medieval
buried soils

vertical
shaft

brick
wall of
Victorian
station

S

medieval
building

baulk beneath modern drain

GL 62.45m

drain

S drain

path

western extent
of granite setts

path

path

GL 61.55m

GL 61.70m

GL 62.22m

0   10m

Fig 53: Site plan showing the station drains, the stanchion pits of the glass canopy and two construction shafts for the main sewer

251

As an economy measure, the framework for the new station was provided using off-the-peg concrete frames more usually used in farm buildings such as milking parlours, leading to the comment that the station was three cowsheds bolted together. However, this provided flexibility for the use of the enclosed space, with brick walls standing no more than 8 feet high, while the gables, both external and internal were glazed to provide the maximum of natural light. The station was founded on a concrete slab, with electrical and other services housed below ground partly beneath Platform 1, with this basement space retained through the recent rebuilding.

Watching brief during demolition of the 1960s station

Between June and August 2015 there was an intermittent watching brief during the demolition of the 20th-century station, particularly during the lifting of the floor slab and subsequent groundworks.

The machine stripping stopped at or near the base of the former rubble and hardcore underlying the floor slab, which had utilised much broken brick and other rubble from the demolition of Victorian outbuildings. As a result, parts of the exposed surface still comprised compressed brick hardcore, while areas of the underlying deposits were patchily visible between these areas.

The area beneath the station can be divided into a series of linear zones running south-north. To the west there were two basement rooms that extended most of the length of the former station, which would have removed any archaeological deposits. They survive beneath Platform 1. To the immediate east of the basements there was a narrow band where truncated orange-brown sand and ironstone natural was visible in patches. No medieval features could be seen cutting into these deposits.

The entire central area comprised only brick rubble and hardcore backfilling where two sunken rail lines had previously extended further south. The southern ends of these two lines had been backfilled when the station was built. To the east, there was a broad strip running south to north, partly under the former station and partly under the former external raised unloading platform where clean and relatively undisturbed, although truncated, ironstone natural was exposed. The only disturbance of the natural was a line of stanchion bases for the concrete frames along the eastern wall of the 1960s station, lying to the west of the concrete revetment at the front edge of the adjacent unloading platform (Fig 54).

Conclusions

The likely and possible implications arising from the excavations in the forecourt of the old railway station have been examined in detail as they arose within the description of the evidence. Below we provide a brief restatement of the principal issues relevant to the broader consideration of the chronology and development of the town and the castle, and the potential for further fieldwork in the future.

Fig 54: Watching brief during the demolition of the 20th-century station in 2015, photographed from the first floor concourse of the new station

The chronology for the construction of Northampton Castle

Whilst it is often stated that the castle was built by Simon de Senlis in the later 11th century, with some even bold enough to provide a specific date, there is in fact no sound documentary evidence concerning the nature or a date for the construction of a castle on this site. As has already been discussed, while it may be likely that Simon began construction of a castle suitable to his status, Northampton was certainly a focus for royal attention as early as 1106, when Henry I held a meeting in Northampton with his brother, Robert, Duke of Normandy (Serjeantson 1908). It is possible that a royal castle was already under construction at this time and perhaps sufficiently complete to provide the location for this meeting.

A broad date range of AD1100–1150 for the construction of the Outer Bailey comes from the pottery dating, with usage of this area through the 12th century also confirmed by radiocarbon dating of hearth debris from the excavated building. There was certainly a royal castle here by 1122, when it is recorded that Henry I kept Easter at the castle in great state, and in 1130 the one surviving pipe roll from this period records land taken into the royal castle from the monks of St Andrew's.

We can therefore suggest a date around AD1120 for the construction of the Outer Bailey, placing it within the reign of Henry I and prior to the period of anarchy that followed his death in 1135. It is suggested that if construction of a motte and bailey castle had been initiated by Simon de Senlis I, then that construction would have been rapidly supplanted by a larger royal castle.

The Outer Bailey

The excavation and the associated watching brief have shown that the Outer Bailey defences in this area comprised a bank comprising upcast Lias clays, which would imply the associate presence of a ditch cut into the clays to supply the material. There was a retaining wall along the front of the bank, which had deep foundations of mortared ironstone. We can assume that on the inside the bank sloped down to ground level, with the excavated building set into the tail of the bank, with that wall provided with deep foundations, while the others were ground laid.

The excavation has also shown the presence of a metalled road heading towards the south-west corner of the Outer Bailey and fragmentary remains recorded during a watching brief have been interpreted as forming part of small gateway, a postern gate, which would have provided direct access between the Outer Bailey and the contemporary West Bridge. The metalled road had fallen out of use by the early 13th century, but the presence of an opening through the Outer Bailey defences at this same location in the mid-19th century, as recorded by Henry Dryden, suggests that the gateway itself may well have survived throughout the history of the castle.

The recorded buildings show that this south-west corner of the Outer Bailey was a busy place during the 12th century. The main building with its wide doorway and large hearth was probably abutted by a lesser structure, perhaps open fronted. The scorched areas may have been fire-basket locations, perhaps to supplement the large hearth within the building that were only brought into use at times of royal visits, when extra capacity was required.

The hearths in the building and the adjacent scorched areas, along with the quantities of pottery from plain large jars, almost invariably with sooted bases, all suggest that these buildings were concerned with cooking, most probably the feeding of men garrisoned within the castle. The presence of high quality meat cuts from a wide range of animals (including red deer), birds (including chicken and goose) and some fish (such as plaice), indicates that even the lower ranks within the castle garrison appear to have benefitted by their royal connections in terms of the range and quality of the meat available.

By the beginning of the 13th century these buildings had been levelled, and were never replaced, which might suggest that in later centuries there was sufficient room to house and feed all the men of the garrison within the Inner Bailey, unless there was merely a move to another part of the Outer Bailey. This latter possibility seems less likely, as in that instance it might be thought that more intensive usage of the road leading to the postern gate would also have continued. At least in the area excavated, we know from the stable soil horizons that sealed the 12th-century deposits that any activity that did place through the later history of the castle left no significant below ground evidence.

The surviving archaeological resource

The Outer Bailey

The forecourt of the former station was the lowest lying point within Northampton Castle, and this in part explains why medieval deposits had survived in this area. Across the northern part of the excavated area all such deposits had been removed, exposing the natural with surviving features cut into it.

To the east lies the raised car park, which includes the area once occupied by the Victorian rectory/school/hotel, where there would have been damage from cellars, but a potential for further medieval remains does still exist over at least the western half of this area.

Further east, adjacent to the west side of St Andrew's Road, there is still an elongated and tree-covered 'mound' that preserves the ground levels as they were until the late 19th century. This area, which is a Scheduled Monument, if excavated could provide more information about activity within the Outer Bailey through time, to compare and contrast with the station site.

The whole area of the raised car park and the Scheduled Area to its east, should therefore be considered to have the potential to contain significant evidence relating to both the Outer Bailey of Northampton Castle and the pre-castle town that was levelled prior to its construction. Trial trenching could be used to establish areas of survival, which should then be either protected or excavated prior to any change of use.

St Andrew's Road and Chalk Lane

The rest of the site of the former castle is considered in greater detail in the overview and the account of the 1960s excavations (Chapman this volume, 137–189), but the main points may be reviewed briefly for completeness.

To the east of St Andrew's Road, the north-east corner of the Inner Bailey remains as it was after backfilling following the excavations in the 1960s, which uncovered parts of the royal apartments, a corner of the Great Hall and a kitchen range, so further potential survives in this area (Chapman this volume 145–151).

To the north, adjacent to the east side of St Andrew's Road, part of the east side of the main northern gatehouse on the curtain wall of the Inner Bailey is known to survive (Chapman this volume 148; Giggins 1999). The area to the north of the castle ditch might contain remains relating to barbican defences in stone protecting the approach to the north gate. Apart from the two semi-circular ditches, which may owe much to refurbishment in the Civil War (Foard 1994), we know nothing at all about any medieval barbican structures, which had probably been lost long before John Speed compiled his map of Northampton in 1610. Recent geophysical and topographic survey in this area has produced some encouraging results that features, including walls, might lie either side of the castle ditch to the north, but the results are too vague to say more than this and cannot provide a date for these possible features (Walford and Chapman 2017: Walford 2018). It has also been suggested that the stone building beneath the Castle Hill mound, may have been an eastern gateway for the castle barbican defences (Chapman this volume, 140).

Not entirely a lost castle

In conclusion, the site of Northampton Castle has been extensively damaged over the centuries. Much of the surviving detail relating to the interior of the Inner Bailey and its buildings and changes to them through time, was lost in the late 19th century, and that gap in knowledge can never be recovered. However, there are a few locations in which buried remains do survive and have the capacity to fill a few of the many gaps in our knowledge.

Apart from the buried archaeological resource, there is a further resource that is also capable of further investigation, the finds recovered during the investigations of both the 19th and 20th centuries. While there is a report on the 1960s excavations (Chapman this volume, 137–189) this deals with the excavated evidence, and only the animal bone and the painted window glass. Other finds are held by Northampton Museums & Art Gallery, but other listed finds have not been located. In addition, the pottery assemblage from the 1960s excavations has not been published, and both the late Saxon and medieval assemblages could have implications for dating both the construction of the Inner Bailey and the chronology of the buildings within it. There is also the large assemblage of worked stone from the doors and windows of the royal apartments that warrants recording, study and publication.

So, both above ground and below ground, there are still more details that can be added to the story of the rise and fall of Northampton Castle, once the seat of kings and a centre of importance within medieval England.

General bibliography

(bibliographies also appear in the relevant specialist sections)

Audouy, M, and Chapman, A, 2009 *Raunds: the origin and growth of a midland village, AD 450–1500: Excavations in north Raunds, Northamptonshire 1977–87*, Oxbow books

Bamford, H, 1981 The worked flints, *in* J H Williams and M Shaw 1981, 126–130

Brown, J, 2008 Archaeological excavation at the corner of Kingswell Street and Woolmonger Street, Northampton, *Northamptonshire Archaeology*, **35**, 173–214

Chapman, A, 1985 *Northampton Castle: A review of the evidence*, Northamptonshire Archaeology unpublished manuscript

Chapman, A, 1999 Excavation of the town defences at Green Street, Northampton, 1995–6, *Northamptonshire Archaeol*, **28**, 25–60

Chapman, A, 2010 *West Cotton, Raunds: a study of medieval settlement dynamics, AD 450–1450: Excavation of a deserted medieval hamlet in Northamptonshire, 1985–89*, Oxbow Books

Chapman, A, 2012 *Archaeological evaluation of the concourse at Northampton Castle Station*, Northamptonshire Archaeology report, **12/188**

Chapman A, 2016 *Excavation at Northampton Station within the Outer Bailey of Northampton Castle, 2013–2015: Assessment report*, MOLA Northampton report, **16/02**

Chapman A, 2018 *Excavation and watching brief within the Outer Bailey of Northampton Castle, 2013–2015*, MOLA Northampton report, **18/117**

Chapman, A, 2021 Late Saxon and Saxo-Norman occupation beneath the Outer Bailey of Northampton Castle, *Northamptonshire Archaeol*, **41**, 79–127

Chapman, A, 2021 Northampton Castle, Part 1: Introduction, pre-castle archaeology, and the history and topogrphy of the castle, *Northamptonshire Archaeol*, **41**, 137–189

CIfA 2014 *Standard and guidance for archaeological excavation*, Chartered Institute for Archaeologists

Dryden, H, 1896 Northampton Castle, *Northamptonshire Notes and Queries*, **6**, 41–44

HE 2015 *Management of Research Projects in the Historic Environment: The MoRPHE Project Managers Guide*, English Heritage

Foard, G, 1994 The Civil War defences of Northampton, *Northamptonshire Past and Present*, **9.1**, 4–44

Giggins, B, 1999 *Northampton's Forgotten Castle*, unpublished MA thesis, University of Leicester

Gough, J, 1984 *The Northampton & Harborough Line*, Oakham, Railway and Canal Historical Society

Law, E F, 1880 The ruins at the Old Castle, Northampton, *Ass Archit Socs Rep Pap*, **15**, 198–2013

Kennett, D H, 1968 Early medieval pottery in the Nene Valley, *Northampton County Borough Museums and Art Gallery J*, **3**, 3–14

Kennett, D H, 1969 Socketed bowls from Northampton Castle, *Northampton County Borough Museums and Art Gallery J*, **6**, 50

Knight, D, Vyner, B, and Allen, C, 2012 *East Midlands Heritage; An updated Research Agenda and Strategy for the Historic Environment of the East Midlands*, Nottingham Archaeological monog, **6**, York Archaeol Trust

Miller, P, Wilson, T, with Harward, C, 2005 *Saxon, medieval and post-medieval settlement at Sol Central, Marefair, Northampton: Archaeological excavations 1998–2002*, Museum of London Archaeology Service (MoLAS) Monog, **27**

NA 2013 *Written Scheme of Investigation for the Archaeological Investoigation of Land within the Northampton Railway Station, Black Lion Hill, Northampton,* Northamptonshire Archaeology

NCC 2012 *Brief for a programme of archaeological investigation of land within the Northampton Railway Station, Black Lion Hill, Northampton,* Northamptonshire County Council

Scriven, R G, 1880 The Earthwork on the site of the Castle at Northampton, *Ass Archit Socs Rep Pap,* **15**, 204–10

Scriven, R G, 1882 Some additional Notes on the Earthwork on the Site of the Castle at Northampton, *Ass Archit Socs Rep Pap,* **16**, 71–72,

Serjeantson, R M, 1908 *The Castle of Northampton*, Journal of the Northants Nat Hist Soc and Field Club, **14**

Sharp, S, 1882 Description of Antiquities found on the site of the Castle at Northampton, *Ass Archit Socs Rep Pap*, **16**, 243–71

Shaw, M, 1985 Excavations on a Saxon and medieval site at Black Lion Hill, Northampton, *Northamptonshire Archaeol*, **20,** 113–138

Soden, I, 1999 A story of urban regeneration: Excavations in advance of development work of St Peter's Walk, Northampton, 1994–7*, Northamptonshire Archaeol*, **28**

Walker, C, 2011 *Archaeological desk-based assessment and impact assessment of land at Castle Station, Northampton,* Northamptonshire Archaeology rep, **11/155**

Walford, J, and Chapman, A, 2017 *Archaeological geophysical survey on the site of Northampton Castle, St Andrew's Road Northampton, May 2017*, MOLA Northampton rep, **17/72**

Walford, J, 2018 *Topographic survey on the site of Northampton Castle, St Andrew's Road, Northampton, January 2018*, MOLA Northampton rep, **18/52**

Williams, F, 1979 Excavations on Marefair, Northampton, 1977, *Northamptonshire Archaeol*, **14**, 38–79

Williams, J H, 1979 *St Peter's Street, Northampton: Excavations 1973–1976*, Northampton Development Corporation Monog, **2**

Williams, J H, and Shaw, M, 1981 Excavations in Chalk Lane, Northampton, 1975–1978, *Northamptonshire Archaeol*, **16**, 87–135

Williams, J H, Shaw, M, and Denham, V, 1985 *Middle Saxon Palaces at Northampton*, Northampton Development Corporation Monog, **4**

Northamptonshire Archaeology, **41**, 2021, 257–304

Excavations at The Green, Northampton 1983: the Anglo-Saxon and medieval phases

by

Michael Shaw

with contributions by M M Archibald, J R Baker, J Bayley, A Cameron, H F Cleere, V Denham, J Evans, A R Goodall, I H Goodall, S Hardy, M Harman, J L Humble, A Locker, D T Moore, G E Oakley, H Richmond, M Robinson, B Spencer, D S Sutherland and J Watson

Summary

The excavations at The Green, Northampton lay immediately south of the earlier excavations at St Peter's Street and St Peter's Gardens which had uncovered evidence of a middle Anglo-Saxon 'palace' complex replaced by extensive late Saxon activity. It was anticipated that additional features associated with the 'palace' complex might be present, along with further evidence for the character and layout of the late Saxon town. In the event a linear ditch in the north-west corner of the site appeared to define the southern boundary of middle Anglo-Saxon activity. Evidence for late Saxon settlement mirrored that uncovered at the earlier excavations, comprising scattered pits and possible sunken-featured buildings, along with postholes, stakeholes and foundation trenches, all heavily disturbed by later activity. Of particular interest from this phase was a finely-decorated bone mount, possibly from a staff. Post-Conquest (c.AD1075–c.AD1275) the site was largely a backyard area with a dense palimpsest of pits, wells and postholes, with some evidence for timber buildings, later replaced in stone, lying alongside Narrow Toe Lane to the west and Freeschool Street to the east. It was only in the later medieval period (c.AD1275–c.1470), however, that sufficient lengths of boundary wall survived to enable property boundaries to be defined. At the northern end of the site the back boundaries of properties fronting on to the south side of St Peter's Street could be recognised, with further properties fronting on to Narrow Toe Lane and Freeschool Street. Two well-preserved stone-built drying ovens lay by the back boundary of the Narrow Toe Lane property. Domestic occupation ceased at around the end of the late 15th–early 16th centuries, with the area given over to large-scale skin processing, evidenced by groups of tanning pits and associated buildings. The evidence relating to the late medieval to early post-medieval tanneries has been published previously, and is only briefly summarised here, with this report documenting the Anglo-Saxon to medieval period occupation, based on a draft report of the early 1990s.

Introduction

The archaeological excavations at The Green, Northampton, were the last major fieldwork project to be undertaken by Northampton Development Corporation's Archaeological Unit. The site lay immediately to the south of two of the previous large-scale excavations: St Peter's Street (Williams 1979) and St Peter's Gardens (Williams, Shaw and Denham 1985), and the excavation was undertaken as part of a research programme into the origins and early development of the town of Northampton (NGR SP 7503 6033, Fig 1).

The excavations were carried out between March and August 1983, under the direction of Michael Shaw with a workforce of 18 people, and were financed with the aid of a grant from the Department of the Environment.

The investigations were undertaken as it was anticipated that middle Anglo-Saxon features associated with the middle Anglo-Saxon 'palace' complex discovered during the St Peter's Gardens and St Peter's Street excavations might be present and that further evidence for the character and layout of the late Saxon town would be revealed. Evidence for medieval occupation was also expected but was accorded a low priority as a number of medieval tenements had already been excavated during the St Peter's Street excavations.

However, a small 16th- to 17th-century tannery or skin-dressing workshop had also been discovered during the St Peter's Street excavations and it seemed possible that further features associated with tanning might be discovered on The Green; if this was the case it was considered important to recover as much information as possible as little was known about the layout of early tanneries and the techniques in use (Shaw 1996 & 2011).

In the event there was only a small amount of evidence for middle Anglo-Saxon occupation and the evidence for late Saxon settlement was unexceptional. A large number of tanning pits of late 15th–17th century date were, however, discovered along the northern half of the site and a number of separate tanneries were identified. Given the results of the excavation, it seemed that only those aspects of the site concerned with the tanning industry needed wide publication, while the results from the other phases merited only regional publication.

The majority of the post-excavation work was carried out before the closure of Northampton Development Corporation in March 1986, again grant-aided by the Department for the Environment. Subsequently, work towards final publication was carried out by the author as

time permitted during employment with Northamptonshire Archaeology Unit (subsequently Northamptonshire Archaeology), within Northamptonshire County Council, in the late 1980s to early 1990s.

Accordingly, the evidence from the late medieval to early post-medieval tannery phase and a discussion of its wider implications, along with a short summary

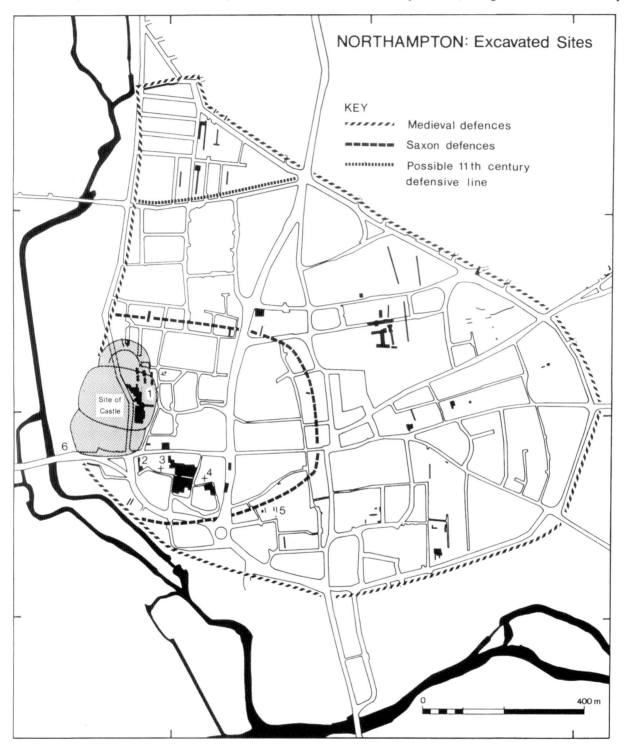

Fig 1: Northampton showing sites mentioned in the text: 1–Chalk Lane; 2–Black Lion Hill; 3–St Peter's Church; 4–St Greogory's Church; 5–St James's Place; 6–West Bridge
(Note: this figure was prepared in mid-1990s and subsequent excavations demonstrated that the southern arm of the late Saxon defences must lie further south)

of the other phases, was published in *Post-Medieval Archaeology* (Shaw 1996). A further report, covering the Anglo-Saxon to medieval phases was never brought to completion. That omission is now filled by the present publication, which presents the draft report essentially as it stood in the early 1990s.

Acknowledgments

The site was subsequently developed for housing. I am grateful to the previous owners, Frincon Holdings and Northampton Borough Council, for access to carry out the excavation. The report was written during and after the closure of the NDC Archaeological Unit and a large number of individuals and organisations must be thanked for enabling the report to be completed under these circumstances. My thanks to: John Williams, who was Chief Archaeologist of the NDC at the time of the excavation, for his advice during the excavation and for his subsequent comments on the text; Simon Hardy, for undertaking much of the preliminary post-excavation analysis as well as acting as an Assistant Supervisor on the excavation; and the contributors of specialist reports. Heather and Ian Lovett prepared the majority of the publication drawings with input also from Ken Connor, Marion Blockley, Alan Williams, Juliette Baxter, Tony Baker and Lesley Hoyland, while the phase plans have been recreated by Andy Chapman. My thanks to the excavation team, especially the supervisors, Dave and Christine Farwell. I am grateful to Alan Hannan and Brian Dix for enabling the report to be completed during my employment with the Northamptonshire Archaeology Unit. The final compilation of this report has been carried out by Andy Chapman in 2020–21 as editor for NAS, utilising the draft text and illustrations prepared by myself in the early 1990s. Andy Chapman would like to thank Northampton Museum and Art Gallery for the loan of the site archive that enabled the compilation of this report.

The Main Report and the archive

The intention behind this report, as with earlier reports produced by the Northampton Development Corporation Archaeological Unit, was to present sufficient information to allow detailed analysis and, if necessary, reinterpretation of the site. The published report contains a description and discussion of the excavation evidence, the finds report, plans and finds drawings. The phase plans show all the positive (walls etc) and negative (postholes, pits etc) features but layers are not included, unless of unusual importance, as they would obscure the features.

As originally conceived, the published report would have been supplemented with a microfiche containing:

- a list of the contexts giving their phase, a description and the finds recovered from them;
- a codified summary of the pottery from each context;
- a sequence diagram for the whole site showing

the relationship of contexts to each other and their phasing.

These have not been published here but they are held in the site archive. The full excavation archive including all finds and site records was deposited with Northampton Museums Service. The museums service archive has now been replaced by a new county archives repository, The Archaeological Resource Centre (ARC), within which the site records will be placed although at the time of writing (August 2021) it has not as yet been accessioned.

The Archaeological and Historical Background

The investigations at The Green formed part of a series of excavations which were undertaken by Northampton Development Corporation's Archaeological Unit between 1973 and 1983 in the south-west quarter of the medieval town of Northampton, around St Peter's Church, in order to elucidate the origins and early growth of the town. Two of the previous sites adjoin the present site (Fig 2). The area immediately to the north was excavated as St Peter's Street (Williams J H 1979) while the area beyond that was excavated as St Peter's Gardens/the Saxon palaces site (Williams, Shaw and Denham 1985). The evidence for the Anglo-Saxon period from these adjacent sites and others in the surrounding area has been assessed in a reconsideration of the archaeological evidence for the origins and early growth of the town (Williams, Shaw and Chapman 2021, this volume 25–77). The author has also produced a recent analysis of the topography and archaeology of the medieval Northampton within a broader study of the origins, growth and development of English medieval towns (Shaw 2021). Hence the background for the Anglo-Saxon and medieval periods need be only briefly summarised here.

Early Anglo-Saxon settlement is witnessed by the discovery of sunken-featured buildings at Chalk Lane (Williams and Shaw 1981, 95–6) and St Peter's Gardens (Williams, Shaw and Denham 1985, 9, 15, 38), associated with quantities of early-middle Saxon pottery. There is no evidence to suggest that the early Anglo-Saxon settlement in the St Peter's area was of a higher status than other settlements in the Northampton area.

However, in the middle Anglo-Saxon period the St Peter's area underwent a transformation in status with the construction in the later 7th to early 8th century of a large timber hall, to the east of St Peter's Church, which was replaced, perhaps in the 9th century, by an even larger stone hall (Williams, Shaw and Denham 1985, 28–35). It would appear that at this period a palace complex in the St Peter's area was acting as an administrative centre for a wider region – presumably a province within the kingdom of Mercia (Williams, Shaw and Denham 1985, 39–42). The stone hall probably survived in use until the late 9th-early 10th centuries (Williams, Shaw and Denham 1985, 43, 55) and its abandonment is possibly due to a reorganisation of settlement under the Danes, who held sway over the Northampton from around 877 until 917 when they surrendered to the English under Edward the Elder.

It is in the late Saxon period that Northampton can first be recognised as a truly urban place. In the area around St Peter's the high status palace buildings are replaced by a rather irregular pattern of timber posthole and sunken-featured buildings apparently set within yards. Evidence for metalworking in iron, copper and silver, along with antler and bone working, and pottery production has been recovered (RCHM 1985, 44).

After the Norman Conquest Northampton underwent a great expansion, and its burgeoning prosperity is reflected in its annual farm (tax) paid to the crown. In 1086 it paid £30.10s, approximately the twenty-fifth highest borough farm, similar to the amount paid by other county towns such as Derby, Nottingham, Ipswich and Worcester. By 1130, however, the farm had more than trebled to £100 and this was raised further to £120 in 1184 so that by the end of the 12th century it was exceeded only by those of London, Lincoln, Winchester and Dunwich. The St Peter's Street excavation provides the clearest archaeological evidence for this period. Timber buildings ranged either side of and fronting onto the newly laid-out St Peter's Street were uncovered (Williams J H 1979, 141–3).

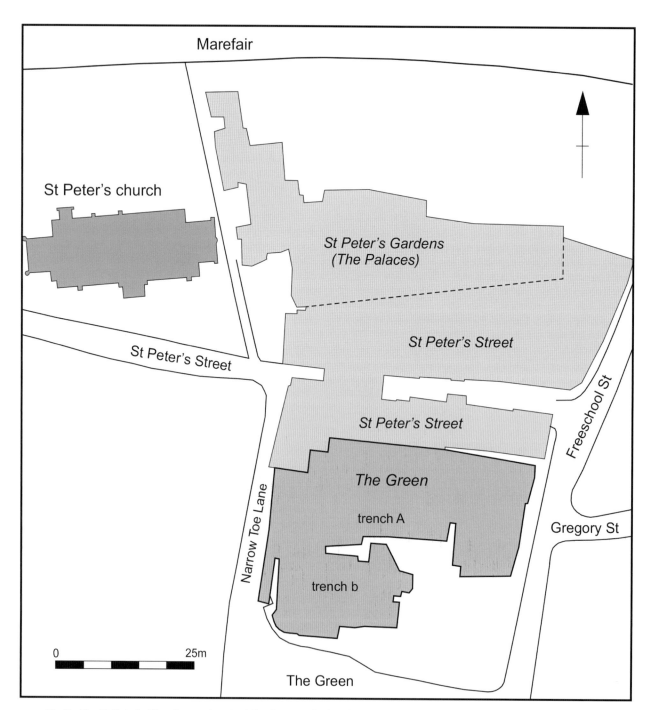

Fig 2: The St Peter's Church area showing The Green and related excavations at St Peter's Street and St Peter's Gardens (middle Anglo- Saxon 'palaces')

The town seems to have already been in decline (Williams 1982, 31) by the late 13th-14th centuries and in a ranking of towns based on the lay subsidy of 1334 Northampton is in 27th place; hence at a time of general urban decline Northampton's would appear to have been greater than most. This decline is not, however, apparent in the archaeological evidence. On St Peter's Street stone buildings began to replace timber ones from the late 13th century onwards and in the early 15th century it is suggested that the whole of the excavated portion of the street was reconstructed in a single action (Williams J H 1979, 145). There was little evidence of large scale industrial activity and the occupation would appear to have been primarily domestic in character.

Ordinary domestic occupation on St Peter's Street ceased around the end of the late 15th-early 16th centuries and the area was given over to large-scale skin processing.

Site location and the urban topography

The Green lies on a gentle south-west facing slope down to the northern arm of the River Nene which lies some 250m to the south-west. It is bordered by Narrow Toe Lane to the west, The Green to the south, Freeschool Street to the east and St Peter's Street to the north. All four streets are shown on Speed's Map of Northampton of 1610 and are assumed to have been in existence from at least the medieval period: the evidence from the St Peter's Street excavations would suggest that St Peter's Street and Narrow Toe Lane originated in the late 11th-early 12th centuries (Williams J H 1979, 143).

None of the street names can be shown to be of medieval origin – the name Freeschool Street must of course post-date the founding of the Free School on the site of St Gregory's Church in 1557. The Green and Freeschool Lane are marked on the Noble and Butlin Map of 1746 (Fig 3a), Narrow Toe Lane and St Peter's Street are so named on the Wood and Law Map of 1847 (Fig 3b).

Tanner Street formerly ran off the west side of The Green, continuing the line of Narrow Toe Lane down to the river, where a mill, generally known as Marvell's Mill, was sited. The parish boundary between St Peter's and All Saint's parishes runs north from the river up Tanner Street and Narrow Toe Lane and then turns east down St Peter's Street before running north again up Freeschool Street. This line presumably marks the former boundary between St Peter's and St Gregory's parishes; St Gregory's parish was incorporated into All Saint's parish in 1557.

The Excavations

Excavation Strategy

It was obvious from the outset that difficult decisions would have to be made in order to achieve the objectives of the excavation within the time and resources available. It was decided that, in order to investigate as large an area as possible of the middle and late Saxon settlements, the medieval levels should be more summarily treated. The medieval occupation of the area had been thoroughly investigated during the St Peter's Street excavations (Williams J H 1979) and the deposits on The Green were thought unlikely to add a great deal to our knowledge of this period, as the area available was situated between the street frontages on St Peter's Street and The Green and was likely to consist largely of backyard deposits.

This strategy was further complicated as the evidence for early post-medieval tanning discovered during the

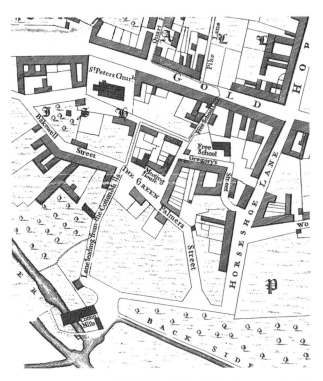
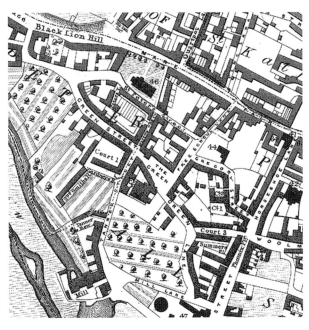

Fig 3: Detail from historic maps: a) Noble and Butlin 1746 and b) Wood and Law 1847

St Peter's Street excavations (Williams J H, 1979, 9 8–103) was considered to be of great significance and it was thought important to establish whether this tannery extended further south into the north-east corner of the present site. Hence the intention was to excavate by machine (JCB 508) down to a level just above the Saxon deposits except in the north-east corner of the site where only the recent overburden was to be removed.

Initially an area of c.675m² (Trench A) was opened. Unexpectedly, tanning pits were recognised by the western edge of the site and accordingly the machining was stopped here at a higher level than originally intended. Elsewhere, there was greater disturbance and the ground was taken down to a lower level by machine. In the eastern half of the trench the ground had been heavily disturbed down to the subsoil. Recent deposits were removed by machine to a level just above the subsoil and the remainder of the recent overburden was removed by spade down to the subsoil. Even at this level modern bricks and other material were pressed down into the subsoil and into any features cut into the subsoil. It had been necessary to remove a large amount of soil from the site using tipper trucks, and it may have been the weight of these when fully laden which had caused this compression of the levels below in this area.

After the completion of Trench A, a further area of c.325m² sq m (Trench B) was opened to the south of the original trench. Again few archaeological deposits remained above the subsoil especially at the south end of the site, facing onto The Green, where the recent buildings had removed all the earlier deposits above the subsoil.

Subsequently, all deposits relating to the early post-medieval tanning complex or to the Saxon period were excavated in detail. Medieval levels were more summarily treated but an attempt was made to establish the nature of any buildings and their plot boundaries, and the general character of the occupation. Deeper pits of late Saxon, medieval and post-medieval date were not fully excavated but were taken down to a depth c.0.8m below the Anglo-Saxon ground surface to avoid contaminating the earlier levels. Hence the dating assigned to the deeper features is based on the artefacts from their upper fills. In practice, given the short life of most of the pits and the broad phasing adopted, this is unlikely to affect the dating, apart from that of longer-lived features such as stone-lined pits and wells; in these cases an attempt was made to gather dating evidence from their linings and construction trenches and a separate date is given for their construction and their final infill.

The Phasing

The deposits on the site have been divided into five broad chronological phases, the two most recent of which have been further sub-divided (Table 1). This phasing relies heavily on the pottery dating as the eastern and southern portions of the site were so heavily disturbed that no stratigraphical links across the whole, site could be made.

Site Chronology

The evidence for Phase 1 is limited, comprising chiefly a number of features with light-coloured fills, from some of which worked flints were recovered.

Phase 2 is characterised by the appearance of the largely hand-made early-middle Saxon pottery (S fabrics in the Northampton Pottery Series – see below).

Phase 3 sees the replacement of the Saxon wares by the predominantly wheel-thrown St Neots-type ware (T1) and Northampton ware (W1).

Phase 4A commences when the early medieval shelly wares (T2) replace T1 as the dominant fabric and is succeeded by Phase 4B when Potterspury ware (W18) appears in a significant quantity.

Phase 5A commences when Cistercian ware (X2a) and German stonewares (YC/YF/YR) are found in the assemblage and is replaced by Phase 5B when late post-medieval/often factory produced, wares (Z fabrics) appear.

These phases are deliberately kept broad as the problems of residuality on a complex urban site occupied intensively over a period of more than a thousand years can mask narrower phasing. Many features, which contained no pottery and had no stratigraphical relationship with dateable deposits, could not be assigned to a single phase. In these cases the features have been regarded as dating from the late Saxon period or later unless there is a particular reason for thinking they might be of an earlier

Table 1: The site phasing and chronology

Phase & Period	Date range	Site activity
Phase 1: Prehistoric and Roman		Sparse features containing worked flint
Phase 2: Early-Middle Anglo-Saxon	c.400–c.850	Boundary ditch and posthole cluster
Phase 3: Late Saxon	c.850–c.1075	Increased activity: SFBs?, wall slots, postholes and pits
Phase 4A: Medieval	c.1075–c.1275	Backyard area with stone walls, pits, postholes and ovens
Phase 4B: Late Medieval	c.1275–c.1470	Backyard area with stone walls (structures can be identified), pits, postholes and ovens
Phase 5A(1): Early Post-Medieval	c.1275–c.1470	The Leather Tanning Complex
Phase 5A(2): Post-Medieval	c.1275–c.1470	(see Shaw 1996, 72–84)
Phase 5B: Post-Medieval to modern	c.1700–to present	See post-medieval maps (summary in Shaw 1996, 84–85)

date. Given the paucity of evidence for occupation prior to the late Saxon period it was thought that it would be misleading to regard undated features as being possibly of Phase 1 or 2 date. Apart from this exception, the phasing has been kept as wide as possible, eg posthole A612, which was found cut into the natural subsoil immediately below modern material, and contained no finds, is regarded as belonging to Phases 3–5B.

The Phase plans

The phase plans (Figs 4–7) are intended to show all features which could belong to that phase. Hence any features which could belong to more than one phase are generally shown on the plan of every phase to which they could belong. The chief exceptions are the mass of undated postholes. Analogy with the adjoining sites has shown that these are most likely to date from Phases 3 or 4A and they are therefore included on these plans only. Disturbed areas are shown by means of a light tint. The context numbers are given on the plans without their trench prefixes, A and B, as these are self-evident. The only exception is where a feature straddles the two trenches, and in this case its trench letter is given as well as the context number.

The Phase plans have been recreated by Andy Chapman for this publication from partial paper copies and photographic negatives of the original drawings, which were not available. A few minor features have been omitted for overall clarity. As it was not possible to number all small features in the dense palimpsests of pits and postholes, some feature numbers that appear in the text, most particularly for small features such as stakeholes and also some postholes or smaller pits, may not be labelled on the phase plans.

Phase 1: Prehistoric-Roman

Gullies and postholes

The most convincing evidence for prehistoric activity on the site comes from the southern half of Trench B (Fig 4). In this area a number of possible gullies (B114, 150, 166, 181), postholes (B152, 155, 178, 211, 222, 249, 250), stakeholes (B172–4, 208) and a possible pit (B177) possessed light-coloured sandy fills. Some were sealed by layers of strong brown sand (B22, 103, 156, 179) from which four worked flints were recovered while a further worked flint came from one of the stakeholes (B173) (Fig 4).

At the north-east end of Trench A, two possible prehistoric sherds were discovered in the fill of a posthole (A692) and this feature, and a number of other postholes (A193, 194, 197, 642, 679–682, 684, 694–5, 698–9, 903, 909, 911–2, 920) and a stakehole (A921) in the same area, may therefore be prehistoric. The majority of these features, however, have a rather darker and a more loamy fill than is usual for prehistoric features in this area of Northampton (Williams and Shaw 1981, 90) and the potsherds may, therefore, either be later in date or residual in their present context.

A further 12 flints were recovered from later contexts giving a total of 17 worked flints from the site as a whole. No features could be assigned to the Roman period and only 11 sherds of Roman pottery were recovered from the site, all of them residual in later contexts.

Discussion

The evidence for prehistoric occupation on the site is extremely limited. The poorly defined gullies, postholes and other features with a light sandy fill can be compared to similar evidence from sites in this area, most notably Chalk Lane (Williams and Shaw 1981, 90–4). A total of 3123 flints were, however, recovered from Chalk Lane compared to the 17 flints recovered from the larger area of the present site; hence any form of prehistoric activity on the present site is likely to have been extremely short-lived, The evidence for Roman activity is even more tenuous; the few potsherds of this date could easily have been brought to the site in building rubble (see Humble 1985a, 70, (M) 75).

Phase 2: Early-Middle Anglo-Saxon (c.400–c.850)

The evidence for early-middle Anglo-Saxon activity is limited, but nevertheless significant: only five early-middle Saxon sherds were recovered, and four of these were definitely residual in their context.

A boundary ditch

A ditch (A280) in the north-west corner of the site appears to have been filled in during the late Saxon period, but it is discussed here as it was probably constructed during the middle Saxon period, as discussed below (Fig 4). The ditch, which ran roughly east-west across the slope of the ground, was 1.5m wide with a rounded bottom, a maximum surviving depth of 0.55m and a fill of strong brown silty loam. A single sherd of early-middle Saxon pottery was recovered from its fill. To the north of the ditch, a complex of postholes (A282–3, 286, 719–22, 728–31, 738–7, 741, 767–71) with predominantly light-coloured sandy fills, are likely to be associated features.

Discussion

The size, fill and alignment of ditch A280, and the cluster of postholes on its northern side, leave little doubt that this was the same feature as a ditch interpreted as a boundary work on the St Peter's Street excavations, where it ran north-south down the slope (Williams JH 1979, 25, 140).

The dating evidence for the feature at St Peter's Street is rather better than that for the ditch on The Green. Six sherds of pottery: three early-middle Saxon, one late Saxon, one late Saxon-Saxo-Norman and one uncertain) and a coin of 10th century date were recovered from its fill (McCarthy 1979, 180; Archibald 1979, 245 (Nu 13)).

Fig 4: The Green: Phase 1, Prehistoric and Phase 2, Early-Middle Anglo-Saxon (c.400–c.850)

Two samples of animal bone from the fill gave radiocarbon dates with modern calibrations (IntCal13) of Cal AD 865–1015 at 62% confidence (Har-1244, 1110±80BP, Cal AD 760–1045 at 90% confidence) and Cal AD 940–1050 at 44% confidence (Har-1454, 1030±80BP, Cal AD 855–1185 at 91% confidence), indicating a date range for the deposition of the animal bone spanning the 10th to early 11th centuries (Chapman in Williams *et al* 2021, this volume, Appendix 2: The Radiocarbon dates, table 3).

Hence a 10th-century date for its final fill can reasonably be suggested. The fact, however, that both the ditch and its associated postholes ran up to the stone hall but not beyond it (see Williams *et al* 1985, 41, fig 24) would suggest that the stone hall was still in existence at the time of the digging of the boundary work perhaps implying that it was associated with a late phase of the palace complex, probably in the 9th century (its construction is likely to post-date that of the stone hall as mortar mixers presumably used in the construction of the latter lie either side of the line of the ditch). Alternatively, the boundary work could be a short-lived 10th-century feature possibly using a ruined stone hall as its continuation to the north.

Whatever the precise date of the boundary work it can be seen that no features definitely associated with the early Saxon (pre-palace complex) occupation of the area or with the middle Saxon palace complex, were discovered to the south of the boundary work, suggesting that occupation of these periods was restricted, in this area at least, to the top of the slope up from the River Nene.

Phase 3: Late Saxon (c.850–c.1075)

The late Saxon period sees a great increase in activity on the site and this is reflected both in the number of features of this date and in the amount of late Saxon pottery recovered from the site. The earliest feature is likely to be the boundary ditch A280, and its associated postholes which, as discussed above, was probably constructed in the 9th century and backfilled in the 10th century (Fig 5).

Pits, postholes and SFBs

The contexts definitely of late Saxon date can be divided into four groups: pits; possible sunken-featured buildings (SFBs); postholes, stakeholes and foundation trenches; and layers. The pits generally gave little clue as to their function and the majority were presumably for the disposal of either rubbish or cess. One pit in the north-west corner of the site (A219), 1.00m wide and 0.8m deep, showed heavy burning and may have been used as a hearth of some sort. At the time of the excavation it was thought that this might be connected with the late Saxon metalworking complex discovered in the area immediately to the north during the St Peter's Street excavations (Williams JH 1979, 74–5). Despite careful examination, however, only one piece of slag was recovered from its fill and the question of its function remains uncertain. Two adjoining pits (A495 and A499) did, however, contain

large quantities of both blooming and forging slag, implying that there was a smelting furnace and associated hearth nearby.

Deposits of sheep's heads and a cat skeleton from pit A459, to the north-west, and cat and piglet bones from pit A754, 4m to the south, might suggest small-scale skin processing in the area. Two features close together in the north (A152, A662), both 0.3m deep with flat bottoms, may be the remains of sunken-featured buildings, but later disturbance precluded a positive identification. From one of them (A152) a particularly fine decorated bone mount with zoomorphic interlace was recovered (WB2, Fig 24). It is tempting to connect such a high status find with the nearby St Peter's Church.

A large number of postholes and stakeholes were discovered. Some were presumably fence lines or ephemeral features but many were probably the remains of timber buildings. The proportion of the site which had been destroyed by later features (over 50% at this phase), however, made the recovery of reasonably complete building plans impossible while the difficulty of assigning a definite date to postholes and stakeholes with little pottery in their fills and with only limited stratigraphical relationships over most of the site has meant that many could not be assigned to a particular phase although analogy with other sites in the same area would suggest that the majority were of late Saxon/Saxo-Norman date (cf Williams JH 1979, 140–3).

A short length of trench (B218), 0.6m wide and 0.3m deep, at the south end of the site which contained a posthole (B213) may be the only surviving portion of a post-in-trench structure. Few layers of late Saxon date survived, although In the southern half of Trench B, there was an extensive area of metalling, B93.1, presumably a yard surface, in the same area as the possible post-in-trench structure.

Discussion

The late Saxon phase stands in complete contrast to the preceding phases, for intensive occupation can now be seen to have spread over the entire site. The nature of the remains fits in well with the evidence from previous excavations in the area in suggesting a pattern of rather irregularly-disposed timber domestic buildings of both posthole and sunken-featured type, with areas of metalling and a large number of pits in their yards. It is not possible to trace the layout of individual properties at this phase as they were not demarcated by boundary ditches or any other surviving feature.

The small number of sherds of Northampton Ware recovered from the site would suggest that the intensification of activity observed on the site in the late Saxon period may have occurred after the floruit of this pottery type in the early to mid-10th century. Hence the spread of occupation down-slope to The Green is likely to have occurred after the abandonment of the boundary work and after the end of the Danish occupation of Northampton.

Fig 5: The Green: Phase 3: Late Saxon (c.850–c.1075)

Phase 4A: Medieval (*c.*1075–*c.*1275)

Once again intensive occupation at this period can be demonstrated. Contexts definitely of medieval date can be divided into: pits, postholes, stone walls and other features indicative of stone structures, ovens/kilns, and miscellaneous (Fig 6).

Pits and stone-lined wells

Pits formed by far the largest group of features; again, few gave signs of any specialist function and most were presumably for the disposal of either rubbish or cess. The majority were unlined; although in one case (A41) a lining was provided where it cut through the fill of an earlier pit, A145. Three pits with stone linings (A90, A330, B118) are likely to have been wells; it is not, however, possible to be positive in this identification as in order to save time and for reasons of safety only their upper fills were removed. This also caused problems with the dating of these features for their upper fills contained material of late post-medieval date. When their linings were removed, however, no pottery later than Saxo-Norman in date was recovered and their excavation is therefore considered to have been undertaken at this period, although they appear to have continued in use, or lain partially open, for a considerable time afterwards.

Postholes

Few postholes could be definitely assigned to this phase. One of a cluster of postholes in the south-east corner of trench A (A122) did contain two Saxo-Norman sherds (post-AD1100) in its fill and it is tempting to suggest that the remainder were also of this date. Given the short life which can be anticipated for timber posts, the pottery from the backfill of the postholes is regarded as suggesting a date for the use of the posts, in which case postholes A184, 105, 106, 187, 111, 116, 122, 123 might form the west and north sides of a structure, postholes A141–4 might represent internal features within the structure and postholes A124, 107, 113, 924, 613, 138, 612, may be a fence line enclosing the property (Fig 6). The west wall of the postulated structure is partially overlaid by a stone wall (A74) which may represent a stone-founded successor to the timber structure (see below).

A further row of postholes (A708, 707, 760, 704, 759, 755) to the west, aligned north-south, was also overlaid by the east wall of a stone building in Phase 4B/5A, and it can therefore be suggested that here too the postholes represent the east wall of a timber building preceding the stone building. It should be emphasised, however, that these postholes cannot be closely dated.

Stone walls

The sequence of building of stone walls on the site is difficult to interpret for a number of reasons: the walls are not generally set down in deep construction trenches unless they are crossing the soft fill of earlier features – hence, given the amount of later disturbance on the site, few long lengths of wall survive; some walls underwent a number of rebuilds and repairs which can be difficult to disentangle; and little dating evidence was found in the walls themselves. To the east, wall A18, aligned west-east, does, however, appear to have been built in this phase, possibly as a boundary between properties fronting onto St Peter's Street to the north, The Green to the south and Freeschool Street to the east. Further east, wall A74, aligned south-north, which runs towards A18 on its south side was also apparently of this phase. Other wall lengths on the same line (A84, 670, 56, 77), which are undated, may be of the same phase. Wall 74 may be the remains of the western, back, wall of a building running parallel to Freeschool Street (Fig 6), which lies 6m to the east. As discussed above, wall A74 runs on the same line as, and indeed partially overlies, the west wall of the postulated posthole building in the south-east corner.

The only other wall definitely of this phase was A469, a short length of wall running north-south at the south end of Trench A, which evidence from later phases suggests may have marked a property boundary. Further evidence for stone walls was provided by a number of foundation trenches: to the west A277; 478; 575; a group to the east 636, 637.5, 639; and B139) where parts of earlier pits had been dug out and backfilled with stone presumably in areas where stone walls passed over the top, and two robber trenches (A654, B123).

The west end of wall A18 overlies a pit (A126) which was filled after AD1200, while four of the foundation trenches (A478, 636, 637.5 and 639) contained post-1200 pottery in their fill. None, however, contained any Potterspury ware (W18). Hence a 13th-early 14th century date is suggested for the first appearance of stone-founded walls on the site.

Ovens

At the west end of the site there were three ovens, A236.2, 268 and 276. None contained any material suggesting that they had an industrial function and a domestic use is therefore suggested for them. The area of the ovens was subsequently, in Phase 4B/5A, enclosed within a building, and it is possible that the ovens themselves lay within a building, the evidence for which has been destroyed by the construction of the later building.

Other features

The miscellaneous group of contexts comprised: layers (A132, 252, 332, 398, 455–6, 524, 606, 629, 641; B102); an area of burnt stones (A529), possibly a hearth or a capping to the underlying pit A539; and a trench/drain (A238).

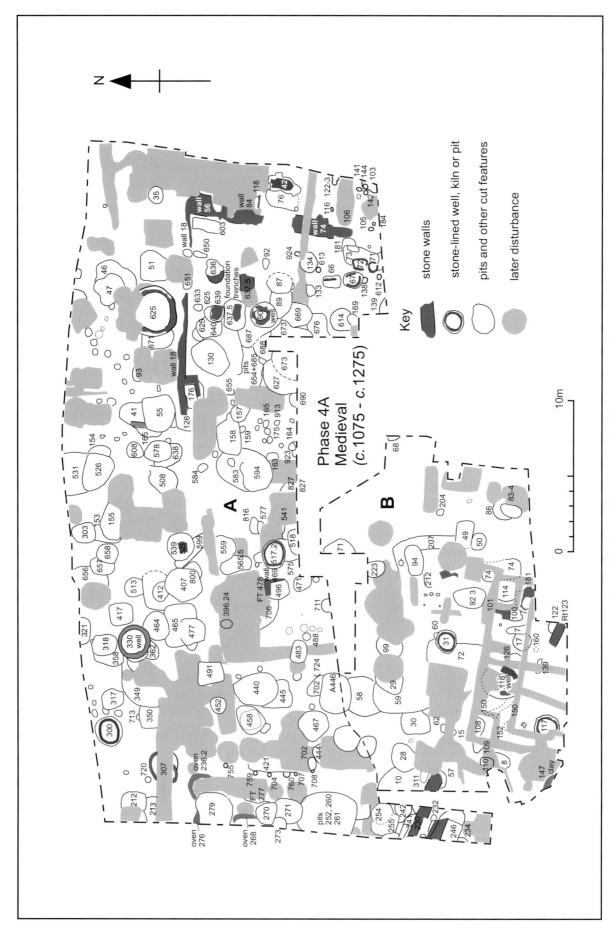

Fig 6: The Green: Phase 4A: Medieval (c.1075–c.1275)

Discussion

The evidence for occupation of this phase confirms that recovered from the St Peter's Street excavations (Williams J H 1979, 141–45). The large number of pits attests that the site at this phase was chiefly a backyard area. The best evidence for buildings of this date comes from the south-east corner of Trench A where a possible posthole building fronting onto Freeschool Street was probably replaced in the 13th-early 14th centuries by a stone-founded building on the same line. Similarly, the row of postholes on the west side of the site may represent the last surviving traces of a timber building fronting onto Narrow Toe Lane.

There was little evidence of industrial activity on the site at this phase, and the occupation appears to have been chiefly domestic in character, though the animal bone assemblage from this phase would suggest some small, scale skin processing.

Phase 4B: Late medieval (*c.*1275–*c.*1470)

Contexts of this phase can be divided into: stone walls and associated features; pits and possible trenches; postholes; layers; and ovens/kilns (Figs 7–11).

Property boundaries

As with Phase 4A, the sequence of stone wall building is difficult to interpret but sufficient survives to allow us to attempt to identify individual properties. The northern end of the site is perhaps divided into three properties fronting onto St Peter's Street by two lengths of wall A773 and A13. These walls continue the line of walls discovered on the St Peter's Street excavation and the properties correspond to Houses 8, 9 and 10 of that excavation (Figs 7 & 8). The southern boundary of these properties is presumably marked by walls A236.1 and A368 on the west side of the site and by walls A18 and A77 on the east side. No evidence was recovered for a wall between these two wall lines in the central area of the site, possibly because there was less earlier disturbance to this area and hence any wall need not have had a foundation trench. Stone foundations A529 set into Phase 4A pit A539 (see Fig 6) do in fact continue the line of A18/77 to the west. So it can be suggested that a wall may have existed at this point in Phases 4A and 4B, running west from AI8 to meet wall A369, in which case stone-lined pits A506 and A507, would have been set against its northern face.

Walls A369 and A457, which continue the line of wall A773 to the south, may mark the eastern boundary of a property fronting onto Narrow Toe Lane (Figs 7 & 8: Property 1). This wall line is interrupted by oven A396 which, although running on the same alignment as the wall line, is offset slightly to the east. This may indicate that the oven was a later insertion into the wall line. The northern boundary would be marked by walls A236.1 and A368 and the southern boundary by walls A205. The western boundary is marked by A351 which lies just off the site to the west but was located in a trial trench (see below). This property provides the best evidence for a

building, though only possibly of this phase (it is dated Phase 4B/5A). It is represented by wall A236.1 to the north, wall A361 to the east and wall A205 to the south. The west wall, A351, lay *c.*0.5m west of the west edge of the trench. It was not possible to excavate this wall as it lay too close to the modern line of Narrow Toe Lane, but its presence and line was confirmed by rapid trial trenches at its north and south ends. The size of the building thus formed was 13m by 6m internally. No evidence of internal arrangements definitely of this phase survived.

At the eastern end of the site another wall line, comprising wall A28 and robber trenches A630 and 631, lay parallel to and south of wall A18. Although the distance of *c.*4.5m between the two wall lines might suggest a building, there are a number of reasons for suggesting that they instead formed a yard: there is no sign of a west wall to complete the building, nor of any floor levels within it; and a stone-lined pit, A52, and a well, A90, had been inserted into the northern and southern wall lines respectively. To the east the possible Phase 4A building fronting onto Freeschool Street (Fig 8: Property 2) may have continued in use.

Pits and wells

The incidence of pit digging can be seen to have declined when compared with the preceding phase; and the pits which do belong to this phase are often stone-lined and were sometimes set against boundary walls (eg pits A52, 404). Well A330 was constructed at this phase and a further six wells are likely to have been in use at this time (A90, 121, 300, 323, B107, 118). Two features (A304, 401) were markedly different from the normal cut features discovered on the site. Both were shallow, rectangular features: A304 was 3.5m long, 1.5m wide, and had a surviving depth of 0.28m and evidence of possible postholes around the edge of the cut. A401 was at least 2.2m long (it was cut away at its northern end), 1.0m wide with a surviving depth of 0.22m. In neither case did the nature of their clay loam fills give any clue as to their function.

The only evidence for posts definitely of this phase were a stone-lined post-pit (A409), 1.0m wide and 0.92m surviving depth, and three stone-lined postholes (A448, 460, 461).

Layers of this phase were chiefly accumulations of loam; no floor levels or metalled surfaces were discovered.

Stone-built ovens/kilns

Five ovens of this date were recognised. Three, A17, A49 and B18, were heavily damaged. Of these, oven A49, to the north-east had a circular chamber, a form usually seen as a domestic baking/bread oven. Oven A17, to the west of oven A49, was badly damaged but appeared to have a rectangular chamber, as associated with drying ovens., as was oven B18, in the south.

Two ovens/kilns, A396 and B20, were well-preserved and unusual forms of a type of feature normally regarded as a drying oven/malt kiln. Oven/kiln A396 was an extremely complex structure of at least two phases (Figs 8–10). At its latest phase a stone-lined pit, 2–3m long

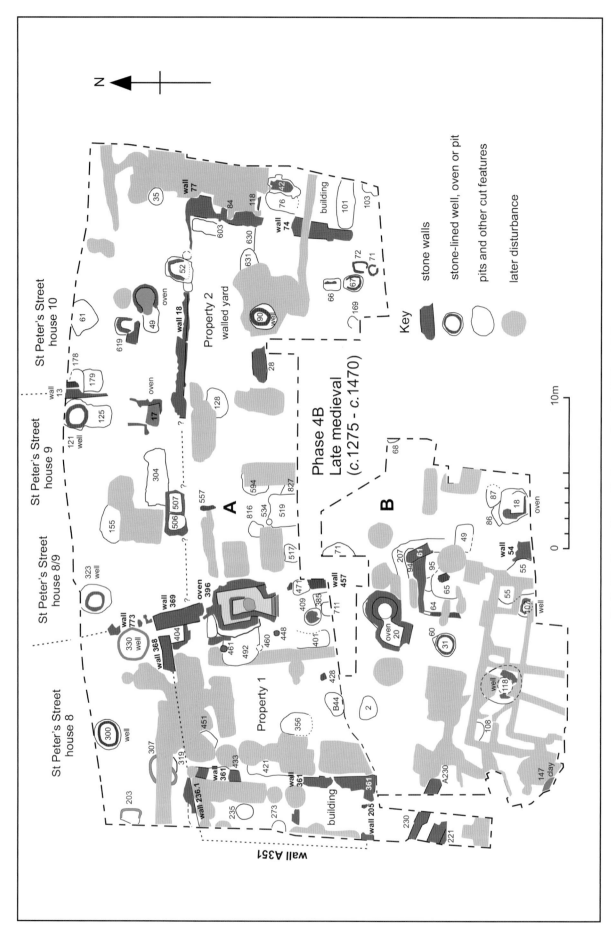

Fig 7: The Green: Phase 4B: Late medieval (c.1275–c.1470)

Fig 8: Rectangular drying oven, A396, looking north, set within an earlier stone-lined pit, with access steps to the stokehole in the foreground

Fig 9: Rectangular drying oven, A396, looking south, with the oven and larger chamber in the foreground, stokehole and access steps in the background

north-south by 2.2m wide east-west, and 0.9m deep, was entered from the south, down two steep steps. Within this chamber was a kiln structure, surviving to a height of up to 0.4m, which consisted of a base of one-two courses of thin ironstone slabs on which rested piers, of ironstone, set at intervals of 0.2m, which supported further ironstone slabs. This structure was set on a floor of large ironstone slabs which had replaced an earlier floor of limestone.

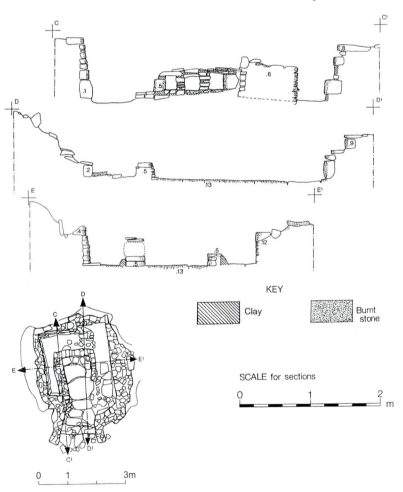

KEY

Clay   Burnt stone

SCALE for sections

0   1   2 m

0   1   3m

Fig 10: Plan and sections of drying oven, A396

271

The internal oven/kiln structure and both floors all showed signs of intense burning. The walls of the oven were battered on the west side and at the west end of the north and south walls. The later structure had so extensively altered the original structure that little can be said about it, it is even uncertain whether it originated as a larger drying oven or as a cellar.

The second drying oven, B20, had a circular firing chamber, which was lined with courses of thin, inward-sloping limestone slabs, measured 1.66m in diameter at the top and 1.00m at the bottom, with a surviving depth of 1.45m and a floor of heavily burnt ironstone slabs (Fig 11). To its south-west was a stoke chamber, 1.5m square and 1.2m deep, lined with limestone and ironstone blocks. The stoke chamber was entered by means of two steep steps on its south side. Soil samples from the lower fills of the oven contained quantities of silicified wheat.

Discussion

At this phase the layout of individual property boundaries on the site can be surmised for the first time. The three properties fronting on to St Peter's Street form the back areas of Houses 8, 9 and 10 of the St Peter's Street excavation (the House 8/9 boundary could not be precisely defined on this excavation). These properties vary in area between 180m^2 and 300m^2 in area. To

Fig 11: Medieval circular drying oven/kiln, B20, looking east with access steps into the square stokehole bottom right

the south of these properties there appears to have been properties aligned along Narrow Toe Lane and Freeschool Street. The boundaries of any properties between the Narrow Toe Lane and Freeschool Street properties and of any properties fronting onto The Green could not be determined. The Narrow Toe Lane property would have been c.230m^2 in area and contained at its western end a building of a similar size and alignment – parallel rather than at right angles to the frontage – to the medieval period buildings fronting on to St Peter's Street (Williams J H 1979, 143–7).

The incidence of pit digging in the yard areas can be seen to fall off dramatically at this phase, and those pits which were dug were generally stone-lined. This phenomenon has been noted previously both in Northampton (Shaw 1984a, 74–5; Williams, Shaw and Denham 1985, 28; Shaw 1985, 123) and elsewhere (cf eg for Southampton, Platt and Coleman-Smith 1975 Vol 1, 34–5).

The two drying ovens/kilns A396 and B20 are both of unusual form: A396 due to the elaborate nature of its internal kiln structure and B20 in having a circular firing chamber. Drying ovens had been found previously elsewhere in Northampton. Two rectangular ones were discovered to the south of St Peter's Street in the 1973–6 excavations (Williams J H 1979, 97) and a further rectangular one, unusually with no sign of a stoke chamber, was discovered during the St Peter's Gardens excavations at the back of a property fronting on to Marefair (Williams, Shaw and Denham 1985, feature Y10, 28, (M)16, fig 47). A further rectangular one was discovered to the north of Marefair in the Marefair excavations (Williams F 1979, 52).

All of these structures, like those on The Green, appear to have been of 15th century date. Soil samples have been analysed from three examples. One from St Peter's Street (G86) produced charred cereal grains, principally of wheat (Williams J H 1979, 97; Keepax et al 1979, 337); one from Marefair produced carbonised seeds, principally of barley, (Williams F 1979, 52; Straker 1979, 78, (M) 156–8); and B20 on The Green produced predominantly charred wheat grains as well as silicified wheat chaff (see Robinson below). Clearly these ovens took a variety of forms and had a variety of functions involving grain processing, though Robinson warns against regarding them as being necessarily drying ovens, and notes that the carbonised and silicified items found may not represent what was being processed.

More recently, a brewing complex has been examined at Angel Street, Northampton, where two drying ovens formed part of a single property (Brown 2021, 61–65 & 320–323), an arrangement similar to Property 1 at The Green. Such drying ovens are not just an urban phenomenon, Excavations at Furnells manor, Raunds, examined a detached malt house associated with the manor house of the 13th to mid-14th centuries, and a detached kitchen/brew house associated with the late medieval manor of the mid-14th to mid-15th centuries (Audouy and Chapman 2009, 98–100 & 105–106, figs 5.39 & 5.45–5.46). At Raunds, West Cotton there was a long sequence of drying ovens from an earth cut oven of the early 12th century through to detached malt houses that formed part of each medieval tenement from the mid-13th century. The

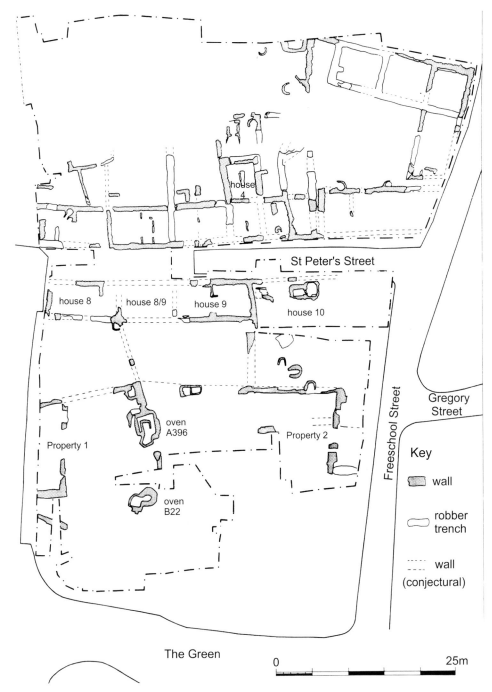

Fig 12: The Green and St Peter's Street, showing late medieval houses, other major features and property boundaries

environmental evidence suggested use both for creating the malted barley for brewing but also a more general, and perhaps equally important use, as grain drying ovens (Chapman 2010, 225–229 & figs 7.74–7.76).

There is little to suggest that the occupation at this phase of the Green was other than domestic in character, though there is, once again, some evidence of small scale skin processing that may pre-date an expansion of the process in the post-medieval period where domestic plots gave way to industrial scale tanneries.

Period 5A: Late medieval–early post-medieval tanneries (*c*.1470–*c*.1700)

The late 15th–17th century tanneries and the associated finds and environmental evidence have been fully published previously (Shaw 1996; Shaw 2011), and only a brief illustrated summary is provided below, extracted from the published report.

Phase 5A (*c*.1470–*c*.1550) comprised the Western, Northern (Phase 1) and North-Western Tanneries (Figs 13, 14 & 16), while Phase 5B (*c*.1550–*c*.1700) comprised the Northern (Phase 2) Eastern and Central Tanneries (Fig

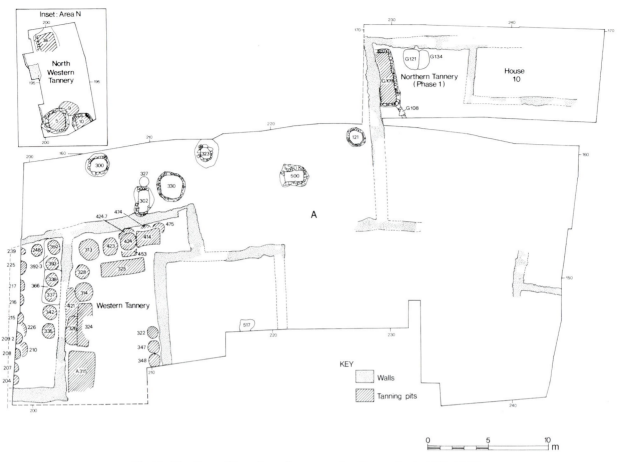

Fig 13: The Green, Phase 5a, early post-medieval tanneries (c.1470–1550)

Fig 14: The Western Tannery, looking south

Fig 15: (left) The Eastern Tannery, looking east

Fig 16: Conjectural reconstruction of the Western Tannery (Ken Connor 1996)

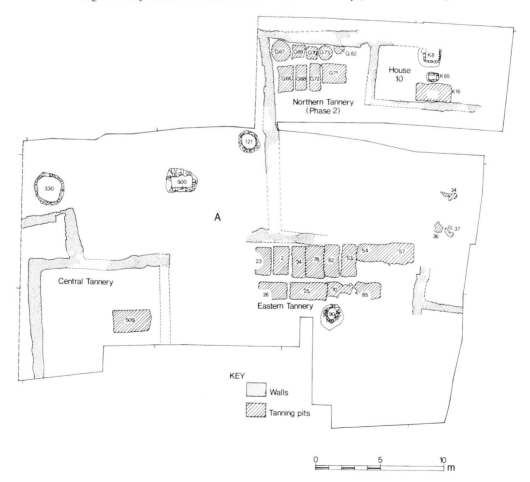

Fig 17: The Green, Phase 5b: the post-medieval tanneries (*c*.1550–1700)

15 & 17), although it is possible that that all three were elements of a single tanning complex.

Each tannery comprised groups of circular and rectangular tanning pits. The animal bone evidence suggests that cattle and horse hides and sheep skins were all being processed, despite contemporary prohibitions of this practice. All the tanneries were small, with the largest, the Western Tannery, comprising 36–37 pits. Many of the pits contained deposits of lime and ash, which were used in the de-hairing process.

Since the 1980s there has been little further work related to the post-medieval tanneries of Northampton. To the west of The Green, excavation of the town defences at Green Street in the mid-1990s identified square clay-lined pits in trench 1 and circular clay-lined tanning pits in trench 4 (Chapman 1999, 38 and 51–53).

The pottery
by Varian Denham

Introduction

A large assemblage of pottery, 17,515 sherds, was recovered from the site. The 15,466 sherds dated from the early/middle Saxon to the late medieval/early post-medieval (Site phases 2–4) are considered in this report (Figs 10–15). The post-medieval pottery, including the early post-medieval pottery from when the site was largely given over tanning (Phase 5), has been previously quantified and described (Denham in Shaw 1996, 85–89).

Most of the pottery recovered from the late Saxon and medieval periods was recovered from rubbish pits and other backyard deposits. It provides useful additional evidence in the study of the ceramics of this period in Northampton.

The Northampton Pottery Fabric Type Series is held by MOLA (Museum of London Archaeology) Northampton, formerly Northamptonshire Archaeology, as part of the County Type Series. The pottery fabric types are coded according to the system in use by NDC Archaeological Unit in the 1970s and 80s, and not those of the current County Type Series.

I am particularly grateful to Mike Shaw, Heather Lovett, Maureen Mellor and Jonathan Humble for assistance in the preparation of this report.

Note: this report, and the subsequent finds reports, are all presented as compiled in the late 1980s to early 1990s.

The pottery fabrics and quantification

The range of fabric types represented in the assemblage is listed in Table 2 and the quantification of the assemblage is presented in Table 4. Reference to previously published fabric definitions are cited in the third column of Table 2: Site code (definitions) and these site codes are related to the site names in Table 3. The prefix (M) to a page number within the text indicates a page in a microfiche section to a published report.

Discussion

All the pottery from the excavation is closely comparable to material from other assemblages from Northampton and reference should be made to earlier publications, as cited in Table 2, for the original definitions and discussions, particularly of fabric types. The report on St Peter's Gardens contains a detailed analysis of 9th- to 12th-century wares (Denham 1985a, 53–7 and (M) 2/5–46) and a full description of the medieval and post-medieval pottery of Northampton (Denham 1985a, 62–3 and (M) 2/49–3/22).

Phases 1–2/3, pre-AD850
Only three sherds were found in contexts which may have preceded Phase 3. These comprised two undiagnostic fragments of possible prehistoric origin (pers comm HM Bamford) from Phase 1 and one sherd of early/middle Saxon date from Phase 2/3.

Phase 3: c.AD850–c.ASD1075 (657 sherds)
The two dominant fabric types were locally and regionally produced St Neots-type Ware (T1) and Northampton Ware (W1), but pottery was imported from East Anglia, the Gloucestershire and Cotswold region, Leicestershire or South Lincolnshire, and Stamford. A small number of high quality wares of probable Continental influence may bear witness to Northampton's widening communications in the late Saxon period.

St Neots-type ware
Fabric T1 and sub-types
An usual range of forms in St Neots-type Ware include small, well made cooking pots with curved rims, globular profiles and slightly sagging bases, and larger straight-sided cooking pots with everted rims (Fig 18, 1–15). Bowls were represented by examples with sharply inturned or hammer-headed rims, and shallow dishes. A spouted bowl and pedestal lamp were also found. Large storage vessels with multiple handles and thumbed decoration on the neck and shoulder (Fig 18, 14) were present in greater numbers than on other sites in Northampton. Only one example of rouletted decoration was recovered (not illustrated).

All sub-types of fabric previously recognised (Denham 1985a, 54) were present, but T1(1) was by far the most abundant, accounting for more than 80% of the definable St Neots-type Ware in Phase 3. This is the most common sub-type of T1 and is chiefly wheel-thrown, calcareous-tempered, thin-walled, purplish-black fabric of 10th and 11th century date which is found throughout the region.

The majority of the pottery was thrown on the fast wheel, and bowls in particular exhibit wire marks on the underside of the bases. Larger vessels, notably storage jars, show evidence of coil construction. It is possible that the pottery was clamp-kiln fired and most is reduced. Cooking pots are frequently heavily sooted from use over an open fire. Bowls may be internally calcined or slipped and presumably served a wide variety of uses in food preparation and preservation.

Table 2: Medieval pottery fabrics (see Table 4 for quantifications)

Fabric code	Familiar name	Site code (definitions)	Origin	Date AD
Early/Middle Anglo-Saxon				
S1	–	M115X	?local	400–900
Late Saxon				
T1	St Neots-type ware	M115X	Local & regional	900–1200
W1	Northampton ware	M115X	Northampton (?10th C)	850–1100
W1/X1	–	M115X	?Northampton	10th century
W32	–	M115X	?local	850–1100
W34	–	M115X	?local (?10th century)	850–1100
W36	–	M115X	?Leicester	850–1100
Late Saxon/medieval				
W2	?Thetford-type ware	M115X	East Anglia	850–1200
W3	Thetford-type ware	M115X	East Anglia	850–1200
W54	–	M115X	?East Anglia	850–1200
X1(1)	Stamford ware	M115X	Stamford, Lincolnshire	850–1250
T11	–	M115X	?Oxon/Glos	900–1300
V5	–	M115X	?Glos/Oxon	900–1300
V8	–	M115X	?Glos/Oxon	900–1300
T1/2	Transitional shelly ware	M115X	?local	1000–1200
W47	–	M115X	Leicestershire	900–1300
W48	–	M115X	?local	900–1300
Medieval				
W4	–	M155X	?Leics/Lincs	1050–1250
X1(2)	Developed Stamford ware	M115:164	Stamford, Lincolnshire	1150–1250
		M139:118		
T2	Medieval shelly ware	M115X	Local & regional	1100–1400
V1	–	M115:157	?Midlands	1100–1400
V6	–	M351	S Northants/Oxon	1100–1400
W7(1)	Oxford Tripod Pitcher	M115:159–60	Oxon	1100–1400
W7(2)	Splashed ware	M115:159–60	Oxon	1100–1400
W7(3)	–	M115:159–60	East Midlands	1100–1400
W7(4)	–	M115:159–60	Bedfordshire	1100–1400
W22	–	M285.68	Source unknown	1100–1400
W29	E Midlands Late Medieval Oxidised ware	M115:163	?local	1350–1600
T2(2)	Lyveden/Stanion ware	M351	Lyveden/Stanion	1200–1400
T6	–	M115:157	Local ?NE Northants	1200–1400
V2	–	M100:135	Potters Marston, Bucks	1200–1400
V3	–	M115:157	?Bedfordshire	1200–1400
V9	–	M285:65	?Nottingham	1200–1400
W8	–	M115:160	SE England	1200–1400
W45	–	M178	Bourne, Lincolnshire	1200–1400
W56	–	M351	Midlands	1100–1500
V7	–	M115:158	?local	1100–1500
V4	Olney Hyde-type ware	M178	Olney Hyde, Bucks	1200–1500
	(Fabric B)			
W11(1)	–	M115:160	?Coventry/?Nuneaton/	1200–1500
			?Nottingham	
W11(3)	–	M115:160	?Coventry/?Nuneaton	1200–1500
W11(4)	–	M115:160	Surrey	1200–1500
W11(5)	–	M115:160	?Surrey	1200–1500
W11(7)	–	M115:160	Midlands	1200–1500
W13	–	M115:161	?N Midlands	1200–1500
W14	Brill-type ware	M115:161	Oxon	1200–1500
W14(2)	Brill-type ware	This report	Oxon	1350–1500
W15	East Anglian Red ware	M115:161	East Anglia	1200–1500

Table 3: Site codes and site names

Site code	Site name (report)
M99	The Horsemarket (Williams 1974)
M100	Greyfriars (Gryspeerdt 1978)
M115	St Peter's Street (McCarthy 1979)
M115X	St Peter's Gardens (Denham 1985a)
M139	Chalk Lane (Gryspeerdt 1981
M178	Marefair (Gryspeerdt 1979)
M285	College Street (Gryspeerdt 1982)
M351	Derngate (Shaw and Denham 1984)
M403	The Ridings (Denham 1984a)
M443	Black Lion Hill (Denham 1985b)
M446	This report

Northampton ware and related types
(Fabric W1 (and sub-types) and related fabrics W32 and W34)

The most common form is the globular pot with everted rim and flat base, although examples of wide jars, spouted bowls and lamp fragments were found (Fig 18, 16–18)..

The majority of sherds fall within the wide range of texture and colour common to this ware, and have the usual quartz and ironstone suite of inclusions. Two shell tempered sherds and one poorly glazed fragment were found, but both, unfortunately were residual in later contexts.

Considerable variation in quality and method of manufacture is evident (Denham 1985a, 55). Little further definition of the complex production and use of this ware is possible given the small size of this assemblage.

High quality wares (origin uncertain)
Fabric W1/X1(1)/Y

Although the majority of sherds are undiagnostic of form three globular cooking pots with everted square rims were identified (Fig 18, 19–20). The fabric lies at the finest extreme of Northampton Ware and is probably a local product. The vessels are well potted, uniformly wheel thrown and fired under oxidising conditions. One or two characteristic traces of red paint were present on undiagnostic body sherds. None of the vessels show signs of sooting.

Calcareous Late Saxon transitional ware
Fabric T1/2

Approximately 13% of the pottery from Phase 3 has some of the characteristics more frequently associated with later shelly wares, in particular a harshness of surface, lack of smoothing and possible higher firing temperature. The forms and fabric of these vessels are in keeping, however, with a 10th-12th century date.

Other wares
Fabrics W36, W2, W3, W54, X1(1), T6, T11, V5, V6, V8, W47 and W48

A small number of sherds of Thetford Ware, Stamford Ware, oolitic-tempered wares from the Cotswold, Gloucestershire and north Northamptonshire regions, and sandy East Midland wares were recovered.

Catalogue of illustrated pottery: Phase 3
Figure 18

1 Cooking pot, St Neots-type ware T1(1), complete profile: 123mm high, rim diam 100mm, base diam 80mm. Phase 3, context A495

2 Cooking pot, St Neots-type ware T1, rim, diam 140mm. Phase 3, context A459

4 Cooking pot, St Neots-type ware T1, rim, diam 160mm. Phase 3, context A459

6 Cooking pot/bowl, sooted, St Neots-type ware T1(1), rim, diam 240mm. Phase 3, context A202

9 Bowl, St Neots-type ware T1, rim, diam 224mm. Phase 3, context A459

11 Bowl, St Neots-type ware T1(1), rim, diam 260mm. Phase 3, context A150

13 Spouted bowl, St Neots-type ware T1(4), rim and spout, rim diam 260mm. Phase 3, context A436

14 Storage jar, St Neots-type ware T1, rim and handles, rim diam 200mm. Phase 3, context A459

15 Cooking pot, St Neots-type ware T1(1), base, diam 100mm

16 Cooking pot, Northampton ware W1, rim, diam 140mm. Phase 3, context A459

17 Cooking pot/bowl, heavily sooted exterior, Northampton ware W1, rim, diam 240mm. Phase 3, context A663.2

18 Cooking pot, Northampton ware W1, base, diam 85mm. Phase 3, context A459

19 Cooking pot, Northampton ware/Stamford ware/ stoneware W1/X1(1)Y, rim, diam 132mm. Phase 3, context B136

20 Cooking pot, traces of red paint (ochre) on outside of rim, Northampton ware/Stamford ware/stoneware W1/X1(1)Y, rim, diam 160mm. Phase 3, context A150

Phase 4a c.1075–c.1275
(8467 sherds)

Despite the upheavals of the Norman Conquest a case for continuity in domestic coarsewares has been argued (Hurst 1976, 342–3). It is evident that many of the forms and fabrics present in 11th-century contexts do persist into the 12th century and the transition to the higher fired, decorative and more varied styles of the 13th century is gradual. It is difficult to quantify with precision the amount of pottery of late Saxon type which is still being produced in the 12th century owing to the problems of residuality in disturbed urban contexts. It is quite probable that as much as 15% of the pottery in Phase 4a is residual, notably fabrics T1, W1 and X1(1). Nevertheless, calcareous late Saxon/early Medieval Transitional Ware (fabric T1/2) is obviously still abundant in this phase (Fig 19, 21–5) and Thetford Ware (Fig 20, 51–3) and other regional wares (Fig 21, 67 and 68) continue to be found.

Whilst vessels produced in this period demonstrate a greater competence: use of glaze and slip, better firing under oxidising conditions, and more stylistic variation; many of the coarsewares are clearly coil-built. No kilns have been identified in the town after AD1075 and it is

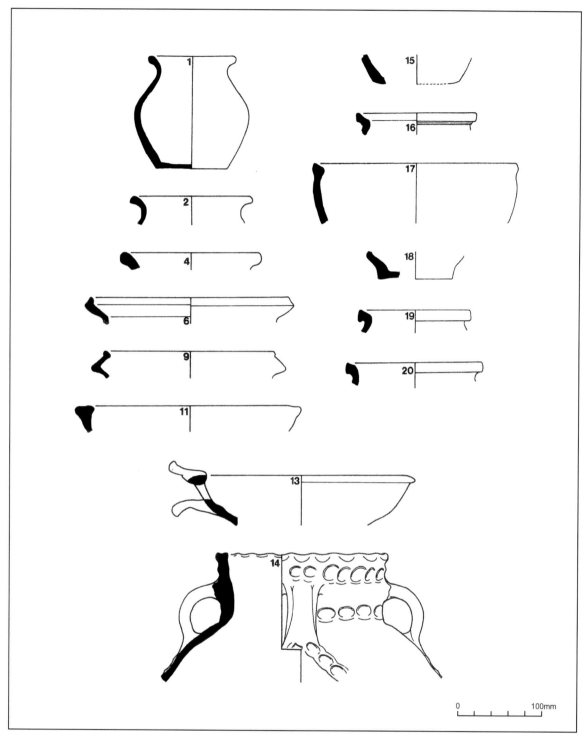

Fig 18: Late Saxon pottery, Phase 3 (1–20)

likely that the majority of the calcareous pottery was being produced in the villages.

At present it is only possible to identify the demise of the urban pottery industry and a decrease in the production of wheel-built and composite vessels sometime during the late 10th to late 11th centuries. More precise dating of these developments, and elucidation of the relationship, if any, between industrial change and political change await regional study.

Calcareous wares
(Fabric prefix T)
Pottery produced in fabrics with a predominance of crushed shell temper accounts for more than 80% of the contemporary assemblage and this is in keeping with the evidence from other excavations in the town. Globular cooking pots with sagging bases occur most frequently, and jugs with either straight or globular profiles and narrow, occasionally rilled necks are common (Fig

279

Table 4: Quantification of pottery: Sherds by Site Phase

Pottery fabrics date/ type code	Site Phases					Total
	2/3	3	4A	4B	Residual	
Early/Middle Anglo-Saxon						
S1	1	-	1	1	2	5
Late Saxon						
T1	–	475	952	167	202	1796
W1	–	35	66	13	18	132
W1/X1/Y	–	6	4	1	3	14
W32	–	-	–	1	–	1
W34	–	1	3	1	–	5
W36	–	2	–	–	–	2
Late Saxon/ Medieval						
W2	–		1		1	2
W3	–	5	13	1	5	24
W54	–	1	1		1	3
X1(1)	–	8	35	10	13	66
T11	–	1	8	1	5	15
V5	–	3	11			14
V8	–	4	2	2	29	37
T1/2	–	87	1154	355	388	1984
W47	–	2	15		1	18
W48	–	1	2		2	5
Medieval						
W4	–	–	1			1
X1(2)	–	–	25	19	3	47
T2	–	–	4986	1286	776	7048
V1	–	–	107	35	42	184
V6	–	–	30	6	1	37
W7	–	–	135	66	35	236
W22	–	–	17	9	13	39
W29	–	–	89	37	4	130
T2(2)	–	–	165	115	86	366
T6		6	144	24	18	192
V2	–	–	9	1	1	11
V3	–	–	91	25	6	122
V9	–	–	7	1	3	11
W8	–	–		1	9	10
W45	–	–	2			2
W56	–	–	4		8	12
V7	–	–	58	16	30	104
V4	–	–		1	2	3
W11	–	–	23	12	19	54
W13	–	–	11	7	8	26
W14	–	–	143	121	91	355
W15	–	–	5	34	62	101
Late Medieval/Early post medieval						
W18	–	–	14	842	845	1701
W20	–	–	–	71	99	170
W29	–	–	1	12	168	181
W50	–	–	–	32	2	34
W16	–	–	–	–	115	115
W21	–	–	–	9	42	51
Totals (Saxon/medieval)	**1**	**637**	**8335**	**3335**	**3158**	**15466**

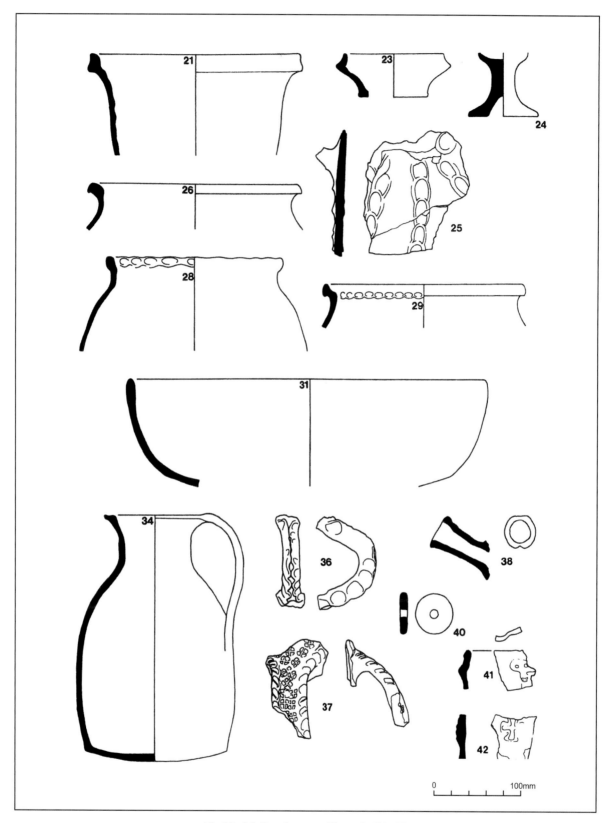

Fig 19: Medieval pottery, Phase 4a (21–42)

19, 21–45). Rims can be curved, square, everted, or of more complex moulded profile. Straight-sided bowls and pedestal lamps with thick walls and moulded stems were recovered together with a pitcher spout and a spindle whorl or counter made from a vessel base. Examples of rouletted decoration on handle and rim was present.

Glazed decorated jugs from the Lyveden/Stanion area (T2(2)) were found, typically with grid-iron or rosette stamps, but one sherd bore a plastic anthropomorphic decoration in a white clay (Fig 19, 41) and another exhibited an unusual cross stamped into white slip (Fig 19, 42). A large group of oolitic tempered sherds from thumbed rim cooking pots and jugs from north-east Northamptonshire were also recovered (Fig 20, 44–5).

Calcareous sandy wares
(Fabric prefix V)
(Fig 20, 46–50 and residual pottery from Phase 5a-B and unstratified contexts)

Only about 5% of the contemporary pottery falls into this category. Most fabrics are likely to be of local origin and the same range of forms is found in these wares as in the calcareous tempered material. Only fabric V3, which probably comes from Bedfordshire, produces unusual forms, most notably large, wide-mouthed bowls with T-shaped rims.

Sandy, and very fine sandy, wares
(Fabric prefixes W and X)
Very little of the pottery was in sandy fabrics. The majority of the sherds derive from glazed jugs, most of which are regional imports from Midland areas, although unglazed body sherds from cooking pots and jugs from a wider catchment area (East Anglia, South-East England) are present in small numbers (Figs 20 & 21, 51–68). Decoration is flamboyant on the glazed jugs, and includes thumbing, rouletting, rilling, combing and stamping over slips and under glaze. The forms include balusters, early cisterns or bunghole pitchers, and globular or tall, straight-sided vessels.

The most notable vessel is a bunghole jar from the Brill/Boarstall kilns (Fig 20, 63). The following notes have been supplied by Maureen Mellor. It is the most elaborately decorated bunghole jar to date from Brill/Borstall kilns. No parallels are known from recent excavations in Oxfordshire and Buckinghamshire. Oxford, the principal market for Brill/Borstall products during the medieval period has many plain bunghole jars (Mellor and Oakley 1984, fig 15.1, 185) in late 15th/16th-century contexts. Excavations of kilns at Brill (Ivens 1981, 105) have yielded plain bunghole jars with archeomagnetic dating to the first half of the 14th century. Maureen Mellor believed this to be too early for bunghole jars – on stratified Oxfordshire sites they date to c.1400. More elaborate vessels were recovered from Chalgrave Moated Manor in South-East Oxfordshire. The demolition levels above the pentice yielded a bunghole jar with combed decoration which was thickly glazed, streaky mottled green, both internally and externally (Typescript c/o Oxford Archaeological Unit CP725/1/1 – Phase 4/2, No.123). Documentary evidence suggests this Manor was demolished c.1485.

The fabric of this vessel is typical of the Brill/Borstall range, although this example is more abundantly tempered than the earlier fine-walled, highly decorated pitchers. The drawing suggests a jar much wider than those found locally (in Oxford). The hole of the spigot was 'peked' through rather than ducked, when the clay was leather-hard. The hole had been reinforced externally.

The general style of decoration with iron-rich red petalled flowers and grid stamped centres in contrasting white clay can be paralleled on earlier highly decorated pitchers (Oxford Castle, *Oxoniensia*, **41** 1976, fig 13, No.13, 261; from Barbican Ditch and other published sites in *Oxoniensia*). But the details of the flower petals on this vessel differ. The earlier petalled flowers were simply red clay smeared onto the surface of the vessel. This technique was apparently refined on the Northamptonshire jar with the aid of a knife which removed the excess clay to highlight the outer edge of the petals. The curvilinear applied strips with stabbed-on grid stamped terminals can be paralleled with sherds from the Boarstall kilns (*Records of Buckinghamshire*, **24**, 1982, 110) and from Oxford (*Oxoniensia*, **45**, 1980, fig15, 20) dated mid-late 13th century.

The thick applied cordons acting as rectangular frames for each rosette are without parallel from amongst the decorative repertoire from these kilns. The glaze varies from orange with mottled green flecks to streaky mottled green (the streaky effect being caused by the bleeding of the iron. The latter is a characteristic of late medieval Brill/Borstall types. The glaze suggests that the vessel was subjected to very uneven firing temperatures, which is perhaps not surprising given the large girth of the vessel.

The extreme scarcity of later medieval fabrics, notably Potterspury ware (W18) and fabrics W20 and W29 would recommend a *terminus ante quem* for the phase before the last quarter of the 13th century, although in view of Mellor's remarks concerning the bunghole jar it may be either that the phase lasted into the 14th century or that the context from which the jar was recovered (pit A261) ought more properly to be placed in Phase 4b (this context also contained a number of Potterspury ware sherds).

Catalogue of illustrated pottery, Phase 4a
Figure 19

21 Cooking pot/storage jar, heavily sooted exterior, Late Saxon transitional shelly ware T1/2, rim, diam 26mm. Phase 4a, context A407

23 Bowl, St Neots-type ware/medieval shelly ware T1(2)/T2, complete profile: height 46mm, rim diam 130mm, base diam 80mm. Phase 4a, context A446

24 Lamp base, heavily sooted, Transitional Late Saxon/ early medieval shelly ware T1/2, base, diam 80mm. Phase 4a, context B10

25 Body, thumb applied strip decoration, Transitional Late Saxon/early medieval shelly ware T1/2. Phase 4a, context A41

26 Cooking pot, traces of external sooting, medieval shelly ware T2, rim, diam 240mm. Phase 4a, context A41

28 Cooking pot, thumbing on interior of rim, medieval shelly ware T2, rim, diam 196mm. Phase 4a, context A673

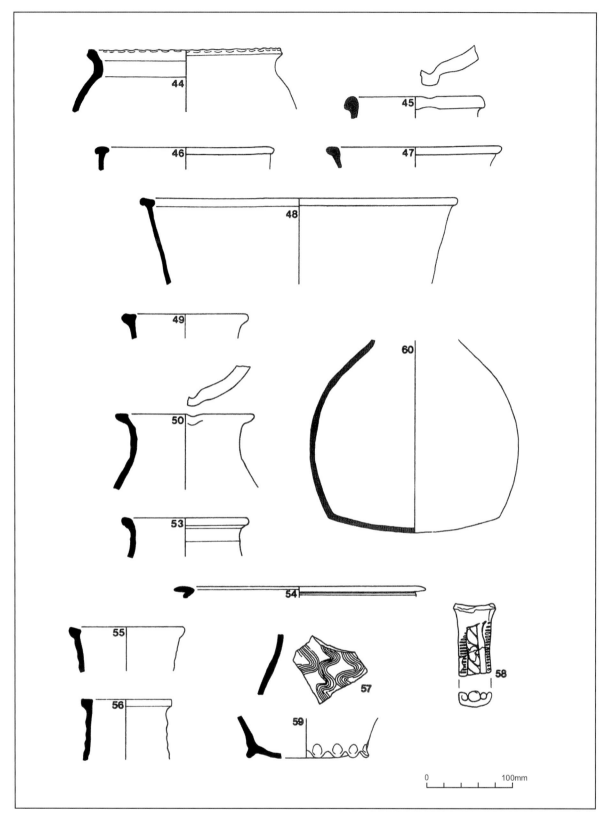

Fig 20: Medieval pottery, Phase 4a (44–60)

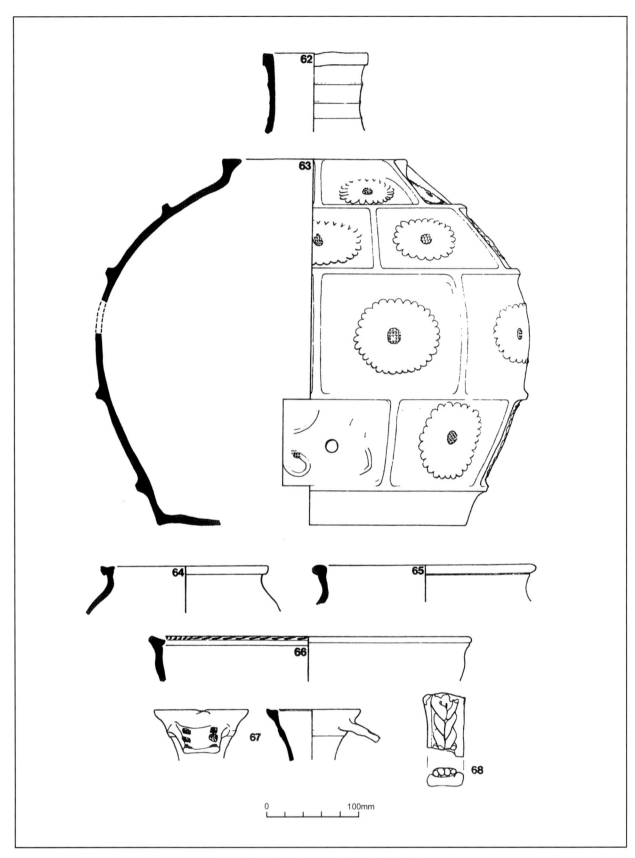

Fig 21: Medieval pottery, Phase 4a (62–68)

29 Cooking pot, thumbing on interior of rim, medieval shelly ware T2, rim, diam 232mm. Phase 4a, context A73

31 Bowl, medieval shelly ware T2, rim, diam 400mm. Phase 4a, context A73

34 Jug, medieval shelly ware T2, complete profile: height 260mm, rim diam 115mm, base diam 158mm. Phase 4a, context A578

36 Jug handle, thumbed strap handle, medieval shelly ware T2. Phase 4a, context A130

37 Jug handle, medieval shelly ware T2. Phase 4a, context A73

38 Pitcher spout, medieval shelly ware T2. Phase 4a, context B10.2

40 Spindlewhorl or counter made from pot base, medieval shelly ware T2, complete, diam 42mm. Phase 4a, context A41

41 Anthropomorphic face in white clay, glazed, Lyveden/Stanion type ware T2(2), rim. Phase 4a, context A51

42 Stamped decoration, possibly from a jug, glazed, Lyveden/Stanion type ware T2(2). Phase 4a, context A446

Figure 20

44 Cooking pot, north-east Northamptonshire (?) T6, rim, diam 220mm. Phase 4a, context A578

45 Jug, north-east Northamptonshire (?) T6, rim, diam 160mm. Phase 4a, context A51

46 Cooking pot, Bedfordshire (?) V3, rim, diam 200mm. Phase 4a, context A61.3

47 Bowl, Bedfordshire (?) V3, rim, diam 200mm. Phase 4a, context A130

48 Bowl, Bedfordshire (?) V3, rim, diam 360mm. Phase 4a, context A407

49 Cooking pot/bowl, Gloucestershire/Oxfordshire (?) V5, rim, diam140mm. Phase 4a, context A638.2

50 Jug, local V7(2), rim, diam 154mm. Phase 4a, context A658

53 Cooking pot, Bedfordshire (?) V3(1), rim, diam 140mm. Phase 4a, context A407

54 Cooking pot, Thetford-type ware W3(3), possibly Roman, rim, diam 285mm. Phase 4a, context A246

55 Jug, glazed, Oxford Tripod Pitcher ware W7(1), rim, diam 130mm. Phase 4a, context A658

56 Jug, glazed, Oxford Tripod Pitcher ware W7(1), rim, diam 100mm. Phase 4a, context A398

57 Body, combed decoration, Splashed ware, Oxon W7(2). Phase 4a, context A539

58 Jug handle, glazed, Splashed ware, Oxon W7(2). Phase 4a, context A407

59 Jug base, heavily thumbed, Splashed ware, Oxon W7(2), base diam 140mm. Phase 4a, context A407

60 Cooking pot, including joining sherd residual in later context A61, Bedfordshire W7(4), base, diam 192mm. Phase 4a, context A41

Figure 21

62 Jug, glazed, Coventry/Nuneaton/Nottingham (?) W11(1), rim, diam 114mm. Phase 4a, context A626

63 Bottle/bunghole jar, glazed, decorated with red clay flowers, petals have knife-cut outer edges, white clay grid-stamped centres; curvilinear applied strips with stabbed-on grid-stamped terminals (see pottery report), Brill-type ware W14(2), rim diam 200mm, base diam 335mm. Phase 4a, context A261

64 Cooking pot, unknown source W22, rim, diam 180mm. Phase 4a, context A626

65 Cooking pot, Leicestershire W47, rim, diam 240mm. Phase 4a, context A638.2

66 Bowl (?) Incised decoration on rim, some sooting on exterior of vessel, East Midlands W49, rim, diam 350mm. Phase 4a, context A387

67 Jug, glazed, Developed Stamford ware X1(2), rim and handle, rim diam 100mm. Phase 4a, context A134

68 Jug handle, glazed, Developed Stamford ware X1(2). Phase 4a, context A303

Phase 4b: c.1275–c.1470 (3364 sherds)

Although there was contamination from residual material, probably in the order of 5–10% of the assemblage, it is reasonable to assume that many of the forms and fabrics of the preceding phase were still being produced and calcareous jugs and cooking pots were common (Fig 22, 69–72). Sandy ware jugs, particularly from Oxfordshire, were also recovered in some numbers (Fig2 22 & 23, 74–78). The most characteristic feature of the assemblage, however, is the rise to prominence of later medieval wares.

Potterspury wares and local late medieval wares
Fabrics W18, W20, W29

The range of forms present in these fabrics is much wider than in the previous phase. Cooking pots, jugs and bowls were still being manufactured in quantity, particularly in the reduced gritty ware (W20) (Fig 22, 79–88). Cooking pots in Potterspury ware, however, frequently have bifid rims and show little sign of sooting, and may well have served an alternative function in the distilling process. Jugs in gritty oxidised fabric W29 tend to respect the forms of earlier phases, but Potterspury jugs are more globular, squatter and almost invariably plain or with limited rilled or combed decoration. Flat-based, wide-mouthed bowls, fish dishes, skillets, chafing dishes, cups, dripping pans and numerous bottles occur in Potterspury Ware, but few were decorated.

Vessels were thrown on the wheel and a thin glaze was applied, but rarely over more than part of the vessel. Pots were fired under well controlled oxidising conditions, and for the first time the vessels show uniformity suggestive of mass production, presumably specifically aimed at the Northampton market.

Fine wares
Fabrics W21 and X2a (Fig 23, 89)

Several sherds of green glazed white wares from the Surrey/Hampshire borders were recovered. All appear to derive from small bowls or lobed cups. Only one fragment of Cistercian ware (X2a) was present and it is probable that this should be regarded as contamination from the subsequent phase where it occurs in abundance. Owing to the lack of fabric X2a it is likely that the phase terminated before the last quarter of the 15th century. It is notable

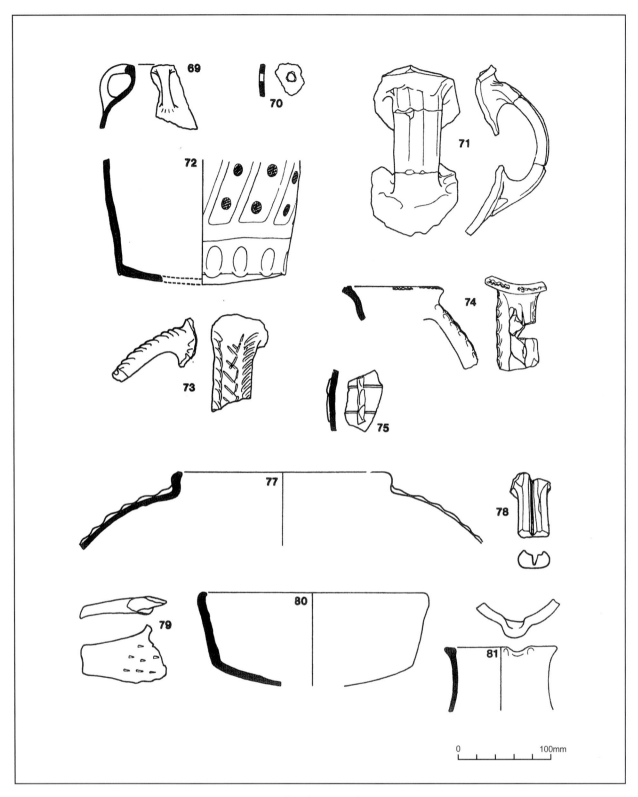

Fig 22: Late medieval pottery, Phase 4b (69–81)

also that the majority of sherds of Surrey white wares was found in Phase 5A despite the smaller quantity of material produced by this phase overall.

A date of *c*.1470 is consequently proposed for the end of Phase 4b.

Catalogue of illustrated pottery, Phase 4b
Figure 22
69   Jug handle, sooted, medieval shelly ware T2. Phase 4b, context A61

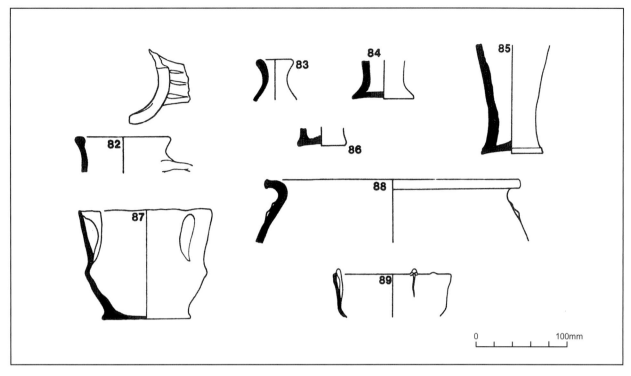

Fig 23:   Late medieval pottery, Phase 4b (82–89)

70   Spindlewhorl (?) Medieval shelly ware T2. Phase 4b, context A179

71   Jug handle, glazed, Lyveden/Stanion type ware T2(2). Phase 4b, context A519

72   Jug base, glazed, Lyveden/Stanion type ware T2(2), base diam 180mm. Phase 4b, context A61

73   Bunghole pitcher handle, glazed, Midlands (?) V1(2). Phase 4b, context A562

74   Jug rim and handle, glazed, Oxford Tripod Pitcher ware W7(1).Phase 4b, context A631

75   Body, jug, horizontal grooved and vertically-applied, thumbed strip decoration, Oxford Tripod Pitcher ware W7(1). Phase 4b, context A179

77   Cooking pot, Brill-type ware W14, rim, diam 240mm. Phase 4b, context A214

78   Jug handle, glazed, Brill-type ware W14(2). Phase 4b, context A506

79   Pipkin/skillet handle, glazed, Potterspury ware W18. Phase 4b, context B20

80   Bowl, Potterspury ware (?) W18, complete profile, rim diam 252, base diam 216. Phase 4b, context A178

81   Jug, Potterspury ware W18, rim, diam 120mm. Phase 4b, context B20

Figure 23

82   Jug, Potterspury ware W18, rim, diam 100mm. Phase 4b, context B20

83   Bottle, Potterspury ware W18, rim, diam 40mm. Phase 4b, context A61

84   Bottle, possibly same vessel as 83, Potterspury ware W18, base, diam 66mm. Phase 4b, context A101

85   Bottle, glazed, possibly same vessel as 83, Potterspury ware W18, base, diam 68mm. Phase 4b, context B20

86   Bottle, base, possibly same vessel as 83, Potterspury ware W18, base diam 54mm. Phase 4b, context A566

87   Cup, Potterspury ware W18, complete profile, rim diam 94mm, base diam 94mm. Phase 4b, context B20

88   Cooking pot, external sooting, East Midlands Medieval Reduced ware W20(1), rim, diam 280mm. Phase 4b, context A125

89   Lobed cup, glazed, Surrey White ware (Tudor Green) W21, rim, diam 130mm. Phase 4b, context A519

The coins and jettons
by M M Archibald

Summary

A total of 14 coins, two jettons, one token and one pilgrim badge was recovered. One of the coins is Roman, two are medieval, one is early post-medieval and 11 are late post-medieval to modern. The coins are generally in a poor condition. A penny of Henry I (Nu2) is of a rare and interesting type. The jettons comprise an English sterling jetton of early 14th century date and a Nuremberg jetton of Hanns Krauwinckel. The token is of lead and probably 15th-16th century in date. The pilgrim badge is of a type known as the vernicle in medieval England and is of 15th century date.

Catalogue

Nu1: Roman mid-4th century AD
Rev: Two soldiers (?) with one standard GLORIA EXERCITVS but not possible to be certain
Wt: 0.40g. (6.1gr) fragment only
Context A14, Phase 5b, SFNu4

Nu2: Henry I, Penny, BMC II
Mint, Lewes
Moneyer, Winred, *c.*1102–4
Obv: + HENRI RE ( )
Rev: + hWINRED ON LE
Wt: 0.34g (5.2gr)
Context B30, Phase 4a, SFNu15
This coin is from the same reverse die as a coin in the British Museum, 1929–8–5–2; the obverse is different. Winred is known at Lewes from William I type III and apparently ceases in this type, II of Henry I. His name is normally spelt without the initial hyper-correct aspirate which also appears before *wen* in names like HWITTA. Owing to the paucity of hoards, little is known about the circulation of the earlier types of Henry I, but they appear to have disappeared from circulation after his first recorded reform of the coinage in 1108. Although a later survival must be borne in mind, this coin is likely to have been deposited *c.*1102–10.

Nu3: "Galley halfpenny"
Obv: illegible
Rev: cross pattee with ?3 pellets in each angle
Wt: 0.19g (2.9gr)
Context A519, Phase 4b, SFNu10
This coin is very badly corroded; about two-thirds survives and it unfortunately fragmented after cleaning. It is certainly one of the small north Italian coins which arrived in England in the early 15th century in the galleys – hence their name.

Editorial note: remainder of catalogue not available

The worked bone, antler and ivory
by Simon Hardy, Mary Harman and Alison Cameron

Summary

Eighteen pieces of worked bone, two of antler and one of ivory were recovered during the excavations. All phases from the late Saxon onwards are represented. The two pieces of antler, both from late Saxon contexts, are a particularly fine decorative mount with zoomorphic interlace (WB1) and a comb fragment (WB2). Three double-ended tools (WB3–5), a pointed tool (WB6), a bobbin or toggle (WB7) and a spindle whorl (WB8) all probably represent textile manufacture; two are from late Saxon contexts (WB3 & WB7).

Among the remaining artefacts are four bone skates (WB9–WB12), three of which are from late Saxon contexts. Bone skates were already well attested in Northampton (cf eg Oakley and Harman 1979, 315), with more recent finds from Northampton Station in 2013 (Hylton in Chapman 2021, this volume, fig 25).

In late Saxon contexts there was no waste antler and only one unfinished bone artefact (a bobbin or toggle, WB20), in contrast to the adjoining sites of St Peter's Street and St Peter's Gardens where substantial evidence for an antler working industry and some for bone working in the late Saxon period was discovered (Harman and Shaw 1985, 75, (M)36).

Catalogue

WB1: Decorated mount; split cylinder with four perforations, one in each corner (Fig 24). The perforations are cut rather than drilled and are conical, widening to the outside. The outer surface is carved with an interlace ornament of six birds with pointed beaks and cloven feet, bordered by a slightly raised edge with diagonal slashes. The ends and edges of the cut are polished, the inner surface is smooth but retains a little of the spongy antler. It is cut from a portion of red deer antler tine. A trace of the curve of the tine is still visible in the long axis.

Two similar mounts have been found in separate excavations at Thetford (Rogerson and Dallas 1984, 182–3, fig 200) in late 10th- to 11th-century contexts. Both are worked from red deer metapodials. They are longer than the Northampton example (54mm and 44mm long) and have three holes rather than two down each side. Margeson (pers comm) suggests that these objects may be mounts from a staff and points out an 11th-century parallel in silver, decorated in the Urnes style, in the Museum of London (*Antiquaries Journal*, **15** (1935), 23). Length: 32mm; Max external diam: 20mm; Max thickness: 3mm
Context A152, Phase 3, SFWB7

WB2: Fragment of a connecting plate from a single-sided composite comb. Semi-circular section; one end broken, the other squared and cut vertically with slightly rounded edges. The back edge is slightly curved, the front straight with saw marks for fine teeth (9 per 10mm). A single iron rivet is situated 19mm from the intact end.
Length: 61mm; Width 14mm; Thickness 14mm
Context (B148) =119, Phase 3, SFWB15

Pointed and double-ended tools, a bobbin or toggle and a spindle whorl

The four tools, all pointed, comprise two double-ended tools (WB3, 4), a probable double-ended tool (WB5) and a possible bodkin (WB6). A bobbin or toggle (WB7) and a spindle whorl (WB8) were also found. All of these objects suggest textile manufacture and have parallels from other sites in Northampton (cf eg Oakley and Harman 1979). Although only two of these finds (WB3 & WB7) were from late Saxon contexts, the earliest occurrence of each form is late Saxon. It is thus possible that some at least of the remaining textile working implements are residual in the contexts from which they were recovered.

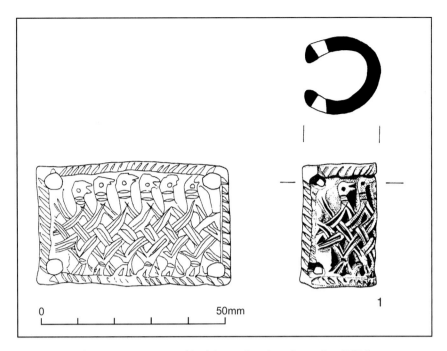

Fig 24: Bone mount with elaborate interlace decoration (WB1)

WB3: Double-ended tool with recto-oval section; one end tapering to a broken point the other chisel like; surface worn to a polish. Fragment from long bone shaft of cattle or horse, possibly a horse splint bone. For similar examples see Oakley and Harman 1979, 312–3, particularly WB54.
Length: 103mm; max width: 8mm
Context A637.2, Phase 3, SFWB5

WB4: Double-ended tool, semi-circular section but with rounded edges slightly curved along long axis; one end worked to a blunt point, the other with a square end and long concave facet; highly polished. Part of the long bone shaft of a large animal. For similar examples see Oakley and Harman 1979, 312–3, WB55.
Length: 89mm; Max width: 14mm
Context (B3) =unstratified, SFWB14

WB5: Pointed tool, possibly originally double-ended but with one end broken; recto-oval in section with slight transverse grooves on one of the flattened surfaces, these so regular as to suggest rolling but are perhaps file marks. It tapers along its whole length, the blunt end broken with slight indication on one flattened surface of the beginning of a spatulate end; surface worn to a polish. Part of the long bone shaft of a large animal, probably cattle or horse. For similar examples see Oakley and Harman 1979, 312–3.
Length: 123mm; Max width: 15mm
Context (B47) =A446, Phase 4a, SFWB12

WB6: Pointed tool; pointed end broken, blunt end pierced by a neatly drilled hole; tapers throughout its length, smooth surfaces except where cancellous bone remains along one side; slight longitudinal striations are probably use wear. Part of the long bone shaft of a large animal, probably horse.
Length: 126mm; Max Width: 24mm; Diam (hole): 5mm
Context A253, Phase 4b, SFWB20

WB7: Bobbin or toggle; crudely perforated by holes cut through the anterior and posterior surfaces of the mid shaft; no wear is visible. Pig right metatarsal with distal epiphysis not fused and missing. For similar examples from Northampton see Oakley 1976, 146, SF95; Oakley and Harman 1979, 313–4; Gryspeerdt et al 1981, 130–2, WB24.
Length: 69mm; Diam (hole): 4mm
Context A495, Phase 3, SFWB8

WB8: Spindle whorl; hemispherical, central perforation slightly conical, widening to top; upper and lower surfaces both abraded (Fig 25, 8). Cattle femur head with epiphysis not fused; quite neatly cut off the proximal end of the femur, the edge of the cut slightly bevelled. For similar examples see Oakley and Hall 1979, 287–8.
Max diam: 35mm; Height 17mm; Diam perforation: 10mm
Context (Al) = unstratified, SFWB2

Skates

Four incomplete skates were discovered. Three are from late Saxon contexts and the fourth from a post-Conquest deposit. They are comparable with skates from a number of other Northampton excavations (Oakley and Harman 1979, 315; Gryspeerdt et al 1981, 130–2, (M) 177–8; Hylton, fig 25, in Chapman 2021, this volume).

WB9: Fragment of a possible skate; cattle left metacarpal, proximal half; the posterior aspect has a small area cut

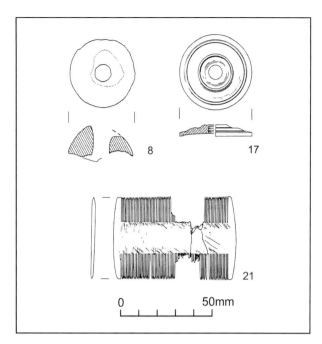

Fig 25: Worked bone: spindle whorl, lathe-turned disc and bone comb (WB8, 17 & 21)

away to produce a flatter surface; the anterior aspect has been cut quite neatly to produce a fairly symmetrical curve; nearly half the articular surface has been removed in the process.
Length: 99mm; Max width: 52mm
Context A150, Phase 3, SFWB24

WB10: Part of a skate, fractured with one end missing; horse right radius, proximal half and part of distal half of shaft; the anterior surface of the proximal articulation has been cut away, particularly at the corners, so that the proximal end of the anterior surface is bevelled off. Part of the anterior surface towards mid-shaft is flattened and polished. On the posterior surface most of the upper part of the ulna shaft has been roughly cut away.
Length: 285mm; Max width: 65mm
Context A320, Phase 3, SFWB17

WB11: Fragmentary skate; horse right metacarpal, part of shaft broken and missing; the anterior surface of the bone is now flat and smooth; at the distal end the cancellous bone is exposed; at the proximal end the uneven cavity is exposed. Part of the posterior aspect of the distal condyle is cut or worn away.
Length: 200mm; Max width: 43mm
Context A459, Phase 3, SFWB19

WB12: Part of a skate; cattle right metacarpal, proximal half, in poor condition; the anterior surface is worn flat; the cancellous bone is exposed at the proximal end and part of the articular surface is worn away; on the medial, and possibly the lateral, side a small area of the bone has been cut away to produce a squarer end; near the mid-point of the shaft the lateral and medial sides have been trimmed off to produce a narrower skate; the distal end is broken off and missing; the proximal anterior surface has a hole,

9mm in diameter, through the centre.
Length: 135mm; Max width: 45mm
Context A640, Phase 4a, SFWB18

Miscellaneous
WB13: Ring; hemispherical in section with bevelled edges, poorly finished; sawn from a section of long bone shaft of cattle or horse, possibly a cattle metatarsal. Outer diam: 23mm; Inner diam: 19mm; Width: 5mm
Context A152, Phase 3, SFWB6

WB14: Pin; one end worked to a point, not broken; the other has the unworked proximal end of the bone as a head. The shaft is polished and slightly curved; goose radius.
Length: 128mm
Context (B3) = unstratified, SFWB16

WB15: Fragment of tube; goose ulna shaft, one end neatly cut across, the other broken; possibly part of a musical instrument or a composite hinge. For similar examples see Oakley and Harman 1979,318, WB103, 104.
Length: 52mm; Diam (external): 9mm
Context B20, Phase 4b, SFWB23

WB16: Perforated peg; Tapering cylinder, broad end straight with two opposed flattened faces pierced by conical hole; both ends cut flat but poorly finished, remainder has slight surface polish; possibly for tightening a threaded cord; part of long bone shaft from large animal. Length: 32mm; Max diam: 6mm; Max diam hole: 2mm
Context A62, Phase 5a, SFWB21

WB17: Lathe-turned disc with central, threaded perforation (Fig 25, 17). One surface convex with two incised grooves near edge and a beading near the centre, this surface polished. Other surface slightly concave with a rim, unpolished. Possibly connected with lacemaking. Possibly from large bone of cattle or more probably horse. [context data missing]

WB18: Perforated disc, probably a button, surfaces rough and deeply incised, probably by sawing, edge quite neatly bevelled. Small central perforation. Part of a long bone shaft of a large animal.
Diam: 18mm; Thickness: 2mm; Diam perforation: 1.5mm
Context (B3)=unstratified, SFWB10

WB19: Fragment of a perforated disc, identical to WB18 but broken in half.
Context (B3)=unstratified, SFWB9

Unfinished Object
Direct evidence for bone working on the site is provided by only one piece, an incomplete bobbin or toggle (WB20) similar to WB7 and also from a late Saxon context.

WB20: Unfinished bobbin or toggle. Pig left metacarpal, distal epiphysis not fused and missing. At the proximal end the lateral surface has been cut away. At the distal end most of the epiphysis and part of the diaphysis has

been removed by multiple cuts to produce an almost flat surface. Small areas have been trimmed off the anterior and posterior aspects to straighten the shaft. No perforation has been made.
Length: 58mm; Max width: 14mm.
Context A305, Phase 3, SFWB22

Ivory

WB21: Incomplete double-sided simple comb with fine teeth (13 per 10mm) on both sides (Fig 25, 21). Ends slightly rounded. The evenness of the work and the thinness of the comb suggest machine manufacture.
Length: 67mm; Width 42mm; Thickness 1.5mm.
Context B9, Phase 5b, SFWB11

The iron objects
by Ian H Goodall

Summary

The iron objects are from contexts of late Saxon date onwards, the most interesting medieval objects being a hinge pivot (Fe13) and barrel padlock case, bolt and key (Fe22–4).

The objects from post-medieval contexts include several from tanning pits; of these Fe9 is a domestic rather than an industrial knife, and knife blades Fe11 and Fe12, though small, could have been used for such purposes as cutting off unwanted scraps from the edge of the skin before tanning. The stout knife, Fe8, may be associated with the tannery, though not found in one of its pits. The finding of a leatherworker's awl, Fe1, may be no more than coincidental.

Catalogue
(Fig 26, 1–28)

Fe1: Awl with expanded stop at junction of curved blade and tang.
Context A505, Phase 5b, SFFe103

Fe2: Tooth from wool comb or flax heckle.
Context B51.2, Phase 3, SFFe266

Fe3: Spade-iron with rectangular mouth, side arm and nailed lug. The grooved edge of the mouth retains part of the wooden blade of the spade.
Context A203, Phase 4b, SFFe1

Fe4–12: Knives, 4–8 with whittle tangs, several with cutting edges worn by sharpening, 9–10 with scale tangs, 11–12 blade fragments, 11 found with part of ?scale tang. 9 has bone scales held by iron rivets, a shaped copper alloy end cap, and riveted non-ferrous shoulder plates.
Contexts 4: B124, Phase 3, SFFe276; 5: A495, Phase 3, SFFe200; 6: A458, Phase 4a, SFFe189; 7: A562, Phase 4b, SFFe177; 8: A517, Phase 4b/5a, SFFe137; 9: A326, Phase 5a, SFFe96; 10: A566, Phase 4b, SFFe169; 11: A24, Phase 5a, SFFe79; 12: A335, Phase 5a, SFFe82

Fe13–15: Hinge pivots. Fe13 has a T-shaped shank retaining the lead caulking run-in to secure it in masonry, whereas Fe14–5 have tapering shanks which were driven into timber or joints in masonry.
Contexts 13: A398, Phase 4a, SFFe136; 14: A519, Phase 4b, SFFe122; 15: A396, Phase 4b, SFFe145

Fe16–20: Strap fragments, all broken.
16: 91x9mm; 17: 38x16mm; 18: 80x17–25mm; 19: 95x17–20mm; 20: 51x23mm.
Contexts 16: B51, Phase 3, SFFe265, 17: A80, Phase 4a, SFFe76; 18: A556, Phase 5a, SFFe170; 19: A340, Phase 5a/b, SFFe90; 20: A340, Phase 5a/b, SFFe94

Fe21: Stud with domed head and broken shank.
Context A327, Phase 5a, SFFe81

Fe22: Barrel padlock case with fin and tube, the bolt-entry end complete. Straight and wavy longitudinal straps strengthen and decorate the case.
Context A73, Phase 4a, SFFe80

Fe23: T-shaped padlock bolt from barrel padlock with shackle. Circular head holds two spines, both broken, but still retaining single and double leaf springs.
Context A177, Phase 3, SFFe176

Fe24: Padlock key with ring bow, shaped broken stem, and non-ferrous plating.
Context A61, Phase 4b, SFFe31

Fe25–7: Horseshoe arms, 25 and 26 with countersunk nailholes, Fe27 with rectangular nailholes.
Contexts 25: (A569) = A559, Phase 4a, SFFe188; 26: A305, Phase 3, SFFe46; 27: A508, Phase 4a, SFFe181.

Fe28–29: Fiddle-key horseshoe nails, the type generally used with horseshoes like Fe25.
Contexts 28: A130, Phase 4a, SFFe198; 29: A508, Phase 4a, SFFe181.

The non-ferrous metal objects
by Alison R Goodall

Summary

The copper alloy objects include two finds of certain Anglo-Saxon date. Cu1 is an incomplete hooked fastener with triangular head; and Cu2 is a pin with a facetted head, decorated with rings-and-dots and an incised cross, the shaft is also decorated. A penannular ear ring (Cu3) is probably also of late Saxon or early medieval date, while the finger ring (Cu6) has similarities with Saxon examples from Thetford (Goodall 1984, 68–69, fig 110, 12–13). The other personal ornaments and dress fittings date from the medieval and later periods. They include the tiny, undecorated annular brooch (Cu4), buckles (Cu7–8), the buckle plates and strap end (Cu11–13) and the lobed suspension loop (Cu14) probably for hanging a purse.

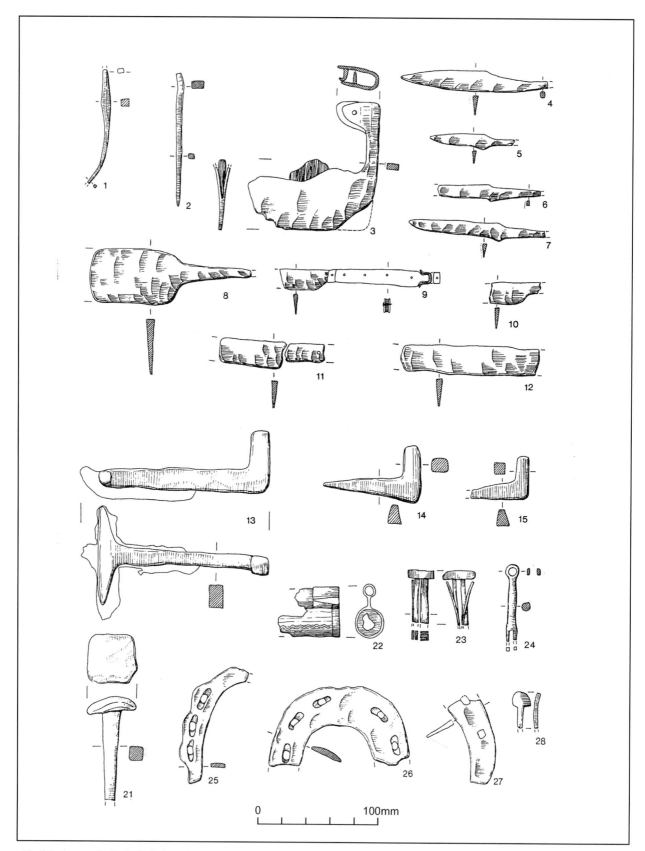

Fig 26: Iron tools (Fe1–3); knives (4–12); hinge pivots (13–15); stud (21); padlock fittings (22–24); horseshoes and nails (25–28)

A rectangular buckle, Cu9, was found in the tanning area but its form suggests a late medieval date rather than during the period of activity of the tannery.

None of the copper alloy finds from the tanning pits can be associated with any of the processes of tanning. Many of them are dress fittings, such as Cu9 and Cu14 and the 11 lace ends from these contexts. Two decorated studs (Cu58–59) also came from the tannery, as did 15 of the 54 pins. The head forms of the pins indicate a date range from the late medieval/early post-medieval period to the 17th/18th centuries.

They may have been used on clothing or to fasten sheets of paper, accounts, etc. in the days before the use of paper clips or staples.

Objects of a more domestic nature include a pair of tweezers (Cu38), needleworking equipment (Cu40–4), the socket from a cream or fat skimmer (Cu50), handles from two spoons or forks not earlier than the 19th century (Cu51–2) and fragments from vessels (Cu53–4). The low proportion of objects connected with food preparation may be significant.

A large number of studs, with heads of two different sizes (Cu60–61) and associated with wood, come from studded coffins of post-medieval date).

Other non-ferrous metal objects include a small pewter shoe buckle (Pb1) and a facetted oval lead weight (Pb2). A plug-like piece of lead (Pb5) retains the impression of a tabby-woven cloth. All of post-medieval date

Catalogue

Figs 27, 1–31 and 28, 36–48

Cu1: Incomplete hooked fastener of late Saxon type with triangular plate and two rivet or stitch holes.
Context A305, Ph3, SFCu30

Cu2: Late Saxon pin with facetted head, decorated with rings and dots and with a cross on the top. The shaft, which becomes rectangular in section, is decorated with a group of incised diagonal lines.
Context A571, Ph3, SFCu112

Cu3: Penannular ear ring with pointed overlapping ends. Probably of late Saxon to early medieval date.
Context A629, Ph4a, SFCu106

Cu4: Small annular brooch frame with recess for pin.
Context A61, Ph4b, SFCu32

Cu5: Brooch pin.
Context Unstratified, SFCu16

Cu6: Penannular finger ring with overlapping ends. Decorated with traced or punched zig-zag line.
Context B74, Ph4a, SFCu140

Cu7: Simple buckle frame with shaped plate.
Context A270, Ph4a, SFCu6

Cu8: Buckle frame with moulded pin and integral forked spacer.
Context Unstratified, SFCu66

Cu9: Rectangular buckle frame decorated with incised diagonal lines.
Context A326, Ph5a, SFCu62

Cu10: Possibly a buckle frame or attachment loop. It would presumably have had overlapping free ends.
Context A73, Ph4a, SFCu41

Cu11: Buckle plate decorated on the front with a punched border and secured by five rivets originally with domed heads.
Context A126, Ph4a, SFCu83

Cu12: Plain buckle plate with five dome-headed rivets.
Context A125, Ph4b, SFCu75

Cu13: Strap end, riveted at top and bottom, with shaped terminal and traced zig-zag lines on front.
Context A435, Ph4a/B, SFCu114

Cu14: Lobed attachment ring, possibly from a belt.
Context A85, Ph5a, SFCu77

Cu15: Rosette-shaped stud.
Context A471, Ph4a/B, SFCu120

Cu16: Solid globular button, broken through and showing insertion of wire loop.
Context A261, Ph4a, SFCu13

Cu17: Probably the shank and loop from a composite button.
Context A626, Ph4a, SFCu108

Cu18: Domed button with iron wire loop.
Context A340, Ph5a, SFCu59

Cu19: Flat-topped button.
Context Unstratified, SFCu12

Cu20–37: Lace ends. Cu31–5 are made from folded sheet metal, the others are rolled. Cu21–2, 26, 29 and 36 seem to be riveted. Cu37 has a shiny black surface coating and comes from a more recent context than all but one of the others.
    Contexts 20, A19, Ph5a, SFCu14; 21, A390, Ph5a, Cu88; 22, A390, Ph5a, Cu89; 23, A390, Ph5a, SFCu79; 24, B35, Ph5a, SFCu132; 25, A78, Ph5a, SFCu42; 26, A248, Ph5a, SFCu5; 27, A424, Ph5a, SFCu98; 28–9, A509, Ph5a, SFCu69–70; 30, unstratified, SFCu35; 31, A26, Ph5a, SFCu36; 32, A26, Ph5a, SFCu27; 33–4, A23, Ph5a, SFCu57; 35, A509, Ph5a, SFCu70; 36, A513, Ph5b, SFCu116; 37, A522, Ph5b, SFCu71.

Cu38: Simple tweezers made from folded strip.
Context A80, Ph4a, SFCu46

Cu39: Fragments of strip, with broad ends, now in several fragments. A519, Ph4b, SFCu92.

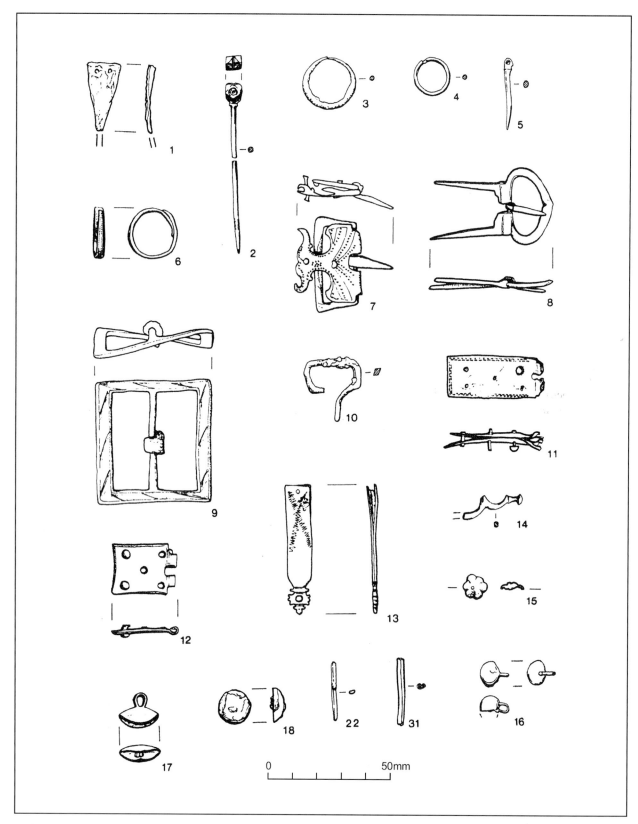

Fig 27: Copper alloy hooked fastener (Cu1) and pin with facetted head (2), late Saxon; ear ring, brooches and finger ring (3–6); buckles (7–12); strap end (13); decorative clothes fittings (14–18) and lace ends (22 & 31)

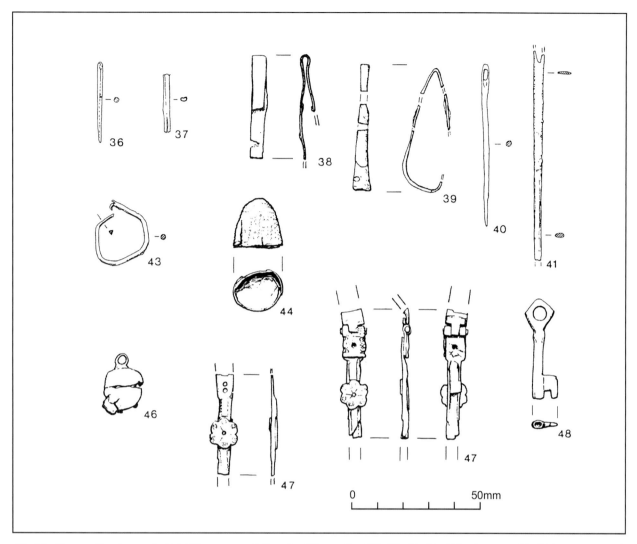

Fig 28: Copper alloy lace ends (36–37); tweezers (38); strip (39); needles (40–43); thimble (44); sheet metal bell (46); ornamental hinge strap (47); casket key (48)

Cu40: Needle with oval eye set in a groove.
Context A377, Ph4b/5a, SFCu73

Cu41: Incomplete needle or bodkin.
Context A329, Ph5b, SFCu51

Cu42: Possibly a broken needle.
Context A390, Ph5a, SFCu78

Cu43: Needle with triangular sectioned tip for working fine leather as in glovemaking.
Context Unstratified, SFCu39

Cu44: Thimble with domed top and pits arranged spirally
Context A528, Ph5b, SFCu97

Cu45: Fragmentary sheet metal bell with strip loop.
Context A619, Ph4b, SFCu110

Cu46: Sheet metal bell with narrow stip loop and corrosion from iron pea.
A309, Ph5a, SFCu52

Cu47: Two ornamental hinge straps, possibly from a casket. Each has applied rosettes, secured by a nail or pin which would also have held the strap onto its base and a rivet which passes through a washer at the back of the strap.
Context (A) Unstratified, SFCu103; (B) A323, Ph4b/5a, SFCu47

Cu48: Casket key with solid stem, simple bit and pierced lozenge-shaped head.
Context A387, Ph4a, SFCu105

The metallurgical evidence

by Justine Bayley, Henry F Cleere, Varian Denham and Michael Shaw

Summary

The evidence for metalworking in the vicinity of the site consisted of: a large quantity (*c.*9.59kg) of ferrous slag, both bloomery tap slag and forging slag, chiefly from late Saxon contexts; two fragments of litharge from late Saxon and early medieval contexts, indicating some sort of precious metal refining; sherds from two crucibles from post-Conquest contexts, both of which had probably been used to melt copper alloys; and ten fragments of copper alloy waste recovered from contexts ranging in date from medieval (Phase 4a/b) to late post-medieval (Phase 5b). The quantity of slag of late Saxon date recovered implies that there must have been a bloomery furnace of slag tapping type and an associated hearth for forging and consolidating the bloom nearby.

Crucibles

Sherds from two crucibles were submitted to the Ancient Monuments Laboratory (AMD for examination and analysis. They are described individually below. Both had probably been used to melt copper alloys; the exact nature of the alloy, however, cannot be determined with any degree of confidence as the metal traces were so weak.

Cr1: Three joining crucible sherds (Fig 29). The crucible was deeply vitrified on the outside and had undoubtedly been used, but only slight traces of metals (copper and possibly zinc and lead) were detected by X-ray fluorescence analysis (XRF).

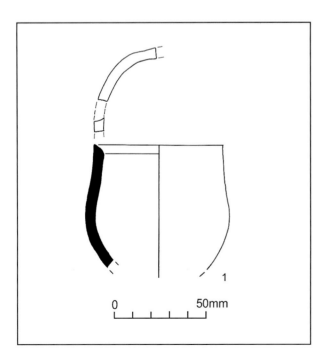

Fig 29: Copper alloy working crucible (Cr1)

Context (A637.4) = 636, Phase 4a, SFPt48, AML850830

Cr2: Body sherd from a crucible. XRF detected lead as well as minor amounts of copper and zinc on the vitrified outer surface.

Context A349, Phase 4a, SFPt49, AML850831

Copper alloy waste

Ten fragments of copper alloy waste were submitted to AML (Ancient Monuments Laboratory) for examination and analysis. They are listed below with individual notes and comments.

CWa1: Copper alloy waste; offcut (?) from the end of a bar.
Context (A533) =519, Phase 4b, SFCu91
CWa2: Copper alloy waste; spill of molten metal.
Context (A533) =519, Phase 4b, SFCu95
CWa3: Copper alloy waste; spill of molten metal.
Context A400, Phase 4b, SFCu100
CWa4: Copper alloy; corrosion (?) products on lump of earth.
Context A313, Phase 5a, SFCu102
CWa5: Copper alloy waste; spilt molten metal (?).
Context A519, Phase 4b, SFCu119
CWa6: Copper alloy waste; droplet.
Context A471, Phase 4a/B, SFCu121
CWa7: Copper alloy waste; droplets.
Context B26, Phase 5b, SFCu129
CWa8: Copper impregnated organic (?) material.
Context B35, Phase 5a, SFCu134
CWa9: Copper alloy fragments.
Context B65, Phase 4b, SFCu138
CWa10: Copper alloy waste; spilt (?) molten metal.
Context B65, Phase 4b, SFCu143
CWa11: Copper alloy waste; metal adhering to a rim piece of a bell mould (cope). The metal has run between the two halves of the mould which cannot have been sufficiently well luted together.
Context B65, Phase 4b, SFCu144

Most of the pieces were examined qualitatively by energy dispersive X-ray fluorescence. The elements detected in each piece are listed below. Those elements appearing in brackets were not significant components of the alloy.
CWa1: copper tin (lead antimony)
CWa2: copper lead
CWa3: copper tin (zinc lead antimony)
CWa5: copper lead (tin zinc antimony)
CWa6: copper (lead zinc)
CWa7: copper tin (lead)
CWa9: copper tin (lead)
CWa10: copper tin (lead)
CWa11: copper tin (lead)

Both its context and composition suggest CWa11 is bell metal, a high tin bronze. Some of the other samples may also be waste metal from the same process

Those containing significant amounts of lead, CWa2 and CWa5, are not suitable for making bells. The zinc and antimony are only present in trace amounts, probably a percentage at most in the metal.

Lead-rich waste

Two samples of lead-rich waste were submitted to AML for examination and analysis, (LWa1, Context A637.2, Phase 3, SFCu61, AML8650283; LWa2, Context A626, Phase 4a, SFCu62, AML8650284). Both samples are fragments of larger masses of litharge and are coloured green by the presence of relatively minor amounts of copper. Traces of silver were also detected on the original surface of the pieces. Comparison with more complete examples suggests the litharge formed as a disc, 20–30mm thick, and about 100mm in diameter. The litharge is a by-product of the recovery of silver from lead by cupellation. Tylecote (1986) has described similar material from Doncaster and suggested its copper content might indicate 'lead soaking' of debased coinage followed by cupellation to recover the silver. Litharge 'cakes' have recently been recognised from several Roman and early medieval sites (Lincoln, Bury St Edmunds Abbey, Southwark, Winchester and Doncaster) and can all be interpreted as indicating precious metal refining of some sort. Their presence in late Saxon and early medieval levels in Northampton is not unexpected as silver was being worked on a substantial scale in the town in late Saxon times (cf eg Bayley 1979). These litharge 'cakes' indicate cupellation on a far larger scale than that suggested by the 'heating trays' which have been found on many late Saxon metalworking sites.

Ferrous slag

A total of 9.59kg of ferrous slag was recovered from the site from all phases from Phase 3 onwards (Table 5). Two types of slag were present: bloomery tap slag and forging slag. Table 5 gives the quantity of ferrous slag recovered from each phase. The evidence clearly attests to ironmaking and ironworking in the vicinity of the site in the late Saxon period. A large proportion of both types

Table 5: Quantities of bloomery tap slag and forging slag

Site phase	Bloomery tap slag (g)	Forging Slag (g)
3	1875	3815
4a	1020	1140
4b	410	515
5a/b	295	235
3/4a	160	–
3/4b	–	20
4a/b	–	10
4a/b to 5a/b	80	15
Total	**3840**	**5750**

Measurements to nearest 5g

of slag recovered from Phase 3 contexts came from pit A495 (44% of the bloomery slag; 78% of the forging slag) while a further 21% of the bloomery slag came from an adjoining pit, A499. Structures associated with metal-working and large quantities of slag were discovered in the area to the north of the present site during the St Peter's Street excavations (Cleere 1979) and the slag from The Green may have originated from there.

The tile and brick
by J L Humble

Introduction

A total of 266 pieces of ceramic tile and six pieces of brick were recovered from the excavation. All of the brick fragments and 248 of the tile fragments were recovered from stratified contexts.

With the aid of a x20 binocular microscope, the fragments were sorted by context chiefly into pre-defined fabric types, and further quantified according to ten form headings: peg, nib, curved indeterminate, ridge, pantile, flat roof indeterminate, roof indeterminate, roof/floor indeterminate, floor and brick. Detailed criteria for recognition of form types have been previously published (Humble 1985a, (M)77). The small size of many of the pieces, however, required the use of a new category, roof indeterminate, as it was often impossible to assess whether the fragment derived from a flat or curved tile.

The fabrics

All of the ceramic building materials from The Green are of medieval or post-medieval manufacture, and residual Roman brick and tile was absent. In Northampton, the re-use of Roman materials would appear to have been a practice confined to building construction during the Saxon period (Humble 1985a).

A gazetteer providing detailed brick and tile fabric descriptions was included in the report for the Riding (Denham 1984c, (M)71–75). Subsequent definitions of newly recognised fabrics can be found in Humble (1985a, (M)81; 1985c, (M)67) and two new fabrics identified in this assemblage are described below:

M10: Roof tile, M446 (The Green); Lyveden (?), NE Northants, medieval
M11: Roof tile, M446 (The Green): Lyveden (?), NE Northants, medieval

Roof tile

At least 90% of the assemblage comprises small fragments of roof tile. It appears that, as demonstrated at other sites in Northampton, brightly glazed peg and ridge tiles in a variety of fabrics were widely in use during the medieval period, ultimately to be superseded *c.*1700 by the employment of nib tiles and pantiles, apparently purchased from a single source, possibly from Lyveden.

It is not possible to relate the roof tile from this excavation to particular building plans, and it is likely that the majority of the material was brought into the area as waste. The range of fabric types present in each phase would suggest that the material derives from a number of structures although the pottery assemblage demonstrates that there was a high degree of residuality, and identification of the contemporary phase component is difficult with such small samples. In addition to conservatism in roofing practices, it could be expected that tiles were widely re-used, and a single roof may have been patched with materials from a variety of sources.

It is likely that fragments classified as flat roof indeterminate from contexts pre-dating Phase 5A derive from peg tiles. These typically have smooth and sanded surfaces, with a partial olive or emerald green glaze, and pairs of round peg holes. Several of the fragments bear traces of mortar torching on the unglazed portion of the upper surface. A tile fragment with curving edge and two peg holes is probably from a hip or valley tile, the first example of this type which has been found in Northampton. Ridge tiles were usually of simple form, but more flamboyant tiles with tooled crests or sockets were also in use.

Elsewhere in England, nib tiles were current from the 13th century onwards (Streeten 1985, 96–7), but in Northampton their appearance appears to have been post-medieval in date (Denham 1984b, 81), and broadly coincided with the introduction of pantiles. At The Green, all five of the nib tiles were recovered from Phase 5b contexts The recovery of peg roof tiles in medieval fabrics, notably in fabric Ml, in post-medieval phases is as likely to be a result of residuality as a reflection of the length of currency of these types.

Floor tile

Only eight fragments of floor tile were found, in two fabrics. One fabric type appears to have been exclusively employed in the production of floor tiles, and it is the only locally produced medieval tile fabric which was not also used for roof tile. It is probable that the 14 tile fragments from Phase 4a (and residual examples of this fabric in later phases) relate to the destruction of a 13th-century floor surface, and this provides the earliest recorded example of this fabric in use in Northampton.

The mammal bones
by Mary Harman

Introduction

Most of the bones were in good condition, though some from the early deposits were less well preserved. All of the bones were looked at and most were identifiable. All the identified bones were listed, with copies of the lists deposited in the archive. In further work on the bones the age of the animals at death was assessed from the state of epiphyseal fusion and of tooth eruption and wear, using for both cattle and sheep the recording system of Ewbank et al (1964, 423–6) and for pigs the system published by Grant (1975, 437–50). The ages are based on the criteria

published by Silver (1963, 250–68). Complete bones and ends of adult bones were measured. Anomalous and abnormal bones were noted and the abnormal bones were sent to Dr J R Baker, see below.

Much of the site was given over to tanning in the early post-medieval period and several features contain specialised assemblages of bones which are likely to be connected with this or with other industries allied to slaughtering and the processing of carcasses. An emphasis on particular bones had also occurred in earlier phases, suggesting that the same industries existed on the site in medieval times. It should be noted that although some features contained groups which are quite clearly extraordinary, features containing only a few bones from similar industrial refuse may not be noticeably unusual and, in an area where pits cut into each other, there may well be ''contamination* by industrial waste in later features; so that, particularly in the post medieval period, there may be a scattering of such waste across the site, masking trends in any ordinary domestic refuse which may have been deposited on the site. This factor should be taken into account as well as the large amount of "normal" residuality on an intensively occupied urban site.

Table 6 summarises the total numbers of bones from different species through the Saxon and medieval phases (2/3–4) and also particular features within those phases that had been treated separately due to the unusual nature of the bone assemblages. The overviews for the medieval phases have previously been published along with the post-medieval bone assemblage in the report on the post-medieval tanneries (see Harman in Shaw 1996, 89–102). These phase overviews are also repeated here to complement the excavated evidence and the finds reports. The 1996 publication also includes detailed tabulated data for phases 3–4a/4b and for features A508 and layer (A637)=132, which are not repeated here. It also provides an overview of such "specialised animal bone assemblages from sites in south-west Northampton and their interpretation" (Harman in Shaw 1996, 100–102).

Prehistoric to early-middle Anglo-Saxon

There are scarcely any bones from layers earlier than Phase 3, and so few from the broad Anglo-Saxon Phase 2/3 that no conclusions can be drawn from these.

Late Saxon, Phase 3

In the late Saxon period, Phase 3, sheep bones are the commonest of the three major domestic meat producing animals, accounting for half of the bones; cattle bones form 35% and pig 15% (Table 6). There is no particular emphasis on any bone or on meat or waste bones in this group, except for one feature, pit A459, which contained an unusual number of sheep's heads, 29 of the 44 sheep bones being from the head; in addition this feature contained most of a cat skeleton, without the head, from a well grown but immature animal. Pit A754 also contained a number of cat bones from at least two animals, and thirteen pig bones from two or three very small piglets,

Table 6: Total number of bones per species, percentage by phase

Phase (date)	Cattle	Sheep	Pig	Horse	Dog	Cat	Other
Anglo-Saxon Phase 2/3 (400–1075)	25 66%	10 26%	3 8%	1 –	–	–	–
Late Saxon Phase 3 (850–1075)	321 35%	452 50%	137 15%	14 –	3 –	18+2 –	1 Red deer 2 Roe deer 3 Fallow deer
Medieval Phase 4a (1075–1275)	1357 31%	2661 62%	309 7%	50 –	11+1 –	60+8 cats & paws	1 Red deer 1 Roe deer 4 Hare
Pit A508	53	875	25	18	–	–	–
Late medieval Phase 4b (1275–1470)	582 42%	679 49%	133 9%	29 –	3+1 –	19+5 –	–
Oven B56	11	98	1	1	–	–	–
Medieval Phase 4a/b	72 46%	74 46%	13 8%	– –	1 –	1+ kitten	–

Percentages not given for features, or groups of features containing specialised deposits

probably only a few days or weeks old. There are a few bones from deer; the identification of the fallow deer fragments is tentative, they may be red deer but if so they must be from small animals.

Medieval, Phase 4a

Phase 4a, post-Conquest medieval, produced the greatest number of bones. The proportion of sheep bones has apparently increased from Saxon times, to 62% of the total, with a consequent decrease for both cattle and pig. Pit A508, considered separately, produced almost entirely sheep bones, particularly heads and feet; pits A73 (cattle: 31; sheep heads and feet: 71, other bones: 27; pig: 7; hare: 1) and A303 (cattle: 68; sheep heads and feet: 27, other bones: 106; pig: 25; dog: 1; cat: 4) contained smaller but similar groups, though there is less emphasis on sheep. These and probably other smaller groups like them, may be partly responsible for the contrast in the proportions of domestic animals between Phase 4a and the other phases, and for the large numbers of sheep head and feet bones. There is also a large number of cattle skull fragments, some of which are horn cores, possibly foreshadowing the concentrations seen in later phases relating to the excavated tannery. Pig bones, however, form less than 10% in this phase, and continue to be less important in later phases than in Phase 3. There are some horse bones, part of a dog skeleton from a well-grown but immature animal, a few other dog bones and very few from wild animals (deer and hare).

Pit A508, as summarised in Table 7, is remarkable for the preponderance of sheep bones, especially the large number of skull and foot bones. More than half of the skulls had been halved, approximately on the sagittal line, though the cuts did not always penetrate the occipital,

and in most the horn cores were either cut off or cut and broken off. Several polled, and single sgurred (or scurred, soft incomplete buds that would otherwise develop into bony horns) and two-horned frontals occurred. A few of the half skulls and some odd occipital bones have small cuts across the condyles or on the occipital just above the condyles, and three of six atlases found have cuts across the ventral surface; these cuts could result from cutting the throat to kill or bleed the animal or from cutting through the muscles, usually under the chin, to pull apart the joint between the atlas and the skull and thus cut off the head using a knife rather than a cleaver. The numbers of vertebrae are: atlas 6; axis 4; other cervical 13; thoracic 13; lumbar 20; and sacrum 6; most of these being halved axially.

Most of the metapodials are incomplete, being represented by either the proximal end with up to half of the shaft attached, or the distal end, again with up to half of the shaft. The unusually large number of phalanges (small bones which are often missed during excavation), presumably accompany these distal ends. Two of the metacarpals and ten of the metatarsals have small cuts across the proximal end, probably from removing the feet. Most of the skulls and feet are from mature or well grown, but immature animals.

This is a puzzling deposit. It is clearly waste relating to slaughtering but may not all be simply slaughtering waste: if it were, it might be expected that the number of fore and hind feet would be approximately double the number of heads, representing the head and all four feet from a number of sheep. However, the figures for metapodials represent the distal ends, those on the left and the right sides representing the proximal ends, and since these may belong together, the minimum number of sheep represented by the feet is 26, whereas the minimum number represented by the skull fragments is 110. The

Table 7: Number of bones of different bird species by phase

Phase	Fowl	Goose	Duck	Other
Phase 3 Late Saxon	35	6	–	1 Jackdaw? Immature: *Corvus monedula*
Phase 4a Medieval	175	143	4	1 Sparrowhawk: *Accipiter nisus*, most of bird 1 Pheasant? *Phasianus sp* 1 Crane: *Grus grus* 2 Dove: *Columba sp* 1 Crow/Rook: *Corvus corone/C.frugilegus*
4A: A303	37	17	–	–
Phase 4a/b	3	7	–	1 Tawny Owl: *Strix aluco*, 1 bird
Phase 4b Late medieval	108	94	4	1 Jackdaw: *Corvus monedula*
4B: A508	38	50	–	1 Dove: *Columba sp*
Phase 4b/5a	18	8	1	–

frontal fragments range from complete half skulls to small but unduplicated pieces of frontal. There are many other skull fragments, which probably belong with these and therefore do not add to the numbers. The maxillae and mandibles are not so numerous but still represent a much larger number of sheep than the metapodials. Many of the skulls had been halved and the horn cores removed, probably so that they could more easily be fitted into the cooking pot: if it were merely to remove the brain, the horn cores would not be removed, and while some obviously bore large horns, few would have had horns suitable for horn work. The feet might be removed before skinning, or with the skin and detached subsequently; it is difficult to find any reason why they should have been cut at mid-shaft. If the feet accompanied the skin and thus represent waste from tanning or tawing it seems odd that the skulls should also be there since many of them were apparently prepared for the kitchen; possibly sheep's head was not a popular dish and these represent unsold stock, surplus from a slaughterhouse. Though there are some meat bones represented in small numbers, this group appears to be mostly waste from an unspecialised slaughtering industry, associated with butchering and some skin processing.

There are a number of cat bones, including some special deposits. Layer (A637)=132 contained bones solely from cats' paws, mostly from mature animals. A left astragalus has cuts on the superior surface, and two each of the metacarpals and metatarsals have cuts at the proximal ends. With such a large number it is difficult to assess pairing, but the consistency in the numbers of bones with the distal epiphysis not fused suggests that about fifteen animals were involved. If the cats had been skinned, the paws would probably be removed with the skin, and these bones might represent the trimming of the skin after it has been tawed.

Another pit, A418, contains a number of cat bones from at least seven animals, all head or limb bones with a few vertebrae: but there are no metapodials or phalanges. As many of the bones are from immature, though well grown, animals this group is unlikely to tie in directly with the paw bones from layer (A637)=132, but could represent the discarded bodies from another batch of cat skins. The front half of an adult cat in A458 has its metacarpals and is probably just part of a casual corpse rather than industrial waste.

The number of bones from different animals found in the late medieval period, Phase 4b, shows a dramatic change in the relative numbers of cattle and sheep bones (Table 6). in Phase 4a there were nearly twice as many sheep bones as cattle bones (excluding the bones from feature A508, which would make the difference more marked), whereas in Phase 4b, even if oven (B56)=B18 is included, though there are slightly more sheep than cattle bones, the difference is far less pronounced.

There is within the general group of features, a large number of cattle skull fragments. Oven B20 had a number of cattle horn cores in the fill. Another oven, (B56)=B18, contained mainly sheep metapodials; they account for 75 of the 98 sheep bones, a further ten being skull fragments, but there were few bones in this feature from any other domestic animals. The sheep bone collection contrasts with those in pit A508 in the comparatively small number of skull fragments, and in that many of the metapodials are complete, not separated into proximal and distal halves. There are very few phalanges; though some could have been missed during excavation this seems unlikely to account entirely for their scarcity, particularly the larger first phalanges.

In pit A203 there are 24 bones from at least five cats; in view of the probable association of cat bones in the earlier phase with skin processing, these bones may also be industrial waste. A single bone from pit A125 presents a more sinister picture, it is a left femur from a young cat of nearly adult size, and there are several small cuts at the proximal end on both anterior and posterior surfaces, as though the animal had been jointed. Much of a dog, with a shoulder height of 0.44–0.47m (*c*.18") was also found in pit A203. The height is calculated from the limb bone lengths using Harcourt's formula (1974, 154).

Late medieval, Phase 4

The bones which can be assigned only to Phase 4 in general are few, and include nothing remarkable apart from some bones from a very small kitten in B207. No bones of wild animals were identified from Phase 4b.

The bird bones

The bird bones were tabulated by phase and, as with the mammal bones, certain features are tabulated individually due to the unusual nature of the assemblages (Table 7).

The fish bones
by Alison Locker

Some 70 fish bones were recovered from deposits dated to the medieval and early post-medieval phases (Table 8). No sieving was carried out, so the results are likely to have been biased in favour of the larger species. As in the medieval deposits at St Peter's Street the majority of the bones were of large deep sea marine fish (cod and ling) though conger eel, herring, plaice and halibut were also represented.

The following species were identified: conger eel (Conger conger), herring (Clupea harenqus), cod (Gadus morhua), ling (Molva molva), plaice (Pleuronectes platessa) and halibut (Hippoglossus hippoglossus). In addition bone fragments that could not be specifically identified were assigned to the groups, large gadoid (probably cod or ling), flatfish indeterminate and unidentifiable. Table 8 indicates the total number of bones identified for each species in each context.

The species recovered indicate the dominance of large deep sea marine fish, ie cod (and ling) in all three phases. This compares well with the evidence from other sites in Northampton; particularly the medieval pits and deposits from St Peter's Street (Jones 1979, 335), and St Peter's Gardens (Locker 1985, 78–9). One freshwater species, pike, however, was found at St Peter's Gardens; while salmonidae (ie salmon or trout) which may have been caught in freshwater were found at both St Peter's Gardens and St Peter's Street. Halibut, a large deep water boreal flatfish, was also identified from a single vertebral centrum from late Saxon deposits from St Peter's Gardens.

The only head bones (apart from one small gadoid parasphenoid) identified from cod are cleithra, these are situated at the base of the skull. Some had been cut by knives, a common find on this bone, and this may be evidence of the beheading of the fish. Jones (1979, 335) has suggested the absence of head bones for ling from St Peter's Street may indicate the import of headless preserved large fish ('stockfish'), this also seems a likely explanation for the large cod and ling from St Peter's Gardens.

Both plaice and halibut would have had to have been preserved, salted or pickled to reach this inland site. Herring is probably under-represented as the small size of

Table 8: Types of fish and fish bones by Phase and Context

Context	CE	HR	CD	LG	GD	PL	HB	FL	UN	Totals
Phase 4A										
A51	–	–	1sk	–	2sk	–	–	–	1	4
A73	–	–	2sk	–	1sk	–	–	–	5	8
A87	–	–	–	–	3	–	–	–	–	3
A303	–	1v	1sk 3v	–	–	–	–	–	–	5
A416	–	–	1v	–	–	–	–	–	–	1
A446	–	–	–	–	1sk	–	–	–	–	1
A508	–	–	1sk	–	–	–	–	–	–	1
A627	–	–	–	1sk	–	–	–	–	–	1
(A727) =452	–	–	–	–	–	–	–	–	1	1
Phase 4A/5A										
A42	–	–	–	–	–	–	–	–	1	1
Phase 4B										
A61	–	–	3sk 6v	2v	9sk 1	1sk	–	3v	2	27
A101	–	–	–	1v	1sk	–	–	–	–	2
A125	–	–	–	–	2sk	–	–	–	–	2
A235	–	–	–	–	–	–	1v	–	–	1
A507	1v	–	–	–	–	1sk	–	–	–	2
Phase 4B/5A										
A323	–	–	1v	–	1sk	–	–	–	–	2

CE = Conger Eel; HR = Herring; CD = Cod; LG = Ling; GD = Lge Gadoid;
PL = Plaice; HB = Halibut; FL = Flatfish; UN = Unidentifiable
v = vertebral centrum; sk = skull fragment

this fish means that it is likely to be missed unless sieving is carried out. Pickled and smoked herring were a staple cheap food during the medieval period.

I would like to thank Jennie Coy (Faunal Remains Project, University of Southampton) for the use of halibut modern reference material.

Bibliography

Archibald, M M, 1979 The coins, counters and a token, *in* J H Williams 1979, 243–6

Armstrong, P, 1977 *Excavations in Sewer Lane, Hull*, 974, East Riding Archaeologist, 3

Audouy, M, and Chapman, A, (ed) 2009 *Raunds: the origin and growth of a midland village, AD 450–1500: Excavations in north Raunds, Northamptonshire 1977–87*, Oxbow books

Bamford, H M, 1979a The worked flints, *in* J H Williams 1979, 290–5

Bamford, H M, 1979b The worked flints, *in* F Williams 1979, 73–4, (M) 122–5

Bamford, H M, 1981 The worked flints, *in* J H Williams and M Shaw 1981, 126–30, (M) 134–57

Bamford, H M, 1985 *Briar Hill excavation 1974–8*, Northampton Development Corporation, Archaeol Monog, 3

Barnard, EF, 1916 *The Casting Counter and the Counting Board, A Chapter in the History of Numismatics and Early Arithmetic*, Oxford University Press

Bayley, J, 1979 The Crucible Fragments, *in* F Williams 1979, 69, (M) 107–9

Bayley, J, 1982 Non-ferrous metal and glass working in Anglo-Scandinavian England: an interim statement, *PACT 7, Part 2*, 487–96

Becker, CJ, 1971 Late Palaeolithic finds from Denmark, *Proceedings Prehistoric Soc*, **37/11**, 131–139

Bedwin, 0, 1976 The excavation of Ardingly Fulling Mill and Forge, 1975–6, *Post-Medieval Archaeol*, **10**, 34–64

Benson, G, 1903 Notes on excavations at 25, 26 and 27 High Ousegate, *York Annual Reports, Yorkshire Phil Soc*, **64**, 64–7

Berry, G, 1974 *Medieval English Jettons*, Spink and Son Ltd, London

Biddle, M, (ed) 1976 *Winchester in the early middle ages: An edition and discussion of The Winton Domesday*, Winchester Studies, **1**

Brinklow, DA, 1984 Walmgate: the archaeology, *in* T P O'Connor 1984, 30–1

Brown, J, 2021 *Living opposite to the Hospital of St John: Excavations in medieval Northampton 2014*, Archaeopress Archaeology

Caldwell, DH, 1976 A group of post-medieval noble burials at Haddington, *Trans East Lothian Antiquarian and Field Naturalists' Soc*, **15**, 25–37

Chapman, A, 1999 Excavation of the Town Defences at Green Street, Northampton, 1995–6, *Northamptonshire Archaeol*, **28**, 25–60

Chapman, A, 2010 *West Cotton, Raunds: a study of medieval settlement dynamics, AD 450–1450: Excavation of a deserted medieval hamlet in Northamptonshire, 1985–89*, Oxbow Books

Chapman, A, 2021, Late Saxon and Saxo-Norman occupation beneath the outer bailey of Northampton Castle, *Northamptonshire Archaeol*, **41**, 79–127

Charleston, RJ, 1975 The Glass, *in* C Platt and R Coleman-Smith 1975, **2**, 204–26

Clark, J E D, Higgs, E S, and Longworth, IH, 1960 Excavations at the Neolithic site at Hurst Fen, Mildenhall,

Suffolk, 1954, 1957 and 1958, *Proceedings Prehistoric Soc*, **26**, 202–45

Clarkson, LA, 1960a The organisation of the English leather industry in the late sixteenth and seventeenth centuries, *Economic History Review*, **13**, 245–56

Clarkson, L A, 1960b *The English leather industry in the sixteenth and seventeenth centuries (1563–1700)*, unpublished University of Nottingham thesis

Cleere, H F, 1979 The metallurgical remains, *in* J H Williams 1979, 278–9

Cook, J, 1986 Northampton Lyngby Axe, *Archaeometry*, **28(2)**, 209

Cox, A, 1979 *Survey of Bedfordshire brickmaking; a history and gazetteer*, Bedfordshire County Council

Cox, J C, 1898 *The records of the borough of Northampton*, **2**, Corporation of Northampton

Cram, L, 1982 The pits and horn cores, *in* C Mahany *et al* 1982, 48–50

Cunliffe, B, 1975 *Excavations at Portchester Castle*, **1**, Society of Antiquaries, London

Cunningham, CM, Farmer, PJ, and Farmer, NC, 1983 A horse and rider aquamanile from Harwich and the significance of Scarborough Ware in Essex, *Essex Archaeol and History*, **15**, 54–67

Davey, N, 1961 *A history of building materials*, Phoenix House, London

Denham, V, 1983 The pottery, *in* JH Williams and C Farwell 1983, 146–50, (M) 6–15

Denham, V, 1984a The pottery, *in* J H Williams and C Farwell 1984, 93–100, (M) 15–48

Denham, V, 1984b The tiles and brick, *in* M Shaw 1984a, 81, (M) 48–53

Denham, V, 1984c The tiles and bricks, *in* J H Williams and C Farwell 1984, 104–5, (M) 70–80

Denham, V, 1985 The pottery, *in* J H Williams *et al* 1985, 46–63, (M) 2/1 – (M) 3/22

Denham, V, 1985 The pottery, *in* M Shaw, 1985, 123–133, (M) 33–54

Drew, JH, 1965 The horn comb industry of Kenilworth, *Trans and Proc Birmingham Archaeol Soc*, **82**, 21–7

Dyer, A, 1979 Northampton in 1524, *Northamptonshire Past & Present*, **6**, 73

Eames, E, 1978 The ceramic tiles, *in* J H Williams 1978, 121–8

Ewbank, JM, Phillipson, DW, and Whitehouse, RD, 1964 Sheep in the Iron Age: a method of study, *Proceedings Prehistoric Soc*, **30**, 423–6

Farley, M, 1982 A medieval pottery industry at Boarstall, Buckinghamshire, *Records of Buckinghamshire*, **24**, 107–117

Freke, D, 1975 Excavations in Lewes 1974, *Sussex Archaeol Collection*, **113**, 66–84

Gardiner, JP, 1985 The flint, *in* A Taylor and P J Woodward 1985, 126–39

Goodall, AR, 1984 Non-ferrous metal objects, *in* A Rogerson and C Dallas 1984, 68–75

Goodall, IH, 1976 The metalwork, *in* O Bedwin 1976, 60–4

Gover, JEB, Mawer, A, and Stenton, FM, 1975 *The place names of Northamptonshire*, Cambridge University Press

Grant, A, 1975 The use of tooth wear as a guide to the age of domestic animals, *in* B Cunliffe 1975, 437–50

Green, HS, 1980 The flint arrowheads of the British Isles, *British Archaeol Reports, British Series*, **75**

Gryspeerdt, M, 1978 The pottery, *in* J H Williams 1978, 133–46

Gryspeerdt, M, 1979 The pottery, *in* F Williams 1979, 57–67, (M) 64–100

Gryspeerdt, M, 1981 The pottery, *in* J H Williams and M Shaw 1981, 108–21, (M) 38–61

Gryspeerdt, M, 1982 The pottery, *in* J H Williams 1982, 68–72

Gryspeerdt, M, Harman, M, and Williams, J H, 1981 The worked bone, *in* J H Williams and M Shaw 1981, 130–2, (M) 173–80

Harcourt, R, 1974 The dog in prehistoric and early historic Britain, *J Archaeol Science* **1**, 151–75

Harden, D B, 1975 Table glass in the Middle Ages, *Rotterdam Papers*, **2**, 35–45

Hare, J N, 1985 *Battle Abbey: the eastern range and the excavations of 1978–80*, Historic Buildings and Monuments Commission, Archaeol Reports, **2**

Harman, M, 1979 The mammalian bones, *in* J H Williams 1979, 328–32

Harman, M, 1983 The mammalian bones, *in* J H Williams and D Farwell 1983, 151, (M) 39–46

Harman, M, 1985 The other mammalian bones, *in* J H Williams *et al* 1985, 75–8, (M) 4/48–63

Harman, M, and Shaw, M, 1985 The worked bone and antler, *in* J H Williams *et al*, 1985, 75, (M) 4/36–46

Haslam, J, 1984 The glass, *in* T G Hassall *et al* 1984, 232–46

Hassall, T G, 1976 Excavations at Oxford Castle 1965–73, *Oxoniensia*, **41**, 232–308

Hassall, T G, Halpin, C E, and Mellor, M, 1984 Excavations in St Ebbe's, Oxford, 1967–76 Part 2: Post-Medieval domestic tenements and the post-dissolution site of the Greyfriars, *Oxoniensia*, **49**, 153–275

Heighway, C M, 1983 Tanners' Hall, Gloucester, *Trans Bristol Gloucestershire Archaeol Soc*, **101**, 83–109

Hodgson, J M, (ed) 1976 *Soil Survey Field Handbook*, Harpenden, Soil Survey of Great Britain (England and Wales)

Humble, J L, 1985a The tile and brick, *in* J H Williams *et al* 1985, **70**, (M) 3/75–84

Humble, J L, 1985b The worked flints, *in* J H Williams *et al* 1985, 71–2, (M) 3/94–8

Humble, J L, 1985c The tile and brick, *in* M Shaw 1985, 134, (M) 63–70

Humble, J L, 1985d The worked flints, *in* M Shaw 1985, 134, (M) 76–9

Humble, J L, and Denham, V, in archive The pottery, in T Yates in archive

Hume, I N, 1961 The glass wine bottle in colonial Virginia, *Journal of Glass Studies*, **3**, 90–117

Hunter, R, 1979 The development of post-medieval St Peter's Street, *in* JH Williams 1979, 134–6

Hurst, J G, 1976 The pottery, *in* D Wilson 1976, 283–348

Ivens, R J, 1981 Medieval pottery kilns at Brill, Buckinghamshire, *Records of Buckinghamshire,* **23**, 102–106

Jenkins, J G, 1973 *The Rhaeadr Tannery*, National Museum of Wales, Welsh Folk Museum, pamphlet

Jones, A G K, 1979 The Fish Bones, *in* J H Williams 1979, 335

Keepax, C A, Girling, M A, Jones, R T, Arthur, J R B, Paradine, P J, and Keeley, H, 1979 The environmental analysis, *in* J H Williams 1979, 337

Knew, E, 1947 *A note on the native tanner of the Sudan and some proposed production developments*, Khartoum

Lindsay, J S, 1964 *Iron and Brass Implements of the English House*, revised Alec Tiranti, London

Locker, A, 1985 The fish bones, *in* J H Williams *et al* 1985, 78–9, (M) 4/72–7

McCarthy, M R, 1979 The pottery, *in* J H Williams 1979, 151–229

Mahany, C, Burchard, A, and Simpson, G, 1982 *Excavations in Stamford, Lincolnshire, 1963–1969*, Society for Medieval Archaeology

Markham, C A, 1898 *The records of the borough of Northampton*, **1**, Corporation of Northampton

Mason, D J P, 1985 *Excavations at Chester 26–42 Lower Bridge St 1974–6 The Dark Age and Saxon periods*, Chester Archaeological Society

Mellor, M and Oakley, G, 1984 A summary of the key assemblages, *in* T G Hassall *et al* 1984, 181–211

Moore, W R G, 1980 *Northamptonshire clay tobacco pipes and pipemakers*, Northampton Museums and Art Galleries

Mosseau, J, 1981 Gobelets et verres a boire, XVe-XVIIe siecle, *in Recherches sur Tours*, **1**, 85–101

Muscott, B B, 1906 Leather, *in The Victoria History of the Counties of England: Northamptonshire*, **2**, 310–7

Mynard, D C, 1976 Excavations on the Mayorhold, Northampton, 1971, *Northamptonshire Archaeol*, **11**, 134–50

Newstead, R, 1939 Records of archaeological finds, ii–v, *J Chester Archaeol Soc, New Series*, **33**, 5–117

Noddle, B, 1980 Polycerate sheep, *Ark* **7**, 156–64

Oakley, G E, 1976 The worked bone, *in* D C Mynard 1976, 145–6

Oakley, G E, 1979a The glass, *in* JH Williams 1979, 296–302

Oakley, G E, 1979b The charcoal and wood remains, *in* J H Williams 1979, 319

Oakley, G E and Hall, A D, 1979 The spindle whorls, *in* J H Williams 1979, 286–9

Oakley, G E and Harman, M, 1979 The worked bone, *in* J H Williams 1979, 308–18

O'Connor, T P, 1982 *Animal bones from Flaxengate, Lincoln, c 870–1500*, Council for British Archaeology for the Lincoln Archaeological Trust, monog, **18**

O'Connor, T P, 1984 *Selected groups of bones from Skeldergate and Walmgate,* Council for British Archaeology for the York Archaeological Trust, **15**, Fascicule **1**

Oswald, A, 1975 Clay pipes for the archaeologist, *British Archaeol Reports, British Series*, **14**

Palmer, N, 1980 A Beaker burial and medieval tenements in the Hamel, Oxford, *Oxoniensia*, **45**, 124–225

Peck, C W, 1964 *English copper, tin and bronze coins in the British Museum, 1558–1963*, 2nd edition, British Museum

Platt, C, and Coleman-Smith, R, 1975 *Excavations in Medieval Southampton 1953–1969*, **1**: The excavation reports, **2**: The Finds, Leicester University Press

RCHME 1985 *An inventory of the historical monuments in the county of Northampton, 5; Archaeological sites and churches in Northampton*, Royal Commission on Historical Monuments (England)

Robinson, M, and Wilson, B, 1983 *A Survey of Environmental Archaeology in the South Midlands*, unpublished typescript

Rogerson, A, and Dallas, C, 1984 *Excavations in Thetford, 1948–59 and 1973–80,* East Anglian Archaeol, **22**

Sanders, G B, and Armstrong, P, 1983 A watching brief on the Beverley high level sewer scheme 1980/1, *East Riding Archaeologist*, **7**, 52–70

Saunders, C, 1977 A sixteenth century tannery in St Albans, *Hertfordshire's Past*, **3**, 9–12

Selkirk, A, 1979 The Nottingham caves, *Current Archaeol*, **69**, 300–3

Shaw, M, 1984 Excavations on a medieval site at Derngate, Northampton, *Northamptonshire Archaeol*, **19**, 63–82 and microfiche

Shaw, M, 1985 Excavations on a Saxon and medieval site at Black Lion Hill, Northampton, *Northamptonshire Archaeol*, **20**, 113.138

Shaw, M, 1996 The excavation of a late 15th century tanning complex at The Green, Northampton, *Post-Medieval Archaeol*, **30**, 63–127

Shaw, M, 2011 Late medieval to early post-medieval tanning: the evidence from Northampton and its wider implications, 117–29, *in* R Thomson and Q Mould, *Leather Tanneries: the archaeological evidence*, Archetype Publications

Shaw, M, 2021 *Approaches to the analysis of the topography, origins, growth and development of English medieval towns: case studies of selected towns and their wider applicability*, University of Birmingham PhD thesis (http://etheses.bham.ac.uk/id/eprint/11081)

Shoesmith, R, 1980 Llangar Church, *Archaeologia Cambrensis*, **129**, 64–132

Taylor, A, and Woodward, P J, 1985 A Bronze Age barrow cemetery, and associated settlement at Roxton, Bedfordshire, *Archaeological J*, **142**, 73–149

Walker, A J, and Otlet, R L, 1985 The Carbon-14 measurements, *in* JH Williams *et al* 1985, 64–6

Whitelock, D, with Douglas, D C, and Tucker, S I, (eds) 1961 *The Anglo-Saxon Chronicle*, Eyre & Spottiswoode

Williams, F, 1979 Excavations on Marefair, Northampton, 1977, *Northamptonshire Archaeol*, **14**, 38–79 and microfiche

Williams, F, and Williams, J H, 1979a The tiles and bricks, *in* JH Williams 1979, 322–6

Williams, F, and Williams, J H, 1979b The ceramic tiles and bricks, *in* F Williams 1979, 77, (M) 140–1

Williams, J H, 1974 A Saxo-Norman kiln group from Northampton, *Northamptonshire Archaeol*, **9**, 46–56

Williams, J H, 1978 Excavations on Greyfriars, Northampton, 1972, *Northamptonshire Archaeol*, **13**, 96–160

Williams, J H, 1979 *St Peter's Street, Northampton Excavations 1973–6*, Northampton Development Corporation, Archaeol Monog, **2**

Williams, J H, 1982 Four small excavations on Northampton's medieval defences and elsewhere, *Northamptonshire Archaeol*, **17**, 60–73

Williams, J H, 1984 From 'palace' to 'town': Northampton and urban origins, *Anglo-Saxon England*, **13**, 113–36

Williams, J H, and Farwell, C, 1984 Excavations in The Riding, Northampton, in the area of Gobion Manor, 1981–1982, *Northamptonshire Archaeol*, **19**, 83–106 and microfiche

Williams, J H, and Farwell, D, 1983 Excavations on a Saxon site in St James' Square, Northampton, 1981, *Northamptonshire Archaeol*, **18**, 141–52 and microfiche

Williams, J H, and Shaw, M, 1981 Excavations in Chalk Lane, Northampton, 1975–1978, *Northamptonshire Archaeol*, **16**, 87–135 and microfiche

Williams, J H, Shaw, M, and Denham, V, 1985 *Middle Saxon Palaces at Northampton*, Northampton Development Corporation, Archaeol Monog, **4**

Williams, J H, Shaw, M, and Chapman, A, 2021 Anglo-Saxon Northampton Revisited, *Northamptonshire Archaeol*, **41**, 25–77

Wilson, D, (ed) 1976 *The Archaeology of Anglo-Saxon England*, Methuen

Wood, J T, 1912 *The Puering, Bating and Drenching of Skins*, London, E and FN Spon Ltd (Kindle edition via Amazon, Good Press 2019)

Woodward, D M, 1968 The Chester leather industry, 1558–1625, *Trans Hist Soc Lancashire Cheshire*, **119**, 65–111

Yates, T, in archive Excavations at Gregory Street, Northampton, 1978–9, unpublished drafts for Northampton Development Corporation

Northamptonshire Archaeology, **41**, 2021, 305–333

The Topography and Archaeology of the Medieval Synagogue and Jewry in Northampton

by

Marcus Roberts

with a contribution from Caroline Sturdy Colls

Summary

The location of the Northampton medieval Jewry had not survived as part of local historical knowledge. From the known locations of medieval Jewries in other towns, it is argued that the Jewry and synagogue in Northampton would have been close to the central business district and local market place. Documentary evidence indicates that it lay in 'Parmentry', named after dealers in English broad cloth, who were resident In Silver Street, and in medieval rentals several Jewish-owned properties are located in relation to the Red Lyon Inn, which stood adjacent to Bradshaw Street. This indicates a location to the north-west of the market place, north of Bradshaw Street and between Silver Street and Sheep Street. Through map-regression, using the Marcus Pierce map of 1632, it is argued the site of the synagogue may be what is now 9 Sheep Street (the Kebabish takeaway), which would have been surrounded with other buildings and homes of the Jewish community. Historical survey indicates that the medieval English synagogue was deeply sunken into the ground, so substantial remains might survive in situ, even where there are later cellars. Through the use of Ground Penetrating Radar (GPR) on the cellars and ground floors of 7 and 9 Sheep Street, it is argued that major parallel linear anomalies beneath the cellar of 9 Sheep Street may be an entry stair and walls, extending as much as 4m (nearly 14 feet) below the cellar floor level, and which could continue well beyond the survey area. An adjacent massive medieval wall in the cellar of the Bear, to the north, could be part of the stair or entry structure at 9 Sheep Street, and might even be a visible section of the synagogue wall, or an adjacent Jewish house. In addition, a GPR linear anomaly below the ground floor rear of 7 Sheep Street might have been part of the southern wall of the synagogue. It is also not beyond question that the structures seen at 9 Sheep Street might even be the galleried entry to a mikveh*, the Jewish ritual bath.*

Introduction

One of my major concerns in my research on the Northampton Jewry has been to identify the location of the medieval synagogue, as well as the boundaries of the Jewry and the major Jewish houses of the community.

At the outset it is important to observe that it is not diffi-cult to locate a medieval English Jewry and synagogue, as the position of these areas is generally completely stereo-typical. All of the major Jewish quarters are immediately adjacent (within *c*.50m) of the heart of the medieval central business district of any town, meaning that they are inevitably next to the most important markets or trading areas, though usually in a position away from the most noisome markets or activities. In the case of towns or cities around a central crossroads they are usually on the central crossroads itself, as in Oxford and Gloucester for example.

As to the synagogues, these are nearly always surrounded by other Jewish dwellings and where possible are set back from the street, for obvious reasons of security and privacy (Jews were explicitly forbidden to allow their 'wailing' to be heard by Christians). Critically, the overwhelming evidence is that medieval Anglo-Jewish synagogues followed the German and French pattern of being sunken or semi-sunken into the ground, so these synagogues would often have their floor level at semi-basement or even basement level, though the build-ings would have an interior loftiness.

It is also important to observe that larger Jewish commu-nities would often have more than one synagogue during their history, and that there were also private synagogues co-existing with communal synagogues. Major Jewish houses of study would also have functioned as synagogues as the two activities have always been conjoined.

More recent research (Hilaby 1993) shows that the synagogues would also have a 'Curia' or Court – often an open court or area surrounded by other communal build-ings, such as lodgings for communal officials, hostelries for Jewish travellers and the bake-house, etc.

It is also important to observe that the Jewish quarters in medieval England were not 'ghettoes' and they were not exclusively Jewish – there would often be some Christian neighbours in the main Jewry, though the majority would have been Jewish.

Therefore, on an *apriori* basis, the medieval Jewish quarter of Northampton will be found at the epicentre of the economic activity of medieval Northampton in the period AD1200–1300. Also, it may be anticipated that there is a good chance that archaeological remains of any synagogue may be met at both cellar and sub-cellar level.

Later medieval rentals clearly show that the Jewry was 'in Parmentry' but this precise location has been lost, though its position in the medieval rental documents after the Drapery, and its appellation after broadcloth sellers, suggests a location just along from the Drapery (Fig 1).

Acknowledgements

This article is based on a lecture to the Jewish Historical Society of England in 1992, with revisions in 2009 and 2012. Following the initial documentary research, an archaeological investigation was conducted in 2009 by Caroline Sturdy Colls, then Technical Director of Survey, Department of Archaeology and Antiquities, University of Birmingham, in a partnership between Marcus Roberts (JTrails) and the University of Birmingham, and directed by Marcus Roberts. The original article has been

prepared for publication by Andy Chapman. Illustrations and photographs have largely been provided by Marcus Roberts, including those of the geophysical survey results by Caroline Sturdy Colls, but Figures 1–3 are by Andy Chapman utilising historic maps and figures from the report on the archaeological works related to the Fish Market and its environs, carried out by Northamptonshire Archaeology, now MOLA (Museum of London Archaeology) (Upson-Smith *et al* 2020, this volume, 335–348).

Identifying the Jewry and Synagogue

Establishing the precise location of the Jewry and synagogue has presented significant difficulties, as my

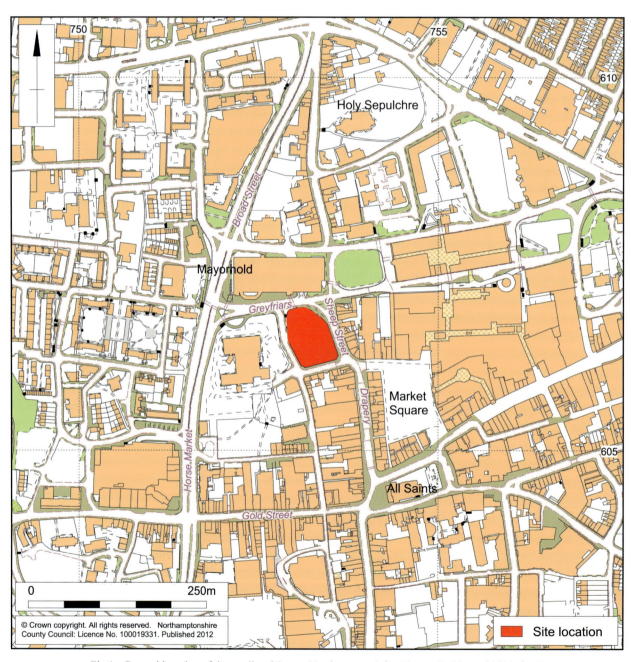

Fig 1: General location of the medieval Jewry, Northampton (after Upson-Smith *et al* 2020, fig 1)

work has shown that there have been significant shifts in the street patterns of the medieval market areas of the town, where the majority of the community lived, worked and offered their prayers. It has also been suggested (Jon Small pers comm) that there was a greater fluidity of property boundaries in Northampton, as compared to towns such as Oxford, where boundaries started being fixed from an earlier period due to the establishment of the colleges. (Editorial note: see Chapman 2021, this volume, 349–359 for further discussion of the issues of the changing street pattern and property boundaries).

Also, the documentary evidence has not always been easy to interpret or reconcile, as the earlier rental and map evidence does not easily converge with early modern traditions as to the site of the synagogue and major Jewish houses, though it may be argued that there is still a critical intersection of evidence.

The area name known as 'Parmentry' (probably named after later dealers 'in parmentry', or English broad cloth) is clearly the Jewry in the medieval rental rolls given the presence of explicit references to the synagogue and some named former Jewish tenants, but the name had disappeared from modern local usage. This has meant that the traditional post-medieval to modern assertion that the medieval Jewry, or 'Parmentry', was in Silver Street was as potentially misleading as it was helpful.

However, documentary and topographical research has indicated the position of the synagogue with a degree of accuracy and historical certainty as being in the near vicinity of the later historic 'Red Lyon Inn', and this defines the general location of the Parmentry and the Jewry (Fig 2b, Noble and Butlin map of 1746). Also, since medieval documents assert that other specific Jewish properties were adjacent, or attached to the synagogue these can be located with relative accuracy as well. Additionally, two other Jewish houses are locatable using other independently verifiable and locatable landmarks, which also conveniently help confirm the other locations given in the reconstruction.

A key evidence in these deductions has been the Marcus Pierce map of 1632, which I believe contains a surviving late medieval 'bird's eye flight map' of the town centre, and which may well provide a depiction of the Jewry and perhaps of the synagogue itself, and enable a more detailed, if speculative, reconstruction of the Jewry as a whole.

The Synagogue and Jewry

The Jewry

The Jewry was known to have existed in an area identified as "in Parmentry", immediately after the expulsion, in so far as the medieval rentals state that the former synagogue was in Parmentry (Northampton Rentals, Edward II and 19–20 Hen VII), and even though unusually, as is common elsewhere, the tradition of the 'Jewry' as a place name does not seem to have survived in Northampton.

We also have a reference to Peytmyn the Jew 'in the North Quarter', who is recorded as the next tenant on from the 'hospice called "le Lyon". The Northampton rentals are not particularly systematic and items are added *ad hoc* to certain heads, so it is only possible that the reference to Peytmyn may belong to Parmentry. However, the 1504 rental does repeat many of the elements regarding the Parmentry that are found in the Edward II rental.

There are numerous references to the properties of Jewish houses and property in royal records and in the Inquest pertaining to the Jewish properties at the Expulsion of 1290 (Exts. and Surv. 143), when there were found to be six private Jewish houses, with the communal property of the Jewry comprising a further five houses, five cottages (with three curtilages attached), the cemetery and the synagogue: a total of 17 buildings, though perhaps three of these were attached to the cemetery outside the Northgate (Roberts forthcoming).

The intramural holding was therefore about 14 houses at the Expulsion. After the Expulsion some of these properties were 'gifted' to named individuals and these names can be found, or implied, in the later rentals. For example to Ralph de Sylveston (a house), also a gift to Simon le Baud may well be the house later in the tenure of Geoffrey le Bawde, and it is entirely possible that the several properties belonging to John le Megre in Parmentry, were of Jewish origin, as he was one of the keepers of the Jewish chirograph chest (which contained the records of transactions between Jews and Christians) in Northampton.

Most of the houses were in Parmentry, but there were other outlying properties in named locations, overlooking or close to the Jewry, in Bearward (Bereward) Street to the north (see Fig 2), Cornhill (Cornchepinge) and in the parishes of All Saints, to the south, and the Church of the Holy Sepulchre on Sheep Street, known colloquially as St Sepulchre's (See Fig 1).

Some forty named Jews can be found in the records of the 13th century, of these approximately twenty-five were householders in the town. The locations of the outlying properties also indicate the general position of the Parmentry; as it is typical to find a few Jewish homes overlooking the main Jewry. It is also important to point out that not all of the houses owned by Jews were their domestic residences, as some were owned as investments, though the ones referred to here are those that were personal residences.

At the Expulsion, the Abbey of St James was initially granted the synagogue, three houses at the entrance of the synagogue, as well as the houses of Sarra de London. However, in 1327 Queen Isabella, wife of Edward II, was granted the income from the Jews' houses in Northampton for life, among other incomes granted for her good service.

There is good reason to think this was a typical English Jewry of the period being an area of predominantly, if not exclusively, Jewish housing right next to the main markets and commercial areas and at a convenient distance to the protection of the castle. The emergence close by of the new Market Square in Northampton in the *c.*12th century, and the growth of the parish of All Saints, may well be indicative in this respect (Fig 1). It is reasonable to think that in the heyday of the Jewry, before the persecutions leading up to the Expulsion, there may have been at least ten to fourteen residential properties – several appropriations of Jewish properties are recorded in official

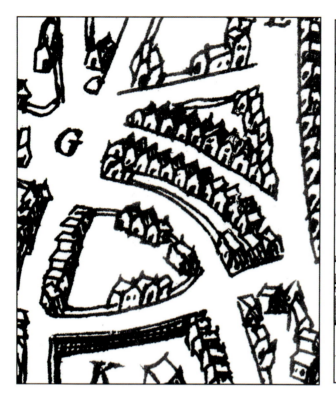

a) John Speed 1610

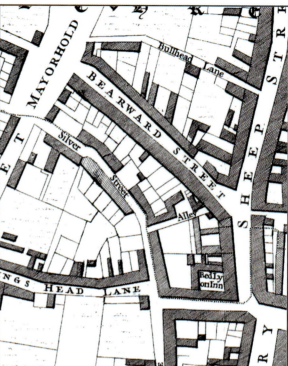

b) Noble and Butlin 1746

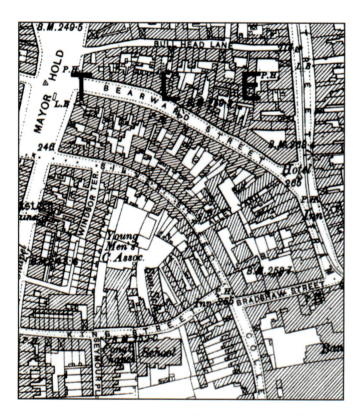

c) Ordnance Survey (2nd edition) 1899

d) Modern, showing the Fishmarket

Fig 2: Comparative maps: a)-c) not to scale, (d) after Upson-Smith *et al* 2020, fig 2

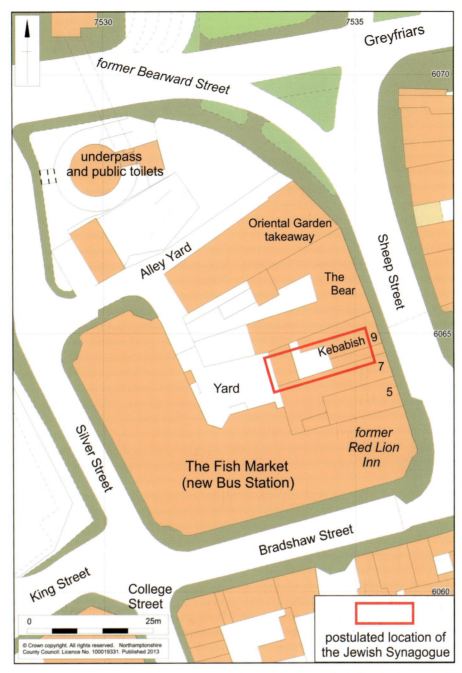

Fig 3: Showing street names and principal buildings referenced in the text, including the former Red Lion Inn

documents before 1290 – at least six or more that could be supposed to be Jewish residences were appropriated in the 13th century – making this latter figure likely.

The synagogue

The synagogue itself was probably the most substantial building in the Jewry insofar as at the expulsion it was valued at £1 – 0s – 9d and one pound of cumin a year. This value included the other five communal buildings, described as "cottages", but the synagogue would have been far in excess of the value of the other properties,

as these are recorded as being at the entrance of the synagogue and were almost immediately torn down after the expulsion. The high medieval valuation of the building suggests a good quality stone building, in that in the same period some of the most expensive properties in Oxford merited 40s a year.

Three Jewish properties in Northampton, including the synagogue, seem to have survived up to the great fire of Northampton in 1675, if not beyond. In 1630 William Raynsford left a house to his daughter Barbara Raynsford, described in the will as a messuage or tenement "somet-ymes called the synagogue of the Jews" and situated in Silver Street. William Raynsford was a leading citizen of the town, being mayor of Northampton in 1585: indeed, several other Raynsfords also served as mayors in the 16th and 17th centuries.

Perhaps the most important testimony as to the survival of the synagogue and Jewish houses comes from Henry Lee, who in 1715 recorded the most notable details of Northampton life from his lengthy career of 53 years as town clerk. His information is vital, as he recalls information from before the Fire of Northampton.

He writes of the Jews that they built themselves various houses in Northampton and goes on to identify three houses including:

> "One where old Menard the Baker lived in the little lane on the south side of the Red Lyon inn, it had a stately hall at the entrance down some stone stairs on the right hand, which hall was very large and open to the roof, as many great houses were in England, the windows on the outside of the house were very small and strengthened with iron bars the whole was a large building; another house built by them was where Mr Pickmer lived when he was Mayor over and against the Ram Inn on the south, which house Mr Thomas Brafield now ownes. The third is the house old Scambler lived in now Mrs Woodford at the end of Silver Street looking in the Mayorhold."

While Lee later continues in his account to mistakenly identify the Holy Sepulchre as the Jews synagogue (a typical error of his time) he definitely relates important local traditions as to the houses of the Jews in Northampton, though it is important to make the caveat that not all traditions of this kind are necessarily accurate and they may contain confusions or translocations. Furthermore, there is a tendency to ascribe unusual architecture to the Jews, as seen in the ascription of the round church of the Holy Sepulchre as the former synagogue. It may also be noted that Lee does not record any of these buildings as being the former synagogue.

On a biographical note, Menard may well be identified as Menard Brown, who was mayor in 1651. This is quite possible, as Francis Pickmer was a contemporary of Menard Brown, being also mayor in 1664.

From these statements it is possible to attempt to establish the locations of the houses mentioned. While there may be some possible dispute as to precise locations, it is clear that most of these properties were in the near vicinity, or directly adjacent to, the later historic Red Lyon Inn.

The house of Menard may be argued to be the identical property as the building identified as the synagogue in Raynsford's will, as both are described in contemporary documents as being in the close vicinity of the Red Lyon (Lee's account and the Deeds for the Red Lyon). Also, and what gives this reference its greater interest, is that it may well link to the medieval reference to the house of Peytmyn the Jew, as next (north?) to the hospice called the 'Lyon', which may well be an early reference to the Red Lyon.

Menard's house is described as being in the little lane to the south of the Red Lyon. The general historical site of the Red Lyon is well known, being on the corner of Sheep Street with modern day Bradshaw Street, this being stated with the caveat that Bradshaw Street is wider and perhaps a little further south than its medieval precursor, which was a small lane not much more than 12 feet (3.66m) wide, and an effective extension of Kings Head Lane towards the market place (see Figs 2b and 3).

It is not entirely clear from Lee's description if the house was the direct and adjacent neighbour of the Red Lyon, on the north side of what became Bradshaw Lane (now Bradshaw Street), or whether it was the near neighbour, just across the lane. In favour of the first position, is the assertion that the building is a forerunner of the 'Old Bake House', which now stands near the corner of Bradshaw Street and College Street.

In favour of the argument is the fact that in the adjacent courtyard (currently part of an Islamic Centre) there are preserved in a modern stone wall some carved stones thought to come from the original building here (Fig 4). One of the stones (top) seems to be an inverted double column base of 13th-century origin, which might have come from the synagogue. A parallel can be made to similar columns at the synagogue in Rouen, France (Fig 5). The other stones are probably from a head of a doorway of c.1500. They have been interpreted as Jewish in origin, by some suggesting the synagogue (Thomas Welsh pers comm).

However, in favour of the second position, we find in 1584, when the deeds of the Lyon Inn were drawn-up, that the tenant was a Mr Blyth and that an annexed part of the property (a building and garden adjacent westwards) had formerly belonged to William Browne, and was situated in Silver Street but separated by a small lane called 'Fleshmonger's End'. He is mentioned in his turn in two entries in the Northampton Borough Records, detailing the positioning of sheep pens in 1582, 1585 and 1594, as living at the sign of the Red Lyon, next to Mr Raynsford. This appears to place the Raynsford property as north of Bradshaw Lane and the direct neighbour of the Red Lyon.

In 1582 and 1585 pens were permitted to be sited from the corner of Mr Blythe's and Wentworth's house "up" to the Holy Sepulchre. In 1594, the order of 1585 was reversed, adding that sheep pens could be sold "from the corner of Mr Blythe's and Mr Wentworth's house down to

Fig 4: Architectural stone inserted in a more recent wall, comprising an inverted double column base of the 13th century and a doorway head of the 15th century

Fig 5: Arrangement of double columns at the synagogue in Rouen, France (from E Privat (ed) 1980, 236–37, figs 6 & 7)

Mr Raynsford's house", leaving a three yard gap across the centre of the street gutter for passage. These directives could be interpreted to suggest that Raynsford's property was either just north of the Red Lyon or to the west.

Also – and this would seem to be significant corroborative evidence – his neighbour to the west up to Silver Street was a William Browne, no doubt a close relative of Menard Browne. The correlation of the exact house, location, and family name is further persuasive evidence as well as its abutment towards Silver Street.

These details show that Mr Blyth's, alias the Red Lyon, was on the corner of Sheep Street with the forerunner of Bradshaw Lane, and that Raynsford's house, the former synagogue, was also on that lane. The crucial indicator is in the use of "up" and "downe" in the directions that are given. The identification of Bradshaw Lane as the street on which Raynford's house lay is ratified in the deed of 1585, which relates that the southern boundary of the Red Lyon was a lane "leading from the Corne market towards Horse Market". The narrowness of Bradshaw Lane is indicated in the record, as there was only three yards [9 feet / 2.74m] of passage between the pens in the lane as opposed to 12 feet in Sheep Street. The lane is not named but it is clear that it is regarded as an extension of Kings Head Lane (now King Street), with only the easternmost end surviving.

The position of Bradshaw Lane is significant in this discussion as it determines the effective southern boundary of the Red Lyon and the synagogue. There is no doubt that the modern day Bradshaw Street is much wider than its forerunner – much wider indeed as can be seen in an examination of the Victorian street line with the post-1921 street line. That it is further south is shown by the fact that the commissioners after the Fire of Northampton allowed a 164 feet [50m] of public ground to be taken "over and against" the Red Lyon. The original line of the narrow lane on which the Synagogue formerly lay in the 1640s is, therefore, probably directly in line with Kings Head Lane and the entry to the Market Place without the staggering of the street line that can be seen today (Figs 2 b-d and 3).

Overall, the analysis so far shows that the medieval synagogue was adjacent to the historic Red Lyon Inn – probably to the north or west, and that the south frontage

of the inn and the line of the street was a little further north than in the modern period. Therefore, this means that the centre of the Jewry can be reasonably accurately identified, and that the Parmentry mentioned in the medieval rental, lay around and about this area. The rental details and the known topography infer that the Parmentry could not have extended any further north than Bereward Street (the modern Bearward Street, largely lost in the 1970s redevelopment, see Figs 2 and 3) and it seems reasonable to think that the extension of Kings Head Lane marked its southern boundary, as the old Drapery is mentioned, which lay just across the lane to the south. The indications are that Parmentry was an area rather than a street, hence the term in the rentals "in Parmentry".

The location of Jewish properties

In order to correctly place the Jewish properties adjacent to the synagogue, the placing of the line of Silver Street, westwards, needs to be determined. The deed of 1584 and the Borough records show that only Raynsford's house seems to separate the Red Lyon from Silver Street (with Fleshmonger's End between the two properties) which seems to indicate that Silver Street was further eastwards than at present. Subsequent map work has also suggested that the frontages of the houses on Sheep Street (former North Street) may have been further eastwards and certainly the street frontage was taken back in 1921 to align the front of numbers 5 – 9 Sheep Street, with the new entry to the Fish Market. There is evidence of cellarage under Sheep Street, which is seen in significant collapses of the road surface and blocked entries to cellars in 7 Sheep Street. The map work undertaken also indicates the possibility of another line further east.

There is every indication that property boundaries and street frontages were not strongly fixed and that the street plan in the heart of Northampton's medieval business district underwent some changes in its main periods of growth from the 10th and 11th centuries onwards, and into the 13th and early 14th centuries, and when the town finally recovered from the depression following the Black Death in the 16th century. Foard (1995) has suggested that a major phase of Norman street planning took place in the 12th century, in particular the development of the market place, but that there were major distortions that took place in Northampton later on.

Excavations at the junction of Woolmonger Street and Kingswell Street demonstrate how Saxon structures were followed by Saxon-Norman structures in just part of the site, while the ground remained largely open and the roads were 'less formally defined'. The street and property boundaries were only formalized in the 13th-14th centuries and a continuous street frontage of properties did not come until much later (Brown 2008).

Similar patterns have been observed elsewhere (such as Oxford) where the street lines and property boundaries have been relatively fluid, as early principal dwelling houses tended to be away from the street frontages, which were gradually built up with smaller commercial parcels developed on the margins of larger plots, with cellarage, until continuous street frontages were built up, with first and second row commercial buildings built back from the frontages. Also, in Oxford a number of significant streets have significantly varied their lines (such as Cornmarket in the 12th century, with a 4m shift) and smaller streets have been created to provide access to buildings (Dodd 2003).

While modern day Silver Street is a northwards continuation of College Street there is no evidence to show that College Street existed before 1300, as this date is its first mention. This may throw doubt on the original line of the street. Also, College Street underwent changes during its history being originally only a narrow ('*strictam*') lane called 'le College Lane' (13 June 36 Hen VI A. 8384). At some point the street was widened, and perhaps realigned. The Drapery, running parallel to College Street has also undergone major changes. By 1556 there is a distinction made between the Old Drapery and the New Drapery in property documents. There is also a medieval street that has disappeared in the near vicinity of the synagogue, Cappe Lane, and the existence of Fleshmongers End, west of the Red Lyon Inn, has already been mentioned.

There are also a number of other smaller Northampton streets which have disappeared from view, and in the north of the central commercial area the top of Bearward Street and Silver Street have both been realigned in the modern period. Thomas Welsh has attributed changes in the line of Silver Street to the eastwards expansion of the Dominican Priory in the 14th century, rather than an earlier origin as the fossilised line of the inner extent of the late Saxon town defences, which others have argued ran between College Street/Silver Street and The Drapery/Sheep Street/Bearward Street (see Williams *et al* this volume, figs 1 & 2).

There is direct evidence showing that the religious houses of Northampton were actively engaged in their own acts of town planning and the making and unmaking of streets. In 1266 the act of street-scaping is caught in time when the Hospital of St John got permission to enclosed a lane called Crakebelle Street, which lay between their church and grange, on the condition that they made a new one towards the street of St John, so that the inhabitants of the lane would have access to the market. This throws potential new light on the action of the Abbey of St James in tearing down the three Jewish houses in front of the synagogue, when they acquired it just after the expulsion – perhaps they were amending the street line at this point for economic reasons? This suggests there is reason to think that some streets were re-planned during the medieval period, after the expulsion, to expand the area available for markets and commercial premises.

Provisional conclusions

We may provisionally conclude from the foregoing analysis that the synagogue was almost certainly adjacent to, or nearly adjacent to, the historic Red Lyon Inn, however, it is difficult to determine if it lay to the west or north of the inn, though it seems less likely that it lay just to the south across the later Bradshaw Lane. However, it may be interjected that the property under discussion could also potentially be the remains of the house of Peytmyn the Jew; not that either argument excludes the other. Also, as another potentially important qualification, this identification with Peytmyn, who was a patron of Jewish learning, could indicate the site of the Jewish house of study which would have functioned both as a synagogue (for its students) and a Talmudic academy. (Editorial note: as previously mentioned, see Chapman 2021, this volume, 349–359 for further discussion of the issues of the changing street pattern and property boundaries).

Additional map work and analysis

The Marcus Pierce map of 1632

In order to further advance the identification of the synagogue and Jewry, we may look at the map evidence to see if this helps the analysis, especially in regard to the contention that street frontages and boundaries may have shifted in the past.

This scenario is supported by a map of the former lands of St Andrew's in Northampton field, produced by Marcus Pierce in 1632 (Fig 6, see RCHME 1985, plate 7). It shows a town-plan whereby Silver Street is further east than at present creating a small area of housing round and about what may be the medieval synagogue – an area that could well answer to the description of the Parmentry.

This remarkable map appears to show an Elizabethan bird's eye view of the town of Northampton, inserted into a later map. It is important as it appears to show former Jewish properties in the Jewish enclave called 'Parmentry'. There were some 15 properties, bounded on the east by Sheep Street. The synagogue is almost certainly the large building behind the four buildings on the south of the plot and it later became a Mayoral residence. This may be the only picture of a medieval synagogue in England. Also, the large building at the very end of Bearward Street, jutting into Sheep Street, is almost certainly '*Bello Fronte*' a former fine, stone, Jewish property that probably belonged to Pictavinus son of Sampson (Fig 6).

While the Speed map of 1610 is ostensibly the earliest map of the town (Fig 2a), it looks likely that Pierce may have provided the detail for his town plan from a lost Elizabethan map or survey – the style is certainly similar to a bird's eye flight map of the type such as Agas' Oxford.

This scenario is likely from the point of view that Pierce's primary concern as map maker in this case was with the fields and acreages outside of the town. Also, it is evident that Pierce's specialty was land surveying – evidenced in his famous Laxton Map, the best known example of his work – it is therefore possible that he used another early map to fill in the town detail to save the labour of surveying.

However, this plan of the town is by all appearances a generally accurately surveyed map – a 'birds-eye flight' map, rather than a bird's eye view – a perspective view map. It contains some good historical detail, such as the only surviving drawing of the destroyed medieval church of All Saints, though this is not to say that the map can be entirely relied upon. However, overlaying this map onto

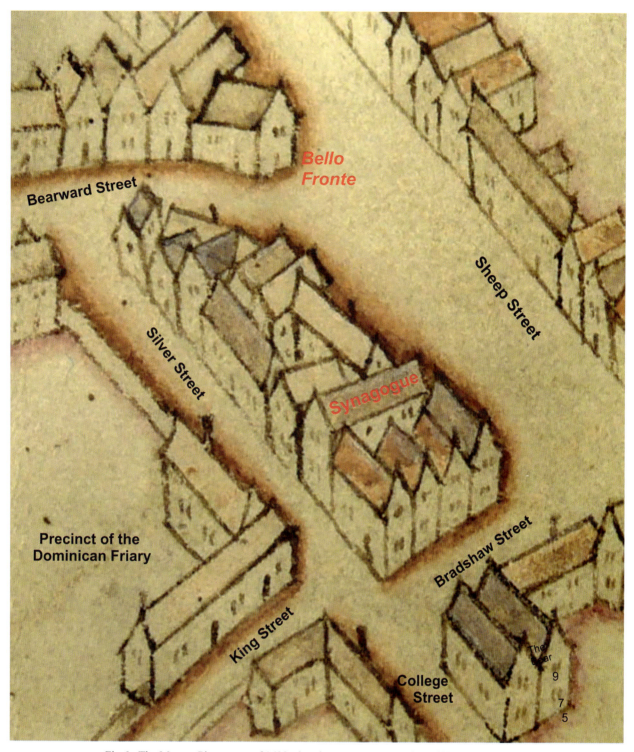

Fig 6: The Marcus Pierce map of 1632, showing street names and possible house locations

satellite imagery shows that the map is quite accurate on a point-to-point basis (suggesting a survey by chain) and reveals genuine historical features, though there are distortions over wider areas showing the map lacked the advantage of the more modern technique of triangulation.

Others have dismissed its portrayal of the Sheep Street area of town as incorrect, as it does not fit with expectations and other map surveys. But this can be resolved

if it is seen as an early map, preceding Speed, and we accept that historic street lines in Northampton did have some fluidity. Also, it does seem to correlate with relict topographical information (historic boundaries, etc) given in the 1880 Ordnance Survey (OS) 25" survey.

The alternative line of Silver Street can arguably be accurately plotted in relict common boundaries, rights of passage and way, and infill buildings in the Drapery area and the area around the former Red Lyon. Also, the small rear entry to the Red Lyon, known as Fleshmongers End, falls on this line and may therefore be part of the relict street line.

The buildings depicted in what can now be tentatively identified as the Parmentry area, can be rationally plotted back on to property walls and boundaries of the Ordnance Survey 25" mapping, assuming that piecemeal development will nearly always leave relict lines and fossilised boundaries of earlier phases of development – broken segments of former larger units and boundaries. Even though the area was extensively re-modelled in the 17th to 20th centuries, the evidence is coherent.

In terms of the best fit for the mapping of Pierce onto the modern landscape, it may be seen that the site of the large building – the possible synagogue – lies just north of the former Fishmarket and the mapping agrees with the assertion that the line of Bradshaw Street is now more southerly than originally and the street has been widened.

Another piece of evidence which reinforces this view is that the "Parmentry", which can be specified on the Pierce map, has some 15 properties (the precise counting depending on whether or how some properties were subdivided or not). Notably the 1504 rental lists fifteen rentable properties or plots, the Edward II rental shows 13 rentable properties, while the Pierce map shows 14 properties. It should be qualified that the King's Rental in Northampton is not a comprehensive list of town properties, as it only covers the property in hand of the king rather than in private hands. However, given the former concentration of Jewish properties here and their confiscation by the king, before and at the expulsion, there is less cause to think that there would be any concentration of private Christian property here.

Houses of the Jewry

In light of the arguments given, several Jewish houses can now be given specific historical locations and a tentative reconstruction of the Jewry as a whole is possible. The general position of the Parmentry is almost certainly the vicinity of the former Red Lyon and specifically it may correspond to the enclave of housing shown by Pierce bounded by Sheep Street to the east and Silver Street to the west, the line of Kings Head Lane to the south and the end of Bearward Street to the north.

The Pierce map shows a large and fine building lying across the 'Parmentry' site and approximately next to the site of the former Red Lyon Inn. The size and orientation of the property, the fact it is central to the 'Parmentry' and that it is fronted by other properties, makes it possible that this is a depiction of the former synagogue, or Peytmyn's house (Fig 6).

In terms of more certain locations Raynsford's house (the synagogue?) was either on the site of the Fishmarket or just to the north of the eastern arm of the Fishmarket. The Jew's house that Lee specifies as abutting directly onto the former Ram Inn can be readily seen on Pierces map, as a large house jutting into the corner of Bearward Street and Sheep Street, though it may also be noted that one commentator has suggested that the Ram is the old

name for the current Bear pub, which brings us back to this specific location next to the Fishmarket again (Thomas Welsh pers comm). However, the First Edition Ordnance Survey map indicates that in the Victorian period a space where this building would have been is directly in front of the Ram Hotel on the junction of Bearward Street and Sheep Street, with the Bear on Sheep Street.

The indication is that the building was eventually cleared to allow for the corner of the street to be widened. In the 1504 Rental we read that at the corner of Le Bereward Street and Sepulchre Street is a house called "*Bello Fronte*" (Beautiful Front). It is not unreasonable to think that this can be identified with the house of Pictavinus son of Sampson, mentioned at the inquest of 1290. It records that Pictavinus, son of Sampson, had a messuage in Sheep Street described as a "bona domus", a good house well-appointed and well built ("bona domus cum aisiamentis omnibus necessari competentibus et bene edificatis"). This would answer the description of "*Bello Fronte*", and the sort of high status house that the later Mayor of Northampton, Francis Pickmer might have lived in (Fig 6).

Despite the possible reservations about the Jewish provenance of "*Bello Fronte*" it does enable a possible identification of the former house of Peytevin the Jew. The 1504 Rental says that "*Bello Fronte*" was opposite the garden of Roger son of Theobald and an earlier entry reads that the house "...late of Peytmyn the Jew..." is "now of the gate of Roger, son of Theobald on the head of Berwardstrete...". The implication clearly is that "*Bello Fronte*" is nearly opposite on the other side of the street to the enclosure and gate of Theobald at the end of Bearward Street. This description seems to fit the topography in Pierce with Peytmyn's house being the tip of the Parmentry and east of the entry to the enclosure behind and to the south of Bearward Street.

It is known that Peytevin the Jew was the son of Magister Aaron, a Talmudic scholar in Northampton. Magister Aaron would have studied at the Talmudic academy in the Jewry, an academy whose existence has been further ratified by the designation of a *Haber Schlomo* or 'scholar Solomon' on the Northampton medieval Jewish tombstone (Fig 7, Roberts 1992 & Jtrails: http://www.jtrails.org.uk/trails/northampton/, viewed May 2021). This is one of only two surviving medieval Hebrew inscriptions in the country, the other at the putative *mikveh* in Bristol. It is likely to have been that of a local rabbi and scholar, confirming the documented scholarly activity in the Jewry. It is in a German style evidencing a Rhennish influence on East Midlands Jews, and is of Barnack stone from the quarries near Stamford.

The 1290 inquest also mentions that the dilapidated house or cottage with a small yard of Gente, who was wife of Sadekyn, went to John de Thorp. In the Edward II rental, the Parmentry lists only one entry for John de Thorp, a tenement. Therefore, this is most probably Gente's house. It is difficult to place this property as the only information about its position is that it comes eighth in the rental, inferring a position no more specific than somewhere (midway?) between the house of Peytevin and the synagogue.

Moving back to the synagogue, the records show that

Fig 7: the medieval Jewish tombstone from Northampton
(photo: Northampton Museums)

there was a close grouping of houses and Jewish property around the synagogue. The 1504 rental states there was a waste plot near to the synagogue. This can be identified with the plot or *placium* of Sampson son of Sampson, one of the leading Jews of Northampton and a signatory of the re-issue cemetery *Starr* (Hebrew for 'contract')*,* the medieval charter leasing land to the Jewish community for a Jewish Cemetery by the Abbey of St Andrew's. His property was confiscated in 1280 and granted to Ralph de Sylveston for 2s a year. It may be that this *placium* was the former Jewish curia or court, adjacent to the synagogue and which would have had communal facilities.

It has also been noted that in 1312–17, in a grant of former Jewish property to the Abbey of St James, there were three communal houses "before the entrance to the school" and also the house of Sarra de London, a Jewess "adjacent to the school". These would provide other communal facilities for the community and perhaps the site of the Talmudic academy though the later facility could equally have been in the house of Peytevin the Jew.

Overall, the reconstruction probably accounts for most if not all of the houses in the Jewry listed at the expulsion. The question arises as to whether they can be placed on the Pierce map of the Parmentry. One way in which this might be done – though it must be emphasized that this is speculative – is to suggest that the southern four houses represent the sites of the former three houses outside the entrance to the synagogue and the empty plot of Sampson, though these three houses could equally have encroached on to Sheep Street. In that case, the large building behind could be a depiction of the former synagogue and the smaller building behind it might be the house of Sara of London. This would reasonably represent the nucleus of

the community. The house of Pictavinus is certainly that abutting the Ram Inn on the corner. The smaller house nearest and opposite the Parmentry can probably be said to be that of Peytevin the Jew. As for Gente's house the small property forming the north side of the courtyard indicated in the centre of the Jewry would fit the description.

The reconstruction of the Northampton Jewry, even taking into account its diminished size before the final expulsion, shows its relative small scale even though it was a large Jewry of the period, comparable to Oxford. The composition of Northampton Jewry revealed in this reconstruction shows that it was a very typical Jewry of the period – being an enclave of predominantly Jewish housing, with some outlying Jewish residences close by, centring on the synagogue and communal facilities while being in the heart of the business quarter of the medieval town, the source of income for the community. The varying quality of housing from the decrepit cottage of Gente, working up to the luxury of Pictavinus's stone house, indicates something of the class structure of the typical Jewry, with a few rich magnates heading the community, working down to the moderately wealthy, such as Sara of London (with her house of one story and a cellar), to the poor such as Gente. As always the presence of scholars at a Talmudic school in the town, impresses one with the quality of literacy, learning and culture in such numerically small and marginalised communities.

It is notable that at the expulsion the Jewish property passed through a number of hands – but mostly to the former bailiffs and administrators of the Jews, such as Ralph de Selveston, Stephen Osberne, and to influential citizens like John le Megre, who was a Burgess and sometime Mayor of Northampton.

The mayoral association with the former Jewish properties is of some interest as both the principal houses of the Jewry, the former synagogue and "*Bello Fronte*" had mayoral residents. It seems possible that Raynsford's house was an unofficial mayoral residence in Northampton as at least two mayors, Raynford and Brown, lived there.

The description of the possible former synagogue by Lee is of considerable interest in light of the recent excavation of an attributed synagogue in Guildford. It is significant as the Northampton synagogue was evidently a single-aisled stone building sunken in the ground and entered by a flight of steps which would probably have had a stone porch. The excavated chamber at Guildford is also stone-built, being a sunken structure with a single aisle entered by flight of steps. In this way it is generally typical of the form of contemporary German and French synagogues and, with other evidence that is emerging, this is pointing to sunken buildings as being the predominant form of medieval Anglo-Jewish synagogues.

As a final note, it is germane to ask whether the synagogue survived the fire of Northampton in 1675, and what was its fate? There is reason to think that the fire of Northampton did not do excessive damage on the west of Sheep Street. That it could have survived beyond this date is tantalizingly suggested by a purchase of a property in Silver Street by a James Brown (a baker) from the Kings Commissioners in 1788. This was in respect of the king alienating himself of Fee farms and otherwise unimprovable rents. Thus, we find a link to the royal rentals again, and a possible link to Menard Brown, one baker, to a James Brown, another baker and possible descendant of Menard Brown.

Modern map projection

Having argued that the houses depicted on the Pierce map were indeed the houses of the Northampton Jewry, we can project the arrangement of these buildings onto a modern base map by overlaying a grid onto the map of 1632 (Fig 9) and then overlying this onto the late Victorian Gough Insurance map (Fig 10) and a modern aerial view (Fig 11).

When the house grid from the Marcus Pierce map is overlaid on the Gough Insurance map (c.1890) it shows a rational correlation between the historic property lines, and has been located on the basis that the contemporary line of Kings Head Lane lay to the north of the modern Bradshaw Street, as argued above.

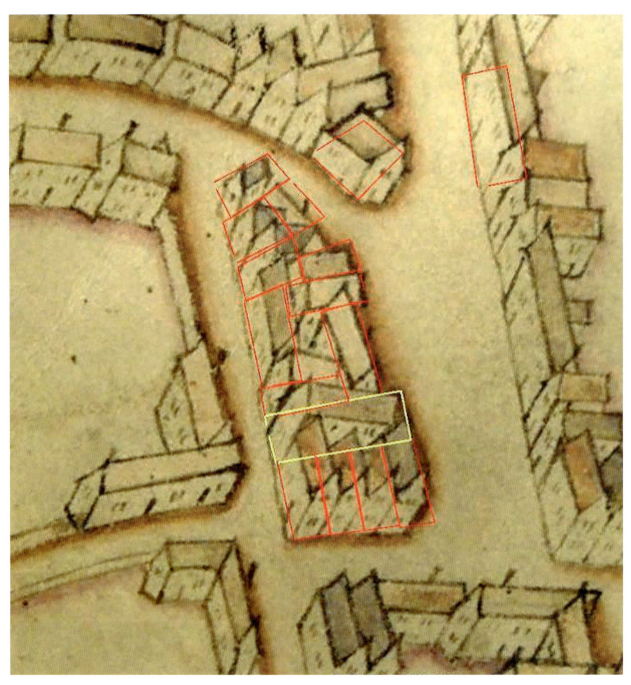

Fig 8: Marcus Pierce Map 1632, with a grid created to overlay on other maps and aerial images
(possible synagogue in yellow, other houses in red)

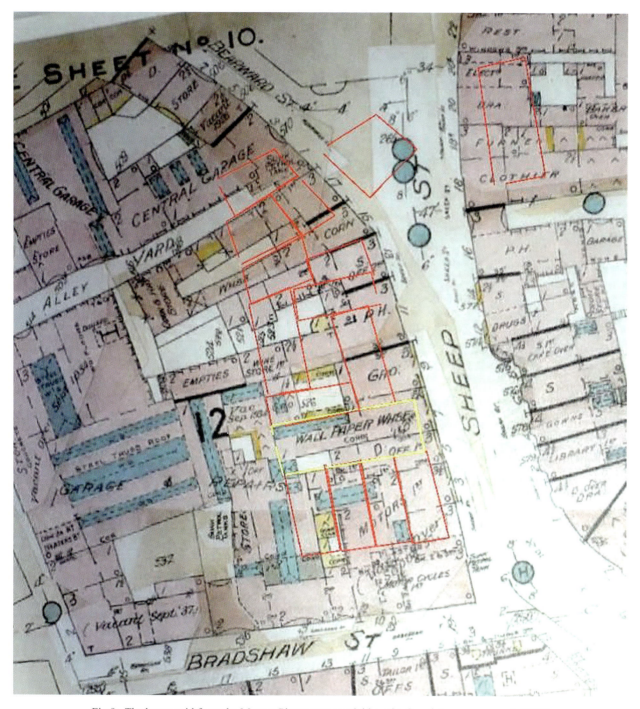

Fig 9: The house grid from the Marcus Pierce map overlaid on the Gough Insurance map (c.1890)

Archaeological Fieldwork and Geophysical Survey of the Parmentry Area

Marcus Roberts with Caroline Sturdy Colls

As a result of the research already undertaken, the opportunity arose to commission a non-intrusive archaeological survey, featuring geophysical survey methods.

The research undertaken had suggested a possible, relatively compact search area, in the heart of the Jewry, with a good possibility of finding medieval features, such

as the walls of the synagogue, the House of Study and other Jewish houses.

Critically, other work conducted elsewhere, as at Guildlford and Rouen, France, had shown that substantial remains of a synagogue were entirely possible, even at sub-cellar level, due to the tradition of constructing sunken or even subterranean synagogues. With rising ground levels over time in town centres of 2–3 metres, substantial sections of synagogue walls had been shown to survive later cellar construction.

The search area offered a number of properties with both

317

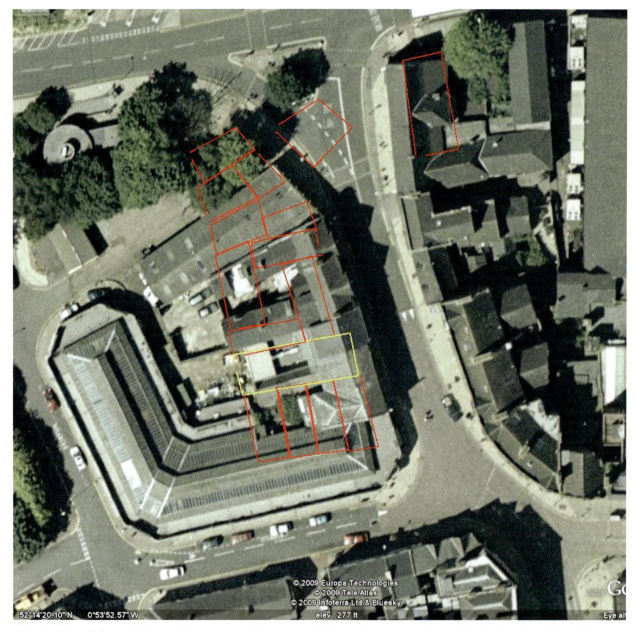

Fig 10: The grid from the Marcus Pierce map overlain on an aerial image showing the former Fish Market (Google Earth images)

intact ground levels and cellars. Access to conduct the survey was granted to 7–9 Sheep Street by Northampton Borough Council and the respective tenants, who offered every assistance. We were unable to search No 7 due to the cellar door being covered with new flooring and extensive dry-rot.

We had wanted to examine the storage cellars under the Fish Market (see Upson-Smith *et al* 2021, this volume 335–348) and the former Police Shooting Gallery under the west of the Fish Market, the former air raid shelter (see Bassir 2015, figs 2–4 and 10–13, which show that this was brick-built as part of the construction of the Fish Market), but access was not possible. We also wanted to survey the cellars of the Bear Inn, using GPR, as well as the area of Sheep Street in front of our main search area, but time did not allow these additional searches.

The Bear Inn cellar

It was possible to examine the cellar of the Bear Inn and this showed a redundant stairway intruded into the wall, but part of the original thickness of the walls is retained as a buttress (Fig 12). The stone steps are cut into the body of an earlier wall and the total wall thickness may be about 6 feet (1.83m) extending into the adjacent property, 9 Sheep Street, the Kebabish. This masonry feature abuts directly to the sub-cellar rectangular feature located by GPR survey in the cellar of 9 Sheep Street, Feature A, as established by measurement (see Figs 15 & 21). This is possibly the remains of either the Synagogue Wall or the adjacent Jewish House.

318

Fig 11: Sheep Street looking north-west, showing the Fish Market, left, and 5 7 and 9 Sheep Street, with The Bear, with its timbered frontage, to the right (photo: M Roberts)

The geophysical survey

The geophysical survey was conducted and reported on by Caroline Sturdy Colls of the Department of Archaeology and Antiquity of the University of Birmingham, mainly using ground penetrating radar (GPR), with a potential search depth of 4m (Fig 13). A measured survey was also undertaken.

While the search areas were in some cases restricted, good results were obtained, though it is impossible to exclude some of the results as potentially false results, as machine artefacts, without further verification by excavation, or a complimentary GPR search following a different search pattern.

Results were found in both 7 and 9 Sheep Street. The search at 7 Sheep Street was both at cellar level (two separate cellar rooms 1 and 2 at the front of the property) and conducted at ground level (at the rear of the property). The search at 9 Sheep Street was conducted entirely in the cellar area, and it was here that the most potentially substantial finds were identified (Figs 14 & 15).

No.7 Sheep Street, Geophysical Survey Results

Cellar 1, to rear of cellar 2

All of the anomalies (Fig 16) probably relate to the above ground features in both of the cellar rooms or uniden-

tifiable areas of general disturbance. There is a notable change of context at a depth of 1.5m though, suggesting an earlier ground level/surface.

Cellar 2, street frontage

The majority of features in this cellar represent irregular areas of slightly elevated dielectric value, thus they are likely to represent areas of mixed disturbance as opposed to significant buried features, such as walls (Figs 17 & 18).

Feature F is visible at a depth of 1.63m across the extent of the survey width. By 2.11m it is still visible but is approximately half its original size. This feature is extremely narrow.

Feature H is visible between 3.06m and 3.44m and represents a circular anomaly. Feature J lies adjacent to it and is similar in nature but is only visible at 3.44m. As these two features lie at the extreme end of the GPR depth range, they are not clearly shown on the section slices, thus making it difficult to define their extent and nature

Ground floor room, to rear of cellar 1

From the schematic summary of the results, several features can be identified (Fig 19). The results without interpretation are also shown (Fig 20).

A: Recto-linear feature, measuring approximately 2m wide by 0.5m long, visible from 0.0m-3.3m, with

319

Fig 12: Possible Remains of Synagogue Wall (or Adjacent Jewish House) in the Cellars of the Bear Inn (photo: M Roberts)

Fig 13: Caroline Sturdy Colls, on right, with assistant, in the cellars of 7 Sheep Street during the GPR survey
(Photo: M Roberts)

high dielectric value, consistent with coal chute down to cellar.

B: A considerable area of disturbance running the full extent of the north side of the survey area. This is possible evidence of a robbed out wall of the medieval synagogue.

D and E: become visible within area B between depths of 1.49–2.03m.

No. 9 Sheep Street (Kebabish), Cellar 3

The GPR survey in the cellar of 9 Sheep Street produced several anomalies (A-F), as described and discussed below.

A: A roughly rectangular feature measuring c.2m by 2m, present from 0.0m to 3.47m (extent of survey depth).

B: Linear feature running the full length of the survey area c.0.75m wide. Present from 0.0m to 3.47m (extent of survey depth). Lies adjacent to feature C. May repre-

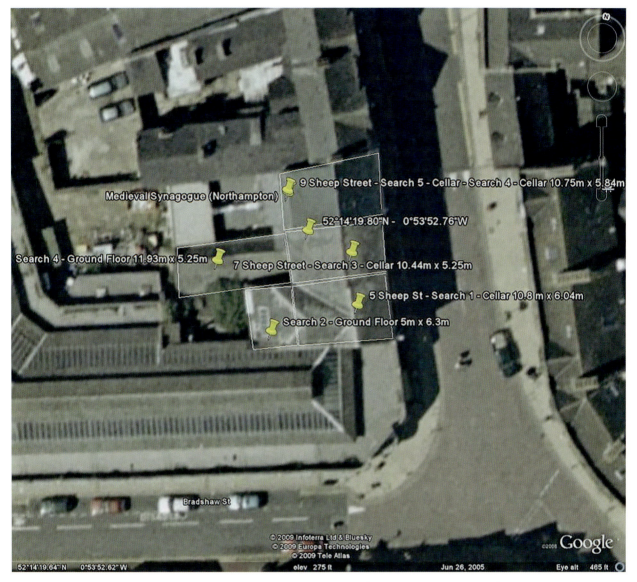

Fig 14: Sheep Street: proposed Survey areas (5 Sheep Street was not surveyed)

sent a false reading caused by machine operating difficulties or a sewer/masonry feature.

C: Linear feature running the full length of the survey area c.0.75m wide. Present from 0.0m to 3.47m (extent of survey depth) but is not as well defined as feature B, to which it lies adjacent. May represent a false reading caused by machine operating difficulties or a sewer/masonry feature.

D: Recto-linear feature, c.2m long and 0.75m wide; visible within area B from 1.49–2.03m, high dielectric value (Fig 22)

E: Recto-linear feature, c1m long and 0.75m wide, visible within area B from 1.79–1.85m, high dielectric value but has small round area of low dielectric value in the centre (Fig 23).

In section, it appears that feature D post-dates the current ground surface (beneath the concrete floor), as disturbance can be seen above it (Fig 22, ---1). Additionally, this feature has been disturbed by a later feature, possibly a bore-hole (Fig 22, ---2). Given its proximity to the drain-pipe of the current building, it is likely that this feature is connected with the drainage system of the property. This is also likely to be the case for feature E (see below).

Discussion

The historical survey indicates that the former Fish Market and the area to the immediate north and south, is almost certainly the site of the medieval Jewry of Northampton, which in its time was among the most important in England and was home to a community who were directly

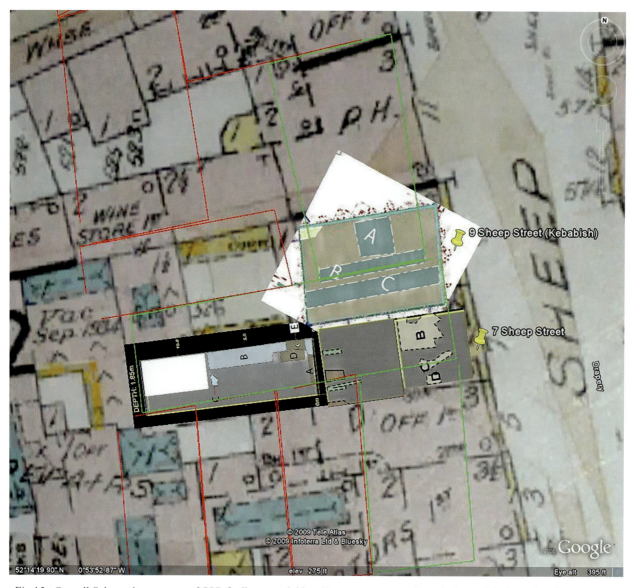

Fig 15: Overall Schematic summary of GPR findings overlaid on Parmentry property boundaries and the late Victorian Insurance Map (Gough *c*.1890)

engaged in the economic activities and growth of the town, and which also contained an important group of Jewish scholars and rabbis at a Talmudic academy, until the untimely General Expulsion of the Jews from England in 1290.

There is good justification to assert that the area around the old Fish Market is the site of the medieval Jewry and that just to the north of the Fish Market, around 5–9 Sheep Street, is the site of the medieval synagogue of the Jews of Northampton, or the Talmudic Academy, which would also have functioned both as a synagogue and a place of learning.

The historical survey also indicates that the unique architecture of the medieval English and Franco-German synagogue, with synagogues sunken into the ground, means that the survival of substantial remains of such buildings are likely to remain *in situ*, except where there are later deep cellars. Also, the cellars of the massively built stone Norman first floor halls, with undercrofts,

favoured by the medieval Jews, are also likely to survive in part, in areas without excessive disturbance.

The hypothesis that the area just to the north of the Fish Market would potentially yield substantial sub-surface remains, was tested, using state of the art Ground Penetrating Radar and 3D software. The GPR survey has appeared to have validated the hypothesis, with a range of findings at both cellar and sub-cellar level, including the finding of what appear to be very substantial sub-cellar remains of thick masonry walls and perhaps an entry stair, extending as much as 4m (nearly 14 feet) below the cellar floor level and which could continue well beyond the survey area.

The identification of what appears to be a directly adjacent massive medieval wall in the cellar of the Bear, which could be part of the rectangular (stair/entry?) structure noted at 9 Sheep Street, tends to support the GPR finds. This section of wall may have been in excess of 2m thick, and now has a later stairway entry intruded into part

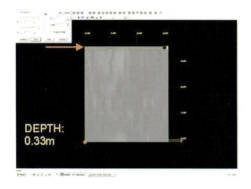

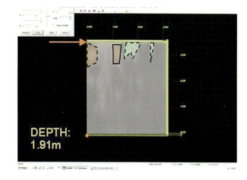

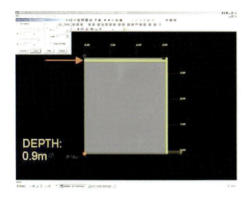

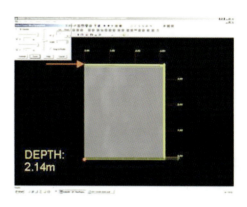

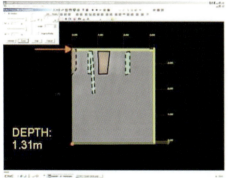

No other disturbances were noted in plan, down to a depth of 3.5m

Start of survey and direction of traverses

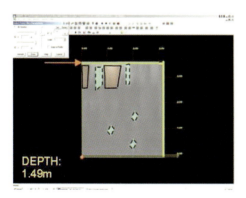

Fig 16: GPR survey results for 7 Sheep Street, cellar 1 (N to right)

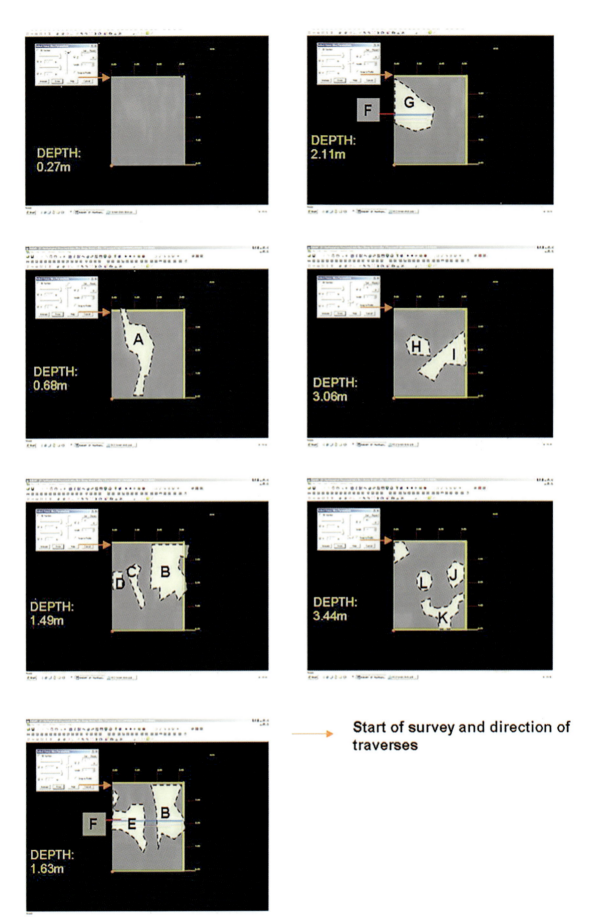

Fig 17: GPR survey results for 7 Sheep Street, cellar 2, street frontage, with interpretation (N to right)

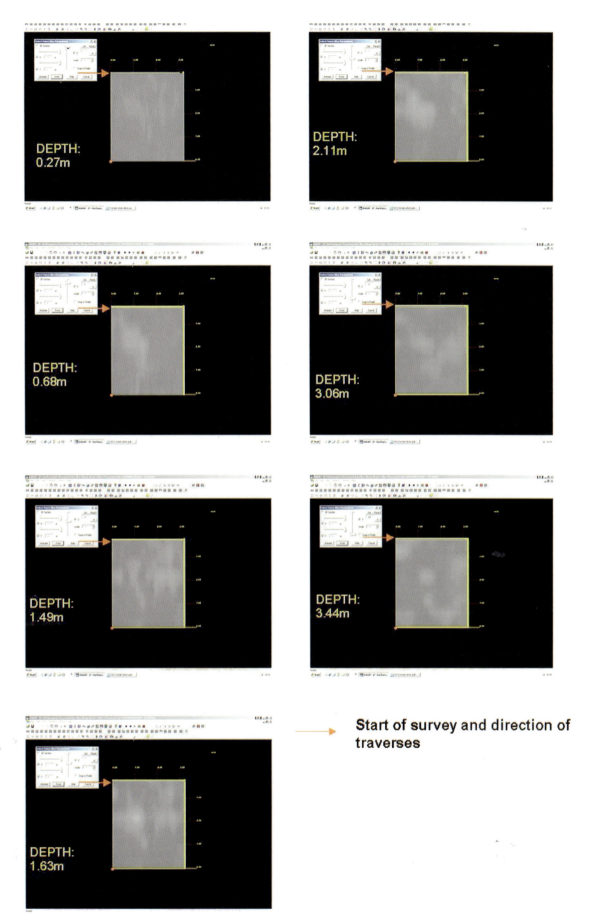

Fig 18: GPR survey results, without interpretation, for 7 Sheep Street, cellar 2: (N to right)

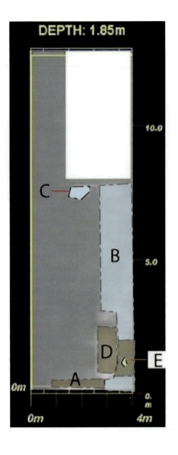

Fig 19: Schematic diagram of GPR results from
7 Sheep Street, rear ground floor (N to right)

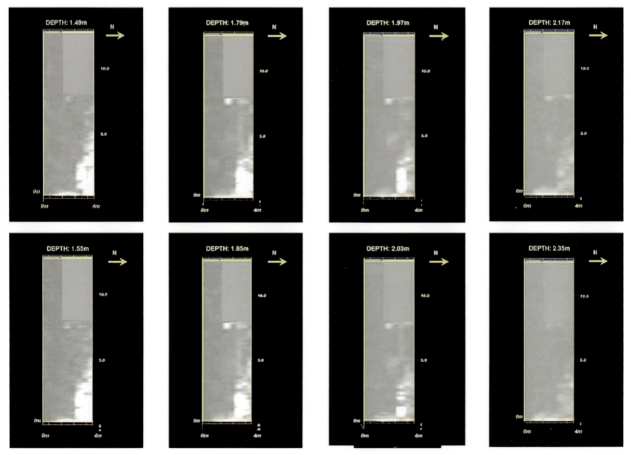

Fig 20: Results of GPR survey from the rear ground floor of 7 Sheep Street

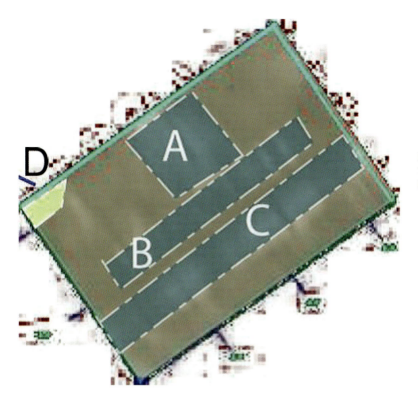

Fig 21: Schematic results of GPR survey from cellar of 9 Sheep Street, showing probable remains of Synagogue

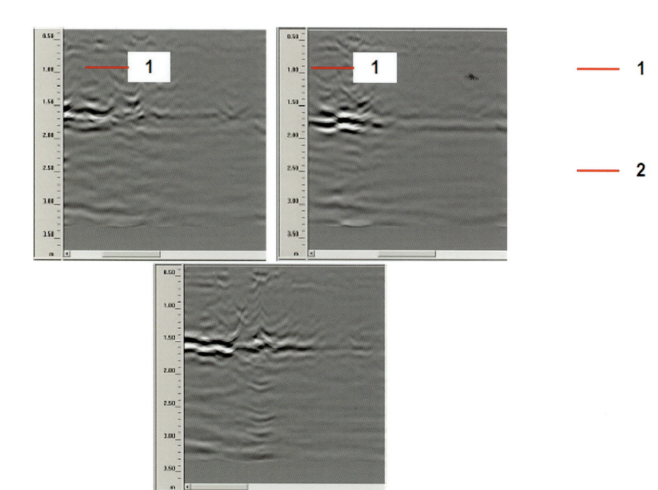

Fig 22: Section showing areas of disturbance relating to feature D, 9 Sheep Street

of it. It seems to be built of a rough type of rag-stone and is clearly discontinuous with the other later stone vaults of the cellars. This might even be a visible section of the synagogue wall, or an adjacent Jewish house.

Of course, it is impossible without further work to eliminate either the possibility of substantial false readings from the radar unit, or that there is some other unaccounted structure to explain the readings, such as a deep sewer not on the borough records. However, these remains as they present themselves seem less likely to

be a survey artefact or domestic sanitary subterranean feature, not least due to their massive size and depth and linked visible archaeology.

If this building were excavated, it may well reveal a significant portion of the medieval synagogue, or Jewish house of learning, which would be a find of both national and inter-national significance. There are only two sites in the UK, which may contain the remains of medieval synagogues, the Upper Room at Jew's Court, Lincoln (Fig 25), which is possibly, but not probably, a medieval

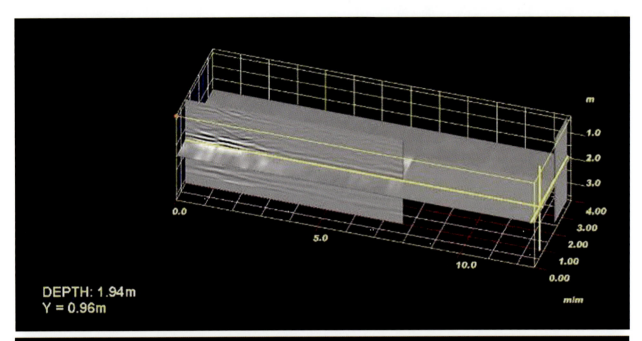

DEPTH: 1.94m
Y = 0.96m

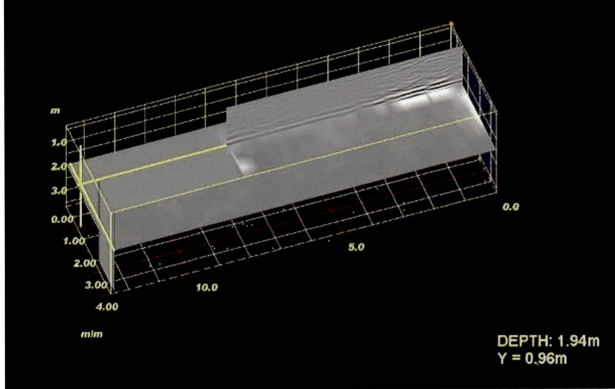

DEPTH: 1.94m
Y = 0.96m

Figure 23 a & b: Three dimensional projections of features D and E at 9 Sheep Street

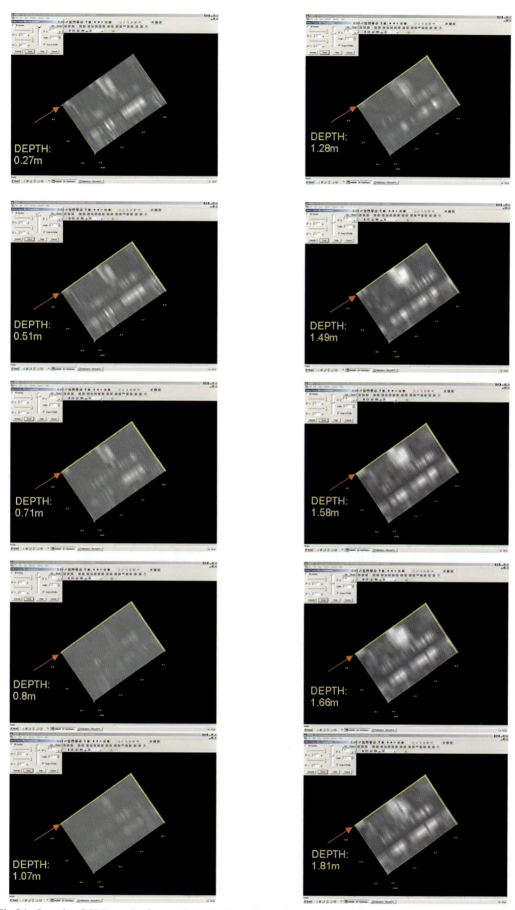

Fig 24: Sample of GPR results from cellar of 9 Sheep Street (Kababish) (original screen-shots, not high-lighted)

synagogue, and the preserved subterranean remains of a probable private synagogue, found at the rear of the High Street at Guildford (now Waterstones) (Fig 26).

In Europe, there are only a small number of remains of such medieval synagogues, including the excavated and preserved House of Study in Rouen, France (Fig 27).

There is also the possibility that the remains of a medieval Jewish ritual bath (*mikveh*) could be found in the area. The *mikvaot*, in the German style, were often substan-

tial Romanesque masonry structures, with galleries and antechambers, descending to a well-chamber, containing a spring of 'living water', at very substantial depths (Fig 28). It is also not beyond question that the structures seen at 9 Sheep Street, might even be the galleried entry to a *mikveh* (which would explain the double wall), as they were quite often combined with a synagogue.

The only confirmed examples of medieval Jewish ritual baths known in England are: Jacob's Well, Bristol and

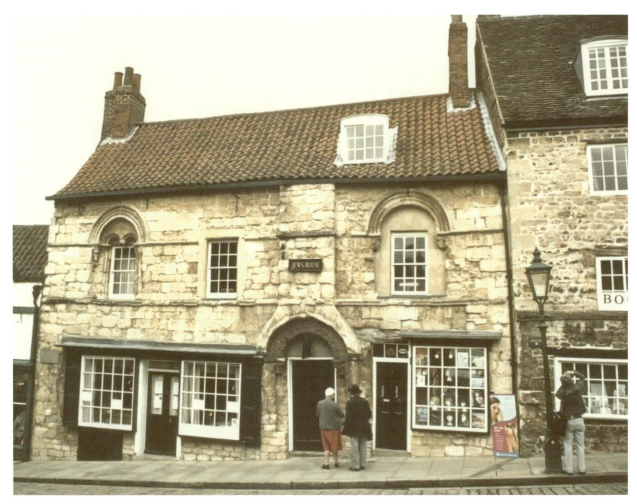

Fig 25: The 'Jew's House' in Lincoln: a Jewish Norman first-floor hall, typical of those built for leading members of the Jewish community. Next door is Jew's Court with its upper room asserted by Roth to be a synagogue (Photo: M Roberts)

Fig 26: Panorama of the synagogue chamber at Guildford, during excavation, showing distinctive use of sedilia and columns (Photo: John Boas, Guildford Museum)

the Milk Street *Mikveh* in the City of London (Fig 29). There are other possible examples at Gresham Street, also in the City, and more recently in the centre of Dunstable, Bedfordshire, excavated by Joe Abrams for Compass Archaeology (Fig 30). Only a small number of medieval *mikvehs* are known in Europe.

The other search areas at Sheep Street also yielded results of interest, including a possible area of robbed-out wall, or a medieval entry at the rear of 7 Sheep Street, which could link to the potential walls at No. 9.

The entirety of the area is of importance, as it is likely to reveal at least some evidence of the rest of the Jewry and it would be the first time that a large area of a single medieval Anglo-Jewry would have been exposed by development. Of course, the GPR work can only indicate larger features and cannot indicate the possible quantity of other smaller archaeological material and artefacts that are likely to be found. Certain classes of artefact (Pepper 1991) have been found to correlate with Jewish areas, which would provide additional evidence as to its prove-nance on any potential excavation.

This entire site would merit a high quality archaeological excavation, should the site be developed, and appro-priate conditions should be attached to the development. Furthermore, if development takes place, any significant remains on the site should at the least, be preserved *in situ*, and if needs be encapsulated by the development, to preserve the remains for the future.

However, and perhaps the most preferable option, is that there is no reason why any significant building, or structure, could not be both excavated and preserved, and interpreted, with full public access, within the new development, and could become a significant visitor attraction in the town. The depth and position of the main potential finds area at the site of the proposed develop-ment make it possible that incorporation of significant finds into the new development could both be practical and cost effective.

On a personal note, I saw the destruction of large areas of Northampton heritage and archaeology during the

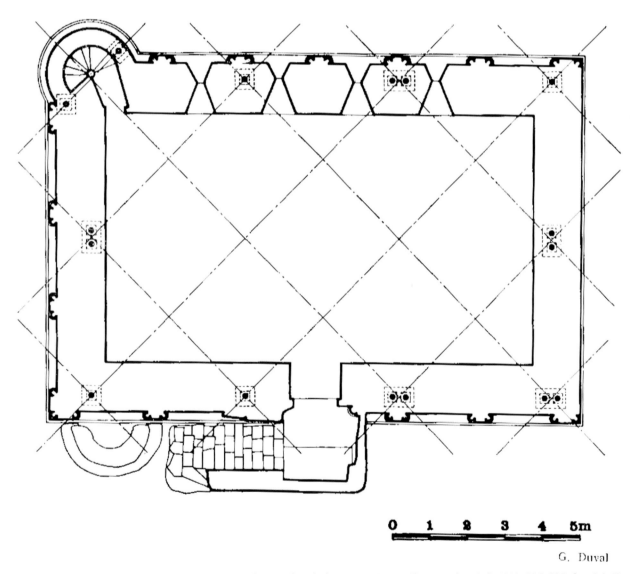

G. Duval

Fig 27: Ground plan of the medieval synagogue/house of study in Rouen, France (*from* E Privat (ed) 1980, 236–237, figs 6 & 7)

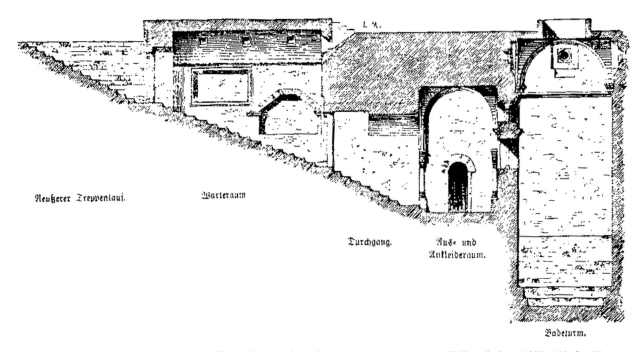

Neußerer Treppenlauf.   Warteraum

Durchgang.   Aus- und
Antleideraum.

Badeturm.

Fig 28: Speyer *Mikveh* in Germany, illustrating massive subterranean stone structures (R Krautheimer 1927, 149, fig 40)

Fig 29: London, Milk Street *Mikveh* (photo: M Roberts)

Fig 30: Possible *Mikveh* in Dunstable (photo: M Roberts)

broad brush developments in the 1970s, when much of the heritage and character of the town was swept away. It may be hoped, and urged, that on this occasion, both heritage and development can be managed, without injury to either, and the potential highly beneficial role of heritage in economic regeneration is recognised and used to advantage for all and that any new findings could enhance local civic pride.

Bibliography

Blair, I, and Watson, B, 2012 Milk Street Mikveh, *London Archaeol,* (13), 4, 109

Brown, J, 2008 Excavations at the corner of Kingswell Street and Woolmonger Street, Northampton, *Northamptonshire Archaeology*, 35, 173–214

Dodd, A, 2003 *Oxford Before the University: The Late Saxon and Norman Archaeology of the Thames Crossing, the Defences and the Town*, Thames Valley Landscapes Monog, **17**

Chapman, A, 2021 An Alternative topography for the medieval Jewry and synagogue, Northampton, *Northamptonshire Archaeol*, **41**, 349–359

Foard, G, 1995 The Early Topography of Northampton and its Suburbs, *Northamptonshire Archaeol*, **26**, 109–122

Hilaby, J, 1993 Beth Miqdash Me'at: The Synagogues of Medieval England, *J of Ecclesiastical Hist* , **44.2**, 182–198

Krautheimer, R, 1927 Mittelalterliche Synagogen, Berlin: Frankfurter Verlags-Anstalt

Lee, F, 1954 A New Theory of the Origins and Early Growth of Northampton, *Archaeol J*, **110**, 164—74

Pepper, G, 1991 An archaeology of the Jewry in medieval London, *London Archaeologist*, **07:01**

Privat, E, (ed) 1980 *Art et Archeologie des Juifs en France Medievale*, Toulouse

RCHME 1985 *An Inventory of the Historical Monuments in the County of Northampton, volume 5, An Inventory of Archaeological Sites and Churches in Northampton*, Royal Commission on Historical Monuments (England)

Roberts, M R, 1992 A Northampton Jewish Tombstone, *c*.1259 to 1290, recently rediscovered in Northampton Central Museum, *Medieval Archaeol*, **36**, Notes and News, 173–177

Roberts, M, forthcoming The cemetery of the medieval Jews of Northampton, *Northamptonshire Archaeol*, **42**

Upson-Smith, T, 2013 *Archaeological investigation and recording at the former Fishmarket and 5–7 Sheep Street, Northampton: January to April 2013,* Northamptonshire Archaeology report, **13/175**

Upson-Smith, T, Walker, C, and Holmes, M, 2021 Archaeological investigation at the former Fishmarket and 5–7 Sheep Street, Northampton, *Northamptonshire Archaeol*, **41**, 335–348

Northamptonshire Archaeology, **41**, 2021, 335–348

Archaeological investigation at the former Fish Market and 5–7 Sheep Street, Northampton

by

Tim Upson-Smith, Charlotte Walker and Mark Holmes

Summary

Northamptonshire Archaeology carried out archae-ological investigation and recording during the demolition of the former Fish Market and 5 & 7 Sheep Street, Northampton, prior to the construction of a new Bus Interchange. Remains of cellars on the Bradshaw Street frontage had been largely removed prior to the construction of the Fish Market in the late 1930s. Below the Fish Market three extant cellars were observed. A further cellar lay under the rear of 5 Sheep Street and there was a stone-lined well under the cellar floor of 7 Sheep Street. Both of these properties were demolished, with only the Sheep Street façades retained. No evidence for the Jewish Synagogue, which research has indicated probably stood close by, was observed, and the infor-mation gained demonstrated that medieval or earlier archaeology survived only in isolated areas between extensive disturbance from the construction of the cellars and walls of post-medieval and modern buildings. An area of intact deposits, including an ironstone wall, beneath 5 Sheep Street pre-dated the existing building and may have been of medieval to late medieval date. A test pit excavated on land to the north of Yard Lane revealed the remains of post-medieval buildings above a quarry pit of post-medieval or earlier date.

Introduction

Northamptonshire Archaeology, now MOLA (Museum of London Archaeology), was commissioned by Northampton Borough Council to undertake archaeolog-ical building recording at the former Fish Market and at 5 & 7 Sheep Street, Northampton. Following the granting of planning permission for the demolition of these build-ings, with only the façades of 5 & 7 Sheep Street being retained, there was a watching brief during the demolition works in early 2013, prior to the construction of a new Bus Interchange (NGR SP 7532 6064, Fig 1).

Building recording of the Fish Market and 3–5 Sheep Street had been carried out by NA in 2012, together with a trial trench at the northern end of the site, north of Alley Yard, to assess the survival of earlier deposits (Bassir *et al* 2012). The Yard in the northern angle of the Fish Market was the only other open area within the develop-ment where it might have been possible to excavate a trial trench, but at the time it was impossible to gain machine access to this area, which also then contained several temporary structures and other materials.

This plot of land is located within Northampton town centre, bounded by Sheep Street on the east, Silver Street to the west, Greyfriars to the north and Bradshaw Street to the south. The development sites comprised the former Fish Market, 5 and 7 Sheep Street, and to the north former public toilets and an underpass, and a small open area (Fig 2). Buildings occupying the north-east corner of the plot, which were to be retained, included 9 Sheep Street, the Kebabish takeaway, which has been identified as the probable site of the Jewish Synagogue (Roberts 2021, this volume, 305–333), The Bear public house, with the Oriental Garden takeaway at the northern end.

The site slopes slightly downwards from north to south and the modern ground surface lies at a height of *c.*78m aOD. The underlying geology is composed of Northampton Ironstone.

Acknowledgements

Northamptonshire Archaeology produced a full client report on all the building recording and the single trial trench (Bassir *et al* 2012), and an edited version of the building report on the Fish Market was published in 2015 (Bassir). They also produced a client report on the watching brief during the demolition works on the Fish Market and 5 & 7 Sheep Street (Upson-Smith 2013).

In order to complement the account of the identified site of the Jewry and the location of the synagogue (Roberts 2021, this volume, 305–333), relevant extracts from the reports prepared by Northamptonshire Archaeology have been brought together to catalogue the archaeolog-ical response, even though these works did not provide any evidence directly relevant to the buildings of the Northampton Jewry or to the synagogue itself. These results will be brought together with the work of Marcus Roberts in a third report that provides a brief overview of the evidence relating to the block that once included the medieval Jewry and synagogue (Chapman 2021, this volume, 349–359).

This report has been compiled by Andy Chapman, formerly of MOLA Northampton. It has been submitted to MOLA for approval, but any errors or omissions are his responsibility. The descriptive texts from the original reports have had only minor editing by Andy Chapman. Illustrations are by Amir Bassir with some additional labelling by Andy Chapman.

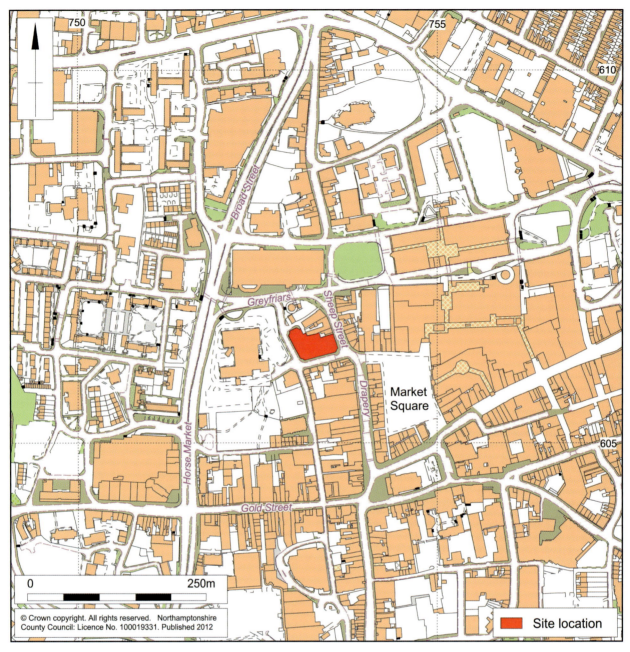

Fig 1: Site location

Historical background for 5 and 7 Sheep Street

by Charlotte Walker

The building at 5 Sheep Street formed the northern two bays of a larger, more imposing, building that had been mostly demolished in the late 1930s to make way for the Fish Market (Fig 3). A report on 5 Sheep Street by Giggins (2011) suggested that the building may have been built shortly after the Great Fire of Northampton in 1675, as the style of the remaining windows bore some resemblance, although less ornate, to those of the Sessions House, which was completed in 1678. Furthermore, it was noted that the central pediment of the original building was decorated with swags above the uppermost windows, and such devices are also replicated on the Sessions House, as well as a shop on the south side of the Market Square. However, this dating has not been proved and the building may date to the later 18th century.

However, there is no doubt that 5 Sheep Street once formed part of the Red Lion Inn. In 1752, the *messuage* at 7 Sheep Street was leased to Joseph Foulkes, a barber and peruke maker, by Robert Dickinson (Northampton Record Office (NRO): 1386/1). It states that *the south part adjoining an inn called the Red Lyon on the south*. The same document states that this *messuage* was to be henceforth known as The Windmill. In 1766 (NRO: 1386/3) it is described as:

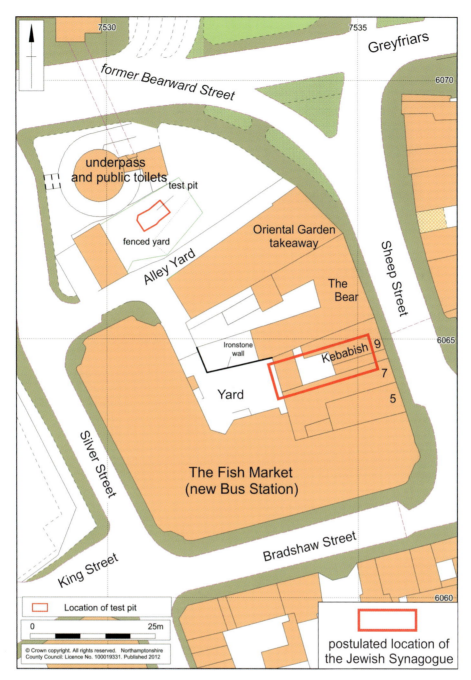

Fig 2: Location of the former Fish Market, 5 & 7 Sheep Street and the test pit

A messuage situate in...Sheep Street or Sheep Market divided from the north part of the messuage or tenement next adjoining and made a distinct dwelling house together with the little yard and necessary house therein lately taken in and laid to the messuage and divided from the yard or backside of the north part by a stone built wall of the height of the Chamber floor being a partition wall; the messuage to be conveyed being used as a public house called by different names and adjoining on the south to the Red Lion....

The plan of Northampton from the Great Election of 1768 shows that the western side of Sheep Street was occupied, from south to north, by Martin Lucas, Richard Foulkes and Thomas Dickinson. This indicates that the Red Lion occupied a large frontage from the corner of Bradshaw Street up to and including 5 Sheep Street. The Red Lion appears to have ceased trading by the end of the 18th century.

By 1788 deeds to the property specify that 7 Sheep Street was formerly a public house *known at different times by different signs* (NRO: ZB2050/19). In 1835, 7 Sheep Street was leased to Robert Page. In 1841, a conveyance states that *the said Robert Page hath lately pulled down the said messuage or tenement and on the site or ground plot thereof erected and built another messuage or tenement and buildings* (NRO: ZB 135/9).

Fig 3: Building 1, 3 and 5 Sheep Street, with No. 5 the north wing at the far right

There is a plan of 3 and 5 Sheep Street, which, though undated, appears to be late 19th century. The plan appears to show the buildings as a single property, however, there is no apparent access between the two. A later pencil line, labelled boundary line, appears to mark a boundary between the two. Part of the boundary wall between the two properties appears to have been the northern side of a corridor with a distinctive kink to bypass a stairway to the cellar. To the rear of the living room was a yard area with a scullery beyond. At the back of the scullery was a coach house with a cellar under, although this appears to have been accessed from No 3 only. There was an entrance to a walled garden from the north of the scullery. The eastern wall of the garden would have formed the boundary for 7 Sheep Street.

In 1885, 7 Sheep Street was sold to Arthur Shemeld, a draper and in 1886 he bought 5 Sheep Street (documents provided by Northampton Borough Council).

In 1889, 5 and 7 Sheep Street were sold to John Brice and Sons. By that date, 5 Sheep Street was still called '*formerly part and parcel of a messuage or Inn called the Red Lion*'. However, by this date No 7 was described as a building which '*had been erected and built many years ago on the site or some part of the site of the said Red Lion*', illustrating some confusion to its past. This error has persisted in later documents.

It seems, therefore, that the merging of the properties probably began during the late 19th century when the Shemelds were in occupation. It is understood that the buildings were remodelled as one shop in 1889, when still occupied by Arthur Shemeld (Welsh 2011). A 1937 plan of 5 Sheep Street shows alterations to be carried out as a result of the construction of the Fish Market. The new external south wall of the building was to be partly reinforced on the ground floor and the same wall on the upper floors was to be entirely rebuilt, with the result that two windows on the first floor would be lost. New roof lights were to be inserted to compensate for the loss of natural light. These results of these alterations were seen during the demolition works (see Fig 6).

There are no plans for 7 Sheep Street, so its early internal layout cannot be defined. Map evidence suggests that in the late 19th century the main building extended as far west as the rear of No 5 (Fig 4a). There was a small yard and to the rear a further small building. To the west of this lay the garden for No 5. This arrangement persisted until at least 1938 (Fig 4b).

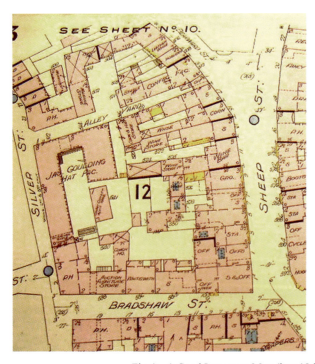

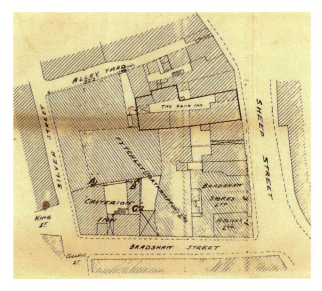

Fig 4: a) Goad Insurance Map (late 19th/early 20th century) b) pre-1930s layout

Recording and watching brief on 5 and 7 Sheep Street

by Tim Upson-Smith

The two bay, three storey façade of 5 Sheep Street was in stone which had been rendered, with modern retail glazed infill to the ground floor (Fig 5). At first floor level there were two sash windows, which had later one-over-one sashes inserted, the second floor retained its six-over-six sash windows with thin glazing bars. These windows had projecting plaster surrounds which extended down from the second floor to create panels above the windows on the first floor. The windows all had projecting keystones. There was a moulded architrave below the eaves.

The facade of 7 Sheep Street was separated from 5 by chamfered quoins. It was of two bays with six-over-six sash windows on the first and second floors. The ground floor, as in No 5, had been modernised with a glass retail unit front. Within the facade of 7 Sheep Street was an entrance to 9 Sheep Street (Fig 5, the white door), which opened into a covered passage, as depicted on the maps (Fig 4).

During the demolition of the rear of 5 Sheep Street, it became clear that the southern half of the facade had been rebuilt in red brick, with the windows provided with concrete lintels, when the adjoining Fish Market was constructed in 1938–9 (Fig 6).

Fig 5: The elevations of 5, 7 and 9 Sheep Street: top, with the entrance to the former Fish Market to the left; bottom, in 2021 with the new Bus Interchange, to the left, and the preserved facades of 5 and 7 with blind windows on the upper floors and restored shop fronts, centre (photo: A Chapman)

Fig 6: The internal facade of 5 Sheep Street, showing the rebuilt southern part (right), with concrete window lintels

7 Sheep Street, the basement

The basement of 7 Sheep Street was divided into four rooms and appeared to have been used as kitchens and food storage. The rooms were of brick and stone, painted and plastered in places. Some more modern brickwork could be seen in the dividing wall of rooms B1 and B4. There was a modern breeze-block wall to the right of the light well in room B2 (Fig 7). Two simple brick fireplaces (FP) were central to the south walls of rooms B2 and B3, with brick chimney flues ascending above. These were later altered to contain cast iron "close ranges" with enclosed ovens, a type that became popular in the late 19th-early 20th centuries. Shelving was inserted into the space between the walls and chimneys.

A light-well built into the west wall of room B2, would originally have been external to the structure. A brick and stone recess built into the east wall of room B3 may have served as a coal chute from outside. A low brick plinth in front of this recess had had a sink on top, which had been removed by the time of the second survey (Fig 7). Rooms B1 and B4 were plain, unfurnished rooms which showed evidence of a mid-level shelf running around the full length of three walls. These rooms were presumably used for storage.

A series of test pits and two footings holes for the temporary supporting works were excavated by hand in the basements of 7 Sheep Street. No archaeological deposits of significance were observed in the test pits. The two temporary footings holes measured 1.6m by 1.8m by c.0.6m deep. No archaeological deposits were observed in the hole in Room B3, with 19th-century fills overlying natural, which was partly exposed (Fig 7).

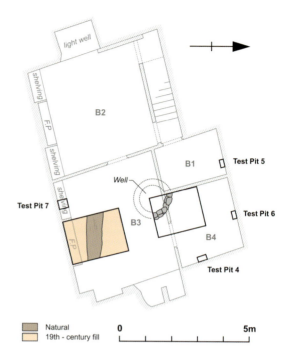

Fig 7: Plan of the basement at 7 Sheep Street

However, a well was exposed under the floors of Rooms B3/B4, once the dividing wall between these two rooms had been demolished (Figs 7 and 8). The well, which lay immediately below the brick floors, was sub-circular, c.0.7m in diameter, and cut through the natural sand and ironstone bedrock. The top of the well was stone-lined and the base was c.1.18m below the floor of the basement at 75.88m aOD. As the well lay under two of the basement walls, it is likely that that it pre-dated the construction of 7 Sheep Street.

5 and 7 Sheep Street, the ground floors

The main access to 5 and 7 Sheep Street was via Sheep Street, and the ground floors had undergone multiple

Fig 8: The well under the basement floor of 7 Sheep Street, looking south-west

Fig 9: Top of ironstone wall (behind ranging pole) exposed in room G1, 5 Sheep Street, with overlying stratified surfaces exposed in section, and continuing down beside the wall, looking west

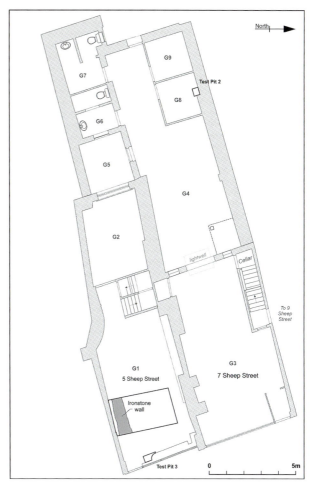

Fig 10: Ground Floor plan, 5 and 7 Sheep Street

phases of modification which had removed most original or early features and fabric. A 19th-century plan of No 5 showed a small shop opening onto Sheep Street with a parlour, store and living room beyond. By 1937 this had been opened up into a single office space with counters and desks. This lay within the room G1 which at the time of the survey measured c.4m by 10m and had modern fittings covering the earlier walls and a lowered, suspended ceiling (Fig 9).

Room G1, 5 Sheep Street

As part of the temporary works a test pit and a footings hole had been excavated through the floor of room G1, but no archaeological deposits were observed. However, the subsequent temporary works excavation revealed a sequence of surfaces overlying the base of an ironstone wall on an east-west alignment. The surviving top of the wall, which was exposed c.0.85m below the present floor level, was constructed in roughly coursed ironstone rubble (Figs 9 and 10). The wall was not related to the current building and is likely to have been an element of an earlier structure. It appeared to have been constructed in a trench which cut through adjacent layers. No dating evidence was recovered.

Rooms G2–G7, 5 & 7 Sheep Street

An arched doorway in the west wall of room G1 led through to room G2, which had been used recently for storage; it is marked as a manager's office on the plan of 1937 and a living room in the 19th century (Fig 10). A roll up security shutter in the west wall provided access to room G5–G7, which were then used as part of 7 Sheep Street. Room G5 was flooded and was suffering severe damp at the time of the survey. The ground floor of No 7 was also suffering from extensive damp problems and was in a state of dilapidation and disrepair. The main shop floor, G3, measured c.5m by 9.5m and provided access to the basement via a stair in the north-west corner of the room.

Room G4 to the west of room G3 was accessed via a square doorway flanked by rectangular windows. The brick lintel of a former doorway or window could be seen on the western face of this wall above the modern doorway. The lightwell to the basement rose to the first floor at this point, indicating that this wall may have originally been an external wall with a yard beyond. To the rear of room G4 were several smaller rooms which were used for toilets and stock storage. These rooms occupied the space of former outbuildings shown on early plans. A door at the westernmost end of room G4 led into the Fish Market yard. Room G7 is shown as a scullery on the 19th-century plan.

The cellars beneath the Fish Market

During the removal of the deep footings of the former Fish Market building four cellars were exposed which retained their barrel-vaulted ceilings. These cellars related to the former public house/hotel which formerly stood on the corner of Sheep Street and Bradshaw Street. The cellars had partially been filled with demolition rubble which is likely to have been sourced from the demolition of the building to make way for the new Fish Market. However, the demolition rubble had only filled the cellars around the former entrances, it could perhaps be imagined that somebody on the site during the construction of the Fish

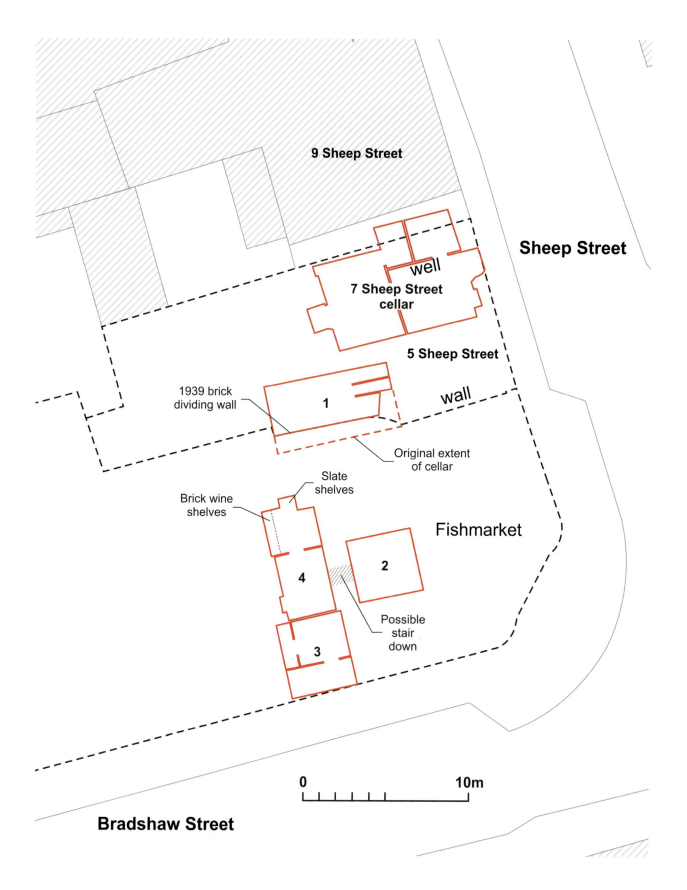

Fig 11: The cellars beneath the Fish Market and 5 and 7 Sheep Street, and the wall and well pre-dating the surviving buildings, with the medieval synagogue possibly on the site of 9 Sheep Street

342

Market had been given the task of filling in the old cellars, and this was achieved by emptying wheel barrow loads down the hole until it was full, which, of course, would leave a pile of rubble spreading out from the hole rising to a mound below the hole that gave the false impression that the cellar had been filled, whilst in reality only a small portion had been.

Cellars 1 and 2 were both at the depth that would be expected immediately below the floor of the ground floor rooms. However, Cellars 3 and 4 were located below these. Due to health and safety constraints it was not possible to gain full access to the cellars, but simple plans and a composite cross section were made with the aid of a laser distance measurer (Figs 11–12).

Cellar 1 was rectangular in plan, c.7.5m by 3.05m (Figs 11–13). The full width of the cellar was not revealed as a brick wall had been built down the length of the cellar, with a bricked-up doorway in it. The walls of the cellar were whitewashed sand/ironstone as was the barrel-vaulted ceiling. This cellar could be accessed via a ladder from 5 Sheep Street, and had seen use during the building's last incarnation as a shop. The brick wall down the length of the cellar was immediately below the outer wall of the Fish Market, so it is clear that the wall had acted as a foundation for the new building whilst allowing the bulk of the cellar under 5 Sheep Street, to continue in use. It became clear during the building recording and subsequent watching brief that the Fish Market building

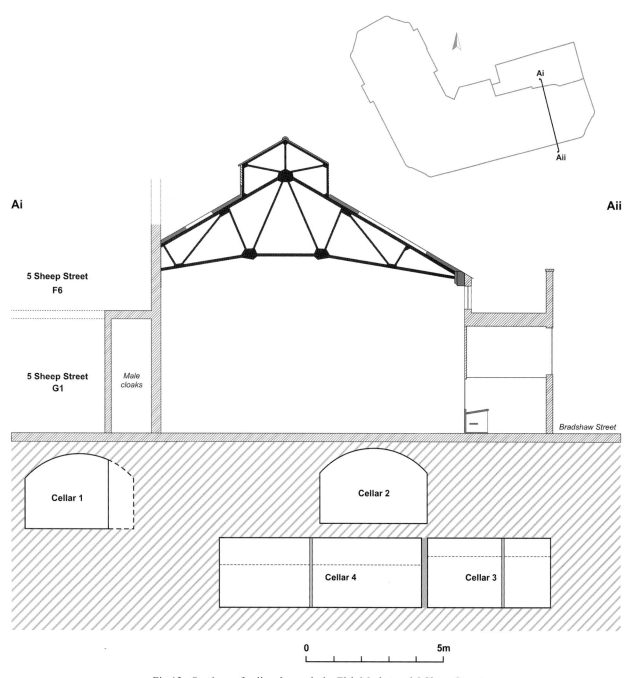

Fig 12: Sections of cellars beneath the Fish Market and 5 Sheep Street

encroached on the southern side of the footprint of 5 Sheep Street, resulting in the rebuilding of the southern gable and the southern part of the frontage.

Cellar 2 was almost square, measuring 3.90m by 3.92m (Figs 11 and 12). Again, the walls were stone as was part of the barrel-vaulted ceiling; however, the central part of the vault had been rebuilt in brick, perhaps suggesting a later repair. There was an opening in the southern wall, which may have had a stair leading down into Cellar 4 where there was a corresponding blocked opening.

Cellar 3 was again almost square, measuring 4.56m north-south by 4.08m (Figs 11 and 12). It was constructed in sandstone/ironstone with a vaulted ceiling. The cellar was split into three rooms by brick dividing walls.

Cellar 4 was rectangular in plan, measuring c.7.3m north-south by c.3.00m wide (Figs 11 and 12). It was constructed from sandstone/ironstone with a barrel vault. Like Cellar 3 it was subdivided into two rooms with a brick partition. Built into the western side were brick shelves for wine bottles (Figs 11 and 14), on the north wall there was a recess with slate shelves.

Some fragmentary walls were observed along the Bradshaw Street frontage which may have been elements of former cellars, although the footings of the Fish Market had made the identification of these walls very difficult.

The ironstone yard wall

An L-shaped length of ironstone and brick wall, c.4m in height, partially enclosing the rear garden of The Bear pub and facing the slope down to the Fish Market yard was also investigated, but was found to be of 19th-century origin (Figs 2 and 15).

Discussion

The investigation and recording during the demolition of the former Fish Market and 5 and 7 Sheep Street and the excavation of the footings for the new Bus Interchange, demonstrated that the site had been heavily disturbed by cellars, along with the air raid shelter under the western arm of the Fish Market, and no evidence was recovered relating to the Jewry or the synagogue, which research has indicated stood in this part of Northampton (Roberts 2021, this volume, 305–333).

The deeper cellars relate to the former hotel which stood on the corner of Sheep Street and Bradshaw Street, and they are likely to have continued in use during the later phases of the building's life prior to its demolition and the construction of the Fish Market in the late 1930s, when they were partially filled.

The cellars observed on the site may have given rise to the many tales of tunnels, as there did appear to be ways between them and entrances into them through holes in their ceilings, which may have been accessed down narrow stairs from the floors above, especially in the case of the deep cellars.

Fig 13: Cellar 1, looking east towards Sheep Street

Fig 14: Cellar 4, showing the brick shelves

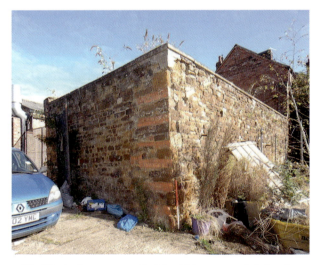

Fig 15: An ironstone wall of the 19th-century, defining the yard to the rear of The Bear

The test pit north of Alley Yard

by Mark Holmes

As part of the archaeological evaluation for the proposed Bus Interchange, a test pit evaluation was required in order to assess the potential of below ground archaeology. Due to the built-up nature of the area only one location was available, and consequently a single test pit was excavated within a fenced compound to the north of Alley Yard (Fig 2). The work was undertaken in October 2012. At the time the compound was used for storage, but it had formerly held machinery for crushing market waste. The concrete base and hard standing for that plant still remained and had to be broken prior to excavation commencing.

The broad aim was to determine the integrity and state of preservation of any archaeological features or deposits that might be present, and specifically to examine the possible survival of a late Saxon town ditch, which on the model first proposed by Alderman Lee and subsequently shown on modern interpretative plans of the pre-Conquest defences (see Williams *et al* 2021, this volume, 26, fig 1and Chapman 2021, this volume, 129–136), should lie between Bearward Street to the north-east and Silver Street to the south-west, at the presumed north-eastern corner of the late Saxon defensive circuit.

Due to the physical constraints of the area, only a test pit measuring roughly 3m by 6m could be excavated (Figs 16 and 17). After hand excavation and recording of the exposed post-medieval structures had been undertaken within a safe working depth, a deeper sondage was excavated by machine with observations and recording being carried out from the trench edge.

The stratigraphic sequence

A great depth of homogeneous soil, possibly infilling a feature such as a quarry pit, overlay the natural ironstone geology. The upper part of this deposit had been cut through by the foundations of a stone building. The building had been later altered with the addition of a brick built cellar and a further wall and yard surfaces before being demolished and the area levelled off (Figs 16–18).

Possible quarry pit

A layer of loose brown sandy clay (20) containing very frequent fragments of ironstone rubble was exposed to a depth of *c*.1.0m in the north-east corner of the trench. No pottery was found and the only dating evidence was a single piece of post-medieval bottle glass. The homogeneous nature of the soil may suggest that it represents quarry backfill. Excavation stopped when the machine bucket hit a hard layer, presumed to be the Ironstone natural. However, in the south-east corner of the sondage a band of light grey clay (21) was observed, but it was impossible to say whether this was redeposited natural clay within the fill or represented *in-situ* natural, possibly lias clay, and therefore the edge of the cut infilled by (20) (Fig 18).

Immediately above layer (20) there was a layer of orange-brown sandy loam with a mixed fill of limestone and sandstone fragments (12), *c*.0.35m thick, possibly

Fig 16: The test pit, looking south-west

former subsoil. It was into this layer that the stone foundations for a building had been cut.

The building

The foundations of a stone-built structure, aligned north-east to south-west, *c*.2.65m wide and in excess of 1.8m long, occupied the eastern half of the excavated area. The western wall foundations, 16, were constructed entirely of ironstone, comprising two rows of roughly faced ironstone blocks, *c*.0.55m wide, with traces of a loose orange sandy mortar. The foundations were *c*.0.55m deep, through layer (12), although no foundation cut was visible.

The southern wall foundation, 15, comprised ironstone blocks, some burnt, laid approximately three stones wide, to a width of *c*.0.78m, bonded with grey sandy clay. The ironstone blocks survived to a depth of 0.20m and sat on a foundation raft of flat ironstone and limestone rubble, 22, which stepped outwards a further 0.28m. Towards the junction with wall foundation 16, these rough foundations changed to more substantial blocks of ironstone, possibly indicating that this was an original return from wall 16 into which later wall 15 had been keyed-in. On top of the wall at its eastern end there was a partial line of surviving red bricks, which may represent the remains of the former upstanding wall.

The main eastern wall foundations lay beyond the edge of excavation but the wider limestone and ironstone rubble raft was visible giving the east-west extent of the structure and suggesting that the surviving walls were forming a room *c*.3m x 2m.

No floor levels survived within the building, but it contained a succession of layers. A possible brick-lined pit, 9, was seen in section in the north-west corner of the building, but lying beyond the trench. It contained layers of ash and charcoal (10).

A short distance to the north of the section edge, a further brick wall was exposed when material from the section fell away from it. How this wall relates to the rest of the building remains unclear but it may have formed the northern wall for the room or it may relate to pit, 9. A mixed layer of ironstone rubble (6) was contained within the structure and presumably represents backfilling of the demolished building.

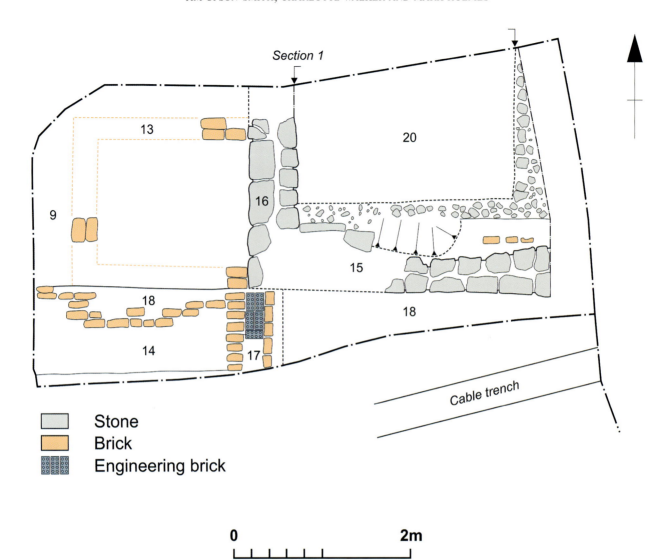

Fig 17: plan of excavated test pit

Later additions

Brick structure 13, 1.99m long by 1.82m wide, was added to the western end of the building. It was infilled with ironstone rubble, which was not removed. There was no obvious entrance and its small size, and the way it had been appended to wall 16, may suggest that it was not an integral structure, a cellar, but perhaps a coal-hole or similar. Brick wall 17 had been appended to the southern end of wall 16, continuing its line southwards.

Bounded by structure 13, to the north, and wall 17, to the south, was a yard surface of red bricks, 14, set edge on but not mortared, with many missing. A further patch of this surface was present to the north of wall 15, apparently overlying and therefore post-dating the destruction levels for the building. The yard surfaces sat upon mixed dark brown sandy clay (18), which may be earlier subsoil.

The whole site was overlain by a layer of brick and stone rubble (3) in which a cut, 2, containing layers of redeposited clay (4) and charcoal (5) had been made. This was in turn sealed by topsoil up to 0.45m deep which covered the site.

Conclusion

Perhaps unsurprisingly for a site in the centre of urban Northampton, the area examined by the test pit had been subject to attrition from a succession of buildings and structures which obscured or had removed earlier features.

The earliest feature was a deposit of ironstone rubble that may have been the fill of a quarry pit. Although the exact nature of the feature could not be ascertained, the homogeneity of the fill would seem to preclude it being the infilling of a feature such as the town ditch. The date of the deposit was not established due to the lack of pottery.

Perhaps of significance was the lack of pottery or other such material from the site in general. The few sherds found were 20th century in date and these came from only the upper levels, and were not retained. There was no residual medieval or other earlier material.

Similarly deep quarry pits, of medieval date, have been located c.75m to the south-west, north of the frontage onto King Street and under the swimming pool at the south-east corner of the hotel complex (Chapman 2001).

Section 1

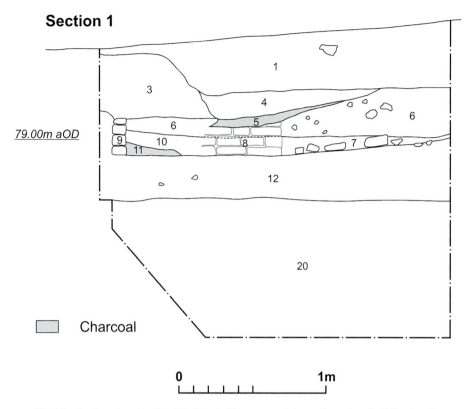

79.00m aOD

☐ Charcoal

0   1m

Fig 18: Section showing the fill of probable quarry pit beneath modern building levels

Fig 19: Possible quarry backfill (20) beneath modern building foundations, looking north-east

Historic maps of the site from 1901 and earlier show that the test pit was located in the backage of buildings fronting on to the former Bearward Street (Fig 2). It is possible that the stone building located in the trench was the western end of one of these buildings, with an open courtyard behind. By 1925 the courtyard appears to have been built over and it is possible that the later brick additions relate to this period. By 1964, the buildings had been demolished and the brick surfaces may be related to a return to an open yard across this area.

Bibliography

Bassir, A, Upson-Smith, T, Holmes, M, and Walker, C, 2012 _Building Recording of the former Fishmarket and 5 & 7 Sheep Street, Northampton, and archaeological evaluation of land at the Northampton Bus Interchange_, Northamptonshire Archaeology report, **12/181**

Bassir, A, 2015 The Fishmarket and Greyfriars Bus Station, Northampton, _Northamptonshire Archaeol_, **38**, _195–219_

Chapman, A, 2001 Excavation at the Moat House Hotel, Northampton, 1998, _Northamptonshire Archaeol_, **29**, 93–101

Chapman, A, 2021 The late Saxon town defences at Green Street, Northampton: a review of the evidence and a radio-carbon date, _Northamptonshire Archaeol_, **41**, _129–136_

Chapman, A, 2021 An alternative topography for the medieval Jewry, Northampton, _Northamptonshire Archaeol_, **41**, _349–359_

Giggins, B, 2011 _5 Sheep Street, Northampton: Historic Building Assessment_

Roberts, M, 2021 The Topography and Archaeology of the Medieval Synagogue and Jewry, Northampton, _Northamptonshire Archaeol_, **41**, 305–333

Upson-Smith, T, 2013 *Archaeological investigation and recording at the former Fishmarket and 5–7 Sheep Street, Northampton: January to April 2013,* Northamptonshire Archaeology report, **13/175**

Welsh, T, 2011 *Document search: The Fish Market as a new bus station,* unpublished document

Williams, J H, Shaw, M, and Chapman, A, 2021 Anglo-Saxon Northampton Revisited, *Northamptonshire Archaeol,* **41,** 25–77

Northamptonshire Archaeology, **41**, 2021, 349–359

An alternative topography for the medieval Jewry, Northampton

by

Andy Chapman

Summary

Marcus Roberts has provided a sound analysis of the documentary evidence to conclude that the medieval Jewry and synagogue at Northampton occupied a block of land between Sheep Street and Silver Street, to the north of Bearward Street, and immediately north-west of the medieval market place. His more detailed analysis by map regression in attempting to locate the probable site of the synagogue was based on a number of assumptions, in particular that the Marcus Pierce map of 1632 was based on a lost map, pre-dating Speed's map of 1610, that recorded a medieval street pattern different in some significant details from all later maps from 1610 onward. The present author was unhappy with a number of the assumptions made and has reworked the map regression based on accepting Speed's map of 1610 and later maps as recording a street pattern that had not changed substantial from the medieval period. The alternative map regression has, however, produced a very similar result: again indicating that the synagogue probably stood on land now occupied by 7 and 9 Sheep Street, but the different set of assumptions indicate that it probably occupied both of these properties and was, therefore, probably substantially larger than indicated in the analysis by Marcus Roberts. The alternative map regression also indicates that the buildings of the Jewry occupied the eastern half of the block between Sheep Street and College Street, with the western half, now occupied by the Bus Interchange, probably largely open ground contemporary with the existence of the Jewry through to the Expulsion of the Jews from England in 1290. The archaeological evidence from the watching brief during the demolition of the Fish Market in 2012 is also summarised and related to the evidence produced by Marcus Roberts on the location of the Jewry and synagogue to bring all relevant evidence together in one document.

Introduction

Primary medieval documentary evidence, mainly property rentals, as analysed by Marcus Roberts (2021 this volume, 305–333), leaves no doubt that the medieval Jewry in Northampton was located to the north-west of the market place, in close vicinity to the later Red Lyon Inn, which appears on the Noble and Butlin map of 1746 on the northern corner of Sheep Street and Bradshaw Street, subsequently the eastern end of the former Fish Market, and now the Bus Interchange (Fig 1: NGR SP 7534 6064).

Having established the general location of the Jewry between Sheep Street and Silver Street, Roberts has taken the analysis a stage further by attempting to locate the synagogue and the houses of various named individuals. Unfortunately, while the town rentals do provide a wealth of information about Jewish property holders and those who later held these properties following the Expulsion of the Jews from England in 1290, the attempt to establish precise locations for individual buildings is fraught with difficulties. This was noted by John H Williams (2014, 167) in his study of the medieval rentals, where "there is…a measure of topographical system in the rental", making it possible to establish likely routes of progression around the town. However, "the rental cannot be used to map late thirteenth century Northampton property by property", as the listed sequences are not necessarily consecutive and, in particular, in not knowing "what properties are not actually listed".

In some cases identifying individual properties can be achieved with a degree of certainty. This is true for the building with the fine front (*Bello Fronte*) as the last house on the northern side of Bearward Street at its junction with Sheep Street. This was probably the fine stone house occupied by Pictavinus son of Sampson (Roberts 2021, this volume 312–313, fig 6). This building was the final entry in the Rental of Edward II for the north quarter, and the progress along Bearward Street was also identified by John Williams as ending at this street junction (Williams 2014, fig 9.1, route V, and 192, V7).

The analysis by Marcus Roberts was carried out before the demolition of the Fish Market in 2012, and in his conclusions he expressed the hope that his work would draw attention to the importance of this block of land in terms of the Jewry and the synagogue, so that any opportunity to obtain supporting archaeological evidence would be taken.

However, while Northamptonshire Archaeology, now MOLA (Museum of London Archaeology), was commissioned by the Borough Council to carry out building recording on the Fish Market (Bassir 2015), in relation to the demolition of the building they were only commissioned to carry out a watching brief during the demolition works. In those circumstances, with the use of heavy machinery for site clearance, opportunities to

Fig 1: Map showing the former Fish Market and the postulated location of the synagogue
(after Upson Smith this volume, fig 3)

make significant archaeological discoveries are inevitably constrained and limited. The discoveries that were made (Upson-Smith *et al*, 2013 and this volume 335–348), will be discussed below and will be related to the analysis by Marcus Roberts and the results of the Ground Penetrating Radar survey, to bring all the available evidence together.

Acknowledgments

As has already been made clear above, this report is totally dependent on the work of others and only exists because of that previous work. This applies particularly to Marcus

Roberts in his analysis of the location of the Jewry and the synagogue, as presented in this volume, as well as his broader work through Jtrails in promoting an understanding of the existence, as well as the location, of the Northampton Jewry, and also the Jewish cemetery, which lay outside the medieval town, which we hope will be subject of a report in a future volume of *Northamptonshire Archaeology*.

The intention is not to be critical of his analysis, but to indicate that even if the assumptions on which it was based are revised, and it is instead assumed that there had been no significant relocation of roads in this area, the alternative map regression has placed the building he identified as the possible synagogue in the same broad location, supporting, and I would hope, strengthening his general thesis.

In addition, this document is also dependent on work carried out by the staff of Northamptonshire Archaeology through building recording, compiling the historical background, and in the limited fieldwork that was possible during the demolition of the Fish Market, as also reported in this volume.

The other purpose of this paper is to bring together strands from both of the previous papers in a single summary that defines what has been lost and what still exists, and in doing so to set the parameters for future work in this area should the remaining properties along the west side of Sheep Street come up for development and provide an opportunity to further explore the site of the medieval Jewry. In particular is the contention that remains of the synagogue may survive even below cellar level, when the presence of cellars on urban sites in Northampton is more usually indicative of the total loss of all earlier deposits and structures, with the cellar floor within truncated natural.

The Marcus Pierce map of 1632 and its reliability

The identification of the *Bello Fronte* at the junction of Bearward Street and Sheep Street, as mentioned above, is an exception due to it falling at the very end of a section of the rental. In his attempt to map at least some of the major properties of the Jewry, and in particular the site of the synagogue, Marcus Roberts turned to the Marcus Pierce map of 1632, which shows the area of the former Jewry and its immediate vicinity in spectacular detail, house by house in three dimensions. This is to assume, of course, that this was meant as at least a schematic representation of the actual buildings that stood there. As described below, comparison with the Speed map of 1610 does provide support for this assumption.

However, the difficulty is that the overall mapped topography on the Marcus Pierce map differs in significant details from Speed's map of 1610, which does tally with later maps of the 18th and 19th centuries. These other sources all show the pattern of double parallel streets that have been interpreted as intra- and extra-mural streets flanking the former defences of the late Saxon town. The street pattern began to the north of Northampton Castle and continued eastwards before turning south (Fig 2). It was first cited by Alderman Lee as a potential fossilisation of the line of the late Saxon town defences (Lee 1954). While there has not been an opportunity to carry out controlled modern archaeological excavation within the double street system to confirm this theory, it is still the favoured archaeological model (Williams *et al* 2021, this volume 25–77). The only excavated length of the early defences lay to the south of the castle at Green Street (Chapman 1999 and Chapman 2021, this volume 129–136).

In the area of the Jewry the double street pattern, as depicted by Speed and later maps, comprised Silver Street forming the north-eastern corner of the intra-mural street, with College Street to the south, while the extra-mural street pattern was Bearward Street forming the outer north-eastern corner and continuing southwards as Sheep Street and the Drapery (Figs 1 & 3). Unfortunately, this north-eastern corner of the double street pattern was largely obliterated in redevelopment through the 1960s and 70s.

In contrast to the parallel streets shown by Speed (Fig 3, left) the Marcus Pierce map shows Silver Street continuing northwards to meet Bearward Street (Fig 3, right). In addition, the block occupied by the buildings of the Jewry appears to be about half the width of the comparable block of land as it appears on later maps. Marcus Roberts has argued that differences between Speed's map of 1610 and the Marcus Pierce map of 1632, can be accounted for by the latter map being based on an earlier lost Elizabethan map, showing a medieval street pattern pre-dating Speed, with medieval College Street lying to the east of where it appears from 1610 onward, halving the width of the plot. It was argued that the street was physically relocated westwards to its modern position, onto land that had formed part of the Dominican Friary until the Reformation under Henry VIII in the 16th century.

However, if the depiction of properties on the maps of both Speed and Pierce are compared, then there is a close consistency between the two maps to the immediate north of the Bradshaw Street. The Pierce map shows four properties end-on to Bradshaw Street, with a large property to the north end-on to Sheep Street, which Roberts has postulated to be the synagogue (Fig 3, right). But this same pattern with buildings end-on to Bradshaw Street and a building to the north end-on to Sheep Street is also shown by Speed (Fig 3, left). The only difference is that the buildings end-on to Bradshaw Street span the entire width of the plot on Speed, while the building to the immediate north and others continuing northwards, span only the eastern half of the plot, with the western half largely open to the frontage.

We must also note that Pierce shows the walled precinct of the Dominican Friary to the west of Silver Street, with a substantial building on the corner of Kings Head Lane (King Street) and Silver Street, while both maps show a building facing onto the southern end of Silver Street, potentially the same building, while the gatehouse to the Dominican Friary faces onto the Kings Head Lane further to the west, as depicted by Speed.

If the building facing onto the southern end of Silver Street is the same building on both maps, it would suggest that that there was no westward relocation of Silver Street (and also College Street to the south) but that in this area of the town the detailed topography of the Pierce map is in error.

What is missing from the Pierce map is the western half of the plot facing onto Silver Street, which is recorded as largely undeveloped in 1610 on Speed's map.

This pattern of a densely occupied frontage to the east while the western half of this block is largely open ground is also shown on the Noble and Butlin map of 1746 (Fig 4b), although by then the western frontage had been developed, but with open ground behind. On the eastern half of the plot, the south-eastern corner, previously comprising houses end-on to Bradshaw Street was the Red Lyon Inn. To the north, the Noble and Butlin map

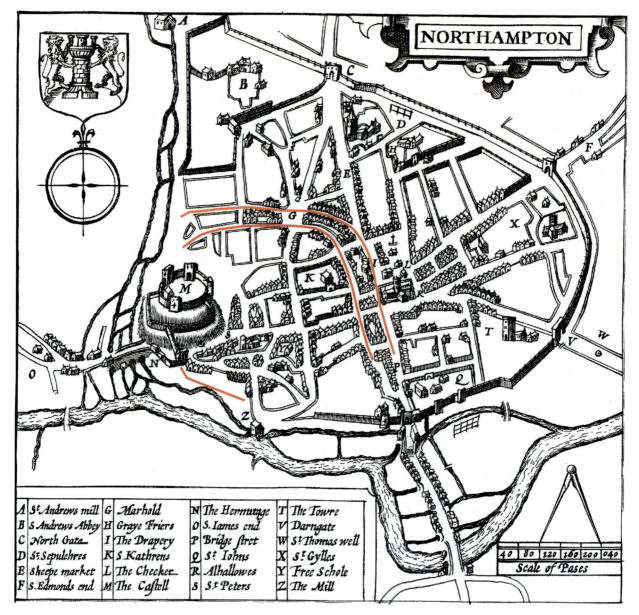

A	S.t Andrews mill	G	Marhold	N	The Hermitage	T	The Towre
B	S Andrews Abbey	H	Graye Friers	O	S. Iames end	V	Darngate
C	North Gate	I	The Drapery	P	Bridge stret	W	S.t Thomas well
D	S.t Sepulchres	K	S Kathrens	Q	S.t Iohns	X	S.t Gylles
E	Sheepe market	L	The Checker	R	Alhallowes	Y	Free Schole
F	S. Edmonds end	M	The Castell	S	S.t Peters	Z	The Mill

Fig 2: John Speed's map of 1610 showing the double street pattern (in red) assumed to define the extent of the late Saxon defences, and the excavated defences at Green Street, south of the castle

also shows a back lane behind the properties that would comprise the area once occupied by the synagogue and related buildings fronting onto Sheep Street. The northern end of this back lane was to survive all the way through to the modern topography, appearing in the 19th century running southwards from Alley Yard (Fig 4c). It was still present following the building of the Fish Market in the late 1930s, when it continued to provide access from Alley Yard to the yards of the buildings fronting onto the northern end of Sheep Street and also to the yard in the angle of the L-shaped Fish Market (Fig 1).

Could this be the lost lane called Fleshmonger's End, referred to by Roberts (this volume, 312), forming a back lane behind the buildings of the Jewry and separating it from the then largely open land on the western half of the plot? It would once have run all the way down to Bradshaw Street, separating the Red Lyon Inn from properties on

the western half of the plot up to Silver Street, with the former course of the lane denoted by the continuous line of property boundaries that continued southwards from the southern end of the extant lane, as clearly shown in the 19th century, to Bradshaw Street (Fig 4c). Later a garage fronting onto Silver Street broke across this boundary by absorbing the full width of the lane into the new property, as shown on the Insurance Maps of the late 19th/early 20th centuries (Fig 6, from Roberts this volume, fig 9).

Having considered the potential realignment of Silver Street/College Street, we must consider another assumption made by Marcus Roberts, the supposed southward relocation of Bradshaw Lane. From the documentary evidence, where the location of various properties are given in relation to the Red Lyon Inn and Bradshaw Lane, it was argued that apparent contradictions of location could be explained if Bradshaw Lane had once lain to the

352

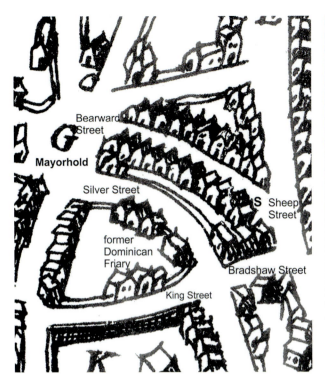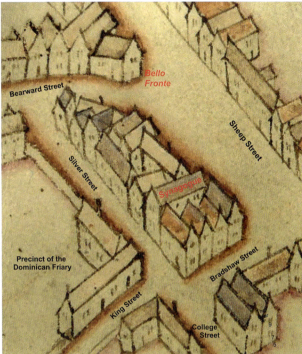

Fig 3: The maps of John Speed 1610, left, and Marcus Pierce 1632, right, showing the comparable depiction of buildings around the junction of Bradshaw Street and Silver Street, and the disparate courses at the northern end of Silver Street

north of the Red Lyon Inn, in line with Kings Head Lane (King Street) to the west (and in effect an eastward continuation of Kings Head Lane), and was later relocated to the south of the Inn, its current location, creating an offset junction with Kings Head Lane (King Street). Beyond inconsistencies in the documentary evidence, a known issue when trying to use rentals to determine the exact location of properties, there is nothing else to suggest that Bradshaw Lane was relocated southwards.

While Marcus Roberts provided recorded exceptions for both the relocation of lanes and for changing property boundaries, and clearly such changes have happened in all towns through time, It could be suggested that these are exceptions to an inherent, and understandable, conservatism towards the maintainance of property boundaries through time. For instance, following the Great Fire of London in 1666, despite the proposal by Wren to escape from the constrictions of the medieval lanscape of narrow roads and lanes, and the mulitude of individal property boundaries; to create a modern plan with wide boulevards and long vistas, it was the retention of the existing townscape and property boundaries that won the day.

Marcus Roberts also makes mention of the fact that the modern streets are broader than their medieval antecedents, which is often the case. This can be illustrated by showing how both Bradshaw Street and Silver Street were widened in the late 1930s, when the Fish Market was built, with the new pavement and the adjacent road overlapping onto the footprint of the demolished houses (Fig 5). As a personal note, having conducted watching briefs during road works/widening in the 1980s along Campbell Street east of Regent Square and continuing down Grafton Street to the west, the northern sides of the roads were already extending across the infilled cellars of former street frontage properties before the 1980s road-widening schemes. This effect creates uncertainty in matching streets for map regression, which is best carried out using the late 19th century Ordnance Survey mapping, as the street pattern was then much closer to the medieval street pattern.

The alternative map transcription

The starting point for reworking the map regression is, therefore, an approach that assumes, lacking sound evidence to the contrary, conservatism both in the layout of the roads and also of property boundaries through time, and certainly so through to the 19th century in the historic centre of the town within the line of the medieval defences. We must, of course, exclude the redevelopment of Northampton from the 1960s onward, which has made many quite drastic changes to parts of the historic road system and the obliteration of many properties and their boundaries in the many large-scale developments that have swept across entire blocks of the previous townscape. The approach has been to replicate the grid of house outlines created by Roberts from the Pierce map (Fig 4d) and to overlay this grid onto the Noble and Butlin map of 1746 and the Ordnance Survey map of 1899 (Fig 4b & c). This figure also serves to show the consistent road layout in this area recorded from Speed to the Ordnance Survey (Fig 4 a, b & c).

a) John Speed 1610

b) Noble and Butlin 1746

c) Ordnance Survey (2nd edition) 1899

d) Marcus Pierce 1632

Fig 4: Comparative plans, showing: a) Speed 1610, with property outlines from the Marcus Pierce map d) transposed onto:
b) Noble and Butlin 1746 and c) Ordnance Survey 1899, with properties outlined in red and the possible synagogue, S,
in green and yellow

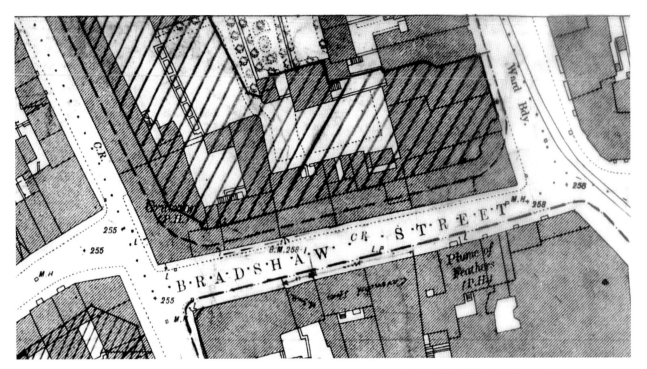

Fig 5: Bradshaw Street, with the Fish Market overdrawn (cross hatched) onto the 1885 First Edition Ordnance Survey map to illustrate the widening of Bradshaw Street in the late 1930s

The location of the synagogue

The outcome of this exercise is of interest in that although the assumptions of a relocated Silver Street and Bradshaw Street have been abandoned, the mapping produces the same broad conclusion as emerged from the map analysis and the Ground Penetrating Radar (GPR) by Roberts, with the most likely candidate for the synagogue identified as modern 7 and 9 Sheep Street (Figs 4c and 6).

The GPR survey had produced evidence for structures surviving below ground and even below cellars, across the northern half of 7 Sheep Street and 9 Sheep Street, while in the cellar of The Bear Inn, adjacent to the square anomaly (Fig 6, A), there was a redundant stairway within a wall about 6 feet (1.83m) thick, "possibly the remains of either the Synagogue wall or the adjacent Jewish House" (Roberts 2021, this volume, 318 & fig 12).

The watching brief of 2012

Along with the demolition of the Fish Market, 5 and 7 Sheep Street were also demolished, although the two facades were retained to maintain the appearance of the Sheep Street frontage (Fig 7, see Upson-Smith 2021, this volume, 339 & figs 5 & 6). The ground floor windows now light a single convenience store that is accessed from inside the Bus Interchange and not from the doors on Sheep Street, which again are there purely to maintain the visual appearance of the frontage.

Despite the limitations of its circumstances, the watching brief of 2012 did produce some hard evidence that is relevant to the discussion of the results of the GPR survey. Beneath the cellar under the frontage of 7 Sheep Street, the only soils surviving under the floor in southern half were dated to the 19th century, with some natural also showing through. More centrally within the footprint there was a stone-lined well shaft cutting natural directly beneath the cellar floor (Fig 8). The well coincides with GPR anomaly B (Fig 6).

It is unusual to find a well on a street frontage, as it suggests that the well may have been within a building, but it is common to find wells of various dates in the yards to the rear of properties. The well pre-dates the then standing building, and is likely to be contemporary with an earlier building on the frontage, so potentially this could have been the synagogue, if it did encompass 7 and 9 Sheep Street.

The adjacent building to the south, 5 Sheep Street, probably lay to the south of the synagogue, where a row of properties are shown fronting onto Bradshaw Street on both maps, Speed and Pierce. The rear rooms of 5 Sheep Street were cellared but not the frontage. In some initial works by the contractor no archaeological deposits were seen, but later works: "revealed a sequence of surfaces overlying the base of an ironstone wall on an east-west alignment. The surviving top of the wall, which was exposed *c*.0.85m below the present floor level, was constructed in roughly coursed ironstone rubble ... The wall was not related to the current building and is likely to have been an element of an earlier structure. It appeared to have been constructed in a trench which cut through adjacent layers. No dating evidence was recovered." (Upson-Smith 20212, this volume, 341 & figs 9 & 10).

There was no further description of the "sequence of surfaces overlying the base of an ironstone wall", but judging purely from the published photograph (*ibid*, fig 9),

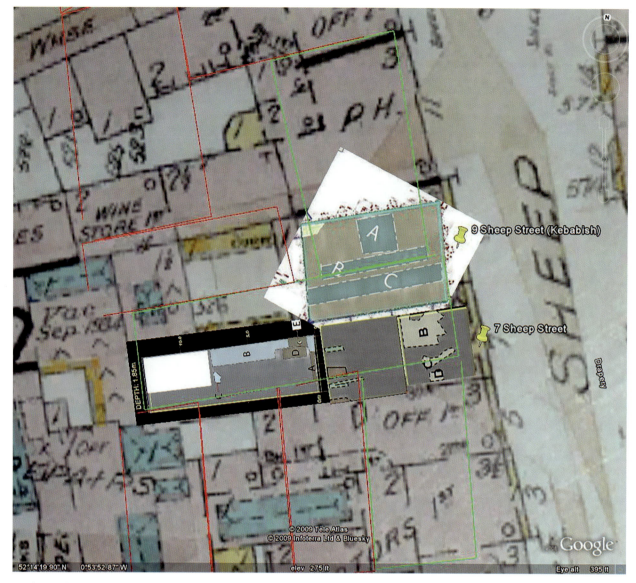

Fig 6: The schematic summary of the GPR results mapped onto the Gough Insurance map, showing the focus on 7 & 9 Sheep Street as the potential site of the synagogue (Roberts this volume, fig 15)

they appear, particularly towards the base of the section, to be finely stratified at least in part comprising thin layers of alternating darker and lighter soils, including a pinkish layer. This could be interpreted as a sequence of floor levels, with laid floors, of clay perhaps, interleaved with dark, probably charcoal-rich, soils that may have come from open hearths, which would also account for the pink scorching and the alternating darker and lighter deposits.

Such an interpretation would imply that these deposits would have been no later than early post-medieval/late medieval in date; as the interpretation offered implies the presence of open hearths reset as each new floor was laid, rather than a fireplace with a chimney. The upper sequence of surfaces overlay the wall, which is described as lying within a construction trench that cut a further sequence of layers, with at least the upper deposit appearing to be similar to the overlying deposits.

This would indicate that the exposed layers were from two earlier structures: with a wall and adjacent surfaces

from an earlier building overlain by the floor levels within a later building. There could also have been earlier phases of activity preserved below the exposed levels, as there is no mention that natural had been reached.

The circumstances in which these deposits were recognised, an excavation by a works contractor related to providing shoring for the retained façades, meant that while the exposed deposits could be recorded, it was probably not possible to carry out any further archaeological excavation to examine this area in detail to further understand and to date these precursor buildings. This was the only significant island of earlier archaeological deposits that was identified. If the presence of this intact sequence had been recognised at an earlier stage of the process of redevelopment, it might have been possible to carry out a full excavation, which might have told us much about the medieval and early post-medieval development of at least one property on the Sheep Street frontage, and this must be seen as a lost opportunity.

Fig 7: The retained frontages of 5 and 7 Sheep Street (Select Convenience), with their now blind windows and closed doorways, and 9 Sheep Street (Kababish takeaway) with the end of the Bear Inn in mock-timbering to the right

As will be discussed below, one of the precursors would have been the Red Lyon Inn and sometime before this the end building of the row of buildings end-on to Bradshaw Street that may have been houses within the Jewry. It is uncertain whether these deposits were left *in situ*. A photograph showing the rear of the facades of 5 and 7 Sheep Street shows supporting walls within the rear cellar of No 5 and these appear continue towards the frontage, suggesting that all levels were reduced to the level of the old cellar floors, probably for ease of construction in the new build (*ibid*, fig 6).

The building recording of the Fish Market included examining the contemporary cellar, which was installed to act as an air raid shelter (Bassir 2015), while beneath the eastern end of the eastern arm of the Fish Market, several cellars were exposed and recorded, including some exceptionally deep cellars beneath the Bradshaw Street frontage (Upson-Smith *et al*, figs 11 & 12).

Consistency of property boundaries

A final issue to consider is the continuity of property boundaries through time, which will be approached by progressing northwards from Bradshaw Street.

Both Speed 1610 and Pierce 1623 show a row of houses end-on to Bradshaw Street (Figs 3 & 9). This row of houses was demolished after the Expulsion of the Jews in 1290, and they were replaced by the Red Lyon Inn (Fig 4b). The analysis of the Historical Records (Walker in Upson-Smith this volume, 336–338) indicates that the Red Lyon Inn had ceased trading by the end of the 18th century, and it was replaced by a single frontage comprising a

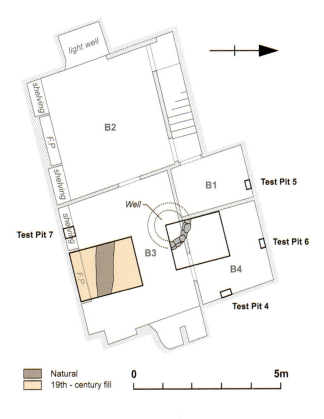

Fig 8: Plan of the cellars of 7 Sheep Street, showing a stone-lined well (from Upson-Smith *et al,* fig 8)

Fig 9: The houses depicted on the Pierce map of 1632, mapped onto the Ordnance Survey map of 1899

central bay with a raised pediment, 3 Sheep Street, and flanking end bays, 1 and 5 Sheep Street (*ibid,* fig 3). This building stood until the southern and central bays were demolished in the late 1930s to make way for the Fish Market. The southern end of the northern bay was also removed, reducing it from two upper stories each with three windows to only two windows. This division even extended into the cellar beneath, were a new blocking wall was built to reduce its width (*ibid*, fig 11). The remaining part of 5 Sheep Street was removed with the construction of the Bus Interchange, but the façade has been retained (Fig 7). The block of land on which the row of houses once stood appears therefore to have continued through to the 20th century as a single property.

It has also been suggested that the synagogue occupied the current No 7 and 9 Sheep Street. There is little doubt that the modern buildings are contemporary, given their identical facades, and that they constituted a single development is indicated by the curious access arrangement, whereby the doorway at the north end of 7 Sheep Street opens into a narrow passageway that actually provides access to the rear of 9 Sheep Street (Fig 7, the white door) (Upson-Smith this volume, figs 4a & 4b).

With the houses to the south and the possible synagogue there are therefore sound grounds for equating these with the modern properties, 1–5 Sheep Street and 7–9 Sheep Street respectively. It is only into the 20th century that the changes of ownership and the merging of properties has created a more complex picture that starts to obscure, and eventually eliminate, the historical connections and the historical property boundaries.

While it has been noted throughout that Bradshaw Street was the southern boundary of the Jewry, the subject of a northern boundary has not been approached. Speed's map of 1610 shows no lanes cutting across between Silver Street and Bearward Street all the way to the Mayorhold in the west, but as in other parts of the town it is likely that minor lanes were merely not depicted. Maps from the mid-18th century onward show Alley Yard between Silver Street and Bearward Street opposite the junction of Bearward Street with Sheep Street. So Alley Yard may define the northern end of the central core of the Jewry. However, as Marcus Roberts points out, the Jewry was not a ghetto, and there are records of nearby Jewish properties on Bearward Street, such as *the Bello Fronte*, they lay nearby but not within the main core of the Jewry around the synagogue.

Conclusions

The analysis and survey by Marcus Roberts was carried out prior to the demolition of the Fish Market, and we have now brought together his conclusions with the results of the archaeological fieldwork that was carried out during the demolition works on the Fish Market prior to the building of the new Bus Interchange.

A different approach was also taken to the map regression, and I believe the results justify this approach especially in supporting both the concept that property boundaries do tend to be long lived aspects of town topography, despite the complex patterns of ownership through time that often serve to obscure that underlying pattern, and also the validity of the double street pattern as a likely fossilisation of the line of the late Saxon defences. The alternative map regression also placed the building identified as the possible synagogue in the same location, supporting, and I would hope, strengthening the general thesis presented by Marcus Roberts.

Exactly what structures, if any, may survive beneath the cellars of No 9 Sheep Street we do not know, but the subsequent archaeological fieldwork has confirmed that one of the recorded GPR anomalies was an archaeological feature, a stone-lined well. It must also be remembered that if No 9 Sheep Street was part of the synagogue, there is the potential for sunken structures that may go deeper than the modern cellars, as has been demonstrated at other synagogue sites in this country and continental Europe, as summarised by Marcus Roberts.

If No 9 Sheep Street and the adjacent buildings are to be redeveloped at some point in the future, every opportunity should be taken to examine and, hopefully, confirm that this was the site of the medieval synagogue within the Northampton Jewry. However, to do so will require something more than a general watching brief during demolition works, and any such programme should target the examination of the potential walls identified in the GPR survey.

Bibliography

Bassir, A, 2015 The Fishmarket and Greyfriars Bus Station, Northampton, *Northamptonshire Archaeol*, **38**, 195–219

Chapman, A, 1999 Excavation of the town defences at Green Street, Northampton, 1995–6, *Northamptonshire Archaeol*, **28**, 25–60

Chapman 2021 The late Saxon town defences at Green Street, Northampton: a review of the evidence and a radiocarbon date, *Northamptonshire Archaeol*, **41**, 129–136

Lee, F, 1954 A New Theory of the Origins and Early Growth of Northampton, *Archaeol J*, **110**, 164—74

Roberts, M, 2021 The Topography and Archaeology of the Medieval Synagogue and Jewry, Northampton, *Northamptonshire Archaeol*, **41**, 305–333

Upson-Smith, T, 2013 *Archaeological investigation and recording at the former Fishmarket and 5–7 Sheep Street, Northampton: January to April 2013,* Northamptonshire Archaeology report, **13/175**

Upson-Smith, T, Walker, C, and Holmes, M, 2021 Archaeological investigation at the former Fishmarket and 5–7 Sheep Street, Northampton, *Northamptonshire Archaeol*, **41**, 335–348

Williams, J H, 2014 *Town and Crown: the Governance of late Thirteenth-Century Northampton,* Northamptonshire Record Society, **16**

Northamptonshire Archaeology, **41**, 2021, 361–385

From medieval quarry pits to a 19th century foundry at Cow Lane (Swan Street), Northampton

by

Claire Finn

with contributions by Paul Blinkhorn, Jim Brown, Andy Chapman, Pat Chapman, Val Fryer, Tora Hylton, Adam Reid, Rebecca Gordon and Philip Armitage

Summary

An area of land was excavated in 2014 at a former car park on Cow Lane, Northampton, now known as Swan Street. The earliest archaeological features dated to the late 12th century and comprised intercutting quarry pits. By the 13th century Cow Lane had been laid out, the quarry pits had been backfilled and the land terraced for occupation.

From the late 13th century, an ironstone wall served as a property boundary and revetment for the terrace. This boundary wall was retained through later periods up to the present development. In the 15th century, on the upslope side of the wall, a number of dwellings were erected with gardens and stone-lined cesspits to the rear; probably with stables and orchards beyond. In the 16th century, these buildings had been demolished, the stonework robbed, and existing pits backfilled to level the land for horticultural use. The 17th and 18th centuries saw renewed domestic activity and the site again became a backyard area, with drains, stone-lined cesspits and post-built structures.

In 1830 the Lion Foundry ironworks was constructed to the north of the revetment wall. Several circular pits, possibly wells, had been backfilled with large quantities of iron and copper slag waste, as well as domestic pottery. The foundry was demolished in the 1960s and replaced by a car park. Below the revetment was a row of three-storey terraced brick houses forming St John's Terrace, built in the mid-19th century. The terrace had two public houses at its eastern end, which were demolished in the late 20th century.

Introduction

A scheme of archaeological observation, investigation and recording was undertaken by MOLA Northampton in November 2014 at the former Swan Street car park, Northampton (Fig 1; NGR SP 7566 6027). A programme of archaeological work was required to preserve earlier settlement remains by record before the construction of a hotel with an undercroft and extensive foundation piling.

The development site occupies an area of *c*.0.2ha within the town of Northampton. The site was divided between two levels; the upper area to the north was previously occupied by a car park, and a lower level to the south that formerly housed a row of office buildings with an apron of car park (Fig 1). The site is bounded to the west by the street, formerly Cow Lane now Swan Street, and to the north and east by further car parking. The no-through-road of St John's Terrace lies to the south. The site is situated across naturally sloping ground, 68–65m above Ordnance Datum (aOD) and faces south across the River Nene. The geology of the site is Northampton Sand and Ironstone at the upper end of the site, with Whitby Mudstone Formation closer to the south (BGS 2017).

Acknowledgements

The work was commissioned by CgMs Consulting, on behalf of their clients Premier Inn. The project was managed by Jim Brown for Northamptonshire Archaeology (now MOLA). The fieldwork was supervised by Jeremy Mordue and was undertaken by James Fairclough, Laura Cogley, Anne Foard-Colby, Chris Pennell, Rob Smith and Gemma Hewitt. Editing and proofreading of the client report (Finn 2015) was undertaken by Rob Atkins and Andy Chapman. Jim Brown, Andy Chapman, Claire Finn and Yvonne Wolframm-Murray provided specialist reports which are summarised for publication. The illustrations are by Amir Bassir and James Ladocha.

Background

The proposed development site lies within the planned medieval town of Northampton on a street formerly known as Cow Lane. The name changed to Swan Street sometime between 1887 and 1901 and the site was terraced on two levels, the upper level housing the site of the Lion Foundry ironworks (Shepherd 2013). Other sites that have been excavated within the vicinity have shown varied levels of preservation, largely due to extensive cellar digging from the 18th century onwards.

The site was evaluated by Northampton Archaeology (now MOLA Northampton) in August 2013 (Brown 2013). The evaluation, consisting of five trenches, identified archaeological deposits that were predominantly late medieval in date, broadly spanning a period between the mid-13th and 15th centuries, with post-medieval deposits of the 16th to 18th centuries overlying them. However, the evaluation also demonstrated that there were areas of the site where there was no potential for archaeological survival owing to the impact of modern cellars, terracing and the foundations of previous buildings.

The site lies within the southern portion of the Norman 'New Borough', established outside the postulated circuit of the Saxon *burh* (Lee 1954), which lay 250m west of the site. Prior to its inclusion in the 'New Borough', the site is thought to have been part of the agricultural hinterland to the Saxon town. This area was probably laid out with streets during the 12th-century

expansion of the town eastward (Foard 1995). Cow Lane may have been amongst these roads, although opinion is divided upon this theory (see Welsh 1996–7). Historic map evidence and data from the Historic Environment Record (HER) indicate that medieval tenement plots occupied parts of the street frontage after this date (Shaw 1985; 1993; Shaw and Steadman 1994; Brown 2008; Brown 2010) (Fig 2).

The first documented appearance of Cow Lane is a reference to Cougate, dated 1275 (Shaw 1984). By 1414, reference was made to four cottages with gardens and thereafter to stables and orchards on the site. At Derngate, a progression of buildings from timber to stone between

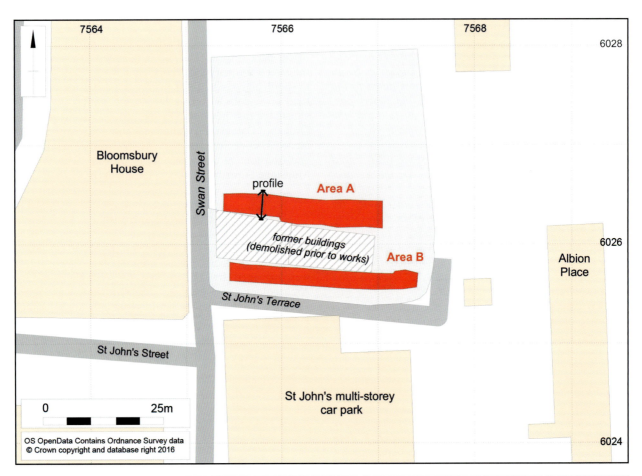

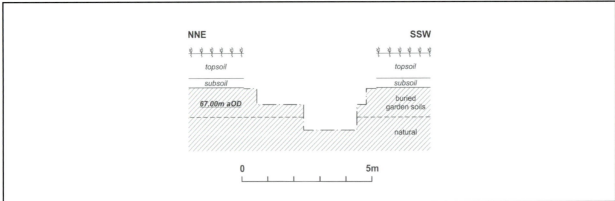

Fig 1: Site location, the excavated areas and profile of Area A

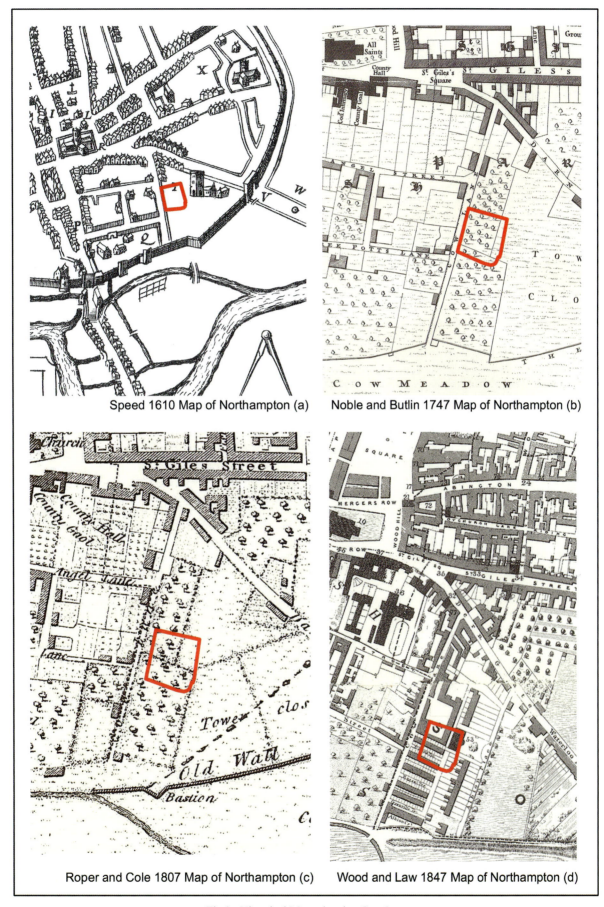

Speed 1610 Map of Northampton (a)

Noble and Butlin 1747 Map of Northampton (b)

Roper and Cole 1807 Map of Northampton (c)

Wood and Law 1847 Map of Northampton (d)

Fig 2: Historical Maps showing Cow Lane

the 12th to 14th centuries were revealed adjacent to the northern part of the street (Shaw 1984).

At the southern end of Cow Lane, excavations on the former St John's car park demonstrated changing land use throughout the period from the late 11th century to the 15th century, where the area alternated between cultivation and low status, ephemeral settlement. This appears to indicate that the area was predominantly used for gardens or fields and occasionally occupied for short periods, in contrast to the permanent and more substantial frontage of buildings on the street to the north. Similar evidence for insubstantial episodic occupation was recorded to the west on the former Northampton High School for Girls site (Shaw *et al* 1992; Hiller *et al* 2002).

The eastern area of the medieval town maintained a largely rural character well into the post-medieval period. Speed's 1610 map shows four cottages still stood at the north end of Cow Lane but that that the southern end remained undeveloped up to the town wall (Fig 2a). Maps from 1747 by Jeffreys, and Noble and Butlin, shows the area was occupied by two orchards (Fig 2b), also recorded by Roper and Cole in 1807 (Fig 2c) and Britten in 1810 (Shepherd 2013, figs 3–4).

The uppermost horizon of the cultivation soils would have been deposited in the 16th-18th centuries, prior to the construction of the foundry. Finds of this period, including Cistercian ware pottery, a jetton and a clay tobacco-pipe, were recovered during the trial trench evaluation (Brown 2013).

Wood and Law's map shows that by 1847 the area to the south of the site had been developed, with parallel streets of housing being constructed perpendicular to Cow Lane (Fig 2d). The gradient of the hillside was fairly steep, dropping rapidly from 68m aOD in the north to 65m aOD in the south and St John's Terrace, the northernmost street, cut a substantial step into the natural contour of the slope. This terracing truncated the archaeological deposits so that the 16th- to 18th-century deposits were largely removed and the soils that lay directly beneath the 20th-century surface layers were predominantly of medieval origin. Twenty-one properties formed the terrace, which contained two public houses. *The Flowing Tankard* occupied numbers 19–21 at the furthest eastern end of St John's Terrace between *c*1845 and 1906 (Fig 3; Plowman 2010, 111–112). *The Old Grey Horse* probably stood at the other end of the street on the corner of St John's Terrace and Swan Street. It traded between 1878 and 1906, after which it was renamed *The Phoenix*. It closed in 1941 (*ibid*).

In September 1830, John Brettell opened an iron foundry called *The Beehive* on Cow Lane, later renamed *The Lion Foundry* (Instone 1970, 4). The foundry was constructed north of the terrace, leading to large-scale vertical truncation of the medieval horizons below (Fig 4).

Site chronology

The site was divided into two areas of open excavation. Area A consisted of a strip *c*30m long by 8m wide to the north of the terrace revetment. Area B was 30m long by 5m wide to the south of this revetment. Archaeological

Fig 3: *The Flowing Tankard*, St John's Terrace in 1894, looking north-east (Northampton Museums and Art Gallery)

deposits were identified at a depth of over 1.0m below the car park surface (Area A; Fig 6) and at a much shallower depth 0.1m below the concrete in front of St John's Terrace (Area B; Fig 7).

Medieval stone quarrying (late 12th to 13th centuries)

The first major activity was the digging of quarry pits, with 28 pits in Area A and five in Area B (Figs 8 and 21). The small size of the open areas meant that a sequence of cuts and pit profiles could not readily be identified, except that multiple quarrying events could be seen (Figs 7 and 8). Pits were primarily sub-circular in plan and the majority were between 0.40m-1.20m in diameter and survived to anywhere between 0.08m and over 1.10m deep. Several of the largest pits, over 6m in diameter, may have been the principal quarries, such as 338, 286 and 317. Smaller pits, between 2.5m-3.0m wide by 0.44m-0.92m deep, like 387, 304, 315 and 349, showed intercut relationships where one quarry was in-filled as the next was excavated.

Waste from the quarrying process was dumped back into the quarry cuts in the form of orange-yellow or brown sandy gravel mixed with lumps of ironstone. The pits were generally filled with one or more dumps of redeposited ironstone quarrying waste, presumably discarded material from nearby pits, mixed with silt or loam garden soil. These layers were generally sterile of finds.

Further quarrying and waste disposal (13th-14th centuries)

Quarry pits (13th century)

The uneven ground left behind by quarry work was levelled out and terraced using domestic waste in the 13th-14th centuries. Overlying the initial quarry fill were multiple dumps of darker sandy silt or clayey silt soil, containing animal bone, charcoal and pottery. Pit [281]

Fig 4: St John's Terrace in 1935, with the foundry behind, looking north-east (Northamptonshire Libraries and Information Service)

Fig 5: St John's Terrace in 1977, showing the dilapidated state of the former Flowing Tankard pub with garage adjacent and the foundry behind, looking north (Northamptonshire Libraries and Information Service)

Table 1: Site phasing and summary

Period	Description
Prehistoric	Two worked flints (residual)
Medieval (Late 12th-13th centuries)	Extensive ironstone quarrying Quarry pits partially backfilled with quarrying waste material
Medieval (13th-14th centuries)	Uneven ground caused by quarrying backfilled with mixed waste, levelled out and terraced Ironstone boundary wall constructed as plot division and revetment for terracing in advance of occupation
Late medieval (14th-15th century)	Garden soil build up Limited back yard activity, with pits and stone-lined cesspits being constructed
Post-medieval (16th-18th centuries)	Stonework robbed from pits and structures, open features filled with waste and ground levelled for horticultural use in 16th century Renewed use in 17th and 18th centuries as backyards, stone footings and postholes for timber structures, drains and cesspits dug, some stone-lined
Post-medieval (19th century)	Foundry constructed 1830 in northern part of the site. A number of circular pits, possibly wells, were backfilled with large quantities of iron and copper slag with some pottery A row of brick terraced houses built on the lower terrace along St Johns Terrace. Each house had a cellar; properties at either end were public houses
Modern (20th-21st centuries)	Site levelled following demolition of the foundry in the 1960s and turned over to car parking. Terrace of houses demolished and replaced by a brick garage, which stood until 2014

Fig 6: Area A (upper layers) cleaned, looking west

Fig 7: Area B, cleaned, looking east

contained a concentration of domestic waste comprising animal bone and pottery, including a large, almost complete, pot of shelly coarseware, which was inverted and dumped into the pit (Fig 10). The pot contained a light grey ashy material with a burnt bone, unburnt bone, charcoal and charred seed from cereals. The base of the vessel was heat damaged and it may have been accidently left on the fire to overcook, ruining the pot and its contents (Blinkhorn pers comm).

Pottery recovered indicates that the majority of dumping dates from between the mid-13th century to the mid-14th century, in some cases continuing until the early 15th century in Area B.

Boundary walls (late 13th-14th centuries)

Once the quarry pits were infilled and the uneven ground surface was levelled, an ironstone wall was built, aligned east-west (Fig 8). The wall was constructed within a vertical sided and flat-based foundation trench. Parts of the wall survived across the site, seemingly as a plot division. The boundary was retained throughout later periods of occupation and a wall was still in existence here prior to the current development. The most substantial parts of the wall were to the east, where it survived as four courses, 0.38m high and 1.10m in length, and between 0.6–1.2m

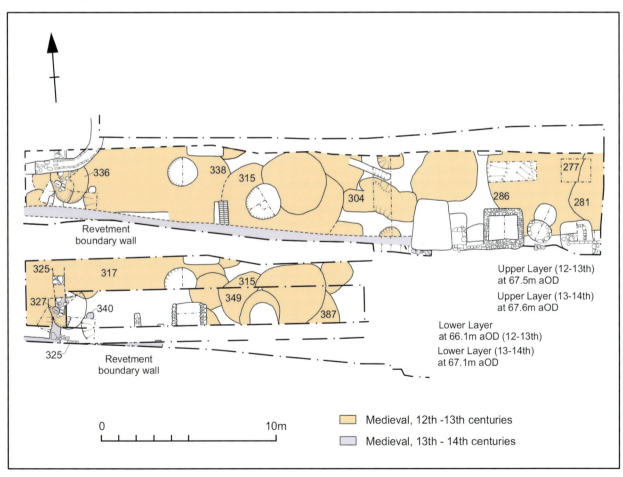

Fig 8: Area A, medieval quarry pits (12th-13th centuries)

367

Fig 9: Section off quarry pits 281 and 277, showing the stratigraphic sequence, looking south

Fig 10: Shattered base of pot with *in situ* content, fill (279) of pit 181 (Scale 20mm)

wide. The facing stones comprised unbonded ironstone, roughly flattened on the exterior surface and with each stone being on average 280m x 160m x 110m. In some areas, only the unbonded ironstone rubble core of the wall survived, with the better facing stones having been robbed away. As well as operating as a plot boundary, the ironstone wall functioned as a revetment for soil levels built up against it in later periods. Two postholes 340 and 327, situated 2m apart, dated to the 13th to early 14th centuries, were situated parallel to, and *c*.1.0m to the north of, the boundary wall. These may represent structural elements associated with the wall, such as a lean-to construction (Fig 8).

A contemporary wall, 325, also stood north to south along the western edge of the site. This wall was cut by a later culvert and only survived as a few stones (Figs 8 and 11).

Later medieval occupation (14th-15th centuries)

A layer of dark grey-brown sandy or silty loam soil built up across the site after the construction of the stone boundaries (119) (Fig 12). The probable cultivation soil had frequent inclusions of ironstone and charcoal, with some clay lenses and rare brick or mortar fragments. Finds from this layer included worked flint, animal bone and a few sherds of early 14th to mid-15th-century pottery, although domestic refuse was not being deposited here on a large scale.

After the soil layer (119) built up, further soils accumulated as the site was used for garden and yard activity and a number of refuse pits and cesspits were constructed (Fig 12), including shallow, circular, earth-cut refuse pits (Fig 13) and deep, rectangular, stone-lined cesspits (Fig 14). Cesspit 378 was constructed of roughly-faced ironstone blocks, with a possible superstructure (Fig 12). Fills contained pottery of early 14th- to mid-15th centuries date, animal and fish bone, faecal concretions and a wide range of wild and cultivated seeds and plant debris.

Post-medieval domestic occupation (16th-18th centuries)

During the 16th century (Fig 14), a layer of compacted light blue-grey clay was laid down, possibly as a yard or floor surface. It was overlain by levelling layers, such as (216), which contained refuse waste of animal bone, 16th-century pottery, broken brick and tile, a copper-alloy pin (SF12) and fragments of lead sheeting (SF13). A second levelling layer (217) was slightly thicker, at 0.22m, and contained a similar range of refuse material, with additional finds of antler, a decorative hook, copper-alloy sheeting and an iron rod (group SF14).

After levelling, a number of features associated with building and back yard activity were constructed and remained in use though the 17th and 18th centuries. This included stone footings and postholes for timber buildings, drains and stone-lined cesspits (Fig 14).

Two large but shallow waste pits were located in the centre of Area A. Both pits contained almost identical fills of soft dark grey-brown clay loam with building rubble of stone and ceramic tiles and domestic waste such as animal bone, shell, charcoal and pottery. Metal finds included two iron nails (SF2), a copper-alloy wire loop fastener (SF1), a fitting and pins (SF3, SF5) and a copper-alloy sheet fragment (SF4). A short section of stone-lined drain on the south-west edge of Area A, (365), is probably of 16th-century date.

Probably contemporary with the 17th-18th century waste pits were several features indicative of timber structures. Four postholes were found in the centre of Area A, giving an L-shaped structure. Two postholes contained stone roof tile as packing material. In addition, an irregular pit, 147, to the north of the waste pits, was filled with white-yellow mortar, probably as a post-pad (Fig 14).

Stone-lined cesspits were also constructed in the 17th and 18th centuries. Pit 213 was a sub-rectangular, 0.90m long and 0.49m wide (Fig 14), with the lining comprising a flagstone floor of roughly cut sandstone blocks, set into a

Fig 11: Area A (lower layers) showing remnants of stone wall 325 and culvert 320, looking north-west

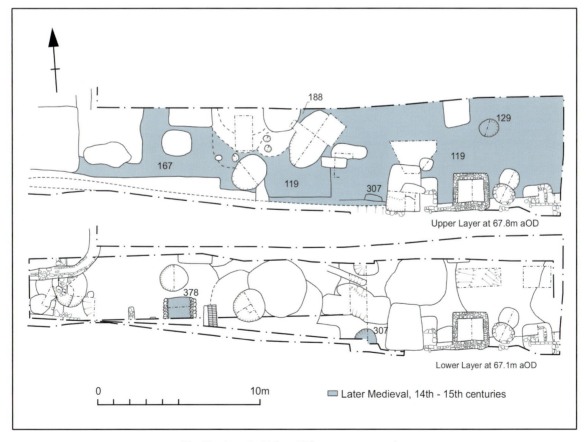

Fig 12: Area A, 14th to 15th-century occupation

Fig 13: Stone-lined pit 378, looking south

animal bone, glass, clay tobacco-pipes and ten sherds of pottery, primarily English stonewares and iron-glazed coursewares of 17th- to 18th-century date.

Another stone-lined pit, 139, was found at the eastern end of Area A. The pit had a layer of solid mortar at its base (Fig 15), perhaps a footing for flagstones, later robbed, and walls of roughly-cut ironstone blocks. The fill of the pit comprised light grey-brown sandy clay silt with large ironstone inclusions, probably from a collapsed superstructure, as well as animal bone, shell, clay tobacco-pipe, red deer antler and pottery.

Many of the stone-lined pits were robbed and had been cut by later features. Pit 213 was recut into a much larger pit, 151, 2.94m long by 1.0m wide and 0.30m deep (Fig 14). The purpose of this larger pit is not known; the clay-rich lower deposit of the fill might indicate that the pit was intended as a cesspit. However, the upper fills of the pit held a large quantity of building waste, including mortar and ironstone fragments, so it may have been the robber cut for the removal of stone from pit 213. Another heavily truncated sub-rectangular pit, 212, cut into (151), was 1.50m wide and 0.11m deep. The fill of grey-blue clay and green-grey sandy silt contained mortar, ironstone, animal bone, glass, clay tobacco-pipe, two copper-alloy pins (SF11), and pottery of the mid-18th-century.

The robbing of wall stone and the infilling of the pits suggests that by the end of the 18th century, the site had lost its domestic function. The infilling of features with

bedding layer of green-grey sandy silt, and four courses of unmortared ironstone wall. A small thimble (SF10) came from the bedding layer. The fill was loose mid grey-brown sandy silt, (205), with inclusions of building waste, mortar, roof and floor tile, and charcoal. Household waste made up a large proportion of the fill, with oyster shell,

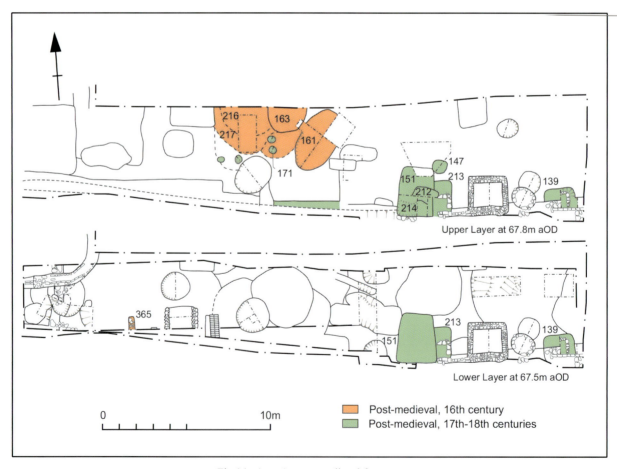

Upper Layer at 67.8m aOD

Lower Layer at 67.5m aOD

0   10m

■ Post-medieval, 16th century
■ Post-medieval, 17th-18th centuries

Fig 14: Area A, post-medieval features

Fig 15: Stone-lined pit 139 and later brick wall 198, looking south

waste might represent an attempt to level the site and much of this material may have been imported from elsewhere.

Industrial deposits (19th century)

By the 19th century, any upstanding structures on the site seem to have been demolished. The robbing of walls and cellars continued, accompanied by additional 19th-century development. The medieval stone wall at the south of the site was dressed with brick cladding, one brick deep on its north side and two bricks deep on its south side, secured with lime mortar. The brick cladding survived in several places, the longest section being 1.8m long; the survival of these brick-clad sections might indicate their use as cellar walls. Several other observable cellars or coal houses had been built up to the boundary wall. Cellar 103 projected 0.70m from the wall and may have had a brick base. An L-shaped robber trench, 159, shows the position of a former cellar wall extending from the boundary. The fills comprised soft yellow-white sandy clay with fragments of stone, charcoal, mortar and a copper-alloy pin (SF6). Similar robbing took place on a length of wall, 178, of which only a few stones remained. Another pit in the western end of Area A, which might also pre-date the foundry, was a rectangular stone-lined pit 181.

The foundry

The *Beehive Foundry* opened in September 1830 (Fig 2; Fig 4). John Brettell had previously co-owned the *Eagle Foundry* on Bridge Street with Edward Harrison Barwell; that foundry had opened in 1823, but only seven years later Brettell had left the partnership under some bad feeling, to be replaced by Thomas Haggar (Instone 1970). Brettell, in the meantime, had set about construction of his own foundry, the *Beehive*, on Cow Lane. At

some point the foundry was renamed the *Lion Foundry*, and by 1850 Brettell had partnered with William Roberts and was now trading as *Brettell and Roberts*. Two years later, Roberts, who lived on Albion Place, had taken over the foundry entirely which he ran for at least a decade. Probably in the last quarter of the century, the foundry was being managed by Henry Mobbs, who also occupied the Vulcan Works on Guildhall Road, producing cast iron items for a group of ironmongers trading as *Mobbs, Snow and Wood*. Mobbs seems to have continued running the Lion Foundry until it closed in 1929 *(ibid)*.

The physical buildings of the foundry lay on the north part of the site, extending as far south as the stone boundary wall. Shortly after the foundry was complete, a row of brick terraced houses were raised to the south of the boundary wall, fronting onto St John's Terrace (Area B) (see Fig 2d). A stone wall of probable medieval date was used as a base for the south-facing front foundation wall, 272, of these houses (Fig 21). The wall here was two bricks thick. Two cellars or coal houses with brick floors, one discoloured with coal dust, were built off the wall on the north side, along with short sections of internal wall (Figs 17 and 21).

The main surviving structural element of the foundry building was a length of brick-lined culvert, 320, that lay at the west end of Area A (Figs 11 and 16). The drain was constructed of red frogless bricks with sandy lime mortar, a single brick thick, with an arched cap 0.20m high. It probably emptied into the main drain running down Cow Lane. The culvert fill comprised mid grey silt at the base, darkening to black at the top. The lower part of the fill contained concreted iron and foundry waste, fragments of stone, brick, bone, 19th- to 20th-century pottery, clay tobacco-pipes, window glass (SF16–19), textile fragment (SF19), a bead (SF20), a pin shank (SF25) and various iron objects, primarily nails (SF24–37).

During the 19th century, a number of pits, some probably earlier wells or cesspits, were used as dumps for foundry waste. Some pits seemed to have been only used by the foundry; pit 137, for instance, contained entirely black silty foundry waste, probably from raking out the furnace, and former well 141 contained loamy layers alternating with dark purple-black tap slag, clinker and ash (Fig 16). The largest slag lump was 0.44m by 0.30m in diameter (Figs 18 and 19).

Other former wells were used both to dump industrial and domestic waste. The most complete example, 177, was *c.*2.0m in diameter and over 3.60m deep. The former well contained multiple layers of black sandy silt containing an abundance of ash, charcoal, building rubble, lumps of slag and metalworking crucible waste, as well as domestic refuse of animal bone, clay tobacco-pipes and 19th- to 20th-century pottery. Pit 183 contained a mix of dark blue-black and dark grey-brown sandy clay with slag, clinker and ash, as well as mortar, large pieces of ironstone, roof slates, wood and house bricks. The fill also contained waste of 19th- and 20th-century household pottery, clay tobacco-pipe, animal bone and bottle glass.

Circular cesspit 143, lined with ironstone, lay at the south-east end of the site. It cut through an earlier foundry waste pit, 141, although it did not contain much foundry material and therefore seems to have been associated

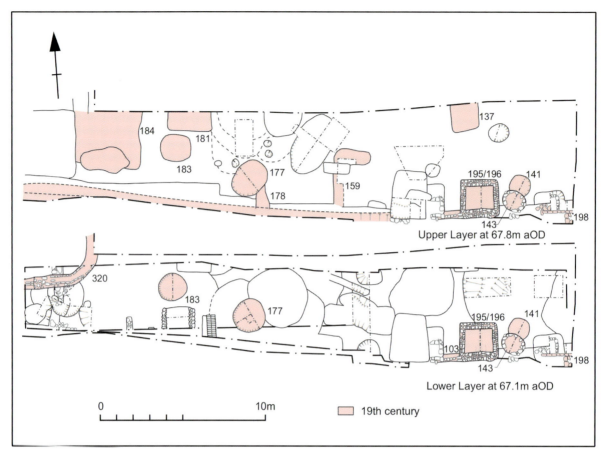

Fig 16: Area A, the foundry (19th century)

Fig 17: Terrace frontage 272 and posthole 223, looking north-east

Fig 18: Slag lump *in situ*, pit 141, looking south

Fig 19: Stone-lined pit 143 (left), cutting earlier pit 141 (right), looking north-west

entirely with one of the properties on St John's Terrace (Fig 19). Adjacent was a substantial rectangular cellar, 195, with the width inside its thick ironstone walls measuring 1.30m (Fig 20). It may have been floored with wooden boards. The contents was primarily highly mixed mid grey and green sandy silt, with building rubble dumped in from the south and all overlain by a deposit of foundry, demolition and domestic waste such as clinker, slag, slate, brick, stone, mortar, wood, animal bone, glass, clay tobacco-pipe and 19th- to 20th-century pottery. The size and contents of this cellar might suggest an association with *the Flowing Tankard* public house that occupied the easternmost properties on St John's Terrace.

Fig 20: Stone-lined cellar 195, looking west

In Area B a line of 15 pits, aligned east-west, were evenly spaced at interval of 1.50m (Fig 21). They were square, rectangular or L-shaped in plan, between 0.64m-1.10m long by 0.45m-1.03m wide and 0.09–0.61m deep, filled with dumps of redeposited topsoil. Their function is unknown, although they may have been post-pits; any

structure in this area was demolished before the foundry and St John's Terrace were built and left no other traces.

Modern remains post-dating St John's Terrace (20th–21st centuries)

The foundry was demolished in the late 20th century, and spreads of demolition material were observed across the site. The most significant depth of foundry material comprised a layer of dark grey-black sandy silt with mortar, coal, slate, brick and ironstone, 0.80m thick (114), which had subsided from behind the revetment wall spilling into the main area (not illustrated). At the west end of Area A was another demolition layer of mixed grey-brown clay, with ironstone, brick and mortar rubble (220; not illustrated).

South of the boundary wall, the western end of the terraced houses was demolished by 1963 and replaced by a brick garage. This was demolished in 2014, although it survived into the present day as a low section of wall four courses high, 5.52m long by 2.15m wide. The last houses in the row to be demolished were numbers 17–21, including the location of the former *Flowing Tankard* public house, which had gone by the late 1980s.

The medieval and post-medieval pottery
Paul Blinkhorn

The pottery assemblage comprises 598 sherds with a total weight of 14,992g. The range of fabric types is typical of medieval sites in Northampton (eg McCarthy 1979), consisting mainly of local wares, along with a small quantity of regional imports from Lincolnshire, Oxfordshire and Nottinghamshire and a few late medieval imports in the form of German Stonewares.

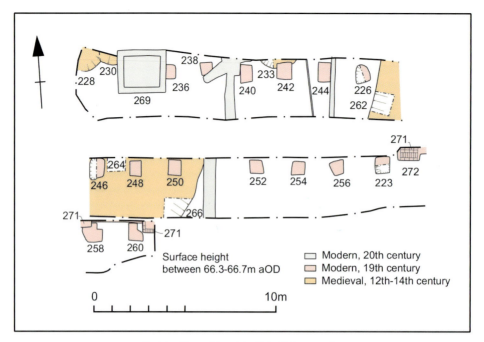

Fig 21: Plan of Area B, 12th-20th centuries

Quantification by fabric types

It was recorded using the conventions of the Northamptonshire Ceramic Type-Series (CTS), as follows:

F200:   T1 (2) type St. Neots ware (AD1000–1200), 5 sherds, 45g

F308:   Nottingham glazed ware (13th century), 1 sherd, 25g

F319:   Lyveden/Stanion 'A' ware (AD1150–1400), 11 sherds, 277g

F320:   Lyveden/Stanion 'B' ware (AD1225–1400), 10 sherds, 85g

F324:   Brill/Boarstall ware (early 13th-16th centuries), 19 sherds, 409g

F329:   Potterspury ware (AD1250–1600), 71 sherds, 709g

F330:   Shelly coarseware (AD1100–1400), 239 sherds, 4235g

F331:   Developed Stamford ware (late 12th-early 13th centuries), 1 sherd, 4g

F342:   North Midlands Whiteware (13th-14th centuries), 1 sherd, 10g

F345:   Oxford ware (mid-11th-14th centuries, 5 sherds, 82g

F360:   Miscellaneous Sandy coarsewares,(12th-14th century), 2 sherds, 20g

F401:   Late Medieval Oxidized ware (AD1450–1600, 34 sherds, 671g

F404:   Cistercian ware (AD1470–1600), 12 sherds, 127g

F408:   Rhenish Stonewares (AD1350–1700), 4 sherds, 30g

F409:   Staffordshire Slipwares (AD1680–1750, 5 sherds, 75g

F410:   Anglo-Dutch Tin-glazed Earthenware (1600–1800), 6 sherds, 70g

F413:   Manganese Glazed ware (AD1680–1750), 11 sherds, 276g

F417:   Nottingham/Derby Stoneware (1700–1900), 3 sherds, 75g

F420:   Westerwald Stoneware (17th-18th centuries), 1 sherd, 21g

F426:   Iron-Glazed coarsewares (late 17th-18th centuries), 28 sherds, 2745g

F429:   White Salt-glazed Stoneware (1720–1780), 2 sherds, 25g

F438:   English Stoneware (late 17th-19th centuries), 11 sherds, 660g

F1000:   Misc (19th- and 20th-century wares), 115 sherds, 4241g

The following, not included in the type-series, was also noted (Young and Vince 2005, 174–5):

F370: Toynton ware (late 13th-14th centuries), 1 sherd, 36g

Chronology

The data in Table 2 shows that there was little activity at the site in the 12th century, with the presence of a few sherds of F200 suggesting it may have had a marginal use at that time. The site then seems to have flourished from the beginning of the 13th century until sometime after the beginning of the 14th century, with the dearth of pottery from the mid late 15th century suggesting that the site was abandoned before then.

The fact that only one small group of ceramic phase M4 sherds (fill 229 of medieval quarry pit 230) can be definitely dated to the mid/late 14th century or later suggests very strongly that the site was no longer used for dumping refuse in this period. The pit fill 229 is dated by a Potterspury ware pipkin handle. It is the only example of a 'developed' later medieval vessel form from this excavation, other than a costrel fragment from a 16th-century context. Potterspury ware pipkins are, however, well-attested finds at other sites in the region (see (Ivens and Hurman 1995, 259; Roberts 1994, 59; King 1994, 197; Blinkhorn 2010, fig 11.34, 217), along with other specialized late medieval products of the industry that were associated with the transportation, storage, preparation, serving and consumption of food and drink. The Brill/Boarstall ware offers much the same picture. The developed forms, fabrics and glazes typical of the later medieval products of the industry (Mellor 1994, 127–32) are entirely absent other than a bodysherd in a late fabric from layer (204) and the costrel from the 16th-century layer 216, with most of the assemblage appearing to be from highly-decorated jugs typical of the 13th-14th centuries. It would appear therefore that, from the pottery, there was an hiatus in activity in terms of pottery deposition starting in the second half of the 14th century and continuing through much of the 15th century.

The groups of pottery dating to the 16th century seem reasonably secure in that, as well as the costrel, there is at least one other sherd of pottery that definitely dates to that time. A fragment of Siegburg Stoneware (F408) from fill 160 of pit 161 has a clear salt glaze, which is very typical of the products of the tradition at that time (Hurst *et al* 1986, 176). After this, there then seems to have been something of a decline from the 17th to early 18th centuries, although it is possible that early modern activity may have removed earlier strata.

The occurrence of the major fabrics per ceramic phase is shown in Table 3. The pattern for the earlier medieval period is largely as would be expected for sites in Northampton. However, the suggestion that the site ceased to be used for dumping waste in the second half of the 14th century is further supported by the relatively low occurrence of Potterspury ware (23.3%) in ceramic phase M4. Certainly, the proportion here is similar to that observed in 14th-century contexts at St Peter's Street in Northampton (McCarthy 1979), with the material not becoming the major ware in most contexts at that site until the 15th century, when shelly coarsewares had fallen from use.

Residuality is fairly low in the late medieval and post-medieval deposits, other than PM3. Just 253g of pottery could be dated to this ceramic phase and around 25% of it is residual, suggesting still further that there were either very low levels of activity at the site in the 17th century, or that these strata have been lost. The 18th and 19th-century groups have very little residual material, suggesting that earlier strata were taken off site when the foundry was built.

The assemblages

Ceramic Phase M1 (12th century)
7 sherds, 1613g
The only pottery that could be dated to this phase, other than six small body-sherds of shelly coarseware from three contexts, is a near-complete jar, also in fabric shelly coarseware (see Fig 14). The vessel has been extensively used, with a thick layer of limescale on the inner surface. Most of the base-pad is missing, with the remaining fragments showing that signs of heavy degradation, which combined with the sooting on the outer surface, suggests the base may have burnt out, or been so damaged that it disintegrated after deposition. It is entirely possible that all the pottery from this phase is later than the bare date suggests, as all the assemblages are small in terms of sherd count, and thus could be lacking contemporary pottery.

Table 2: Ceramic phase chronology, occurrence and defining wares

Phase	Defining wares	Date	Sherds	Weight (g)
M1	Shelly coarseware Sandy coarsewares	12th century	7	1613
M2	Lyveden/Stanion 'B' ware Brill/Boarstall ware	Early to mid-13th century	58	995
M3	Potterspury ware	Mid 13th to early 14th centuries	117	978
M4	Typology	Early 14th to mid-15th centuries	148	2030
M5	Medieval Oxidized ware	Mid to late 15th century	0	0
M6	Cistercian ware	Late 15th to early 16th centuries	3	16
M7	Rhenish Stonewares	16th century	57	1005
PM1	Anglo-Dutch Tin-glazed Earthenware	Early to mid-17th century	0	0
PM2	Staffordshire Slipwares	Mid to late 17th century	0	0
PM3	Manganese Glazed ware English Stoneware	Late 17th to early 18th centuries	12	253
PM4	White Salt-glazed Stoneware	Earl to late 18th century	38	951
MOD	Misc. 19th and 20th-century wares	19th century +	158	7152
Total			**598**	**14993**

Table 3: Pottery occurrence per ceramic phase by fabric type, expressed as a percentage of the total weight per phase, major fabrics only

Ceramic Phase Fabric	M1	M2	M3	M4	M6	M7	PM3	PM4	MOD
Shelly coarseware	100%	98.1	67.9	42.2	0	12.4	9.5	0	0.2
Lyveden/Stanion 'A' ware	0	0	0.5	13.3	0	0	0	0	0
Oxford ware	0	0	0	4.0	0	0	0	0	0
Lyveden/Stanion 'B' ware	–	0.5	5.2	0.2	0	0.4	0	0	0
Brill/Boarstall ware	–	0.3	11.2	10.0	0	9.1	1.2	0	0
Potterspury ware	–	–	14.1	23.3	0	6.6	7.5	0	0.2
Late Medieval Oxidized ware	–	–	–	–	31.3	58.7	7.5	2.0	0.5
Cistercian ware	–	–	–	–	68.7	10.6	0	0.8	0.1
Anglo–Dutch Tin–glazed Earthenware	–	–	–	–	–	–	0	5.1	0.3
Staffordshire Slipwares	–	–	–	–	–	–	0	7.9	0
Manganese Glazed ware	–	–	–	–	–	–	0	28.9	0.1
Iron–Glazed coarsewares	–	–	–	–	–	–	73.9	39.6	30.5
English Stoneware	–	–	–	–	–	–	0.4	4.9	8.6
White Salt–glazed Stoneware	–	–	–	–	–	–	–	2.6	0
Misc. 19th and 20th century wares	–	–	–	–	–	–	–	–	59.3
Total (g)	1613	995	978	2030	16	1005	253	951	7152

Shaded cells = residual material

The pottery from this phase, as is often the case in Northampton, is entirely dominated by shelly coarseware (eg McCarthy 1979, 216), along with a few sherds of glazed jugs in the form of Lyveden/Stanion 'B' ware and Brill/Boarstall ware. The sherd of North Midlands Whiteware, from the base of another glazed jug, also occurred during this period. No other pottery types were noted. Just five rimsherds were noted, all in shelly coarseware. Three were from jars and two from bowls, which is a fairly normal pattern for the period.

Ceramic Phase M3
(mid-13th to early 14th century)
117 sherds, 978g

This assemblage is again dominated by shelly coarseware, although the proportion is somewhat lower (67.9%) than in the preceding phase, mainly due to the introduction of Potterspury ware (19.3%) and an increase in the occurrence of Brill/Boarstall ware (11.2%). Lyveden/Stanion 'B' ware represents 5.2% of the material, along with single sherds of Lyveden/Stanion 'A' ware and developed Stamford ware. A single residual sherd of St. Neots ware was also present.

The Lyveden/Stanion 'B' ware, Brill/Boarstall ware and developed Stamford ware are all fragments of glazed jugs, with the Potterspury assemblage comprising jars, bowls and jugs. Thirteen rimsherds were present, one of which was from a Potterspury jar, and the rest from shelly coarseware vessels. Of these, two were from bowls and one was from a pedestal lamp, with the rest being from jars. This is again a fairly typical pattern of vessel consumption.

Ceramic Phase M4
(14th to mid-15th century)
148 sherds, 2030g

As discussed above, it seems highly likely that very little pottery from this phase dates to after the mid late 14th century. Shelly coarseware is still the major pottery type (42.2%), with Potterspury ware increasing to 23.3%, which is typical of 14th century assemblages in the town. Brill/Boarstall wares declines slightly to 10%, but Lyveden/Stanion 'A' wares are well-represented, making up 13.3% of the phase assemblage, although just four sherds of the 'B' ware are present. One of the Brill/Boarstall jugs has a thumb-frilled base, which is unusual for the products of this particular tradition, but other examples are known, usually of 14th-century date (Mellor 1994, 127). Oxford ware is fairly well-represented in this phase, making up 4% of the group, including a sherd from a glazed jug from layer 119 which has a near-identical decorative scheme to that of a largely complete vessel from West Cotton that was securely stratified in a pit of mid late 13th-century date (Blinkhorn 2010, fig 11.38, 231). It is probably residual; as such pottery does not appear to have carried on in use beyond the end of the 13th century in Oxfordshire (Mellor 1994, 71). The single sherds of Toynton ware and Nottingham Glazed ware also occurred in this phase, as did two residual sherds each of St. Neots ware and sandy coarseware.

Just eight rimsherds were noted, two of which were a jar and a bowl of Potterspury ware. The sherd from the Potterspury ware pipkin also occurred in a pit of this date. The other six rimsherds are all shelly coarseware, from three jars, a bowl, a lamp and a jug. Shelly coarsewares jugs are very rare in the later part of the life of the industry, and the example from this phase may well be residual, although a rimsherd with a very similar form occurred in a 14th-century context at West Cotton (Blinkhorn 2010, fig 11.24, 165). A large fragment of the base of a shelly coarseware storage jar with applied strip decoration was also noted. The sherd is very worn, and is either residual or was very old when finally disposed of, either of which is possible as storage vessels often had a very long life.

Ceramic Phase M6
(late 15th to early 16th century)
3 sherds, 16g

This group comprised just three small sherds from two different contexts. It is entirely possible that it is all residual.

Ceramic Phase M7 (16th century)
57 sherds, 1005g

Most of the assemblage (73.9%) comprises late medieval oxidized ware, which is typical of late-medieval sites in the region. Four rimsherds are present, three of which were from large bowls and the other from a jar. This is a typical pattern for the tradition. Cistercian ware, mainly in the form of cups or multi-handled tygs, is also well-represented (10.6%). Potterspury (6.6%) and Brill/Boarstall wares (9.1%), made up most of the rest of the assemblage, although as nearly 13% of the whole assemblage is residual, some of these long-lived wares may be redeposited. Three sherds of German Stoneware (F408) are also present, including a fragment of a Siegburg drinking vessel with a clear salt glaze, a typical 16th-century product of the industry. Also noted is a fragment of a rather unusual flat-backed costrel (water-bottle) in Brill/Boarstall ware. Such vessels are known from Oxford, albeit rarely, in the late 15th-16th centuries (Mellor 1994, fig 77, 8).

Ceramic Phase PM3
(late 17th to early 18th century)
12 sherds, 253g

All the pottery came from two contexts, and over one quarter of it is residual. The major ware is the utilitarian iron-glazed earthenware, along with small quantities of English stoneware. No other pottery occurred. This suggests that there was very little surviving evidence for activity at the site during this period, with the complete lack of Staffordshire finewares (F413, F409) or tin-glazed earthenware (F410) suggesting that it was all of an industrial or utilitarian rather than domestic nature.

Ceramic Phase PM4
(early to late 18th century)
38 sherds, 951g

All the pottery from this ceramic phase came from just four contexts. Residuality is very low, just 2.8%. Iron-Glazed coarseware is once again the main ware type, but makes up a much lower proportion of the group at 39.6%. Manganese wares in the form of tankards and chamberpots, typical products of the industry, are well-represented (28.9%). Other fine tablewares in the form of plates, jugs, tea-bowls, tankards and dishes of Rhenish stonewares Staffordshire slipwares, Anglo-Dutch tin-glazed earthenware, and white salt-glazed stoneware) are also present.

The group is a very typical assemblage from a reasonably well-to-do urban household of the period.

Ceramic Phase MOD (19th-20th centuies)
158 sherds, 7152g

Residuality is again very low at less than 3%. The assemblage mainly comprises mass-produced refined white earthenwares, many with blue transfer decoration, along with iron-glazed earthenware pancheons and English stoneware storage jars. It is again a very typical domestic assemblage of the period.

Building materials
Pat Chapman

Tiles

Six stone roof tile sherds, four of limestone and two of sandstone, weigh 3.9kg. These tiles would be medieval to early post-medieval in date. A tiny fragment of Welsh slate came from foundry waste pit 141.

The assemblage of 27 fragmentary roof tile sherds, from 10–20mm thick, weighs 2.73kg. These are plain and glazed flat tiles, one glazed ridge tile and one pantile. Twelve sherds come from pit 161; the remainder are mainly single sherds from a range of features and layers.

The majority of the fabric is slightly coarse orange-brown sandy clay with the occasional dark grey to black core, similar to Lyveden/Stanion ware. The tiles are 13–18mm thick, and three have pulled nibs. There is a fine sandy orange clay fabric, including the ridge tile, and plain tiles 20mm thick. Three sherds, 11mm thick, in a fine silty pink-buff and pale orange fabric are similar to Potterspury ware. The lead-glazed ridge tile has a wavy line and the remains of a crest. The roof tile is medieval to early post-medieval in date, apart from the pantile sherd in pit 177, which would date from the early 18th century onwards.

Five small sherds of ceramic floor tile made from sandy orange clay, weigh 365g. One sherd, 20mm thick, from pit 161, has a trace of dark green glaze along one edge. Three sherds, 18–24mm thick, from pit 264, have worn green-glazed surfaces. The sherd from layer (216) is 30mm thick with chamfered edges and a black glaze.

A fragment from a sandstone slab, 75mm thick, with one smooth surface and a small fine-grained limestone sherd from a paving tile, 22mm thick, come from pit 161.

Bricks and mortar

Four lumps of brick from pit 141 were all semi-vitrified from being subjected to intense heat. Three lumps of brick were found together in the foundry waste pit 141, weighing 1125g, and one additional piece, weighing 1210g, came from an earlier fill. One brick was originally white, 75mm thick, with the remnant of a stamp *.UR*. on the surface and not in a frog, possibly a Stourbridge firebrick. The other fragments are ordinary handmade bricks 65mm and 110mm wide.

Forty-three small rounded pieces of white limestone mortar with black flecks and two small lumps of grey limestone mortar, together weighing 55g, come from sample 3 from fill 321 of brick culvert 320.

Discussion

The ceramic and stone roof tiles and the floor tiles would be associated with the medieval and early post-medieval buildings in the surrounding area. These mostly come from pit [161]. The bricks are associated with the foundry waste.

Clay tobacco-pipes
Tora Hylton

A small group of 47 clay tobacco-pipe fragments were recovered comprising 12 complete or fragmented pipe-bowls and 36 stem fragments, which span the late 17th-18th and 19th centuries. The majority of the assemblage was recovered from two contexts; the stone-lined cesspit 195, probably belonging to the public house *the Flowing Tankard*, as well as from a robber cut 214 for another cesspit 213. Smaller quantities of pipes were found in ten other contexts. Ten of the bowls are sufficiently complete to enable dating and they have been classified according to Oswald (1975, 37–41) and Moore (1980). Chronologically the earliest bowl represented is a fragment decorated with a narrow band of rouletting just below the lip of the bowl, a decorative motif used until c.1710 (Moore 1980, 6). It was recovered from fill (208) of 16th to 18th-century robber cut 214.

Typologically, the remaining ten bowls equate to Oswald's type G24, which provide an early 19th-century date (c.1810–40). All the bowls are decorated, nine with a simple motif of oak leaves (*ibid*, fig 9, 20), and one with a fluted motif (*ibid,* fig 9, 28). One bowl and one stem/spur fragment are furnished with the maker's initials 'F S', for Francis Street, who had workshops in Gregory Street and Horseshoe Street (*ibid*, 25).

The stem fragments measure up to 155mm long. Changes in manufacturing technique ensured that there was a regular reduction in the diameter of the bore between c.1620 and 1800. The size of the majority of bores, measured by 64's of an inch, indicates a date in the 19th century. A smaller number measure 6, 7 & 8/64's suggesting an earlier date for the stem fragments (like the bowl fragment above). These early stems were recovered from two layers in cesspit 213, the fill of robber cut 214, the fill of pit 212 and the fill of one pit in the linear posthole alignment in Area B.

Glass
Claire Finn

Glass was recovered from six contexts, and mainly comprised bottle glass. Pieces from three mouth-blown olive green wine bottles dating between the late 18th to early 19th centuries came from square stone-lined cesspit 195. A mouth-blown concave-necked wine bottle of the 18th century came from robber cut 214. Other bottle glass dating to the 19th century came from fill of waste pits 212 and 183 and the foundry culvert 320.

A more unusual vessel also came from waste pit 183. This was the base of a very thin milk glass vessel with a folded-in raised foot, splayed-out body and pontil mark. This vessel was probably a tea or coffee cup, with or without a handle, in milk glass to imitate porcelain. Three glass small finds (SF16–18) were recovered from soil sample 3 from the fill of the foundry culvert 320, including very tiny fragments of post-medieval window glass, as well as small pieces of bottle glass from multiple bottle types.

Metalworking and other post-medieval debris
Andy Chapman

Samples of metalworking debris were retained from deposits of post-medieval date, and these presumably derive from the Beehive/Lion Foundry that occupied part of the site from 1830 until the mid-20th century. The fills of pit 141 contained furnace waste, slag and clinker: from fill (140) there are two large pieces of dense glassy grey-green tap slag with occasional air bubbles and fluid surfaces that retain the shape of the narrow channel, 100mm wide, into which the slag had been allowed to flow (Fig 22).

Fills of pit 141 produced pieces of ferrous furnace slag, with some adhering to bricks from part of the furnace structure, which was perhaps a brick-lined outflow channel at the base of the furnace.

The fill of stone-lined pit 196 contained one piece of vesicular iron slag, weighing 152g, and two small fragments of black-green glassy slag, weighing 40g,

Fig 22: Glassy iron smelting tap slag, pit 141 (Scale 50mm)

typical of material from post-medieval iron furnaces. From post-medieval layer (217), there is a single piece of undiagnostic iron slag, weighing 115g, from either a furnace or a hearth.

The fill of brick culvert 320, produced 390g of ironpanned ferrous debris, one very small piece of glassy slag and 184g of coke clinker.

From fill (176) of well 177, there were sherds from a metalworking crucible, with walls 12mm thick and 135mm in diameter at the rim, with a pouring lip (Fig 23). The inner surface contains remnants of green copper minerals, indicating that this crucible was used for casting objects in copper alloys, probably bronze and brass. The fill also contained a single lump of ironpanned ferrous debris.

Fig 23: Crucible from well 177 (Scale 50mm)

This assemblage is all consistent with the functioning of a post-medieval iron foundry, with the crucible indicating that copper-alloy casting was also being carried out.

Other finds
Tora Hylton

Around 43 registered finds were recovered from Cow Lane (Table 4). Twenty of these were iron objects, mainly nails, and a further 17 finds were of copper alloy. Four small finds of glass are discussed elsewhere.

Of the iron finds, many are undiagnostic due to corrosion, although some very large nail shanks or iron rods are visible (SF14, SF33–SF34). There is a horseshoe nail with expanded head and ears (SF21) (Clark 1995, 87, fig 76). A piece of clay tobacco-pipe stem was found fused into a lump of iron corrosion products in fill (321) of the brick culvert 320, from whence a large proportion of the small finds originated.

Ten copper-alloy wound wire or spherical-headed small pins were found, of Williams group H2 (1979, 261, fig 230), dating from the 16th-17th centuries (*ibid*, 260).

Notable amongst the copper-alloy finds is a hooked tag on a decorated backplate, from layer (217) (SF14; Fig 24). This was probably used for fastening clothing (see Margeson (1993, 17, figs 71–75). Another copper-alloy clothes fastener, a small wire-loop fastener (SF1), was recovered from waste pit 161 (*ibid*, 20, figs 98–101). A thimble of the 16th to 17th-century (SF10) was recovered from stone-lined cesspit 213 with machine-knurled indentations.

Other noteworthy finds include a small, annular black bead, possibly of stone (SF20, 321), and a small fragment of textile (SF19).

Fig 24: Copper-alloy hooked fitting, (SF14) layer 217, (height 51mm)

Mammal bone
Adam Reid and Rebecca Gordon

The work at Cow Lane produced a relatively large assemblage, with a total of 7.5kg of animal bone hand collected from 41 different contexts, and a further 0.5kg recovered from seven wet-sieved soil samples. The assemblage contains a variety of domesticate taxa, with some evidence for butchery and craft working, as well as the utilisation of wild animal species.

The medieval phases (12th to 16th century)

There are 131 fragments from medieval contexts (28%). The majority of the represented taxa are domesticates, with the exception of a small number of bones from horse, dog, fallow deer, rabbit and possibly hare. Fallow deer and hare are well-known high status animals in the medieval and post-medieval period.

A total of five possible cases of butchery were noted – two chop marks on a large mammal-sized rib fragment from demolition layer (101), a cleave mark on a cattle talus recovered from fill (160) of pit 161, two chop marks on a large mammal-sized rib fragment from fill (160) of pit 161, several chop marks on a sheep/goat metacarpal from layer (204) and a chop mark on a large mammal-sized pelvic fragment from fill (279) of pit 281.

Table 4: Catalogue of registered finds

SF No	Fill /cut/ type	Description
SF 1	160/161/ pit	Wire loop fastener: copper alloy. L: 14mm, W: 9mm, Th: 1.5mm
SF 2	160/161/ pit	Nails: iron, x2.
SF3	160/161/ pit	Fitting: copper alloy. Fragmentary, circular with flaring edges. W: >21mm, Internal diam: 12mm.
SF4	162/163/ pit	Folded sheet fragment: copper alloy. Undiagnostic.
SF5	160/161/ pit	Copper alloy. Two small pins with wound wire heads, Oakley type H2. L: 25mm, Diam of head: 3mm; L: 30mm
SF6	158 /159 construction cut	Pin: copper alloy. Spherical head. L: 43mm, Diam of head: 3.5mm
SF7	170/171/ posthole	Pin: copper alloy. Wound wire head, type H2. L: 27.5mm, Diam of head: 2.3mm
SF8	178/179/ wall	Pin: copper alloy. Spherical head. L: 44mm, Diam of head: 4mm.
SF9	184/ layer	Pin: copper alloy. Wound wire head, type H2. L: 32mm, Diam of head: 3mm.
SF10	207/213/ cesspit	Thimble: copper alloy. Incomplete thimble with machine-knurled indentations. Dia: >19mm
SF11	219/19/ layer1	Pins: copper alloy. Wound wire heads, type H2. L: 31mm, Diam of head: 2.5mm; L: 26mm, Dia of head: 2mm
SF12	216/ layer	Pin: copper alloy. Wound wire head (H2). L: 26mm, Diam of head: 2mm
SF13	216/ layer	Sheet: copper alloy. Fragment, undiagnostic. L: 42mm, W: 10mm, Th: 1.5mm
SF14	217/ layer	Decorative hook: copper alloy. Hook rising from back plate formed of a serrated circle with two lozenge-shaped prongs extending from the top (Fig 23). L: 51mm, W: 31mm, L of hook: 17mm Sheet fragment: copper alloy. L: 21mm, W: 10mm, Th: 1mm. Iron rod: iron. Undiagnostic. L: >110mm, W: >18mm
SF15	219/119/ layer	Iron object: iron. Undiagnostic.
SF16–18	321/320/ culvert	Glass
SF19	321/320/ culvert	Woven fabric: textile
SF20	321/320 culvert	Bead: stone? Small annular black bead. Ex dia: 8.5mm, Int diam: 4mm.
SF21	282/286/quarry pit	Horseshoe nail: iron, with expanded head and ears. L: 29mm, Diam of head: 15mm
SF22	374/ 378/ cesspit	Iron corrosion: iron, slag
SF23	278/281/ pit	Nail shank (?): iron
SF25	321/320/ culvert	Pin shank: copper alloy. L: 16mm.
SF26	321/320/ culvert	Iron object: iron
SF27	321/320/ culvert	Nail shank: iron
SF28	321/320/ culvert	Nail shank: iron
SF29	321/320/ culvert	Clay tobacco-pipe and iron object: tobacco pipe fused to iron corrosion products
SF30	321/320/ culvert	Nail: iron. Nail attached to a small stone by corrosion deposits
SF31	321/320/ culvert	Nail: iron
SF32	321/320/ culvert	Nail: iron
SF33	321/320/ culvert	Iron bar: iron. L: 96mm, W: 20–30mm
SF34	321/320/ culvert	Iron rod: iron rod fragment with curved profile
SF35	321/320/ culvert	Nail shank: iron
SF36	321/320/ culvert	Object: iron / stone. Amorphous lump / small stones and corrosion
SF37	321/320/ culvert	Nail shank: fused to stone
SF38	278/281/ pit	Plate fragment: iron. Undiagnostic.
–	282/286/ quarry	Glass
–	314/315/ pit	Strip: copper alloy. Strip with vestige of perforation hole at one end. L: 72mm, W: 11mm, Th: 4mm

The post-medieval phases
(16th century onward)

Identifications were provided for 65 of the hand collected fragments recovered from post-medieval contexts (56%). This represents a much higher proportion than for the medieval phases and is a reflection of the difference in the quality of preservation between the two periods. All of the represented species are domesticates with the exception of one fragment of dog bone from fill (299) of pit 300, rabbit bone recovered from fills (112) of foundation cut 113 for wall 198 and fill (208) of pit 214, fallow deer bones from fill (208) of pit 214 and fill (210) of pit 212, and fallow deer antler from fill (138) of pit 139. A tine of the antler sawn through is indicative of craft-working.

A large number of microfaunal remains were recovered from the sieved material from the foundry culvert 320, including several mandibles and long bones.

Mammal teeth

Five mammals could be confidently assigned an age category based on the eruption and subsequent wear of the mandibular teeth. One of the cattle was aged between 8–18 months, three sheep/goat were aged between 6–12 months, 1–2 years and 2–3 years and one pig was 7–14 months.

Bird bone
Rebecca Gordon

Following the initial assessment of the animal bone, the bird and fish bone remains were subjected to further analysis. Bird bones were identified to taxon and species where possible. Birds that could not be identified were recorded as large and medium bird. The bird assemblage was small with a total of 45 fragments recovered. Overall, most of the bird remains were in a good state of preservation. Gnawing marks were observed on three specimens, which were similar to cat gnawing (Moran and O'Connor 1992).

The vast majority of the birds identified were chicken, along with a small number of goose bones and one pigeon. Most of the bones derived from adults, although there were some juvenile chickens and one juvenile goose bone. The presence of juvenile domestic birds on an archaeological site is suggestive of on-site breeding. Most of the elements which belonged to chicken were long bones. One chicken humerus had a cut mark on the proximal end and another chicken was identified as male based on the spur on the tarsometatarsus.

Fish and amphibian bone
Philip L Armitage

The fish bone assemblage was small with the majority of bones having been recovered from environmental samples. Despite this, a number of different species were identified, totalling 17 individuals present, comprising edible fish species and small amphibians. Much of the assemblage came from late medieval stone-lined cesspit 378, including one near-complete articular of a cod. One Atlantic cod vertebra fragment from fill (278) of pit 281 showed evidence of burning.

The only identifiable fish bone material from a post-medieval context was an Atlantic cod vertebra from the fill of a modern pit 223. An unidentifiable bone was also recovered from early post-medieval layer (217).

Shells
Jim Brown

There are 26 individual shells, weighing 267g. The majority of the shells (22) are European flat oysters, *Ostrea edulis*, the remaining four are blue mussels, *Mytilus edulis*. Both of these species are common sources of food and occur naturally along the coasts of the British Isles. One mussel and one oyster shell come from medieval pit 378, while all the others were recovered from post-medieval deposits of the 16th-18th centuries.

Plant macrofossils and other remains
Val Fryer

Soil samples for the retrieval of the plant macrofossil assemblages were taken from across the excavated area, and seven were submitted for assessment. Following the initial assessment, full quantification and analysis was undertaken on four of the seven samples: sample 4, fill (335) of 13th-century pit 336; sample 1, quarry pit fill (282) of 13th- to 14th-century pit 286; sample 2, fill (278) of 13th- to 14th-century pit 281; and sample 5, fill (374) of 14th- to 15th-century cesspit 378; both reports have been integrated below.

Results

Cereals/chaff, seeds of common weeds, wetland plant macrofossils and tree/shrub remains are present at a low to moderate density within all seven assemblages. Preservation is variable; whilst some cereals and most seeds are well preserved, others are severely puffed and distorted, probably as a result of combustion at very high temperatures. Some material also appears rounded and abraded, possibly indicating that it was either exposed to the elements for some considerable period prior to burial, or suffered mechanical damage as a result of the disturbance of features during the intensive reuse of the area.

Oat, barley, rye and wheat grains are recorded, with wheat being predominant in most instances. Both bread wheat and rivet wheat type rachis nodes are recorded, along with a limited number of unusually small (probably immature) wheat grains. Wheat would have been well suited to production on the slightly clayey base rich local soils (Cranfield University online Soilscapes database), and although it was rarely used whole for human consumption, it was a staple crop when milled for the production of flour. Most of the wheat grains from the

Cow Lane assemblages appear relatively robust, although the sample from pit 336 does include a number of unusually small, rounded specimens, which it is assumed are derived from immature spikelets. Although cereal chaff is generally very scarce, bread wheat type rachis nodes with diagnostic crescentic glume inserts are recorded, along with one poorly preserved rivet wheat node with persistent glume bases. Rivet wheat is first recorded during the early part of the medieval period, but as it complemented the main bread wheat crop, producing a flour best suited to the making of biscuits, it rapidly became established across large areas of the Midlands and East Anglia.

Oats are also reasonably common, although in the absence of the diagnostic floret bases, it is impossible to state whether wild or cultivated varieties are present. The sample from quarry pit fill 286 includes a number of small grains, all of which are possibly derived from tertiary spikelets. Whilst much of the current material is probably present as a contaminant of the main wheat crop, oats were regularly used as animal fodder and were also toasted (as 'groats') for human consumption. Rye grains, with elongated embryos and distinct dorsal ridges, were recorded at a low to moderate density. Rye has been noted from other sites within medieval Northampton (for example St. Peter's Walk, Carruthers 1999, although it tends to occur most frequently within deposits of Late Saxon date. Barley grains are surprisingly scarce, and the few specimens that are recorded are very poorly preserved. However, none appear to have the asymmetry typical of a six-row variety. Although all four assemblages include cotyledons and/or fragments of large legumes, none retain intact testae or hilums and they cannot, therefore, be clearly identified.

Other potential crop plant remains include a possible mineral replaced field bean, additional indeterminate large pulse (cotyledon fragments and a possible fragmentary hempseed, although identification of the latter is far from certain. Some specimens from the quantified samples which are more rounded, may be peas, but none appear to be sufficiently robust to be identified as beans.

Seeds of segetal weeds and grassland herbs are present throughout, although scarce within the fill of burnt cooking pot from (279) and culvert [320]. Taxa noted most frequently include stinking mayweed, orache, brome, cornflower, small legumes, goosegrass, medick/clover/trefoil, grasses and dock, with corn cockle, brome and cornflower being also identified in the quantified samples.

Wetland plant macrofossils are generally scarce, although occasional sedge and spike-rush nutlets are recorded particularly in the quantified samples. Tree/shrub macrofossils are relatively scarce, but do include fragments of charred hazel nutshell, mineral-replaced elderberry seeds and desiccated bramble 'pips' and fig seeds. Charcoal/charred wood fragments, including a number of larger pieces, are present throughout, but other plant macrofossils are relatively scarce. However, charred bracken pinnule fragments are recorded within the assemblages from pits [336] and [378].

Fragments of black porous and tarry material are present within all seven assemblages being especially common within the assemblages from quarry pit fill (336) and cesspit 378. Although most are probable residues of the combustion of organic remains (including cereal grains) at very high temperatures, the pieces within culvert 320 are distinctly hard and brittle, probably indicating that they are by-products of the combustion of coal. Coal fragments are also abundant within the same assemblage. Other remains include fragments of bone, ferrous globules (probably derived from the 19th-century iron works), mineral-replaced arthropod remains and faecal concretions, with the latter being particularly abundant within fill (375) of pit 378.

Discussion

With the exception of the sample from the foundry culvert and burnt cooking pot from (279), the assemblages are reasonably uniform in composition and it would appear most likely that much of the material within them is derived from a common source. However, by the mid-13th to 14th centuries, archaeological evidence suggests that refuse was being dumped into the disused quarry pits at the southern edge of the medieval town, some of which were subsequently disturbed by later building and/or gardening activities. While domestic refuse in the form of cereals, bone fragments, fish bones and eggshell is almost certainly present within the current assemblages, it is thought most likely that some of the seeds are derived from the use of grasses and grassland herbs as litter, bedding or flooring materials, which were subsequently burnt when soiled. Other seeds may be indicative of late stage cereal processing, which would have involved the removal by hand of any larger items of a similar size to the grains which had persisted within batches of cereal imported into the town from the agricultural hinterland.

Within the seed assemblage, the presence of stinking mayweed almost certainly suggests that cereals and most particularly the wheat were largely being grown on the fertile clay loam soils to the south east and south west of the town, although occasional seeds of sheep's sorrel, a weed of free-draining acid sand soils, are also recorded. Small legumes are present/common within some assemblages, a pattern which has now been noted from numerous other sites of medieval date. All are probably related to the rotational cropping of leguminous plants as a means of improving soils left impoverished by over production and inadequate application of animal manure. In addition, the presence of bracken also indicates that areas of heathland were being exploited for their valuable raw materials.

The material within the burnt cooking pot (from fill (279) of pit 181) is almost certainly derived from a domestic source similar to the other assemblages, although a far lower density of material is recorded. The contents may suggest possible food remains, but this has been infused with intrusive material and contaminated by other waste dumped nearby. As noted above, the later culvert (sample 3) appears to be largely filled with coal and coal by-products, most of which are probably derived from either domestic hearth waste or the industrial activities which took place on the site during the early modern era. A small number of charred cereals and seeds are also present, but these may again be residual.

In summary, many of the current assemblages would appear to be derived from domestic and/or agricultural refuse, much of which was originally deposited during the medieval period but subsequently disturbed by later activity. If late stage cereal processing was occurring on or near the site, this may imply that the Swan Street area acted as a focus for the importation of grain into the medieval town, an activity possibly facilitated by the nearby River Nene.

Quantification discussion

Four samples were selected for in-depth analysis; from fill 335/336, 13th-century pit; quarry pit fill 282/286, 13th to 14th century; quarry pit fill 278/281, 13th to 14th century; and cesspit fill 374/378, 14th to 15th century. These are broadly similar in composition, although there are subtle differences which may be indicative of specific activities which were occurring on or near the site. The earliest assemblage, from 13th-century fill (335) of pit 336, is grain dominant, with wheat being particularly abundant. However, the quality of the material is generally poor, with the inclusion of a number of immature grains, which were probably harvested while they were still unfit. Such material would have a tendency to sprout in store, thereby severely compromising the entire batch of grain. Other contaminants, in the form of cereals, pulses and large weed seeds, are also present and it is suggested that the palatability of any flour milled from this material would have been severely impaired. It would, therefore, appear most likely that this assemblage is derived from the final stage of the processing of a batch of wheat, comprising material which was removed by hand immediately prior to the use of the grain. Whether this process was carried out on an *ad hoc* basis by the occupants of the site, or whether it is indicative of a more established agricultural process is unknown, but it would appear that the resulting 'dross' was either used as tinder/kindling or was deliberately burnt, possibly in a bonfire, hence the relatively poor preservation of the material.

By the 13th-14th centuries, a number of quarry pits, which had previously occupied much of this area towards the south edge of the town, were increasingly being used for the deposition of refuse. Samples 1 and 2 are both from such refuse deposits (within pits 286 and 281 respectively), and it is noted that the assemblages are reasonably similar in composition, possibly suggesting a similar source for the remains. In both instances cereals are common, but perhaps unusually, oats are predominant. Whether this is significant is unclear, as the oats could simply be present as contaminants of a main wheat crop. However, it is noted that a number of the grains are large and well developed, possibly suggesting that they are derived from cereal which was deliberately being grown for either human or animal consumption. The weed assemblages are moderately diverse, with seeds of both segetal weeds and grasses/grassland herbs being relatively common. The grassland herbs are most likely to be derived from litter, fodder, bedding or flooring materials which were burnt after use. However, the relative abundance of possible early stage cereal processing detritus is unusual

within an urban context, where it would, perhaps, be anticipated that the occupants were largely reliant upon the importation of semi-cleaned or prime grain. Segetal weeds are certainly relatively scarce from other sites within the southern part of Northampton (Carruthers 1998–9), although a malting oven at Kingswell Street to the west of the current site (Fryer 2008) does contain material indicative of the use of processing waste as fuel for the oven. However, near contemporary evidence from sites within Norwich (Murphy 1988) does suggest that some limited crop processing was occasionally undertaken within certain urban centres, albeit (in the Norwich example) at the periphery. The taphonomy of these two refuse assemblages is, therefore, likely to be complex. However, as small quantities of possible culinary detritus are also present within both samples, it is suggested that the remains are largely derived from mixed rubbish deposits, although it is unclear whether this material was being generated locally or whether it was being dumped from elsewhere within the medieval settlement.

The exact nature of the assemblage from late medieval stone-lined pit 378 is difficult to define for a number of reasons. Firstly, the assemblage is small and limited in composition; cereals and seeds are present, but often as single specimens. The few remains which are recorded are generally poorly preserved, with the grains in particular being severely puffed and distorted. Such preservation is typical of material burnt in an uncontrolled manner, possibly within a bonfire. In addition, the material is fragmented and abraded, with the charcoal in particular being highly comminuted, possibly suggesting either pre-depositional exposure to the elements or damage caused by post-depositional disturbance. Finally, it would appear that many of the features of this date had been disturbed by later building and/or gardening activities, resulting in an unknown degree of residuality and/or contamination. Notwithstanding these issues, the assemblage is unusual as it contains mineralised faecal material along with mineral replaced seeds and stem fragments. Unfortunately, the faecal residues are so comminuted that it is impossible to state whether they are derived from human sewage or animal dung, but given the context, it is, perhaps, most likely that the pit did primarily function as a cesspit.

In summary, three of the four assemblages selected for analysis appear to be derived from small quantities of refuse, which were deliberately dumped within an area of the town which may have been somewhat under developed, at least during the earlier part of the medieval period. The fourth assemblage, from stone-lined pit 378, also contains similar refuse, although it is suggested that this feature was primarily intended to function as a cesspit. As the data set is so limited, and as the taphonomy of the assemblages is potentially very complex, it is difficult to state with any degree of certainty how representative the remains may be of activities which were occurring within the near vicinity. However, it is suggested that some limited processing of cereals may have been occurring nearby, with the grain possibly arriving within the town via the nearby River Nene. As such activities were a potential nuisance (being 'messy', a focus for rodent infestation and a serous fire hazard), it is, perhaps, not surprising that they were being undertaken within an area which was somewhat peripheral to the main focus of the medieval settlement. It would appear that the cereals represented within the assemblages were largely being grown on the local base rich soils, probably as part of a cropping regime including the rotational cultivation of small legumes. Wheat was almost certainly a mainstay of the local economy, although oats, rye, barley and large pulses were also probably being grown in their own right.

Discussion

Activity on land at Cow Lane took place as three main episodes between the medieval period to present, interspersed with periods of abandonment and dereliction.

Quarrying

The earliest significant activity was quarrying which took place in the late 12th century onwards, followed by the infill of pits. As noted above, the waste from the ironstone extraction process was dumped back into the pits very quickly after the stone was quarried. After the pit was no longer in use for quarrying, sandy silty clay mixed with domestic pottery and waste was dumped into them. This resulted in the levelling and terracing of the land, although this was not a uniform process. Some pits indicated that quarrying was happening contemporaneously with dumping in other areas of the site. Ironstone was extensively quarried in Northampton during the 12th century, and numerous other excavations in the locality have uncovered quarrying activity, including Derngate (Shaw 1984, 72, 74), Black Lion Hill (Shaw 1985, 122), Kingswell Street (Brown 2008, 188, fig 10), St John's Street and Fetter Street (Brown 2010, 16, 27; Brown 2021).

Pottery recovered from the quarry fills indicates that the majority of dumping dates from between the mid-13th century to the mid-14th century, with some dumping probably continuing to take place until the beginning of the 15th century. As dumping seems to have begun soon after the extraction of the ironstone, quarrying probably took place periodically from the late 12th or early 13th centuries onwards as a periodic process of extraction over a long period rather than a systematic, organised strategy. This date contemporary with other quarrying events in the area; at St John's Street, quarry pits were excavated from the Saxo-Norman period to the early 13th century (Brown 2010, 26), and quarrying defined plot boundaries between Kingswell Street and Woolmonger Street from the 13th to 14th centuries (Brown 2008, 188). This activity follows on from the major expansion of the town that took place in the 12th century. However, at Cow Lane, as with quarrying at Black Lion Hill (Shaw 1985, 118) and Derngate (Shaw 1984, 74), quarrying is suggestive of small scale interventions rather than on a commercial scale. Quarrying at Cow Lane may be associated with the layout of the roads in this part of town, including Cow Lane itself, which was perhaps established in the third quarter of the 13th century.

Occupation

After the pits were levelled and the site terraced, a boundary wall was constructed, aligned east-west across the site. Small wooden structures may have been related to the wall in this period, surviving as postholes. At the end of the medieval period, the area was probably cultivated as back yards, with a build-up of sandy silt soil and loam, mixed with a small scatter of domestic pottery. Medieval soils are likely to have been a gradual accumulation of cultivation material, which is consistent with observations from nearby sites at Derngate (Shaw 1984), St John's Street (Shaw 1993), Fetter Street (Brown 2010, Brown 2021), St John's car park (Shaw and Steadman 1994) and the former Northampton High School for Girls (Shaw et al 1992; 1993; Hiller et al 2002). The cutting of numerous refuse pits and cesspits also formed part of this backyard activity. These varied between shallow earth-cut pits and larger stone-lined constructions. Some limited terracing also took place to the west of the site, and during the following post-medieval period, further levelling and flooring events raised the terrace level. The function of the site remained broadly unchanged during the post-medieval period, with evidence for backyard timber buildings, drains, cesspits and wells.

This form of land use continued until the end of the 18th century, when upstanding structures were demolished, wall stone and pit lining stones were extensively robbed and some pits were infilled. Contemporaneous with the construction of the iron foundry in the early-mid 19th century, a medieval stone wall was clad with brick and a number of cellars or coal houses with brick floors were adjoined to the wall on its north side. Pits and earlier wells were infilled with waste from the foundry workings. A row of brick terraced houses were constructed fronting onto St John's Terrace, with cellars and back yard waste pits, some of which post-dated the foundry layers. This terrace was depicted on Ordnance Survey maps of 1886 and 1925, which show the houses each had a yard at the front and a smaller yard to the rear, with the properties backing onto stone boundary wall. The uncovered cesspits would have occupied much of this yard space. A large square stone-lined cesspit might relate to the former public house which stood at the end of St John's Terrace.

At the turn of the 20th century, Cow Lane was renamed Swan Street. The foundry and houses of St John's Terrace were both demolished, and demolition waste spread across the site. A brick garage was constructed in the footprint of the terrace, which stood until 2014, and the land to the north was used for car parking.

Bibliography

Blinkhorn, P, 2010 The Saxon and medieval pottery, in A Chapman (ed) *West Cotton, Raunds. A study of medieval settlement dynamics: AD450–1450. Excavation of a deserted medieval hamlet in Northamptonshire, 1985–89,* Oxford, 259–333

Brown, J, 2008 Excavations at the corner of Kingswell Street and Woolmonger Street, Northampton, *Northamptonshire Archaeol,* **35,** 173–214

Brown, J, 2010 *Medieval and post-medieval remains at Angel Street car park, Northampton,* Northamptonshire Archaeology rep, **10/107**

Brown, J, 2013 *An archaeological trial trench evaluation at Swan Street car park, Northampton, July 2013,* Northamptonshire Archaeology rep, **13/147**

Brown, J, 2021 *Living opposite the Hospital of St John: Excavations in medieval Northampton 2014,* Archaeopress Archaeol

Carruthers, W, 1999 Charred plant remains and the arable environment, *in* I Soden 1999 A story of urban regeneration: Excavations off St Peter's Walk, Northampton 1994–7, *Northamptonshire Archaeol,* **28**, 108–112

Clark, J, 1995 *The medieval horse and its equipment: Medieval finds from excavations in London,* Museum of London

Finn, C, 2015 *Archaeological Investigation and Excavation at Cow Lane, Northampton: November 2014,* MOLA Northampton rep, **15/79**

Foard, G, 1995 The early topography of Northampton and its suburbs, *Northamptonshire Archaeol,* **26**, 109–122

Fryer, V, 2008 Plant Remains, *in* J Brown 2008, 209–210

Hiller, J, Hardy, A, and Blinkhorn, P, 2002 Excavations at Derngate, Northampton, 1997–2000, *Northamptonshire Archaeol,* **30**, 31–62

Hurst, J G, Neal, D S, and Van Beuningen, H J E, 1986 *Pottery Produced and Traded in North-West Europe 1350 – 1650,* Rotterdam Papers, **6**

Instone, E, 1970 Northampton Iron Foundries, *Bulletin of Industrial Archaeology,* **8**, 2–8

Ivens, R J and Hurman, B, 1995 The Medieval Pottery, *in* R Ivens, P Busby and N Shepherd *Tattenhoe and Westbury: Two Deserted Medieval Settlements in Milton Keynes,* Buckinghamshire Archaeol Soc Monog, **8**, 241–302

King, N A, 1994 Medieval and Post-Medieval Pottery, in R J Zeepvat, J S Roberts, and N A King *Caldecotte, Milton Keynes: Excavation and Fieldwork 1966–91,* Buckinghamshire Archaeol Soc Monog, **4**, 197–207

Lee, F, 1954 A New Theory of the Origins and early growth of Northampton, *The Archaeol Journal,* **110**, 164–74

Margeson, S, 1993 *Norwich Households: Medieval and Post Medieval Finds from Norwich Survey Excavations,* East Anglian Archaeol, **58**

McCarthy, M, 1979 The Pottery, *in* J H Williams 1979, 151–242

Mellor, M, 1994 *Oxford Pottery: A Synthesis of middle and late Saxon, medieval and early post-medieval pottery in the Oxford Region,* Oxoniensia, **59**, 17–217

Moore, W R G, 1980 *Northamptonshire Clay Tobacco-pipes and Pipemakers,* Northampton Museums and Art Gallery

Moran, N C, and O'Connor, T P, 1992 Bones that cat gnawed upon: a case study in bone modification, *Circaea,* **9 (1)**, 27–34

Murphy, P, 1988 Plant macrofossils, in B Ayers *Excavations at St. Martin-at-Palace Plain, Norwich, 1981,* East Anglian Archaeol, **37**, 118 – 125

Oswald, A, 1975 *Clay pipes for the Archaeologist,* British Archaeol Rep British Series, **14**

Plowman, J, 2010 *Northampton public houses and their signs,* Azlan Publications

Roberts, J S, 1994 Caldecotte Village, *in* R J Zeepvat, J S Roberts, and N A King *Caldecotte, Milton Keynes: Excavation and Fieldwork 1966–91,* Buckinghamshire Archaeol Soc Monog, **4**, 59–96

Shaw, M, 1984 Excavations on a medieval site at Derngate, Northampton, *Northamptonshire Archaeol,* **19**, 63–82

Shaw, M, 1985 Excavations on a Saxon and medieval site at Black Lion Hill, Northampton, *Northamptonshire Archaeol,* **20**, 113–138

Shaw, M, 1993 *Archaeological evaluation at St John's Street, Northampton 1990,* Northamptonshire Archaeology rep, **861**

Shaw, M, and Steadman, S, 1994 Life on a medieval backstreet: archaeological excavations at Swan Street, Northampton 1989, *Northamptonshire Archaeol,* **25**, 143–147

Shaw, M, Steadman, S, and Webster, M, 1992 *Northampton High School for Girls, Derngate: Archaeological Evaluation- Stage 2– Fieldwork,* Northamptonshire Archaeology report

Shaw, M, Steadman, S, and Webster, M, 1993 Northampton, Derngate, Northampton High School for Girls (SP758 603), *Medieval Archaeol,* **37**, 278

Shepherd, N, 2013 *Archaeological desk-based assessment at Swan Street, Northampton,* CgMs Consulting, **NS/15308**

Welsh, T, 1996–7 Northampton alternatives: Conjecture and counter-conjecture, *Northamptonshire Archaeol,* **27**, 166–176

Williams, J H, 1979 *St Peter's Street, Northampton: Excavations 1973–1976,* Northampton Development Corporation Archaeol Monog, **2**

Winder, J M, 2011 *Oyster shells from archaeological sites: a brief illustrated guide to basic processing,* unpublished, https://oystersetcetera.files.wordpress.com/

Young, J, and Vince, A 2005 *A Corpus of Anglo-Saxon and Medieval Pottery from Lincoln,* Lincoln Archaeol Studies, **7**

Websites

Northampton Museums 2015 http://www.northampton.gov. uk/museums, https://www.flickr.com/photos/northampton_ museum/sets/72157623474349430,

BGS 2017 British Geological Survey Geoindex http://www.bgs. ac.uk/geoindex

Northamptonshire Archaeology, **41**, *2021, 387–402*

The history and development of Northampton County Gaol and Northampton Museum & Art Gallery

by

Amir Bassir

Summary

The former County Gaol, Northampton, later home to Northampton Museum & Art Gallery and County Council offices, was subject to comprehensive historic building recording survey ahead of proposed redevelopment. The report describes the development of the county gaol and the subsequent phases of redevelopment, and in particular the establishment of the museum and art gallery. The buildings and later alterations to them are described in detail with photographs illustrating both major features and structural details, particularly windows.

Introduction

The former County Gaol, Northampton, which at the time of writing housed the Northampton Museum & Art Gallery in its eastern wing, fronting onto Guildhall Road, was subject to a comprehensive historic building recording survey ahead of a proposed scheme of redevelopment (NGR SP 7558 6040, Figs 1–5). This work will see the expansion of the museum into the adjacent range which until recently housed County Council staff. The County Gaol was constructed in 1846 and comprised two wings with accommodation for 150 inmates. Following closure in 1880 the east wing was converted to a museum, and the west wing was later converted to a Salvation Army barracks, both conversions resulting in the loss of the majority of the original internal layout. The west wing was later re-converted for use as County Council offices.

Acknowledgements

The project was funded by the Northampton Borough Council. Project management, fieldwork and reporting were carried out by Amir Bassir for MOLA (Museum of London Archaeology) Northampton. The client report containing a detailed description of the building and the adjacent County Offices is available through the Northamptonshire Historic Environment Record and online through the Archaeology Data Service (ADS) (Bassir 2017).

Historic Background
The County Gaol

Early County Gaols

During the 14th century, various acts of parliament had established a judicial system in which magistrates were chosen by the king from the land-owning classes and were given powers to hold sessions of court. These sessions, held every three months, became known as the Quarter Sessions and the magistrates, also called Justices of the Peace, could both hear cases and pass judgement on the same. Serious criminal cases were passed to the assizes; bi-annual circuits presided over by Keepers of the Peace. Northamptonshire was part of the Midland Circuit which also encompassed Derbyshire, Leicestershire, Nottinghamshire, Rutland, and Warwickshire. Northampton Castle served as the country gaol and Assize and Quarter Sessions were held there up to 1570 (Cowley 1998).

The Elizabethan Poor Law of 1601 and subsequent statutes required the construction of Houses of Correction in each county, and Northampton had such an establishment by 1634 (Markham 1885, 5). This is referred to in a deed of 1671 in which it is stated that Lord Christopher Hatton had set aside sums of money for the purchase and repair of the Bell Inn at Northampton, and the erection of new buildings principally for the purpose of a House of Correction. "In this deed it is also expressly stated that the property was then used not only for a House of Correction, but also for a gaol" (*ibid*, 7). As to the location of the Bell Inn, Markham suggests that "the Hatton family had a residence over the property, lying between the old Bell Inn and the George Inn" (*ibid*, 8). The Victoria County History states that the House of Correction was "in or near the old Bell Inn, across the road from the south-east corner of All Saints Churchyard" (VCH 1930, 35).

"Work was eventually started to provide a permanent building, but in the great fire of Northampton in September 1675, this partly completed Sessions House was burnt to the ground, together with the gaol. So in 1676 work was started again on building a new Sessions House in George Row" (Cowley 1998, 142).

The Sessions House in George Row

The architecture of the Sessions House is attributed to architect Henry Bell and surveyor Edward Edwards, working alongside a committee. The building housed two court rooms, judge's office and judge's chambers and underground passages that enabled prisoners to be brought from the cells directly to the dock. It was located on the site of the former gaol which had been destroyed in the fire of 1675, though it has been noted that the cellars of the Crown Court probably incorporate fabric of the pre-fire gaol (Giggins 2012). The adjacent property, to the west side of Sessions House, was owned by Sir William Haselwood who built a house which he leased to the county magistrates as the new County Gaol. This property was purchased for the County in the year 1691. The arrangement of these buildings may be seen on Noble and Butlin's map of 1749 (Fig 1).

The late 18th and 19th century rebuilding

Towards the late 18th century it was decided to rebuild both the County Gaol and the House of Correction.

> Because of the reforms of the prisons following the work of John Howard, in 1792, a new county gaol building was started, just to the rear of the existing one. It cost £16,000 and housed 140 criminals and 30 debtors. The old buildings were still kept on, but as Turnkey's Lodge, and day rooms and exercise rooms and yards (Cowley 1998, 161).

The new gaol was constructed 1792–94 by Mr Bruttingham, architect, to a plan by Mr Howard. It had an I-plan form comprising a linear range with perpendicular terminals with yards between (Fig 2). The building was rendered with neo-Classical proportions and the elevations were fairly plain with little decorative work except that formed by the arrangement of stonework around the door and window openings.

In 1819, the adjoining property to the east of Sessions House was purchased for use as Judge's Lodgings during assize sessions. The land to the west of the old gaol, formerly used as an Infirmary, proved too costly to purchase and so two properties to the east of the gaol, one adjoining the judge's lodgings, and comprising houses and gardens were purchased instead. In the year 1823 an Act of Parliament was passed for the building of Gaols and Houses of Correction, and several other Acts were passed which required the Northampton magistrates to enlarge the old gaol. In the year 1840 the County took the matter in hand, and the Right Honourable John Charles Spencer, and the Rev Edward Robert Butcher made a Presentment to Quarter Sessions that the Gaol and the House of Correction were not large enough (Markham 1885). A new gaol was constructed on the recently purchased land (Fig 3) and was described by Whelan as follows:

> [it was built] at an expense of £25,000, under the supervision of Mr J Milne, then the county architect. It was opened in July 1846 and will accommodate

150 prisoners…The building is composed of two wings, which form a right angle with each other, their point of junction affording a means by which the whole can be seen; the cells are thirteen feet one inch in length, six feet eleven inches in width, and nine feet eight inches in height from the floor to the crown of the arch; a water closet and metal basin, supplied from a reservoir of water at the control of the prisoner, are in every cell; and there are twenty exercising yards for the male prisoners arranged upon a radiating plan (Whelan 1874, 155).

The gaol was accessed from St Giles Square, via a three part gatehouse building with central arched entrance, labelled as *Gaoler's House* on Markham's Plan (Markham 1885). The gatehouse was later remodelled and served as a bank and County Fire Offices, and subsequently as a public house, currently named The Old Bank.

The only known contemporary depiction of the gaol's internal layout prior to the late 19th-century alterations is a first floor plan of the gaol labelled as "first floor plan of the proposed alterations at the Northampton County Gaol" (Fig 6). The drawing also includes surrounding buildings such as the Judge's Lodgings, County Hall, the remains the former female gaol and the surrounding enclosure wall (NRO Map 5432). The gaol is shown as having rows of cells along the walls, separated by a central corridor with galleried walkways connected by spiral stairs, and with an open space formed at the intersection of the two wings. It can be seen that the rooms located at the north of the building were larger than the gaol cells and it is possible that these may have served as store rooms and gaolers' rooms. Roughly central to the north-south wing, two of the cells are depicted as each having small square-shaped features which may represent lavatories or perhaps washing facilities. Of interest is a short westward projection opposite to the intersection of the two wings. This feature is also shown on the 1847 map of Northampton by J. Wood and E F Law (Fig 3) but it appears to have been demolished by 1860 (Fig 4). This projection mirrored the eastern area of the wing and had angled walls to the main elevation.

A statute, passed in 1865, merged the titles of Gaol and House of Correction to the Appellative of Prison. The responsibility of running gaols and of their maintenance had, up to the mid-19th century, been the responsibility of the County or Borough. An Act of 1877 transferred this responsibility to the Secretary of State instead of sheriffs and magistrates, and also gave the Secretary of State power to discontinue any prison.

In consequence of this Act, and of there being two gaols in Northampton, namely the County and the Borough, on the 10 December 1879, the Secretary of State made an order that Her Majesty's Lower Prison at Northampton… should be discontinued on and after the 1 January 1880; and by reason of this order the Prison Commissioners conveyed the dismantled prison on the 28 August 1880, to the Clerk of the Peace for the use of the County. For which the prison the County paid £9157 12s. 0d.

At the June Sessions of 1880 it was resolved to sell the late County Gaol, with the house occupied by the Governor of the Gaol, and the Chief Constable's House; and at an adjournment of the Sessions held on the 21 August, 1880, the Clerk of the Peace reported that Mr J Watkin had offered the sums of £5500 for the Gaol, £3000 for the gaoler's residence and £3000 for the Chief Constable's House. This offer was accepted, and the whole of the properties were accordingly conveyed to him.

Mr Watkin then sold the eastern part of the prison to the Town Council, who converted it into a Museum and Reading Room. The southern part of the building is then [1885] used as Barracks for the Salvation Army, who held meetings there almost nightly; the gaoler's residence is used as a Tradesmen's Club; and the old portion of the prison (which was at one time used as a Militia Storehouse), is now changed into a row of dwelling houses, and dignified by the name of Angel Terrace (Markham 1885).

"The old County Gaol was sold to Mr J Watkins in 1880, who sold the portion now used as the Museum and Art Gallery to the Town Council. The remainder of the property was bought by the Salvation Army in 1889 [author correction: 1884] and purchased from them by the County Council in 1914. The Salvation Army remained in occupation as tenants till early in 1928" (VCH 1930, 35).

A description of the alterations made to the gaol following its takeover by the Salvation Army in 1884 is provided in a newspaper article covering the opening of the new barracks:

The "Army", after being established in the town for about five years, found it necessary to secure a more commodious and more convenient place for use than the old "Barracks" near the Midland Station, and the portion of the old County Gaol running parallel to Guildhall Road was hired for the purpose. The necessary alterations were commenced a few months ago, and completed last week. Three rows of cells, which in the old building were placed one above the other, have been removed, and a spacious hall thus made that will rest about two thousand people. At the back there is a gallery calculated to comfortably hold three hundred and fifty, and in the front there are two platforms, one about a foot higher than the other, and behind these raised seats for the band, choir etc. The hall is high, and lighted by gas, fixed within a few feet of the ceiling. At the back there is a smaller hall, seating about 700 people and 16 rooms that can be used as head-quarters of the division. The public entrance is from Guildhall-road, and a private one for the soldiers from Angel-lane. The cost amounted to between £800 and £900, and the place is taken on a lease of 21 years, at the rate of £120 per year, with the option of extending it for 14 years afterwards at a slightly increased rent (Supplement to the Northampton Mercury, Saturday, July 12, 1884, 2).

In order to accommodate the large galleried halls required by the Salvation Army, the majority of the gaol cells above the lower ground floor level, and their associated walkways, were fully removed, creating a three-storey space which was open to a ceiling at eaves level. The slightly larger gaol rooms at the north of the building were retained however, as were a number of the former gaol cells at lower ground level, though the partitions between the cells were opened through to allow for the creation of larger rooms. The southern part of the gaol was partitioned to create the rear of the large hall, with school rooms to the south. Stairs were added at the east and west sides of the building to allow access between the balconies which ran around the rear and sides of each of the two halls. The balconies were supported from the walls by ornamental metal brackets.

Following the purchase of the gaol by the County Council in 1914, the Salvation Army retained use of the building as tenants. There appears to have been some limited use of the gaol by the Council's Education Department, with book stores in the south end of the lower ground floor level, and offices at the north end of ground and first floor levels. In addition, the building also housed a mineral water factory in the basement and in smaller buildings constructed in the space between the former County Gaol and the Female Gaol. Between the years 1894–96 the mineral water factory was operated by Edwards & Co., and was succeeded in 1898 by Francis Dilks who used the building until 1910 (Morgan and Starmer 1977).

Expansion in the 20th century

From 1899 and into the 1920s, the County Council created several new blocks on the site to house its increasing staff numbers and new departments.

In 1928 the increasingly urgent accommodations problem was faced by moving further into the old County Gaol. The old gaol block...was converted into offices at a cost of £22,000. This took overspill staff, including officers from the Education and Public Health Department. It also housed in the early 1930s the new Public Assistance and Building's Departments (Bradbury 1989).

Elevation drawings and plans of the gaol as existing prior to the late 1920s and early 1930s conversion works were carried out by the architect J W Fisher of Talbot Brown and Fisher (NRO ref: TBF173). In the lead up to the conversions a number of architectural drawings showing the proposed internal layouts and exterior elevations were produced (NRO ref: NAP 670–674).

The earliest drawings, dating to 1926, were produced by the Education Surveyor of the County Education Offices (G H Lewin) and J W Fisher of Talbot Brown and Fisher (NRO ref: TBF 173), and show a rough pencil estimation of internal layout, overlain on the existing layout. The east elevation proposed the almost complete replacement and enlargement of the existing small gaol windows, and depicts modillions at the eaves. The proposed elevated walkway entrance is a large and highly decorative element with a pair of roundel windows above. This design was carried forward in Lewin's drawings of 1927 and 1928. It is clear that Mr Lewin intended for the elevations to have, as far as the intended internal layout allowed, a uniform and consistent scheme of fenestration, comprising regularly spaced rows of windows with occasional smaller windows to accommodate stairwells. The use of modillions at the eaves, and the large decorative eastern

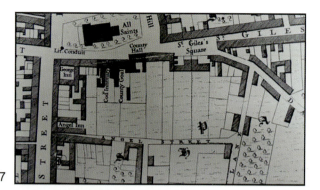

Fig 1   Noble and Bultin's map of 1747

Fig 2   The former County Gaol, later the female
prison, built 1792-94 (Local Studies Library)

Fig 3   J. Wood and E. F. Law's map of 1847, showing
the new gaol alongside the former County Gaol

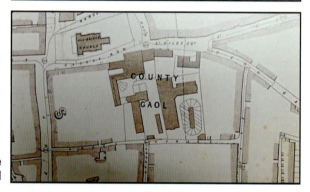

Fig 4   W. W. Law's map of 1860, showing the
straightening of the western wall of the gaol

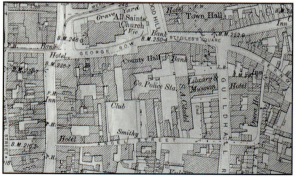

Fig 5   Ordnance Survey map of 1901, showing
the museum and library extensions and the new
terraced houses along Guildhall Road

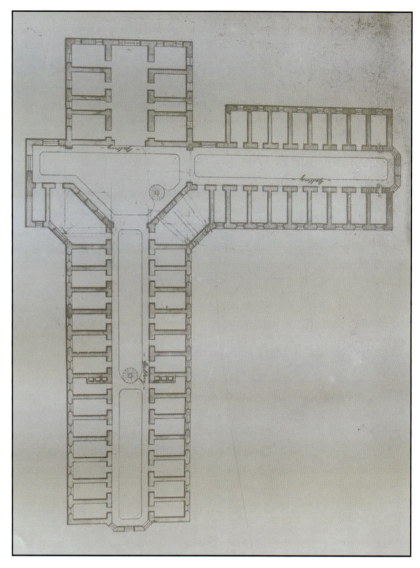

Fig 6   Undated plan of the first floor of the gaol (NRO ref: Map 5423).
Note the projecting western area

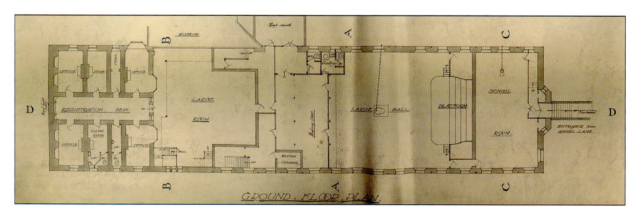

Fig 7   1926 ground floor plan of the west wing, showing the
Salvation Army layout (NRO ref: TBF 173)

entrance were retained and the modillions continued and the south elevation. The original southern bay window was proposed to be remodelled, or more likely re-built, and it was also proposed that the half-round window in the south gable pediment be replaced with a Serlian-style window with exaggerated keystone.

The proposals were refined and consolidated in plans and other drawings by J W Fisher dated 1928 and 1929 (NRO ref: TBF 173). In these drawings the upper part of the elaborate eastern entrance was reduced in scale and the roundels dropped from the design to be replaced with regular windows. This design assumed an open walkway between the buildings rather than the current covered one which diminishes the intended element.

It can be see that the main elements of the proposed internal layout, such as the lavatory block with its open-top atrium, the main stair with lift, and the placement of the larger and higher status rooms at the south of the building, were essentially part of the proposed design by at least 1926 and were little altered in subsequent revisions. The only main element of the interior which was altered between design and construction was the positioning of the ancillary staircase which was moved from the eastern side of the building to the western side. The latest set which were found during this research date to December 1931 and are signed by G H Lewin (NRO ref: NAP 657–700).

Comparing the proposed elevation drawings with the building as existing, it is clear that the intention to almost completely re-fenestrate the building was not carried through into practice. The southern bay window is quite plain with none of the decorative elements which were proposed, and the modillions shown on the drawings were not added. It is probable that this is due to budgetary constraints. The east-facing elevation would have been most publically visible in the 1930s and was uniformly and consistently re-fenestrated, more in-keeping with the intended design. The south elevation was less publically visible and a uniform façade less easily imposed due to the need to accommodate elements such as the staircases. As such it retains a mix of window types and designs, some original to the gaol, others dating to the late 19th century, and some installed during the County Council's conversions.

Northampton Museum & Art Gallery

The Museums Act of 1845 allowed local authorities to establish and maintain museums. Prior to this, collections were largely in private hands and were at risk of dispersal. The drive to create a museum in Northampton began in the 1860s, headed by Sir Henry Dryden and members of the Architectural Society (Moore 2015). Despite favourable public opinion and meetings, no museum was created until August 1866. This was located in the Town Hall and filled two rooms with an extensive loan collection but was troubled by a small budget, a result of the Public Libraries and Museums Act of 1855, which allowed Councils to raise a one penny rate for museum maintenance.

With the expansion of the library which now accompanied the museum, larger premises were obtained in Guildhall Road. Part of the old County Gaol building was purchased and reconstructed, allowing the library to be transferred in 1883. This was followed by the museum, which opened here in a rather inaccessible upper room in April 1884 (Moore 2015).

The east wing of the gaol remained essentially unaltered in outline between the years 1860 and 1885, with the exception of an extension at the eastern side of the building which passed through the former prison boundary wall and acted as an entrance from Guildhall Road (Fig 38).

By 1898 the building had been expanded by the construction of a new L-plan block at the north-west corner of the building to house the library. In the mid-1920s the construction of the purpose built Central Library on the site of a former tram depot on Abington Street allowed the building to be repurposed as a museum and art gallery.

The buildings were subjected to a scheme of alterations in the early 1930s, roughly concurrent with changes to the west wing of the gaol. Plans of the proposed alterations are dated to April 1931 and attributed to Alfred Fidler, Borough Engineer (NRO map 5433). The proposals show stores and lavatories in the basement, and existing Exhibition and Museum Rooms and stores at ground and first floor levels. The proposed extensions created a roughly square plan, filling in the available space around the existing, slightly irregular plan which had been created in the late 19th century. The alterations also necessitated the re-fronting of the range to a harmonious, unified design.

The museum was expanded to the north in the early 1960s by the construction of rooms and a full height stairwell. This was probably also accompanied by some internal rearrangement to the building.

Building descriptions
The West Range / County Gaol

The building

The western wing which, unlike the east wing, is fully visible, presents plain red brick elevations with grid-like fenestration and very little by way of decorative embellishment (Figs 12–19). Except for localised alterations such as around window openings, the brickwork comprises hand-made, kiln-fired bricks, often with horizontal skintle marks, arranged in English Bond.

The eastern elevation has a regular scheme of fenestration comprising equally-spaced windows over four floors (Fig 12). That of the west elevation is less regular as the openings needed to accommodate internal features such as stairs, an external overhead link corridor to the adjacent building, several doors at ground level, and an external fire exit (Fig 16).

Many of the original gaol windows survived the Salvation Army alterations that removed most of the internal layout. However, very few now remain as most of the former window openings were enlarged during the 1920s/30s alterations in order to provide more light to the offices.

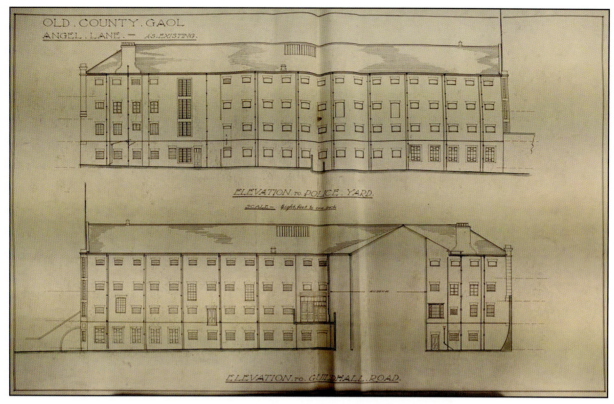

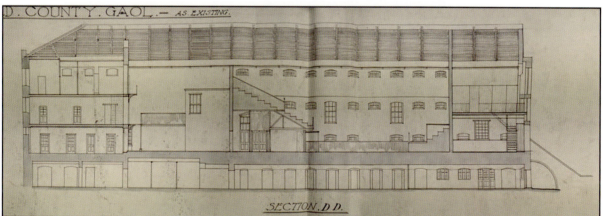

Fig 8   1926 Elevations and section of the west wing prior to remodelling (NRO ref: TBF 173)

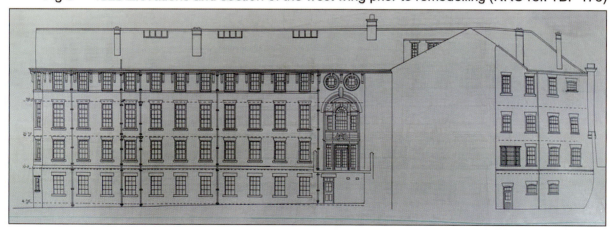

Fig 9   1927 Proposed east elevation (NRO ref: TBF 173)

Fig 10   Proposed design for the raised walkway entrance
with revisions in red (NRO ref: TBF 173)

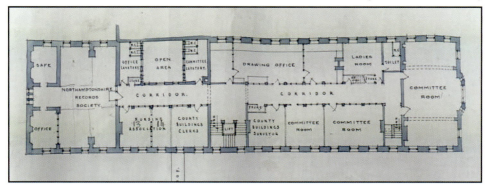

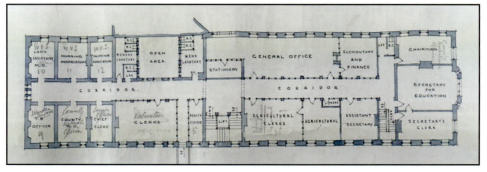

Fig 11   1931 proposed plans of the first floor (bottom)
and second floor (top) (NRO ref: NAP 657-700)

394

The primary window types are as follows:

Original gaol windows: are small, deeply recessed windows with spayed sills and reveals and several have single piece cast-iron security bars held within the external opening. These survive at the north end of the west wing basement level and were formerly the dominant window type at ground floor, those of the floors above being slightly shorter.

The short angled wall at the intersection of the two wings contains pairs of small windows, these having pivoting metal-framed windows which can be pushed outwards a short distance to allow for ventilation. It is uncertain if these are original or are Salvation Army period replacements.

By 1860 a western projection to the gaol was removed and the wall straightened. The projection, having been removed and the wall made good, had a new tier of mullioned windows inserted across four floors, of which only that the basement level now remains. These windows formerly lit a stair and a galleried three-storey room beyond. A tier of windows of the same design are located at first and second floors of the north elevation of the west wing. A ground level former porch and giant order pilasters of the same material are also found on the same elevation and it is possible that the north elevation was remodelled concurrent with the removal of the western projection. All of the small gaol windows on the north elevation had been blocked by the 1920s.

The majority of windows were installed during the 1920s / 1930s remodelling and conversion of the building, replacing the small gaol windows which largely survived the late 19th-century conversion. These comprise un-horned sash windows, either six over six, or six over nine. They have short flat-arched heads and concrete sills. At ground floor the windows are set in blue brick external surrounds with rounded edges and have metal frames with top and bottom pivoting panels.

A 1928 estimate for the conversion (NRO ref: TBF173) provides a list of proposed alterations including the removal of a bay window of the south elevation, enlargement of existing windows and providing new window openings including sashes.

The gallows or hanging shed

The former gallows or hanging shed was located at the far northern end of the west elevation and its former location is marked on the brickwork there (Fig 19). Following Enclosure in 1779, Northampton's gallows, which previously were located in Abington, were moved, by order of the Commissioners, to a site on the Northampton Heath, now called the Northampton Racecourse. Hangings were publically visible and something of a spectacle, with crowds lining the route which the condemned took from the gaol to the execution site. Concerns about the size of the crowds and the unruly nature of these events led to the building, in 1819, of a new gallows at the rear of

the County Gaol (Cowley 1998, 149). This 'new drop' became redundant following the abolition of public hangings in 1868 which required executions to be carried out inside prison walls, and so a new 'hanging shed' was built against the north-west corner of the gaol.

The structure comprised an 8m long platform elevated *c*.2.8m from current ground level. The platform was supported by four iron brackets that projected from the brickwork of the wall. These brackets have been sawn off flush with the wall and remain visible. Truncated stone steps descend from the gallows platform to the remains of a stone platform with a wooden doorway adjacent. It has generally been held that it was through this door that the condemned were led from the gaol to the gallows (Fig 17).

The Ordnance Survey map of 1885 (*not reproduced*) shows a continuous platform spanning between this doorway and the opposite boundary wall, with a set of steps adjacent to the gallows, rising from the ground to the platform. A sunken lane is shown leading to the platform at its western side, with a further set of steps rising to the platform. This lane partly survives, though much reduced in length. The condemned door is not visible from the other side as the doorway has been fully blocked in brick. Adjacent to the door is a circular cast-iron bell pull. The stone-built flight of steps leading to a doorway to the garden of the Judge's Lodgings is not shown on any map until the Insurance map of 1928 (*not reproduced*).

The lower ground floor

The lower ground floor level retains the greatest survival of original cell partitioning outside of the museum area, having undergone less modification following the Salvation Army acquisition of the building, and being relatively little modernised following the 1930s office conversion (Figs 21–29). As seen in the museum basement, the basement of the west wing is set out as a tripartite arrangement of a central corridor flanked by smaller rooms. The plan of 1926 (TBF173) labels the southern part of the building as book storage with a librarian's room, and the central corridor labelled as *Packing Place*. The bulk of the rooms are not labelled, however it is known that a mineral water factory operated out of the basement until at least 1912. The Insurance Map of 1928 (*not reproduced*) labels the north part of the basement as offices. The mineral water factory is not listed on this map and likely ceased operating at this site by this date.

The southern entrance is located within the projecting central bay and comprises a raised double-door with concrete steps, flanked by two pairs of windows. The doors open to a central corridor with a red tile floor and a jack or barrel vaulted roof, with arched doorways leading to rooms along the east and west sides of the building (Fig 24). As noted in the basement of the east wing, there are two room or cell types, these being distinguishable by their ceilings which are either groin or jack vaults (Fig 26). The majority of cell partitioning walls were removed by 1926 to create larger rooms along the east and west walls, and the newly created openings were made good with wide arches to retain ceiling support. No fixtures or fittings relating to the former gaol use were in evidence in any of the rooms. The central corridor formerly stretched beyond its current limit but had been partitioned by 1926, and was later halved longitudinally to create two separate and parallel corridors.

Entering the gaol from the west, a hallway or corridor runs alongside the lift and opens into a lobby area with a circulation space which provides access to a walk-in safe or strong room, the eastern car park entrance, and doorways to the southern corridor. The safe was created as part of the County Council's conversions and occupies one cell. It features a sturdy steel or iron door bearing the manufacturer's plaque *John Tann Ltd Maker 117 Newgate Street London*. The Tann family produced safes and iron chests from the late 18th century, and significantly expanded their business in the 19th and 20th centuries.

The northern area of the lower ground floor, until recently, served as staff canteen with kitchen and food stores. The central part of this floor housed power, heating, ventilation, and lift apparatus, as well as the full height atrium. The canteen encompassed the central corridor as well as the former flanking cells or rooms which have been opened up (Fig 25). The corridor here is half the width of that to the south, being *c*.2.5m wide. It has a quarry tile floor and a vaulted ceiling which spans the full width of the corridor. The rooms formerly located to each side of the corridor are longer than the cells elsewhere and may have served a different function. The north-western room formerly had a *chute covered with grating* (1926 plan) which connected to the exterior of the building.

Of interest are two unusually narrow spaces formed between the former cells, these spaces also having their own small windows and individual vaulted ceilings but being too narrow for use as cells. These small rooms also existed at ground floor level and on the 1926 plan are labelled as *lavatory* and *coal* (TBF173).

A doorway in the north-east corner of the canteen leads to a *c*.10m-long underground passage located externally to the building, which, at its eastern end, opens to an external stairwell adjacent to the Old Bank Public House.

The first floor

The first floor is the only part of the gaol for which there is a known plan showing the layout prior to Salvation Army modifications (Fig 6). This comprised ranges of identical narrow cells along the east and west walls of the main range, with galleried walkways leading to a large open space at the junction of the two wings, with larger rooms, possible gaoler's rooms and staff facilities, located in the northern part of the building.

Following the closure of the gaol and conversion to Salvation Army barracks, the ground, first, and second floor cells were fully removed except for at the north end of the building, and the newly opened spaces were utilised as large halls with galleried seating, balconies and stages between ground and second floor levels. In order to allow access from Angel Street to the ground floor level a stair was built against the south elevation. The southern part of the building was partitioned to form *School Rooms* at ground and first floor levels, with an internal stair between the two, located in the south-east corner of the rooms. The first floor school room was double height and extended to the roof.

Following the County Council conversions the levels were re-floored and large open-plan office spaces and smaller enclosed rooms were created. The floor levels are carried on RSJs (Rolled Steel Joists) installed between each window and supported on two rows of columns. Access between the floors is via a main stair and lift located centrally at the western side of the building, and a secondary or emergency stair well in the south-west corner.

The cells or rooms at the north end of the gaol retained their original form until the 1920s and were used by the Salvation Army as offices, cloak room and store. The corridors between these rooms were partitioned and also converted to functional rooms. The narrow rooms between the main cells, marked as coal stores and lavatories on early plans, were incorporated into the adjacent rooms to enlarge them.

A three-storey lavatory block was created adjacent to a full-height enclosed atrium which allowed for natural light and better ventilation to these rooms. The atrium is un-roofed and is accessible only from the basement (Figs 28–29). The bathrooms have been modernised but they formerly had well-made panelled stalls. At first level, on the west side of the building, opposite the lavatory block, are finely built, good quality, semi-glazed and panelled office partitions with a passage way that formerly allowed elevated access to the adjacent County Council building but which is now blocked in brick and plastered internally.

The second floor

The second floor retains the lowest survival of original gaol partitioning, these having been removed almost completely by the Salvation Army alterations. Elevation drawings of 1926 show that this floor had retained an almost complete complement of original gaol windows. The current windows were enlarged vertically in both directions and the only external trace of the original windows is in the moulded bricks from which the original lintels sprang.

At the southern end of the second floor level is a large room, labelled as *Committee Room* on the plan of 1931 (NRO ref: NAP 657–700). The room is spacious and well-lit by windows to the south, east and west. The central area of the room has a raised, lath and plaster barrel-vault ceiling which accommodates a Diocletian window located above the central bay window. The Diocletian window pre-dates the bay window which was re-built during the 1930s alterations. A similar window is also located in the end gable of the eastern wing and it is probable that these windows are original to the gaol, predating the Salvation Army alterations.

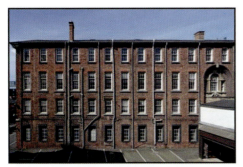

Fig 12   The east elevation of the west gaol wing

Fig 13   The south elevation of the west wing

Fig 14   Looking west along the covered passage,
note altered windows to the right

Fig 15   The 1930s elevated access porch and windows

Fig 16   The southern end of the west elevation

Fig 17   The north-west corner of the gaol adjoining the stone
boundary wall with door to judges lodgings and blocked doorway

Fig 18   The north elevation of the west wing

Fig 19   The position of the former hanging shed platform

Fig 20   The former northern entrance

Fig 21   Chamfer-moulded cast-stone mullioned window

Fig 22   Detail of window with iron bars

Fig 23   Example of the gaol windows

Fig 24   The basement central corridor, looking south

Fig 25   Basement, the north-west rooms, latterly staff canteen

Fig 26   Example of the former basement cells

Fig 27   Arched passageway at the north-east of the west gaol wing

Fig 28   View of the atrium

Fig 29   The west wing lavatory block atrium

The East Range / Northampton Museum & Art Gallery

The basement

At the time of this article the museum's basement encompassed the full footprint of the east wing of the gaol, as well as the 1930s and 1960s extensions. The basement comprises three linear, roughly equal sized spaces, the central space being effectively an open gallery used as an art store, while the flanking spaces are or were formerly subdivided into smaller rooms and cells and also used as storage spaces as well as staff kitchen and lavatories (Figs 40–42).

The former rooms or cells were simple rectangular spaces measuring 4m x 2.1m, and a height of 3m from the floor to the shallow jack or barrel-vaulted ceiling. It is evident that not all of the rooms at this level were in use as cells as many of the spaces were double the width of the standard gaol cells with simple brick groin vaults. Several of the standard cells have also been opened up into larger rooms and can be distinguished by their jack vault ceilings (Fig 40). In the north-west corner of the basement is a square room with an adjacent corridor from which a quarter turn stair provides access to ground floor level. The stair sits disjointedly within the building so that a small arched alcove is created at its rear and a gap is created between the stair and the wide archway of the corridor.

No windows remain in the room or corridor. Where these would be there are full-height blind niches with arched headers and capped shouldered jambs below sill level. The brickwork of the jambs has a cleaner, more mechanical quality compared to the rougher brickwork of the building and appears to be making good an alteration. If the former cell windows were converted into doorways and later blocked, it is unclear why so many doors were required. Where doors remain, the shouldered jambs are also present, however the door is set back from these and the surround is flush.

Both wings of the gaol had full height bay windows at the distal elevations. The window of the museum range can be seen on insurance maps between the dates 1889 to 1928 but ceases to be shown from 1937. The lower portion of this window survived into the 1930s and is shown on the proposed basement plan of 1931. It is unclear how this window functioned following the creation of the Museum and Library as two-storey extensions were built against this elevation. At basement level it retained window openings and had a central door, but was removed and the wall made good at the upper floors.

The northern area of the museum basement is of two phases; an initial Library extension dating to the 1880s, and a rectangular block dating to the 1930 expansion of the museum. Beyond these is a narrow corridor formed against a brick retaining wall, and to the north of this is the 1960s extension. The retaining wall has a sloping buttress at its base which spans the full length of the corridor and into the adjacent yard where the wall rises to second floor level to compensate for the significantly higher ground level at the north (Fig 43). The yard is fully enclosed by the eastern wall of the gaol's west wing, the northern retaining wall, and the museum buildings at the east and south.

The ground and upper floors

The ground, first and second floor levels are largely open plan, comprising spacious galleries and exhibition spaces and very little of the gaol layout survives (Figs 44–49).

From Guildhall Road the visitor entrance is into the eastern 1930s extension (Figs 38–39), in which there are two offices (formerly Clerk's and Curator's offices), and a short corridor with door to the basement. A porter's room and a packing room were originally in the extension but have been removed. The current stud partition walls postdate the 1930s phase of works which shows the walls had been light panels with large windows, very likely similar to those seen at first floor level within the gaol.

The area within the former gaol is divided into a two-storey lobby-cum-exhibition space housing the main stair, a large square exhibition space also of two storeys, and a smaller single-storey exhibition room at the west. Within these rooms are cast iron columns, fluted, and rising from toroidal column bases on inverted cushion plinths. At the apex are simple bell capitals. Foundry marks, largely illegible due to heavy paint, are located on the plinths and are identified as the eagle badge of the Rice & Co Ironfounders of Northampton (Fig 46). The Eagle Foundry was located on the Phipps Brewery premises on Bridge Street. The foundry had been purchased by Sir Pickering Phipps Rice in the 1860s and produced a range of domestic, commercial and industrial components including fire goods, railings, grates and lamp posts.

The main ground floor museum space is roughly square, measuring c.13.5m x 13.5m, and is fully contained within the gaol wing, encompassing five cell bays. Following change of use from gaol to museum, the original small cell windows were significantly enlarged by dropping the first floor window sills to the level of the ground floor window sills, creating tall openings spanning between two former floor levels. The construction of the additional exhibition room at the north of the museum in the 1930s would have rendered the northernmost windows obsolete, however, the proposed plan does not indicate any alterations to the windows and they are shown as being open. The blocking of these windows appears to have taken place sometime after the 1930s and uses modern common brick. Given that the museum was again expanded in the early 1960s it is probable that the blocking is associated with that phase of works.

Discussion

English prison reform began as a gradual process from the 18th century at which time there was a marked increase in prison building to accommodate a growing population of incarcerated men, women and children. An increasing population in rapidly industrialising towns led to a growth of slums in which poor living conditions and crime were common.

Fig 30   The ground floor level landing

Fig 31   Ground floor, west wing, steel framed window

Fig 32   Detail of iron quadrant stay

Fig 33   Windows overlooking the atrium

Fig 34   The first floor panelled offices

Fig 35   The main ground floor office space

Fig 36   First floor offices

Fig 37   The southern second floor office

Fig 38   The museum facade to Guildhall Road

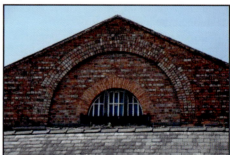

Fig 39   The eastern gable window of the gaol

Fig 40   The north-west room of the museum basement

Fig 45   Internal view of gaol window in the museum

Fig 41   Former northern rooms, now a corridor
in the museum basement

Fig 46   Detail of column base with the mark of the Eagle Foundry

Fig 42   The museum basement, former kitchen

Fig 47   Detail of stair balustrade

Fig 43   The battered retaining wall at the north of the museum

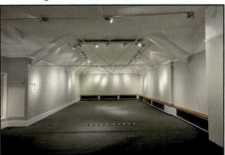

Fig 48   First floor museum space with steel roof trusses

Fig 44   The museum lobby and stair

Fig 49   Detail of horned sash with chain

There was no uniform system of discipline or management in English prisons during the 1830s...In its search for a new direction in prison management, the British Government looked to the USA, where two systems of discipline had developed. Both sought to prevent communication between prisoners...one by total silence and the other by complete separation. The prisons in which the two regimes were imposed differed fundamentally in their design and the architecture of each became inextricably linked with their respective systems of discipline (Brodie *et al* 2002, 84).

"The Prisons Act of 1835 leant towards the separate system, and it was enthusiastically endorsed by two of the Prison Inspectors whose posts the Act established" (May 2006). In 1839 the removal of legal limitations to the length of time that solitary confinement could be enforced allowed for this system to be implemented and Pentonville Prison was built in 1840–2 with 520 separate cells. This was a model prison with five radiating wings converging at a central hall. Northampton Gaol, which opened in 1846, was modelled on Pentonville Prison and was set out as two galleried wings of four levels each with rows of narrow cells along the walls, and could accommodate 150 prisoners. The cells each had a small barred window and were fitted with a water closet and metal basin. Larger rooms were located at the north end of the west wing and at basement level in the east wing. Exercise was controlled and limited to twenty exercise yards housed within a sub-rectangular walled enclosure with radiating partitions.

The gaol operated for a fairly short period of time and was closed following a statute of 1865 under which responsibility for the running of gaols was transferred to the Secretary of State. Very little of the internal gaol layout now remains, except at the basement levels which have been least altered since the closure of the gaol. No fixtures of fittings relating to the gaol were noted and from ground level up the cells were wholly removed to accommodate the museum and library and the Salvation Army barracks. The rooms at the north end of the west wing appear to be largely original to the gaol, though with some minor alterations. Probably it was not deemed necessary to alter these rooms due to their larger and more practical size.

The conversion of the east wing to a Museum, Library and Reading Room, resulted in the loss of the original layout except for parts of the basement level. Several of the gaol windows remain at basement level (Fig 45), but those of the floors above were enlarged in the 1920s and 1930s.

In the west wing, although the interior had been almost fully remodelled, a great many of the small gaol windows still remained by the 1920s. It was originally proposed that this wing be fully re-fenestrated with a homogenous scheme of sash windows enlarging and replacing all earlier windows. Fortunately this wholesale re-fenestration was not implemented and a few earlier windows still remain at the northern end of the west elevation (Figs 22–23).

The creation of the Northampton Museum in 1883 in part of the old gaol, represented a publically accessible and systematic housing of antiquities, and moved away from the private curio collection approach which had previously been a fashionable gentleman's hobby and was prone to dispersal of artefacts and collections. The setting up of a museum was enabled by the Museums Act of 1845 and was driven by Sir Henry Dryden and members of the Architectural Society. The east wing of the gaol was remodelled to house a public reading room with museum above and the library was located in a new extension which faced Guildhall Road. The library was transferred to a purpose built facility on Abington Street, and in the early 1930s the museum and the east wing were again subject to alterations and given a new façade.

Bibliography

Bassir, A, 2017 *Historic Building Recording and Archaeological Observation at the Northampton Museum & Art Gallery and the Old Gaol, Northampton, Northamptonshire,* MOLA (Museum of London Archaeology) Northampton rep, **17/107**

Bradbury, J, 1989 *1889–1989 Government & County, A History of Northamptonshire County Council,* University of Bristol Press

Brodie, A, Croom, J, and O' Davies, J, 2002 *English Prisons, An Architectural History,* English Heritage

Moore, R, 2015 The Development of Archaeology in Northamptonshire to 1980, *Northamptonshire Archaeol*, **38**, 5–21

Cowley, R, 1998 *Guilty M'lud! The Criminal History of Northamptonshire,* Peg and Whistle Books

Giggins, B, 2012 *The Sessions House, Northampton, Observations 2012,* Academia, available online at https://www.academia.edu/20401838/Northampton_Sessions_House_Historic_Building_Assessment?auto=download [accessed 13/02/2018]

Markham, C A, 1885 *History of the County Buildings of Northamptonshire,* Taylor and Son

May, T, 2006 *Victorian and Edwardian Prisons,* Shire Publications

Morgan, R, and Starmer, G, 1977 *Froth and Fizz,* Northampton Museums and Art Gallery

NRO NAP 670–674 *Proposed Conversion of Old Gaol into Offices* Northamptonshire Record Office

NRO NAP 657–700 *Northamptonshire County Council County Buildings, Northampton* Northamptonshire Record Office

NRO Map 5423 *First Floor Plan of the Proposed Alterations at the Northampton County Gaol* Northamptonshire Record Office

NRO MAP 5433 *Proposed Alterations and Additions to the Museum Guildhall Road* Northamptonshire Record Office

NRO TBF173 *Old County Gaol, Angel Lane, Northampton 1926 Alterations etc,* Talbot Brown and Fisher Collection, Northamptonshire Record Office

Pevsner, N, Bailey, B, Cherry, B, 2013 *The Buildings of England: Northamptonshire,* Yale University Press

Supplement to the Northampton Mercury, Saturday July 12 1884, *Opening of New Salvation Army Barracks*

VCH 1930 *The Victoria History of the County of Northampton,* **3**, St Catherine Press

Whelan, F, 1874 *History, Topography and Directory of Northamptonshire,* Francis Whelan & Co

Northamptonshire Archaeology, **41**, 2021, 403–409

Northampton Notes

Medieval chess pieces from Northampton

by

Andy Chapman

Introduction

Today Northampton is a medium-sized provincial town, but in the medieval period the presence of the royal castle saw it rise to prominence as a town favoured by frequent royal and noble visits, with parliaments and other meetings of state taking place in the castle (Chapman 2021a, this volume 137–189). It is therefore of no surprise that chess, the medieval board game of the nobility, was not just being played in the town but that in the later 12th century there was a workshop that was fashioning chess pieces in antler to provide new chess sets for potential customers.

The discovery of two discarded unfinished chess pieces in antler (Fig 1) along with quantities of partially worked antler debris during excavations at Angel Street, Northampton has increased the number of medieval stylised chess pieces from Northampton to three, with the previous single example recovered during the clearance of the ruins of Northampton castle in the late 19th century (see Fig 3).

The chess pieces from the excavations at Angel Street and the workshop in which they were made are described

and discussed at length in the site report (Brown 2021: Chapman 2021b, Brown and Finn 2021, Atkins *et al* 2021). The intention of this shorter article is to provide more detailed illustrations of the two pieces from Angel Street, and to set them alongside the previous discovery from the castle, which is currently on display at Northampton Museum and Art Gallery. Thanks must go to MOLA (Museum of London Archaeology) Northampton Office, for whom I was working at the time the Angel Street pieces were discovered, allowing me the opportunity to handle them soon after recovery.

Chess in medieval Europe

The game of chess came into Europe from India through contact with the Arab world, probably as early as the 10th century, and by the 12th century it had become established as the popular game at the upper levels of European society (Eales 2002, 39–48 and Riddler 1995). The finest pieces were usually fashioned in ivory and were figurative and elaborately decorated, such as the famous chessmen found on the Isle of Lewis, Scotland in the 19th century (Stratford 1997; Caldwell and Hall 2014), now one of the star attractions of the Anglo-Saxon gallery at the British Museum, alongside the Sutton Hoo ship burial.

Stylised chess pieces

To supply the wider market with chess sets smaller pieces were made from antler, bone or jet, often decorated with patterns of ring-and-dot motifs along with incised lines encircling the base and running over the top. These simple chess pieces followed the stylised Arabic forms, although in Europe simple figurative elements, such as ring-and-dot eyes, were often added (Fig 2).

The king and queen (Fig 2, left) comprise a cylindrical or square base with the upper part cut back to form a throne represented by an inverted, flat-topped V-shape. They are also fitted with a small knob or cylindrical head on top, frequently elaborated and given stylised or even semi-naturalistic facial features. The only difference between the two would be the larger size of the king, so a single piece could be either a king or a queen.

Fig 1: the head of a king/queen and the bishop from Angel Street (Scale 10mm)

The bishop (Fig 2, second left) has only been referred as a bishop in literature since the 17th century, although it had been portrayed as such on figurative pieces, such as the Lewis chessmen, since the 12th century. It was previously known in the west as the aufin or alfin, from the Arabic *Alfil*. The Arabic portrayal of the Indian elephant comprised two forward projecting humps, the stylised tusks, set on a cylindrical body. In part of a group of exceptionally large stylised pieces in whalebone, from Witchampton Manor, Dorset (Dalton 1927), there is a bishop where the horns have been replaced by a pair of sub-rectangular, heads with faces, similar to the single, but plain, head on a knight within the same group. The Witchampton Manor bishop provides a parallel for the paired heads on the bishop from Angel Street, below.

The knight (horseman) (Fig 2, centre) depicted by an abstract head set on a cylindrical body is the most easily recognised piece, as the basic form has survived into the modern standard Staunton set, as established in the mid-19th century, as a stylised horse's head.

The Arabic *rukh,* westernised to rook (Fig 2, second right), was a camel-mounted soldier represented by an abstract form of the Persian chariot, depicted by a deep V-shaped notch on a plain rectangular or oval block. This turreted top may have resulted in Europeans mistaking it for a castle. The illustrated example, from Tempsford Park, Bedfordshire, is unusually elaborately decorated, with a total of 156 ring-and-dot motifs (112 single and 44 double), on both faces and sides and also the surfaces of the curving, V-shaped notch (Chapman 2000 and 2005).

The pawn (foot-soldier), even in otherwise ornately carved sets, is always portrayed as a simple block or pillar with minimal elaboration, as in this previously unpublished example from a medieval settlement at Ketton Quarry, Rutland, excavated by Northamptonshire Archaeology (now MOLA Northampton) (Fig 2, photograph right), which stands 29mm high and is decorated with incised lines around the base and over the domed top, with each of the ten lines centred on a flattened facet and terminating above a ring-and-dot motif. There is a similar pawn from The Prebendal Manor, Nassington (Chapman 1999).

The majority of these stylised chess pieces stand 35–45mm high, with smaller pawns at 25–35mm. At the extremes, the Witchampton Manor whalebone bishop stands 105mm high, while the smallest example known to the author is from Wallingford, Oxfordshire found during excavations in 2015 (Lindsey Bedford pers comm). It stands only 21.8mm high, but is still decorated with incised lines and groups of ring-and-dot motifs on the body and across the plug in the top. It is dwarfed by the bishop from Angel Street (Fig 3), and at this size the entire set could have been an easily portable 'pocket' set. (Thanks to Lindsey Bedford who brought the piece to Northampton for me to see and comment on, which enabled the direct physical comparison to be made).

Archaeological discoveries

Stylised chess pieces have been occasional finds from archaeological excavations since the mid-19th century, with early examples being a rook in bone from Woodperry, Oxfordshire (J W 1846, fig 17) and a knight and pawn in jet from Mote Hill, Warrington, Lancashire (Kendrick 1852). Since then urban sites, particularly London, have produced examples along with rural manor houses, abbeys and castles. However, a more crudely fashioned knight in animal bone from a potter's tenement at Lyveden, Northamptonshire, suggests that the game was not entirely restricted to the upper levels of medieval society (Bryant and Steane 1971, 66–67, fig 19a & plate 18).

These chance finds are most often single pieces, often complete, recovered at the place where they were used, presumably through accidental loss. While the Northampton Castle bishop conforms to this pattern, the pieces from Angel Street appear to be unique in being incomplete or unfinished as a result of being discarded at the workshop where they were being manufactured.

The pieces and fragments of pieces from Witchampton Manor are still the only example of multiple pieces from a single set recovered at one time. In this instance there

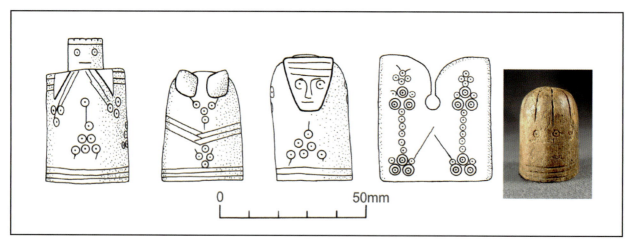

Fig 2 The basic forms of medieval stylised chess pieces: king/queen, bishop, knight, rook and pawn (after Chapman 2005, fig 2, and photograph of a pawn from Ketton Quarry, to scale)

Fig 3: The exceptionally small bishop from Wallingford compared to a more typical piece, the bishop from Angel Street, Northampton (Scale 10mm)

stylised forms and the range of variability and complexity around the basic shapes, a few published pieces have been misidentified, for example a very simple and plain stylised king/queen from Milton Keynes which was published as "little doubt" that it was "indeed a chessman", possibly a bishop although "alternatively it may be a king or queen" (J Leveson Gower 1994, 33–35, fig 18).

It is also notable that whilst pawns would necessarily make up 50% of all pieces manufactured, they are significantly under-represented among the recovered pieces, indicating that either they were not as often lost, which seems unlikely, or that they these small and sometimes plain pieces may have gone unrecognised in past excavations or even within some recovered finds assemblages.

A Bishop from Northampton Castle

During the destruction of Northampton Castle in 1879–80 to make way for a new railway station and goods yard (Chapman this volume 137–189), a chess bishop in antler, with its characteristic paired horns, representing the tusks of an elephant, was among the finds recovered. The Northampton Castle bishop is oval in plan with a domed top, where the spongy tissue has been replaced by a plug. It stands 37mm high, by 29–33mm in diameter, and is decorated with incised lines and clusters of ring-and-dot impressions on the front and sides (Fig 4).

The piece was illustrated by Sharp (1882, plate 5) in his account of the finds from the castle, and it also appeared in the study of the castle by Rev R M Serjeantson (1908, 58); unfortunately the printers inverted the piece so that it was sitting on its horns but Serjeantson was able to add a marginal note correcting this error before publication. Henry Dryden had also taken an interest in this piece immediately after its discovery and presented it, along with other comparable examples, at a meeting of the Royal Archaeological Institute in June 1882, as recorded in the Archaeological Journal (Dryden 1882), at a time when few pieces had been recovered and fewer published.

is little doubt that this constituted a deliberate deposit of pieces, and the burnt fragments may suggest that there had been an intention to destroy them that at least partially failed. In one fashion, Northampton can now join Witchampton in being the first site to produce more than one piece from a single workshop.

I am not aware that anyone has compiled a full gazetteer of all known stylised chess pieces from England. Having published a short paper on stylised chess pieces based on over 40 examples that I had records of at the time (Chapman 2005), several additional examples were made known to me directly as a result of that article, and I am aware of several more that have been found since. So perhaps some 60–70 medieval stylised chess pieces in antler, bone and jet have been found in England to date.

The recovered pieces represent all the four major characters in a range of forms from some of the most highly stylised examples worked in jet to some where the figurative elements have almost taken over from the stylised forms. One word of warning is that given these

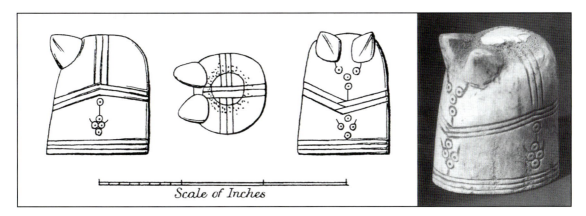

Fig 4: The bishop from Northampton Castle (after Dryden 1882: photograph Northampton Museum and Art Gallery)

The King/Queen and Bishop of Angel Street

The medieval chess workshop

At Angel Street, Northampton we have the first identified location for a workshop manufacturing chess pieces (Brown 2021). The workshop was in timber, defined by large post-pits, and it is dated to the mid to late 12th century (Brown and Finn 2021). Quantities of discarded offcuts from both red deer and fallow deer antlers were found in both contemporary deposits and redeposited into some later contexts, with some pieces chamfered in preparation for further working.

The king/queen

The first piece found at Angel Street was a small circular stylised head in antler, 25mm high and 15mm in diameter (Fig 5). The flat top had been cross-cut to form a simple crown, with a deep central hole into the spongy tissue, which had probably held a hard antler plug, now lost, with the cross cuts probably once carried across this plug. The face is marked by ring-and-dot eyes on the flattened facets on either side of an angled nose. It was probably discarded because in fashioning the facet for the right side of the face the spongy core of the antler was exposed, making it impossible to set a ring-and-dot right eye in the correct position, opposing the left eye, although a partial misplaced eye, too low and too close to the nose, was added, perhaps in an attempt to salvage the piece. The lower part of the head, with its cut tapering, would have been inserted into the top of a larger cylindrical body to form either a King or Queen, as in Figure 5, where it is set on a body from London, Seal House (Egan 1998, 292 & fig 221, no 956).

The bishop

In the last week of excavation a second and more complete chess piece was recovered. It was fashioned on a cylindrical length of antler and stands 42mm high and 28–32mm in diameter. The front has been cut back to form a pair of projecting rectangular heads (Fig 6).

During manufacturing it would appear that an extra sliver of antler was accidental taken off the inside edge of the right-hand face, producing a disparity in width that is probably the reason why this piece was discarded. Prior to being discarded, a large antler plug had been inserted into the top, and a small square edge of antler had been driven into the base, but this had probably caused further splitting of the spongy tissue. While some plain pieces have been discovered, it is more likely that if the piece had not been discarded they would have gone on to decorate the body with incised lines and ring-and-dot motifs. The deep gouge on the body is likely to be damage subsequent to it being discarded.

The projecting heads have replaced the more usual stubby horns in symbolising the tusks of an elephant, taking us back to the origins of chess in India and the middle-east. As noted above, there is a large bishop in whalebone from Witchhampton Manor, Dorset that provides a parallel for using paired stylised heads instead of horns to represent the tusks (Dalton 1927).

Conclusions

The identification in Northampton of a workshop that was involved in producing chess pieces in antler in the later 12th century is a significant addition to the early history of chess in England. That it was identified in Northampton may be a surprise to those who were unaware that this medium-sized provincial town, with few visible historic structures, was then in its medieval heyday, with a much visited royal castle as a centre for parliaments and other meetings of state, as well as several religious houses. This was exactly the right place for an enterprising craftsman in bone and antler to look towards a potential market for chess sets among the titled lords and their retinues who were then regularly gathering in Northampton, with an ability to play a good game of chess perhaps becoming as essential then as playing a good game of poker, bridge or whist has been at the appropriate levels of modern society (Fig 7).

Bibliography

J W 1846 Antiquities found at Woodperry, Oxon, *Archaeol J,* **3**, 116–24

Atkins, R, Brown, J, and Finn, C, 2021 Chess pieces, bone and antler carving in Northampton, *in* J Brown 2021, 319–320

Brown, J, 2021 *Living opposite to the Hospital of St John: Excavations in medieval Northampton 2014*, Archaeopress Archaeology

Brown, J, with Finn, C, 2021 A carver's workshop opposite the Hospital of St John, *in* Brown 2021, 46–51 & figs 2.10–2.13

Bryant, G F, and Steane, J M, 1971 Excavations at the Deserted Medieval Settlement at Lyveden, A Third Interim Report, *Northampton Museum and Art Gallery Journal,* **9**

Caldwell, D H, and Hall, M A, 2014 *The Lewis Chessmen: New Perspectives*, National Museums Scotland

Chapman, A, 1999 A stylised chess piece from the Prebendal Manor House, Nassington, Northamptonshire, *Northamptonshire Archaeology* **28**, 135–9

Chapman, A, 2000 A stylised chess piece from the moated enclosure at Tempsford, *South Midlands Archaeology* **30**, 7–8

Chapman 2005, Gaming pieces, *in* A Maull and A Chapman 2005 *A Medieval Moated Enclosure at Tempsford Park*, Bedfordshire Archaeol Monog, **5**, 79–80, fig 6.3,13 & plate 15

Chapman, A, 2005 *Medieval Stylised Chess Pieces*, The Finds Research Group AD700–1700, Datasheet, **35**

Chapman, A, 2021a Northampton Castle, Part 1: Introduction, pre-castle archaeology, and the history and topography of the castle, *Northamptonshire Archaeology*, **41**, 137–189

Chapman, A, 2021b Antler working debris and worked chess pieces, *in* J Brown 2021, 200–204, figs 3.22–3.28

Dalton, O M, 1927 Early chessmen of whalebone excavated in Dorset, *Archaeologia*, **77**, 77–86

Dryden, H E L, 1882 Proceedings of Meetings of the Royal Archaeological Institute, June 1, 1882: Exhibit of Chess and Playing Pieces, *Archaeol J,* **39**, 421–2

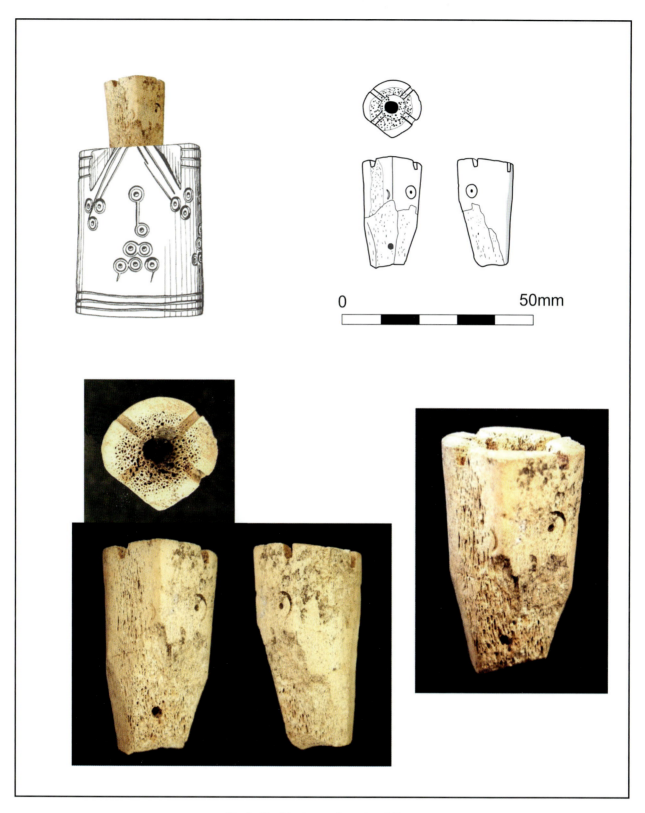

Fig 5: The king/queen from Angel Street

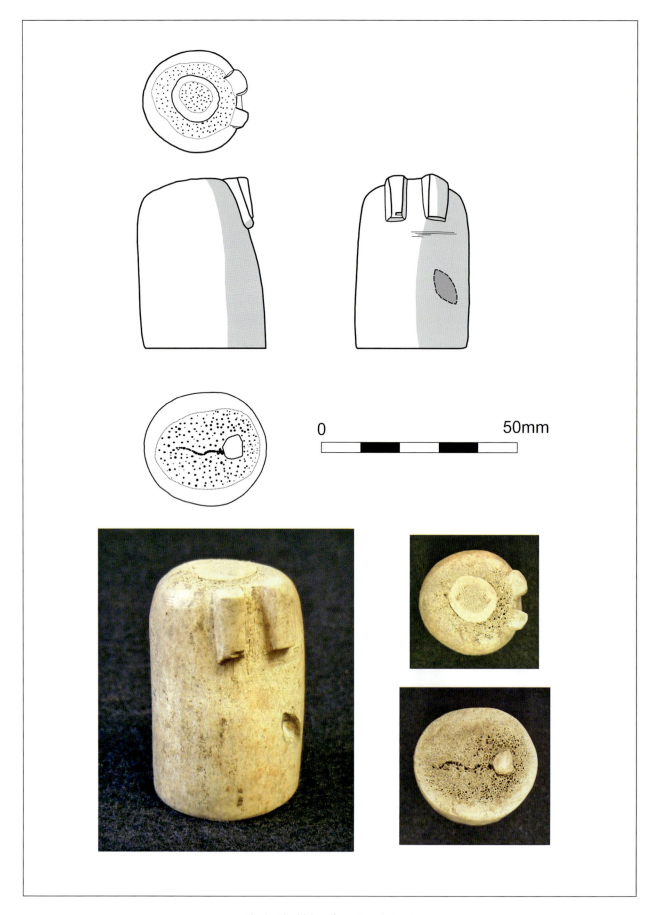

Fig 6: The bishop from Angel Street

Fig 7: Playing chess in the medieval hall at Tempsford, Bedfordshire by Alex Thompson (née Thorne)

Egan, G, 1998 Chess pieces, in G Egan, *The Medieval Household Daily Living c.1150– c.1450*, Medieval Finds from Excavations in London, **6**, 291–4

Eales, R, 2002 *Chess: The History of a Game*, Hardinge Simpole chess classic

Kendrick, J, 1852 An account of excavations made at the Mote Hill, Warrington, Lancs, *Proceedings and Papers of the Hist Soc of Lancashire and Cheshire,* **5**, 59–68

Leveson Gower, J, 1994 Antler Gaming Piece, *in* D C Mynard 1994 Excavations on medieval and later sites in Milton Keynes, 1972–1980, Buckinghamshire Archaeol Soc Monog, **6**

Maull, A, and Chapman, A, 2005 *A Medieval Moated Enclosure at Tempsford Park*, Bedfordshire Archaeol Monog, **5**

Riddler, I D, 1995 Anglo-Norman Chess, *in* J Alexander Voogt, de (ed) 1995 *New approaches to board games research: Asian origins and future perspectives,* Leiden, 99–109 http://www.academia.edu/4603178/1995_Anglo_Norman_Chess (accessed 22/08/2021)

Serjeantson, R M, 1908 *The Castle of Northampton*, Northamptonshire Nat Hist Soc

Sharp, S, 1882 Description of Antiquities found on the site of the Castle at Northampton, *Associated Architectural Societies Reports and Papers,* **16**, 243–71

Stratford, N, 1997 *The Lewis Chessmen and the enigma of the Hoard*, London: British Museum Press

Northampton Castle's Postern Gate

by

Graham Cadman

Introduction

The following notes were compiled by Graham Cadman in his former role within Northamptonshire County Council (NCC), Historic Environment Record team (HER).

Northampton Castle's Postern Gate, moved to its present position in Victorian times (NGR SP 7484 6041), remains the best known and most visible vestige of the town's once proud royal castle. The Gate is **located** on Black Lion Hill close to the town's new railway station entrance on the approach to historic West Bridge. The south elevation of this fine but forlorn looking stone-built monument will be familiar to passers-by, though increasingly hemmed in by road signs. Its resolutely closed green painted wooden door leads only to a security grill and beyond a short flight of steps to the station car park's own security fencing. This and adjoining trees partially obscure this northern elevation which was not designed for show and is little visited apart than for maintenance access.

The Postern Gate and its adjoining stone walls are Grade II Listed (National List for England entry number 1371878). The Gate structure has been owned by Northamptonshire County Council (NCC) since 1974 when it was acquired from Northampton Borough Council following local government reorganisation. NCC subsequently improved the site and carried out repairs including the removal of nearby advertising hoardings. The gate was further restored by the County and Borough council's in 1992–93. It is nowadays managed and maintained as one of the County Council's County Heritage Sites.

Originally a small side entrance set in the curtain wall of the inner bailey on the west side of the medieval castle, the gate was dismantled in 1879 as the castle was being demolished to make way for the railway station (Chapman 2021, this volume, 137–189). The gate was rebuilt on its present site. Constructed of mixed ironstone and limestone, it includes some masonry from the original castle postern gate. Coursed stone is present above the entrance arch together with a stone gable, parapets and ornamental kneelers. This form is repeated at the rear of the gateway which has a roof structure comprising a solid substructure of stone with rafters sunk into it and a covering of large limestone roof slates. The design is essentially Victorian Gothic 'which gives it the appearance of a detached Victorian rectory porch' (Giggins 2011). This impression is strengthened by the painted plank door, a replacement for an earlier one.

Authenticity

Research by historic buildings specialist Brian Giggins (2011) for the County Council compared the present monument with 19th century photographs made of the original before demolition along with a detailed drawing produced by antiquarian Sir Henry Dryden prior to its relocation (preserved in the Local Studies collection at the Central Library). Giggins concluded that when the arches are looked at in detail it can be seen that the majority of the stones were not re-erected 'in the same relative positions'. Of the three masons marks known to have existed only one now survives. A stone that was on the left hand side of the arch has been moved to the right hand side and another stone has been turned upside down. The former contains two holes drilled to take an iron staple. Graffiti on the left hand side of the present arch does not continue on to the next stone suggesting that the stone was re-cut to fit the present position. The weathering on the present

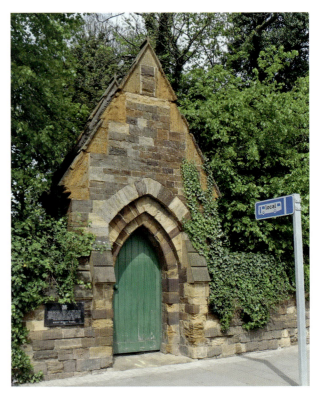

Fig 1: Postern Gate south elevation, May 2015, with encroaching ivy and trees (G Cadman)

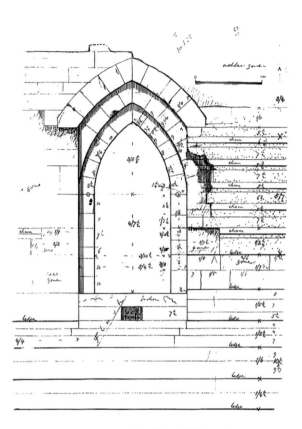

Postern. Black Lion Hill. Northampton.

Fig 2: South elevation of the Postern Gate,
drawn by Brian Giggins 1990

Northampton Castle ~ West Postern

Based on a drawing by Sir H. Dryden

Fig 3: Dryden's mid-19th century drawing of the original gate
in situ (from Giggins 2011)

stones indicates that a large amount of new or re-cut stone was used in the Victorian reconstruction.

Giggins concluded that it is probable that the present monument contains medieval masonry and that some of it may be correctly positioned in the entrance archway. The adjoining walls may also incorporate original stone from the castle. There are, however, a large number of stones in the arches of the gate which have not been precisely relocated and the majority of the structure does not reflect the location of the original postern masonry. In the light of this' he suggested that the present monument might be viewed as a Victorian memorial to the destruction of the castle rather than a rebuilding of the medieval postern gate.

Significance

Northampton Castle's Postern Gate is of historic and some archaeological significance as well as being of community value:

It is by far the most publicly recognised surviving part of Northampton Castle. It is highly visible, adjoining historic West Bridge and the town's railway station. It is known to generations of Northampton people and is seen by many thousands of local people and visitors every year. As such it has great communal value.

It also has some historic significance in terms of its association, albeit indirectly, with the individuals and events associated with the medieval castle and directly, with local antiquarian and public interest in the castle during the Victorian and later eras.

It is of historic interest as a Victorian memorial to the destruction of the town's castle. The Gate's presence today, results from antiquarian and public interest and concern. The demolition of the castle and the construction of the new railway station re-awakened Victorian interest in the castle. In 1878 work had commenced on levelling the majority of the site of Northampton Castle to construct a goods yard for the London & North Western Railway Company. The castle became the focus for a campaign led by the Rev'd Baker to preserve part of the castle's walls within the new redevelopment scheme. In the event the railway company would only agree to a lesser scheme, with their moving and partial reinstatement of the Postern Gate to its present location. For the first time in the modern era, there was public clamour to safeguard part of the town's heritage.

The present Monument does contain some medieval masonry even if much of the stonework was replaced

411

with modern stone during the Victorian relocation and rebuilding. The Gate therefore retains some architectural and archaeological significance even though it has been physically divorced from its original architectural and archaeological context.

The Postern Gate makes a contribution to the context of the medieval castle and to its subsequent demolition and partial replacement by Northampton railway station. Whilst it no longer occupies its original position in the inner bailey wall, it does help contribute to public awareness that a castle once stood hereabouts and helps provide a historic context for the present railway station. Being located just inside the conjectured line of the castle's outer bailey wall and ditch, the monument also helps visibly mark the approximate southern limit of the castle.

The monument also has value as a focus for future public recognition, presentation and understanding of the castle and the historic town of which it forms a part.

References

Chapman A, 2021 Northampton Castle, Part 1: Introduction, pre-castle archaeology, and the history and topography of the castle, *Northamptonshire Archaeol*, **41**, 137–189,

Giggins, B, 2011 *The Postern Gate, Black Lion Hill, Northampton,* Unpublished report for NCC HER (Compiled 1990 and reproduced with minor corrections in 2011)

Northamptonshire Archaeology, **41**, *2021, 413–414*

Northampton Town Mill

by

Graham Cadman

The following notes were compiled by Graham Cadman through his former role within Northamptonshire County Council (NCC), Historic Environment Record team (HER).

Northampton Town Mill (NGR SP 7500 6013) operated as a cotton, paper and corn mill over many centuries before its demolition in the late 1920s. It was known at different times as Town Mill, Marvill's Mill, Perry's Mill, Edward Cave's Mill, Gibson & Forbes Mill & Cotton Mills (Starmer 2002). During 2014 its site was the subject to observation and updated reporting to Northamptonshire Historic Environment Record (HER) (Cadman 2014), as summarised in this note. Existing HER records include cotton mill (HER 1160/38), mill building (1160/38/2) and mill leat (1160/38/3).

The former mill was located towards the north end of what is nowadays Towcester Road, close to its junction with Tanner Street, Northampton (Fig 1). A modern road bridge (approx. centre SP7500 6013) here takes Towcester Road across the Brampton Arm of the River Nene linking its north bank with Foot Meadow to the south. The HER records that fragments of ironstone walls and a displaced bored wooden pipe several metres long were observed (by Andy Chapman for Northamptonshire Archaeology) during trenching works in 1985 on the 'southern approach road' hereabouts. Today, a narrow strip of ragged, mortared mixed brick and stone work (centred on SP75000 60128) extends approximately 7.5m under and adjoining the south side of the modern bridge. There are indications that this masonry continues to the west, buried under the present river bank. Is this part of the mill walling identified by B Giggins in 1997 (HER 1160/38/2)? Adjoining the west side of the north abutment of the bridge is a small area of cast concrete and mortared brickwork (SP75007

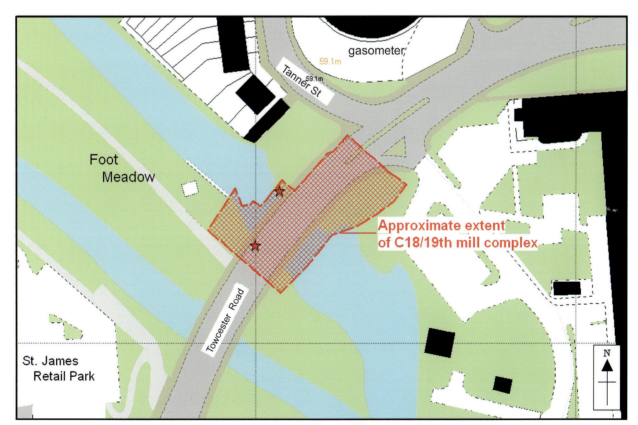

Northamptonshire County Council Licence No. 100019331, Published 10/02/2014

Fig 1: Approximate extent of the 18th and 19th century Northampton mill complex, depicted in red on modern OS map utilising the first edition OS 1:2,500 scale mapping. Red stars mark approximate location of surviving brickwork (Note that the gasometers and houses on Tanner Street, to the north, were demolished in 2013/2014)

60145), also possibly associated with a late phase of the mill? If confirmed, these remains will constitute the last visible traces of Northampton Town Mill along with the modified line of the old mill race, visible for a couple of hundred metres to the east of the modern road bridge.

The full extent of buried archaeological remains associated with the mill's multiple phases of use has not been determined. Whilst construction of the modern bridge and river management works will have caused extensive destruction, the surviving riverside masonry indicates at least some fragmentary survival potential. Any remains represent a heritage asset potentially of high importance given that the mill has been identified as the '*world's first true cotton mill*' (Bates 1998, 57) as well as being claimed as '*... the first water-powered cotton mill in the world*' by Starmer (2002, 94). Redevelopment hereabouts should accordingly take careful account of this potential and ensure that the opportunity is not lost to recover evidence from and commemorate the presence of one of the town's otherwise lost historic industrial landmarks.

References

Bates, D L, 1998 Cotton-spinning in Northampton: the Gibson & Forbes Mill, 1785–1806, *Northamptonshire Past & Present*, **51**, 57–75

Cadman, G, 2014 *Note for Northamptonshire Historic Environment Record (HER). Northampton Town Mill, 11 February 2014*, unpublished note NCC HER

Starmer, G, 2002 *Northamptonshire watermills survey 2001–2002*, Unpublished 2 volume survey commissioned by NCC & held by Northamptonshire Historic Environment Record (HER)

Northamptonshire Archaeology, **41**, 2021, 415–416

Northampton, Historic Jetties

by

Graham Cadman

A note of two Northampton 'jetties' or alleys has been passed to Northamptonshire Historic Environment Record (HER) following recording and observation by Graham Cadman, and the modified version published here was offered to *Northamptonshire Archaeology*, 6/01/2017.

> Collins Street to Wilby Street: NGR SP 7654 61002 to SP76863 60982
> Wilby Street to East Street: NGR SP 76850 60979 to SP76809 60969

Ninety-five and forty-two metres long respectively, these historic highway features were built in the Abington area of the town during Victorian times and represent integral parts of the expanding town's residential suburbs. Their line follows that of an earlier path or track, present on J Wood and EF Law's Town of Northampton Plan of 1847.

Both form part of the adopted highways network and continue to be used, though accessibility is occasionally impaired by weeds, rubbish dumping and episodes of anti-social behaviour. Regular, ongoing maintenance is essential to help retain these old pedestrian routes within the town and to support their ongoing, active public use.

Jetties in one form or another have been familiar features in Northampton from medieval times onward. Jeyes Jetty located within the medieval town centre is one well known early example. All are distinctive features of Northampton's evolving townscape and can be regarded as heritage assets in their own right, contributing to the character and sense of place of the Victorian and earlier town. That between Collins and Wilby streets also contributes to the setting of the adjoining Billing Road Cemetery within Billing Road Conservation Area.

Postscript: Jeyes Jetty, June 2020

Jeyes Jetty is an historic feature of the town centre topography, running between the Drapery and College Street (Figs 2–4). Planning permission and Listed Building Consent was granted in early June 2020 for the installation of lockable gates at both ends of Jeyes Jetty effectively closing this town centre historic public right of way or jetty to public use. Repeated incidents of anti-social behaviour and crime led to Northampton Borough Council's proposal to close using a Public Spaces Protection Order.

In the opinion of the writer closure is a retrograde step. Characterful but increasingly scarce heritage assets in the historic town, such as Jeyes Jetty warrant cherishing with the adoption of imaginative, sustainable ways to tackle threats to their continued public use and enjoyment. Is treating them as nuisances meriting public exclusion, the best way of helping conserve such elements of Northampton's historic environment in the 21st century?

Fig 1: View east from Wilby Street, Northampton to the jetty which runs through to Collins Street
(G Cadman, 7 August 2014)

Photographs of Jeyes Jetty by Graham Cadman, 10 September 2020

Fig 2: The eastern entrance to Jeyes Jetty sits unobtrusively beside the Timpson shop and under the south end of 6 & 7 The Drapery, which is Grade II Listed, a rough ashlar clad building of the 18th century where Philadelphus and John Jeyes opened their pharmacy business, which continued operating on this site until 1969

Fig 3: The eastern entrance to Jeyes Jetty from The Drapery

Fig 4: College Street western entrance to Jeyes Jetty with modern sign arch

Northamptonshire Archaeology, **41**, *2021, 417–418*

A 3D model of the Greyfriars Bus Station, Northampton

by

Amir Bassir

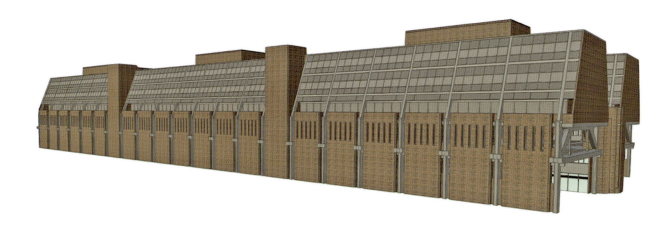

Fig 1: Screen shot showing 3D view of the exterior of Greyfriars Bus Station

Fig 2: Screen shot showing view into the bus lanes

The 3D model

In North*amptonshire Archaeology*, 2015, **38**, 205–219, there was a building recording report on the former Greyfriars Bus Station, Northampton, which was closed in 2014 and demolished in 2015 (Bassir 2017).

As an extension of that work, based upon historic building survey information and the original design drawings, a 3D image has been produced by Amir Bassir, formerly Historic Buildings Officer at MOLA (Museum of London Archaeology), in Google SketchUp.

The 3D image of both the outside and the inside of the building (see screen shots, Figs 1 & 2), may be explored online through Sketchfab.com at: https://sketchfab.com/models/66ebff2a3f584fa09f9fcb8eb67b6cc4 (accessed 6/7/2021).

Here you can wander around the eerily empty building devoid of people, buses and internal fittings.

Bibliography

Bassir, A, 2015 The Fishmarket and Greyfriars Bus Station, Northampton, *Northamptonshire Archaeology*, **38**, 195–219

County Notes

Social distancing and leprosy: a medieval example from Raunds

by

Andy Chapman

Introduction

Social distancing is a phrase we all know from our experiences through much of 2020 and 2021 as well, but as a response to a threat of contagion the process has a much longer history. This example is taken from a recent analysis of burials including an individual from the churchyard at Raunds, Furnells, excavated in the late 1970s, where the original osteological diagnosis of probable leprosy has been confirmed by recent obtained DNA evidence (Boddington 1996, Kerudin *et al* 2019).

The church and cemetery at Raunds, Furnells had formed part of the holding of a late Saxon thegn, and it became a small manor house complex following the Norman Conquest (Audouy and Chapman 2009). The earliest church dates to the mid-10th century, being an addition to a timber hall and associated buildings constructed within a series of ditched plots in the second quarter of the 10th century, following the Late Saxon re-conquest of the Danelaw. Burial continued through the 11th century, with a larger church added by the middle of the 12th century. By the end of the 12th century interment in the cemetery was probably confined to the occupants of the western manor house (Audouy and Chapman 2009, table 3.1).

Acknowledgements

Thanks are due to Jo Buckberry of the Biological Anthropology Research Centre, School of Archaeological and Forensic Sciences, University of Bradford, which houses the skeletal assemblage from Raunds, Furnells, who kindly provided copies of the two papers referenced in this article (Kerudin *et al* 2019 *and* Craig *et al* 2010). The photographs of burial 5046 are from the Raunds, Furnells archive, formerly held by Northamptonshire Archaeology, Northamptonshire County Council, and due to be housed at the new Northamptonshire archaeological archive at Chester Farm, Northamptonshire. The article has been prepared by Andy Chapman, who in the late 1970s was site supervisor for the excavation of the cemetery firstly under original project director Andy Boddington and subsequently Graham Cadman.

Leprosy

Leprosy is one of the oldest diseases known to humankind, with the oldest skeleton displaying such lesions from Rajasthan in northwest India dating to 2000BC. The disease appears to have been uncommon in Europe until the medieval period, and In Britain the prevalence of leprosy peaked in the 13th century AD. It declined during the 15th century AD before becoming uncommon again from the 16th century AD onwards, possibly because of improved social conditions combined with the development of enhanced resistance to the disease among the human population (Kerudin *et al* 2019, 1).

In life post-leprosy disfigurements have caused sufferers to be subject to social discrimination, referred to as leprosy stigma. In the past this was driven by misunderstandings regarding transmission of the disease, but discrimination still persists today in some parts of the world

In skeletons, manifestations of the disease can be observed in the hands, feet, facial bones, tibiae and fibulae of affected skeletons. "About 5% of leprosy cases develop skeletal changes, and the lesions used in osteological assessment of the disease can be ambiguous. An important adjunct to palaeopathological analysis has therefore been provided by the detection and sequencing of *M. leprae* DNA, which is sometimes preserved in archaeological skeletons displaying osteological lesions, and has also been occasionally detected in skeletons free from such lesions" (Kerudin *et al* 2019, 2).

The original interpretation of burial 5046, a young man aged 17–25 years at death, as an individual possibly suffering from leprosy was based on Rhinomaxillary changes (bone erosion and absorption around the upper jaw and the palate and nasal bones) as well as and new bone formation, most clearly evident in the thickening of the lower half of the right femur (Figs 1 & 2). Recent analysis of DNA obtained from burial 5046 has confirmed the original interpretation that this individual had suffered from leprosy.

However, it is now also possible to define sub-types of leprosy, and the incidence of these through time and space can be used to track the spread of leprosy into and across Europe.

Fig 1: Raunds, Furnells, Burial 5046 (Raunds, Furnells archive)

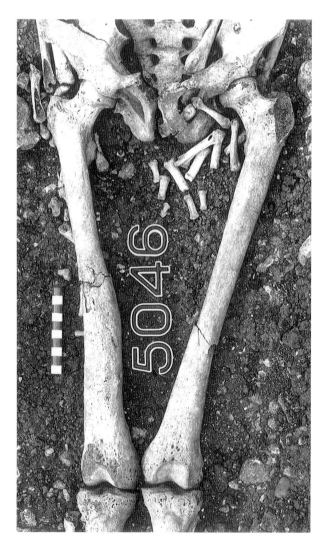

Fig 2: Burial 5046, showing obvious periosteal bone formation on the right femur (Raunds, Furnells archive)

Burial 5046 was of subtype 3K, which:

"has not previously been reported in Britain. In modern *M. leprae*, this subtype is associated with East Asia, in particular Japan, China, the Philippines and New Caledonia… Among ancient specimens it has been detected in a Turkish skeleton from the 8th–9th centuries AD, three skeletons from Hungary, from the 7th–10th centuries AD, and another from 11th–13th century AD Denmark. The R5046 skeleton is from a similar period (10th to mid-12th centuries AD) as these other European detections, but is the most westerly in location, and hence the most distant from the modern distribution of the subtype. The distribution pattern raises the intriguing possibility that the individual represented by skeleton R5046 did not contract leprosy in Britain but instead had travelled to continental Europe and/or Asia and contracted the disease there. It has previously been suggested that human mobility along the Silk Route was responsible for bringing subtype 3K to eastern Europe from its supposed centre of origin in East Asia" (Kerudin *et al* 2019, 5–6).

Above I have quoted part of the conclusion from the published report, which then goes on to speculate that during the Anglo-Saxon period, up until the 10th century AD, there was extensive travel between Britain and continental Europe, especially of educated clerics, and this suggests the possibility that leprosy of subtype 3K was transmitted to Britain and other parts of western Europe by people who had travelled to the Holy Land and back via Vienna and along the Danube to Constantinople, traversing Hungary, Serbia and Bulgaria (Kerudin *et al* 2019, 6).

However, there may be a simpler explanation. Raunds lay within the Danelaw and the church and the adjacent residence of a *thegn* from the 10th century onward had been preceded by a farmstead, dated to the mid-9th to early 10th centuries, labelled the Anglo-Scandinavian farm as a result of the presence of horse harness fittings and gaming pieces showing Scandinavian influence (Audouy and Chapman 2009, 66).

It may be that our young man, burial 5046, was of Scandinavian decent and had acquired this strain of leprosy either directly or through family connections as a result of their known travels down the Danube and on to Constantinople, where they formed the core of the Varangian Guard through the 10th and 11th centuries. We may also note that following the Norman Conquest some Anglo-Saxons who had suffered at the hands of the Vikings and the Normans left the country to seek their fortunes elsewhere, and by the end of the 11th century Anglo-Saxons outnumbered Scandinavians within the Varangian guard (*Varangian Guard*, Wikipedia: accessed 27/04/2021).

Social distancing in the Raunds, Furnells cemetery

It has been established that burial 5046 had suffered from leprosy, and we have speculated that he may have been of either Scandinavian or Anglo-Saxon decent with links to travellers to Constantinople, who may have

been responsible for the transmission of this eastern strain of leprosy into Western Europe in the 10th to 11th centuries.

If we now consider his burial site within the Furnells cemetery, it can be seen that he lay at the southernmost end of the penultimate row in the south-east corner of the cemetery, and therefore in one of the most isolated positions possible, and therefore a potential example of social distancing in death (Fig 3).

A previous study had already identified the south-east corner of the churchyard as containing a high proportion of burials probably of lower status individuals (Craig and Buckberry 2010). This conclusion was based on the analysis of physical stress markers visible on the bones, such as *cribra orbitalia*, linear enamel hypoplasia (LEH) and *tibial periostitus*, as indicative of poor health and therefore probable lower social status, and lacking grave elaboration, with marker stones and stone or timber coffins argued to be indicative of higher social status.

The spatial analysis showed a concentration of high status burials immediately south the church and a concentration of burials exhibiting stress markers in the south-east corner of the cemetery. While there was an absence of coffined burials or elaborate stone coverings or markers in this area, there was a high incidence of burials with stones set around the head. This prompted

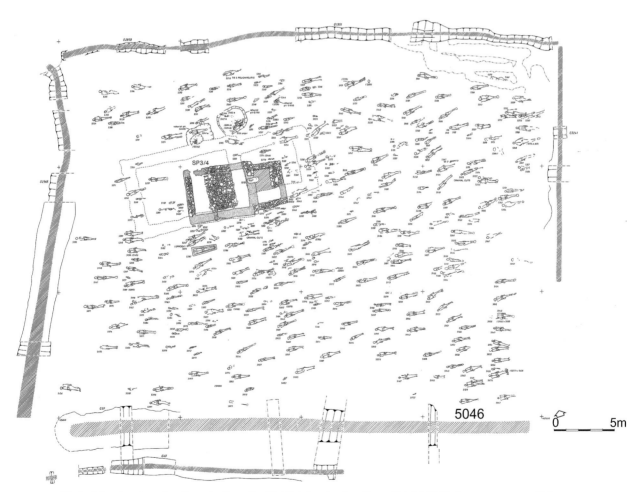

Fig 3: The churchyard at Raunds, Furnells, highlighting the location of burial 5046, the young man with leprosy
(after Boddington 1996, fig 25)

the conclusion that stones set around the head were not a marker of high status, but perhaps a low status cheap alternative to more elaborate stone arrangements, which may explain why they are such a common feature within Anglo-Saxon cemeteries.

Conclusions

In conclusion, not only did our young man have a short life probably blighted by the obvious physical disfigurements caused by leprosy, which would have left him shunned in life, but even in death he was relegated to the furthest corner of the churchyard along with others of poor health and low status. This was probably social distancing to a location where those more fortunate had no need to either pass close by to risk contamination from the inevitable diseases of poverty, or even to be reminded of their existence.

Bibliography

Audouy, M, and Chapman, A, (ed) 2009 *Raunds: the origin and growth of a midland village, AD 450–1500: Excavations in north Raunds, Northamptonshire 1977–87*, Oxbow books

Boddington, A, 1996 *Raunds, Furnells: the Anglo-Saxon Church and Churchyard*, English Heritage Archaeological Report, **7**

Craig, E, and Buckberry, J, 2010 Investigating Social Status using evidence of Biological Status: A case study from Raunds, Furnells, *in* J Buckberry and A Cherryson (eds) 2010 *Burial in Later Anglo-Saxon England, c. 650–1100 AD*, Oxbow Books

Kerudin, A, Muller, R, Buckberry, J, Knusel, C J, Brown, T A, 2019 Ancient *Mycobacterium leprae* genomes from the mediaeval sites of Chichester and Raunds in England, *Journal of Archaeol Science*, **112**, 1–6 (DOI: https//doi.org/10.1016/j/jas.2019.105035)

Northamptonshire Archaeology, **41**, 2021, 423–427

A late medieval pottery kiln at Glapthorn

by

Gill Johnston

Summary

A third late medieval pottery kiln has been found in Upper Glapthorn, located in the same deserted area of the village as the Gypsy Lane kilns (Johnston et al 1997). This third kiln is half the size of the other two and it is possible that firing was limited to two or three events. Products of all three kilns are considered to be similar: wheel thrown late medieval coarse wares mainly for dairying and brewing, plus crested ridge tiles. All of these types have parallels in the later Stanion/Lyveden 'D' ware tradition (Blinkhorn 2008). Kilns 1 and 2 were also firing lime in between pot firings, but this was not the case for Kiln 3. It has not yet been possible to find any parallels for this dual use.

Introduction

At Glapthorn, Northamptonshire, a late medieval pottery kiln, Kiln 3, lies 100m south of the Gypsy Lane kiln in a field on the other side of the road at TL9064 0250 (Fig 1), on the same geology of Blisworth clay overlying a shelly Cornbrash and stone. A discrete area of burnt stone and red burnt clay was noted. Twenty years ago the parch marks of a cottage sized rectangular building were visible 100 metres to the west but much of the stone was removed when a new farmer acquired the land. This area of the village has been deserted since before 1614 (Map, NRO 4526).

The first kiln was discovered in 1984, Leacroft, lying in a village garden, the second, Gypsy Lane kiln, is situated in a field half a mile to the east. These kilns had made use of earlier buildings and were associated with workshops and both were firing large amounts of lime between pot firings. Both kilns were considered to have been in use for several years judging by the huge quantity of wasters produced.

Kiln 3, the subject of this note, was discovered during a field walking exercise, when a discrete area of red burnt limestone stone and burnt clay was noted, preceding preparation to plant Miscanthus, a crop which will cover the site for 15 years once planted and which potentially might have caused severe damage during preparation.

A kiln at Glapthorn, though it is not clear which, has been securely dated by documentary references and coin evidence to AD 1483, when an accounts book of the Duke of Buckingham's manor, at that time in the tenure of John Mores/Morrice lists materials for repair of the manor: 'To the potter for six score crestis…12 shillings'.

A rental in the same book (page 17) lists Walter Brassbrygge, potter, paying 11s. for two cottages, 'which he says are in decay' (Johnston *et al* 1997). The name 'Brassbrygge' is perpetuated in Bracebridge Hill and Bridge in the modern village.

The pottery recovered from all three kilns accords with the Lyveden/Stanion 'D' ware tradition dated AD 1350–1500, (Blinkhorn 2008).

Acknowledgements

Some urgency was involved in recording this kiln and thanks is due to the farmer Mr Bruce Wilkinson for his compliance and assistance. Members of the Middle Nene Archaeology Group (MidNAG) were responsible for the excavation and recording, namely Stephen Upex, Carmel and Paul Crawley, Bob Seaton, Olive Main, Chris Stanley, Andrew Brewster, Sarah Botfield and Andrew Roberts. David Burdett did the machining.

The excavation

An area 7m x 8m was cleared, using a JCB mechanical excavator, to the base of the topsoil revealing a clear circle of burnt stone set into a layer of small limestone rubble which may represent a deliberately laid surface partially encircling and partially spread over the remains of the kiln. The stoke-pit to the west was apparent and an area of clean brown silty soil had settled in the western end where the contents had sagged. Plough ridges were visible and had disturbed the stones of the pedestal and removed part of the interior edge of the wall on the south side.

As no dating material or pottery was mixed with the upper fill of the firing channels it was considered necessary to section both the firing channel and stoke-pit (Figs 2 and 3). The kiln was filled to ground level with stone rubble, much of it showing burning and red burnt luting clay from between the stones of the superstructure. It became clear that the kiln had been demolished deliberately and backfilled with the remaining rubble and burnt clay, the best stone presumably being removed and saved for other purposes.

The kiln had an internal diameter of 1.45m, with an entrance or stokehole at the west end, 0.60m wide and 0.60m long, this being the thickness of the entrance. The walls of the kiln had been mortared with pale yellow

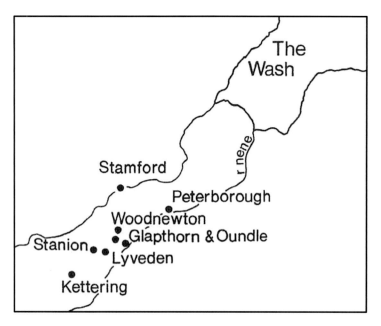

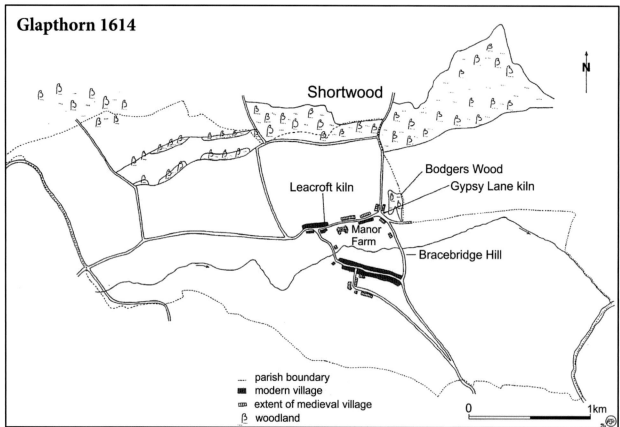

Fig 1: General location plan and location of excavated kilns based on map of 1614

chalky clay and only the base layer remained. The northern side of the wall was only one stone deep with a backing of smaller stone set in pale yellow clay to a width of approximately 0.60m; to the east the true width of the wall remained as a double skinned wall, 0.60m wide which was mortared with the same material; on the south side only the inner ring of stone had survived. The structure was therefore a complete circle with single stokehole

inserted into it. Two heavily burned large stones formed the sides of the stokehole entrance.

The pedestal in the centre of the kiln was rectangular, only one stone thick, 0.45m high, 0.80m long, 0.60m wide and 0.47m deep. The main body of the pedestal had been formed when the firing channels were dug out of the extremely shelly natural Cornbrash, which could be scraped away quite easily by hand. However, it had

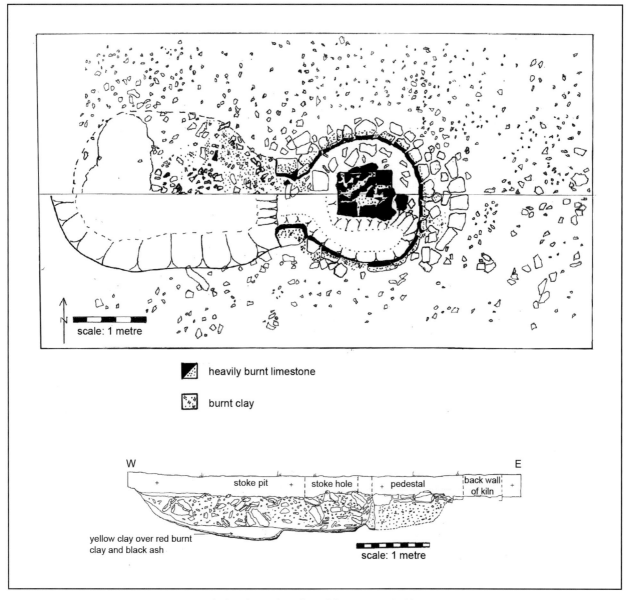

heavily burnt limestone

burnt clay

yellow clay over red burnt
clay and black ash

Fig 2: Plan and section of the excavated Kiln 3

enough strength to support the weight of the stone walls of a kiln. Heavy burning of the pedestal and sides of the firing channel was evident and an ash layer in the base confirmed this.

At the back, the eastern end of the kiln the firing channels were not connected. The side which was excavated formed a blind end which was 100mm below the top of the pedestal, sloping steeply down towards the base of the channel. At its deepest the channel was 0.47m below the top of the pedestal.

The stoke-pit was 3.0m long, up to 2.2m wide and 0.60m deep. A step, 100mm high, lay 0.50m from the entrance, cut into the clay floor of the pit. The fill of the stoke-pit was mainly demolition rubble with a thin layer of black ash and red, lightly fired clay, covering the base. A very thin layer of wasters covered the entire base of the kiln and stoke-pit, layer 10.

The pottery

The stratified pottery from the bottom layer of the interior of the kiln and stoke-pit, layer 10, comprised only 3.0kg of wasters from pottery vessels and ridge tiles. These are similar to those from the other two kilns, wheel thrown Late Medieval Reduced and Oxidised wares, now dated AD 1350–1500 (Blinkhorn 2008), and is therefore considered to be of the same date, ie c.AD 1483 (Figs 4 and 5).

Very little pottery was observed in any other context. The small collection of sherds from the layers at the base of the topsoil and probably associated with habitation in the area were of late Stamford ware (AD 950–1250) and medieval shelly wares of the Stanion /Lyveden tradition (AD 1200–1500), both of which are very common in this area.

Fig 3: The excavated kiln, looking east

Discussion

This latest kiln in Glapthorn is unusual in that it appears to have either been cleaned out very thoroughly or alternatively, had not been fired more than a couple of times. Both the other kilns had been fired many times without being cleaned out and the ash layers had been allowed to build up until they completely filled the firing channels beneath the floor of the chamber.

The construction of this kiln differs from the other two kilns in that the firing channels and pedestal had been formed by scooping out the shelly Cornbrash and then building a circle of stones around the rim to form the walls and adding a layer of stones on top of the pedestal. There was no evidence of a clay lining in the firing channels as this would be quite unnecessary, consequently the Cornbrash had been subject to intense heat. The kiln was also half the size of the other two kilns and had never had a back stokehole. No pot bank has been noted anywhere in the vicinity

The pottery matches the dating for the sites of the other two kilns in the village both of which were making use of earlier buildings. What appeared to be a yard surface covered the demolished kiln but there was no firm evidence of this kiln being associated with a building.

Fig 4: Late medieval pottery sherds from Kiln 3

Layer list

+   Rubbly, pebbly layer at base of silty topsoil.
1   Soft, red burnt clay and stone layer in south side of firing channel below +.
2   Brown silty soil lying in a depression at the west end of the stoke-pit above 10.
3   Stone layer, large stones, many burnt, lying in a matrix of burnt clay at west stokehole entrance and continuing through it up to the front of the pedestal, above 4 but probably part of it.
4   Large structural stones, squared off, heavily burnt at entrance to kiln in the stokehole below 2 and 3. These are demolition.
5   Stony area E of kiln above 7.
6   Clean chalky natural clay at west end of excavation below 10.
7   E of kiln. Layer of larger randomly placed stones below 9.
9   Rubble layer around north side of kiln in a clay matrix, seals the kiln and stoke-   pit.
10 Deeper level in the stokehole and stoke-pit consisting of red burnt clay, larger burnt stones and pottery wasters.
11 Very thin layer of ash and charcoal covering the entire base of the kiln channel and stoking area, lying above burnt natural within the kiln.

Bibliography

Blinkhorn, P, 2008 The pottery, in P Chapman *et al* 2008, 236–255

Chapman, P, Blinkhorn, P, and Chapman, A, 2008 A Medieval Potters' Tenement at Corby Road, Stanion, Northamptonshire, *Northamptonshire Archaeol*, **35**, 215–270

Johnston, A G, Foster, P J, and Bellamy, B, 1997 The Excavation of Two Late Medieval Kilns with Associated Buildings at Glapthorn, near Oundle, Northamptonshire, *Medieval Ceramics*, **21**, 13–42

Fig 5: Late medieval pottery, including bung-hole jars and open bowls, and crested ridge tiles from other Glapthorn kilns

Northamptonshire Archaeology, **41**, 2021, 428–429

Pottery wasters at 1 High Street, Stanion

by

Graham Cadman

Limited archaeological rescue recording was undertaken during the digging of the foundations for a domestic garage at 1 High Sreet, Stanion, Northamptonshire, in late March and early April 2019 (Fig 1: SP 91491 86975). This work identified further evidence for medieval Lyveden/ Stanion pottery production in the village (see Chapman *et al* 2008).

Dumped material with traces of a possible burnt structure were recorded and provide further evidence that pottery production extended along at least part of the High Street, though the form that this took, whether as an outlier or southern continuation of the main concentration of kilns and associated features recorded to date in the Corby Road and Little Lane area, remains to be tested.

Initial analysis of approximately half (61.6kg) of the pottery recovered confirms the presence of wasters of jars and bowls and strip-decorated glazed and stamped jugs along with a small number of glazed and crested ridge tiles, several facemask sherds and straight pulled pipkin handles and one fish-dish. The majority of the pottery examined is, not surprisingly, Stanion ware mostly with a characteristic green glaze and oolitic limestone tempering; also present is a small amount with a distinctive white fabric and a green glaze, which has previously been noted from excavations in Stanion (Fig 2, from Chapman *et al* 2008, 248–9, figs 23 and 29, ST13 & ST14).

Pottery analysis continues of the remainder of the assemblage by members of the Northamptonshire Archaeological Field Group.

References

Chapman, P, Blinkhorn, P, and Chapman, A, 2008 A medieval potters' tenement at Corby Road, Stanion, Northamptonshire, *Northamptonshire Archaeol*, **35**, 215–270

Fig 2: Medieval jugs from Stanion in an uncommon white fabric with a green glaze (from P Chapman *et al* 2008, fig 23)

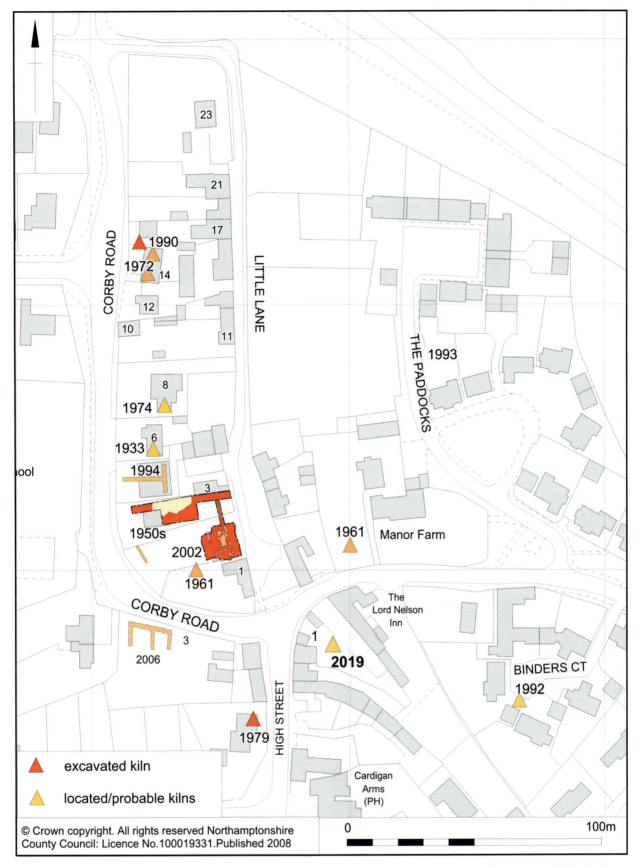

Fig 1: Stanion, showing location of 1 High Street, south of Corby Road and Little Lane (after P Chapman *et al* 2008, fig 4)

Northamptonshire Archaeology, **41**, *2021, 430–431*

A medieval Rhenish '*Blaugrau*' cooking-pot handle from the Prebendal Manor, Nassington

by

Paul Blinkhorn and Jane Baile

A recent re-assessment of some of the Anglo-Saxon and medieval pottery from the excavations at the Prebendal Manor, Nassington, Northamptonshire (TL 06320 96131, see Baile *et al* 2021) has brought to light a fragment of an unusual pottery find in the county, a handle from a small Rhenish Greyware cooking pot of the 12th-13th century (Fig 1).

It is the only earlier medieval imported sherd known from the site, and was originally misidentified as Pingsdorf-type ware, an entirely different type, albeit from a similar geographical source. It was unstratified, and occurred during pre-excavation cleaning in Area 1 1984.

The basic pottery type, generally known as "Rhenish Greyware', is also commonly referred to as *Blaugrau* or 'Paffrath' ware (eg Brown 2002, 34), with the latter name coming from perhaps the best-known manufacturing centre, near Cologne (Jennings 1981, 26), although they were also made at a number of other centres in north-west Europe. These handled vessels were traditionally known as "ladles" (Dunning *et al*. 1959, 56), but they are now generally considered to be a form of cooking-vessel, as many of them exhibit exterior sooting consistent with such as use (Vince 1985, 39). They are fairly well-known in King's Lynn (Clarke and Carter 1977, fig 102, 34–6), the most probable port of entry for the Northamptonshire

examples. Certainly, Grimston ware, which was made just outside King's Lynn, is known from Nassington, showing that there was contact between the two places.

Finds of imported medieval pottery of this date are fairly rare in Northamptonshire, and Nassington is just the fourth site to have produced Rhenish *Blaugrau* vessels of this type. The only other places where they occurred were Castle Lane, Brackley (Blinkhorn in archive), Angel Street, Northampton (Blinkhorn 2021) and Deene End, Weldon (Blinkhorn 2003). None of these sites appear to have been of "ordinary" status. Brackley Castle Lane produced unusually large quantities of pottery from the Coventry area, where these Rhenish vessels also occur (Ratkai and Soden, in archive), suggesting that the tenements, which were near the castle, were occupied by wool merchants with connections to that city. Deene End, Weldon was an iron-smelting site, probably under monastic control (M Aston pers comm), and as well as producing a fragment of a *Blaugrau* vessel it also yielded a sherd of Pingsdorf Ware. Angel Street, Northampton (Brown 2021) has produced the largest collection of imported medieval pottery of any site in the town, with wares from the Rhineland, France, the Low Countries, and Spain, and seems likely to have housed merchants in the medieval period. It also produced Pingsdorf Ware.

The Nassington vessel continues the pattern of occurrence at places in the county of greater than normal wealth and status (Baile *et al* 2021). It is well-attested from the historical record that Nassington was a prebend attached to Lincoln cathedral. The manor was well endowed and in 1254 was valued at £30 (*taxio p 39b),* one of the highest within diocese. Many of the prebendaries were the king's clerks often engaged with the king's affairs in France and Rome, and Ranulf de Nassington, the first known prebendary, may have been a Norman. In the 13th century John Romyen, Peter de Sabello, Raymond de la Goth, Ramon de San Salvatore were all appointed to the prebend. Many of them never set foot in Nassington, but the combination of the wealth of the site and its relative proximity to King's Lynn via the nearby River Nene was probably sufficient to attract merchants from the coast. A cooking vessel such as this would have been of no great status, and so while it may simply have been a novelty for the manorial kitchen, it is also possible, given the nature of the place, that some people of continental origin were there, and that this represents a personal possession. It is certainly an interesting addition to the small known *corpus* of imported medieval pottery from excavations in the county of Northamptonshire.

Fig 1: Handle from a Rhenish Greyware (*Blaugrau* or 'Paffrath' ware) vessel

Bibliography

Baile, J, Hill, N, and Gardiner, M, 2021 The Development of a Manor House over the Longue Durée: Nassington Prebendal Manor, Northamptonshire, *Archaeol J*, (DOI: 10.1080/00665983.2021.1886431)

Blinkhorn, P, in archive *Pottery from Castle Lane, Brackley*, Northamptonshire Archaeology Archives

Blinkhorn, P, 2003 The Pottery, *in* A Thorne, A medieval tenement at Deene End, Weldon, Northamptonshire, *Northamptonshire Archaeol*, **31**, 116–19

Blinkhorn, P, 2021 Pottery, *in* J Brown 2021 *Living opposite to the Hospital of St John: Excavations in medieval Northampton 2014*, Archaeopress Archaeol, 152–191

Brown, D H, 2002 *Pottery in Medieval Southampton c 1066–1510,* Southampton Archaeol Monog, **8**

Brown, J, 2021 *Living opposite the Hospital of St John: Excavations in medieval Northampton 2014,* Archaeopress Archaeol

Clarke, H, and Carter, A, 1977 *Excavations in King's Lynn, 1963–1970,* Soc Med Archaeol Monog Ser, **7**

Dunning, G C, Hurst, J G, Myres, J N L and Tischler, F, 1959 Anglo-Saxon pottery: a Symposium, *Medieval Archaeol*, **3**, 1–79

Jennings, S, 1981 *Eighteen Centuries of Pottery from Norwich,* East Anglian Archaeol, **13**

Ratkai, S, and Soden, I, in archive *Warwickshire Medieval and Post-Medieval Pottery Type-Series*

Vince, A G, 1985 The Saxon and Medieval Pottery of London: A review, *Medieval Archaeol*, **29**, 25–93

Northamptonshire Archaeology, **41**, *2021, 432–433*

Northamptonshire and the Heritage at Risk Register 2020

by

Graham Cadman

Introduction

Historic England published their Heritage at Risk (HAR) Register 2020 on 15 October. Their aim is to work with owners, friends groups, developers and other stakeholders to find solutions for 'at risk' historic places and sites across England. This year's Register includes 59 entries in Northamptonshire.

Heritage at Risk sites can come in many forms; from grand to simple buildings and structures, to large visible earthworks and less visible buried remains. Many issues threaten these sites, from environmental to human impact. This year's Register thus includes buildings and structures (confined to Listed Grades I and II* only) , places of worship, archaeological sites, battlefields, wrecks, parks and gardens, and conservation areas across England known to be at risk as a result of neglect, decay or inappropriate development.

Since its launch in 1998 the Heritage at Risk programme and its annually published Register has focused attention on those places in greatest need. Its audience is wide-ranging and includes local authorities, owners, developers, the general public, and buildings preservation trusts. Working in partnership, Historic England looks to find imaginative solutions for historic places and sites at risk. The outcomes of research and the annual Register help prioritise where to focus expertise and limited funding. Some of the buildings and structural scheduled monuments identified as being neglected, broken and unloved in earlier editions of the Register are now thankfully safe. Others are on the way to being rescued whilst others still await help.

The 2020 Register contains 59 entries for Listed buildings and structures, places of worship, archaeological monuments and Conservation Areas across Northamptonshire. Sound progress is being made with some; others sadly remain in poor or declining condition. Thankfully, no registered battlefields or parks and gardens are currently identified as being at risk in the county.

You can find out what's at risk across England by searching the Heritage at Risk Register: https://historicengland.org.uk/advice/heritage-at-risk/.

Details of all Northamptonshire entries are available in the Heritage at Risk Midlands Register 2020 at: https://historicengland.org.uk/images-books/publications/har-2020–registers/mid-har-register2020/.

Previous years' Heritage at Risk Registers are available to download on the Historic England website: https://historicengland.org.uk/.

Summary of Northamptonshire HAR 2020: by local authority

Corby

Church of St Leonard, Rockingham, Rockingham

Daventry

Church: Old Church of St John the Baptist, Moulton Lane, Boughton,

Five Listed churches: Church of All Saints, Church Lane, Clipston; Church of St Denys, Clipston Road, Kelmarsh; Church of All Saints, Daventry Road, Norton; Church of St Michael, Stowe IX Churches; Church of St Peter and St Paul, Church Lane, Watford.

Weedon Barracks: seven II* Listed entries for enclosure, bastion and canal walls and the West Lodge.

Gate arch: south of south front of Manor House, Winwick Manor, Winwick

Three Scheduled Monuments: all identified as vulnerable to arable ploughing: Univallate hillfort 250m south and a bowl barrow 300m south east of Castle Dykes Farm, Farthingstone; Two bowl barrows and a henge 600m east of Mill Hill Farm, Naseby; Site of Bannaventa, Norton / Whilton.

East Northamptonshire

Five buildings or structures:
Apethorpe Palace, Apethorpe; Ashton Mill, Oundle Road, Ashton; Barnwell Castle, Barnwell; Lilford Hall, Lilford-cumWigsthorpe; Dovecote on site of manor house and gardens, Wakerley.

Five Listed churches:
Church of St Nicholas, Main Street, Bulwick; Church of St Peter, Main Road, Lowick; Church of St Peter, Berrister Place, Raunds; Church of St Lawrence, Church Street, Stanwick; Church of St Mary Magdalene, Main Street, Yarwell.

Two Scheduled Monuments at risk:
Arable ploughing, Crow Hill Iron Age hillfort with associated settlements, Irthlingborough; Roman villa, Little Addington.

Kettering

One Listed Building:
Dovecote, north east of Newton Field Centre, Newton and Little Oakley.

Northampton

Listed buildings:
8, 8a, 9 and 9a, George Row (Northampton & Country Club);

Church of St Andrew, Church Walk, Great Billing, Billing.

Scheduled Monument: Multivallate hillfort at Hunsbury Hill.

Conservation Area: St Crispin Hospital, Upton.

South Northamptonshire

Two Listed buildings: Terrace gardens, Castle Ashby Park, Castle Ashby; Stable block and outbuildings at Wakefield Lodge, Potterspury.

Seven Listed churches: Church of St Mary, Horton, Hackleton; Church of St John the Baptist, Church Road, Boddington; Church of St Peter and St Paul, Church Lane, Chacombe; Church of St Luke, Banbury Lane, Cold Higham; Church of All Saints, Church Lane, Croughton; Church of St Peter and St Paul, Church Street, Nether Heyford; Church of St Mary, Thenford; Church of St John the Baptist, High Street South, Tiffield.

Scheduled Monuments: Astwell Castle Farm (Gatehouse Tower), Helmdon; and six plough or tree/scrub threatened Scheduled monuments – Roman villa, Chipping Warden and Edgcote; Roman villa south east of Cosgrove Hall, Cosgrove; Roman villa north of Road Hill Farm, Harpole; Roman villa south east of Stokegap Lodge, Stoke Bruerne; Sulgrave bowl barrow, Sulgrave; Former World War I National Filling Factory, Banbury, Warkworth.

Conservation Area: Old Stratford

Wellingborough

Listed building: Chester House, Higham Road, Irchester – description includes the information that – 'Works were delayed when the main contractor went into liquidation; completion and public opening is planned for summer 2021'.

Listed churches: two – Church of St Mary, The Green, Orlingbury; Church of St Peter and Paul, Main Street, Sywell.

Scheduled Monuments: two – site revealed by aerial photography north of Easton Lodge, Easton Maudit; Romano-British settlement and pottery kilns west of Ecton North Lodge, Ecton / Sywell.

Conservation Area: Wellingborough Town Centre

Northamptonshire Archaeology, **41**, 2021, 434–436

Portable Antiquities Scheme in Northamptonshire 2018

by

Eleanore Cox

In 2018 the Portable Antiquities Scheme recorded 1151 objects from Northamptonshire. These break down into periods as follows:

Period	No of objects
Mesolithic	67
Neolithic	51
Bronze Age	66
Iron Age	18
Greek & Roman Provincial	1
Roman	460
Early Medieval	22
Medieval	221
Post-medieval	233
Modern	8
Unknown	4

These objects and coins represent the range and variety of archaeology across the county. There were 17 cases of Treasure from the country during 2018: these are recorded on the schemes database (www.finds.org.uk). Some of the most notable unique identifications are:

NARC-76492A – a group of three gold Iron Age staters found in close proximity dating between 50 BC – AD 40; NARC-87D452 – an incomplete gold biconical spacer bead of probable early medieval date; NARC-183002 and CAM-357103.

Finds of note

From the parish of Deanshanger (Fig 1: NARC-49AFF5), a dispersed hoard of 17 palstaves, 30 socketed axes and five pieces of casting waste. The hoard is of Middle to Late Bronze Age date (1500–800 BC). The palstaves are attached to a split haft, with stop ridges to prevent slipage. They are of slender looped form and are in good

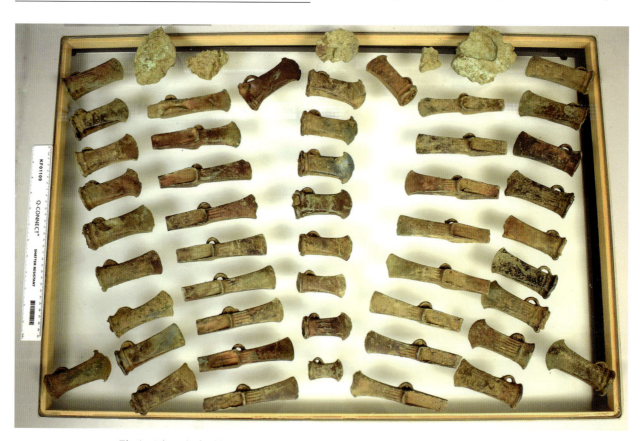

Fig 1: A hoard of Middle to Late Bronze Age palstaves and socketed axes (scale 0.3m)

condition. The socketed axes are predominantly square mouthed, to take a squared haft, with integral loops and differing degrees of flaring to the blade edge. Some have impact damage to the socketed end. There are also five pieces of casting waste ranging in weight from 84–995g.

From central Kettering found around 1930, as a surface find by a gentleman, while playing as a child (Fig 2: NARC-41B49<u>9</u>), a copper alloy As of Claudius I (AD 41–54), dating to *c*.AD 41–50 (Reece Period 2). S-C reverse type depicting Minerva advancing right, holding shield and brandishing a javelin (Cf. RIC I (2nd ed), 128, no 100). This is an official or good quality contemporary copy. Contemporary copies of this issue appear frequently in Britain and typically copy RIC I (2nd ed), 128 & 130, no 100 and no 116.

Ongoing study by Robert Kenyon suggests that a number of this issue, identified as contemporary copies were in fact of Roman auxiliary mints which operated at Lyons (Gaul) and in Spain. This example is probably from the Lyon I, à la Grosse Tête mint, although may be Mint of Rome. This issue of coinage can be associated with Claudius I military expansion into Britain in AD 43.

From the parish of Crick (Fig 3: NARC-0FF365), a copper alloy strap end of early medieval date (AD 875–1100). The object is of openwork design in the Winchester style, with both zoomorphic and plant-scroll decoration. The moulded decoration takes the form of two vertically-arranged birds, facing each other with a plant of three stems between. Each snout curves upwards to form the lower outer edge of the frame. The remaining central upper portion depicts the sub-ovate head of a serpent or bird with two curvilinear plant stems above and beyond the recessed portion.

The Winchester style is derived from illuminated manuscripts. It originated in Britain and Ireland and came across the continent during the 7th-9th centuries. The style incorporates zoomorphic, curvilinear and anthropomorphic aspects from across continental Europe.

From the parish of Lowick (Fig 4: NARC-EECB11), a glass bottle seal of post-medieval date (AD 1700–1800). The seal depicts a stag or deer head facing left, with a diagonal linear "rope" below and enclosed within a beaded circle. The glass is heavily patinated with a dark green patina in some places and a multi-coloured opalescent patina predominant on the reverse.

Around 1636 English law prohibited the sale of wine in glass containers. Individuals were encouraged to have private bottles made with their own seals which they then took to a wine importer who filled them with wine from a cask. Bottles were also provided with a seal for several reasons such as to indicate the contents of the bottle, to commemorate a well-known person, or to identify the owner of the bottle.

The Finds Liaison Officer

The Finds Liaison Officer holds regular Finds Events in Northamptonshire. For more information on these you can email flo@northamptonshire.gov.uk.

More information regarding the recording of objects found by members of the public can be found on the Portable Antiquities Scheme website at www.find.org. uk. Information regarding items of potential Treasure and the schemes work can also be found on the website. The Schemes database can also be found on the website for more information on objects and coins found in Northamptonshire since 1999.

Bibliography

Needham, S P, Lawson, A J, and Green, H S, 1985 Early Bronze Age hoards, Associated Finds Series monog, British Museum Press

Fig 2: Coin of Claudius 1 associated with the Roman military expansion into Britain in AD 43

Fig 3: An early medieval strap end

Fig 4: A glass bottle seal of post-medieval date

Abdy, R, Franz Mittag, P, forthcoming *Roman Imperial Coinage: Volume 1* (2nd Edition). Spink, London

Boon, G C, 1988 Counterfeit coins in Roman Britain, *in* Casey, J, and Reece, R, (eds), *Coins and the Archaeologist* (2nd edition), London, 102–88

Besombes, P-A, and Bompaire, M, 2005 *Trésors Monétaires XXI*

Ashmolean Museum, British Archaeology at the Ashmolean Museum: https://britisharchaeology.ashmus.ox.ac.uk/east-oxford/ob-bottle-seal.html

Northamptonshire Archaeology, **41**, 2021, 437–439

Portable Antiquities Scheme in Northamptonshire 2019

by

Eleanore Cox

In 2019 the Portable Antiquities Scheme recorded 1130 objects from Northamptonshire. These break down into periods as follows:

Period	No of objects
Mesolithic	76
Neolithic	55
Bronze Age	8
Iron Age	16
Roman	628
Early medieval	58
Medieval	383
Post-medieval	288
Modern	13
Unknown	5

These objects and coins represent the range and variety of archaeology across the county. There were 28 cases of Treasure from the country during 2019, these are recorded on the schemes database (www.finds.org.uk) with some of the most notable's unique ID's here: NARC-18E7E4, NARC-AB669F, NARC-0352D0, NARC-363257, BH-77E5FF, NARC-97BAA7, NARC-86A788, NARC-DE2466, NARC-9E9B75 and NARC-6CFD25.

Finds of Note

From the parish of Deanshanger (Fig 1: NARC-53510E), a copper-alloy contemporary copy of an As, known as a limes falsum, of Otacilia Severa dating to the period AD244–249. CONCORDIA AVGG reverse type depicting Concordia seated left holding patera and cornucopiae.

As Mint of Rome. RIC IV, 94, no. 203d. The bust on the obverse is facing right. However, official asses of this issue have busts facing left. A Limes Falsum is a contemporary imitation from the northern borders of the Roman Empire. They are often of the As or Dupondius denominations.

From the parish of Brigstock (Figs 2–3: NARC-1C1272), a silver and gold sword pommel of early medieval date (AD 900–1120), of Petersen type O. The pommel is composed of five lobes, which decrease in width and height from the tallest in the centre. The lobes are joined at the rectangular base. From the lower edge of the base is a V shaped projection on both sides. The projection has three deeply incised chevrons on one face, and two on the other. The pommel is extensively decorated; the outer aspects of the lobes have an incised design filled with niello. All lobes have a recessed sheet of decorated gold, front and back. The three central lobe inset sheets are decorated with a fine gold beaded wire in a basket-hatching style interspersed with gold pellets. On the two outer lobes gold recessed sheets are decorated with a central pellet and a spiral of fine beaded wire. Between each of the lobes is a strand of beaded wire flanked by shorter lengths of repeating oblique beaded wire.

From the parish of Irchester (Fig 4: NARC-BDC51E) a copper alloy seal matrix of medieval date (AD 1200–1400). The object is conical in form. At the opposing end to the handle is a circular matrix. The lower face is engraved with a bust of a tonsured monk, facing right with a chalice in front. Around the central motif, between the inner and outer border, is an inscription which reads *SI DNI hENR' DE NOWERS*. The inscription should probably be expanded to read *SIGILLUM DOMINI HENRICI DE NOWERS*, which appears to refer to Seal of Lord Henry

Fig 1: A Roman coin from Deanshanger

Fig 2: Early medieval silver and gold sword pommel from Brigstock

Fig 3: Views of all surfaces of the sword pommel from Brigstock

of Nowers. This surname is recorded elsewhere in the late 12th and early 13th century (DES, under Nowers) and appears to come from Noyers in Eure, France.

Sealing was used for authenticating documents for around 300 years in medieval Britain. Though initially limited to the higher ranks of the church and state, the use of seals became more general from the 11th century onward and by the end of the 13th century tradesmen and peasants also possessed them.

From the Abthorpe area (Fig 5: NARC-FBC935), a gold signet (or seal) finger-ring of post-medieval date

(AD 1600–1700). The bezel is decorated with a heraldic design. The arms are 'chevron charged with three escallops, two ram heads flanking a crescent chief, and a rams head right base'. All of the details on the upper surface are in the negative so that any impression made into sealing-wax would appear in relief.

This is a common form of post-medieval signet ring, dating from late 16th to 17th centuries.

Clive Cheesman of the College of Arms comments:

> 'A family of this name [Benson], using these arms, lived at Charwelton and Dodford, and at least one of the family moved to Towcester... [In the] *History of the County of Northampton,* **1**, 296; you will see that George Benson (d 1687, aged 88), of Towcester,

Fig 4: A medieval copper alloy seal matrix from Irchester

Fig 5: A post-medieval gold signet ring from Abthorpe

was third son of Richard Benson of Aylesbury in Berkshire. The crescent indicates a second son, so the ring cannot have been made for him. It could have been made, of course, for *his* second son, but his will is available and it looks as if he only had one son – though there may have been others who died young. But in any case I think the style of the ring is early 17th century rather than late, so it is more likely perhaps to have been made for someone of George Benson's own generation. This would suggest his brother Henry, who was the second son; he lived at Charwelton and was High Sheriff of Northants in 1658 and 1659.'

The Finds Liaison Officer

The Finds Liaison Officer holds regular Finds Events in Northamptonshire. For more information on these you can email flo@northamptonshire.gov.uk.

More information regarding the recording of objects found by members of the public can be found on the Portable Antiquities Scheme website at www.find.org. uk. Information regarding items of potential Treasure and the schemes work can also be found on the website. The Schemes database can also be found on the website for more information on objects and coins found in Northamptonshire since 1999.

Bibliography

Mattingly, H, Sydenham, E, and Sutherland, C H V, 1949 *Roman Imperial Coinage, Volume IV: Gordian III–Uranius Antoninus*, Spink, London

Baker, G, 1822 *History of the County of Northampton*, Victoria County Hist, **1**, London

Petersen, J, 1919 *De Norske Vikingesverd*, En typoligisk-kronologisk studie over vikingetidens vaaben

Obituaries

Paul Woodfield (1933–2020)

Clive Trevor Paul Woodfield Dip Arch RIBA MCIfA was born in Birmingham November 1933 and died in his sleep of a heart issue, aged 86, in Stony Stratford, 24 April 2020. In a life well-lived he, and his late wife, Charmian (1929–2014), had a significant influence on archaeology in the county. This was recognised in the case of Paul Woodfield when he was appointed a Vice President of Northamptonshire Archaeological Society. Paul published over 30 books, articles and notes over a near fifty-year period (1963–2010) including ten articles and notes in *Northamptonshire Archaeology* (see below).

Paul Woodfield trained as an architect and was elected to RIBA in 1961, but also was fascinated by archaeology from an early age. He worked in the late 1950s on excavations at Verulamium and this is where Paul met Charmian. Paul was primarily an architect and worked in Coventry city's Planning and Architecture Department in the 1960s and later became Deputy County Architect for Radnorshire in 1968. In 1972 he became head of Building Conservation with Milton Keynes Development Corporation and this continued to 1985. It was during this time he wrote the book on Historic Buildings of Milton Keynes which was published soon after he left in 1986 (see below). Paul then worked for English Heritage including for a period as its head of Central Architectural Practice in London and later for CADW.

Paul lived in Towcester in the 1970s and Charmian and Paul's children attended Sponne School. In his time at Towcester Paul designed a rear extension for the listed medieval Chantry House, a building bequeathed to the Towcester parish church, which was converted into the Parish Office with two meeting rooms opened in 1987.

Some of Paul's architectural legacy has been saved as a collection of 78 measured drawings produced by Paul between 1970 and 2004 and these can be accessed at https://historicengland.org.uk/images-books/photos/collection/PWD01.

The catalogue of his work produced by ADS: (https://archaeologydataservice.ac.uk/library/browse/personDetails.xhtml?personId=5183.

They show new buildings and conversions of old buildings with which he was involved. Most of these projects were in Northamptonshire, Buckinghamshire and Bedfordshire. Paul had been involved in some prestigious projects including preparing the drawings for the Lincoln Cathedral Bishop's chair. Paul was interesting in restoring buildings. At Berwick, where Charmian and he had a second home, he is remembered for restoring a number of listed buildings including The Merchant's House on Palace Green.

During and after 'retirement' from architecture, Paul was involved in many archaeological projects including building recording. In this capacity he was one of a number of single independent archaeologists principally involved in evaluations. This sometimes led on to an excavation, for example, at Delapré Abbey when a series of Roman pottery kilns were uncovered (published in *Northamptonshire Archaeology* in 2010). He was also interested in popular publication, and with Charmian he wrote the guide book to English Heritage's Lyddington Bede House, Northamptonshire.

The Woodfields principal home for many years was at 107 High Street, Stony Stratford, which was a very interesting and impressive large detached High Victorian town house which was built by, and was the home of, the architect Swinfen Harris, and is itself a listed building. Anyone visiting the Woodfields at this elegant place would have to pass a large board in their front garden which declared it was 'a nuclear free zone'. Many people have a memory of the eccentricity, in that great British tradition, of the Woodfields – that was part of their charm. The Woodfields were always kind and receptive, involving themselves in a host of people and organisations, mostly in their own time. This ranged from metal detectorists (they helped record the important Bronze Age hoard from Monkston Park, Milton Keynes, now on display at the British Museum), to local archaeological institutions and historical societies such as the Towcester Historical Society.

Publications

Woodfield, P, 1963 A Norman Tympanum found in Coventry, *Archaeol J,* **43 (2)**, 293–294

Woodfield, P, 1963 Yellow glazed wares of the seventeenth century, *Trans & Procs Birmingham Archaeol Soc,* **81**, 78–87

Webster, G, and Woodfield, P, 1966 The 'Old Work' at the Roman public baths at Wroxeter. *Antiquities J,* **46 (2)**, 229–239

Woodfield, P, 1966 Barcombe Hill, Thorngrafton, *Archaeologia Aeliana Series 4*, **44**, 71–77

Woodfield, P, 1967 Bronze Age implements in Coventry Museum, *Trans & Procs Birmingham Archaeol Soc,* **82**, 92–93

Woodfield, P, and Savory, H N, 1972 A new Bronze Age axe from Cefnllys, Radnorshire, *Trans Radnorshire Soc,* **42**, 85–86

Woodfield, P, 1973 The houses of Radnorshire. Part Va,Town houses of Knighton, *Trans Radnorshire Soc,* **43**, 50–63

Woodfield, P, 1976 An intaglio from Wroxeter, *Britannia,* **7**, 284–285

Woodfield, P, 1978 Roman architectural masonry from Northamptonshire, *Northamptonshire Archaeol,* **13**, 67–86

Seaby, W A, and Woodfield, P, 1980 Viking stirrups from England and their background, *Medieval Archaeol,* **24**, 87–122

Woodfield, P, 1981 The larger medieval houses of Northamptonshire, *Northamptonshire Archaeol,* **16**, 153–196

Woodfield, P, 1983 The palace of the bishops of Lincoln at Lyddington, *Leicestershire Archaeol and Hist Soc Trans,* **57**, 1–16

Woodfield, P, 1986 *A Guide to the Historic Buildings of Milton Keynes*, Milton Keynes Development Corporation

Woodfield, P, 1991 Early buildings in gardens in England, *in* A E Brown (ed) *Garden Archaeology: Papers presented to a conference at Knuston Hall, Northamptonshire, April 1988*, Council British Archaeol, Research Rep, **78**, 123–137

Woodfield, P, 1992 An Anglo-Saxon stone from the church of St Lawrence, Towcester, *Northamptonshire Archaeol,* **24**, 102–105

Clayton, M, and Woodfield, P, 1993 Coordinated project information and conservation works, *English Heritage Scientical Technology Review,* **2**, 3–5

Woodfield, P, 1995 The Dark Ages, and the Anglo-Saxon period, *in* J Sunderland, and M Webb (eds), *Towcester: the story of an English county town*, Towcester Local Hist Soc, 51–59

Alcock, N W, and Woodfield, P, 1996 Social pretensions in architecture and ancestry: Hall House, Sawbridge, Warwickshire and the Andrewe family, *Antiquities J,* **76**, 51–72

Mynard, D C, Woodfield, P, and Zeepvat, R J, 1996 Bradwell Abbey, Buckinghamshire: research and excavation, 1968 to 1987, *Records Buckinghamshire,* **36**, 1–61

Woodfield, P, and Ivens, R J, 1998, A further mid sixteenth century pottery kiln at Potterspury, Northamptonshire, *Northamptonshire Archaeol,* **28**, 160–162

Woodfield, P, and Ivens, R J, 2000 Potterspury, SP 7604 4322, *Post-medieval Archaeol,* **34**, 293–6

Woodfield, P, 2001 A further pilgrim badge of the Pietà or Our Lady of Pity, from Towcester, *Northamptonshire Archaeol,* **29**, 204–206

Woodfield, P, and Woodfield, C, 2001 A probable pre-Reformation find from Potterspury. *Northamptonshire Archaeology,* **29**, 207–208

Woodfield, C, and Woodfield, P, 2001 An unusual pottery find from Towcester. *Northamptonshire Archaeol,* **29**, 212–213

Woodfield, C, Woodfield, P, and Hylton, T, 2002 Other finds, in R Atkins, and A Chapman, Excavation of Roman settlement at Sponne School, Towcester, 1997, *Northamptonshire Archaeol,* **30**, 27–28

Tracy, C, and Woodfield, P, 2004 The Adisham 'reredos', *J British Archaeol Association,* **156**, 27–78

Woodfield, P, 2005 The sculptured stone, and other architectural elements from the deserted site of Wolfage, at Park Farm, Brixworth, *Northamptonshire Archaeol,* **33**, 153–156

Woodfield, P, 2005 various reports in C Woodfield, *The Church of Our Lady of Mount Carmel and some conventual buildings at the Whitefriars, Coventry,* Archaeopress monograph, 48–9, 54–55, 56–7, 58, 154–165, 286, 298–99,297 and 361–63

Woodfield, C, and Woodfield, P, 2005 *Lyddington Bede House,* English Heritage

Woodfield, P, 2008 The church of St Peter Stantonbury, Milton Keynes, *Records of Buckinghamshire,* **48**, 161–183

Woodfield, P, 2010 The Delapré Roman Kiln Field, Northampton, *Northamptonshire Archaeol,* **36**, 97–113

Rob Atkins and Brian Giggins

Frances Williams (1952–2019)

Frances Williams, who was born in Wolverhampton on 26 March 1952, was much involved with the Northamptonshire Archaeological Society in its early days, during and following its transition from the Northamptonshire Federation of Archaeological Societies. She was Secretary 1975–78, Meetings Secretary 1981–83 and Newsletter Editor 1978–83.

From an early age Frances had had an interest in archaeology, and in 1973 she graduated from Birmingham University with a BA in Ancient History and Archaeology. At the end of her second year, with a departmental travel bursary, she set off with two fellow students for six weeks in Egypt. Following in the footsteps of Amelia Edwards and others, the three young ladies made their independent, intrepid way up and down the Nile visiting sites and museums. This was 1972, fifty years ago, sometime before mass tourism arrived in Egypt. She went on to gain, also at Birmingham University, an MA in Archaeological Publication, supervised by Philip Rahtz, which resulted in her publication of 'Excavations at Pleshey Castle' (BAR 42, 1977).

Frances had met her future husband John on an excavation in Colchester in the summer of 1971. In the September John became archaeologist at Northampton Development Corporation, and about the same time her parents moved to Long Buckby. Frances then began digging as a volunteer on excavations at Northampton when she was home from university. Between 1972 and 1980 she worked in a variety of capacities for Northampton Development Corporation's Archaeological Unit, including between 1976 and 1980 as a full-time Field Officer and in 1979–80 also as Finds Administrator. Among her various roles she was a supervisor on the Overstone Roman site, and then excavations within Northampton at St Peter's Street and Chalk Lane; she co-directed the Marefair excavations (F Williams 1979, Excavations at Marefair, Northampton,

NA **14**), and contributed in a variety of ways to the Unit's post-excavation work and publications.

Frances and John were married during the St Peter's Street excavations in 1973. With the arrival of son Gareth in 1980 and daughter Joanna in 1983, Frances gave up full-time employment. She had already undertaken some adult education work in archaeology for the University of Leicester and now developed this further.

When the family moved to Lancaster in 1984 she again undertook adult education teaching for the University of Liverpool and the WEA, and following a further move to Kent in 1989 for the University of Kent. From the mid-1990s, in response to government policy, flexible pathways were defined for mature students, leading to the award of degrees via stepping stones of certificates and diplomas. Frances developed and taught with great success for many years a course on Ancient Egypt and its relationship with other east Mediterranean civilisations, demonstrating the breadth of her interests. She was now also teaching at the University's campus at Canterbury, and she was supervising students writing disserta-

tions on Egyptological topics as the final stage of their degree studies. When archaeology was incorporated with Classical studies in a new university department, Frances had the opportunity to introduce Egyptology to younger students studying full-time, while also co-supervising postgraduate research.

In more recent years, with increasing fees severely reducing university adult education provision, Frances 'went private' in providing courses in Egyptology and developed a dedicated following in Kent. 1997 saw her first Time Travellers' expedition to Egypt – to Luxor and Denderah, and over the next twenty years she continued to lead study trips to Egypt.

Frances was a founding member of the Institute of Field Archaeologists (1984), now the Chartered Institute for Archaeologists.

Frances died on 12 June 2019 from lung cancer, never having smoked. She is survived by her husband and two children.

John H Williams

Burl Bellamy (1942–2020)

Gill Johnston is very sad to report the death, on 19 July 2020, of her friend and long-standing archaeological colleague Burl Bellamy (b Kettering 1942). Burl has been member of NAS for many years, often attending the AGM despite the winter trek from the other end of the county. He was a member of the Northamptonshire Field Group, and a keen and knowledgeable member of the archaeological community in Northamptonshire.

Burl was taken under the wings of Denis Jackson and Pat Foster in the mid-1970s and has since spent many weekends and holidays helping on excavations. He also spent many years fieldwalking the countryside around his home in Geddington, developing a deep knowledge of the landscape and woodlands of Rockingham Forest. He has produced articles for *Northamptonshire Archaeology* and other journals on the historic landscape, most recently for NAS an overview of the Lands and Landscape of Fineshade Abbey (*NA* **38**, 2015).

He was always ready to assist in any way and particularly useful was his ability to delve through document archives and to use historic plans and maps to explore changing patterns of land use.

Burl enjoyed a full and active life, he loved cayaking with his sons and has cycled in the Alps for many years. He is survived by his loving wife Val and three sons and their families.

Gill Johnston

Patrick Foster (1942–2020)

In January 2020, the family of Pat Foster posted the news on Facebook that Pat had passed away following his long battle with cancer, which Pat had recorded on his Facebook posts together with a stream of interesting and thought provoking news items, often marking his despair at the current state of the world.

His family wrote:

> "To all friends, colleagues, relatives and everybody who would want to know, Patrick passed away today in the morning. He died at home, peacefully, and with his loving wife at his side. Try not to be sad. Join us in thoughts and celebration of one long, full and wonderful life."

Pat Foster died on the 17 January 2020 and his funeral was on the 25 January.

Pat Foster was born in Kettering in 1942 attending the Henry Gotch School and then Kettering Technical College. From there he was conscripted into the Royal Artillery. On leaving the army he worked for the Kettering Tyre Company rising to senior management.

However, it may have been time in the army on the Scottish islands that sparked his deep interest in the natural world and archaeology. He learnt the skills of archaeology working with his great friend Dennis Jackson and became a superb excavator and also a very good archaeological illustrator. He played a significant part in recording Northamptonshire's archaeology over many years and was a long-standing member of NAS, even following his departure to work as an archaeologist in the Czech Republic.

Pat recorded a large number of sites authoring or co-authoring articles and notes in the journal from 1972 to 2000, and without his work a notable amount of archaeological knowledge would have been lost. An example of his work and dedication can be seen in the *Bulletin* that preceded *Northamptonshire Archaeology*, **7**, 1972, under Wellingborough (SP 89206945) *"This site was found on 13th July 1971 while checking road scraping ... working in the evenings and at weekends R Harper and P Foster recorded and excavated a number of features..."*. Pat worked with many people still active in the archaeology of the county, who have fond memories of him …

> "*Both he and Dennis introduced me to practical archaeology, and I look back fondly to the times I joined both of them on sites around Corby. At that period, I remember that he was working as a manager of a tyre fitting depot but it was archaeology that dominated his interests. His enthusiasm for the subject was infectious and I have not seen his speed with a trowel repeated! I owe both of them a debt of gratitude*".
>
> Brian Giggins

> "*Pat has been ill for some time and anticipating this for at least a year. Pat Foster took me under his wing and introduced me to the Northamptonshire Field Group when I was new to the area. This led to many happy and exciting projects with Pat, Burl Bellamy and Dennis Jackson over a period of 30 years. Pat then left the country to live in Czech Republic where he continued his archaeological career until the end of his life. I am grateful for everything he taught me and remember him for his generosity his enthusiasm and his and energy.*"
>
> Gill Johnston

Compiled by Andy Chapman

Lesley-Ann Mather (1965–2020)

Lesley-Ann Mather, Northamptonshire Archaeological Advisor, Northamptonshire County Council, died in early December 2020, at the age of only 53, from bowel cancer.

Lesley-Ann came to Northampton aged around 11 and attended Thomas Becket Catholic School, Northampton. After school she first studied Economics at Edinburgh University before changing to Archaeology.

After graduation she joined Northamptonshire Archaeology in 1993 and stayed for more than two years, working on a series of sites mostly in the county, which included Daventry town centre for Iain Soden and DIRFT (Daventry International Rail Freight Terminal) for Andy Chapman. Anyone who worked with her experienced a very hard-working person with a marvellous sense of humour who was extremely enthusiastic with a high commitment to archaeology.

She experienced Field Archaeology with several different units after leaving Northampton in 1996: working for Albion Archaeology, Bedford; followed by Edinburgh and then BUFAU (Birmingham University Field Archaeology Unit) from 1997. For BUFAU she worked on two large excavations in the county at Grange Park, Northampton and again at DIRFT, this time as a Supervisor. DIRFT was a challenging clay site with numerous intercutting features excavated during a very

cold and wet winter. Despite these dreadful conditions she seemed to love it – at least that is what she told Rob Atkins and Andy Chapman when she gave them a site tour!

She later moved into Development Control Archaeology, firstly for Leicestershire in 2000 before moving to Bedfordshire and then, in 2009, she became Northamptonshire County Council Archaeological Advisor, a post she held until her untimely death. Lesley-Ann took over at a time when the county had not had a Development Control Archaeologist for some time, following the departure of Myk Flitcroft, so she came into post after a period in which Northamptonshire had become notorious in the archaeological world for setting a precedent that if had become an example for other planning authorities, could have endangered the whole process of commercial archaeology.

Lesley-Ann therefore had the tricky task of bringing archaeology back into the local planning process. Soon she had an assistant, Liz Mordue, and over a number of years they re-established Northamptonshire as a place of sound archaeological practice. At site meetings with contractors Lesley-Ann keenly fought the corner for doing justice to the archaeology, assisted by her ability to find levity even in the tensest of meetings. She also pushed for publication of archaeological sites she had been monitoring, as with the recent excavation at Angel Street, Northampton.

She, with other partners, instigated the first version of the deposition guidelines in 2014 for the future Northamptonshire Archaeological Resource Centre, and she would have been delighted that after more than 20 years Northamptonshire finally does have a new dedicated archive repository, The Archaeological Resource Centre (The ARC) at Chester House Estate (Irchester Roman town).

Lesley-Ann was an extrovert with many interests outside archaeology including being a long-term supporter of Celtic (and locally watched Rushden & Diamonds over many years). She loved motor cycling often turning up to site meetings on a bike, went on skiing holidays, was a Labour supporter politically and enjoyed a good drink at the pub. Despite her many years as a planning archaeologist, she loved to keep up her field site experience. Firstly, in Italy, and later at the Ness of Brodgar, Orkney, she helped on site with her partner, Andy during the summer holidays for more than two decades.

Archaeology has lost, far too young, a staunch and unstinting advocate, but above all a nice and genuine person.

Rob Atkins

Richard Ivens (1950–2020)

Dr Richard Ivens BA PhD FSA MCIfA died, after a short illness, in Banbury on 1 May 2020.

Richard Ivens was born in Banbury in April 1950. He was proud of Northamptonshire, the County where he had deep roots as his family had lived in Northamptonshire/ Warwickshire for many generations. His connection with Northamptonshire and its past grounded him. He grew up in Kings Sutton and was educated at Magdalen School in Brackley, where swimming lessons took place in a medieval fish pond. Although he started as a geography undergraduate at Queen's University in Belfast he quickly changed to archaeology and stayed on at Queen's as a post-graduate. Archaeology became his all consuming passion.

In a career which spanned more than four decades he had lived and worked in several counties in England, including for a short time in Puxley, South Northamptonshire, as well as two decades in Northern Ireland and Eire. Over this time he held posts at The Queen's University, Belfast, where he had been a research assistant to E M Jope, and the Institute of Irish Studies. During his time there he published several articles in various Irish journals.

Richard also worked for the Milton Keynes Archaeological Unit and was the main author of the Tattenhoe and Westbury monograph (1995), published in the Buckinghamshire Archaeological Society series. After the Milton Keynes unit closed Richard set up on his own largely working on evaluations, mostly in the South Midlands area including many sites in Northamptonshire. He was also instrumental in publishing Martyn Jope's archive, while teaching in the University of Nottingham and the writing up and editing old research excavations for publication filled the latter part of his career.

Richard had an enormous attention for detail and organisational capacity allied to a sharp mind and great insight. Work always started with precise observation of individual sites or artefacts. Richard demanded that any statement be based on evidence, whether he was concerned with someone else's publication, a student's essay, or widely held beliefs. He was totally prepared to put his own works to the same rigour. He saw himself as a historian who used archaeological data in addition to historic data and spent much of his time on documentary research. Richard had no time for the compilation of lists ("postage stamp collection") or abstract schemes of development ("fairy tales").

His main interest was always in the medieval period and he will be remembered for publications that include pottery kilns from Brill, Buckinghamshire and Potterspury, Northamptonshire (the latter comprised articles in volumes 26 and 28 of *Northamptonshire Archaeology*). Richard was also a keen member of the Castles Studies group and published articles on Deddington Castle, Oxfordshire, a ringwork at Killyliss, County Down, Ireland, and in Northamptonshire he co-ordinated work on the records and finds from excavations at Sulgrave Castle.

Richard was a kind and warm hearted person, who worked with, and made friends with many people in the county with a deeply whimsical and dry sense of humour. He was generous with his time, teaching and assisting others, no matter what their status, colleagues, students and volunteer. He was a member of many local groups as well as the Council for British Archaeology (South Midlands).

Publications

Ivens, R, 1980 *Patterns of Human Activity in the Southern Midlands of England: Archaeological and Documentary Evidence*, Unpublished Queen's University of Belfast PhD thesis.

Ivens, R, 1981 Medieval Pottery Kilns at Brill, Buckinghamshire, *Records of Buckinghamshire, 23*, 102–106

Ivens, R, and Jope, E M, 1981 Some Early products of the Brill Pottery, Buckinghamshire, *Records of Buckinghamshire*, **23**, 32–38

Ivens, R, 1982 The Medieval Pottery from Excavations at Temple Farm, Brill, Buckinghamshire, *Records of Buckinghamshire*, **24**, 144–170

Ivens, R, 1983 Deddington Castle, Oxfordshire: A Summary of Excavations 1977–1979, *South Midlands Archaeology*, **13**, 34–41

Ivens, R, 1983 Tullylish, *Rescue News*, **11**

Ivens, R, 1984 De Arte Venandi cum Avibus: an archaeological and historical introduction, *J Banbury Historical Soc*, **9.5**, 130–137

Ivens, R, 1984 Killyliss Rath, Co. Tyrone: A Report on Excavations in 1982, *Ulster J Archaeol*, **47**, 9–35 and fiche

Ivens, R, 1984 Movilla Abbey, Newtownards, Co. Down: Excavations in 1981, *Ulster J Archaeol*, **47**. 71–108 and fiche

Ivens, R, 1984 Deddington Castle, Oxfordshire, and the English Honor of Odo of Bayeux, *Oxoniensia*, **49**, 101–119

Ivens, R, 1984 A Note on Grass-marked Pottery, *J Irish Archaeol*, **2**, 77–79

Ivens, R, 1985 Medieval Building Trades, *J Banbury Historical Soc*, **9.8**, 222–236

Ivens, R, 1985 Salvage Excavations at Tully, Omagh, Co. Tyrone, *Ulster J* Archaeol, **48**, 144–149 and fiche

Ivens, R, Simpson, D D A, and Brown D, 1986 Excavations at Island MacHugh 1985 – Interim Report, *Ulster J Archaeol*, **49**, 99–102

Ivens, R, 1987 The Early Christian Monastic Enclosure at Tullylish, Co. Down, *Ulster J Archaeol*, **50**, 55–121 and fiche

Ivens, R, 1988 Secrets of a hilltop: Dunmisk, Co. Tyrone, *in* A E Hamlin and C J Lynn (eds), *Pieces of the Past*, Belfast, Department of the Environment for Northern Ireland, 27–29

Ivens, R, 1988 Saints scholars and smiths: Movilla Abbey, Co. Down, *in* A E Hamlin and C J Lynn (eds) *Pieces of the Past*, Belfast, Department of the Environment for Northern Ireland, 50–52

Ivens, R, 1988 Around an early church: Tullylish, Co. Down, *in* A E Hamlin and C J Lynn (eds), *Pieces of the Past*, Belfast, Department of the Environment for Northern Ireland, 55–56

Ivens, R, and Simpson, D D A, 1988 Excavations at Lislear, Barronscourt, Co. Tyrone, *Ulster J. Archaeol.* **51**, 61–68

Ivens, R, 1988 Notes on medieval coarse pottery in the Ulster Museum, *Ulster J Archaeol*, **51**, 127–134

Ivens, R, 1988 A note on medieval pottery from Cave Hill and the archaeology of caves, *Ulster J Archaeol*, **51**, 132–134

Ivens, R, 1989 Dunmisk Fort, Carrickmore Co. Tyrone, Excavations 1984–86, *Ulster J* Archaeol, **52**, 17–110

Ivens, R, 1989 D.M.V.'s at Shenley Brook End and Tattenhoe, *South Midlands Archaeology*, **19**, 15–18

Ivens, R, 1990 The deserted village of Westbury by Shenley, *South Midlands Archaeology*, **20**, 21–22

Ivens, R, 1991–2 Medieval Pottery Studies in Ulster: the future, *Ulster J. Archaeol*, **54–55**, 160–161

Ivens, R, and Henderson, J, 1992 Dunmisk and glass making in Early Christian Ireland, *Antiquity*, **66**, 52–64

Ivens, R, 1993 The Shenleys, *in* R A Croft and D C Mynard 1993 *The Changing Landscape of Milton Keynes*, Buckinghamshire Archaeol Soc Monog, **5**, 131–141

Ivens, R, 1993 Tattenhoe, *in* R A Croft and D C Mynard 1993 *The Changing Landscape of Milton Keynes,* Buckinghamshire Archaeol Soc Monog, **5**, 159–164

Ivens, R,, Busby, P, and Shepherd, N, 1995 *Tattenhoe and Westbury two deserted medieval settlements in Milton Keynes 1984–1990,* Buckinghamshire Archaeol Soc Monog, **8**

Ivens, R, and Jope, E M, 1995 A Later Medieval Pottery Kiln at Potterspury, Northamptonshire, *Northamptonshire Archaeology*, **26**, 141–48

Ivens, R, and Jope, E M, 1998 Excavations at the Rath at Ballymacash, near Lisburn, County Antrim, *Royal Irish Academy*, **98C**, 101–123

Ivens, R, and Woodfield, P, 1999 A Further Mid Sixteenth Century Pottery Kiln at Potterspury, Northants, *Northamptonshire Archaeology*, **28**, 160–2

Ivens, R, 1999 (Ed for E M Jope) The Saxon and Medieval pottery from Alexander Keiller's Excavations at Avebury, *Wiltshire Archaeology Magazine*, **92**, 60–91

Ivens, R, 2000 and Woodfield, P A, Potterspury, SP 7604 4322, *Post-medieval Archaeology*, **34**, 293–6

Ivens, R, 2001 Crannog and Everted-Rim Pottery, *Ulster J Archaeol*, **60**, 57–62

Ivens, R, and Mynard, D C, 2002 The Excavation of Gorefields: a Medieval Nunnery and Grange at Stoke Goldington, Buckinghamshire, *Records of Buckinghamshire*, **23**, 19–101

Reports on Developer Funded Archaeological Investigations

1995–2009 Approximately 150 reports on archaeological evaluations, watching briefs, desk-based studies, medieval pottery, etc, prepared in conjunction with Planning Applications.

Forthcoming

Ivens, R, Simpson, D D A, *et al* forthcoming The re-excavation of Island MacHugh, Barronscourt, Co. Tyrone in 1985–86, *Ulster J Archaeol*

Ivens, R, The Pottery forthcoming, *in* F J Crone and F McCormick Excavations at Marshes Upper, Co. Louth, *Louth Archaeol J*

Dr Isabel Lisboa

Adrian Challands (1944–2020)

Adrian Challands who has died at the age of 76, was the Archaeological Officer for Peterborough Development Corporation, working from the Field Centre of the Nene Valley Research Committee, which was established during the development of the city from 1969. He was one of its longest-serving members. He was also a member of both NAS and the Middle Nene Archaeological Group (MidNAG). Following the winding up of the Peterborough Development Corporation, Adrian became an archaeological consultant: he surveyed many sites and produced specialist reports for Cambridge Archaeological Unit.

A full obituary is available on the website of the Nene Valley Archaeological Trust: https://www.nenevalleyarchaeology.co.uk/post/obituary-adrian-challands

Christopher Taylor (1935–2021)

Chris Taylor, who died on 28 May 2021, was the leading recorder and analyst of English landscapes, especially medieval, in the second half of the 20th century.

Born in Lichfield in 1935, Chris took a degree in History and Geography at what became the University of Keele, followed by a diploma at the Institute of Archaeology. Between 1957 and 1960 he was already working as a summer assistant at the RCHM Salisbury office, and joined the Commission full-time in 1960, working on several volumes: West Cambridgeshire (1968), Peterborough New Town (1969), Dorset II-IV (1970–72), and North-East Cambridgeshire (1972).

However, as recalled by Paul Stamper, Chris was frustrated with the inherited RCHM focus on discrete 'sites', and was troubled by what to do with the numerous fenland sites in north-east Cambridgeshire. These were very numerous: pumping engine remains, lodes, probable Roman canals, drains of various dates and field systems of medieval, 17th-century and later dates. Merely to list these and describe them was useless. So Chris pushed for, and got, permission to write an introductory history of the fenland landscape, explaining how it had been drained and farmed since Roman times to the present day, an early example of turning 'sites' into landscapes.

Chris then turned to Northamptonshire and, with the barest assistance, turned out the six Northamptonshire volumes between 1975 and 1985 (although the staff of the then NDC contributed much to the final Northampton volume). These volumes are still a valuable starting point and reference for examining any part of Northamptonshire today.

He also extended his hugely impressive and influential range of personal publications covering fieldwork techniques, and studies of fields, farmsteads, villages and gardens. The small but seminal Shire volume on The Archaeology of Gardens was rich with examples drawn from Northamptonshire of what was effectively the study of an entirely new class of earthwork.

Chris retired from the RCHM after 33 years in 1993, which gave him the freedom to work on further stimulating books and papers, attendance at conferences, and generous advice to all who sought it. He was elected FSA in 1968, FBA (Fellowship of the British Academy) in 1995, and in 2013 was awarded the Academy's John Coles Medal for Landscape Archaeology.

It is probably quite difficult to get hold of now, but his *National Trust History: Cambridgeshire and Mid Anglia* (1984), is a fine example of how he used material first encountered in his days of 'listing and recording', while bringing in the results of excavation and other survey work from across Northamptonshire, Bedfordshire and Cambridgeshire to create a popular overview of the human shaping of the Mid Anglia landscape through time, in a highly readable and well-illustrated publication.

For a number of us who were working for Northamptonshire Archaeology in the mid-1990s there are also the personal memories of a training course led by Chris over a couple of bitterly cold and snowy days across the village and garden earthworks at Wothorpe, Cambridgeshire (Taylor, C, 1997 An Archaeological Field Survey of Wothorpe, Cambridgeshire, PCAS, 1997, **85**, 161–70).

Andy Chapman (extensively quoting from a longer obituary by Paul Stamper for the Society of Antiquaries online magazine Salon, There is also an obituary in the *Guardian*, written by another well-known medievalist Chris Dyer: https://www.theguardian.com/science/2021/jul/09/christopher-taylor-obituary)

Recent publications

by

Andy Chapman

Northampton

Living opposite to the Hospital of St John: Excavations in medieval Northampton 2014
Jim Brown
Archaeopress Archaeology and MOLA Northampton
Paperback; 362 pages; 205 figures, 91 tables
Printed ISBN 9781789699364:
Printed Price £60.00 (No VAT)
EPublication Price £16.00 (Exc. UK VAT)

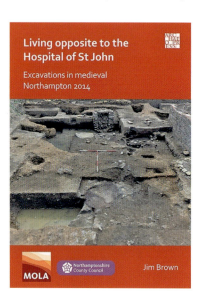

This volume presents the results of archaeological investigations undertaken on the site of new county council offices between St John's Street and Angel Street, Northampton in 2014 by Northamptonshire Archaeology, now MOLA (Museum of London Archaeology) Northampton. In parts of the site there were intact sequences of medieval urban development that extend from the 12th century with quarry pits and a timber-built workshop producing chess pieces in antler, through the stone-built frontages of the high medieval period, with yards to the rear that contained pits, wells and stone-built malt drying kilns, producing the malted barley for brewing.

This is the first monograph publication of an excavation within the town since 2005 and the excavations by MOLAS that preceded the construction of Sol Central on Marefair. It is therefore an important event in the archaeology of Northampton. It also forms a companion and complementary volume to this journal, extending the archaeology of the medieval town beyond the limits of the original Saxon core and the castle, and complementing the articles o the Jewry and synagogue.

While the account of the site and its finds is to be recommended, a disappointing aspect to this volume is that Figure 1.2, which is intended to provide the broad context for medieval Northampton (a plan that has subsequently had even wider coverage through appearing in the popular magazine Current Archaeology, **377**, Aug 2021) contains numerous errors of detail. Rather than creating a modern summary of the current state of knowledge, it is actually based on a plan from 1985 that appeared in the Royal Commission volume on Northampton (RCHM 1985, 49, fig 7), which contained some long recognised errors, while other aspects needed changing to follow more recent discoveries, often made by Northamptonshire Archaeology itself, and these corrections have not been made.

A major error is the placing of the Dominican Friary to the immediate north of Gold Street when it should be the plot to the north of St Catherine's and west of the Jewry and synagogue. Similarly, The church of St Mary (by the Castle) is shown too far north, following the claim by Dr Alexander in the 1960s that the medieval building he excavated beneath Castle Hill could be equated with St Mary's church, when documentary evidence and Speed's map of 1610 show the correct location further to the south. In the same area, the Chalk Lane excavations (Site 18) lay west of Chalk Lane beneath the levelled bailey bank of the castle, not two streets to the east of the castle. Sites carrying a street name, such as Kingswell Street (Site 2), have all been labelled on the street itself, rather than the appropriate plot adjacent to the road, and the St Peter's Street excavations, central to the understanding of the middle Anglo-Saxon palaces, have been labelled at the southernmost extent of the series of excavations, The Green, as published in this volume.

Returning to my home territory, so to speak, the castle and its environs: the plan of the castle that has been overlaid on the base map is certainly a little too far to the north, as here it overlaps onto Bath Street while to the south it stops short of Black Lion Hill, and it is probably a little too large as well, as to the west the inner bailey overlaps with the water courses that flanked its western side. To the south-west, the line of the late Saxon and medieval defences was established as lying to the west of Green Street in my excavations of 1995, while this plan shows the line to the east of Green Street, so the whole south-western arc of the defences is too far to the north-east.

For a reliable context for Northampton you should refer to the plans that have been produced by Michael Shaw for his PhD thesis, see below, some of which also appear in this volume within the article *Anglo-Saxon Northampton Revisited*. Figure 1 shows all the excavated areas within the town, with all the digital data newly created, and Figure 2 references the major street names and the site names, a total of 36 interventions rather than the 22 listed by MOLA. The medieval churches and religious houses are listed and catalogued in Figure 5.21 of Michael Shaw's thesis.

Approaches to the analysis of the topography, origins, growth and development of English medieval towns: case studies of selected towns and their wider applicability
Michael Shaw 2021
University of Birmingham PhD thesis

This is not yet a published volume, but it may have been published by Archaeopress by the time this volume is available. For those who can't wait, the two volumes (text and illustrations) can be downloaded through University of Birmingham e-thesis repository, with the following link: https://etheses.bham.ac.uk/id/eprint/11081/?fbclid=IwAR032LBOI_F1vxNX6_Iu9AZ2n0PqCnMCrsfuFhLPDAp-C1ErSxFLk_72XV0

The aim of this PhD thesis was to take a broad critical look at the strengths and weaknesses of the various strands of evidence and the associated methodologies available for analysing the development of English medieval towns. This is achieved through the use of several case studies, one of which is Northampton (where Mike worked as a field archaeologist for both the Northampton Development Corporation and Northamptonshire Archaeology within the NCC in the 1970s and 80s, see The Green, this volume), as an example of a larger town with a considerable body of archaeological evidence to supplement map, documentary and topographical studies.

The Northampton elements of this study arc separate from, but overlaps with and extend the study of the pre-Conquest origins of Northampton that appear in this volume (Williams *et al* 2021) into the post-Conquest period. The two papers will be essential reading for anyone wishing to understand both the origins of Northampton and its growth through the medieval period. In relation to Northampton, Chapter 5 provides an overview and discussion of the evidence, while Appendix 1 provides a gazetteer of the evidence, with the town broken down into a set of plan units, and including plans of many of the medieval excavated sites.

As already noted in relation to the MOLA volume, this study by Michael Shaw also contains accurate mapping of the previous excavation sites that are set within the street plan and the known religious houses and other documented elements of the medieval town.

Northampton: 5000 Years of History
Mike Ingram, 316 pages, 44 illustrations
Northampton Tours Publications, 2020
Printed by and available from Amazon, £19.99

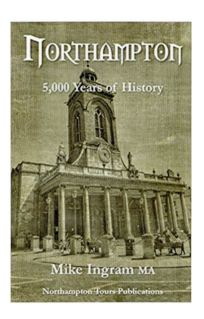

Overviews of the history and archaeology of Northampton do not come along all that often, so this volume warrants a lengthy review, especially within a Northampton-focussed journal and also when parts of the content make it quite a difficult to review without providing some quite detailed comments on its shortcomings and errors.

If you want 1000 years of Northampton history, from the Norman Conquest onward complete with details of visiting medieval kings and their battles, and much more as well, then this a volume that can be recommended with only a few reservations: at over 300 pages but relatively few illustrations it provides plenty of good historical reading matter. There are also pleasing aspects for the more recent history of the town, especially the extensive coverage of the radical past of Northampton, now sadly in the past, in both a broad overview chapter on radicalism and a chapter devoted to the life of Charles Bradlaugh, Northampton's famous and pioneering radical MP.

However, from an archaeological perspective, if you are hoping for a sensible account of the first 80% of those claimed 5000 years of history, you will be sadly disappointed. The first 3500 years of that history fly by in an opening chapter of six pages, including a half page illustration. The next 500 years, from the end of the Romans to the Norman Conquest takes only a little longer, a whole nine pages.

And the half page illustration to Chapter 1 is a view of the Chalk Lane car park, claiming that "*this is where Northampton began*", with the introduction telling us that "*Northampton is over 5,520 years old...older than Stonehenge...it began as a small Neolithic farm or settlement on what is now Northampton's Chalk Lane car park*". This is taking myopic local chauvinism to a ludicrous extreme. The sizeable worked flint assemblage from Chalk Lane is not an indicator of a settlement specifically at that location, but a product of chance survival and excavation. Most archaeological sites in Northampton are, of course, a palimpsest of the past 1000+ years of pit digging, wall foundations, cellars and drains, with the earliest deposits usually cut to pieces and surviving on only small isolated islands (look at the report on The Green in this volume, figs 4–7 to see this in action). At Chalk Lane the presence of the bailey bank of the castle had prevented this from happening for much of the past 900 years, so all the underlying pre-Conquest soils were in relatively pristine condition for an urban site. There was also the time, in those pre-commercial archaeology days, to investigate more of those early buried soils. On surrounding sites, such as St Peters Street, the worked flints are scattered and sparse residual finds in later deposits. The huge numerical disparity between Chalk Lane and nearby sites is therefore at least partly a product of site taphonomy, the varying histories of subsequent damage since the deposition of the flints at those sites. It is, of course, true to say that these numbers do indicate a significant presence of people across this western side of Northampton at various times from the Mesolithic through to the Bronze Age, as noted in an article in this volume. But this does not necessarily place the origin of occupation precisely at the Chalk Lane car park or make Northampton older than Stonehenge.

To keep the review relatively short I will focus on only a few of the many other issues with the archaeological coverage. But firstly, on the positive side, I will say that most of the significant archaeological sites do at least get a mention, which must be unique for a publication by an historian.

There are a number of small but annoying inaccuracies, of which I will mention just one, as it relates to a site that I excavated: the claim that the pre-Conquest defensive bank, as excavated at Green Street, was "faced with wood or stone and topped with a wooden palisade" (page 14). Yes, the clay bank had a wooden revetment along the front, later replaced by a stone revetment, but the only surviving thing that sat on top of the bank was the post-Conquest stone wall of the medieval defences. The placing of a wooden palisade on top in the text appears to be purely an assumption by the author based on what he thinks it should have looked like.

There is also a major issue that must be considered in some detail, and that is the claim that Castle Hill, which lies to the north-east of the castle, as mapped and recorded through the 18th and 19th centuries, was actually an original castle motte with a shell keep on top. The archaeological evidence from the excavations of 1962, as published in this volume, has demonstrated that the mound in fact dates to the Civil War refurbishment of the castle defences. Lacking this publication, I can accept that the motte interpretation can still be proposed as a theory. What I find unacceptable is to produce a map of the medieval town, repeated several times (fig 6, page 23; fig 9, page 55 and fig 11, page 63), where fictitious walls have been drawn in to link the known and recorded inner bailey of the castle to Castle Hill. Also, the 'mound to the immediate north of the Chalk Lane car park', is not one of the towns 'muckhills', it is an archaeological spoil heap from the excavations of the early 1960s. It is Castle Hill that later became a town muckhill.

I must also take exception to Mike's comment on page 8 that "many of these important [archaeological sites have] not been made public, [as] they lie behind expensive paywalls or in some cases, not even written yet." While commercial archaeology has many faults, and developers may block publicity during excavations through fear of delays to the development or unwanted night-time visits from metal detectorists, the majority of field archaeologists are keen to bring their work to the public. But taking a complex archaeological site to publication is a much harder task than excavating the site in the first place, and the pace of development throughout my career always meant that new fieldwork took precedence over analysis and report writing, which is why I'm now spending my retirement catching up with my accumulated backlog. It also requires money, and in some unfortunate cases there are sites that deserve publication but now have no budget to pay for the necessary work, and a commercial archaeological unit does have to be run as a viable business, or it goes out of business.

In my experience many, although I have to note not all, of my fellow commercial archaeologists have gone beyond their own working hours and personal "pay walls" by putting in extra hours to see sites through to publication. It is not part of some conspiracy to hide archaeology from the public. There is also much online through the *Archaeology Data Service* (ADS), and you can always get in touch with the archaeologists themselves, as we are generally keen to provide information when it is asked for.

Finally, I must also note that for a work of history it is remarkable that the volume contains no bibliographic referencing at all, so you can only accept the story told at face value and have no direct means of finding any of the source material, either archaeological, and there is much that is evidently from the pages of *Northamptonshire Archaeology*, or historical, despite the history sections containing numerous direct quotations. This is a particular failing when the text is presented without any evident qualification between factual records and the authors own interpretations.

In his introduction, Mike states that, "*a number of myths have crept into the town's popular history, this book will hopefully set them all straight*". I'm afraid that ambitious claim has not been fulfilled.

Northampton in 50 Buildings
Lorna Talbott, 96 pages, numerous colour photos
Amberley Publishing, 2020, £14.99

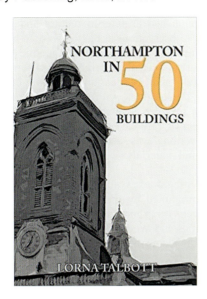

This is part of an Amberley series, *X town/city in 50 buildings*, and can be described in the famous and most useful phrase from Science Fiction author Douglas Adams as, 'mostly harmless'. You can always quibble about the odd omissions in such a publication; I would have liked to see a few of the more recent buildings, even though now lost, such as the old Art Deco Fish Market and also the Greyfriars Bus Station. For all its failings the old bus station played a significant part in the lives of all older Northamptonians, and deserves more than a passing superficial reference as the "mouth of hell": trotting out a description invented to help justify its demolition following decades of council neglect. It has been replaced by a bus interchange too small to serve the entire town, where the buses pollute the air around the narrow and constricted street access, while the old bus station site sits empty and derelict.

But to return to the book, it does cover a wide range of buildings, and while public and corporate buildings feature highly it does include some little gems, such as the 'Swiss chalet' of No 1 Victoria Gardens. The photography of the buildings is competent but given the turnover of the series it is not top quality architectural photography, with many stretched perspectives and leaning walls. But for anyone who wants a broad overview of the major buildings of Northampton ranging in date from the castle to the new International Academy, which opened in 2018 (and I haven't yet seen it), it is a good starting point.

However, as you might expect in a wide-ranging series aimed at a popular market, the research has been less than comprehensive, so don't treat the accompanying text as the gospel truth. From an archaeological viewpoint, the middle Saxon timber 'palace', flanked by the original churches of St Peter and St Gregory, should be the starting point for significant buildings of Northampton, and the true creation of the town, but here credit goes to the Danes in the 9th century. And, of course, we have the old chestnut rolled out yet again that the castle was not only built by

Simon de Senlis, but as a 'fortified dwelling in 1084'. It amazes me how undocumented events can acquire such precise attribution and dating. But as I said at the beginning, as a poplar production it is a good buy and 'mostly harmless'.

Excavation reports

The Development of a Manor House over the Longue Durée:
Nassington Prebendal Manor, Northamptonshire
Gardiner, M. Baile, J, & Hill, N, 2021
Archaeological Journal, **178**
DOI: 10.1080/00665983.2021.1886431
PDF from Taylor & Francis Online, £35.00

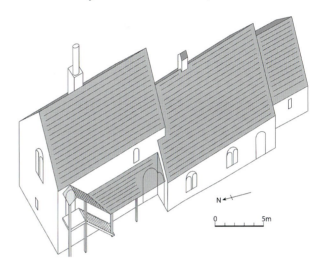

Like the reports on Faxton and Orton Meadows, Peterborough reviewed below; this is another long awaited report. Excavation beneath the floors of the Prebendal Manor House at Nassington revealed the remains of part of a timber hall and chamber of the 11th century which was replaced *c*.1200 on almost exactly the same site by a stone hall and chamber (as reconstructed in the report, see above). This report provides an overview of the history of the manor house and its development through time as revealed by excavation, illustrated with plans, reconstructions and photographs of the excavated site.

The development sequence at Nassington is paralleled by the development of the manor houses at Raunds, Furnells and Raunds, West Cotton, but while these sites were abandoned in the late medieval period to be investigated by conventional methods of excavation, what makes Nassington unique is that the latest hall is not only still standing, but still occupied, and Jane Baile was literally excavating beneath the floors of her own house. It is also appropriate that this review should appear in the same volume as the obituary of Patrick Foster, as he was a key figure in the original excavations in the 1980s. A later stage of excavation was the subject of an episode of *Time Team*. This report is required reading for anyone interested in the development of the medieval manor house from late Saxon timber halls onward.

PS: For those of us who are not historians, the Longue Durée (the Long Term in English), is from a branch of French historical study that gives priority to long-term historical structures (in this case the lifeline of a single manor house), rather than history built from localised short-term events, such as wars, which are seen as the domain of the chronicler and the journalist (Longue durée – Wikipedia, accessed 10/07/21). It is also the concept that lies at the root of attempts to teach Big History, again escaping from nationalism and localised short-term events to see the boarder patterns that have brought us from the Big Bang to today, or As Douglas Adams (author of The Hitch Hiker's Guide to the Galaxy) put it, Life the Universe and Everything.

Faxton: Excavations in a Deserted Northamptonshire Village 1966–68

Butler, L, and Gerrard, C, 2020
Society for Medieval Archaeology Monograph, **42**
Paperback £30.79
Hardback £120.00

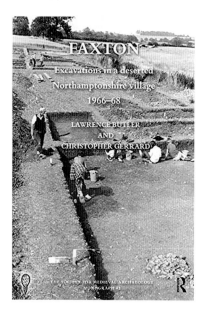

Volumes produced by the Society for Medieval Archaeology are available from Routledge in a variety of formats, hardback, softback and eprint. If you are a member of the SMA and would like to purchase from Routledge at a discounted price you need to use the discount code which can be found in the SMA Newsletter.

'The village of Faxton in Northamptonshire was only finally deserted in the second half of the 20th century. Shortly afterwards, between 1966 and 1968, its medieval crofts were investigated under

the direction of archaeologist Lawrence Butler. At the time this was one of the most ambitious excavations of a deserted medieval settlement to have been conducted and, although the results were only published as interim reports and summaries, Butler's observations at Faxton were to have significant influence on the growing academic and popular literature about village origins and desertion and the nature of medieval peasant crofts and buildings. In contrast to regions with abundant building stone, Faxton revealed archaeological evidence of a long tradition of earthen architecture in which so-called 'mud-walling' was successfully combined with other structural materials.

The 'rescue' excavations at Faxton were originally promoted by the Deserted Medieval Village Research Group and funded by the Ministry of Public Buildings and Works after the extensive earthworks at the site came under threat from agriculture. Three areas were excavated covering seven crofts. In 1966 Croft 29 at the south-east corner of the village green revealed a single croft in detail with its barns, yards and corn driers; in 1967 four crofts were examined together in the north-west corner of the village in an area badly damaged by recent ploughing and, finally, an area immediately east of the church was opened up in 1968. In all, some 4000m² were investigated in 140 days over three seasons.

The post-excavation process for Faxton was beset by delay. Of the 12 chapters presented in this monograph, only two were substantially complete at the time of the director's death in 2014. The others have had to be pieced together from interim summaries, partial manuscripts, sound recordings, handwritten notes and on-site records. Building on this evidence, a new team of scholars have re-considered the findings in order to set the excavations at Faxton into the wider context of modern research. Their texts reflect on the settlement's disputed pre-Conquest origins, probable later re-planning and expansion, the reasons behind the decline and abandonment of the village, the extraordinary story behind the destruction of its church, the development of the open fields and the enclosure process, as well as new evidence about Faxton's buildings and the finds discovered there. Once lauded, then forgotten, the excavations at Faxton now make a new contribution to our knowledge of medieval life and landscape in the East Midlands'

This volume should sit on your book shelves alongside the Raunds volumes, as major studies conducted on Northamptonshire sites into the origins and form of the medieval village.

Coton Park, Rugby, Warwickshire: A Middle Iron Age settlement with copper alloy casting

Chapman, A, 2020
Archaeopress Archaeology
Printed Price £35.00 (No VAT).
EPublication (PDF format),
Price £16.00 (Exc. UK VAT).
(https://www.archaeopress.com/ArchaeopressShop/
Public/displayProductDetail.asp?id={893CFC78–
7D42–454D-AEBA-36828EEECCA7})

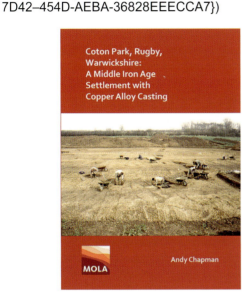

While Coton Park is not in Northamptonshire, the site is only some 8km from the Iron Age metropolis at DIRFT (Daventry International Rail Freight Terminal), so the results are relevant to Iron Age studies in Northamptonshire. This is particularly so as the extensive discussion includes an overview of Iron Age pottery typology and chronology that is largely based on Iron Age ceramics in Northamptonshire, building on and extending the pioneering work of Dennis Jackson. There is also a study of the transition from the saddle quern to the rotary quern, which is dated to the period 250–200BC, coinciding with an increase in the size of storage jars, often scored ware jars, in response to the increased production capacity of the rotary quern. In addition, there is an overview of the Iron Age roundhouse and the nature of the surviving evidence on our often plough-denuded sites across the midland counties. This draws extensively on some of the better preserved sites excavated by Dennis Jackson in Northamptonshire (Brigstock, Aldwincle and Wakerley) which serve as exemplars for the range of evidence that may survive. Finally, Coton Park produced a substantial quantity of copper alloy casting debris, crucibles and fragments of lost-wax investment moulds, which provide useful comparisons for similar material that is often recovered from other Iron Age settlement sites but typically in much smaller quantities.

The author would also like to thank Warwickshire-based archaeologist Stuart Palmer for his whole page review published in Current Archaeology, **366**, September 2020, 56.

A Romano-British Settlement and Cemetery at Higham Road, Burton Latimer, Northamptonshire

Luke, M, and Barker, J, 2020
Albion Archaeology monog, **4**
Price not stated, contact Albion Archaeology for details.
(https://www.albionarchaeology.co.uk/burton-latimer)
Email: albion.archaeology@centralbedford.gov.uk

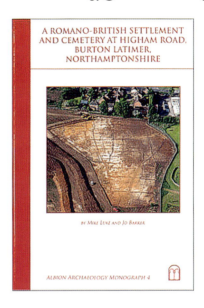

This is a report on investigations into a Romano-British settlement at the site of the a new housing development in Burton Latimer. As well as revealing the remains of an extensive rural settlement, the excavation also identified forty-seven contemporary graves; an unusually large number for a rural community.

Thirty of the graves were contained within a cemetery, with two separate clusters accounting for most of the remainder. Two of the people had been decapitated, while nine were buried face-down. One of the burials was a woman of possible African heritage.

The settlement was founded in the late 1st century AD and continued throughout the Roman period, with up to eight building tentatively identified. The plant remains and animal bones point towards a mixed farming regime, with evidence for craft activities as well. The small number of personal items may suggest a lack of "wealth" or high "status", but the presence of late Roman glassware and part of a copper-alloy figurine counterbalances this. More than 300 coins were found as well, including a hoard of at least 100 that were found historically, while a small number of finds with military associations offer further indications of links beyond the immediate community.

Bourton Way, Wellingborough and Station Road, Higham Ferrers: Two Middle Iron Age Settlements overlooking the River Nene in Northamptonshire

Luke, M, and Barker, J, 2020
Albion Archaeology monog, 5
Price not stated, contact Albion Archaeology for details.
(https://www.albionarchaeology.co.uk)
Email: albion.archaeology@centralbedford.gov.uk

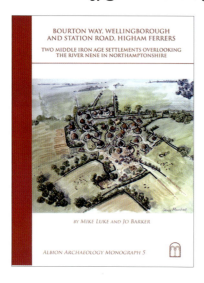

This volume, as it says on the cover, reports on two middle Iron Age settlements in the Nene valley, one near Wellingborough and the other near Higham Ferrers, both of which are elements of more extensive settlements that have seen previous excavations, as detailed below.

The Bourton Way site, near Wellingborough, is part of an extensive open settlement, containing smaller scale enclosed elements and connected with boundary systems and a trackway that extend into the broader landscape. These are assigned the ugly term – agglomerated settlements. The previously excavated elements have been published within the journal as *Great Doddington: an Iron-Age enclosure*, D Windell 1981, *Northamptonshire Archaeol*, **16**, 65–72, and *Excavation of an Iron Age settlement at Wilby Way, Great Doddington*. A Thomas and D Enright 2003, *Northamptonshire Archaeol*, **31**, 16–59. The overall scale of this site approaches the extensive Iron Age landscape examined at DIRFT (Daventry International Rail Freight Terminal), G Hughes and A Woodward 2015 *The Iron Age and Romano-British settlements at Crick Covert Farm, DIRFT Volume I,* and R Masefield (ed) *et al* 2015 *Origins, Development and Abandonment of an Iron Age Village, DIRFT Volume II,* both volumes Archaeopress Archaeology.

The Station Road site, Higham Ferrers was more limited in extent, comprising lengths of enclosure ditch and some pits, which formed the north-eastern margin of a more extensive area of Iron Age settlement, which lay beneath a larger and more significant Roman settlement, also previously partly excavated, (=S Lawrence and A Smith 2009, *Between villa and town: Excavations of a Roman roadside settlement and shrine at Higham*

Ferrers, Northamptonshire, Oxford Archaeol Monog, **7**.

The discussion includes a few not particularly useful comparative plans of roundhouses defined by drainage ditches (fig 2.8) and even less useful comparative plans of post-ring houses (fig 2.9), especially as one example (Crick, RG58) is actually a classic wall-trench roundhouse with doorway post-pits at the entrance. The partial post-ring is set between the wall slot and the drainage ditch, so these are likely to have had some other function. For a very similar structure at Coton Park, Rugby, it was suggested that these outer postholes may have held the ends of the principal rafters, and the Coton Park report also includes an extensive overview of the form and structure of the local Iron Age roundhouses (A Chapman 2020, see review above, 28, 126–139, figs 10.4–10.6).

Prehistoric Burial Mounds in Orton Meadows, Peterborough

D F Mackreth
East Anglian Archaeology, **173**
170 pages
ISBN 9780952810537

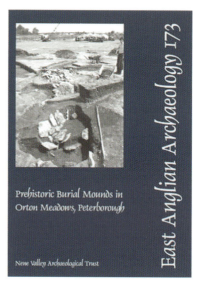

I first heard about this site in the late 1970s while I was involved in the excavation of the Briar Hill Neolithic causewayed enclosure, Northampton. When I was writing the report on the Neolithic oval mound at Tansor in the late 1990s I managed to obtain a draft copy of the text. So this is another site that we have been awaiting for many decades.

Lakes were due to be dug at Orton Meadows in the Nene valley, to improve flood management following construction of the Peterborough Eastern Bypass. This led to the excavation of two burial mounds which lay on the north bank of an old course of the river. A round barrow, found by David Hall in the 1970s, was still visible as a slight bump in the ancient water meadows. When archaeological excavation began, a subtle change in the vegetation nearby revealed another, older, burial monument. Work was intermittent, held up by lack of funds and only completed under a government unemployment scheme.

Both burial mounds span the period from the Neolithic to the Middle Bronze Age with evidence that they shared a sequence of development. Iron Age weaponry and currency bars were recovered from the old course of the Nene and there was evidence that ritual or religious practice continued at the round barrow into Early Saxon times. The focus of the cult may have been the tidal effect on the Nene.

Cultivation in open fields up-stream during the Late Saxon and medieval periods led to silting of the valley bottom, almost completely covering the burial mounds, the process coming to an end progressively through the eighteenth century. The burial mounds were effectively sealed by alluvial deposits accumulating over the last thousand years, and almost untouched by any post-medieval disturbance.

General

A Medieval Life: Cecilia Penifader and the World of English Peasants before the Plague

Judith M Bennett. 2020
University of Pennsylvania Press: The Middle Ages Series
Paperback: 192 pages, illustrated: £20.52
ISBN: 0812224698
(2nd edition: revised, with new illustrations)

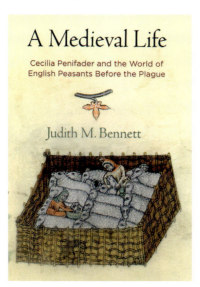

A Medieval Life **offers a biography of one woman, a portrait of her world, and an introduction to historical method. It is particularly relevant to the Northamp**tonshire reader, as that one woman lived her life within the manor of Brigstock, which then took in both Brigstock and Stanion, so the study brings to life the bare bones of our archaeological work using the extensive surviving records to take us on a journey through the daily life of peasants, and particularly women, in the early 14th century.

Each chapter includes a new section on how medievalists today are studying such topics as puberty, morals, courtship, and climate change. The illustrations are largely taken from the famous Luttrell Psalter to provide a parallel visualisation of those lives, and one figure, page 128, features an assemblage of medieval Stanion pottery previously published in *Northamptonshire Archaeology*, 2008, **35**, page 217. The final chapter explores some of the different ways in which historians, for better and for worse, have understood medieval society.

If you want to follow Judith M Bennett's exploration of the life of women in the medieval world, here are some other titles that might be of interest: *Ale, Beer, and Brewsters in England: Women's Work in a Changing World, 1300–1600;* as well as *History Matters: Patriarchy and the Challenge of Feminism;* and *Singlewomen in the European Past, 1250–1800 (Early American Studies),* Judith M Bennett and Amy M Froide. The broad thesis of Judith M Bennett's writing is that the development of the future of feminism should be founded on well-informed knowledge of the past, something that, of course, holds true for understanding any aspect of our lives in the modern world.

The only negative comment would be that her archaeological background is a little dated in providing the reader with the upland, Dartmoor, long house as the model for the medieval peasant home, when it has long been shown that this is not applicable to lowland England. Similarly, dwarf walls with cruck frames and wattle and daub infill are also not obligatory when good building stone is readily available, as in much of Northamptonshire, especially so around Brigstock, so close to the limestone quarries of Barnack.

The Battles and Battlefields of Northamptonshire

Mike Ingram and Graham Evans
Northamptonshire Battlefields Society
price £9.99, 155 pages

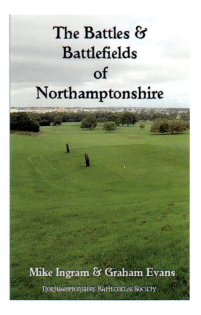

This is available from the Northamptonshire Battlefields Society and Amazon. Subjects include 'All Roads lead to Northampton': the Boudicca Revolt: The Baron's Wars: The Wars of the Roses: The Midland Revolt: The English Civil War including the Siege of Grafton Regis and Naseby: The Black Watch Rebellion and the Battle of Waterloo (you will have to read the book to find out more about that link) and much more. All profits go to the Society to help fund activities.

Northampton in the Great War,
Your Town & Cities in the Great War
Turton, K, 2016
Pen & Sword Military

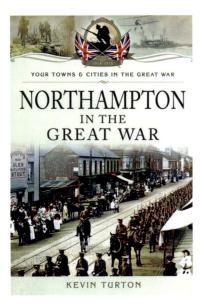

Northamptonshire at War 1939–45,
Your Town & Cities in the World War Two
Turton, K, 2017
Pen & Sword Military

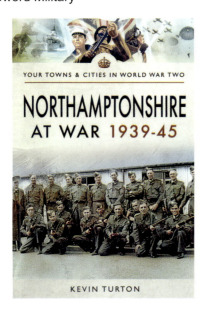

As Britain seems destined to be continuously replaying the two World Wars (sometimes one might think as a substitute for a meaningful future) here are two offerings from the same author, Kevin Turton, covering both. Kevin, according to the cover blurb, has written thirteen books covering history and true crime, and now writes from his home in Northamptonshire

For the Great War Kevin sets the broader scene and also provides a wealth of local material to show the impact of war directly and indirectly on daily life and business life, and the changes that occurred as the war progressed. He focusses on Northampton but frequently strays beyond to cover particular aspects. The text is profusely illustrated with 72 images in its 139 pages, featuring contemporary photographs and extracts from contemporary adverts and newspapers, and only occasionally locations as they are today.

For World War Two he follows the same approach, although with 30 illustrations in 122 pages it is far less profusely illustrated, and some of the included material again shows locations as they are today. You would have thought it would have been possible to at least match the Great War in terms of relevant local images, especially given that the whole county is being covered, and perhaps a little less background research was carried out in preparation for this publication.

That said, both are well presented examples of the local town/county at war genre and provide ample material to satisfying the evident interest in such material. If I had to make a recommendation it would have to be for the Great War volume, where the quantity and range of illustrations do so much to bring the period to life around the excellent text.

Both are priced at £12.99 and are available from www.pen-and-sword.co.uk.

Specialist studies

Fit for Purpose? Organic Residue Analysis and Vessel Specialisation: The perfectly utilitarian medieval pottery assemblage from West Cotton, Raunds
Dunne, J, Blinkhorn, P, Chapman, A, and Evershed, R P, 2020
Journal of Archaeological Science, **120**, 105178
(https://doi.org/10.1016/j.jas.2020.105178)

In the previous journal (NA 41, 2019, 207), we listed an article published in the *Journal of Archaeol Science* looking at the results of residue analysis on the pottery from West Cotton, Raunds in relation to the medieval peasant diet. This year we have a further article based on that residue analysis. This time the residue analysis is related to vessel type and how the residues within the fabrics help define the usage of particular vessel types, while the distribution of these vessels across the site is related to use within either kitchens or as tableware.

New insights into Neolithic milk consumption through proteomic analysis of dental calculus
Charlton, S, Ramsoe, A, Collins, M, Craig, O E, Fischer, R, Alexander, M, and Speller, C F, 2019
Archaeological and Anthropological Sciences, **11**, 6183–6196
(https://doi.org/10.1007/s12520–019–00911–7)

A new study relating to the origins of dairy consumption within European populations used skeletal material from three British Neolithic sites, the causewayed enclosures on Hambledon Hill, Dorset, the Hazleton North chambered tomb, near Cheltenham, Gloucestershire, and the Banbury Lane Middle Neolithic monument, Northampton, as briefly reported in NA 37, 2012 (Yates et al 2012, 19–28).

Northamptonshire Archaeology online

It has been a long journey, but all back issues of *Northamptonshire Archaeology* are now available online, free to all, with the Archaeology Data Service (ADS). The process began in the 2000s in getting the old paper journals scanned to pdf format, this cost the society a little over £1000.00. Having achieved that, the Council for British Archaeology (CBA) had set up an online Archaeology Library (ArchLib) and NAS joined, together with a few other county societies. For a few years pdf copies of articles were available online, but the library never grew as hoped, and was poorly advertised by the CBA so it became lost and forgotten on their website, and was eventually closed down through lack of use.

However, we had always planned to go to the ADS anyway, as this has become the national centre for archae-ological digital archives. In order to get online though, you must compile all the metadata and record it on a spreadsheet, which for 41 volumes containing over two hundred main articles, over a hundred notes, the annual roundups and various other contributions, resulted in a spreadsheet containing 1416 lines of data, and a lot of columns per line.

The 2004 monograph, *The Archaeology of Northamptonshire*, was used as a trial run of the system, so that was the first volume to become available on ADS, on this link: https://doi.org/10.5284/1050887.

Through lockdown in 2020 the spreadsheet was completed and forwarded to ADS who created the online library. This has cost NAS a little over £2000.00, which covers the setting up of the journal on the system and its future curation. For additional fees, we will also be able to add future issues as well, with a built in delay following publication before they become freely available to all.

The journal is available on this link: https://doi.org/10.5284/1083067; and you can download copies of any older issues that you don't have as paper copies. Remember, there is a full index available from the NAS website as a pdf download, or from the editor as NAS196674@gmail.com

Oxford Archaeology Library of reports: Northamptonshire

Reports on projects in Northamptonshire carried out by the various branches of Oxford Archaeology are available in pdf format from the OA online library: https://library.oxfordarchaeology.com/2871/

Northamptonshire Archaeology and MOLA (Museum of London Archaeology) Northampton: online

Copies of client reports for work in Northamptonshire (and elsewhere) carried out by both Northamptonshire Archaeology and its successor MOLA Northampton are available online, as pdf files, from the Archaeology Data Service (ADS), listed separately under the names Northamptonshire Archaeology and MOLA Northampton.

Northamptonshire Archaeology, **41**, *2021, 458–466*

Archaeology in Northamptonshire 2018

Summaries for MOLA (Museum of London Archaeology) Northampton
Compiled by Yvonne Wolframm-Murray

The sites listed include investigations undertaken in 2018 and some earlier works reported on in 2018.

Prehistoric

A43 Moulton bypass, land between roundabouts at Overstone Road and Spinney Hill

SP 79458 66305 and SP 78877 65072
Evaluation, MOLA

An archaeological field evaluation on land to the east of the A43 at Moulton, comprised thirty trenches. Archaeological features consisted of ditches, possibly Iron Age in date, a probable Saxon sunken-featured building, an adjacent undated well and five drains (two of stone and three of brick). Adam Reid and Adam Meadows OASIS 317729

Earls Barton, Phase 1E at Earls Barton Spinney Quarry

SP 85230 62150
Evaluation, MOLA

Archaeological trial trenching comprised 19 trenches which revealed a series of shallow ditches on various alignments, either undated or Iron Age and Roman in date. One ditch contained a large quantity of heat affected stones whilst another, curvilinear in plan, had not been visible on the geophysical survey. Paul Sharrock. OASIS 319279

Earls Barton, Earls Barton Spinney Quarry

SP 845 621
Geophysical survey, MOLA

A magnetometer survey of 19ha of land at Earls Barton Spinney Quarry, identified extensive archaeological remains, which included possible prehistoric ring ditches, a pit alignment, enclosures and roundhouses of probable Iron Age or Roman date and a possible Iron Age or Roman field system. Adam Meadows. OASIS 312161

King's Cliffe, Jack's Green

TL 038 974
Geophysical survey and evaluation, MOLA

An archaeological geophysical survey of *c.*6ha detected an area of possible industrial activity and a large number of ditches defining enclosures, a trackway and boundaries. Graham Arkley. OASIS317028.

An archaeological trial trench evaluation produced a low density of archaeological remains but included a probable Iron Age pit alignment and part of an Iron Age enclosure. An extensive irregular boundary ditch of uncertain date and two undated parallel boundary ditches or possible

trackway drainage ditches were also recorded. A small number of pits and postholes were also present, which may be of Iron Age date, although direct dating evidence was limited. Alex Shipley OASIS 330831

Kislingbury, land at Rothersthorpe Road

SP 469787 259088
Evaluation, MOLA

An archaeological evaluation, comprising eight trenches, followed a geophysical survey that had defined positive magnetic anomalies forming rectangular enclosures and sub-divisions and a ring ditch. All eight trenches contained archaeological features, with 24 ditches recorded and several showed evidence of having been re-cut indicating that they had been maintained or modified over time. Quantities of pottery and animal bone recovered from some ditch sections suggested that there had been domestic occupation nearby. In contrast, other ditch sections produced fewer artefacts and these may represent enclosures. It is like that these features represent a late Iron Age settlement located just to the west of a previously excavated Iron Age settlement. Christopher Jones. OASIS 320291

Moulton, Moulton Heights

SP 79030 67440
Evaluation, MOLA

The second phase of the archaeological trial trench evaluation on land at Moulton Heights, Moulton, comprised fifty-five trenches targeted on known cropmarks and geophysical anomalies. Archaeological features comprising predominantly ditches and pits were encountered in thirty-four trenches. The features were mainly boundary and enclosure ditches related to prehistoric and Roman settlement sites. A small assemblage of prehistoric and Roman pottery was recovered. Kamil Orzechowski, OASIS 323216

Northampton, south-east of Grange Park

SP 770 542
Geophysical survey, MOLA

On land south-east of Grange Park, Northampton a geophysical survey identified a small enclosure complex of probable Iron Age to Roman date, and a group of probable prehistoric monuments including three ring ditches and a pit alignment. Graham Arkley. OASIS 326492

Raunds, land at Midland Road

TL 00547 73216 and TL 00373 73288
Excavation, MOLA

Archaeological excavations undertaken on land at Midland Road, Raunds located a small middle Bronze

Age cemetery comprising five cremations. Three of the cremations were urned but the vessels were severely degraded by the wet conditions, and were in clay-like state. The remaining two cremations were unurned. Jonathan Elston. OASIS 315011

Upper Stowe, land adjacent to Sheepfold Grange, Main Street

SP 6468 5662

Evaluation, MOLA

Five trial trenches were excavated, with a late Iron Age ditch in one trench. Yvonne Wolframm-Murray. OASIS 337846

Wellingborough, HMP Wellingborough

SP 890 659

Geophysical survey and evaluation, MOLA

On the line of a proposed new access route to HMP Wellingborough, a geophysical survey and subsequent trial trench evaluation recorded seven middle/late Iron Age ditches, a roundhouse and two pits. These remains are probably part of the same settlement found in previous work to the south of the development area. Medieval to post-medieval furrows were also recorded. Graham Arkley and Carol Simmonds. OASIS 330408

Wellingborough, Stanton Cross

SP 915679 and SP 911695

Geophysical survey, MOLA

A geophysical survey of *c.*70ha of land to the east of Wellingborough, was undertaken ahead of the proposed Stanton Cross development scheme. The survey covered two irregular parcels of land, extending from north of Finedon Road to south of Irthlingborough Grange. Two extensive sets of archaeological remains were identified, each appearing to be broadly late prehistoric to Roman in date, with various enclosures and other occupation features present. A large palaeochannel, perhaps Pleistocene in date, was also present. Graham Arkley. OASIS 335121

Roman

Wellingborough, Stanton Cross

SP 915679 and SP 911695

Geophysical survey, MOLA

A geophysical survey of *c.*70ha of land to the east of Wellingborough, was undertaken ahead of the proposed Stanton Cross development scheme. The survey covered two irregular parcels of land, extending from north of Finedon Road to south of Irthlingborough Grange. A Roman road was traced intermittently over more than 1.5km. Elsewhere there were a number of linear ditches and two pit alignments. Graham Arkley. OASIS 335121

Saxon

A43 Moulton bypass, between roundabouts at Overstone Road and Spinney Hill

SP 79458 66305 and SP 78877 65072

Evaluation, MOLA

An archaeological field evaluation comprising of thirty trenches took place on land to the east of the A43 at Moulton. Archaeological features comprised a probable Saxon sunken-featured building, an undated well adjacent to two small stone drains, and three other drains, including one of brick. Adam Reid and Adam Meadows. OASIS 317729

Medieval

Badby, Church of St Mary the Virgin

SP 5597 5874

Watching Brief, MOLA

Archaeological investigation was undertaken during work to the nave, along the churchyard path and in the south porch. The Church lies towards the southern end of the village within an area thought to have Anglo-Saxon origins. The surviving architecture in the church dates from the 14th century with various alterations in the 15th, 18th and 19th centuries. The church has retained its graveyard, although it closed to burials in 1886. There were three soil horizons below the 16th-century porch, with 12 articulated burials, showing long term use for burial in this area (Fig 1). None of the burials can be dated, except to say they pre-date the porch. The number of sub-adult burials in this location is significant, with seven of the skeletons between neonatal and teens in age. The practice of burying young children in close locality to the church has been recorded at other sites, including Raunds, Furnells in the late Saxon/Norman period. It was possible they were buried in this location as it was believed that closeness to the church and rain falling from the roof of the church onto the burials had a greater sanctifying affected on them. One of the child burials had a pillowstone (Fig 2). Beneath the churchyard path were the remains of 27 individuals dated between the medieval and Victorian periods. The most interesting finds were a pewter paten and chalice fragment found with one of the burials, items placed with the interment of priests, a practice that generally occurred countrywide between the 13th and 16th centuries. The work within the nave showed that two of the medieval pier bases still displayed some of the original mortared stone foundation, which may represent part of an earlier church structure. Much late 19th century restoration work was also observed. Tim Sharman, Kamil Orzechowski and Carol Simmonds. OASIS 328082

Editorial note by Andy Chapman: the size and upright positioning of the stone associated with the early child burial at Badby church (Fig 2) might suggest it was a grave marker rather than a pillowstone. While not common at the Raunds Furnells late Saxon/Norman cemetery, a few burials, particularly those close to the Norman coffin and the presumed location of the church door, had the head and/or the foot end marked by rough-hewn upright

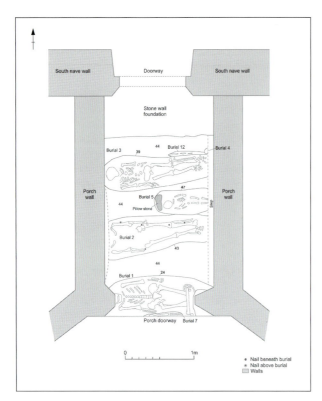

Fig 1: Badby Church porch, plan of the earliest of three levels of graves, including a child burial (see Fig 2)

Fig 2: Badby Church porch, child burial with pillowstone/ grave marker, head to west

stones (eg Boddington 1996, 45–46, figs 56 &57: *Raunds Furnells: The Anglo-Saxon church and churchyard*, English Heritage monog).

Irthlingborough, Addington Road
SP 9505 7092
Geophysical survey (earth resistance survey), MOLA
A previous magnetometer survey and trial trench excavation had found evidence of medieval settlement in this area, and the purpose of the resistance survey was to provide further information about the layout and extent of these remains. Only one archaeological feature, most

probably a metalled track surface, was clearly detected, although some less distinct anomalies of possible archaeological relevance were also present in the data. Adam Meadows. OASIS 306589

Long Buckby, land at 8 Harbidges Lane
SP 623 676
Strip, map and sample, MOLA
Sparse medieval (*c.*12th century) to modern features were found at 8 Harbidges Lane. The site lay at the rear of former backplots which fronted both Harbidges Lane to the east, West Street to the north and medieval settlement remains directly to the south (see Reid 2019, *Northamptonshire Archaeology,* **40**). The *c.*12th-century western plot boundary gully of Harbidges Lane may have been found, and this suggests that Harbidges Lane may have been laid out in this period. The low quantity of features recovered from all periods may imply that these peripheral backplot areas could have been used for horti-culture/agriculture. Adam Meadows. OASIS 305976

Northampton, land at Mereway, Wootton Park
SP 75368 57823
Evaluation, MOLA
Furrows indicative of medieval ridge and furrow cultivation, possible pits and tree root disturbance from a hedgerow where identified during a trial trench evaluation. Esther Poulus. OASIS 334699

Northampton, land west of Upton Lane, Upton Park
SP 7205 5955
Geophysical survey, MOLA
A geophysical survey of *c.*1.5ha of pastureland detected remnants of medieval to early post-medieval ridge and furrow cultivation and two modern pipelines. John Walford. OASIS 333739

Raunds, land at Midland Road
TL 00547 73216 and TL 00373 73288
Excavation, MOLA
The client report on the archaeological excavations undertaken on land at Midland Road, Raunds in 2016 was completed in 2018 (see *Northamptonshire Archaeology*, **39**, 2017). Activity during the late 11th century AD represented peripheral settlement remains. Two timber structures lay in the far north-east of the area. During the 12th to 13th century the settlement pattern changed with the formation of larger enclosures that replaced the smaller paddocks. Peripheral areas became more agricultural and livestock orientated. Towards the frontage, next to Midland Road, a large cluster of postholes were present from which only one sherd of medieval pottery was recovered. In the 13th century to 14th century the area underwent further reorganisation. Five rectilinear ditched plots were larger and more regular in layout than the former paddocks. The main boundary ditches were aligned north-east to south-west. A manorial farm complex developed in the south-west corner of the site during this period with a stone-built circular dovecote standing a little way back from the frontage on Midland Road with

Fig 3: Raunds, Midland Road: the medieval circular dovecote overlain by a post-medieval square dovecote

a probable malt oven structure adjacent to it, and a large pond (Fig 3 and *ib id*, 258, fig 3). By the 14th century the enclosures and field systems appear to have gone out of use with the manorial complex on the Midland Road frontage expanding. The circular dovecote was demolished around the 16th century and replaced with a square dovecote of similar size, with a yard on the south-west side, shared with a malthouse. A stone rubble trackway separated the dovecote from a possible field shelter with a cobblestone yard area, a pitched limestone yard surface with surrounding boundary wall, and a large stone barn to the north. The dating of the buildings is problematic with the absence of occupation deposits and the use of the buildings resulted in little datable material surviving. The fields surrounding the manorial farm were given over to ridge and furrow cultivation and appear to have been used regularly for sport shooting with lead pistol shot being found across the site in the subsoil. Jonathan Elston. OASIS 315011

Rushden, Eastern SUE development site

SP 974 668

Geophysical survey, MOLA

A magnetometer survey across the site of the proposed Rushden Eastern Sustainable Urban Expansion (SUE), covered *c.*215ha of land and revealed six discrete archaeological areas, including a possible medieval or post-medieval enclosure. Medieval ridge and furrow cultivation was also detected across the majority of the survey area. Graham Arkely. OASIS 297550

Wellingborough, HMP Wellingborough

SP 890 659

Geophysical survey and evaluation, MOLA

On the line of a proposed new access route to HMP Wellingborough, a geophysical survey and subsequent trial trench evaluation recorded medieval ridge and furrow in the western area of the site. Graham Arkley and Carol Simmonds. OASIS 330408

Post-medieval

Blisworth, Buttermilk Hall Farm

SP 73601 51116

Historic Building Recording, MOLA

A programme of historic building recording at Buttermilk Hall Farm, Blisworth, was undertaken prior to the conversion of a barn and stables to a residential dwelling (Fig 4). The origin of the farm lay in the mid-18th century; by the early 19th century, maps show an L-shaped plan comprising the threshing barn, stables and a cowshed connecting the barns and farmhouse. The Ordnance Survey Map of 1885 depicts the development of the farm into an F-shaped plan with the addition of an open animal shelter. Over the next century only small alterations had been made, which included the addition of a pigsty, the enclosing of the open animal shelter, renewal of the roofs and replacement of the doors and windows. Yvonne Wolframm-Murray. OASIS 317145

Canons Ashby, Canons Ashby House

SP 57720 50645

Historic Building Recording, MOLA

Between October and December 2017 a programme of historic building recording was undertaken at Canons Ashby House, a National Trust property. This work sought not only to provide a detailed record of the house, but also to examine the sequences of development of alteration which were undertaken in the nearly 500 years since its construction (Figs 5 & 6). Recording comprised a complete photographic survey of the external elevations and all accessible rooms and roof spaces, and a drawn record which included doors and windows, timber-framing, roof trusses, and sections, elevations and plans. A laser survey was also carried out which allowed the house to be mapped to a high level of detail, and an aerial drone survey provided high level photographs from which a full photogrammatic model of the house exterior was produced.

The house comprises four interconnected ranges enclosing a central courtyard and stands adjacent to the former Banbury Lane drovers' route. Adjacent to the house are formal gardens and pasture fields leading to a small lake. The remains of a former medieval priory are located a short distance away from the house and provided some of the building material for its construction.

The present house was expanded and modernised by John Dryden in the period 1551–1584 around a farmhouse which forms the north-western corner of the building and possibly parts of the east range. This survey suggests that the farmhouse comprised a two-part structure with a storied bay at the north containing parlours, and a possible hall to the south. The extension by John Dryden resulted in an H-plan house with tower. This formed the basis for later developments which expanded the structure into a courtyard plan form. Later developments, particularly in c.1710, altered floor levels, room layout and access, fenestration, and overall aesthetics and decoration. Amir Bassir. OASIS 322973

Editorial note: The full client report on Canons Ashby House is the finest presentation of building recording that I have seen. It runs to 296 pages and contains 285 illus-

Fig 4: The farmyard at Buttermilk Hall Farm, Blisworth, with the threshing to the rear and the stables to the right

Fig 5: An aerial view of the four interconnected ranges, enclosing a central courtyard, of Canons Ashby House, along with part of the formal gardens, left, and Banbury Lane, right

trations, which include photographs, plans and elevations, mostly in colour, ranging from whole frontages down to details of individual doorways, windows and associated fittings. I would encourage anyone with a specific interest in Cannons Ashby or a general interest in the art and craft of building recording to get hold of copy, as it gives great pleasure just working through the mass of beautifully

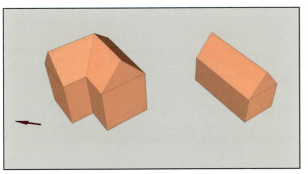

Wylkyns Farm, farmhouse with detached building

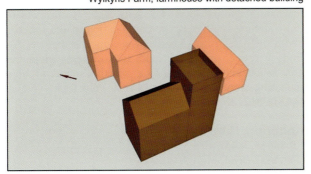

New Tower House by John Dryden

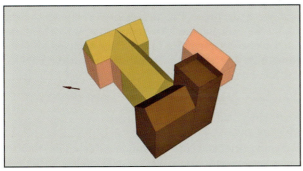

Tower House joined to the farm house which was extended one bay

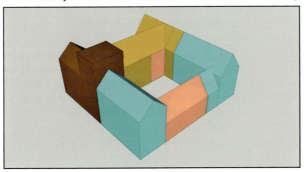

Two new wings added, detached building likely rebuilt in stone and modified to fit new ranges

Fig 6: Reconstruction of the development of Canons Ashby House from the mid-16th century to the early 17th century

presented images and illustrations. Unfortunately, it is not yet available online through the Archaeology Data Service (ADS) Library of Unpublished Fieldwork Reports, but might be available directly from MOLA Northampton, providing they have permission from the National Trust. If seriously interested in obtaining a copy, contact Rob Atkins on: ratkins@mola.org.uk).

Earls Barton, Earls Barton Spinney Quarry
SP 845 621
Geophysical survey, MOLA
Geophysical survey located medieval to early post-medieval ridge and furrow and a post-medieval or modern brick culvert. Adam Meadows. OASIS 312161

Hardwick, Manor House, Manor Farm
SP 85110 69763
Watching Brief and Historic Building Recording, MOLA
Archaeological observation and recording was carried out during the excavation of the foundations of a new extension at Hardwick Manor House. The house was constructed in the 14th century with modifications in the 15th and 16th centuries. The former great hall, which stood on the eastern side, was destroyed in the 17th century, but an evaluation trench located a possible wall foundation cut, which contained a pottery body sherd dated to the 15th century. Beyond this main wall, remains were found to suggest that there had been another building with external walls, possibly brick or stone with internal timber walls. A building recording survey took place on an existing extension, which had a 1775 date stone below a window. This was a single-storey brick extension with a cellar and a thatch roof, which was expanded in 1887 to form a two-storey building with a slate roof. Yvonne Wolframm-Murray. OASIS 334465

Kislingbury, land at Rothersthorpe Road
SP 469787 259088
Evaluation, MOLA
A post-medieval boundary and ridge and furrow cultivation remains were found during an archaeological evaluation comprising eight trenches. Christopher Jones. OASIS 320291

Northampton, Barnes and Becks Meadows
SP 76906 59443
Watching brief, MOLA
Electrical improvement works on land within the boundary of the Registered Battlefield of Northampton 1460 (NHLE 1000028) were observed. The works were carried out through a methodology that ensured minimal ground disturbance. No archaeological features were observed, although metal detection survey recovered six post-medieval finds dating to the c.16th to 17th centuries. Ian Fisher and Carol Simmonds. OASIS 309644

Northampton, Northampton Castle, St Andrew's Road
SP 7490 6056
Topographic survey, MOLA
A topographic survey of part of the site of Northampton Castle was undertaken to compare the results with those

of a spot height survey undertaken in 1956. This led to the identification of several locations where there were variations in level, presumably due to recent landscaping of the site. Graham Arkley and Mark Burch. OASIS 314351

Northampton, Wootton Park School
SP 770 542
Geophysical survey, MOLA
A geophysical survey at Wootton Park School detected medieval or post-medieval ridge and furrow cultivation, and other anomalies which relate to modern services, landscaping and sports pitches. John Walford. OASIS 328458

Northampton, land south-east of Grange Park
SP 770 542
Geophysical survey, MOLA
On land south-east of Grange Park, Northampton, a geophysical survey identified an area of post-medieval settlement with possible medieval antecedents. Graham Arkley. OASIS 326492

Upper Stowe, land adjacent to Sheepfold Grange, Main Street
SP 6468 5662
Evaluation, MOLA
In three of the five trenches excavated there were post-medieval stone deposits, and one of these corresponded with the location of a possible kiln identified by previous geophysical survey. Yvonne Wolframm-Murray. OASIS 337846

Unknown/Modern

Bradden, Water Lane
SP 464644 248144
Watching Brief, MOLA
A programme of archaeological investigation and recording was carried out during groundworks for the footprint of a new building and associated services. Only two undated archaeological features were identified: a small posthole and pit. Christopher Jones and Esther Poulus. OASIS 322273

Burton Latimer, 23 Regent Road
SP 8954 7489
Evaluation, MOLA
Four trenches were excavated but none contained archaeologically significant features. Two sherds of unstratified medieval pottery were recovered from the subsoil, whilst 19th/20th-century pottery and glass were recovered from a pit. Yvonne Wolframm-Murray. OASIS 329848

Cold Higham, on land adjacent to the Old Rectory, Church Lane
SP 66228 53563
Watching brief, MOLA
A programme of archaeological observation, investigation, recording and analysis was conducted in an area heavily truncated by modern landscaping. Two features were not disturbed, and these comprised an undated pit

which contained the partially articulated skeletal remains of an adult horse, and a stone wall constructed with lime mortar. This wall foundation was near the north-western edge of the excavation area and aligned with the extant wall of an adjacent outbuilding, and had presumably extended from it to form the boundary to a yard. Liam JS Powell. OASIS 321804

Corby, land at Weldon Park
SP 935 897
Evaluation, MOLA
An archaeological field evaluation comprised 74 trenches. One undated ditch was recorded. A previous magnetometer survey had indicated the likely presence of ridge and furrow on the site, but this has not been confirmed by the evaluation. Kamil Orzechowski. OASIS 329612

Irthlingborough, Nene Business Park
SP 95364 71024
Watching Brief, MOLA
The area for development was stripped of soils down to the natural ground level. The only features observed in the watching brief were the continuation of the furrows and a ditch seen in the earlier trenching on the site. No finds were recovered. The south side of the development area was heavily disturbed by a spread of modern rubble including stone, concrete and brick. Christopher Jones. OASIS 312135

Kettering, Hazelwood Lane
SP 86615 78457
Watching Brief, MOLA
During an archaeological observation, investigation and recording, the stone and brick footings of three buildings were identified. Two phases of development of the site in the 18th and the 19th centuries were recorded; the latter phase corresponded to buildings depicted on maps from 1826 and 1886. Other features included a cobbled surface, pits, a possible well, a posthole, and later drains and surfaces. Yvonne Wolframm-Murray. OASIS 314592

Kettering, William Knibb Centre
SP 8708 7891
Watching Brief and Historic Building Recording, MOLA
A buried Second World War air raid shelter at the late 19th-century William Knibb Centre, Montagu Road, Kettering, was uncovered. The structure comprised a grid of interconnected tunnels, lined and sealed with pre-cast concrete slabs set into a pre-cast concrete frame. The shelter appears to be a variation of a common type of shelter, of which several examples have been uncovered in association with schools, where they were intended to accommodate several hundred children for short periods of time in the event of an air raid. These were very utilitarian structures, simple in design, which were not intended for prolonged occupation, most providing only latrines and wooden benches. Excavation was required due to safety concerns after the structure had been investigated via a series of test holes and with a remotely operated vehicle with on-board camera. Amir Bassir. OASIS 308398

King's Cliffe, Jack's Green

TL 038 974

Geophysical survey, MOLA

An archaeological geophysical survey of c.6ha detected a possible former stream channel and some remains probably associated with the Second World War King's Cliffe Airfield. Graham Arkley. OASIS 317028

Moulton, Moulton Heights

SP 79030 67440

Evaluation, MOLA

A second phase of the archaeological trial trench evaluation on land at Moulton Heights, Moulton, comprised fifty-five trenches targeted on known cropmarks and geophysical anomalies. The presence of a post-medieval drainage system was recorded in south-western corner of the evaluated area. Kamil Orzechowski. OASIS 323216

Moulton, Moulton College Hydroponic Greenhouse site

SP 770 673

Geophysical survey, MOLA

A magnetometer survey was undertaken on c.4ha of land prior to the proposed construction of a hydroponic greenhouse. The survey detected one undated pit, as well as ridge and furrow dating from the medieval to early post-medieval period. Graham Arkley. OASIS 323353

Northampton, next to St Edmund's Terrace, St Edmund's Road

SP 76115 60782

Watching brief, MOLA

Works on a building plot adjacent to St Edmund's Terrace uncovered walls, buried soils and a possible well, all dating to the 19th and 20th centuries. Jonathan Elston. OASIS 334779

Wellingborough, HMP Wellingborough

SP 890 659

Evaluation, MOLA

In the north-east part of the site a trial trench evaluation found an undated linear feature, a drain and several furrows. A possible fragment of medieval roof tile was recovered from one of the furrows. No other artefacts were recovered. Ester Poulus. OASIS 337157

Wellingborough, HMP Wellingborough

SP 890 659

Geophysical survey and evaluation, MOLA

On the line of a proposed new access route to HMP Wellingborough, a geophysical survey and subsequent trial trench evaluation recorded a modern boundary ditch in the western area of the site. Graham Arkley and Carol Simmonds. OASIS 330408

Wellingborough, Stanton Cross

SP 915679 and SP 911695

Geophysical survey, MOLA

A geophysical survey of c.70ha of land to the east of Wellingborough was undertaken ahead of the proposed Stanton Cross development scheme. The survey mapped parts of several backfilled quarries and former tramways associated with the ironstone industry during the late 19th to early 20th centuries. Graham Arkley. OASIS 335121

Negative sites

Castle Ashby, The Falcon Hotel

SP 85995 59549

Watching Brief, MOLA

Between June and September a programme of archaeological observation, investigation and recording were part of a larger project which focussed on historic analysis of the Falcon Hotel and the impact of the present development on the existing heritage assets within Castle Ashby. The current works were limited to the observation of the groundworks related to construction of new extensions to the north-west and the north–east of the existing building. During the observation no archaeological features, surfaces or finds were present, probably as the result of deep disturbance related to earlier demolition works. Amir Bassir. OASIS 330110

Chelveston, The Airfield, 20MW energy battery storage facility, Chelveston Renewable Energy Park

TL 01334 68672

Watching brief, MOLA

No archaeological remains were encountered within a watching brief within the present development area. This part of the site lay outside of the area of Iron Age and Roman activity identified to the south. Christopher Jones OASIS 332363

Higham Ferrers, Saffron Moat

SP 95828 68698

Watching Brief, MOLA

The installation of a new information and display board at Saffron Moat, Higham Ferrers, required a programme of archaeological observation, investigation and recording. No archaeological finds were recovered and no archaeological features were observed. Ian Fisher. OASIS 310205

Irhlingborough, Nene Business Park

SP 95364 71024

Watching brief, MOLA

The area for development was stripped of soils down to the natural ground level under constant archaeological supervision. The south side of the development area was heavily disturbed by a spread of modern rubble including stone, concrete and brick, the only features observed were the continuation of the furrows and ditch seen in the earlier trenching. No finds were recovered. Christopher Jones. OASIS 312135

Spratton, Spratton Hall School

SP 71669 70556

Watching brief, MOLA

Archaeological observation, investigation and recording were carried out during the groundworks for tennis courts, changing room pavilion and test pits. The areas investigated had previously been levelled and terraced by landscaping for the existing playing fields which had destroyed any archaeological deposits that may once have existed. James Fairclough and Christopher Jones. OASIS 324463

Towcester, Towcester South, Phase 1a development

SP 70800 47170

Watching brief, MOLA

Between March 2017 and April 2018 a programme of archaeological observation, investigation and recording was carried out during groundworks. The applied methodology ensured minimal ground disturbance. No archaeological features were observed, despite Iron Age and early Roman features being identified in previous geophysical survey and trial trenching. Ian Fisher. OASIS 316457

Towcester, Wood Burcote

SP 6968 4729

Watching brief, MOLA

An archaeological observation, investigation and recording took place during the installation of a new path. The works consisted of ground surface reduction by up to 0.35m onto subsoil. Ian Fisher. OASIS 321811

Wellingborough, HMP Wellingborough

SP 890 659

Watching Brief, MOLA

An archaeological observation and recording of the site took place during the removal of deep foundations of the former 20th-century prison. These extensive former foundations had penetrated to depth greater than the archaeological horizon. As a consequence, no archaeological features or overburden comprising topsoil or subsoil deposits survived. Carol Simmonds. OASIS 334639

Archaeology in Northamptonshire 2019

Summaries for MOLA (Museum of London Archaeology) Northampton
Compiled by Yvonne Wolframm-Murray

Prehistoric

King's Cliffe, Wansford Road, land at Rockingham Forest Park

TL 03831 97470

Excavation, MOLA

An excavation uncovered part of a possible pit alignment. A four-post structure in this same area was dated to the Iron Age. Part of a middle Iron Age settlement comprised two enclosures as well as numerous intercutting circular or sub-circular pits (Fig 1). Adam Douthwaite and Adam Reid. OASIS 361720

Fig 1: King's Cliffe Enclosures 1 and 2, and intercutting quarry pits

Northampton, Overstone, A43 Moulton Bypass

SP 79458 66305 to SP 78877 65072

Evaluation, MOLA

In March 2018 and February 2019 trial trench and test pit evaluations carried out on land between the roundabouts at Overstone Road and Spinney Hill found a curvilinear Iron Age enclosure ditch. Adam Reid, Alex Shipley and Adam Meadows. OASIS 346672

Overstone, Sywell Road, land at Overstone Farm

SP 79731 66211

Geophysical survey and evaluation, MOLA

A geophysical survey identified three ring ditches and several linear features. The presence of the ring ditches was confirmed in the evaluation, and a single pottery sherd, prehistoric in date, and animal bone was recovered. The other features were undated. James Fairclough. OASIS 384109

Raunds, land north of Brick Kiln Road

SP 9943 7402

Excavation, MOLA

An excavation, comprising two areas totalling 0.04ha, revealed an isolated pit in each area, one of which was dated to the mid-late Iron Age during the previous evaluation and four parallel undated ditches. Simon Markus. OASIS 342097

Towcester, Towcester South, Trial Trenches 13–2

SP 7040 4761

Evaluation, MOLA

Features dated to the late Iron Age comprised ditches, a gully, a posthole and pits, four of which had bases lined with limestone,. Chris Pennell. OASIS 377983

Towcester, Tiffield Park

SP 6942 5014

Geophysical survey & evaluation, MOLA

A geophysical survey of *c.*26ha of land identified a probable prehistoric ring ditch, several sets of enclosures likely to date from the Iron Age and Roman periods. The evaluation confirmed pits, gullies and ditches associated with enclosures of Iron Age to Roman date. John Walford and Jonathon Elston. OASIS 349101, 375088

Wellingborough, HMP Wellingborough, Doddington Road

SP 890 659

Excavation, MOLA

Two phases of the late Iron Age ditches, probably 1st century BC, comprised part of a field system of two or more boundary ditches, several postholes and two pits, followed by a probable sub-rectangular enclosure that cut the boundary ditches. Chris Pennell and Yvonne Wolframm-Murray. OASIS 343957

Wellingborough, Wellingborough East, Area 3

SP 7880 5890

Excavation, MOLA

There was a landscape of multi-period remains. A Neolithic causewayed enclosure was only partially excavated (Figs 2 & 3) and an isolated pit contained Neolithic pottery. Iron Age settlement comprised at least eleven sub-circular

enclosures and seven ring ditches as well as associated features such as pits (Fig 3). The pottery assemblage indicates that the use of this settlement spanned the 3rd to 1st centuries BC with a continuation into the early 1st century AD. Carol Simmonds and Tracy Preece. OASIS 351637

Fig 2: Wellingborough, Neolithic causewayed enclosure ditch during excavation

Fig 3: (Below) Wellingborough East, the Eastern area all periods of activity from the Neolithic causewayed enclosure onward

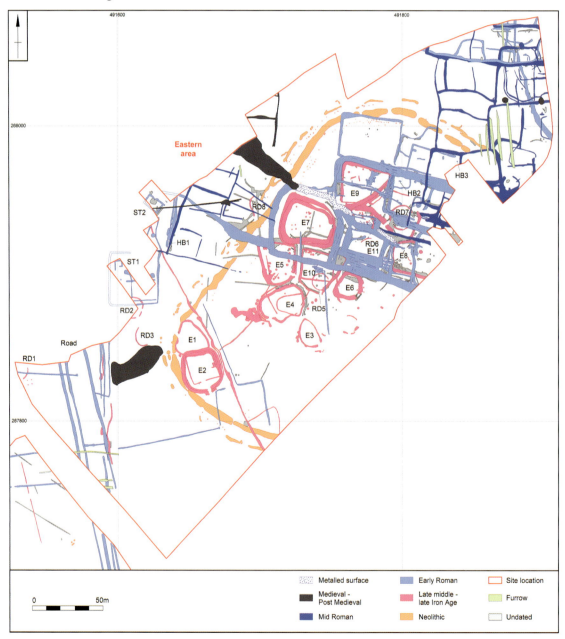

Wellingborough, Stanton Cross, Flood Relief Zone 5

SP 910 699, SP 925 674

Geophysical survey & evaluation, MOLA

The geophysical survey of *c.*13.5ha identified a group of sub-circular enclosures, roundhouses and pits and another group of rectilinear enclosures. A curving ditch, perhaps part of a very large enclosure, was also identified. Evaluation in one area recorded middle to late Iron Age enclosures, ditches and pits. John Walford, Alex Shipley, Adam Douthwaite. OASIS 368034, 372914, 349270

Roman

Northampton, Brackmills, land at Brackmills Point – Decathlon

SP 7880 5890

Topographic survey & excavation, MOLA

An archaeological topographic survey and excavation revealed a large and complex series of features indicative of a multi-period settlement spanning the late Iron Age to late Roman periods. The site had been first identified during geophysical survey and trial trench evaluation. A pit alignment was the earliest feature. There were a series of enclosures and boundary ditches as well as pit

Fig 4: Brackmills Point, Roman pottery kiln 1, with scattered kiln bars

Fig 5: Brackmills Point, Roman pottery kiln 2

groups, timber and stone-built roundhouses, substantial rectangular stone-built structures, burials, pottery kilns and a drying oven (Figs 4–5). A large finds assemblage comprises pottery, animal bone, environmental remains, ceramic and stone building material as well as coins and other metal artefacts. Settlement appeared to have largely ceased by the end of the 4th century AD, although there was a single sunken-featured building of early medieval date. Chris Chinnock. OASIS 349958

Northampton, Overstone, A43 Moulton Bypass

SP 79458 66305 to SP 78877 65072

Evaluation, MOLA

In March 2018 and February 2019 trial trench and test pit evaluations were carried out on land between the roundabouts at Overstone Road and Spinney Hill, as part of the A43 Moulton bypass. There was a large sub-rectangular Roman enclosure. Adam Reid, Alex Shipley and Adam Meadows. OASIS 346672

Pytchley, land at Butcher's Lane

SP 85933 74479

Watching brief, MOLA

A watching brief revealed a small number of ditches, dated to the 3rd/4th centuries AD, which may define part of a Roman field system. A small number of pits and postholes are likely to also date to this period. Paul Beers and Chris Chinnock. OASIS 347172

Towcester, Bell Plantation

SP 68710 49822

Evaluation & excavation, MOLA

This work extended the known extent of the expansion of the northern suburbs of *Lactodorum*. A previous trial trench evaluation had revealed the presence of a middle to late Roman inhumation (now radiocarbon dated) and other Roman features. A small excavation found a probable early Roman boundary which was later redefined as well as quarrying within the area. In the middle Roman period a routeway headed towards Watling Street, aligned perpendicular to it. A cluster of postholes lay directly to the north of the routeway and may suggest structure(s) had once fronted this route. A watering hole/well, backfilled with a notable quantity of later 2nd-century AD domestic waste and a little industrial material, lay directly to the south of the routeway. By the middle–late Roman period this occupation and routeway was replaced by a possible enclosure, defined by three ditches, which may have been parallel to Watling Street. A small quantity of 3rd-century pottery was recovered and it is likely that occupation had ceased by the 4th century. Adam Douthwaite and Yvonne Wolframm-Murray. OASIS 359083

Towcester, land at Bickerstaffes Road (Water Lane)

SP 69179 48486

Evaluation, MOLA

Features of Roman date, consisting of two ditches, a pit, a metalled surface and stonework, may represent the edge of the *agger* of the Alchester Road or a stone structure. The metalled surface was quarried at some later date. The features produced a large quantity of pottery and metal finds, including imported amphorae, a well-preserved late 2nd-century Roman coin and a cosmetic spoon. Alex Shipley. OASIS 364821

Towcester South, Trial Trenches 13–2
SP 7040 4761
Evaluation, MOLA
A cremation, dating to the Roman period was excavated. Chris Pennell. OASIS 377983

Wellingborough, Wellingborough East, Area 3
SP 7880 5890
Excavation, MOLA
The site revealed a landscape of multi-phased archaeological remains including the late Roman period (see Fig 3). In the early to mid-1st century AD, a rectilinear enclosure system was established. Other features comprised paddocks, evidence for buildings with stone footings, a metalled surface defining a trackway and part of the Irchester Roman road. Two inhumations and one unurned cremation burial were also identified. Occupation continued until the late 3rd to the mid to late 4th century. Carol Simmonds and Tracy Preece. OASIS 351637

Wellingborough, Stanton Cross, Flood Relief Zone 5
SP 910 699, SP 925 674
Geophysical survey & evaluation, MOLA
The geophysical survey of *c.*13.5ha identified a group of sub-circular enclosures, roundhouses and pits and another group of rectilinear enclosures. Evaluation in one area recorded a possible Roman road. John Walford, Alex Shipley, Adam Douthwaite. OASIS 368034, 372914, 349270

Medieval

Brackley, 2 Bridge Street
SP 58438 36752
Watching brief, MOLA
After the demolition of a stone barn a watching brief was conducted during the digging of foundation trenches for three buildings. Four pits, two medieval and two undated, were recorded. One pottery sherd from a pit was broadly dated to AD1100 to 1400. Environmental analysis from another pit produced wood, molluscs, seeds and insects, the beetle taxa suggesting a degree of household refuse, and being waterlogged with foul water, and therefore probably left open for some time. Chris Pennell. OASIS 353799

Bugbrooke, land south-west of The Firs
SP 6720 5693
Geophysical survey, MOLA
The geophysical survey indicated medieval or post-medieval ridge and furrow cultivation and quarrying. Graham Arkley. OASIS 364702

Ecton, Leathermills Sluice
SP 8313 6154
Excavation, MOLA
An excavation at Leathermills Sluice was undertaken in advance of restoration work to the existing sluice and ancillary structures. There were parts of a 13th-century stone-built mill building with internal dividing walls and a surviving floor. The medieval watermill was replaced by a slightly larger mill structure in the 16th century, which continued in use until the early to mid-19th century when it fell into disuse and was eventually demolished (Fig 6). A third undated rectangular structure was sited close to the medieval mill building. This building had no visible internal features and its function is unclear. The excavated structures were explored sufficiently to characterise them but were not fully excavated, instead being re-buried to preserve them *in situ*. Stephen Morris and Mark Holmes. OASIS 345782

Fig 6: Ecton, Leathermills, vertical view from drone

Fotheringhay, Fotheringhay Castle
TL 062 929
Aerial & geophysical surveys, MOLA
Ground Penetrating Radar and magnetometer techniques, combined with a new analysis of resistivity data surveyed in 1991, has provided evidence of a tower on the motte and buildings and yards or rubble in the inner bailey of Fotheringhay Castle (Fig 7). The ground plan of buildings within the inner bailey is at variance with the only known depiction of the castle before its demolition in the late 17th and 18th centuries. The reason for this discrepancy is uncertain but could suggest either that the drawing is inaccurate, or that an otherwise undocumented phase of post-medieval buildings was constructed after the demolition of the castle. Only selected excavation would provide dating evidence for the buildings. Survey to the north and east of the castle has also identified historic remains including hollow-ways, tenements, foundations of small buildings one of which may be a dovecote and the moat surrounding the outer courts of the castle. Stephen Parry. OASIS 349811

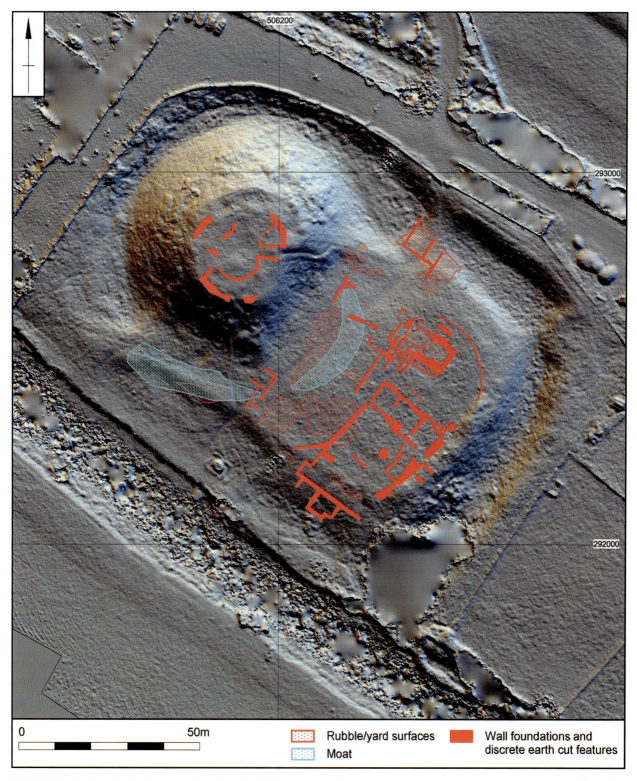

Fig 7: Fotheringhay Castle: interpretation of geophysical survey over lidar base survey, showing a tower on the motte and buildings within the inner bailey

Northampton, St Andrew's Road, Northampton Castle
SP 74916055
Evaluation, MOLA
Archaeological works in the inner bailey of the former Northampton castle were designed to evaluate the survival of archaeological features prior to a potential forthcoming community excavation. A test pit at the south-east end of the site uncovered a surviving wall face relating to the castle. Alex Shipley. OASIS 373095

Northampton, Overstone, A43 Moulton Bypass
SP 79458 66305 to SP 78877 65072
Evaluation, MOLA
In March 2018 and February 2019 trial trench and test pit evaluations were carried out on land between the roundabouts at Overstone Road and Spinney Hill, as part of the A43 Moulton bypass. An early–middle Saxon sunken-featured building (SFB) produced a pinbeater, used in the manufacture of textiles. Adam Reid, Alex Shipley and Adam Meadows. OASIS 346672

Paulerspury, Kennel Lane
SP 722 454
Geophysical survey, MOLA
The geophysical survey indicated evidence for medieval or post-medieval ridge and furrow cultivation. No further features of archaeological interest were detected. Graham Arkley OASIS 367575

Pytchley, land at Butcher's Lane
SP 85933 74479
Watching brief, MOLA
A watching brief revealed a single inhumation, buried in a prone position, cut into the upper fill of one of the Roman ditches. The burial has been radiocarbon dated to the mid-7th to early 8th centuries AD and may relate to other early medieval burials previously excavated in the vicinity. Paul Beers and Chris Chinnock. OASIS 347172

Thrapston, land at Haldens Parkway
TL 0103 7887
Evaluation, MOLA
An evaluation identified medieval/post-medieval ridge and furrow as well as four undated postholes. Chris Pennell. OASIS 357105

Warmington, 18–20 Chapel Street
SP 0778 9123
Watching brief, MOLA
The earliest archaeological features observed dated to the mid-12th to late 15th centuries included postholes from a medieval building which had existed along the present roadside. A series of gullies and some pits were located within the southern and eastern half of the site. Paul Sharrock. OASIS 373616

Towcester, Tiffield Park
SP 6942 5014
Geophysical survey & evaluation, MOLA
A geophysical survey of c.26ha of land and evaluation identified medieval to early post-medieval ridge and furrow cultivation. John Walford, Jonathon Elston. OASIS 349101, 375088

Wellingborough, works at Area 14
SP 90921 68483
Watching brief, MOLA
The remains of ridge and furrow cultivation were present. Adam Reid.

Wellingborough, Stanton Cross, Flood Relief Zone 5
SP 910 699, SP 925 674
Geophysical survey & evaluation, MOLA
The geophysical survey of c.13.5ha identified features including ridge and furrow. John Walford, Alex Shipley, Adam Douthwaite. OASIS 368034, 372914, 349270

Post-medieval

Cogenhoe, land at Manor Works, 50 Church Street
SP 83110 60889
Watching brief, MOLA
Post-medieval pits and an undated ditch were seen during a watching brief. The earliest cartographic evidence for the site is the Ordnance Survey map of 1885, showing the buildings that are still present. Jonathan Elston. OASIS 342316

East Haddon, land at Dairy Farm, Church Lane
SP 66670 67731
Evaluation
MOLA
An evaluation comprising two trenches revealed post-medieval/modern quarry pits. Extraction of clay in the countryside for locally made brick and tile was not uncommon. Finds recovered from one of the backfills dated to the 18th-19th centuries. Yvonne Wolframm-Murray. OASIS 351342

Ecton, Leathermills Sluice
SP 8313 6154
Excavation, MOLA
An excavation at the Leathermills Sluice was undertaken in advance of restoration work to the existing sluice and ancillary structures. An upstanding 19th-century barrel-arched, stone-built boat house/shelter lay to the west of the post-medieval mill. The excavated structures were explored sufficiently to characterise them but were not fully excavated, instead being re-buried to preserve them *in situ* (see Fig 6). Stephen Morris and Mark Holmes. OASIS 345782

King's Cliffe, Wansford Road, land at Rockingham Forest Park

TL 03831 97470

Excavation, MOLA

There were a series of post-medieval trackways and boundary ditches in the area (see Fig 1). A number of other undated features are also likely to relate to the post-medieval and/or modern use of the site. Adam Douthwaite and Adam Reid. OASIS 361720

Northampton, Overstone, A43 Moulton Bypass

SP 79458 66305 to SP 78877 65072

Evaluation, MOLA

In March 2018 and February 2019 trial trench and test pit evaluations were carried out on land between the roundabouts at Overstone Road and Spinney Hill. A possible post-medieval well and five adjacent stone-lined drains were found. Two undated palaeochannels on the south side of the site following the valley, may represent sections of the same feature. A single undated ditch was also recorded. Twenty test pits were also excavated in and around the woodland located along the eastern side of the A43, north of Spinney Hill roundabout. No archaeological remains were found at this location. Adam Reid, Alex Shipley and Adam Meadows. OASIS 346672

Preston Capes, The Old Rectory

SP 57488 54887

Evaluation, MOLA

An evaluation in the proposed area of two new ponds revealed the remains of a post-medieval pit in the area of the small pond. An earthwork bank likely formed part of post-medieval landscaping. Christopher Jones. OASIS 350368

Towcester South, Trial Trenches 13–2

SP 7040 4761

Evaluation, MOLA

Post-medieval ridge and furrow was investigated. Chris Pennell. OASIS 377983

Modern/unknown

Broughton, 5 Church Street

SP 8348 7572

Watching brief, MOLA

No finds or features were observed in a watching brief during the digging of foundation trenches. The thickness of the subsoil recovered suggested it had either been imported onto the site, or that it may have derived from flattened medieval cultivation earthworks. There was no evidence that the medieval village extended as far south as Church Street. Adam Reid. OASIS 364305

Bugbrooke, land south-west of The Firs

SP 6720 5693

Geophysical survey, MOLA

The geophysical survey indicated a large area of disturbance in the north-west which could be attributed to the construction of either the nearby Grand Union Canal or bridge, or possibly to the demolition of the former Swan public house. Graham Arkley. OASIS 364702

Corby, land at Weldon Park

SP 935 897

Mitigation, MOLA

Mitigation re-found a pit located in a previous evaluation, but no further archaeological features were identified. Chris Pennell. OASIS 376828

Daventry, 7–13 Warwick Street

SP 57036 62403

Watching brief, MOLA

No archaeological remains were found during the re-development of the site. However, the possibility of identifying archaeological features was reduced due to a large portion of the groundworks having been carried out prior to archaeological visit. Paul Sharrock and Carol Simmonds. OASIS 360496

Earls Barton, Whites Nurseries

SP 8460 6280

Evaluation, MOLA

There were two small irregularly-shaped features most likely of natural origin. A machine-cut pit was also observed as well as service pipes, these modern features almost certainly related to greenhouses which had once occupied part of the development area. Kamil Orzechowski. OASIS 374262

Gretton, land at 9 Station Road

SP 89638 94162

Evaluation, MOLA

There was intense disturbance from the reducing and levelling of the site, construction and destruction of a building. Modern pottery was recovered from the layers of demolition. Gemma Hewitt. OASIS 350668

Hargrave, Nags Head, 4 Moor Cottages

TL 03869 70819

Watching brief, MOLA

No archaeological remains were found during a watching brief on house footings and service trenches for a single residential building. Paul Sharrock. OASIS 363038

Kettering, land at 163 Beatrice Road

SP 86989 80240

Watching brief, MOLA

A watching brief was undertaken after the demolition of the existing building, a single bungalow with garage. The four new dwellings will be built within the footprint of the former bungalow and garages. No archaeological features or finds were found. Ian Fisher. OASIS 347253

Kislingbury, The Mill

SP 69413 59436

Building recording, MOLA

A programme of historic building recording encompassed the mill building, the cottage, and associated outbuildings; all non-designated heritage assets. At the time of recording the buildings had been partially demolished and works had commenced. There was continuous mill activity from at least the 17th century, and perhaps much earlier as Kislingbury is recorded as having a mill from Domesday, however, a direct link to the site is undetermined. The cottage and barn represent the earliest structures in their Northampton sandstone construction. However, they have now been stripped and there is little to determine their original form. The mill and associated outbuildings date from the mid/late 19th century and represent a growth in the mill activity. The expected growth in wealth is represented in the building of the main house not long after. Electricity overtook traditional milling techniques in the early 20th century and as a result milling ceased here during the First World War. Their use as workshops in the mid/late 20th century has stripped them of most of their original features, as well as the original milling machinery. Lauren Wilson. OASIS 356052

Northampton, Billing Brook Road
SP 7936 6431
Evaluation, MOLA
The trial trench evaluation revealed numerous land drains and disturbed ground resulting from nearby construction works and modern landscaping activities. No archaeological finds or features were identified. Adam Meadows. OASIS 365835

Northampton, Duston, 9 Holyrood Road
SP 73722 6108
Watching brief, MOLA
A watching brief undertaken during the excavation of the foundation trenches revealed no archaeological features or finds. Ian Fisher. OASIS 347260

Northampton, Kingsthorpe, Mill Lane
SP 74646284
Evaluation, MOLA
There were no archaeological remains. A pottery sherd of late 17th or early 18th-century date was found in the topsoil. Yvonne Wolframm-Murray. OASIS 368520

Rothwell, 9–11 High Street
SP 81458 81115
Watching brief, MOLA
Five test pits were observed and recorded. In one test pit part of the foundations of an undated wall could be seen,

and in another was the layer of an old metalled surface. Yvonne Wolframm-Murray. OASIS 377909

Warmington, 18–20 Chapel Street
SP 0778 9123
Watching brief, MOLA
Modern activity included a boundary ditch and spreads/ foundations related to the creation and demolition of a working men's club which existed prior to these works. Paul Sharrock. OASIS 373616

Towcester, Tiffield Park
SP 6942 5014
Geophysical survey & evaluation, MOLA
A geophysical survey of c26ha of land and evaluation identified an historic parish boundary and the remains of a short-lived late 19th-century iron works and railway. Some very intense anomalies of uncertain origin were also detected. John Walford, Jonathon Elston. OASIS 349101, 375088

Wellingborough, works at Area 14
SP 90921 68483
Watching brief, MOLA
A modern boundary ditch and a post-medieval quarry pit. No other archaeological finds or features were present. Adam Reid. OASIS (website not in use due to virus)

Wellingborough, Stanton Cross, Flood Relief Zone 5
SP 910 699, SP 925 674
Geophysical survey & evaluation, MOLA
The geophysical survey of c.13.5ha identified a tramline associated with local ironstone extraction industry in the modern period. Other features detected by the survey included ridge and furrow, palaeochannels, former ironstone quarries and a modern pipeline. John Walford, Alex Shipley, Adam Douthwaite. OASIS 368034, 372914, 349270

Northamptonshire Archaeology, **41**, 2021, 475–480

Archaeology in Northamptonshire 2020

Summaries for MOLA (Museum of London Archaeology) Northampton
Compiled by Yvonne Wolframm-Murray

Prehistoric

Courteenhall, Milton Malsor & Blisworth
SP 74629 54319
Evaluation, MOLA
This evaluation was largely concentrated in the vicinity of previously identified Iron Age and Roman activity. The archaeological remains largely comprised Iron Age and Roman ditches, pits and two potential kilns. Part of a Late Iron Age La Tène bowl with curvilinear impressed decoration was recovered from one of the ditches. Rachel Clare. OASIS 405960

Higham Ferrers, Chelveston Road School
SP 970 685
Geophysical survey, MOLA
Geophysical survey was undertaken as, following previous investigations, it was thought that part of an Iron Age and Roman linear settlement would lie close to the south-eastern corner of the pitch. The results of the survey showed that, whilst this was indeed the case, the detectable archaeological remains lay entirely outside of the development footprint (Fig 1). John Walford. OASIS 409122

Fig 1: Higham Ferrers, Chelveston Road School: geophysical survey in progress

Higham Ferrers, Newton Road
SP 9710 6840
Geophysical survey, MOLA
Geophysical survey of *c*.5ha of land identified Iron Age to Roman settlement remains comprising a series of enclosures and roundhouses alongside a boundary ditch. The remains are part of a linear settlement which previous archaeological works have shown to extend at least 1km west from the present survey area, beneath the A6 and towards the grounds of Ferrers School. Graham Arkley. OASIS 383836

Northampton, Upton Park, south of Weedon Road
SP 7140 5970
Excavation, MOLA
The excavation targeted anomalies identified during the geophysical survey and trial trench evaluation. There were two palaeochannels, possible feeders of a Pleistocene glacial lake, which formed in the Nene Valley. The palaeochannels were *c*.60m wide and *c*.100m apart, running roughly north to south, truncated by two late Bronze Age/Iron Age pit alignments and a Roman trackway. A round barrow ring ditch was 26m in diameter, 1.50–2.90m wide and up to 0.76m deep (Fig 2). The ditch fills produced few finds, but the fill of a recut on the eastern side comprised dark brown-grey sandy silt overlain by mid to dark grey-brown sandy silt. These deposits produced a large amount of worked flint and a small amount of pottery, including a small sherd of fineware Beaker pottery. Set into the top of the filled barrow ditch was an unurned cremation within a pit, with the cremation deposit containing small amounts of hazelnut shell and

Fig 2: Upton Park, Northampton, Bronze Age round barrow during excavation

Fig 3: Upton Park, Northampton, base of an early Bronze Age domestic Beaker from a pit, decorated with lines of incised fingernail impressions (Scale 10mm)

significant quantities of charcoal. Within the ring ditch there was a single feature, a small pit, undated. In another part of the excavation an isolated pit produced part of the base, 80mm in diameter, and the flaring lower body of a coarseware domestic Beaker vessel with the lower body decorated with four unevenly spaced rows of oblique fingernail impressions, with the direction reversing in each row to create a simple herring bone pattern (Fig 3).

To the north of the barrow were two sinuous roughly parallel pit alignments, aligned north-east to south-west for a recorded length of *c*.50m (Fig 4). The southern alignment continued for a further *c*.420m in same direction, while the northern alignment diverted to the north-west and continued for another *c*.440m. In a later phase some of the pits were cut by small lengths of ditches and gullies which may have been due to a restructuring of the boundary. Most of the pottery recovered from the pits was in a poor condition, highly fragmented with post-depositional abrasion, and can only be broadly dated to the Iron Age. These pit alignments are related to previously excavated lengths of pit alignment to both the west (Carlyle 2010, figs 3–6) and the east (Foard-Colby & Walker 2010, fig 5; Walker and Maul 2010, figs 5, 8 & 9).

Fig 4: Upton Park, Northampton, diverging pit alignments, looking west with Weedon Road to the north

Carlyle, S, 2010 An Iron Age pit alignment near Upton, *Northamptonshire Archaeology*, **36**, 53–73

Foard-Colby, A, and Walker, C, 2010 Iron Age settlement and medieval features at Quinton House School, Upton, Northampton, *Northamptonshire Archaeology*, **36**, 53–73ouse

Walker, C, and Maul, A, 2010 Excavation of Iron Age and Roman settlement at Upton, Northampton, *Northamptonshire Archaeology*, **36**, 9–52

Yvonne Wolframm-Murray and Jim Burke. OASIS 43922

Towcester, Towcester South, Trenches 22–50
SP 7040 4761
Evaluation, MOLA

Features mostly comprised ditches and pits, with some material suggesting these features predominantly dated to the earlier part of the late Iron Age. Additional features tentatively identified included two possible cremations and an inhumation burial. Amelia Fairman, Yvonne Wolframm-Murray and Chris Pennell. OASIS 500699

Wellingborough, Stanton Cross (Plot 17)
SP 915 685
Geophysical survey, John Walford

The geophysical survey followed on from similar works conducted by MOLA on other parts of the development site between 2016 and 2019. It detected dispersed archaeological remains of probable Iron Age and Roman date, including a small ditched enclosure in the north of the field. OASIS 402295

Wollaston, east of Hookham's Path
SP 9150 6265
Evaluation, MOLA

A cluster of features, probably parts of enclosures, largely dated to the late Iron Age period. The presence of a small quantity of early Roman pottery would imply possible continuity into this period. Adam Reid. OASIS 397292

Roman

East Northants Resource Management Facility Proposed Extension
TL 00308 99890
Evaluation, MOLA

Two ditches, identified by the geophysical survey, may have formed part of a larger late Roman enclosure in use for a relatively short period, perhaps for stock management. The animal bone assemblage indicates that cattle and sheep/goat are the majority species of livestock. Potential evidence for small-scale charcoal production was also encountered, though the date of this activity remains unknown. A sparse artefactual assemblage was recovered, leaving the majority of the features undated. Camilla Collins. OASIS 408127

Northampton, Fraser Road
SP 78926 64669
Geophysical survey & evaluation, MOLA

Undated features comprising five ditches and five postholes may have been part of a Roman field system recorded during an excavation conducted in 2013 to the west of the site at Booth Rise. Levente Balasz. OASIS 407124

Northampton, Upton Park, south of Weedon Road
SP 7140 5970
Excavation, MOLA

A Roman trackway was traced for nearly 900m. If it continued further to the east, the trackway would have met perpendicularly the projected route of a main road from Duston Roman town. It comprised two sinuous ditches, aligned east to west, *c.*6.5m apart and 0.30–0.85m wide by up to 0.15m deep. Where the trackway crossed the remains of the palaeochannel, a cobbled surface had been constructed, presumably to consolidate the ground. Yvonne Wolframm-Murray and Jim Burke. OASIS 43922

Silverstone, land at Dadford Road
SP 66567 42456
Evaluation, MOLA

Two ditches were identified, one of Roman date and the other was undated, but pre-dated the ridge and furrow. Gemma Hewitt. OASIS 408257

Wellingborough, Stanton Cross (Plot 17)
SP 915 685
Geophysical survey, MOLA

The geophysical survey followed on from similar works conducted by MOLA on other parts of the development site between 2016 and 2019. It detected a short length of probable Roman road in the west, and a pattern of other ditches which may be elements of a former field system. Some traces of medieval ridge and furrow cultivation were also detected. John Walford. OASIS 402295

Medieval

Courteenhall, Milton Malsor & Blisworth
SP 74629 54319
Evaluation, MOLA

Two medieval ditches were noted, the remnants of furrows were present. Post-medieval and modern landscaping and waste disposal was also noted across the site. Rachel Clare. OASIS 405960

Courteenhall, Segro Logistics Park Flood Compensation Area
SP 74945 53585
Evaluation, MOLA

Very few features of archaeological interest were identified, with most of the archaeological remains relating to medieval ridge and furrow cultivation. The site is external to the foci of Iron Age and Roman occupation identified to the north within the proposed development area for the Segro Logistics Park. Paul Sharrock. OASIS 500662

Everdon, Church of St Mary
SP 59452 57451
Watching brief, MOLA

The Church of St Mary, Everdon, is a Grade I Listed Building, dating to the early 14th century. Medieval settlement remains lie to the south and east of the church. During the watching brief four burials and a deposit of disarticulated bone were observed. Three of the burials were articulated and lying on an east to west alignment. One disarticulated burial and a disarticulated bone deposit were found close to the north-west footpath and had been disturbed and reinterred during the rebuilding of the footpath during the 20th century. The burials form one of the final phases of interment in the area immediately surrounding the church before the graveyard was extended to the south. No grave cuts were visible in section and no charnel was encountered, suggesting that the grounds had been raised during landscaping after the burials had taken place. Mary Ellen Crothers. OASIS 418263

Northampton, Upton Park, south of Weedon Road

SP 7140 5970
Excavation, MOLA
Medieval drainage ditches and field systems relating to part of the medieval settlement of Upton lay within the eastern part of the development area. Yvonne Wolframm-Murray and Jim Burke. OASIS 43922

Silverstone, land at Dadford Road

SP 66567 42456
Evaluation, MOLA
Ridge and furrow was seen on the site. Gemma Hewitt. OASIS 408257

Towcester, Towcester South, Trenches 22–50

SP 7040 4761
Evaluation, MOLA
Medieval features dating to AD 1100–1400 and the remnants of ridge and furrow were noted. Amelia Fairman, Yvonne Wolframm-Murray and Chris Pennell. OASIS 500699

Wellingborough, land at Wellingborough North

SP 87702 70523
Evaluation, MOLA
There was a ridge and furrow system along with late medieval field boundary ditches. Alex Shipley. OASIS 388099

Post-medieval

Long Buckby, Sharpes Lane, Castle House

SP 6262 6756
Watching brief, MOLA
Three foundation trenches were observed and recorded. The upper fill of a ditch, an ironstone wall foundation and a cobbled yard surface, all of post-medieval date, were exposed and recorded. Yvonne Wolframm-Murray and Paul Thompson. OASIS 407038

Northampton, St Mary's Court and Berkeley House

SP 75129 60594
Evaluation, MOLA
Six test pits were excavated in green areas surrounding residential flats due to be demolished in the centre of Northampton within the bounds of the late Saxon burh

and within an area of known medieval remains identified by other archaeological works in the surrounding area. There were deeply stratified deposits in all of the test pits, mostly consisting of layers. Due to the depth of these deposits the natural substrate was not encountered in any of the test pits, which lay beyond the limits of safe working practise. The earliest recorded remains within the test pits comprised soil layers, which varied in date from the medieval through to the 19th century. Sealing or cutting those deposits there were structural remains dating from the early–middle 18th century with 19th and 20th-century remains in four test pits. A typical urban finds assemblage was recovered consisting of pottery, glass, animal bone, clay tobacco-pipes and ceramic building materials. In addition, there are finds that primarily comprised post-medieval dress accessories recovered from a fireplace. James Fairclough. OASIS 389834

Oundle, St Osyth's Lane, The Angel

TL 04247 88065
Building recording, MOLA
Building recording was undertaken at The Angel prior to works being undertaken on the building (Figs 5 and 6). The site comprises No. 4 St Osyth's Lane, a former public house, and a Grade II listed building. St Osyth's Lane runs south-east from the Market Place and is mentioned in Oundle's Conservation Area Appraisal as retaining modest vernacular cottages. The building is in two distinct ranges that the list description dates to 18th century (north) and early 19th century (south). Although the current story of the building is a commercial one, the use of this site as a public house is relatively modern. The level of alteration and continuous small-scale development, as well as the stripping-out of the building on its conversion to a public house, has removed extensive historic fabric. However, despite this it is clear that the south range and north range originated as two separate structures with their own rear ranges and yard access via an alleyway between them, now blocked. Lauren Wilson. OASIS 382246

Fig 5: Oundle, The Angel; the street frontage showing the two component properties

Fig 6: Oundle, The Angel; the yard with later extensions to the frontage

Silverstone, land at Dadford Road
SP 66567 42456
Evaluation, MOLA
Post-medieval plough furrows were identified across the site. Gemma Hewitt. OASIS 408257

Towcester, Towcester South, Trenches 22–50
SP 7040 4761
Evaluation, MOLA
Post-medieval materials were found in two different single trenches Amelia Fairman, Yvonne Wolframm-Murray and Chris Pennell. OASIS 500699

Modern/Unknown

Ashton, 15 Roade Hill
SP 76575 50058
Watching brief, MOLA
A watching brief took place during groundworks related to the footings excavation of a new dwelling located within the footings of a previously demolished building. No features or finds were recorded. It was noted that the ground level of the northernmost part of the developed plot had been reduced prior to the monitoring. Kamil Orzechowski. OASIS 402759

Astcote, 2 High Street, Manor Farm House
SP 67672 53179
Evaluation, MOLA
Evaluation on land west off the High Street revealed remodelling of the land, indicating that there may originally have been a pronounced terrace towards the west end of the plot that had been levelled and smoothed to a gentle slope by the deposition of imported soils and limestone rubble. Topsoil and subsoil overburden revealed infrequent sherds of medieval pottery. Jim Burke. OASIS 395538

Clipston, land at Naseby Road
SP 71020 81613
Evaluation, MOLA
A brick and ironstone wall and two modern ditches of the early 20th-century were investigated and recorded. Christopher Jones. OASIS 390081

Cottesbrooke, land at Cottesbrooke Hall
SP 71087 73733
Watching brief, MOLA
A watching brief was carried out during the excavation of four pits c.2.0m by 1.2m to facilitate the passing through of an underground service. No archaeological features or artefacts were recovered. Ester Poulus. OASIS 390667

Courteenhall, Milton Malsor & Blisworth, Rectory Farm
SP 74629 54319 & SP 75143 54412
Building recording, MOLA
The report covers two foci of historic agricultural buildings, comprising five barns within a rural setting, with historic building recording undertaken on two barns. These may represent one farm complex, or equally could relate to different ownerships. Barn 2 is the earliest, appearing on cartographic sources from the 1820s. Barn 1 dates from the 19th century and although has some constructional similarities with Barn 2, represents a different phase of development, perhaps associated with the need for more storage space within the farm. Barn 5 is an early 20th-century stable range with trough and hayrack. Barns 3 and 4 are late 20th century in date and correspond to the date at which Barn 1 was converted to other usage. Overall this is an interesting example of continued farming and how changing demands within agriculture is reflected within the change, addition or extension of historic buildings. Lauren Wilson. OASIS 405604

Foster's Booth, Watling Street East, land north of the Red Lion
SP 66726 53946
Watching brief, MOLA
Prior to the construction of a row of three terrace houses, an initial visit comprised three hand-dug test-pits one of which contained a thin, dark organic layer. A second visit during the excavation of the footings revealed a probable pit containing a similar dark and organic matter. No other features or finds were present. Paul Beers. OASIS 400980

Higham Ferrers, Castle Fields
SP 9614 6885
Watching brief, MOLA
A watching brief within Higham Ferrers castle (SM13607) saw no archaeological features, but four modern layers were recorded in small hand-dug trenches. The deepest deposits, up to 0.45m below modern ground level, comprised 20th-century allotment soils overlaid by make-up/levelling layers all containing a mixture of 18th-20th century pottery, brick and tile, two pieces of medieval roof tile, modern metal and glass debris. The deposits were all sealed by a topsoil and turf layer. Stephen Morris. OASIS 407721

Middleton Cheney, land at Thenford Road
SP 50770 41820
Evaluation, MOLA
The shallow remains of ridge and furrow cultivation, the remains of post-medieval quarrying and backfill and a modern ditch, the remains of demolished farm buildings and evidence of the new development were recorded. Jim Burke. OASIS 390500

Paulerspury, land to the north of Gray's Close
SP 72551 45772
Evaluation, MOLA
No archaeological features were identified. Jim Burke. OASIS 395689

Rothersthorpe, 20 Church Street
SP 71463 56617
Watching brief, MOLA
No archaeological features, remains or deposits were uncovered. Paul Thompson. OASIS 396101

Wood Burcote, Sheppards Farm
SP 69561 47087
Evaluation, MOLA
A single ditch was dated to the early to mid-19th century. Adam Reid. OASIS 500874